MONEY AND BANKING:
Analysis and Policy

MONEY AND

CHARLES R. WHITTLESEY
ARTHUR M. FREEDMAN
EDWARD S. HERMAN

WHARTON SCHOOL OF FINANCE AND COMMERCE
UNIVERSITY OF PENNSYLVANIA

BANKING: Analysis and Policy

The Macmillan Company, New York

Collier-Macmillan Limited, London

Fourth Printing 1965

Earlier editions, entitled *Principles and Practices of Money and Banking*,
copyright 1948 and 1954 by the Macmillan Company.

Library of Congress catalog card number: 63-9237

The Macmillan Company, New York
Collier-Macmillan Canada, Ltd., Toronto, Ontario

Printed in the United States of America

Design: N. Sylvester

PREFACE

This volume is a completely rewritten version of *Principles and Practices of Money and Banking* by Charles R. Whittlesey. Since that work first appeared in 1948 there have been substantial changes in financial conditions, ideas, and practices. For example, in 1948 the Exchange Stabilization Fund, established at a time of monetary crisis in the 1930's, was to all appearances dead and buried. By 1961 it had been exhumed and was again in active operation. When the second edition of that volume appeared in 1954 the world was struggling with the problem of dollar shortage, and a number of distinguished economists were warning us that this was to be regarded as a permanent state of affairs. Yet before the decade was out our problem was one of a dollar surplus, with a persistent tendency toward erosion of the country's gold reserves. When the work on this volume was started there was widespread concern over inflation. By the early 1960's this threat appeared to have receded.

Such is the pace of change in the problems of monetary economics. Nor does the record suggest any convincing reason for supposing that comparable developments will not occur in the future. All this is part of the challenge which monetary economics presents to both student and teacher. To those so bold (or so filled with conceit concerning their powers of enlightenment) as to write textbooks, it presents self-evident difficulties. To address attention primarily to current problems risks becoming out of date. To treat the subject historically not only risks loss of reader interest but seems also to shirk responsibility for contributing, however modestly, to a solution of issues that press upon us.

What has been done in this volume is to concentrate upon what appear to be the more enduring aspects of the subject, and to treat the rest as elements of an evolutionary process that reaches backward into the past and forward into the future. Historical evidence is offered not as an end in itself but as a means of illuminating principles and illustrating the origin and development of institutions, problems, and policies.

The book follows a seven-part sequence which proceeds from basic concepts and institutions, to instruments of monetary management, to monetary theory, and then to stabilization policy and international finance. A short introduction to monetary analysis is included in the first chapter with a view to providing an early orientation which will suffice until the student reaches the more extensive treatment of theory in Part V.

Long experience in the teaching of monetary economics has persuaded us that monetary and fiscal analysis are best understood after an explanation of money and credit, money markets, the mechanism of commercial banking, central banking, and related elements of the framework of finance. It is helpful to be able to move

v

from the instruments of monetary management to monetary analysis and then to policy without interruption.

We have endeavored to maintain perspective on what is of lasting interest in the study of monetary matters. At the same time we have undertaken to cover all significant modern developments in the field. Monetary theory is developed somewhat more fully than is usual in textbooks in this field, and is designed with a view to clarifying policy issues. This emphasis reflects the conviction that economic theory, carefully formulated and tested, is an indispensable aid to an intelligent understanding of current problems and to a wise application of policy. Theory, properly understood, is not only the most useful but also the most durable tool that can be placed in the hands of the student of monetary economics.

We have treated inflation and fiscal effects as integral parts of aggregative analysis, and not as something to be brought in *ad hoc* in the policy section of the book. Income and interest theory are integrated by means of a graphic approach which we feel to be pedagogically superior to the Hicksian I-S and L-M framework. We have also given attention to the determinants of the structure of interest rates and to suggested mechanisms through which monetary actions influence economic activity, including availability, wealth, and liquidity effects.

Other features of the volume which are worthy of note are the discussion of the national debt as a means of discretionary control and as an automatic stabilizer; the treatment of the organization and operation of money markets; the discussion of the banking structure and its regulation, including bank entry and the problem of mergers; and the emphasis on changes in simple balance sheet accounts as a tool for understanding monetary and banking operations.

Although an introductory course in Economics is not a binding prerequisite for the use of this volume we have taken advantage of the fact that students usually have had such a course before taking Money and Banking. The text was designed to be used for a one semester course in Money and Banking at the University of Pennsylvania. With some supplementary material it could be readily adapted for a two semester course. For those who find the present coverage too extensive for treatment in one semester, exclusions will be a matter of desired emphasis. Of the institutional materials, Chapters 10, 11, 26, and 27 could be omitted without serious disruption of the presentation. Instructors wishing to give less emphasis to monetary theory may find it convenient to exclude at least the first two sections of Chapter 18.

We have sought, by means of brief selected bibliographies and occasional footnotes, to indicate where users of the book can turn conveniently for supplementary guidance and for data relating to current developments. To remain abreast of future events in this area will require intelligent post-graduation reading and thinking. The purpose of this book is to contribute to the will as well as to the ways of achieving both.

We are indebted to numerous friends in academic and banking circles including the Federal Reserve System. Especially are we obligated to colleagues at the University of Pennsylvania. Among those who have read parts of the book and offered constructive suggestions are Professors Arthur I. Bloomfield, Andrew F. Brimmer, W. Carlton Harris, E. Gordon Keith, Morris Mendelson, Paul F. Smith, and Fred M. Worley. They are, of course, in no way accountable for imperfections which have survived their efforts.

CONTENTS

PART TWO: COMMERCIAL BANKS AND RELATED INSTITUTIONS

of a monopoly bank (or banking system) with an external drain—Time deposits, financial intermediaries, and demand deposit expansion—Actual versus potential deposits: the role of excess reserves—Expansion limits of an individual bank within a system of many banks—Qualifications relating to the expansion of the individual bank

Open-market operations—Changes in reserve requirements
—Limits to Federal Reserve credit expansion
THE SELECTIVE INSTRUMENTS OF CREDIT CONTROL: Margin re-
quirements—Control of consumer credit—Control of real
estate credit
PSYCHOLOGICAL MEANS OF CONTROLLING CREDIT: Moral suasion—
The Voluntary Credit Restraint Program

LIST OF FIGURES

LIST OF TABLES

PART ONE

Money and Credit

1

MONEY AND THE ECONOMIC SYSTEM

Money is the epitome of paradox. It is at once the most and the least important of economic goods. We are told that money makes the marc go and that the love of it is the root of all evil. On the other hand, we do not use it to eat or to wear or directly to produce other economic goods (though some societies have found it possible to do these things with their money). But its possession enables us, so we ordinarily think, to do all these things better. At other times, as in inflation or deflation, money may be a source of disruption and disorganization. And clearly, among its other properties, money provides inspiration, second perhaps only to love, for contrivers of paradox and aphorism.

So unique was money formerly thought to be that it was customary to differentiate the forces determining its value from those of all other economic goods. Today, despite acknowledged differences, we are inclined to emphasize, rather, the similarity of money to economic goods, viewing assets as a continuum that shows a common thread uniting real assets, such as butter and buildings, income-yielding claims, such as Treasury bills and bonds, and money, such as dollar bills and demand deposits. And we have come to believe that the really important problems of money relate to the stream of money payments rather than to the quantity of money itself—what one writer has spoken of as money on the wing in contrast to money sitting.

WHAT IS MONEY?

A distinguished British authority on money and central banking who was an official of the British Treasury for many years starts one of his books with the statement:

> Money is one of those concepts which, like a teaspoon or an umbrella, but unlike an earthquake or a buttercup, are definable primarily by the use or purpose which they serve.[1]

This functional approach to defining money can be illustrated by an example from American monetary history.

During the War Between the States when there was a great dearth of small change in the North, many individual businesses and organizations had copper one-cent pieces minted to their order which were then paid out to circulate widely throughout the country. These coins bore various designs, some advertising a merchant's wares, some urging the election of a particular candidate for office, and others bearing nothing more than a patriotic phrase or symbol. Although they were of the shape, size, and material of the one-cent pieces issued by the government, they were obviously based on no legal right of issue. They carried no promise to pay, and they were not legal tender (i.e., a legally enforceable means of discharging general monetary obligations). Nevertheless, they were accepted without question in current transactions and, in general, performed all the services ordinarily performed by one-cent coins. Because they did the work of money, they clearly must be considered to have been money.

A functional approach lends itself readily to a definition of money in terms of its crucial work of serving as a medium of exchange. In the present volume, the term "money" will be used to designate anything commonly accepted as a means of payment for goods or in the discharge of other types of business obligation (such as the meeting of interest payments on a debt). This definition, which conforms fairly closely to colloquial usage, permits us to divide the universe of valuables into those that we "spend" (money) and those that we purchase in the process of spending (non-monetary claims, such as stocks and bonds, and goods, such as haircuts and automobiles).

With money defined in this way, the test of what is money is independent of matters of form or physical substance; it turns on nothing more than whether or not the item in question customarily functions as a means of payment. Thus coins and non-interest-bearing paper claims (together comprising what we will refer to as "currency" or "pocketbook money") issued by the United States Treasury or by one of the twelve Federal Reserve Banks (e.g., silver certificates, Federal Reserve notes, and metallic quarters and pennies) qualify as money without question since they are all commonly accepted as means of payment. On the other hand, a gold watch or a government bond does not meet our criterion of money since, although valuable, they are not commonly accepted or used as means of paying for goods or liquidating business obligations.

The overwhelming bulk of trade in the United States is carried on by

---

1. R. G. Hawtrey, *Currency and Credit* (London: Longmans, Green, 1928), p. 1.

means of checks drawn against demand deposits at commercial banks. According to our means of payment test of what constitutes money, as well as by widely accepted usage, such demand deposits (or "checking accounts") are money. These deposits consist of book entries recording bank promises to pay currency on demand to their customers. They are *not* stocks of coin or paper money placed in the bank by bank customers and held by the bank pending disposition by depositors.[2] Although deposits do sometimes arise out of placing currency in a bank, the bulk of these bank liabilities come into being in connection with the receipt by banks of checks written on other banks, or by additions to customers' checking accounts which banks make in exchange for bills or interest-bearing promissory notes received from customer-borrowers.

There is a common tendency to regard currency as *real* money and demand deposits as an inferior and somewhat dubious kind of money. The superiority of currency is usually urged on the ground of an alleged more universal acceptability. It is probably true that checks written on demand deposits are unacceptable in more transactions by number than is currency, partly because of uncertainty as to the existence of a demand deposit equal to the value of the proffered check and partly because of the convenience of currency in retail transactions, the expense and inconvenience of cashing checks, occasional distrust of banks, and the usefulness of currency for illicit transactions and tax evasion. On the other hand, in most transactions involving sums of money in excess of let us say $1,000, currency would be so inconvenient as to be practically unusable, even though not literally unacceptable. There can be little doubt that for these sizable transactions, as well as for many others, demand deposits are preferable to currency. Demand deposits are held by the public (preferred) in a ratio of about $4 of deposits to $1 of currency and *spent* in a ratio of over $9 of deposit money to $1 of currency. Since this public preference for deposits has increased secularly for generations, it is clearly very questionable to regard currency as a superior form of money. It may be more sensible to view both currency and demand deposits as full-fledged money, each with attributes that appeal to money holders for certain purposes.

The question may be raised why we do not count checks rather than demand deposits as money. One reason is that it is the ultimate transfer of the demand deposit between the accounts of payer and payee that fully completes the transaction. The check is the means of transferring a deposit account, and its acceptability depends on the belief that the payer has an

---

2. The word "deposit" is misleading in this respect since it suggests that a deposit consists of that which is placed in the bank rather than the bank's liability to a customer. The student who wishes to do so can readily verify by reference to the consolidated balance sheet of commercial banks in the United States, published in the Federal Reserve Bulletin or the Annual Reports of the Federal Deposit Insurance Corporation, that currency holdings of commercial banks (recorded as "vault cash") in recent years have been less than 2 per cent of their total deposit obligations.

account which may be debited by the amount of the check, permitting a corresponding credit to the account of the payee. A second important reason for considering demand deposits rather than checks as money stems from a desire to distinguish between the stock (or supply) of money in existence and the rate at which it is used (or the *velocity* of circulation of money). The stock of money is the amount existing at a moment of time (as would appear in the balance sheets of all economic units). The total money expenditures in a given time period, the *flow* of money, will be some multiple of the average amount of money existing over the period. Since for many purposes we are interested in the flow of expenditures for output, and, since the flow may change because of a change in either the stock or the size of the multiple (velocity) referred to, clarity of thought requires that we be aware of the distinction. The volume of demand deposits in existence at any particular time corresponds reasonably well to the stock of checking account money. On the other hand, the volume of checks outstanding at any particular time is a measure of the rate at which orders are being written to transfer checking accounts, rather than the volume of means of payment available for use at the time.[3] Moreover, the volume of checks outstanding has the limitation of being unmeasurable—we cannot tell that checks have been written until they are deposited in banks by their recipients, at which point they cease to be checks outstanding.

In addition to their demand liabilities, commercial banks typically hold a smaller but still very substantial volume of time deposits for the accounts of their customers. Do they fit our definition of money? In some respects time and demand deposits seem to resemble each other closely. Both are liabilities of the bank, and some of us may think of our checking and our savings accounts more or less interchangeably as accounts in which we may deposit funds that we do not require for the time being or to which we may turn if we desire to draw out additional currency. The bank must pay out currency on demand to owners of checking accounts but is permitted to delay in paying on time deposits; however, this option is seldom exercised and makes little difference to the average depositor (though it does to the banker who finds in it one reason for holding longer term securities against time than against demand deposits).

By far the most important difference is that time deposits are not transferable by check. Unlike demand deposits, they are not used as a means of payment. They are therefore not money as we have defined it. They are created only by someone placing currency or checks with the bank. As we shall see later, this is not necessarily true of demand deposits. If the depositor wishes to use his time deposit, the bank must provide him with

---

3. Even if the rate of use of deposits is increased (or decreased) this will mainly affect transfers between existing deposit holders without altering the total. There may be moderate alterations in the totals because of time lags in the collection of checks. However, these may be taken into account in estimates of aggregate demand deposits.

currency or demand deposits. Demand deposits but not time deposits constitute the unique and distinctive contribution of commercial banks to the money supply.

A final (and more difficult) issue concerns the relationship of gold and gold certificates to our concept of money. Since 1933 gold coin, gold bullion, and gold certificates have been barred by law from internal circulation as means of payment within the United States. From the standpoint of the domestic economy of this country, gold items are therefore not money. However, gold is the ultimate means of payment of international obligations and conforms to our definition of money from the broader perspective of the world economy. This suggests that a general definition of money does not yield an unambiguous money supply aggregate that fits all the purposes for which we might want a money stock total. For some purposes we may wish to include the gold stock in the money supply; for other purposes we might want to know only the supply of domestically usable money; and more often we will want to know the stock of domestic money in the hands of the public. We return to this issue in Chapter 3 in discussing the composition of the money supply of the United States.

MONEY AND THE UNIT OF ACCOUNT

The concept basic to all monetary systems is the "unit of account,"[4] the primary unit of measurement, in terms of which values are generally calculated, accounts kept, and contracts written. In the United States the unit of account is the dollar; in Mexico it is the peso, in Italy the lira, in India the rupee, and so on. In most countries efficiency enforces a single unit of account. In Great Britain, however, dual units survive, the pound and the guinea, and at various times in our history we have had dual units of account (one of the most notable was the Civil War period when some accounts continued to be kept in terms of the gold dollar despite the disappearance of gold from circulation in favor of the heavily issued greenbacks).

In a highly developed economy such as that of the United States the number of available goods is large and the number of value relations that are potentially of practical importance to individual and business transactors is very large. Without some means of simplifying and reducing this vast number of possible value relationships a modern exchange economy would be impossible. A unit of account permits the value of all goods and claims to be expressed in terms of a single common denominator. Each has a single price attached which is some fraction or multiple of the unit of account,[5] and the relative values of all such items are given by the ratios of their prices

---

4. Sometimes referred to as the "money of account" or "standard of value."
5. An ice cream soda is worth a "quarter," a phonograph record, $4.98.

expressed in this standard unit. The resultant *system* of prices greatly simplifies the problem of comparing values and thus greatly increases the possibility of intelligent calculation in the purchase of goods and claims, the keeping of accounts, and the reckoning of the economic position of a family or a business enterprise.

What is the relationship between the unit of account and "money" as defined above? It is frequently asserted that one of the functions of money is to serve as the unit of account or standard of value. But people do not quote prices, keep accounts, and write contracts in terms of those specific items (nickels, $10 bills, or a $350 deposit) which correspond to our definition of money. Values are calculated in terms of *the dollar*, a unit of account. Our system of definitions will be tidier if we regard the unit of account as an abstract unit in terms of which prices are expressed and contracts written, and money as those specific things that actually circulate as means of payment.[6] The items which serve as means of payment are uniquely related to the abstract unit of account: they are expressed or defined in terms of that abstract entity as fixed fractions or multiples. Money, being defined in terms of the unit of account, always has an invariable price in terms of that unit. A quarter is defined as one-fourth of a dollar and always passes in circulation at that money price; a $5 Federal Reserve note always passes at five times the value of the dollar. On the other hand, goods and most non-monetary claims have prices that are subject to variation. A package of cigarets or a haircut or a government bond may change in price; a quarter or a $5 bill cannot.

The invariability of the *price* of money does not, of course, mean that money has an unchanging *value*. In the fundamental economic sense of purchasing power, or command over goods in exchange, the value of money is clearly subject to change, and, in fact, inflation and deflation are usually defined as decreases (inflation) and increases (deflation) in the value of money. However, the fact that money is expressed or defined in terms of the unit of account makes it impossible to *measure* changes in the value of money by changes in its money price. Money prices may be used to measure changes in the value of television sets or common stocks, but not a $10 bill.

If we wish to measure changes in the value of money itself between any two dates, it is necessary to select an appropriate sample of goods and obtain

6. This distinction may be elucidated by considering the unit of account as "the *description* or *title* and the money . . . the *thing* which answers to the description . . . The difference is like that between the King of England (whoever he may be) and King George." J. M. Keynes, *A Treatise on Money* (New York: Harcourt Brace, 1930), Vol. I, p. 4. Keynes also cites another example that may clarify this distinction. "A District Commissioner in Uganda to-day, where goats are the customary native standard, tells me that it is a part of his official duties to decide, in cases of dispute, whether a given goat is or is not too old or too scraggy to constitute a standard goat for the purposes of discharging a debt." (*Ibid.*, p. 13.) In this instance, there is a standard goat that is a purely conceptual unit of account, and a number of actual goats that conform more or less adequately to the standard, and which can therefore be used as means of payment.

information concerning their quantities and prices on those dates, from which we can then construct *index numbers* of the prices of goods in our sample. Thus, if the index number of prices in year 5 is 120 as compared with 100 in the base year, this means that a unit of money can buy only 83 per cent ($100 \div 120 \times 100$) as much of the items in the sampled collection of goods in year 5 as compared with the base year. In other words, in terms of this index the value of money fell by approximately 17 per cent between these two years. It will be noted that the value of money varies inversely with the price index: a rise in the index signifies that a given amount of money will buy fewer goods than before, while a fall in the index indicates that it will command more.

Substantial fluctuations in the value of money are of particular importance in economies that make extensive use of fixed-dollar contracts. The volume of money contracts in the United States, as measured by the net private and public debt outstanding, amounted to more than $800 billion in the early 1960's. The terms of these contracts do not normally vary with changes in economic conditions. This means that in cases of substantial increase in the value of money (deflation), debtors are obligated to pay their creditors fixed-dollar sums with a purchasing power substantially greater than that of the dollars received when the debts were incurred. In the picturesque language of D. H. Robertson, "A downward swoop of the level of prices reveals like a flare a line of struggling figures, caught in their own commitments as in a barbed-wire entanglement."[7] In the contrary case of a significant decline in the value of money (inflation), debtors are able to liquidate their obligations to creditors with dollars of less value than those originally borrowed. In cases of extreme inflation, the wealth of creditors may be wiped out as "debtors pursue their creditors and pay them without mercy" (as was said of the behavior of debtors in the Revolutionary War). It follows that changes in the value of money necessarily alter the distribution of real income and wealth between debtors and creditors.[8] Other important effects of inflation and deflation on the creation and distribution of output are discussed below in Chapter 20.

MONEY, ASSETS, AND LIQUIDITY

Money and Wealth

For purposes of monetary analysis, assets may be divided into *real assets*, on the one hand, and *claims* on the other. The latter category in-

---

7. D. H. Robertson, *Money* (New York: Harcourt Brace, 1929), p. 15.

8. The conflict of interest between debtor and creditor under conditions of change in the value of money has had important political repercussions in America from the colonial period to the present. Little sense can be made of Shays Rebellion, the Greenback and Populist movements, and the history of bimetallism and the gold standard without recognition of this underlying conflict.

cludes those which we have agreed to call money, and financial assets such as promissory notes and bonds. In the administration of his assets, an individual (or firm) may choose from among real assets, money, or non-monetary claims of a wide variety, weighing their relative advantages and disadvantages in order to achieve a preferred combination.

An automobile is an example of a real asset. Over its lifetime this asset yields a flow of transportation services to its owner-user. In contrast, the promissory note given to a bank by the owner of the automobile, enabling him to acquire it, is a claim. The owner of this claim (the bank) has a contractual right to a series of money payments, including interest and principal, from the automobile owner. The note is thus an asset of the bank but a liability of the debtor. While this note and similar financial instruments may be regarded as part of the wealth (or net worth) of their holders, they do not enter into the aggregate net wealth of the community as a whole. For if we consolidate the balance sheets of all economic units in a system, each financial instrument issued and held internally as an asset would correspond exactly to an obligation owed elsewhere in the system and thus would cancel out. It is clear, therefore, that, apart from net external debts or claims, which we are ignoring here for simplicity,[9] the aggregate net wealth of a nation is its stock of real assets.

It follows from this relationship between claims and wealth that changes in the quantity of money, or the volume of public or private claims, do not correspond to alterations in the wealth of the community. An increase in the public debt or a sharp break in common stock prices does not directly reduce community real assets; they merely alter the value and proportions of outstanding claims against wealth. This *may* result in indirect repercussions on the rate of production of real assets, but it is important to recognize that the immediate effect of changes in the value of claims (including money) is not on the aggregate wealth of the community but rather on its distribution.

Money, the very symbol of wealth, is thus not the substance of wealth. For the most part, modern moneys in domestic circulation consist of pure claims rather than commodity stocks.[10] They derive their utility not from being literally consumed, like food, or from being worn, like diamonds, but from their power to exchange for other things. The maintenance of the

9. A debt held *externally* which is not offset by a claim held elsewhere in the community must be considered negative wealth and subtracted from gross assets to arrive at a proper measure of net wealth. Similarly, claims against foreigners increase the total net wealth of the community.

10. Over 98 per cent of the money in circulation in the United States is made up of entries on the books of banks (demand deposits) plus paper currency, and the remainder in the form of coin contributes to the net wealth of the community considerably less than its monetary value if entered at commodity value. The gold stock of the United States has a current market value amounting to many billions of dollars, but it is not available for domestic circulation. It is part of community wealth, but it is not part of the domestic money supply.

value of money thus turns on being able to get rid of it—for goods and other claims—without significant loss. As a specialized claim, accepted by social convention because of its usefulness in mediating exchanges, money is largely excluded from any listing of the items comprising community wealth. With the exception of commodity money, money always involves a promise to pay (a debt) and a claim against the issuer by the holder of the money (a credit); these debts and credits disappear along with other claims in the process of computing the net worth of the community.

Money and Liquidity

As a claim, money has two distinctive characteristics that influence public attitudes toward holding it as compared with alternative assets. The first is that money ordinarily provides no income. If we own a mortgage on a piece of land, a share of stock, or a savings account, they will ordinarily afford us a flow of money receipts in the form of interest or dividends (and possibly capital appreciation). Money yields no such income flow, and it is important to bear in mind that holding money thus involves a sacrifice of real and money income that could be obtained by shifting from money to goods or income-yielding claims.

A second distinctive characteristic of money, and the one that causes us to desire to hold at least some of our assets in this form, is its "power of universal command" over goods and other claims. This of course derives from the fundamental nature of money as a generally acceptable means of payment; it can be converted into other things quickly and without sacrifice of capital value. The extent to which an asset approaches money in ease of convertibility and freedom from risk of capital loss may be referred to as its degree of "liquidity."[11] If we own a house appraised at $15,000 and a demand deposit of $15,000, both are worth the same amount and are presumably exchangeable for $15,000 worth of other things. The deposit, however, could be used directly to obtain an equivalent value of other goods; the house, on the other hand, would have to be converted first into money, with considerable delay and potential capital loss depending on the desired speed of transfer, the state of the market for houses during that period, and luck in finding a buyer interested in this particular residence. Thus the demand deposit is extremely liquid, the house relatively illiquid.

All assets have the quality of liquidity to some degree, and it is possible to conceive of a liquidity scale as of a given time (and for each individual) according to which we might order all existing assets. At the top of the scale would be money itself. Just below money would be such claims as time deposits, fixed-price government securities such as E-bonds, and call

---

11. The expression "liquidity" is a figure of speech in which money is treated as the analogue of a liquid in a physical sense—it can presumably "flow" more readily than other assets through markets and the economic system.

loans, all of which are readily convertible into money with only minor delays. Only slightly less liquid would be 90-day bills issued by the United States Treasury, which fluctuate very little in market value and are fully redeemable in a short time. Still further down the scale we would encounter longer term bonds and stocks, subject to larger fluctuations in market prices, inventories of standard commodities, furniture and household equipment, real estate, and, near the bottom, specialized industrial equipment with little or no second-hand market (such as a fender press for a special make of automobile). The assets at the top of our list down through Treasury bills are very close to money in degree of liquidity; for purposes of storing readily available purchasing power they are important money substitutes. They are frequently called "near-moneys" to indicate this ready substitutability.

Reasons for Holding Money

As a result of its general power of command over other goods— its high degree of liquidity—money is held for three general purposes. First, since there is an imperfect gearing of money income payments (usually weekly or monthly) and ordinary outlays (made daily or several times per week), a large part of the money holdings of individuals and business firms is merely to bridge the gap between receipts and expenditures. The demand for money for such a purpose may be called the "transactions demand" for money, and the corresponding cash balances, "transactions" balances. The transactions demand for money is likely to depend primarily on methods of income payment and expenditure and the value of transactions taking place during a given period (which will tend to vary closely and directly with the national income). If a community were suddenly to change from a system of monthly to weekly income payments, the average size of money holding would fall and the demand for money for transactions purposes would decline. If aggregate money incomes rose, transactions demand would rise along with the likely increase in average money transactions. Since methods of payment and expenditure change slowly it is probably reasonable to view the transactions demand for money in relatively short periods as primarily dependent on changes in the volume of transactions or income.

A second reason for holding money is to enable the individual or business to meet unforeseen contingencies that reduce money inflow or augment money outlays, with a minimum of delay and cost. The demand for money for this purpose is commonly referred to as the "precautionary demand" or "contingency demand," and the corresponding balances may be referred to as "precautionary" or "contingency" balances. An individual might be required to meet a sizable and unexpected hospital bill on relatively short notice. Without a precautionary balance he might be compelled to borrow or dispose of earning assets on whatever terms the market dictates at the moment. Or an individual or business might suddenly be faced with a favorable opportunity to buy, such as a bankruptcy sale of appliances or inventory. A margin of reserve funds would be very useful in permitting a transactor to take advantage of such unpredictable opportunities.

The demand for money for precautionary purposes is a reflection of uncertainty as to the future course of income and necessary or desirable expenditures; the size of this demand is likely to depend heavily on the degree of individual and business uncertainty at any particular time. In periods such as the early 1930's after the stock market crash and the onset of a serious depression, and in the late 1930's when an outbreak of war seemed imminent, the uncertainties besetting the public were great and the demand for contingency balances relatively high. In the period after World War II the demand for such balances was low, owing in part to widespread optimism about the future course of demand and prices and also because of the more extensive commitment of the government to defense and stabilization policies.

Finally, since the future prices of assets are always somewhat uncertain, individuals may hold at least a part of their assets in the form of money because the present rewards for holding non-monetary assets are not considered adequate to compensate for the risk of a fall in asset prices. This is referred to as the "speculative motive" for holding money, and the corresponding money holdings, "speculative" balances. Transactors holding money in the expectation of price declines are commonly referred to as "bears," and those holding non-monetary assets in expectation of price increases are called "bulls." Bears may not only hold money in expectation of price declines, but they may also "sell short," i.e., they may sell promises to deliver a specific quantity of a non-monetary asset at a certain price at some future date, in exchange for money now. The bear is speculating that he will be able to buy the relevant asset at a price lower than that now prevailing, thus enabling him to cover his commitment at a profit to himself. Market prices of assets are affected by changes in the degree of bearishness or bullishness of actual or potential buyers and sellers. A sudden shift in sentiment that causes a larger number of buyers and sellers to expect price declines (to become bearish on the price of that asset) will tend to reduce the willingness of asset owners to hold that asset at its going price. The demand for this asset declines and the supply increases, thus reducing the equilibrium price.

THE ROLE OF MONEY

The Importance of Money in the Economic System

There have been and still are societies without a commonly accepted medium of exchange. But these have been localized subsistence economies with small populations and little specialization of economic function. In more populous societies, where the division of labor is elaborate and the economy complex and highly interdependent, money is indispensable. This is a consequence of the relationship between specialization, markets, and money so well described by Adam Smith in *The Wealth of Nations*. The growth of specialization, i.e., the division of labor, was put forward by Smith as the fundamental source of increases in productivity and wealth. This relationship was attributed to the increase in worker skill resulting from concentration on a simple operation, the saving of time formerly lost in passing from one kind of work to another, and "the invention of a great number of machines which facilitate and abridge labour, and enable one man to do the work of many."[12]

The growth of specialization, in turn, was shown to be dependent on the size of markets, with large markets stimulating and narrow markets retarding the extension of the division of labor. In the words of Adam Smith, "When the market is very small, no person can have any encouragement to dedicate himself entirely to one employment, for want of the power to exchange all that surplus part of the produce of his own labour, which is over and above his own consumption, for such parts of the produce of other men's labour as he has occasion for."[13] This is a reciprocal process. The expansion of outputs seeking market outlets enlarges the markets for other products so that specialization stimulates, in addition to being stimulated by, increases in the size of markets.

After establishing this important relationship between the division of labor and the size of markets, Adam Smith turned to the question, "Of the Origin and Use of Money." Here he wished to show that wide markets, and hence a highly developed system of subdivided labor, presuppose a concurrent development of some specialized instrument for mediating exchanges. He noted that in the absence of money, producers would be compelled to engage in direct or indirect barter with other producers in order to obtain other goods.[14] But successful barter transactions require a degree of coordination of wants between transactors as to quality, quantity, and time and place of goods to be exchanged that is likely to necessitate considerable labor in seeking out and striking a bargain with other traders. By splitting barter transactions into purchases and sales which are independent of one another, money eliminates the need for a coincidence of

12. Adam Smith, *The Wealth of Nations*, Cannan edition (New York: Random House, Modern Library, 1937), p. 7.

13. *Ibid.*, p. 17.

14. Smith actually went farther than this in illustrating his point: he asserted that in the early phases of the development of specialization, prior to the invention of money, "exchanging must frequently have been very much clogged and embarrassed in its operations." Since there is no way by which we can know how effectively exchanges were being carried out just prior to the invention of money (if this could be dated), Smith's speculations on this matter must be regarded as purely conjectural.

desires as a condition for a successful exchange and greatly reduces the time and effort that would otherwise be expended in marketing. This contributes to economic efficiency and is essential to the development of regional, national, and international markets that have fostered and sustained the mass production methods of modern industrialized countries.

An effectively operating monetary mechanism is a necessary but not a sufficient condition for a highly productive economy. The latter depends primarily on the existence of a favorable combination of "real" factors—a skilled and energetic work force, abundant and readily accessible natural resources, and a large stock of up-to-date capital equipment. These factors are so important in influencing economic welfare that many economists of the nineteenth and early twentieth centuries looked upon money as a "veil" which tends to obscure real relationships but has no independent effect on economic activity. In the words of John Stuart Mill,

> There cannot . . . be intrinsically a more insignificant thing, in the economy of society, than money; except in the character of a contrivance for sparing time and labour. It is a machine for doing quickly and commodiously, what would be done, though less quickly and commodiously, without it; and like many other types of machinery, it only exerts a distinct and independent influence of its own when it gets out of order.[15]

Within the past generation or so economists have increasingly taken the view that the classical economists as exemplified by Mill went too far in de-emphasizing the role of money as a determinant of economic welfare. To some extent this has been a result of increased recognition of important features of the economy affecting the role of money (such as inflexible prices and wages and the existence of uncertainty) which Mill tended to ignore. It has also been due, in part, to observation from experience among Western capitalist economies since 1914 that monetary mechanisms tend to be "out of order" more frequently than was envisaged by earlier economists. This was particularly evident in the United States in the inflation and sharp deflation during and after World War I (1918-1921), in the Great Depression of the 1930's, and in the significant inflationary episodes following World War II (1946-1948, 1950-1952). Chronic monetary disorder has been evident not only in most individual economies, but also in the machinery of international exchange since the disruption of the international gold standard during World War I.

With the growth of economic interdependence, national and international, and the increase in wealth among the highly industrialized societies, economic instability has become a more pressing economic problem. Increased interdependence has widened the ramifications of fluctuations in incomes and prices, while greater wealth has increased both living standards

15. John Stuart Mill, *Principles of Political Economy*, Ashley edition (New York: Longmans, Green, 1926), p. 488.

and the importance of economic security as a goal of economic activity. This has tended to shift the focus of economic theory from the problem of the allocation of resources in a fully employed economy to a concern with short-period determinants of the level of economic activity. At the same time, the cold war competition between the United States and the Soviet Union and the growing concern with the extreme poverty of a large part of the world's population have directed increased attention to the conditions of long-term economic growth.

While this has tended to bring about a longer time perspective in economic analysis, there has also been increased recognition of the fact that since longer periods are composed of a series of linked shorter periods, short-run instability may have adverse repercussions on economic growth over more extended periods. The size of the money stock and the changing attitudes of the public and business toward holding and spending money are important determinants of short-run instability. From the standpoint of understanding and regulating both instability and economic growth, therefore, it is important "that we do use the mechanism of money, and that we have learnt so imperfectly to control it."[16]

An Introduction to Monetary Analysis

In the traditional view, the effects of a change in the money stock were conceived as simple and direct. An increase in the supply of money, leading to more money in the hands of the public than they needed or were willing to hold to mediate transactions, was thought of as resulting in an increase in total expenditures for output.[17] Since a full employment level of output was assumed to be the normal state of affairs, any increase in monetary expenditure would result in a rise in the price level. A decrease in the money supply, following the same analysis, would lead to a shortage of balances in relation to the volume of monetary expenditures, a reduction of expenditures in an attempt to build up balances to the desired size, and, given the level of output, a fall in prices.

Thus the line of argument ran from a change in the money supply, to a corresponding change in the flow of monetary expenditures, to a corresponding change in the level of prices. Except during periods of adjustment, the effects of monetary change were conceived as purely nominal. That is, all price tags would be written up or down, but the substantive elements of the economy would be essentially unaffected—real output and employment, real wealth, the rate of growth, levels of interest rates and

---

16. D. H. Robertson, *op. cit.*, p. 1.

17. It was assumed that the rate of turnover, or velocity of circulation, of money would be unaffected by changes in its quantity and could be assumed to be constant. Independent changes in volocity were recognized as a potential source of change in total expenditures, which would have effects similar to those of changes in the money stock.

real wages, and the relative values of goods and services. All these were explained in the branches of analysis called the "theory of value" and the "theory of distribution," whereas the province of monetary theory was the price level.

In recent years this form of the traditional analysis has been extensively modified. In part the change has stemmed from a new range of objectives growing out of new issues and problems—stability of employment and economic growth, as opposed to preoccupation with stability of the price level. In part it is a product of theoretical sophistication which has re-examined the classical premises and, in an attempt to make the analysis relevant to the problems of the modern era, has extended its conditions to include the effects of uncertainty and imperfections of competition in factor and output markets.

In this somewhat more complicated analysis, the sharp distinction between money and other assets becomes blurred so that money as an asset differs only in degree from those claims classified as "near-moneys," somewhat more from those lower in the liquidity scale, and so on through the entire hierarchy of assets. The motives for holding money become more complex, while the results of change in the money stock become less certain and less direct. Monetary theory becomes a part of general economic analysis, concerned with both the real and nominal effects of monetary change.

In explaining the effect of a change in the money supply, the traditional theory traces a direct relationship between the stock of money and the level of total expenditures, while in modern analysis monetary change affects expenditure through more complex and indirect channels. Monetary change is conceived as affecting the price of financial assets (therefore interest rates), which in turn affects consumption and investment expenditures and thus total spending. Any increase in expenditures for output appears in the markets for goods and services as an increase in demand. The specific results will depend on conditions of supply in the related markets. To the extent that supply is responsive to an increase in demand (elastic), as with extensive excess capacity and unemployment, we should expect the primary effect to be an expansion of output with accompanying price rises of lesser importance. To the extent that supply is unresponsive (inelastic), we should expect the importance of these effects to be reversed.

In this analysis, although an increase in the money supply will tend to be expansionary and a decrease contractionary, the degree of effect may be widely variable over time under diverse circumstances. The effect would depend directly on (1) the degree of bond price (i.e., interest) change induced, (2) the extent to which easier credit terms may encourage additional borrowing and spending, (3) the sensitivity of consumption spending to changes in the market price of securities, and (4) the degree to which output tends to expand in response to an increase in demand.[18] Clearly, there is no easy, short, or simple guide to monetary analysis.

Finally, some of the effects of monetary change would be "real," with implications for welfare, e.g., changes in output, employment, interest rates, and conceivably the rate of economic growth. In these respects the effects of monetary change are more than nominal, and money is more than a "veil." But these results should not be exaggerated. Money is not wealth, and money must exert its influence within the limits of productive possibilities as conditioned by resources and technology. It is possible, indeed likely, that the effects of monetary change may be weak under easily conceived circumstances, as might be implied by particular combinations of influences listed in the previous paragraph. And even where significant, if supply is inelastic the forces of monetary change may spend themselves primarily in influencing prices as in the economic world of John Stuart Mill.

SELECTED BIBLIOGRAPHY

DAY, A. C. L., and S. T. BEZA, *Money and Income*. New York: Oxford University Press, 1960, Chapters 1 and 2.

ELLIS, HOWARD S., *German Monetary Theory*. Cambridge: Harvard University Press, 1934, Part I.

HAWTREY, R. G., *Currency and Credit*. London: Longmans, Green, 1950, Chapter I.

KEYNES, J. M., *A Treatise on Money*. New York: Harcourt, Brace, 1930, Book I.

ROBERTSON, D. H., *Money*. London: Nisbet, 1948, Chapter I.

SHAW, E. S., *Money, Income, and Monetary Policy*. Homewood, Ill.: Irwin, 1950, Chapter I.

---

18. Each of these relationships, in turn, may be influenced by a variety of forces which require more extended analysis.

2

MONEY TYPES AND
STANDARDS

In this chapter we examine the various kinds of money and the principal ways in which they may be classified, the nature, types and significance of monetary standards, and the historical development of money types in Western societies.

KINDS OF MONEY

The index of a well-known book on primitive money lists 170 objects and materials which have been used as money, ranging alphabetically from adzes to yarn.[1] Included are such diverse items as slaves, gunpowder, cigarets, woodpecker scalps, dog teeth, and cowrie shells. They range in weight from elephants and the stone money of Yap in the South Pacific to the feather money of the New Hebrides. For generations salt has circulated as money among the natives of Ethiopia, without being supplanted by the gold and silver coins or paper claims of the traders with whom the natives came into contact. To the westerner who is accustomed to other monetary forms, these types of money seem strange and unsatisfactory, but to the people who use them they appear natural and quite serviceable. The wide variety of acceptable monetary substances, past and present, and the continuous gradual change in the composition of money within our own society suggests that there is no such thing as a "natural" money appropriate to all times and places.

Physical Types

One of the most familiar ways in which to classify money is on the basis of physical form. According to this criterion, there are three prin-

1. Paul Einzig, *Primitive Money* (London: Eyre and Spottiswoode, 1949).

cipal kinds of money: (1) metallic coins, (2) paper money, and (3) deposit money. The first two categories, coins and paper money, are commonly grouped together and designated as "currency," or by the descriptive titles "hand-to-hand money" or "pocketbook money." Deposit money we have already seen to be demand liabilities of commercial banks which are transferable by check.

The physical characteristics of these three kinds of money have an important bearing on their uses and quantitative importance in the money supply. Metallic coins are bulky and relatively inconvenient to transport, and they may be easily lost or stolen. In the United States, as in most highly developed countries, they are used only in retail trade in the form of coins of small denomination (one dollar and less).[2] Confined to this narrow sphere, coins constitute a relatively minor fraction of our money supply (less than 2 per cent), but they play a distinctive and indispensable role in retail trade. In the United States they are issued exclusively by the Treasury, which does so on notice from the Federal Reserve Banks that their stocks of particular denominations are running low.

Paper money in the United States is issued in denominations of $1 to $10,000, with two-thirds of the dollar volume in denominations of $20 or less. In terms of volume outstanding, paper money is considerably more important than coin, but it is still essentially a larger denomination complement to coin in retail trade. It has the advantage over coin of being less bulky and more flexible in denomination, but it is bulkier and less safe than deposit money. Although the right to issue paper money was held by commercial banks chartered by the United States (national banks) until 1935, at present only the Treasury and Federal Reserve Banks possess this power. The Federal Reserve Banks issue over 90 per cent of all paper money and 85 per cent of the total dollar volume of currency outstanding; the Treasury provides the remainder. Since the smallest denomination of paper money now issued by the Federal Reserve Banks is the $5 bill, the Treasury is the principal issuer of small denomination currency, supplying all coins and $1 and $2 bills, as well as some $5 and $10 bills.

Deposit money issued by commercial banks constitutes almost four-fifths of the money stock in the hands of the public. Because it is transferable by check, it is the least bulky of the three kinds of money. It is completely flexible with respect to amount held and transferred, and it is the safest type of money. Because of its flexibility and safety, deposit money is predominant in mediating financial and other business transactions. And it is important in retail trade where larger sums of money are involved.

---

2. See Table 2-1, page 22, for a listing of the coins now issued by the United States Treasury.

Full-bodied and Token Money

Another classification, useful for the analysis of monetary standards and problems connected therewith, rests on the relationship between the value of monetary objects *as money*, on the one hand, and their value in their best alternative uses, on the other. A silver dollar, for example, which contains 412.5 grains of metal, 90 per cent of which is silver and 10 per cent copper, has a monetary value of one dollar, given by the face value of the coin. The value of this quantity of silver and copper in their best alternative uses depends on the market quotations of these metals. If the market values of the metals included in this coin add up to one dollar, the silver dollar would be referred to as *full-bodied money*, which may be defined as money whose value is not substantially greater than that of its component materials. Since the market value of the metals included in the silver dollar is less than a dollar, this coin falls into the category of *token money*, i.e., money whose value as money is appreciably greater than that of the matter of which it is composed.

Full-bodied money is usually encountered only where a country has a commodity standard such as the gold standard, with the standard commodity circulating in the form of coin. For example, prior to the withdrawal of gold from circulation in 1933 gold coins were full-bodied money in the United States. That is to say, melted down and sold as gold they would have yielded a sum approximately equal to the face value of the melted coins. The conditions under which a full-bodied money such as existed under our pre-1933 gold standard can be established and maintained, and the advantages and disadvantages of having a full-bodied money are discussed below in connection with monetary standards.

All money in domestic circulation in the United States today is token money: in every instance its value as money exceeds the market value of its component materials by a substantial margin. For paper money the commodity value of the money stuff is negligible, and with deposit money we attain the ultimate in token quality since there is literally no component material. Coins are the only money in domestic circulation in the United States that have any substantial commodity value. Nevertheless, their token character may be seen from Table 2-1, where the money value, commodity content, and commodity value of our circulating coins are given for a date in the early 1960's. This table shows that in no case was the commodity value of our circulating coins as much as 75 per cent of the monetary value at which these coins circulated. In the case of the nickel the commodity value of the coin was less than 10 per cent of its value as money.

Why will people accept at face value money which is without equivalent worth in commodity markets? Basically they do so because they know it will be accepted freely by others in the normal operation of an exchange

TABLE 2-1. Monetary Value, Commodity Content, and Commodity Value of Circulating Coins in the United States, September, 1960

Coin	Gross Weight in Grains	Components	Market Value of Commodity Contained in Coins (in Cents)
Dollar	412.5	90% Silver 10% Copper	70.9
Half dollar	192.9	90% Silver 10% Copper	33.1
Quarter	96.45	90% Silver 10% Copper	16.6
Dime	38.58	90% Silver 10% Copper	6.6
Nickel	77.16	75% Copper 25% Nickel	0.4
Penny	48.00	95% Copper 5% Tin and Zinc	0.2

economy. The money function is important, and claims which have negligible commodity value but which carry out this function effectively circulate readily at much higher monetary values as a result of an implicit social convention. To each money is acceptable and valuable because it is known that it will be accepted by others.

In order to ensure public acceptance of token money, governments must control the quantity of money so as to maintain reasonable stability in its value. In most countries today this requires that the monetary authorities restrict their own issuance of money and exercise direct and indirect controls over money issued by commercial banks (demand deposits),[3] according to some end or ends deemed central to monetary policy.[4]

Public acceptability of token money may at times be encouraged by providing for redemption of money in some standard commodity at the discretion of the holder. At a certain stage in economic development when the state is weak and the social convention precarious, the redemption privilege may be useful for assuring the general acceptability of money. Under modern conditions, however, where the relationship of token money to a commodity such as gold has become remote, it is the convention of general acceptability, however this originated, which makes money valuable, not its redeemability in gold. Where gold is in substantial demand as a "reserve" of monetary systems, it may be truer to say that the value of gold depends on its use as money than that the value of money depends on the value of gold.[5]

---

3. It should be obvious that if there is a possibility of overissue of token money by governments, the threat would be much greater still if private parties were permitted to issue token money without restraint. For an example of conditions under virtually unregulated private rights of money issue, see Chapter 11.

4. For example, to seek reasonable price-level stability, or high levels of employment, or a rapid rate of economic growth, or some combination of these ends.

5. D. H. Robertson, writing in a period when gold coins still circulated in a number

Legal Tender Money

Certain kinds of currency are usually endowed by government with legal tender powers, for the dual purpose of increasing their acceptability and clarifying the legal position of debtor and creditor in discharging obligations calling for money payments. Legal tender is that money which a creditor has no legal right to refuse if offered by a debtor in fulfillment of a general monetary obligation.[6] The refusal by a creditor to accept an offer of legal tender money does not discharge the debt, but in most states it releases the debtor from further interest payments and from penalties for default of contract from the time of the offer and refusal of payment.[7]

Until 1933 the various currencies in circulation in the United States had legal tender powers to varying degrees. Gold coins and gold certificates were legal tender to an unlimited degree, and silver dollars were legal tender unless specifically excluded by contract. United States notes ("greenbacks") were also legal tender except for payment of custom duties and interest on the public debt. Other paper money issued by the Treasury, Federal Reserve Banks, and commercial banks was acceptable by the federal government for ordinary tax payments but was not legal tender in private transactions. Subsidiary coins (half-dollars and smaller denominations) were legal tender for only limited amounts.[8]

---

of countries, imagined the following little speech by an angry five-pound note that had just been accused of being "a little flimsy and anaemic" as compared with a gold coin:

"And let me tell you this, too, if a great many of those haughty gold coins were to lose their money job simultaneously, they wouldn't be worth as much as they flatter themselves they would, not by a long way. They think men run after them so because they're strong and handsome, and so it was, when men were savages. But the chief reason men run after them now is because they're *money*. If one of them gives up the money profession while the rest stick to it, he's worth what he was before, because he can always get a money job again. But if they all got the sack at once, goodness knows where they'd be: for this dentistry yarn has worn a bit thin—there aren't all that number of rickety teeth in the world." *Op. cit.*, pp. 49-50.

6. If a contract calls for payment in some specific good or form of money, this is not a general monetary obligation and the offer of legal tender will not fulfill the contract. In the United States prior to 1933, many billions of dollars of contracts called for the payment of a certain physical quantity or number of dollars worth of gold. With the withdrawal of gold from circulation in the United States in 1933 such contracts became unenforceable. At that point Congress abrogated all contractual gold payment requirements, making them payable in legal tender money.

7. In the Colonial period and during the time of the American Revolution, non-acceptance of legal tender sometimes resulted in forfeiture of debt. Marco Polo reported that in China in the thirteenth century, the refusal to accept imperial money was punishable by death.

Why should a creditor ever refuse to accept legal tender? For one thing, in a serious inflation legal tender money may depreciate to such an extent that its acceptance by a creditor may be tantamount to cancellation of the debt. A second reason for refusal to accept legal tender money may be its momentary inconvenience. For example, a businessman may not wish to accept payment of a large sum of legal tender currency after banking hours because of the possible danger of loss through theft.

8. Fractional silver coins—half-dollars, quarters, and dimes—were legal tender for a debt up to ten dollars; minor coins—nickels and pennies—were legal tender for obligations of 25 cents or less.

By the Legal Tender Act of June 5, 1933, the Congress abolished all differences in legal tender powers among circulating currencies. According to this legislation:

> All coins and currencies of the United States (including Federal Reserve notes and circulating notes of Federal Reserve banks and national banking associations) heretofore or hereafter coined or issued shall be legal tender for all debts, public and private, public charges, taxes, duties and dues, except that gold coin when below the standard weight and limit of tolerance provided by law for the single piece, shall be legal tender only at valuations in proportion to their actual weight.

How important is the granting of legal tender powers in making money generally acceptable? Normally it is not a very significant factor, as we may infer from the steady growth in importance of demand deposits, which are not legal tender. We tend to accept all kinds of money indifferently, and it is only when the monetary system is subject to serious strain that the question of legal tender rights becomes of widespread public interest. Even under conditions of breakdown, however, it is by no means certain that the legal tender money will be accepted and non-legal tender money rejected. In the German inflation of 1922-1923, non-legal tender money such as privately issued paper and foreign currencies tended to be substituted for the rapidly depreciating mark, which became increasingly unacceptable despite its legal tender qualities. Legal tender powers may increase the acceptability of a money to some degree, but the grant of such powers is neither a necessary nor a firm assurance of acceptability.

MONETARY STANDARDS

The concept "monetary standard" relates to the nature and conditions of issue of the ultimate money of the system. The latter, commonly referred to as "standard money," is that money in which the monetary authority itself may ultimately discharge its obligations. (In other words, it is the legal tender money applicable to the debts of the monetary authority.) To be on a particular monetary standard is to have that form of money as the standard money. Thus under a gold standard circulating currencies which are debts of the monetary authority (or which are convertible into such debts, as in the case of commercial bank notes and deposits) are redeemable on fixed terms in gold; i.e., gold is the standard money with which the monetary authority must discharge its debt obligations.

There are two main types of monetary standards—commodity standards and non-commodity or paper standards. Each of these types of standards may be divided into subclasses as follows: [9]

---

9. This schedule includes well-known actual and proposed monetary standards but is not offered as all inclusive.

Commodity Standards {
  Monometallism
  Bimetallism
  Symmetallism
  Composite commodity money
}

Paper Standards {
  Free
  Controlled
}

Commodity Standards

The best-known commodity (and monometallic) standard is gold, although, as was noted earlier, many other metals and other substances have served, at one time or another, as the standard money. The operating mechanics of the gold standard are representative of any monometallic standard and contribute to an understanding of other monetary standards as well. To be "on the gold standard" is to maintain equality between the monetary value of the currency and the value of a given weight of gold in a free market. The various provisions for establishing and maintaining the gold standard have their justification as a means to this end. It is not the means but the end—that of maintaining equality between the value of currency and a stipulated amount of gold—that constitutes the essence of the gold standard. This end is ordinarily achieved by maintaining *interconvertibility* between circulating currencies and gold. Interconvertibility means that currency is redeemable in gold and gold is exchangeable for currency, each at a fixed ratio between gold and currency. The effect of maintaining interconvertibility is to assure an equality of value (i.e., purchasing power) between a unit of currency and a specific quantity of gold. since any departure from this relationship would induce corrective responses under free-market conditions.

For example, before 1933 the dollar was defined as 23.22 grains of pure gold, and the federal government was prepared to coin gold (or to provide other forms of currency) in unlimited quantities, though subject to a nominal charge, at the rate of one dollar for every 23.22 grains of gold offered to it. This was equivalent to establishing a fixed purchase price of $20.67 per ounce of gold (there are 480 grains in an ounce), and this became the minimum market price for gold since nobody would sell gold for less as long as the government would buy it or permit it to be coined at the rate of $20.67 per ounce. With a fixed purchase price an increase in supply would simply cause gold to be converted into money at a faster rate. This would tend to increase incomes, expenditures, prices, and costs, including the cost of producing gold, and, since the *price* of gold is fixed, the rise in costs and a decline in what it would buy would eventually retard gold output and the influx of new money. Thus under the gold standard an inflationary increase in the rate of gold production tended to be self-limiting.

On the other hand, if the market price of gold tended to rise above $20.67, circulating coins would be melted down and used in non-monetary applications, and the government would redeem circulating currency from its own stocks of gold. By reducing the volume of gold in monetary use and increasing the amount available in commodity markets, any substantial rise above the established price would be prevented. Under these conditions an ounce of gold could be converted into currency or sold as a commodity for approximately the same sum; it follows that the maintenance of interconvertibility is also a means of assuring that circulating standard commodity money is full bodied.

The gold standard is said to be international when countries maintain interconvertibility between domestic currency and gold and allow the free export and import of gold. The effect of interconvertibility is to maintain equality of value between currency and gold within the country; the effect of free export and import of gold is to maintain equality between the value of gold in the country and its value outside the country. These two conditions constitute the requirements of the international gold standard for the simple reason that when they are observed the identity in value between currency and gold in the world market is assured, and without them a continuing identity in value is improbable if not impossible.

A number of different types of gold standard have existed at one time or another. They differ primarily in the provisions governing interconvertibility between currency and gold. The most familiar type is the gold coin standard which existed in this country until 1933. Under the gold coin standard, currency was interconvertible with gold on the initiative of anyone and in quantities as small as the smallest gold coin available. Under the gold bullion standard, on the other hand, currency is convertible into gold only in large amounts, and there may be the further qualification that only certain specified groups, such as foreign central banks, may exercise the privilege of redemption in gold.

By the Gold Reserve Act of 1934, the Secretary of the Treasury, subject to approval by the President, was given unusual power in the administration of the gold standard. He was authorized to "purchase gold in any amounts, at home or abroad . . . at such rates and upon such terms and conditions as he may deem most advantageous to the public interest."[10] At one time qualifications such as these would have been considered inconsistent with adherence to a true gold standard, which assumed a fixed price for gold. Nevertheless, the 1934 Act is generally accepted as having placed the United States on a "modified" gold bullion standard. It is this that constitutes our present monetary standard.

Under the gold exchange standard, currency is convertible not into gold coin or bullion but into drafts payable in the currency of some country

10. *The Federal Reserve Act* as amended through December 31, 1956 (Washington: Board of Governors of the Federal Reserve System, 1956), pp. 194-95.

which is on the gold standard. Since foreign exchange payable in gold will be approximately equal in value to gold, the gold exchange standard assures an equality of value between domestic currency and a fixed weight of gold and is consequently a genuine form of the gold standard.

Bimetallism exists when two metals are standard money at a fixed ratio in terms of one another. Unless the relationship is firmly fixed, we might have a dual standard but not bimetallism. The legally established ratio between the two metals is known as the mint ratio.

Under symmetallism the standard would consist of a single metallic unit in the form of a combination of different metals in legally established proportions. The standard money would be the combination of metals rather than a single metal or pair of metals. The composition of the combination would be rigidly prescribed with a view to providing greater stability of value than would be possible with one metal only.

The proposed composite commodity money resembles symmetallism, but the standard unit, instead of consisting of metals only, would be made up of an assorted list of staple commodities. As in symmetallism, these different commodities would be combined in fixed proportions.

Identity between the purchasing power of currency and that of the standard unit or units would be maintained under bimetallism, symmetallism, and composite commodity money by the same device as it is under the gold standard, namely, by means of interconvertibility and free export and import of the standard commodity or commodities. Neither symmetallism nor composite commodity money has actually been applied in practice.

Non-commodity or Paper Standards

In a country on a paper standard, money is not convertible on fixed terms into any specific commodity or collection of commodities. Such a standard is sometimes called an *inconvertible* paper standard, an expression which is redundant since the term "paper standard" necessarily implies inconvertibility with any standard commodity. A *free* paper standard is distinguished from the controlled type in that exchange dealings between that currency and foreign currencies are relatively unrestricted; exchange rates are allowed considerable latitude to fluctuate, although the government or some other official organization may undertake to exercise a steadying influence, as through the operations of an exchange stabilization fund.

With a *controlled* paper standard, exchange dealings, and consequently exchange rates in terms of foreign currencies, are strictly regulated. During the 1930's when the German reichsmark was a controlled paper standard currency, international economic transactions such as foreign trade, travel, and capital movements were subject to the most rigid and arbitrary regulations. Instead of a single free-market quotation for the reichsmark in terms of the dollar, there were a dozen or more different quotations, each applying to a particular type of transaction and all established by bureaucratic methods. Various degrees of controlled paper standards continued after World War II; even as late as the 1960's some fifteen of the sixty-seven countries affiliated with the International Monetary Fund maintained multiple exchange rates.

The Importance of the Monetary Standard

The question of what is the best monetary standard has been perhaps the most bitterly contested of all monetary issues. During the earlier part of the nineteenth century the controversy centered around the relative merits of various types of commodity standard, particularly gold, silver, and bimetallism. During the second half of the nineteenth century the competing standards were gold, bimetallism, and paper. The gold standard became firmly entrenched both within the United States and internationally in the late nineteenth and early twentieth centuries. Nonetheless, World War I brought about its widespread abandonment, and the rehabilitation of the gold standard between 1918 and 1929 was slow and incomplete. The Great Depression of the 1930's was accompanied by an even more general abandonment of the gold standard and by a more profound questioning of its theoretical and practical merits. The standards which have been established since the breakdown of the 1930's do not fit easily into the categories of paper or commodity—they contain elements of both in varying proportions.[11]

Why has the question of the monetary standard been such a source of controversy? Basically, because people hold strong and very different views as to desirable monetary policy, and because the choice of a monetary standard may call for particular lines of monetary action or circumscribe the range of discretion of the monetary authorities. Where the money supply is tied by law or strong tradition to a stock of commodity (or commodities), it is subject both to a physical limitation and to the necessity of maintaining an environment conducive to "confidence" on the part of money holders in the redeemability of token money. Critics would argue that maintenance of convertibility may get in the way of other desirable objectives. For example, during a period of declining income and employment a stabilizing policy would require *expansionary* monetary and fiscal policies, while maintaining or improving the ability to meet prospective gold drains might require, on the contrary, a *contractionary* policy. Under these circumstances the choice might be fuller employment *or* the gold standard. It is the potential strength—and at the same time weakness—of commodity standards that they necessarily limit the range of discretionary monetary policies.[12]

11. See further, Chapter 3.

12. In addition to reducing the discretionary power of the monetary authority some writers have maintained that a commodity standard has a deflationary bias on the ground that deflationary policies improve the reserve position of the monetary authority,

Undesired deflationary pressures will exist in a commodity standard at a time when the stock of standard commodity is increasing sluggishly as compared with the expansion of economic activity and the growth in the demand for money. This was the situation in the United States for most of the period between the close of the Civil War and the end of the nineteenth century. It is also possible for the stock of the commodity used as standard money to expand more rapidly than is consistent with price level stability because of discoveries or improvements in technical processes, as was so under the international gold standard from about 1896 to 1914.

With "debt money" there is no physical limitation to the volume that may be issued so that the prevention of excessive creation of money under a paper standard depends on the stability of the society and the intelligence and sense of responsibility of those with the power to influence monetary policy. The classic examples of monetary breakdown—in Germany in the early 1920's and in China, Greece, and Hungary in the middle 1940's— occurred when these conditions were not met. The historical evidence and certain aspects of the budgetary process in contemporary democratic societies (welfare and log-rolling pressures for increased expenditures, the disagreeableness of tax increases, and the possibly greater political inexpediency of permitting unemployment rather than moderate inflation) suggest that paper standards may be expected to have an inflationary bias. It should be noted, however, that historical evidence on the inflationary character of paper reflects to some degree the fact that under conditions of extreme political and economic disorder commodity standards are invariably abandoned, leaving the more flexible paper standard to bear the brunt of a difficult situation. The paper standard may permit the subsequent inflation, but its causes are usually more deeply rooted.

Advocates of commodity standards such as gold are likely to fall into one or more of three groups: (1) creditors, who have a vested economic interest in a high value of money and consequently are likely to favor monetary standards that sharply restrict its supply; (2) those engaged in or affiliated with the gold mining business; (3) those who doubt the capacity of governments to prevent inflationary increases in the money supply without some firm rule such as the gold standard provides compelling such limitation, or who prefer reliance on "natural market forces" to government regulation on ideological grounds.

Opponents of commodity standards (advocates of a managed paper standard) are likely to include the following: (1) debtors, who have a vested economic interest in a decline in the value of money; (2) those who favor

---

whereas expansion always poses the threat of a weakening or exhaustion of reserves. The alleged deflationary bias is attributed, in part, to the fact, that deflationary policies tend to improve a country's balance of payments—the lower prices and incomes stimulate exports and retard imports, and thus either increase international monetary reserves or tend to reduce their rate of outflow. Moreover, tight money and higher interest rates would tend to improve the reserve position of the monetary authority by attracting foreign balances and reducing domestic commercial bank expansion.

rules such as stabilization of the price level or the quantity of money, rather than the rules implicit in a commodity standard; (3) those who feel that the arbitrary limitations imposed on monetary and fiscal policies, and the possibility of inappropriate fluctuations in the money supply under a commodity standard, are much too high a price to pay for restraints on governmental abuse.

MONETARY DEVELOPMENT

Usefulness Versus Uselessness

Early money was often, though not always, some useful substance. The ox of ancient Greece was thoroughly useful. So was the original drachma of the later period of Greek history (*drachma* means "handful," in this instance a handful of iron nails). The pound and such corresponding forms in other languages as livre and lira arose when more exact measures of weight were adopted. Pound sterling signified a particularly accurate and reliable pound weight of silver.

In the evolution of the money material there seems to have been a tendency to move from the more useful substance to the less useful and more ornamental. The close relation between money and ornamentation is attested by the popularity of silver and gold, two of the most ornamental of metals. It is further illustrated by the frequent use of coins as ornaments —a practice which serves to explain the issuance of coins with holes in them to make them suitable for stringing and the great number of old coins in which holes have been punched to facilitate stringing.

There are good reasons for regarding uselessness in a money substance —uselessness, that is, except for purposes of ornamentation—as a virtue. These reasons are supported by logic as well as by history. First, in a grave emergency like famine or war a necessity, such as cattle or grain, would be consumed even though it were the standard money. Whatever the merits of this arrangement from other points of view, it is a serious disadvantage from the monetary standpoint since it would mean the destruction of the medium of exchange. Second, necessities tend to be characterized by inelastic demand. As a result, their value is subject to greater fluctuation than that of luxuries. Stability of value is a virtue in the money material; luxuries, because of their more elastic demand, tend to meet this test more successfully than necessities.

From Commodity Money to Debt Money

From the various terms—pecuniary, pound, and lira—which recall the commodity origins of money it is a long step to the expressions "bank note" and "dollar bill," for both note and bill are words relating to debt. This step from terms denoting physical assets to terms implying debt is of great significance in the history of money. Whereas all the other terms show a steady progression in the development of commodity money, "note" and "bill" represent a sharp break with the past. They reflect a stage of monetary evolution when money which represented an actual physical asset had been left behind and pure claim (debt) money had emerged.

The contrast between commodity money and debt money is clearly illustrated by the terms "pound sterling" and "bank note." The first originally meant, as was mentioned above, a given weight of a specified substance— silver. Bank note, on the other hand, merely meant a bank's promise to pay some other type of money on demand. It was a bank's promissory note.

For a long time, debt money retained a link with the past in the form of legal and other connections with some commodity base—usually gold. That is to say, the bank note was a promise to pay some sort of commodity money. In the course of time even this connection became more tenuous or disappeared. In many countries of the world, debt money now stands alone without even the pretense of commodity backing. Moreover, debt money has assumed a variety of forms, of which demand deposits or "checkbook money" is now the most common.

The evolution from commodity money to debt money was accomplished only gradually. For the most part, moreover, the process was haphazard and accidental. Ordinarily, legislators did not meet together and work out some new monetary standard. Instead, the monetary standard originated spontaneously (oxen, wampum, gold, gold exchange), and later the legislators enacted into statutory law what economic forces and custom had already brought about. Usually the laws both here and abroad lagged far behind events. The gold standard existed in England for a hundred years before it was accorded legal recognition. Throughout most of the history of the United States the *de facto* monetary standard differed from the *de jure* standard—from 1792 to 1879 this country, *de facto*, was successively on the silver standard, the gold standard, and the paper standard, but nominally (i.e., in terms of the metals defined as standard) we were on a bimetallic standard until 1873 and then on the gold standard.

A change from one type of commodity money to another, though important, did not involve a major shift in the basis of monetary policy. Whether a country used silver or gold, the total volume of money and changes in its amount were still subject to the limitations imposed by the physical character of the money substance. Thus the basis of the automatic regulation of the volume of money remained, even though the particular commodity used as money was different. Adoption of debt money as the standard, on the other hand, removes the basis of the automatic regulation of the money supply by means of market changes affecting the money commodity. While it would be possible to devise a system of debt money which would operate automatically, the effect of the spread of debt money was to diminish the influence of automatic forces and to increase greatly the role of monetary management throughout the world. It is important to observe that the rise of monetary management came about largely by default, i.e., through countries being "driven off" commodity standards rather than by deliberate choice in the sense that management was desired or preferred.

Changed Conceptions Concerning Desirable Monetary Qualities

It may be inferred from the foregoing discussion, as well as from everyday experience, that evidences of the commodity origin of money have largely disappeared. We no longer encounter gold money, and even silver money circulates, as paper money does, at a monetary value above that of the commodity it contains. The commodity origins of money continue, however, to exert an influence on many of our prevailing monetary conceptions. One example is probably the familiar nostalgia for the old-fashioned form of the gold standard. Another is the fact that it is still customary for many textbooks to list the well-known qualities of a desirable money material which were suggested by Jevons in the nineteenth century, namely, portability, divisibility, homogeneity, cognizability, durability, and stability of value. And more likely than not, it is maintained that gold possesses these qualities in greater degree than any other material.

The idea that gold money is more easily recognized than paper money is a survival from the days when the art of engraving was in a primitive stage. Today, the quality of good paper currency is at least as readily discernible as the quality of coins. Paper, whether in the form of currency or checks, is far more portable than any metallic money. Divisibility is perfectly accomplished by the simple method of printing larger or smaller denominations.[13] Gold, on the other hand, is not divisible into small denominations in anything but a purely technical sense; gold coins of a value appreciably under $5.00 would be so small as to be unusable because of the risk of loss. Moreover, when the costs of printing and replacement are compared with the costs of minting and abrasion, the economy of using paper money, even if not its durability, is fully comparable with that of gold or silver.

Only with respect to the final characteristic—value independent of the money use—can paper be said to be definitely inferior to gold, and even here the practical inferiority of paper is open to question. It is far from certain that the value of gold, apart from the value set and maintained by the monetary authorities, is of a very stable character. And if the value of money is subject to regulation by the monetary authorities, it becomes a

13. The almost infinite divisibility of paper money is seen by contemplating the value of a Hungarian one-pengo note after World War II when one quadrillion pengos were worth 25 cents in American money.

question whether the money substance any longer needs to possess an independent value of its own.

SELECTED BIBLIOGRAPHY

CARLILE, W. W., *The Evolution of Modern Money*. London: Macmillan, 1901, Part II, Chapters I-III.

EINZIG, PAUL, *Primitive Money in Its Historical and Economic Aspects*. London: Eyre & Spottiswoode, 1949, Introduction and Book I.

HAWTREY, R. G., *Currency and Credit*. London: Longmans, Green, 1950, Chapter II.

HERSKOVITS, M. J., *Economic Anthropology*. New York: Knopf, 1952, Chapter XI.

JEVONS, W. S., *Money and the Mechanism of Exchange*. New York: Appleton, 1892, Chapters V-IX.

NUSSBAUM, ARTHUR, *Money in the Law*. Brooklyn: Foundation Press, 1950.

SPAHR, SPROUL, and the Douglas and Patman Committees, on Gold and the Monetary System. In L. S. Ritter (ed.), *Money and Economic Activity*. Boston: Houghton Mifflin, 1961, Chapter II.

ROBERTSON, D. H., *Money*. London: Nisbet, 1948, Chapters III-IV.

WHITTLESEY, C. R., *International Monetary Issues*. New York: McGraw-Hill, 1937, Chapters I-III.

3

THE PRESENT MONETARY
STRUCTURE OF THE
UNITED STATES

The Constitution of the United States conferred upon Congress the power to coin money and to "regulate the value thereof." These words may safely be assumed to have referred to the value of the dollar relative to gold or to gold and silver, i.e., "mint parity," the official valuation of the monetary unit in terms of the standard metal or metals. It did not refer, as is sometimes supposed, to the value of money in the sense of its purchasing power over commodities.

Regardless of the interpretation intended by the framers of the Constitution, the provision has not been clearly or strictly construed. Congress, it is true, has passed laws for the issue of particular types of money and has enacted other laws specifying the legal standard. On the other hand, Congress granted authority to the President which enabled him to establish a *de facto* paper standard during the War Between the States. Even wider monetary powers were turned over to the President and the Secretary of the Treasury in 1933. Moreover, banking laws have made it possible for private institutions to issue certain types of circulating medium. When all is said and done, however, it remains true that ultimate power over money, banking, and central banking still rests with Congress.

LEGAL AND ADMINISTRATIVE ORGANIZATION

The Treasury Department embraces the Director of the Mint, who is in charge of the minting of coins, and the Bureau of Printing and Engraving, which manufactures paper money. Also under the Treasury is the Comptroller of the Currency whose principal duty, apart from certain responsibilities with respect to Federal Reserve notes (our principal form of currency), is the supervision of national banks.

The Federal Reserve System is an organization structurally unconnected with the Treasury under the general administration of a board of seven members with headquarters in Washington. It comprises twelve semi-governmental Federal Reserve Banks situated in strategic financial centers throughout the country. The twelve Federal Reserve Banks together with the Board of Governors in Washington are the American equivalent of a central bank and correspond to the Bank of England and other central banks abroad. The Federal Reserve System embraces nearly half the country's commercial banks by number and five-sixths by assets. These are the so-called member banks; they maintain close and vitally important relations with the Federal Reserve Banks.

The Federal Deposit Insurance Corporation was established by the Emergency Banking Act of 1933 and was changed to its present form by legislation enacted two years later. It is federally organized and administered and embraces approximately 98 per cent of all commercial banks. The insured banks hold over 99 per cent of all deposits in commercial banks, though only a little over half of these deposits are covered by insurance. Any deposit in an insured bank is guaranteed against loss up to $10,000, and all deposits in insured banks, including amounts in excess of the $10,000 limit, are subject to an annual assessment to defray the costs of insurance. In addition to taking over the affairs of insured banks in case of failure and handling liquidation proceedings, the FDIC assumes a considerable part of the responsibility for examining and supervising insured banks, and in other ways as well seeks to prevent banks from failing.

The different states charter and supervise banks other than those included in the national banking system. Banking requirements established by state laws vary widely, the standards of some of the states being virtually as high as those imposed by the federal authorities, while those of other states are considerably lower. There are thus fifty-three different banking authorities in the United States—the fifty states plus the three federal organizations. A large number of the country's banks are under three separate jurisdictions —the three federal authorities (Comptroller of the Currency, Federal Reserve System, and the FDIC) or two federal (Federal Reserve System and FDIC) and a state. Only a relatively few are under a single jurisdiction, that of a state. These are the so-called "nonmember, uninsured banks," state banks which remained outside the FDIC.

THE MONETARY STANDARD

The present monetary standard of the United States does not fit easily into a classification based solely on the distinction between paper and commodity standards. Although we shall follow the convention of calling it a "modified gold bullion standard," it might also be described as a modified paper standard with some continuing attachments to gold. Since gold neither circulates as money nor is obtainable by domestic holders of money, standard money for internal purposes in the United States consists of paper issues of the monetary authorities. The abandonment of gold coinage and circulation and the elimination of interconvertibility between gold and domestic money have loosened the tie between gold and the money supply and freed the monetary authorities from restrictions on policy that would follow from a closer attachment to gold. Moreover, such gold movements as still take place between countries no longer govern as they once did the volume of circulating money in the respective shipping and receiving countries. This is due in large part to the fact that monetary authorities have ceased to regard the size of gold reserves as the principal guide to monetary policy; in fact, actions to offset the monetary effects of gold movements in the interests of strictly domestic considerations have become commonplace among the monetary authorities of the leading Western powers.[1]

On the other hand, the United States Treasury maintains a fixed purchase price for gold at $35 an ounce, and all monetary gold and additions to the gold stock must be sold to the Treasury. The Treasury pays for newly purchased gold by writing checks for the required sums on its deposit accounts at the Federal Reserve Banks. This increases the money supply and the reserves of the commercial banks by the amount of the acquired gold. Against the gold thus purchased the Treasury issues an equivalent amount of gold certificates to the Federal Reserve Banks as a means of replenishing the Treasury's deposit accounts at the Reserve Banks. The gold certificates are reserves of the Federal Reserve Banks, so that a Treasury purchase of $1 of gold increases the money supply, bank reserves, and central bank reserves, each by $1.

The United States Treasury also stands ready to redeem gold at $35 per ounce, but ordinarily only in fairly large amounts, in bullion form, and to the order of foreign central banks. Thus, although the general public cannot obtain gold in exchange for circulating currencies, external losses of gold may be sustained by the monetary authorities, which directly affect the money supply and the volume of reserves held by commercial banks and the Federal Reserve Banks. These effects, and the problems raised by a large outflow of gold such as that suffered by the United States in recent

---

1. The typical view may be seen in the Annual Report of the Board of Governors of the Federal Reserve System for 1959, where one of the principal functions of Federal Reserve open-market operations was stated to be "to offset the possible disturbing effects of a variety of seasonal and other market factors that recurringly create or absorb bank reserves. Over the year 1959, the most important market factor absorbing bank reserves was the further outflow of gold from the country" (p. 3). For a further discussion of the "rules of the gold standard game" and the growth of offsetting policies, see Chapter 23.

years, are no longer as important as they were when the money stock was tied more closely to gold, but they cannot be ignored.

THE MONEY SUPPLY OF THE UNITED STATES

When used without qualification, "money supply" will refer to the total stock of domestic means of payment which is owned by the "public," i.e., by individuals, business firms, and state and local governments. We exclude from the money supply of the United States the monetary gold stock, which serves as an international money but is not permitted to circulate within the country; gold certificates, which function as reserves for the twelve Federal Reserve Banks but likewise are not allowed to circulate as domestic means of payment; and currency and demand deposits owned by the Treasury, the Federal Reserve Banks, and the commercial banks, which are money-issuing institutions holding these funds partly as reserves to support publicly owned demand deposits.[2]

As was mentioned earlier, the money supply of the United States consists entirely of *token* issues of currency and demand deposits. The aggregate volume of these issues has expanded enormously during the present century with the most rapid growth taking place in time of war (see Figure 3-1). At the end of World War II the money supply was over sixteen times as great as at the turn of the century. The rate of growth in circulating medium was far more rapid than the increase in population or business activity. In 1945, currency and demand deposits totaled $673 per capita, compared with only $76 in 1900. At the beginning of the 1960's the per capita figure was $764.

The growth in circulating medium has been by no means steady or uniform. As is to be expected, the total, particularly of demand deposits, declined during depressions. The effect of war, on the other hand, was greatly to expand the total and to stimulate the growth of currency considerably more than of deposits. Thus the ratio of currency to deposits which had been falling steadily until 1914 rose from 1915 to 1920, and the same experience was repeated between 1940 and 1945.

The rise in the ratio of currency to deposits that occurred from 1930 to 1933 was caused by bank failures and general lack of confidence in banks. The rise in the proportion of currency to deposits after 1914 and 1940, however, seems to be a characteristic war phenomenon. Various reasons are given for the relatively greater use of currency in time of war: incomes tend to rise more rapidly among "blue-collar workers" who make least

---

2. These exclusions are based partly on the fact that the policy sections of this book are concerned primarily with spending decisions of the public. Also, inclusion of both the cash holdings of money issuers and the monetary superstructure supported by these holdings would involve double counting.

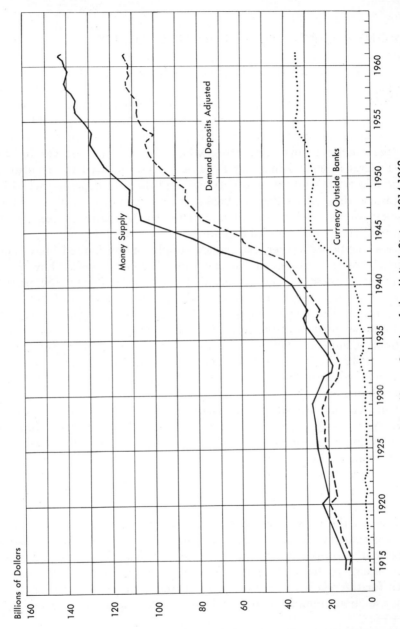

Billions of Dollars

Money Supply

Demand Deposits Adjusted

Currency Outside Banks

Figure 3-1. Money Supply of the United States, 1914-1962.

Source: Data from the *Federal Reserve Bulletin.*

use of banks; banking connections are disrupted by the shifting about of persons in the service and in war industries; high taxation leads to evasion by payments in currency rather than by checks; black markets encourage the use of currency rather than checks.

Currency

At the end of April 1962, total currency issued in the United States and held outside of the Treasury and Federal Reserve Banks was $33.2 billion. This total is broken down into specific issues in Table 3-1.

TABLE 3-1. Currency in Circulation* in the United States, April 30, 1962

Kinds of Currency	Dollars in Circulation* (millions)	Issuer
1. Federal Reserve notes	27,997	Federal Reserve Banks
2. Silver certificates	2,000	U.S. Treasury
3. Subsidiary silver coin	1,638	U.S. Treasury
4. Minor coin	621	U.S. Treasury
5. United States notes	316	U.S. Treasury
6. Standard silver dollars	353	U.S. Treasury
7. In process of retirement	235	U.S. Treasury
Total	33,160	

* Excludes currency held by the Treasury and Federal Reserve Banks, but includes currency holdings of commercial banks.
Source: *Federal Reserve Bulletin.*

It may be noted that the bulk of this sum, an amount equal to 85 per cent of the total volume of currency outstanding, consisted of Federal Reserve notes. The next most important categories were silver certificates, silver dollars, subsidiary silver coin, and minor coin. The remaining types of currency were the relics of earlier monetary legislation. United States notes are the greenbacks which originated during the War Between the States. Currency "in process of retirement" includes national bank notes, Federal Reserve Bank notes, Treasury notes of 1890, and gold certificates. Most of these issues have been lost, destroyed, or absorbed as collector's items.

Federal Reserve notes and Federal Reserve Bank notes, despite the similarity in names, are two distinct forms of currency. The difference between them turned on provisions governing their issuance. Federal Reserve Bank notes, in contrast to Federal Reserve notes, never constituted a major part of the currency supply.[3]

The complexity of the currency structure, however clumsy and illogical

3. A sudden expansion in their volume occurred in 1943 as a result of the issue, because of the wartime shortage of labor and materials for the printing of currency, of several hundred millions of notes which had been printed many years before and subsequently held in storage.

it may appear, is of relatively little consequence; the backbone of the currency system is Federal Reserve notes and small coins. As long as these function satisfactorily, the system as a whole can be regarded as a success by the test that really matters—that of performance.

The particular denominations of currency in circulation as well as the proportion of the total money supply which is held in the form of currency are governed by the actions of individuals. Changes in the total of all currency outstanding or of any particular denomination occur automatically: at any given moment commercial banks, the Reserve Banks, and the Treasury are merely the agents through which the preference of individuals is expressed. "Neither the Federal Reserve Banks nor the Treasury has under ordinary circumstances any direct way of keeping in circulation a larger amount of currency than the public requires or of reducing the amount of currency that the public needs to finance its current operations."[4]

The action of the public in choosing to hold more or less currency or more or less of particular denominations is likely to be influenced by such factors as the physical volume of trade and the prevailing level of prices, the methods by which trade is conducted—as by check or cash—the types of economic activity pursued, and the volume of demand deposits. At times it may be affected by such factors as confidence in the banks and changes in the distribution of the national income among different groups of the population. Methods of Treasury financing, whether by taxation, borrowing from individuals, issue of paper money, or borrowing from banks, may exert an indirect effect on the factors that influence the behavior of individuals.

Demand Deposits

Almost 80 per cent of the money supply of the United States is made up of demand deposit accounts of the public in commercial banks. This understates the importance of checking accounts in the total volume of money payments since the average rate of turnover of deposit money is higher than that of currency. It is estimated, as was noted earlier, that over 90 per cent of the total volume of money payments in the United States is made with deposit money as the medium of exchange.

In computing the net demand liabilities owed by commercial banks to the public (i.e., "adjusted" demand deposits in the language of Federal Reserve publications), we must make some substantial deductions from the total or "gross" demand deposits shown on the books of commercial banks. As can be seen in Table 3-2, adjusted demand deposits of the public are the aggregate of bank demand deposits, less interbank demand balances, demand balances of the Treasury at commercial banks, and "cash items in process of collec-

---

4. Board of Governors of the Federal Reserve System, *Banking Studies* (Washington: 1941), p. 310.

tion."[5] All three of these deducted items are claims of money-issuing institutions against one another, which would cancel out in a consolidation of the balance sheets of all money issuers. When they are subtracted from the total demand deposits of commercial banks, the remainder consists of the net demand claims against commercial banks of non-money issuers, i.e., the public.

TABLE 3-2. Gross and Adjusted Demand Deposits of Insured Commercial Banks, December 31, 1961

Class of Demand Deposit	Dollars (Millions)
1. Individuals, partnership and corporations*	128,901
2. States and political subdivisions	12,149
3. U.S. Government	5,934
4. Interbank, foreign ond domestic	17,738
Gross demand deposits	164,722
Less:	
1. U.S. Government	5,934
2. Interbank, domestic	16,440
3. Cash items in process of collection	20,677
Adjusted demand deposits	121,671

* Includes certified checks, officers' checks, and related items. For an explanation of these items, see pp. 57-58.
Source: *Federal Reserve Bulletin.*

The bulk of the demand deposits of the "public" are owned by individuals, partnerships, and corporations, whose holdings by type of owner are shown in Table 3-3. The most striking features of this table are the predominance of personal accounts of individuals in *number* of accounts and the great importance of non-financial business in *dollar amounts* of deposits held. Personal accounts of individuals contributed 79 per cent of the number and 30 per cent of the dollar amount of the demand deposit accounts of individuals and business concerns; non-financial businesses accounted for less than 10 per cent of the number of accounts and 50 per cent of their dollar volume. It is clear that the average size of account of non-financial businesses is considerably larger than that of the individual depositor.

An analysis of the size distribution of demand deposit accounts of individuals, partnerships, and corporations made a few years ago disclosed that the 102,000 demand deposit accounts of $100,000 or more (which were almost exclusively business balances) accounted for over four times the dollar

5. Cash items in process of collection consist mainly of checks which have been deposited in the banks of their recipients but which have not yet been received by the banks of those drawing the checks. They constitute an element of double-counting in the deposit totals resulting from the time lag involved in the collection of checks: until the account of the drawer of a check is debited, the sum being transferred appears simultaneously on the accounts of the banks of the drawer of the check and its recipient. This source of duplication, generally known as "bank float," can be allowed for by subtracting from gross demand deposits the estimated total of those items received by banks but not yet collected.

TABLE 3-3. Demand Deposits of Individuals, Partnerships, and Corporations, for Insured Commercial Banks, By Type of Holder, January 25, 1961

Type of Holder	Number (Millions)	%	Amount (Billions of dollars)	%
All holders	58.4	100.0	109.0	100.0
Domestic business	6.2	10.7	64.2	58.9
Corporate	2.3	3.9	49.5	45.4
Non-corporate	4.0	6.8	14.7	13.5
(Financial business)	0.5	0.8	10.0	9.2
Corporate	0.3	0.4	8.2	7.5
Non-corporate	0.2	0.3	1.8	1.7
(Non-financial business)	5.8	9.9	54.2	49.7
Corporate	2.0	3.4	41.2	37.8
Non-corporate	3.8	6.4	12.9	11.9
Non-profit organizations	3.0	5.1	5.3	4.8
Farm operators	2.8	4.8	4.1	3.7
Individuals—personal	46.2	79.2	32.4	29.7
All other	0.1	0.2	3.1	2.8

Source: Federal Reserve Bulletin.

volume of demand deposits held by the 41.6 million deposit owners (mainly individuals) with accounts of $1,000 or less (see Table 3-4). Balances of $25,000 or over, which were less than 1 per cent of deposit accounts by number, accounted for 54 per cent of the total volume of individual and business demand deposits. Since these large balances are more active than the smaller accounts, the proportion of deposit transactions carried out by businesses were presumably greater than the share of business firms in the volume of deposit holdings. The predominance of business deposits and other deposits of large size suggests that the behavior of deposits is likely to be shaped largely by businesslike considerations of economic advantage. This fact will prove to be useful in explaining the relationship between the demand for money and other assets and ultimately interest rates.

TABLE 3-4. Demand Deposits of Individuals, Partnerships and Corporations,* for Insured Commercial Banks, By Size of Accounts, January 28, 1959

Size of Account	Number Thousands	Per Cent	Amount Millions	Per Cent
Under $1,000	41,585	80.9	$ 9,107	9.2
$ 1,000-$ 5,000	7,270	14.1	15,754	15.9
5,000- 10,000	1,313	2.6	9,080	9.2
10,000- 25,000	776	1.5	11,669	11.8
25,000- 100,000	366	0.7	16,527	16.7
100,000 and over	102	0.2	36,735	37.2
Total	51,412	100.0	$98,872	100.0

* Excluding deposits of nonprofit organizations, trust departments of banks, and foreigners.
Source: George Garvy, Deposit Velocity and Its Significance (New York: Federal Reserve Bank of New York, 1959), p. 42.

What is the significance of the fact that our circulating money is now predominantly demand deposits rather than bank notes as was the case before the Civil War? In terms of outward appearance the differences are considerable, yet legally and economically bank notes and demand deposits are essentially similar. A circulating note issued by a bank, such as those now originating with the Federal Reserve Banks, is a promise to pay a specified sum of money upon demand. Such a note may circulate for long periods of time, being used to exchange goods and pay debts, without once returning to the issuing bank for fulfillment of the bank's promise to redeem it in some other kind of money. Similarly, in the case of a bank whose demand deposits give it a commitment to pay money on demand, a large volume of payments may be effected by means of checks drawn against the deposits. But if the movement of checks in and out of the bank is fairly even, all this may be accomplished without the bank being called upon at any time to pay out more than an insignificant proportion of the other types of money which it has promised it would pay if requested.

The legal obligation of the bank to pay money on demand and the high probability that, for the most part, the obligation will not materialize are substantially the same for bank notes and demand deposits. The chief distinction between them is in physical form: bank notes are formally engraved or printed certificates made out for designated amounts. Demand deposits, on the other hand, are merely book entries acknowledging a commitment to pay. They circulate by means of checks made out on printed forms in amounts and at times determined according to the convenience of the depositor. While the matter of form might seem to be of relatively minor consequence, it accounts in large measure for the fact that the privilege of issuing bank notes was long subject to strict regulations and finally was taken away from commercial banks entirely, while the privilege of establishing demand deposits against which checks could be drawn has been accorded to banks with great freedom. Legislators have been fully conscious that bank notes were money, but with few exceptions the monetary character of demand deposits has been recognized obscurely or not at all.

NEAR MONEYS

A review of the present monetary structure of the United States would be incomplete without some attention to the size and composition of the stock of "near moneys." These we have seen to be liquid assets held by the public, which are not used directly as means of payment but are regarded by their holders as close substitutes for money as assets because of their price stability and ease of transfer into money proper. They consist mainly of debts of the federal government and the principal private financial institutions. Some of the more important of these debts are time deposits of commercial and mutual savings banks, shares in savings and loan associations, shares and deposits in credit unions, policy reserves in private life insurance companies, United States savings bonds, and Treasury bills. As was noted in Chapter 1, there is no sharp break between these highly liquid assets and others slightly less liquid so that any precise line of division between near money and other liquid assets in somewhat arbitrary.

The changing composition and volume of eight kinds of near moneys may be seen in Table 3-5. And in Table 3-6 the stock of near moneys over time is

TABLE 3-5. Non-Money Liquid Assets of the Public for Selected Years, 1940-1960 (Billions of Dollars)

			Year End		
	1940	1945	1950	1955	1960
Commercial bank time deposits	15.8	30.1	36.3	48.4	71.3
Savings bank time deposits	10.7	15.3	20.0	28.2	36.3
Savings and loan shares	4.3	7.4	14.0	32.2	62.2
Credit Union shares	0.2	0.4	0.8	2.4	4.9
Postal Savings deposits	1.3	2.9	2.9	1.9	.8
Policy reserves of life insurance companies	27.2	38.7	54.9	75.4	98.5
U. S. Savings Bonds	2.8	42.9	49.6	50.2	47.2
U. S. Treasury bills	1.3	17.0	13.6	22.3	39.4
Total	63.6	154.7	192.1	261.0	360.6

Source: Derived from *Federal Reserve Bulletin.*

compared with changes in the stock of money proper and the gross national product (GNP). It will be observed that particularly rapid growth occurred between 1940 and 1945 in the two near moneys that are debts of the federal government, United States savings bonds and Treasury bills. The rise in the ratio of near money to GNP during World War II together with the even more rapid increase in the money supply indicates a substantial rise in the liquidity of the public, which contributed significantly to the postwar inflation.

The most notable increases in the volume of near moneys since 1945 have been in shares of savings and loan associations and credit unions, although substantial gains were also made in time deposits at commercial and savings

TABLE 3-6. Relationships between Money Supply, Near Moneys, and GNP, for Selected Years, 1940-1960 (Billions of Dollars, Except as Noted)

			Year End		
	1940	1945	1950	1955	1960
Money supply	42.3	102.3	117.7	138.2	143.8
Near moneys	63.6	154.7	192.1	261.0	360.6
Near moneys as percentage of money supply	150%	151%	163%	189%	251%
GNP	101.4	215.2	284.6	397.5	504.4
Money supply as percentage of GNP	42%	48%	41%	35%	29%
Near moneys as percentage of GNP	63%	72%	67%	66%	72%

banks, policy reserves of life insurance companies, and Treasury bills. While the money supply increased by little more than a third between 1945 and 1960, the aggregate volume of near moneys more than doubled. Thus the importance of near moneys in the total stock of liquid assets increased significantly relative to money during this period. During the period extending from the end of 1955 to June 1959 when a generally "tight money" policy was in effect in the United States, the money supply increased only about 1 per cent. During the same period the stock of near moneys, on the other hand, increased 25 per cent. The declining ratio of money supply to GNP is readily apparent.

Recent discussions have focused on two related aspects of the role of near moneys in monetary economics. First, since they are close substitutes for money, relative increases in the stock of near moneys increase the flexibility of the public in its spending decisions. The link between income and expenditures is loosened since, on the one hand, part of income may be utilized to accumulate near money, or, on the other hand, expenditures in excess of income may be financed by reducing holdings of near moneys. If the public decides, as it did at the outbreak of the Korean conflict, that prices are likely to go up and goods would become unavailable, those with idle balances may spend them directly on commodities and services, and, in addition, those holding near moneys may use them to finance an increase in expenditures by exchanging them for remaining idle balances, thus increasing the rate of turnover of the money stock. On the other hand, in times of declining activity and falling incomes near moneys may act as a cushion, serving to maintain spending at a higher level than would otherwise prevail.

The second aspect of near moneys which has been subject to considerable attention in recent years stems from the fact that the institutions which issue them are outside the scope of direct regulation by the monetary authorities. Since near moneys have monetary significance and since their relative volume has substantially increased, the question must be raised whether monetary controls can be adequate in the absence of restraints upon the financial institutions which issue these non-money liquid claims.

SELECTED BIBLIOGRAPHY

BOARD OF GOVERNORS OF THE FEDERAL RESERVE SYSTEM, Banking Studies. Washington: 1941, pp. 39-83, 295-319.
————, *Federal Reserve Bulletin.* (See current issues for full data on the money supply and many near moneys.)
————, *The Federal Reserve System.* Washington: 1961, Chapters 1-5, 9-12.

————, "The Monetary System of the United States," *Federal Reserve Bulletin* (February 1953), pp. 98-109.

GOLDSMITH, R. W., *Financial Intermediaries in the American Economy Since 1900*. Princeton: Princeton University Press, 1958, especially Chapters I and II.

SHAW, E. S., *Money, Income, and Monetary Policy*. Homewood, Ill.: Irwin, 1950, Chapter II.

SIMMONS, E. C., "The Relative Liquidity of Money and Other Things," *American Economic Review* (1947), pp. 308-311. (Reprinted in American Economic Association, *Readings in Monetary Theory*.)

4

CREDIT AND CREDIT INSTRUMENTS

Credit instruments may be thought of as constituting, along with money, the stock in trade of banks and other financial institutions, by which financial operations are carried on. The present chapter describes primarily the nature and functions of credit and credit instruments and the major types of credit instruments that are relevant to an understanding of banking and the financial system. A final section examines briefly the nature and effects of credit in the economic system and the conditions upon which its smooth functioning chiefly depend.

NATURE AND FUNCTIONS OF CREDIT INSTRUMENTS

For a transaction to give rise to debt or credit, it must involve a commitment to pay money. The borrowing of a coat, the renting of a car, or the checking of a suitcase at a railroad station do not represent pecuniary claims, and, consequently, they are not to be regarded as creating debts. Moreover, the obligation to pay money cannot be narrowly restricted. If a person is obligated to return the identical pieces of money left with him, the contract is one of safekeeping and not one of debt. At one time the so-called "gold clauses" in certain types of bonds gave a creditor the right at maturity of the bond to demand payment in gold coins. This was, of course, a debt in the accepted sense since payment could be made in any gold coins. It would not have constituted debt if the exact coins had been specified. That would have made it a contract for the sale of certain gold coins, not a debt.

Debt and Credit

A debt, then, is an obligation to pay money, and credit is a right to receive money.[1] Indeed, one person's legal right to receive is simply the other side of another's legal obligation to pay. Quantitatively, debt and credit are identities, the one being looked at from the viewpoint of the person who owes and the other from the viewpoint of the person who is owed. The relation between the two terms is the same as that which exists between "purchase" and "sale." Both sets of words refer to the same thing, but in each case it is looked at from opposite points of view. Because we may speak of a given transaction as either purchase or sale does not mean that there is other than a single transaction. Nor does it alter the fact that the total of all sales and all purchases in a community must be identical. So it is likewise with debt and credit.

Sometimes it is necessary to choose between the terms "credit" and "debt" because the obligation or the claim aspect is important, as when we speak of the government debt or a line of credit. Here again there is an exact analogy with "purchase" and "sale": the word we choose depends on which aspect of the transaction we wish to emphasize. In many contexts, however, it is entirely a matter of custom that the one term rather than the other is employed. This is true, for example, in the expression "credit instruments," which could be referred to as accurately and sometimes with greater meaning as "debt instruments."[2]

Credits or debts may rest on (1) oral understandings, (2) open book accounts, or (3) written agreements. When the obligation to pay money is expressed in proper written form the document is known as a "credit instrument." The reason for having credit instruments is that credit, like other rights, is intangible, but, again like other rights, it may be of very great value. In order to buy and sell credit, it is necessary to incorporate it in such a form that it can be more readily exchanged. The document which we speak of as a credit instrument might be thought of as a package in which the salable commodity "credit" (a right to receive money) is wrapped up for convenience in handling.

Checks drawn against demand deposits (and also the circulating notes issued by the Federal Reserve Banks) are unique among credit instruments. Technically, checks are rights to currency payable by the bank on which they are drawn, but, as was noted in an earlier chapter, they are customarily accepted in payment for goods and services and in discharge of debt

---

1. Various other meanings are attached to the word "credit," especially including the quality of faith or confidence which presumably underlies dealings in credit instruments. It is customary, for example, to speak of "credit standing" or of a "poor credit risk." For brevity this and other uses are omitted from the present discussion.

2. Recognition of the reciprocal character of debt and credit should be sufficient to disabuse us of the common belief that an increase in credit is *per se* desirable and an expansion of debt *per se* undesirable.

without any intention of exchanging them for the amount of currency specified on the face of the check. Because demand deposits perform the work of money they are generally regarded as money.[3] This is not true of promissory notes, bonds, and real estate mortgages, for example, which constitute claims to money but are not themselves ordinarily used to discharge debts.

Credit Instruments as a Device for Transferring Control over Money

The primary function of credit instruments is to allow control over money to be transferred, enabling users to have it and thereby to command resources at the time that suits them best. An individual who expects to receive money in sixty days but urgently needs money now may be able to obtain it at once by offering his promise to pay money (ordinarily a somewhat larger sum) in two months. In effect, he has pushed forward by sixty days his ability to employ money to command goods and services. The lender, in turn, surrenders his use of the money now in return for the right to have money in sixty days. In effect, he has deferred by two months his ability to command goods and services. Because of the payment of interest or discount, the borrower must content himself with a slightly smaller total of dollars in return for the convenience of having the use of money at once, and the lender is rewarded with a slightly larger total of dollars as compensation for waiting.

In many cases, of course, the transfer of money is indirect or implicit rather than actual. A promise to pay in sixty days for goods received today, for example, does not involve the physical transfer of money from seller to buyer, but it does mean that the buyer is allowed to retain use of money for another sixty days or—what amounts to the same thing—to avoid scraping together now the money required to pay for the goods purchased. The effect, therefore, is the same as though actual money had been handed over in payment for the goods and then returned to the purchaser to use as he wished for the next sixty days. By means of such actual and "constructive," i.e., implicit, transfers of money, credit instruments permit command over goods and services to be shifted over time.

The actual techniques of effecting the transfer of control over money are likely to vary with different types of credit instruments. In the original sale of a government bond, for example, a sum of money is transferred from a lender to the government. As a result of the transaction, the government receives money in the present and the lender, that is, the purchaser of the bond, gets the right to receive specific amounts of money at interest dates and at the time the bond matures. If the bond changes hands later, what is exchanged is the right to receive these specific future sums.

When a store sells goods on credit, as by charging them to a customer's

---

3. As was mentioned before, it is customary to count the demand deposits as money rather than the checks drawn against them.

account, the store really exchanges its wares for the right, indicated by the charge account, to receive money from the customer at some future time. If the store is unwilling or unable to wait as long as suits the customer, it may transfer the claim to a bank or other lending institution in exchange for cash or for a credit instrument of shorter maturity.

Much the same applies to installment credit. An automobile or refrigerator sold on the installment plan is exchanged, in effect, against rights to future payments from the purchaser. These rights are more precisely and formally specified than in open book accounts. For this reason it is easier to discount such credits with other lenders if the original seller of the merchandise does not wish to carry them. Probably the most significant feature of installment credit is the ease with which claims to future money may be created or transferred through this medium. In the past a good deal of attention has been directed toward the possibility that this very element of ease might result in an expansion of installment credit beyond a point that was in the best interest of the borrowers and of society. At different times it has been feared that a sudden increase in the volume of installment credit would aggravate inflationary price tendencies. Such fears are based on the belief that an expansion in these claims to *future* money would tend to increase the *current* demand for certain types of goods, such as automobiles, electrical goods, and jewelry. It explains why the authorities on some occasions have restricted installment credit as a move to combat inflation.

In real estate transactions, real property is usually exchanged for a certain amount of cash plus a mortgage or mortgage bond. Such a transaction represents a combination cash-and-credit operation. The property is exchanged for a stipulated amount of cash available at once plus the right to further amounts of cash which will be made available at specified times in the future.

Perpetual annuities such as the Consols of the British government are an unusual and interesting form of credit instrument. They consist of interest-bearing obligations with no date of maturity. These securities, like all the others, represent claims to money in the future, but the peculiar feature about them is that there is no provision for the repayment of a principal sum. Instead, they are claims to a perpetual series of interest payments. Similarly, the various forms of commercial paper such as notes, drafts, and acceptances differ in details of origin, maturity, and safeguards, but they share one feature in common—all represent rights to money in the future.

TYPES OF CREDIT TRANSACTIONS

Transactions involving the purchase and sale of credit are of great importance and bewildering variety in contemporary industrial economies. It may be useful, therefore, to consider some of the ways in which credit transactions are frequently classified and the rationale of such usage. Some of the commonly encountered bases of classification of credit transactions are shown in Table 4-1.

TABLE 4-1. Classifications of Credit Transactions

Classifying Principle	Main Classes	
1. By Purpose	Consumption Production Speculation	Commercial Investment
2. By Type of Creditor	Bank Other Financial Institutions Business (Trade) Individual	
3. By Maturity	Demand (Call) Short Intermediate Long	
4. By Type of Debtor	Private Governmental (Public)	
5. By Type of Instrument	Open book Draft Promissory note	
6. By Other Characteristics of the Transaction	Negotiated (Private Placement) Open market (Public Issue) Negotiable Registered Secured (Collateral) Unsecured	

This table suggests that the categories established by business usage refer to ways of looking at credit transactions rather than types of credit as such. The fact that the classifications are not exclusive—i.e., they are extensively overlapping—means that the various categories cannot be added to get a meaningful total. No meaning attaches, for example, to the sum of bank credit plus trade credit plus consumption credit. The same example suggests that consumer credit is not a different *kind* of credit as compared with, say, bank credit, but may be the same transaction viewed in another way. Similar comment is appropriate for popular terms such as "investment credit," "commercial credit," "long-term credit," etc.

Qualifying expressions used to describe credit instruments such as "government" bond, "trade" acceptance, "banker's" bill, "collateral" loan, and "short-term" note, may help us to some extent in identifying among whom, how, or on what conditions transfers of claims to money take place. Other terms, such as "productive" and "consumptive," far from being descriptive of their ultimate economic effects, may turn merely on a matter of form or of the immediate use for which the proceeds are employed. In other instances, the meaning of the terms attached to credit and credit instruments, and even the overtones of approval or disapproval which they carry, rest on nothing more substantial than long-established custom. The conventialized meanings of the particular terms should be borne in mind: a qualifying term often cannot be taken literally as describing the true character of the instrument.

In the merchandising of any commodity, the package in which it is marketed is dictated by two factors, namely, the nature of the commodity and the anticipated desires of the prospective purchaser. This is as true of credit as it is of groceries. A real estate mortgage, a check, or a registered government bond represent a "bundle" of this important commodity credit, and each is in the form which is best suited to its particular characteristics. Differences in their form are largely traceable to differences in the nature of the underlying credit operation. Such differences as are indicated by the adjectives "registered" bond and "negotiable" instruments arise out of the need of adjusting the form of credit instruments to the wishes of prospective buyers. Registration protects the owner against the danger of loss, theft, or destruction of the credit instrument. Accordingly, the incorporation of this feature brings within the scope of the market for credit instruments those investors (individuals, businesses, and institutions) who demand this kind of protection. In short, although the descriptive terms attached to credit transactions and credit instruments may be misleading, the distinguishing features of different types of credit instruments stem not from arbitrary decisions or chance but from the fact that these features are essential in order that the instruments may conform to the needs and wishes of issuers and prospective purchasers.

Negotiability

Negotiability signifies that a "holder in due course" of a credit instrument possesses a perfect title to it.[4] Negotiability gives the holder in due course the same rights to a credit instrument that a person has in the possession of currency. (An innocent person who is paid stolen currency acquires a secure title to it.) Embodiment of the feature of negotiability greatly reduces the risk attached to the acquisition of a credit instrument and correspondingly increases its marketability. It is essential to the ready use of checks and contributes to the important position occupied by bills of exchange and promissory notes in the portfolios of commercial banks.

---

4. The conditions of being a holder in due course are that:

    1. The instrument is complete and regular upon its face.

    2. He became the holder before it was overdue and without notice that it had been previously dishonored, if such was the fact.

    3. He took it in good faith and for value.

    4. At the time it was negotiated to him he had no notice of any infirmity in the instrument or defect in the title of the person negotiating it.

The requirement of a negotiable instrument developed out of practices going back hundreds if not thousands of years. They became part of common law and eventually were codified into essentially standard form.[5] For an instrument to be negotiable it must be:

1. in writing;
2. signed by the maker or drawer;
3. an unconditional promise or order to pay a definite sum of money;
4. payable on demand or at a fixed or determinable future time;
5. payable to order or bearer.

The origin of these requirements of negotiability rests not on any legal basis, even though in the course of time they have come to be confirmed by statute. They arise rather out of simple economic necessity: unless these features are present in a credit instrument the average individual or businessman could not acquire it with the assurance of being able to dispose of it again if desired. Without that assurance he might be unable or unwilling to acquire the credit instrument. With it he is willing to accept title because he has confidence in being able to transfer valid title to others.[6]

The requirements of negotiability, in short, are merely those conditions which enable the instrument to be negotiated (i.e., to be transferred in a way that conveys perfect title upon the holder). They are designed to place credit instruments, to this extent, on a footing comparable with money. That simple fact explains both what the requirements are and why.

SELF-LIQUIDATING CREDIT INSTRUMENTS

Let us assume that a manufacturer of cotton textiles obtains a loan from a bank for the purpose of buying raw cotton. The cotton is fabricated and the cloth sold for enough to pay off the loan at the end of the sixty days, plus enough to cover other expenses and provide a profit on the transaction. This is a self-liquidating productive loan whose distinguishing feature is the cycle from cash at the beginning of the transaction, into commodities during the process of manufacture and sale, and back into cash at the end of the transaction. In a successful self-liquidating loan the completion of the operation which gave rise to the loan provides the funds for discharging it. What is most noteworthy about this type of loan is that the money transferred to the borrower facilitates a productive process that generates its own repayment.

In customary usage, the term "self-liquidating" ordinarily appears in connection with "short-term, self-liquidating commercial paper." It is important

---

5. They were embodied in the Uniform Negotiable Instruments Act, first passed in England in 1882 and later adopted throughout the United States.

6. The technical term for transfer of title is "negotiation"; hence the word "negotiability."

to recognize that the quality of being self-liquidating is not peculiar to that class of instruments. The terms "short-term" and "commercial" are as significant as "self-liquidating" in identifying the nature of such credit instruments, and it is not to be inferred that only commercial paper is self-liquidating.

The concept of a cycle from cash back to cash, which is the essence of a self-liquidating commercial loan, applies also to many types of investment instruments. An issue of 20-year bonds might be floated, for example, to provide a million dollars to build a hydroelectric installation. Let us suppose, first, that the proceeds from the operation of the plant are sufficient to pay interest on the bonds and build up a sinking fund which is used to retire the bonds at the end of the twenty years, and, secondly, that the plant is entirely worn out or obsolete at that time. This would constitute a self-liquidating transaction in the same fundamental sense as the loan to the textile producer, the principal difference between the two being the length of time each had to run. In each, the funds to redeem the obligation would have been provided as a matter of course through completing the operation which gave rise to the obligation in the first place. While such a long-term issue of bonds would, in a literal sense, be self-liquidating, it is not the kind of transaction to which the term is customarily applied.

Credit instruments which are not self-liquidating can be of as high quality as those which are, and they may be no less desirable from the standpoint of social welfare. Government bonds redeemed out of taxation or by floating a new issue are not self-liquidating, nor is a consumer loan. A consumption loan used to defray the costs of a college education may be repaid out of the higher income made possible by that education. But since the higher income is not viewed as inherent in the operation, the loan is not classified as self-liquidating. Furthermore, while such a loan might be of great benefit to the individual and to society, it is nevertheless classified as a consumptive rather than a productive loan.

CREDIT INSTRUMENTS OF MAJOR IMPORTANCE TO BANKING

Notes, Drafts, and Governments

Notes, drafts or bills of exchange, and governments comprise the "Big Three" of bank assets. The last of the three, governments, is a relative newcomer, at least in its present proportions, but it is now the most important in dollar volume.

Traditionally, the lending operations of banks were based on two kinds of short-term credit instruments, the promissory note and the draft or bill of exchange. The promissory note has generally been more familiar in the United States and the bill of exchange in England. Both are credit instruments embodying the usual requirements of negotiability. The main difference between them is that one is in the form of a promise to pay and the other is in the form of an order.

A typical promissory note contains, in addition to name of place, date, and signature, a statement such as:

"Sixty days after date I promise to pay to the order of John Smith the sum of $1,000."

It is very likely to stipulate the payment of interest at a specific rate, but this is not always included. Promissory notes vary widely with respect to amount, the time to maturity, and the credit standing of the maker. All these factors help to determine the rate of interest at which banks and others are willing to lend money on them.

The most familiar example of a draft is an ordinary bank check. Other drafts and bills of exchange[7] conform to the same general pattern. A typical draft, for example, might contain, in addition to name of place, date, and signature, such words as:

"Sixty days after date pay to the order of James Jones the sum of $1,000," together with the name and address of the person or company to whom the order is directed. This would be a "time draft" since it provides for a lapse of time before payment. If the order were to say "on demand" or "at sight" instead of using such an expression as "sixty days after date," it would be called a "demand draft" or "sight draft."

Drafts, unlike promissory notes, customarily do not provide for an explicit payment of interest. The buyer of such a non-interest-bearing obligation is not prevented, however, from earning interest on it. When a bank, for example, acquires such a credit instrument it customarily determines what it will pay for the instrument by subtracting interest for the period from date of purchase until maturity from the face amount. This process is known as "discounting." It results in the payment of a rate of interest on the actual proceeds of the transaction which is slightly higher than that nominally paid. This may be seen by comparing two credit instruments due in sixty days, one of them bearing interest at 6 per cent and the other non-interest-bearing:

	Interest-bearing Loan	Discount
Value at maturity	$1,010	$1,000
Interest charged by bank	10	10
Proceeds to borrower	1,000	990
Effective rate of interest	6%	6.06%

7. The two terms are used more or less interchangeably, though at one time drafts were generally thought of in connection with domestic trade and bills of exchange in connection with foreign trade.

The reason why discount entails a higher effective rate than simple interest is that the actual proceeds are less because of the fact that interest is deducted in advance, as shown in the illustration. In entering the value of a loan or a discount on the books of the bank, either one is figured at its face value. In the example given, each would be entered at $1,000 even though the present value of the discounted bill is only $990. The effect of this practice is to *overstate* the current value of discounted obligations among the assets of banks. On the other hand, the practice of entering interest-bearing notes at par is to *understate* their current value, since their worth gradually rises above par as a result of the accumulation of interest due.

To a certain extent, the inaccuracies inherent in carrying both discounts and interest-bearing loans at face value tend to offset one another. The main justification for the policy, however, is one of practical necessity: to show current value on the books of the bank at all times would call for revaluing each asset every day, since each day alters the interest factor which is present in every earning asset. The policy of carrying assets of this character at face value is standard practice and, even though somewhat arbitrary, is fully understood and allowed for by banking specialists.

A draft, it will be noted, is a demand for payment and does not involve any commitment on the part of the drawee (the person or firm ordered to pay) to honor the drawer's order to pay. Checks are a form of draft (sight draft) which it is generally assumed that the drawee will pay, but for ordinary drafts originating in trade this assumption cannot so easily be made. In order to convert a time draft into a binding commitment, the drawee may therefore make and sign an appropriate notation on the bill; thereafter it is known as an "acceptance."

The other major group of bank assets consists of "governments," and embraces different classes of obligations of the United States Treasury.[8] The various classes of Treasury securities range from bonds which are issued with the longest maturities, through notes and certificates of indebtedness, to bills which have the shortest maturity, approximately ninety days at time of issue. It is to be observed that to the extent that banks hold bonds until maturity it is possible for some of the bonds in their portfolio to have as short a period to run as any of the notes or bills which they hold. Today, for example, a large proportion of governments with less than five years to run—even a considerable proportion of those within one year of maturity—are classified as bonds. A 20-year bond that has been held nineteen years, for example, would be in that category.

On the balance sheet of banks it is customary to include all promissory

---

8. At one time it was customary to include the securities of other governmental units under the heading of "governments." It is the general practice of bankers today to classify such obligations as "municipals" and to restrict the "government" classification to Treasury securities.

notes and drafts[9] under the heading of "loans and discounts" or just "loans," and all governments under the heading of "investments." It may seem surprising that Treasury obligations such as bills, even though bought on a discount basis, are listed not under "loans and discounts" but under "investments" along with interest-bearing bonds. It is even more worthy of note that the "investment" category, which one might expect to consist entirely of long-term assets, contains instead a large proportion of Treasury obligations with only a short time to run to maturity. In fact, "investments" include Treasury bills which are, generally speaking, the most liquid of a bank's assets other than cash, along with other assets which are not so liquid.

Checks, Certified Checks, and Cashier's Checks; Endorsement

Demand deposits which are transferred by checks drawn on commercial banks have come to be the principal type of circulating medium in the United States and other Anglo-Saxon countries. The wide use of checks is the result of inherent advantages which they possess. First, they facilitate, in various ways, the keeping of records. A check can be transferred by simple endorsement on the back and the endorsements provide a record (not necessarily complete) of the hands through which the check has passed. In addition, the Federal Reserve Banks, together with many other large banks, may make and retain photographic copies of both sides of checks which pass through their hands. Of particular importance, a cancelled check, when returned to the drawer, constitutes a receipt for the payment made.

Second, checks are extraordinarily convenient in that they can be made out at just the time and in the exact amount desired and can be transported with equal ease regardless of their value. A third advantage, not unrelated to the preceding, is that they add greatly to the safety of doing business since they dispense with the necessity of holding large sums of currency, and both payer and payee are safeguarded in case of loss or destruction of checks in a way that would not be possible if currency were employed.

A certified check differs from an ordinary personal check in that it bears a notation by a qualified officer of the bank declaring that the check is valid and will be honored in full. At the time of certification, the account against which the check is drawn is debited to make sure that the full amount required will be available when the check is presented for collection. Certified checks are employed where the drawer is not well enough known for his personal check to be accepted freely, or where it is desired to avoid delay which might be entailed in the clearing of an ordinary check. Similar considerations dictate the use of cashier's (or treasurer's) checks and banker's drafts, the first consisting of checks drawn by a bank against itself and the second of checks drawn by a bank against that bank's deposit account in

---

9. Except checks on other banks, which are treated as cash or as "cash items in process of collection."

another bank. A business or individual who desires to use a cashier's check pays the issuing bank for it by currency or check at the time of issue, and ordinarily a small fee is charged for the bank's services. Both certified and cashier's checks are of superior quality, but the high quality of checks in general is attested by the fact that most check transactions are carried on by ordinary checks and these special types are resorted to only under exceptional circumstances.

Checks are ordinarily transferred or payment for them is acknowledged by "endorsement," a procedure that may also be employed in the case of other negotiable instruments. While endorsement is not legally necessary for unnamed holders through whose hands the check may pass, it is nevertheless customary to ask them for endorsement. Such endorsements provide a more complete record, and, unless an endorsement is "qualified" (see item 4 below), it imposes a secondary liability upon the endorser in case, for any reason, the drawee fails to pay.

There are four principal types of endorsement:

1. Blank. Consists of merely signing the holder's name. The instrument then becomes payable to bearer. Example: "James Brown."
2. Special. Names the person to whom the instrument is transferred. Example: "Pay to the order of John Smith," (signed) "James Brown."
3. Restrictive. Not only names the person to whom the instrument is transferred but also limits payment to him alone. Thereupon the paper ceases to be a negotiable instrument since it cannot be transferred further. Example: "Pay to John Smith only," (signed) "James Brown."
4. Qualified. Limits the further liability of the endorser. Example: "Pay to the order of John Smith without recourse," (signed) "James Brown."

Collateral Loans

The right of a creditor to receive money in the future is frequently safeguarded by the debtor's pledging collateral security of some kind. The security pledged for collateral loans usually consists of real estate; bonds and stocks (stock exchange collateral); and bills of lading, warehouse receipts, and trust receipts (merchandise collateral). The pledging of collateral serves a double purpose. First, the fact that the only way the security can be redeemed is through paying the loan gives the debtor an extra inducement for carrying out the obligation. Second, in case of default the creditor can dispose of the pledged security to discharge the claim. In effect, there are two sources to which the creditor can look for discharge of the credit instrument he holds—the debtor himself and the security which has been given as collateral. Seizure of collateral does not, however, release the debtor. He is still liable in case, for example, liquidation of the collateral does not provide sufficient funds to discharge the debt in full.

A survey conducted a number of years ago indicated that of all bank loans to business enterprises, over three-fifths by number and over two-fifths by dollar amount were secured by the endorsement of others or by the pledge of specific collateral. The type of collateral most commonly pledged was real estate, followed by bonds and stocks and warehouse receipts, with assignments of title, accounts receivable, life insurance, chattel mortgages, and trust receipts occupying a relatively minor position.

Margin. A further factor of safety is introduced by the fact that the market value of the collateral pledged is always expected to be greater than the face value of the loan which is secured. The difference between the market value of the collateral and the amount of the loan which is granted with it as security is known as "margin." With a 40 per cent margin the loan would equal 60 per cent of the market value of the collateral; with a 75 per cent margin the loan would be 25 per cent of market value. The size of the margin which is required differs according to the character of the collateral and the stability of the market price of the securities or merchandise involved, as well as according to other special factors—not excluding how good a bargain the borrower is able to drive with the lender.[10] If the margin shrinks through a decline in the market value of the collateral, the borrower may be required to post additional collateral or to reduce the face amount of the loan. In the case of stock market loans, if the borrower is unable to maintain the required margin or to provide additional margin when called upon to do so, the loan becomes immediately payable. If it is not then paid, the bank is empowered to sell the collateral and apply the proceeds toward retirement of the loan.

It might seem that no loss could possibly be incurred by banks on loans of this type. Actually, their record is by no means perfect. In periods of crisis the scramble to liquidate collateral may be so general that not every bank is able to get out from under in time. Even collateral loans may become "frozen." It then becomes a question of nursing the loan along in the hope that the debtor may be able to pay out, or of waiting for a reversal of market conditions to restore the value of the collateral. Needless to say, the sale of collateral to protect loans serves to aggravate a downward movement of prices. When prices later begin to improve, the liquidation of securities or other property acquired through default may continue for some time to exert a depressing influence.

Substitution of collateral. Collateral loan agreements ordinarily give the borrower the privilege, without disturbing the loan itself, of substituting different collateral from that which was pledged when the loan was made. New collateral which is substituted for old must, of course, maintain adequate margin and be of satisfactory quality. The reason for providing for the substitution of collateral is that otherwise the asset pledged as collateral would be immobilized for the duration of the loan. In that event, the owner

10. As will be explained later, margin requirements on stock market loans are controlled by the Federal Reserve with a view to influencing stock market activities.

might be prevented from disposing of it in such a way as to derive a profit or avoid a loss.

The lender has no reason to object to changes in collateral so long as the protection afforded him is maintained, and it is presumably to his long-run interest to facilitate those operations which are financially advantageous to the one who owes him money. Moreover, unless this degree of flexibility were afforded, the borrower would be less willing to enter into collateral loan agreements. As in the case of other features of credit instruments, the provision for substitution of collateral represents a logical adaptation of business practice to the requirements of the situations which this particular type of instrument is expected to meet and the functions it is designed to perform.

Merchandise collateral or documents of title. Reference was made above to the use of merchandise collateral in connection with lending operations. Thus a number of different types of documents are in current use which enable goods in process of being sold or manufactured to serve as collateral for securing loans. Such a document, since it does not call for payment in money, is obviously not a credit instrument. It is, rather, a "document of title," to be used in the transfer of rights to goods themselves. It is more comparable to a rental lease.

A *bill of lading* is a receipt, issued by a carrier, such as a railroad, steamship company, or airline to show ownership of goods in transit. By discounting a draft secured by the bill of lading, the seller of the goods is able to obtain funds without waiting until the transaction is finally completed. At the same time, the lender of the money, e. g., the bank which discounted the draft, has the protection afforded by the claim (bill of lading) to the goods being shipped.

When the goods arrive at their destination the bill of lading must be forthcoming if the buyer is to obtain possession of the goods from the carrier. If it is not convenient for the buyer to pay the draft outright he may arrange, upon "accepting" the draft, to obtain the bill of lading and transfer the goods to a warehouse, giving the lender a *warehouse receipt* as security for the loan. In effect, the collateral for the loan would have been changed from a bill of lading giving title to goods in transit to a warehouse receipt carrying title to goods in storage.

Still another kind of substitution of collateral may take place before the transaction is finished. If the buyer is relying upon the proceeds of the sale of the goods to provide funds for paying off the acceptance, it is necessary to find some means of enabling him to obtain possession of the goods in order to effect their sale. This is accomplished by surrendering the warehouse receipt in exchange for a *trust receipt*. The warehouse receipt enables the buyer to take possession of the goods, but the loan is still protected since the trust receipt gives the lender legal title to the goods and a claim on the money received from their sale.

At each stage of the operation just described, the loan was secured by a document adapted to that particular stage, i.e., by a claim on goods in transit (the bill of lading), on the goods stored in a warehouse (the warehouse receipt), or on the proceeds of the sale of the goods (the trust receipt). The element of faith ("credit," in the underlying sense of confidence in the obligor) was present in each instance, and the form of the document employed was accommodated to the particular circumstances, as was also the body of law and convention which has been built up to safeguard the interests of both borrower and lender. The basis of the security afforded by each of the documents was the value of the goods to which they related. Because the future price of goods is seldom certain, the amount of the loan extended on the basis of merchandise collateral such as has been described is normally somewhat less than the nominal worth of the goods.

Term Loans

The so-called "term loan" occupies an intermediate position between the ordinary promissory note and an investment security such as a bond. The rise of term loans in the latter 1930's is attributable in part to the experience of the depression when many businesses which had come to rely on short-term borrowing found themselves severely embarrassed as a result of the tightening of credit conditions. Another factor in its growth in popularity was the fact that the term loan permitted substantial sums to be borrowed without going through the formalities which were imposed by the newly enacted Securities and Exchange legislation in the flotation of other types of securities. Once established, it continued to enjoy considerable favor, especially among institutional lenders such as banks and insurance companies.

Term loans are business loans with a maturity of over one year. They may run for as long as fifteen years. Term loans usually contain an amortizing feature whereby current payments cover interest and in addition provide something toward reduction of principal. The amortizing feature helps to lessen risk by reducing the size of the obligation embodied in the more distant claims. Most term loans as measured by dollar value are not secured by any particular property or other collateral. They have been used to provide funds for a great variety of productive purposes, e.g., to supply working capital, to modernize equipment, to obtain rolling stock, to add to fixed capital.

One of the major advantages of term loans is their flexibility. They are flexible in the sense that the loan contract is readily adjustable. As a result, the amount of a loan may be increased or reduced, or the period lengthened or shortened, by means of simple negotiation between borrowers and lenders. They are also flexible in that the series of annual payments of interest and principal provided for under a term loan contract make it possible to divide a particular term loan among different types of lending institutions. In a representative term-loan agreement, for example, the funds may be supplied jointly by a bank and an insurance company with the bank taking the shorter maturities and the insurance company, for whom liquidity is of less concern, the longer maturities. In such a contract, the rate of interest earned by the insurance company on its share of the loan is ordinarily somewhat higher than that earned by the bank on its share.

Other Types of Credit Instruments

Mortgages, which are, of course, collateral loans backed by real estate, represent a substantial share of bank assets. The increase in lending on real estate is partly attributable to the expansion of time deposits for which assets of a less liquid type than those held against demand deposits are regarded as suitable. It has been influenced by the rise of family formation and home ownership. And it has also been favored by government guarantees provided under the Veterans Administration and the Federal Housing Administration. Mortgage loans now usually incorporate the amortization feature, which, by contributing to both safety and liquidity, has greatly increased their attractiveness to banks.

Personal loans and installment sales credit constitute a relatively new field of commercial bank operations but one which has become of great importance. The former consist of rather small, generally unsecured, notes of individuals, and the latter consist chiefly of personal notes, collateraled by claims on durable consumer goods sold on the installment plan, by far the most important being new and used automobiles. Both personal and installment loans are customarily of the amortizing type. Interest rates, when figured on the basis of unpaid balances, are high compared with other types of credit, but so also are costs of handling, largely because of the relatively small size of the individual transaction. Losses, on the other hand, have proved surprisingly small. In the case of consumer sales credit, the lender is effectively safeguarded by the size of the margin, the right of repossession of the property in the case of default, and insurance policies covering such contingencies as theft, destruction, and damage to the property.

Banks hold a limited volume of bonds, other than obligations of the Treasury, chiefly municipals and high-grade corporates. Except for the stock of Federal Reserve Banks, which member banks own as one of the requirements of membership in the Federal Reserve System, and a few other minor cases, the only stock held by national banks and most state banks is that which was acquired through seizure of collateral to protect loans going into default. Since stocks represent shares in the concern issuing them rather than an obligation to pay specified amounts on account of interest and principal, they are not regarded as suitable earning assets for banks to hold. Banks are required to liquidate such unauthorized assets within a reasonable period of time, six months being specified for national banks and many state banks.

THE CREDIT SYSTEM

The Layering of Claims

The expression "layering of claims" refers to the system of inter-relationships that make up the credit structure. What this expression is intended to suggest is the idea of one claim being superimposed upon another. For example: a customer owes a store on a charge account; the store is indebted to the wholesaler; the wholesaler has accepted a draft drawn on him by a manufacturer; the manufacturer may have taken out a term loan at a bank; the bank owes its depositors; and so on. A body of relationships such as this may be expected to continue in substantially similar form, despite constant churning within the structure, as long as business activity is maintained at approximately an even level. Thus as one obligation is paid another takes its place. An old charge account is succeeded by a new one; one acceptance or one term loan is replaced by another.

Inseparable from the layering of claims where one debt is superimposed, as it were, upon another is what amounts to a continuous flow of payments arising out of this system of interrelated claims. The general effect is as though one debt as it matured were so dovetailed with another farther up the scale of layering that the same money could be passed along in discharging one debt after another. This is, of course, a highly simplified description of the way the credit system works. Nevertheless, it reflects reasonably accurately the actual operation of a smoothly functioning credit economy, and it helps to explain the disturbances that occur throughout the economy when something happens to interrupt the flow of payments anywhere along the line. Such an interruption, when sufficiently general, is spoken of as a "credit crisis."

Maintenance of the Continuity of Credit Relationships

The credit system in a modern economy, then, is to be thought of as an interconnected, interdependent body of contractual engagements to pay and be paid. Efficient operation of the system requires a continuous flow of money payments as stipulated in credit instruments and other credit agreements. But continuity implies not only the fulfillment of outstanding loan contracts but also the avoidance of a sudden contraction in the total volume of credit. A certain amount of net contraction of credit may signify nothing more than a readjustment in the manner of conducting business as when, for example, a merchant shifts from holding large inventories to a policy of hand-to-mouth buying. But in many situations if one creditor in a series of layering of claims should insist upon getting cash and holding on to it the effect would be to impair the prospect of payment being received by subsequent creditors in the series. And a wholesale attempt to contract credit would have extremely disturbing consequences. It would signify a reduction in the current demand for goods and services at the existing level of prices and would seriously interfere with the fulfillment of outstanding loan contracts. The economic stagnation of the early 1930's was undoubtedly aggravated by the generalized attempt to contract credit.

A major requirement of successful credit administration at the level of the individual business is an accurate estimate of the expectations of others and of their prospects for fulfillment. It involves a recognition, implicitly at least, of expectations that enter in at various stages of the layering of claims. But it also requires that the continuity of credit relationships not be disturbed unduly by an unexpected contraction of credit elsewhere along the line.

The goal of wise credit administration at the level of central bank operations, and of governmental policy in general, is the pursuit of policies that help to preserve stability in the structure of credit. This signifies maintaining the continuity of money payments from old debtors to old creditors and from new creditors to new debtors. It implies avoiding sudden variations in the volume of credit outstanding. It recognizes that fulfillment of the obligation by one businessman may be what makes possible the fulfillment of the obligation of another businessman. One of the main purposes of a central bank, as will be seen later, is to be able to move into the credit structure in the role of lender of last resort. This is essentially a matter of maintaining the continuity of credit relationships in a time of crisis.

Credit and Economic Stability

Credit is an extraordinarily useful feature of the economic system. The fact that it is a means of transferring control over money makes it an indispensable adjunct to the use of money. It has contributed enormously to the productivity of the capitalistic system, the speed with which that system incorporates technological advances, and its responsiveness to changes in human wants.

At the same time, the growth of credit has undoubtedly added to the potential instability of the economy. The fact that it facilitates the transfer of control over money, which is the basis of its great usefulness, is the very feature that has contributed to excessive demand and inflation at one time, and insufficient demand and deflation and unused resources at another. For the transfer of the use of money by means of credit may tend to make total demand greater at a time when it is already excessive and to reduce demand when it is already too small. Such perversity of behavior is not, fortunately, the invariable rule; there have been times when the use of credit has helped to promote the stability of demand and business activity.

Broadly speaking, of course, the aim of public policy is to promote the benefits of the use of credit and to restrain its potentially harmful effects. Public policy seeks to accomplish these ends by means that will not interfere unduly with consumer choice and private initiative. But some interference is inevitable, and—to make the task more difficult—no objective standards exist to tell the authorities what degree of interference is proper and what degree is excessive. The most rudimentary guide which the authorities can observe is to attempt to maintain the continuity of credit and view with questioning and caution any sudden, substantial change in the structure of credit and credit relationships.

APPENDIX:
PRICE—YIELD RELATIONSHIPS

This appendix provides a brief discussion of specialized concepts related to fixed-income securities (i.e., debt or credit instruments) and arithmetic relationships that link prices and yields in the money or capital markets in which they are exchanged. Such securities represent the obligation of debtors to make (and correspondingly, the right of creditors to receive) one or more money payments in the future. The *principal* is the face amount of the security (equal to the sum originally received by the debtor if he issued the instrument at par). It is normally the number of dollars that will be received at the *maturity* or expiration of the instrument. The *"coupon"* or *contractual rate of interest* is the rate stipulated in the security agreement, usually on an annual basis. A 3 per cent bond is one that carries a "coupon" of 3 per cent a year on its face or par value.

The principal, maturity, and contractual rate may be viewed as defining the size and timing of the stream of promised payments. Thus a ten-year, $1,000, 3 per cent bond at date of issue represents a series of payments of $30 a year at the end of each of ten years and of $1,000 at the end of the tenth year. (After five years have elapsed, however, the same instrument represents a promise to pay $30 at the end of each of the next five years plus $1,000 at the end of the fifth year.)

In some cases, as exemplified by Treasury bills, where the instrument specifies only an obligation to make a single payment, there is no contractual rate. In other cases, there may be no lump-sum payment, but only a sequence of equal payments over time, as in the case of annuities or of amortization payments used to retire a home mortgage.

Market Price and Yield

The *market price* of a security represents the public's current evaluation placed on the stream of anticipated future payments. We have today a complex of many different securities carrying different coupons and maturities and, what is more confusing, often carrying different coupon rates with the same maturity date. The market prices of securities, reflecting these differences, vary greatly, but the prices alone provide poor guidance to investors and borrowers as to the more desirable issues. For example, is a 4 per cent, 10-year bond selling at $98 a better buy than a 3½ per cent, 12-year bond selling at $95? What is needed is a means of comparison; this is provided in the concept, "*yield to maturity.*"

Yield to maturity is the average annual percentage return which an individual would receive on his investment if he were to buy a particular security at the quoted market price and hold it to maturity. An understanding of yield to maturity requires a familiarity with the concepts *capitalization* (or *present value*) and *discounting*. If $100 were invested today at 5 per cent, the amount accumulated at the end of a year would be $100 plus $100 × 0.05, or $100 (1 + 0.05), or $105. If this amount were invested at 5 per cent for another year, the amount at the end of the second year would be $105 + $105 × 0.05, or $105 (1 + 0.05), or $100 (1.05)^2. This is equal to $110.25. Following the same process, investing this amount for another year at 5 per cent would give $100 (1.05)^3, or $115.76. Thus, the result of accumulating $100 for three years at 5 per cent as given by the equation:

$$\$100\,(1.05)^3 = \$115.76.$$

In this equation $115.76 is the *amount*, $100 is the *present value* of $115.76 due in three years, and 5 per cent is the rate of accumulation or discount.

If both sides of the equation are divided by $(1.05)^3$, then

$$\$100 = \frac{\$115.76}{(1.05)^3}.$$

This indicates that $115.76 due at the end of three years when discounted at the rate of 5 per cent, compounded annually, gives the value $100. This, the present value, also called the "capitalized" value, is seen to be that quantity which when accumulated at the given rate over the period equals the given final amount.

In general terms, where P is the present value, i is the rate of accumulation or discount, and A is the amount at the end of n periods,

$$P(1+i)^n = A, \quad \text{or} \quad P = \frac{A}{(1+i)^n}.$$

Given the number of periods separating P and A, if we know A and i, we can determine P. This is called the discounted value of A. If we know P and i, we can determine A. This is the accumulated amount of P. If we know P and A, we can determine i. This is the rate of discount or accumulation, or "yield."

Although we have discussed accumulation, discounted values, and yield for a single deferred payment, the analysis is similar where there are multiple payments. In principle, each can be handled separately, and simply consolidated. For example, if $100 is due at the end of two years, and another $100 at the end of three years, at 5 per cent the discounted value of these payments is

$$P = \frac{\$100}{(1.05)^2} + \frac{\$100}{(1.05)^3} = \$90.70 + \$86.38 = \$177.08.$$

If, however, we knew P and the payments to be made at the end of two and three years, we could determine the rate of discount i.

The yield is neither a contractual rate nor a market price; it is an imputed or calculated value. To calculate the yield of an instrument we need to know the contractual elements defining the payments stream—the face amount, contractual rate, and maturity—and the market price. On the other hand, if we know the payments stream and the yield which an instrument must provide to make it competitive with others, we can deduce the market price it must command. Yield and price change over time in a fixed relationship.

The distinction between the coupon rate and the yield (also termed the "market rate") should now be clear. The coupon rate is a constant, established in the loan agreement and used to determine the periodic payments over the life of the loan. The yield is a variable, which depends on the fixed-payments stream and the price which the security commands in the market.

Price-Yield Relationships for a Treasury Bill

These relationships may be illustrated by assuming, first, a bill promising $100 at the end of one year. If it can be bought for $95, what is the return or yield for holding it one year? It is the appreciation taken as a percentage of the original investment ($5/$95 × 100) or about 5.3 per cent. Alternatively, if the market rate of interest on comparable obligations were 5 per cent, what would be its current price? In principle, we must find a value such that when we add to it 5 per cent of itself the sum is $100. In this case the result is slightly more than $95 ($95.24).[11] Thus the market for bills may be described either as establishing a price of $95.24, or a yield of 5 per cent.

With a yield of 8 per cent the price would fall to $92.59 and with a rate of 2 per cent, the price would be $98.04. Similar relationships would

---

11. Where P is the market price of the instrument, under the conditions of the problem:

$$P + 0.05P = \$100, \text{ or}$$
$$P(1 + 0.05) = \$100, \text{ and}$$
$$P = \frac{\$100}{1.05} = \$95.24.$$

prevail among prices and yields of the usual 90-day Treasury bills. At 5 per cent per annum $100 due in three months is worth $98.77; at 8 per cent it is worth $98.04; and at 2 per cent it is worth $99.50. Thus we find that, given the maturity value, the price varies inversely with the prevailing market rate of interest or yield. Changes in market prices also imply inverse movements of market yield.

Price-Yield Relationships for a "Consol"

These relationships may be further clarified by considering a very different type of security, namely, a "Consol," which is a promise to make a series of payments in perpetuity. It may be viewed therefore as an example of an interest-bearing security with an infinitely deferred payment of principal. What is priced is simply a series of annual payments: a 5 per cent $100 Consol represents a promise to pay $5 a year forever. What it is worth in the market depends on yields of comparable instruments, and reciprocally, the yield that can be obtained by purchasing such an instrument depends on the purchase price. If the market yield is 5 per cent, anyone investing $100 can get an income of $5 a year. It follows that a 5 per cent Consol would sell at par, for competition would prevent any price from being maintained which was higher or lower. At 2 per cent, however, an investment of $100 would command only $2 per year. The Consol with a return of $5 per year would therefore provide the same yield when its price was 2½ times as high, or $250. At 8 per cent, the Consol would sell at $62.50.

Market Prices and Maturity

The contrast in price movements of a 90-day Treasury bill and a Consol associated with given interest changes is clearly seen from our two examples. For the Consol, a movement of the interest rate from 2 per cent to 8 per cent implies a change in market price from $250 to $62.50. The corresponding price change in the case of the Treasury bill is only from $99.50 to $98. In both cases market prices and interest rates move inversely; but the degree of change is vastly different. In general, the relative effect of a change in interest rates on the present value of any promised payment depends on how long it is deferred.[12] A security represents simply a series

---

12. As noted above, the present value (P) of $100 deferred one year at 5 per cent is 100/1.05. In general, as we have seen, where a quantity (A) is due at the end of n periods in the future, and the appropriate yield or market rate of interest is i, the present value or price (P) is given by the relation:

$$P = \frac{A}{(1+i)^n}.$$

Since the factor $(1+i)$, which appears in the denominator, is multiplied by itself a number of times (n), which depends on the number of periods A is deferred, the rela-

of such payments. It is the greater average duration or period of deferment of long-term instruments which accounts for their greater fluctuation in current price in response to current changes in market rates of interest.

Most securities are neither as short as bills nor as long as Consols. But the same principle of valuation holds. The degree of fluctuation in market price is directly related to maturity. The longer the maturity date of a security the closer it approaches Consols in extent of possible price fluctuation; the shorter it is the more it resembles bills in the narrowness of price fluctuation. This fact is of great consequence in the management of portfolios by investment officers and in the control of credit by central banks.

Reconciliation of the Coupon Rate with the Market Yield

The maturity structure of rates, as revealed by Table 4-2, indicates that different rates prevail for different maturities. A bond agreement

TABLE 4-2. Yields, Coupon Rates, and Prices of United States Government Obligations of Various Maturities, June 26, 1962

Maturity (in years)	Coupon Rate (per cent)	Price*	Yield (per cent)
¼	—	99.30	2.82
1	2½	99.12	3.01
2	3	99.22	3.12
3	2⅝	95.08	3.33
4	3	98.00	3.49
5	3⅝	99.17	3.69
7	4	101.00	3.82
9	4	100.12	3.93
12	3⅞	99.04	3.94
18	4	100.04	3.97
23	3¼	90.16	3.83
28	3½	91.21	3.98
33	3	86.04	3.72
36	3½	90.22	4.00

* Price is the "bid" price in dollars and 32ds.
Source: *Wall Street Journal*. Similar data are published daily in most newspapers.

tive influence of a change in i on P will be greater the greater is n. Consider the following tabulation showing the influence of a change in i from 4 per cent to 6 per cent on the present value of $100 due alternatively in fifty years and in one year.

Maturity	Present Value of $100 discounted at	
	4%	6%
50 years	$14.07	$ 5.43
1 year	$96.15	$94.34

A rise in rate from 4 to 6 per cent reduces the present value of a payment due in one year by 2 per cent. But it reduces the present value of the payment due in fifty years to less than half its former value.

or indenture, however, provides for the same payment in every year, notwithstanding the fact that with the passage of time actual maturities will become shorter and shorter, moving eventually to periods ordinarily associated with rates of yield considerably below the coupon rate.

How, then, is a coupon rate of say 4 per cent reconciled with a market rate of, let us say, 2 per cent when only one year remains to maturity? The answer is suggested by the discussion above: the bond will sell at a premium such that the coupon of 4 per cent less the premium (which disappears when the bond reaches maturity) will leave a net yield just equal to the yield indicated for that period. This principle applies, in fact, throughout the entire life of the bond. It is by means of a change in market price, i.e., by a premium or discount from par, that the yields on bonds are brought into conformity with changes in market rates even though coupon payments remain constant.

SELECTED BIBLIOGRAPHY

GREEN, T. F., JR., *Practical Summary of Negotiable Instruments*. New York: Longmans Green, 1928.

HAWTREY, R. G., "Credit," *Encyclopaedia of the Social Sciences*. New York: Macmillan, 1933.

ROBINSON, ROLAND I., *et al*, *Financial Institutions*. Homewood, Ill. Irwin, 1960.

SPENCER, W. H., and C. W. GILLAM, *A Textbook of Law and Business*. New York: McGraw-Hill, 1952, Chapter IX.

PART TWO

Commercial Banks and
Related Institutions

5

NATURE, FUNCTIONS
AND OPERATIONS OF
COMMERCIAL BANKS

The meanings attached to the word *bank* cover a wide, and widening, range. At one extreme it is used to refer to a reserve fund used in gambling; at the other it is applied to the most conservative investment banking house. The term is applied most frequently, however, to commercial banks, and henceforth we shall use "bank" and "commercial bank" as synonymous. Where we refer to other financial institutions with which the term is associated, we shall identify them by descriptive adjectives, as, for example, savings bank or investment bank.

It was noted previously that the bulk of the money supply of the United States is made up of demand deposit liabilities of commercial banks. Accordingly, an understanding of the nature and activities of commercial banks is essential to an adequate grasp of the workings of our monetary system. We must keep in mind, however, that, although banks are important issuers of money, two sets of governmental institutions, the Treasury and the Federal Reserve, also possess important monetary powers. As we shall see later, monetary management consists largely of actions by the monetary authorities to influence the activities of commercial banks.

In the present chapter, we examine the nature of commercial banks and the kind of business in which they engage, the structural framework of banking and bank regulation in the United States, the process by which commercial banks create money, and the traditional theory of commercial banking. In the following chapter we consider the limits to deposit expansion by the commercial banking system and the individual commercial bank. In Chapter 7 we look at the special problems involved in the management of the assets and liabilities of commercial banks.[1]

1. Issues relating to the banking structure, such as branch versus unit banking, bank mergers, and the regulation of entry into the banking business, are discussed in Chapter 27.

FUNCTIONS OF COMMERCIAL BANKS

Financial institutions in general are distinguishable from other types of business by the nature of their assets, which consist largely of claims on other institutions and individuals. Commercial banks are most sharply differentiated from other financial institutions by the character of their principal liabilities. Only commercial banks hold demand deposits. The demand deposit accounts of commercial banks comprise the bulk of the money supply, and, inasmuch as the public obtains additional currency through commercial banks by converting bank money into pocketbook money, the first important function performed by banks may be described as the *administration of the money supply*. Banks maintain demand deposit accounts for their customers and convert deposit money into currency (or vice versa) at the discretion of the latter; they periodically transmit statements to customers showing all transactions involving deposit balances; and they participate in an elaborate clearing mechanism that permits checks to be collected quickly and with a minimum of work.[2]

A second major function of commercial banks, which derives from the fact that demand deposits serve as money, is that of *money creation* (and destruction). When commercial banks acquire earning assets, the demand deposit accounts of those selling or transferring these assets to the banks are increased,[3] and when banks reduce their holdings of earning assets demand deposits are decreased. Variations in the earning assets of commercial banks are the most important direct source of changes in the money stock. Banks are unique among non-governmental institutions as administrators of demand deposits and as money issuers.

A third major function of commercial banks is that of *lender*, with banks serving both as intermediaries between savers and borrowers and as lenders of newly created funds. Commercial banks thus influence not only the size of the money stock, but also the allocation of funds and thus the direction and use of resources within the system as a whole. Banks are obviously not the only lending institutions, but they are among the most important both in terms of total lending activity and as the predominant lenders in the fields of consumer finance and of lending to small- and medium-sized commercial, industrial, and agricultural businesses.

The overall importance of commercial banks as lenders may be gauged

---

2. The clearing machinery in which the commercial banks and central bank of the United States participate is discussed in Chapter 12.

3. This assumes that the seller of assets desires in exchange a demand deposit rather than currency. This assumption is quite reasonable since a large proportion of money transactions are carried out entirely by deposit transfers. Furthermore, as may be inferred from our definition of the money supply, even if the transaction does involve currency the direct effect on the money supply is the same as if only deposit money were involved. See below, pp. 83-84.

by their aggregate holdings of financial assets and their net acquisitions[4] of financial instruments in recent years, in comparison with that of other financial intermediaries. At the end of 1961 insured commercial banks in the United States had loans outstanding of $127.8 billion, and held $89.7 billion in securities, $56.2 billion in cash assets,[5] and $6.7 billion of miscellaneous assets, for an aggregate of $277.4 billion. This total may be compared with that for mutual savings banks which then had assets of $42.8 billion, savings and loan associations with assets of $82.1 billion, and life insurance companies with assets of $126.6 billion.

A second important indicator of the overall significance of an institution as a lender is its contribution to the flow of funds into credit markets. From 1957 to 1961 a net sum of $146.7 billion was advanced to borrowers via the acquisition of credit and equity instruments by the three principal categories of lending institutions, commercial banks, insurance companies, and other savings institutions. The totals supplied by each group were remarkably even, being $49.4, $48.9, and $48.4 billion respectively.[6] The annual contribution varied substantially, however, in the case of banks (from a low of $5.1 to a high of $14.9 billion) and was most stable (at a rising rate) for the insurance sector.

The Commercial Banking Business

The term "commercial" bank is a holdover from an earlier period when banks were predominantly short-term financiers of goods in transit and inventories of traders and merchants. This designation was not as inappropriate in 1900 as it is today, but even then investments were over one-fifth of banks' earning assets and banks were more sharply distinguishable from other financial institutions as demand deposit administrators and money creators than as commercial lenders. The term commercial has become increasingly anachronistic, particularly since 1929, as banks have diversified their activities to a point where many of them are properly referred to as "department stores of finance."[7]

---

4. "Net" acquisitions of financial instruments are the total value of such instruments acquired *less* the value of financial instruments sold during the same time period.

5. Cash assets include cash items in process of collection, vault cash, interbank deposits, and deposits with the Federal Reserve Banks. The total of cash assets given here is substantially greater than that shown below in Table 5-1. The difference lies chiefly in the entry for items in process of collection. It is attributable primarily to the practice known as "window dressing" whereby banks endeavor to improve their apparent liquidity position at the year-end. The usual procedure is to draw checks on one another on the last day which appear as items in process of collection but cancel out upon presentation.

6. Cf. "Summary of Principal Financial Flows," *Federal Reserve Bulletin*, July 1962, p. 901.

7. As early as 1940 an unduly strict adherence to the conception of a bank as a commercial lender led one financial writer to the doleful conclusion that commercial banks "have largely gone out of the banking business." See Robert B. Warren, *The Search for Financial Security* (New York: Columbia University Press, 1940), p. 32.

An indication of the variety of business activities engaged in by commercial banks may be obtained by examining a statement of assets and liabilities of all commercial banks (Table 5-1). This table does not tell the whole story, of course, since banks perform other important services, such as providing facilities for the safekeeping of valuables or serving as trustee for individuals, businesses, and other organizations, which absorb considerable manpower and yield substantial revenues but do not show up directly on the balance sheet. Nevertheless, the balance sheet yields a great deal of information as to the business activities of banks. It may be seen that in addition to administering demand deposits commercial banks have a substantial volume of time and savings deposit liabilities owing to members of the public. Banks also provide customers who anticipate difficulty in using their personal checks with credit instruments that are more acceptable because of explicit assurance of payment by the bank, e.g., certified and cashier's checks, letters of credit, and travelers' checks. In brief, banks provide their customers with a full complement of depository services.

TABLE 5-1. Assets and Liabilities of Insured Commercial Banks in the United States, March 26, 1962

Assets			Liabilities		
Type	Amount (millions)	%	Type	Amount (millions)	%
I. Cash	$ 44,992	16.5	I. Deposits	$234,830	88.0
II. Loans (net)	125,828	47.2	A. Individuals, partnerships and corporations (payable on demand)	110,387	
A. Commercial and industrial	44,940				
B. Agricultural	6,535		B. Individuals, partnerships and corporations (time deposits)	77,585	
C. For buying securities	5,766		C. U. S. Government	7,057	
D. To financial institutions	9,029		D. States and subdivisions	17,308	
E. Real Estate	30,705		E. Banks and foreign governments (including postal savings)	16,958	
F. Other loans to individuals	27,862				
G. Other loans	3,630		F. Certified and officers' checks, etc.	3,536	
H. Valuation reserves	—(2,639)				
III. Investments	89,022	33.7	II. Miscellaneous	9,282	3.5
A. U. S. Government obligations	64,094		III. Capital accounts	22,478	8.5
B. Obligations of states and subdivisions	21,480				
C. Other securities	3,448				
IV. Other assets (buildings, fixtures, other real estate, etc.)	6,748	2.6			
Total assets	$266,590	100.	Total liabilities	$266,590	100.

Source: Derived from FDIC, *News Release*, July 17, 1962.

A-1   A-2

From the asset side of the balance sheet, we see that banks invest a considerable proportion of their assets in United States Government obligations and other securities; that they lend heavily on real estate and to individuals; and that they have a sizable volume of loans outstanding for financing agriculture, security purchases, and other financial institutions (mainly finance companies). The largest single subdivision of loans is "commercial and industrial" loans. Banks remain important lenders for short-term working capital purposes, although a considerable proportion of the items included in this category are longer term loans that bear little relation to the traditional commercial loan.

It is important to bear in mind that commercial banks are profit-seeking businesses, trading their own debts (deposits) for the higher yielding debts of others (notes, bills, and longer term securities). With few exceptions banks are corporations, owned by stockholders who are interested in the size of earnings and dividends, and whose welfare is a major concern of bank management. It is true that banks are closely regulated by law and by supervisory authorities as to volume and type of reserves, kinds and proportions of loans and investments that may be made, accounting practices, and other matters. Member banks and insured non-members are forbidden to pay interest on demand deposit accounts, and the Board of Governors of the Federal Reserve System, the Federal Deposit Insurance Corporation, and state bank supervisors impose ceilings on the interest rate paid on time and savings deposit accounts.[8] Nonetheless, neither bank profits nor the rates charged by banks on loans and investments are subject to governmental regulation;[9] they are determined by economic forces operating in particular credit markets.

Banks are usually managed conservatively, partly because of regulatory limitations on asset holdings and entry, but also because of the force of a tradition antagonistic to speculative risk-taking and aggressive methods of soliciting business. However, conservative management can be two-sided —it may mitigate speculative excesses and the cruder forms of monopolistic exploitation, but it may also tend to impede risk-taking activities, and it

---

8. Since February 1, 1936, when the FDIC first imposed limits on interest paid on the time and savings deposits of insured non-member banks, these rates have been the same as those imposed by the Board for member banks. At the beginning of 1962, the maximum interest rates payable on time and savings deposits by insured commercial banks were raised to:

For savings deposits	3½ percent
Time deposits payable:	
In 12 months or more	4 percent
In 6 but under 12 months	3½ percent
In 90 days but under six months	2½ percent
In less than 90 days	1 percent

9. Apart from the usury laws, which vary widely between states, and are, by and large, of limited significance because of their high-rate limits and the relative ease with which they may be evaded.

may contribute to attitudes inconsistent with a desirable degree of banking competition.

The Structure of Commercial Banking in the United States

The commercial banking structure in the United States is unique among industrialized countries in its high degree of decentralization. Most economically developed countries have banking systems dominated by a few very large institutions with numerous branch offices. In England and Wales, for example, nearly all the domestic banking business is in the hands of eleven branch banks, and over 85 per cent is carried on by the "Big Five"— the Midland, the Westminster, Barclays, Lloyds, and the National Provincial —with much of the remainder done by two smaller branch systems. In Canada there were only nine banks in 1958, operating a total of 4,556 domestic banking offices. In the United States, on the other hand, the "unit" or single office bank is still predominant despite the great increase in branch banking, particularly since World War II. On January 1, 1962 there were 13,432 banks in the United States, of which 10,948 were unit institutions and 2,484 branch banks (i.e., banks operating two or more offices). These 2,484 branch banks conducted business at a total of 11,077 branches, so that while under 20 per cent of the banks in this country were branch banks, 55 per cent of the 24,509 banking offices were operated by these multiple office banks.

Although there are a great many banks in the United States, a surprisingly large percentage of the banking business is conducted by a relatively small number of institutions. In 1962 the sixty-one banks with deposits of $500 million or more (0.5 per cent of the total number of banks) held 43 per cent of all demand deposits and the same per cent of the dollar volume of commercial bank loans. At the opposite end of the size spectrum, the 10,266 banks with deposits of $10 million or less (73 per cent of bank numbers) held only 13 per cent of all demand deposits and bank loans.

Since most depositors and smaller borrowers have little choice but to do business with local financial institutions, the degree of competition in the banking business depends to a great extent on the number of bank offices in local communities rather than on national aggregates of bank office numbers. A recent investigation disclosed that 45 per cent of the banking offices in the United States were located in communities with no other banking office, 20 percent had one competitive office, and only 19 per cent were located in communities with nine or more competitive banking offices. Many banks, of course, must compete with other financial institutions as well as with banks in contiguous and even more distant locations. Development of improved transportation and faster communication have widened areas of competition. But the prevalence of small numbers of banking offices in economically significant local markets suggests that banking services are sold under far less competitive conditions than might be inferred from national totals of banks and bank offices. We will return to questions relating to the banking structure in Chapter 27.

We have seen in Chapter 3 that there is a complex structure of regulatory authority concerned with commercial banking in the United States, with three federal and fifty state agencies having jurisdiction over these institutions. Table 5-2 indicates the distribution of the number and volume of demand deposits of commercial banks according to the various categories of regulatory authority. The division between national and state banks relates to the political jurisdiction under which banks are organized, chartered, and regulated. National banks are organized under federal law. and are subject to regulation solely by federal authorities. State banks are

TABLE 5-2. Classification of Commercial Banks in the United States, December 31, 1961

| | Number of Banks | | Demand Deposits | |
	Number	Percent	Dollars (millions)	Percent
National banks	4,513	33.6	89,966	54.3
State and private	8,918	66.4	75,813	45.7
Total	13,431	100.	165,779	100.
Member banks	6,113	45.5	142,170	85.8
National	(4,513)	(33.6)	(89,966)	(54.3)
State	(1,600)	(11.9)	(52,204)	(31.5)
Non-member banks	7,318	54.5	23,609	14.2
Total	13,431	100.	165,779	100.
Insured Banks	13,108	97.6	164,721	99.4
Non-insured banks	323	2.4	1,058	0.6
Total	13,431	100.	165,779	100.

Source: Data from *Federal Reserve Bulletin.*

organized and chartered to do business under state law and are subject to state (and usually some federal) supervisory authority. The division of regulatory authority antedates the formation of the Federal Reserve System and the FDIC, and to it we may trace the origins of the multiple banking authority that is one of the distinctive characteristics of the banking system of the United States.

With the establishment of the Federal Reserve System in 1914 it became possible for the same bank to be subject to two separate supervisory agencies; national banks were required to be members of the Federal Reserve System and state banks were permitted to become members if they could meet the conditions of membership. Thus national banks were under the Comptroller of the Currency and the Federal Reserve, state banks under the Federal Reserve and the state banking authority. Not quite half of the commercial banks are members of the Federal Reserve. These include, in addition to all national banks, about one-fifth of the state banks. Since member banks include most of the larger banks in the country, the deposits of member banks comprise about 85 per cent of the total.

With the formation of the Federal Deposit Insurance Corporation in 1935 it became possible for the same bank to become subject to three separate supervisory agencies. Since all member banks must be insured with the FDIC, both national banks and state member banks are subject to a triple authority. More important, the FDIC extended the scope of regulation by federal authority well beyond its previous limits, since many state non-member banks desired deposit insurance. At the end of 1961 there were 6,995 non-member insured banks with demand deposits of 22.5 billion and only 323 non-insured banks with demand deposits of 1.1 billion (less than 1 per cent of total demand deposits).

This regulatory structure is cumbersome and wasteful, even though steps have been taken to reduce the overlapping of regulatory action. In practice the incidence of supervision is less burdensome than might appear. Primary responsibility for national banks rests with the Comptroller of the Currency and primary responsibility for state banks, regardless of membership in the Federal Reserve System or the Federal Deposit Insurance Corporation, rests with the state authorities. Furthermore, a high degree of cooperation has been effected among the federal agencies. Thus national banks are examined by the Comptroller of the Currency but not by the Federal Reserve Banks or FDIC. State member banks are examined by the Federal Reserve (as well as by the state authorities) but not by the Federal Deposit Insurance Corporation. Insured nonmember banks are examined by both the Federal Deposit Insurance Corporation and the state authorities, and non-insured state banks by the state authorities alone.

THE PROCESS OF MONEY CREATION

Commercial banks, as has been noted, are both intermediaries and money creators. In the former capacity they transfer resources given them by shareholders and depositors to borrowers, much the same as insurance companies, savings banks, and other financial institutions do. When an insurance company, for example, receives a check for $20,000 in payment of an insurance premium, it can lend this sum by buying an earning asset such as a corporate bond. Banks can do this and more, since they have the power to lend out not only the cash transmitted to them, but also deposit money which they create in the process of lending. It is this power to lend newly created funds that most sharply distinguishes the lending process of commercial banks from that of other financial intermediaries.

In general, the intermediary and money creation activities of banks are so closely intertwined as to be indistinguishable. Cash received by banks is rarely loaned out directly; ordinarily it becomes part of a pool of cash reserves that serve to support the banks' outstanding deposit liabilities. It enables the banks to acquire additional loans and investments in exchange for deposits, which involves the banks in both intermediary and money creation activities.

Cash Flows and Deposit Changes

From the standpoint of the commercial banking *system* demand deposits may increase (or, by reversing the transactions, decrease) for any one of three main reasons. First, the public may transfer currency to a bank in exchange for an equivalent addition to demand deposits. Second, the Treasury or Federal Reserve Banks may create new money claims which are deposited with banks, thus increasing demand deposits. Finally, the banks may create demand deposits on their own initiative by exchanging such deposits for earning assets.[10] In the first two cases deposits increase as a consequence of a net inflow of cash (currency or deposit claims against the Federal Reserve Banks) to the banks. Deposits which originate in this way, and which are therefore accompanied by an increase in the net cash assets of the banking system, will be referred to as *primary deposits*. In the third case, the deposits arise out of the lending operation itself and result in no net addition to bank cash. The deposits so created will be referred to as *derivative deposits*, as they derive from the lending process of commercial banks. It is in the establishment and destruction of derivative deposits that banks actively create and destroy money.

In order to illustrate the principal ways in which primary deposits are established, let us assume, first, that Mr. Faust, a customer of the Mephisto State Bank (a member bank), decides to transfer to the bank, in exchange for a demand deposit, the sum of $1,000 in currency previously held for safekeeping in a wall safe. The balance sheet of the bank would be altered by an addition to cash assets and a corresponding increment to demand deposits:

MEPHISTO STATE BANK

Assets		*Liabilities*	
Cash	+$1,000	Demand deposits	+$1,000

The money supply would be unchanged, since the addition to demand deposits is offset by an equal decline in currency held by the public. The currency in Mr. Faust's wall safe was part of the money supply as we have defined it; currency held by a commercial bank is not. Since bank cash has

---

10. Demand deposits may also increase as a result of a shift by depositors from time to demand deposit accounts. This is of some importance, but at this stage in the discussion it is convenient to regard such transactions as involving withdrawals of currency from banks and, shortly thereafter, redeposits of currency.

increased by the same amount as demand deposits, and since banks need to hold cash reserves that are only a fraction of outstanding deposit liabilities, this transaction has increased the lending power of the banking system.

Let us consider, secondly, a case where new money claims are issued by the Federal Reserve Banks in the process of buying securities (open-market operations). For convenience we shall assume that Mr. Faust sells a $1,000 government bond to the Federal Reserve Bank of New York. Mr. Faust receives a cashier's check for $1,000 drawn on the Federal Reserve Bank; this he transfers to the Mephisto State Bank in exchange for an equivalent addition to his demand deposit. The bank now owns a claim against the Federal Reserve Bank which it will use to increase its cash assets in the form of either additional currency or a larger deposit account with its Federal Reserve Bank. Assuming that the latter course is chosen (which is most likely), the net result is as follows:

FEDERAL RESERVE BANK		MEPHISTO STATE BANK	
Assets	*Liabilities*	*Assets*	*Liabilities*
Government bonds +$1,000	Deposits of Mephisto State Bank +$1,000	Deposits with Federal Reserve Bank +$1,000	Demand deposits +$1,000

In this example the money supply is increased by $1,000, in the form of additional demand deposits of the commercial banks; the increase, however, resulted from action by the Federal Reserve Bank, not the commercial banks. The new deposits are primary deposits because they came into existence as a result of an inflow of additional cash assets to the commercial banking system.

The Lending Process and the Creation of Derivative Deposits

Let us now suppose that a businessman, needing funds to acquire a stock of inventory, asks the Mephisto State Bank for a loan of $25,000. After the loan is granted, the balance sheet of the bank would show a $25,000 addition to the bank's assets in the form of notes receivable, and an equivalent addition to the deposit liabilities of the bank.[11]

MEPHISTO STATE BANK	
Assets	*Liabilities*
Loans +$25,000	Demand deposits +$25,000

11. This assumes a loan in which interest is collected at maturity. If, as is more common, the loan were "discounted," a note payable in three months at a rate of 4 per cent per annum would realize only $24,750 for the borrower. "Loans" would still go up by $25,000, but deposits would increase by $24,750 and a liability account "income collected but not earned" by $250.

In this case the bank has acquired an income-yielding asset in exchange for rights granted the borrower to draw checks on the bank for an equivalent sum. The bank has exchanged its own non-interest bearing debt for an interest-bearing obligation of its customer. This exchange of debts has its rationale in the bank's quest for income and its customer's need for an acceptable means of payment. Simply by expanding its debts in the form of demand deposits the bank was able to increase its earning assets and at the same time supply the businessman with the ready funds he desired.

It will be noted that this transaction results in an increase in the money supply since demand deposits have risen without any offsetting change elsewhere in the system. In other words, the bank has loaned money that it created in the very process of lending. This process of money creation is sometimes referred to as the "monetization of credit," as the credit instrument of the borrower (a promissory note) has been converted into money by its exchange for the newly created derivative deposit.

Let us now assume that the bank decides to acquire a $5,000 government bond for its investment portfolio. After arranging for the purchase from a dealer, the bank would write a cashier's check for the cost of the bond and convey it to the seller. In the simplest case the seller of the bond would bank with the institution acquiring the bond, depositing the check to his account. Then the seller would have increased his demand deposit by the amount of the check, and on the other side of the balance sheet the bond holdings of the bank would be increased by the same amount.

BUYING BANK

Assets	*Liabilities*
Bonds +$5,000	Demand deposits +$5,000

We see that the process of acquiring a bond has increased the money supply exactly as in the case of the loan.

Typically the seller of a bond will do his banking at an institution other than the buyer bank, in which case the seller's bank will increase its demand deposits and cash assets at the expense of the buyer bank. Assuming that the seller has deposited in his own bank the cashier's check received from the buyer bank, and that this check has been cleared, the net effect of the transactions will be:

BUYING BANK		SELLER'S BANK	
Assets	*Liabilities*	*Assets*	*Liabilities*
Bonds + $5,000		Cash +$5,000	Demand
Cash −$5,000			deposits +$5,000

It will be noted that demand deposits have increased by the value of the purchased bond, as in the previous case. In this instance, however, the demand deposit first appears on the accounts of a bank other than the one acquiring the bond so that the bond purchase by a bank results in the establishment of a demand deposit in another bank. By the same line of reasoning, the sale of a bond by a bank will result in the reduction of the demand deposit of the buyer in his bank. (The student should show this by making the appropriate balance sheet entries.)

Interbank Deposit Transfers

The principal source of day-to-day fluctuations in the demand deposits of *individual* commercial banks is neither primary nor derivative deposit changes. It is interbank deposit transfers, i.e., the shift of existing demand deposits between commercial banks. As checks are written on existing deposits they are transferred from bank to bank in a never-ending process. Deposit totals for the system are not altered by these transfers, but they may affect the deposits of individual banks to a significant extent.

Interbank deposit transfers may be illustrated by assuming that our depositor, Mr. Faust, deposits at his bank a check for $500 sent him by Mr. Wilcox, drawn on the First National Bank of Mephisto. Mr. Faust's bank obtains a claim on the First National, in exchange for which it credits his account for the $500. For simplicity let us suppose that the claim is collected in currency by a messenger walking across the street and presenting the check to the other bank. The First National then debits Mr. Wilcox's account by the amount of the check and the two banks adjust their cash accounts, thus completing the set of transactions. The changes in the balance sheets of the two banks are as follows:

MEPHISTO STATE BANK		FIRST NATIONAL	
Assets	*Liabilities*	*Assets*	*Liabilities*
Cash +$500	Demand deposits +$500	Cash −$500	Demand deposits −$500

It should be observed that here, as in the case of the depositing of currency in the bank, there is no change in the money supply. The increase in demand deposits in one bank is offset by a corresponding reduction of the demand deposits in another institution. It should also be noted that in this case, in contrast to instances where primary deposits are established, there is no increment to the cash assets of the commercial banks taken together, but rather a transfer of cash between banks. These interbank transfers are of major importance to the banks involved and significantly affect the behavior of individual banks. But they do not affect system totals as do primary and derivative deposits.

THE TRADITIONAL THEORY OF COMMERCIAL BANKING

Enough has been said to indicate that the essential feature of commercial banking is the holding of liabilities in the form of deposits payable on demand, and, against these, the holding of resources in the form of interest-bearing obligations which are payable, usually not on demand but at some future time. The former represent the debts of the bank and the latter the debts of individuals, business concerns, and governments. As observed earlier, bank assets now include a significant proportion of government bonds and other securities. Traditional thought on the subject of banking was based upon the assumption, however, that the earning assets of commercial banks would be of commercial origin and this assumption still strongly influences the conduct of the banks.[12]

The role of commercial banking as traditionally conceived can best be indicated by an illustration. Let us suppose that a wholesaler buys a shipment of clothespins and in return gives the manufacturer his promissory note or accepts a draft drawn by the manufacturer. The note or acceptance is made payable in sixty days, since the dealer anticipates that by that time the proceeds of his sale of clothespins will provide funds for meeting it. The manufacturer, however, needs ready cash and cannot wait sixty days for his money. Accordingly he takes the note or acceptance to his banker who "discounts" it for him; that is, the bank allows him the face value of the note less interest to maturity. The banker does this by crediting the checking account of the manufacturer, and the latter draws against this credit as he sees fit. When the note falls due it is collected by the bank rather than by the manufacturer.

The result of this series of arrangements is that the bank has exchanged its own highly acceptable credit, in the form of the checking account balance, for the less well-known credit of the clothespin dealer which was in the form of the latter's note or acceptance. Commerce and industry were served, since the merchant secured a stock of goods he otherwise might not have been able to get, and the manufacturer sold an order he otherwise might not have been able to sell. The interest on the discounted note constituted the bank's reward for the economic service it performed, and in the end—as in every textbook idyll of this sort—all parties benefited. And the "invisible hand" of the economic harmonists moved on to other good deeds.

---

12. The historical preference of bankers for self-liquidating commercial paper was amusingly illustrated by Governor Benjamin Strong in testimony presented before the Joint Committee of Agricultural Inquiry during the 1920's: "Lord Rothschild once was asked how he told a good bill when he had it presented for discount—in the early days the Rothschilds were the largest buyers of bills in Europe—and he said he always put his tongue to it to see whether it had a little flavor of salt. The idea was that he didn't want to buy a bill that hadn't moved across the ocean in a vessel carrying a shipment of goods." Joint Commission of Agricultural Inquiry, Washington, Government Printing Office, 1922, Vol. 11, p. 517.

Assumed Adjustment of Money Supply to "Needs of Trade"

In this idealized description, the banking process, through the medium of self-liquidating commercial paper, was held to be firmly rooted in trade and industry. This relationship is emphasized in the name *commercial* banking.[13] It was assumed that an expansion of bank credit was highly desirable since it presumably accompanied and facilitated an expansion in the volume of goods produced and exchanged. But more especially it was believed that the process of creating demand deposits by discounting self-liquidating commercial paper would increase or decrease the money supply in step with the volume of business.

The reasoning behind the traditional theory of commercial banking was that an increase in production and trade presumably would give rise to a larger volume of commercial paper. By the discount of this commercial paper at banks, demand deposits would be increased and thus the desired result—the expansion of the money supply in accordance with the growth in the volume of business—would be achieved. Similarly, if business was declining, less commercial paper would be drawn so that as old notes and bills matured and were paid they would not be replaced by an equal quantity of new notes and bills. Consequently, the total of discounted loans in the portfolios of banks would decline and with it the stock of money.

The traditional theory assumed, in effect, that the changes in the quantity of commercial paper would be proportional to changes in the volume of business transactions. By lending only on such paper the quantity of money was expected to change automatically with changes in the volume of trade. Thus by creating deposits against good self-liquidating commercial paper the banks were expected to provide a system of credit accommodation for business that would be automatic, safe, and adapted to that vague ideal, "the needs of trade." The role of banks was presumed to be passive, reflecting and facilitating changes in business but not inducing them. The traditional theory may be summarized as saying that by confining bank earning assets to short-term productive business loans, i.e., by regulating the *quality* of bank assets, an appropriate *quantity* of money would be assured.

An Appraisal of the Traditional Theory

There can be little doubt that in making short-term, self-liquidating, working capital loans commercial banks perform a useful lending function which they are well fitted to carry out by their size, geographic position, and tradition. Furthermore, loans made on self-liquidating commercial paper have proven to be profitable and, for the most part, safe, although as we shall see in Chapter 7 their contribution to the liquidity of

---

13. The traditional theory is also sometimes referred to as the "commercial loan theory," or the "real-bills doctrine."

bank assets is easily exaggerated. Nevertheless, the doctrine that an appropriate quantity of money would be automatically assured simply by regulating the *quality* of bank assets in accordance with the criteria of the traditional theory must be rejected as fallacious.

It is difficult to establish precise standards for an appropriate or ideal quantity of money. Broadly, the concept refers to a money stock that changes in a manner consistent with full employment, acceptable economic growth, and reasonable stability of the price level. On this test one difficulty with the traditional doctrine arises from its focus on a narrow sector of the economy. If the expansion of inventory investment justifies an increase in the money supply, it is not easy to see why increases in other components of production should not require increases in the money stock as well. This would include increases in fixed capital goods as well as consumers goods. In short, the criteria of an appropriate money supply noted above suggest that it should grow at about the same secular rate of increase as total output. But the traditional theory links the growth of money to a special kind of financial instrument generated by particular forms of investment. In so doing it suggests a false guide for adjusting the stock of money to the needs of business.

A second major difficulty with the traditional theory is its implicit neglect of the problem of independent changes in the velocity of circulation of money. Such changes alter the volume of expenditures that will be associated with a given stock of money. If we assume a sharp increase in the velocity of circulation of money from an initial condition of full employment, the money stock consistent with full employment without inflation will be smaller than the existing stock of money. This would not be true from the standpoint of the traditional theory—in fact, as we shall see below, from that vantage point the appropriate stock of money will be larger than previously.

A third major weakness of the traditional theory is its tying of the money supply to the money *value* of inventories to be financed by bank loans, when this value itself depends in part on the size of the money supply. Thus, in a period of deflation a reduction in the value of inventories to be financed would reduce the value of commercial paper offered to the banks, which in turn would cause a contraction of the money supply. The reduction in the money supply would cause a further decline in prices, and the downswing would be further reinforced. In an inflationary period, on the other hand, a rise in the price level would mean a rise in the value of inventories, which would justify an increase in the volume of bank loans. The resultant increase in the money supply would contribute to a further upward movement in prices, and the inflation would be reinforced by the interaction between the money supply, the price level, the value of inventory stocks, and the value of commercial paper discounted at the banks. The essential point to note here is that the linking together of the money supply and the *value* of commodity stocks provides a built-in mechanism to sustain any upward or downward movement of the price level and economic activity.[14] It should be obvious that a system in which money can be created and destroyed on this basis cannot be depended on to produce appropriate fluctuations in the money supply.

Up to this point the discussion of the traditional theory has suggested that it is wrong in principle. That is to say, if banks followed the traditional theory to the letter the proper volume of money would result only by accident. Actually, banks never did confine their lending exclusively to the categories prescribed. And with the rise of bank holdings of government securities during and after the Great Depression, banks became less passive lenders than previously. With an increased willingness to buy and sell securities to compensate for cyclical fluctuations in the volume of commercial loans held, banks have increasingly violated a basic premise of the traditional theory. However, as we might have expected from our brief examination of the internal logic of the traditional theory, the result of this increased activity of commercial banks in securities markets has been an increase in the stability of the money supply.

These are by no means all the criticisms that could be brought against the traditional theory of commercial banking, but they are enough to illustrate its shortcomings. Despite its inadequacies, the traditional theory has exerted great influence on banking thought and legislation. It is still employed as a point of reference: banking as it actually operates is often compared with the idealized pattern described in the traditional theory.

SELECTED BIBLIOGRAPHY

Federal Deposit Insurance Corporation, *Annual Reports*.

HAWTREY, R. G., *Currency and Credit*. London: Longmans, Green, 1950, Chapter VI.

MINTS, L. W., *A History of Banking Theory*. Chicago: University of Chicago Press, 1945, Chapters I-IV, XIII.

ROBERTSON, D. H., *Money*. London: Nisbet, 1948, pp. 99-107.

SAYERS, R. S., *Modern Banking*. London: Oxford University Press, 1960, Chapters 1-2, 10.

SHAW, E. S., *Money, Income, and Monetary Policy*. Homewood, Ill.: Irwin, 1950, Chapters III-IV.

WHITTLESEY, C. R., "Banking Principles and Practices," *Encyclopaedia Britannica*, 1959 ed.

---

14. It should be noted that a commodity standard provides a link between the money supply and a *physical quantity* of some commodity. The physical stock of a commodity is obviously limited in a way in which the *value* of a stock of commodity is not.

6

COMMERCIAL BANK
DEPOSIT EXPANSION

We have seen that commercial banks actively create money in the process of acquiring earning assets. Since additional earning assets result in increased income, banks have an incentive to expand their deposits and earning assets to the limits fixed by law, regulatory authority, and current standards of prudence in bank management. In this chapter we shall consider in detail the factors limiting the expansion of deposits and the manner in which they operate.

The main factors limiting bank deposit expansion may be grouped under three headings: (1) the volume of cash reserves held by the commercial banks; (2) the minimum ratio of reserves to deposits imposed by law, regulation, or current standards of bank prudence; and (3) the drain of cash to other banks or out of the banking system in the process of deposit expansion. We shall examine each of these limiting factors in turn, and then consider how they operate to restrict, first, the expansion of deposits by the commercial banking system, and, second, deposit expansion by an individual bank within the system.

BANK RESERVES

The fundamental role of reserves in limiting deposit expansion calls for a detailed analysis of the meaning and significance of bank reserves. The usual connotation of reserves is something saved or held back for a particular purpose, as for use in an emergency. It is in this sense that we employ it in speaking of reserves of troops or of food reserves. At one time the expression bank reserves conveyed the same general idea, that of a stock of ready cash to meet abnormal demands. Today, however, only a limited part of the funds classified as bank reserves are of this character.

The Meaning of Bank Reserves

In discussions of banking the expression "reserves," used without qualification, ordinarily refers to the cash assets of a bank. This includes currency held in the vaults of the bank ("vault cash"), demand deposits held with other commercial banks (interbank or correspondent balances), demand balances held by member banks (and some non-members) with the Federal Reserve Banks, and cash items in process of collection. The cash assets of insured commercial banks in the United States amounted to $56 billion at the end of 1961, or approximately one-fifth of bank assets. They were divided among the four components as shown in Table 6-1.

TABLE 6-1. Cash Assets of Insured Commercial Banks, December 31, 1961

Type	Amount (in Millions)	Per cent
Vault cash	$ 3,693	6.6
Deposits with Federal Reserve Banks	16,918	30.2
Demand balances with other banks	14,147	25.2
Cash items in process of collection	21,424	38.0
Total	56,182	100.0

Source: FDIC, News Release, July 16, 1962.

Frequently encountered in writings on banking is the distinction between "primary" and "secondary" reserves. In this usage, primary reserves refer to reserves as we have defined them in the preceding paragraph (i.e., as cash assets). Secondary reserves are earning assets of commercial banks which can be exchanged for cash with little delay or loss in capital value, such as Treasury bills. The concept of secondary reserves is less precise than that of primary reserves since no sharp distinction can be made between such reserves and still less liquid earning assets. Nonetheless, the concept is analytically useful and of considerable importance in bank asset management, as banks typically rely to a significant extent on their holdings of highly liquid non-cash assets for meeting abnormal cash demands of customers. When the word reserves is used without qualification, however, it will refer to primary rather than secondary reserves.

It is well to bear in mind that just as there is a distinction between commercial and central banks, so there is a corresponding distinction between the reserves of each. The reserves of commercial banks will be referred to as "bank reserves," and for the member banks of the Federal Reserve System, "member bank reserves." The reserves of the Federal Reserve Banks will be referred to as "central bank reserves." The present chapter is concerned only with "bank reserves" and "member bank reserves."

Legal and Non-Legal Reserves

The cash assets of commercial banks may also be subdivided into legal and non-legal reserves. Legal reserves are those assets of a bank that may be counted as reserves for the purpose of meeting a state or federal reserve requirement. Non-legal reserves are all other cash assets of banks: they are the residual that remains when legal cash reserves are subtracted from total cash assets.

For banks that are members of the Federal Reserve System, legal reserves consist of deposits held with the district Federal Reserve Bank plus bank vault cash. Before 1959, only deposits with a Federal Reserve Bank could serve as legal reserves of member banks. During that year, however, Congress authorized the Board of Governors to permit member banks to count some or all of their vault cash as part of their legal reserves. In a series of steps, beginning in December 1959, the Board modified its reserve requirement regulation to permit increasing proportions, and then, in November 1960, all vault cash to be counted as legal reserves. This innovation was designed, in part, to adjust for the fact that many banks, particularly smaller country banks, had found it necessary to hold relatively large amounts of vault cash for operating purposes. Permitting vault cash to be counted as legal reserves is one way in which these differences may be taken into account in fixing reserve requirements.

Non-member bank legal reserves differ according to the laws of the fifty states, but they commonly include (1) vault cash, (2) balances with other banks, and (3), in some states, securities issued by states or by the United States Treasury.

It should be noted that the terms "legal reserves" and "required reserves" are not synonymous. Legal reserves are those reserves that are in a form permitting them to fulfill the requirements of law, but banks need not limit these holdings to the amounts currently required. In fact, it is a common and useful practice to subdivide legal reserves into required and excess legal reserves. Required legal reserves are that part of legal reserves which a bank must hold, given its deposits and the applicable legal reserve requirements; excess legal reserves are the quantity of legal reserves over and above those that are required. Figure 6-1 describes the changes in volume of total, required, and excess legal reserves of member banks for the period 1930-1962 inclusive.

Since for all practical purposes a bank or a banking system must have excess legal reserves in order to expand deposit liabilities,[1] the volume of excess legal reserves is an important indicator of the potential lending power of commercial banks. It is possible, however, that while some banks have excess reserves, others have been under such heavy pressure for loans or

---

1. The Federal Reserve permits member banks to reduce their ratio of legal reserves to deposit liabilities below the required ratio for short periods, but this is not likely to provide the basis for any significant expansion of deposit liabilities.

cash that they have borrowed substantial sums from the Federal Reserve Banks. Thus a given amount of excess reserves might be accompanied at one time by negligible bank borrowing, and at another time by a substantial volume of borrowing. Because of the existence of pressures on borrowing banks to contract commitments, the willingness of the aggregate of banks to expand credit and the degree of ease or tightness in the money market are better measured by the difference between excess legal reserves and bank borrowings from the Federal Reserve Banks. When excess reserves

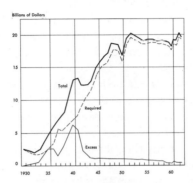

Figure 6-1.   Member Bank Reserves,
1930-1962.

Source: Adapted from the *Federal Reserve Chart Book.*

exceed borrowings this difference is termed "free reserves." It is of course possible that the volume of member bank borrowing at the Reserve Banks may exceed the total of excess legal reserves, in which case "free reserves" are negative. In this instance it is common to speak of the volume of "net borrowed reserves" of the commercial banks. Changes in the volume of free and net borrowed reserves 1952-1962 are shown on Figure 6-2.

As was noted earlier, non-legal reserves are a residual item derived from total cash reserves by subtracting legal cash reserves. It follows that for member banks of the Federal Reserve System, non-legal reserves include (1) demand balances with other banks (interbank or correspondent balances), and (2) cash items in process of collection.[2] Non-legal reserves are sometimes designated "working reserves," but this terminology implies a functional distinction between legal reserves and other cash assets that is not warranted by existing practice.

The Functions of Bank Reserves

Bank reserves serve a wide variety of purposes. One of their major functions is simply *to enable banks to carry out the normal banking*

2. In the unlikely event of a reduction in the proportion of vault cash declared by the Board to be eligible as legal reserves, some part of vault cash might once again become part of non-legal reserves.

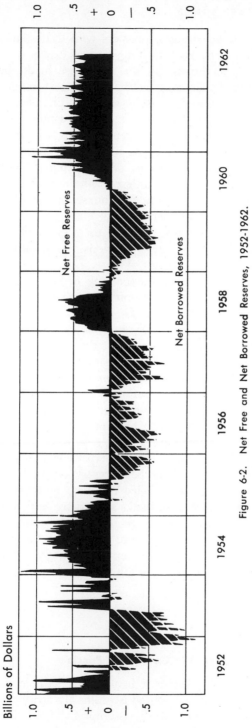

Figure 6-2. Net Free and Net Borrowed Reserves, 1952-1962.

Source: Board of Governors of the Federal Reserve System.

routine—cashing checks, providing customers with drafts and other instruments for making payments, and meeting normal drains of cash to other banks. This function is performed by the vault cash in the bank itself, by deposits held with other banks, and by the legal reserves held in the form of deposits with a member's Federal Reserve Bank. The amount of balances which a bank sees fit to maintain for routine purposes is subject to a considerable element of discretion. Substantial sums, for example, may be left on deposit with correspondent banks not because they are expected to be used directly but rather as a means of compensating these banks for services rendered or possibly to be rendered. The depositing bank thereby feels free to call upon its correspondent for counsel or any of a wide variety of banking services and accommodations.

Cash reserves over and above those held to meet minimum reserve requirements or employed in current operations are usually held for the purpose of *meeting abnormal demands*. They are, therefore, reserves in the everyday sense of the word. At times the lack of attractive opportunities to lend or invest has led banks to accumulate large balances of idle funds in their vaults and on deposit with other banks, including the Federal Reserve Banks. Such balances are hardly reserves in the usual sense; instead of being ready funds awaiting an emergency, they are idle resources awaiting more active utilization. They are not so much funds held in readiness for some future contingency as funds temporarily out of employment.

A third major function of bank reserves is to serve, in conjunction with legal or customary minimum ratios of reserves to deposits, to *limit the amount of commercial bank deposits*. The joint operation of reserves and minimum reserve ratios in containing deposit expansion is considered below in the discussions of reserve ratios and bank expansion limits.

A fourth function performed by bank reserves may be inferred from the fact that balances among member banks which result from the deposit of checks drawn on various different banks are largely settled through debits and credits to reserve accounts. Thus reserves perform the function of a *settlement fund*. It is one of the important services of the Federal Reserve Banks and their branches to serve as centers for an extraordinarily effective check-clearing and settlement organization.

THE RESERVE RATIO

Fractional Reserves: The Goldsmiths' Principle

The quantity of reserves a bank needs to hold in order to be able to meet claims as they are presented is ordinarily a rather small fraction of its liabilities to the public. Indeed, the assumption of liabilities in the form of bank notes or deposits greatly in excess of the cash available for redeeming these promises has always been the cardinal feature of commercial banking. It is made possible because the obligation to pay on demand is an obligation to pay *any* authorized money and not the particular coins or circulating notes which may have originally established the deposit. This is what enables the commercial banker to operate with so much greater freedom than a baggage office.

London goldsmiths in the seventeenth century are supposed to have discovered that it is safe to hold reserves amounting to only a fraction of the liabilities assumed. Thus the practice of holding fractional reserves is sometimes said to be based on the Goldsmiths' Principle. This familiar principle amounts to saying that banks may safely promise to pay total sums considerably in excess of the cash actually on hand for meeting such promises.

There are several reasons why fractional reserves are ordinarily adequate for carrying on the business of banking, and these reasons constitute the bases of the Goldsmiths' Principle. The most important reason is that some of the claims will probably not be presented at all, and very rarely, if ever, will even a very large proportion be presented at the same time. Second, some of the checks drawn on a bank will be redeposited by customers of the same bank, so that reserves are not actually taken from the bank. Third, new deposits will be bringing cash in at the same time that withdrawals are taking it out. Fourth, the maturing of loans and investments, which can be controlled to some extent by a conscious spacing of maturities, provides a continuous inward flow of cash. Finally, some of the assets of the bank can be converted into cash with little or no loss if funds obtained from the other sources are insufficient.

The exact amount of reserves that may be needed to support any particular volume of deposit liabilities cannot be precisely determined. Indeed, the amount varies with different banks and with the same bank at different times. Calculations of appropriate reserve ratios quite properly include allowance for a considerable margin of safety. A number of factors influence the proportion of reserves likely to be considered desirable. One of the most obvious is the liquidity of the bank's earning assets, which relates to the ease of obtaining additional cash in case of need. Another factor is the probability of a sudden increase in the presentation of claims on the bank, as in the case of a run. The prospect of a sudden increase in withdrawals may be influenced by legal safeguards, by the stage of the business cycle, and by foreign or domestic disturbances.

Another basic factor bearing on the necessary volume of reserves is the extent to which the banking resources of the country are capable of being mobilized in time of emergency. The importance of this factor was demonstrated following the establishment of the Federal Reserve System. Largely because of the way in which total reserve funds were made more elastic and mobile, reserve ratios were substantially reduced with no apparent sacrifice in safety. Finally, there is the important question of the quality of bank management. The less competent the management, the higher would reserves presumably need to be in order to provide the same degree of safety for deposits. It is not to be supposed, however, that a less competent management would, in fact, carry higher reserves.

For many years the trend of the ratio of reserves to deposits was downward. Furthermore, a reduction of the ratio where this could be achieved without a loss of security was long regarded as one of the goals of banking policy. It appealed to the banker as economically desirable, since it signified a reduction in the proportion of non-earning assets, and, from the standpoint of society, it suggested that gold and other basic reserve money were being more fully and hence more economically utilized. The problem during these years was to determine how large a stock of reserves was needed to assure the safety of deposits.

After 1933 both total reserves and the ratio of reserves to deposits in the United States rose greatly. The idea of economizing on the amount of bank reserves was abandoned as an objective of public policy. For many years the reserve ratio was influenced practically not at all by concern over the safety of deposits. The ratio of reserves to deposits rose from 23 per cent in 1932 to 42 per cent in 1940 largely as a result of the tremendous influx of gold from abroad and the limited demand for credit, in the face of which bankers and banking authorities felt more or less powerless. The action of the central banking authorities in raising the level of reserve requirements in 1936, 1937, and 1941 was designed to reduce the inflationary potential of the increased volume of bank reserves. Despite this action, large excess reserves continued into the period of World War II (see Figure 6-1).

The Minimum Reserve Ratio as a Limit to Deposit Expansion

Even a bank which held a complete monopoly of commercial banking in a country would not be free to expand deposits indefinitely. In order to be able to redeem deposits on demand (or on short notice) it would have to hold an amount of reserves directly related to the volume of its deposit obligations. It follows that an ultimate limit to the expansion of bank deposits is set by the minimum ratio of reserves to deposits. This minimum may be fixed by law, regulatory authority, custom, or by considerations of banking prudence. Even in the absence of any legal regulation of reserve ratios, if bankers feel that they must have a certain minimum proportion of reserves to deposits, the maintenance of this proportion will limit deposits much as does the maintenance of a minimum ratio set by law.

Banks in the United States are subject to minimum ratios of reserves to deposits that are prescribed by law (in the case of many non-member banks) or regulated within limits fixed by law (for member banks and some non-members). Since 1933 the Board of Governors of the Federal Reserve System has had the power to raise and lower the minimum reserve ratios of member banks between previously fixed percentages and approximately twice those levels. In the early 1960's the Board could alter the required ratio of reserves to net demand deposits between 10 and 22 per cent for reserve city banks, and between 7 and 14 per cent for country banks.[3] For time deposits the limits were 3 and 6 per cent for both classes of banks. Current reserve requirements of member banks may be found in the *Federal Reserve Bulletin,* a monthly publication of the Board of Governors of the Federal Reserve System.

A legal reserve requirement tends to impair the availability of bank reserves. For example, a bank which has $100,000 of reserves, free and unrestricted, can use them whenever the need arises. If a law should then be passed compelling the bank to have $100,000 on hand at all times, it would no longer be free to use the money when it wished, and the money would cease to be a reserve for an emergency. By analogy, one may consider the effect of requiring each fire station always to have a fire truck in the station house. Reserves for an emergency must be capable of use when the emergency arises; otherwise they are reserves for something other than this particular contingency.

It would be incorrect to suppose that legal reserve requirements completely destroy the availability of the required reserves. There are various ways in which reserves, even though required, may in fact be utilized. A member of the Federal Reserve System is allowed to let its legal reserves fall below the requirement, provided that at another time it holds extra reserves sufficient to bring the average amount held throughout the period (which varies from weekly to semi-monthly) up to the required ratio. In addition to this possibility, any reduction in deposits frees reserves by a fraction of the amount withdrawn. Thus with a 20 per cent reserve requirement, every decline of five dollars in deposits frees one dollar of reserves.

Finally, banks may draw down reserves below the level set by law, provided they are willing to accept certain penalties. As long as reserves are deficient the bank may not make new loans, it may not pay out dividends, and it may be subject to a fine. Thus the latitude which the law does tolerate introduces some flexibility into the provisions for required reserves, but chronic failure to meet reserve requirements could lead to further

---

3. Before 1962 commercial banks were classified as country, as reserve city, and as central reserve city banks. This classification originated in a period before the establishment of a central bank in recognition of the importance of interbank deposits as bank reserves and the tendency of such deposits to be pyramided upward from rural banks to city banks to banks in the major money market cities of Chicago and New York. It was written into the National Banking Act for the purpose of fixing different reserve requirements for banks at differing levels of this pyramid. Central reserve city banks comprised the downtown banks of Chicago and New York; reserve city banks, the downtown banks in the other principal financial centers; country banks, all other member banks, whether located in rural areas or cities. In 1962 the category "central reserve city banks" was merged into "reserve city banks." See further, pp. 211-212.

sanctions against the offending bank, even to the extent of expulsion from the System.

Despite these qualifications it remains true that the effect of the minimum reserve requirement is to restrict the use of some part of bank reserves as an immediately available resource for lending and render them important primarily as a limitation on the expansion of deposits. This restraining function is clearly seen at times when the authorities raise the level of reserve requirements. The purpose of such action is invariably to restrict the potential expansion of bank deposits.

Thus the principal function of a legal minimum reserve ratio is to control the expansion of bank liabilities. A requirement that legal reserves of 20 per cent be held against demand deposits limits deposit expansion, with the minor exceptions noted, to an amount not greater than five times the legal reserves held. By the same token, if 100 per cent reserves were required, no expansion of deposits through the lending process would be possible.

CASH DRAINS

A third major limitation on the expansion of bank deposits results from cash drains. In the broadest sense a cash drain refers to any kind of cash loss suffered by a bank. Such losses influence bank expansion by reducing the quantity of bank reserves so that strictly speaking only two factors limit deposit expansion—the volume of bank reserves and the minimum legal reserve ratio. However, it is convenient to consider cash drains separately in order to distinguish clearly between an initial quantity of cash reserves and the changes in the volume of reserves that result from the expansion process.

If a drain of cash out of one bank results in a gain of cash by another bank, we refer to this as an *internal drain*, since the cash remains within the banking system. This type of drain is also sometimes described as an *interbank drain* or *clearing drain*, emphasizing that the movement of cash is between banks and appears as an adverse clearing balance against the institution undergoing the cash drain.

A second major type of cash drain, in which cash is lost from the entire system of banks, is commonly referred to as an *external drain*. In this case either currency is withdrawn from the banks into hand-to-hand circulation, or reserves are drawn down as a result of an export of gold to settle foreign balances. An external drain is a movement of reserves away from the banking system and is thus the opposite of a primary deposit (described in the previous chapter), which is a movement of publicly held currency and new money issues of the monetary authorities, and therefore of reserves, *to* the banking system.

Both the internal and external cash drains may be subdivided according to whether the loss of reserves is *sporadic* or *regular*. A sporadic drain is relatively unpredictable and is not related in systematic fashion to some other important variable. A regular cash drain is one that occurs in a predictable pattern in relation to changes in some other important variable, such as the time of year or the level of business activity.

A sporadic internal drain might occur, for example, if an unusually large number of checks were written on a bank as a result of a series of fortuitous decisions by its regular customers, so that on several succeeding days this bank suffered an adverse clearing balance. A sporadic external drain might result from a shift in public attitudes as to the desirable division of money holdings between currency and demand deposits. The most striking examples of this type of drain have occurred when depositors have come to believe that their banks were in financial difficulties, with resulting "runs" on banks, i.e., widespread attempts to shift from deposits to currency. The possibility of a sporadic cash drain is of course an important determinant of bank holdings of reserves and other liquid assets. As such it may influence the desired ratio of reserves to deposits and thus the expansion of deposit liabilities.

Seasonal factors are a major source of cash drains. The movement of currency out of banks into hand-to-hand circulation during the Christmas season is a regular external drain. The gradual drawing down of accounts between harvests by customers of a bank located in a one-crop town is a regular internal drain. These are temporary losses, gradually offset by the post-Christmas inflow of currency and the postharvest buildup of farmer deposits that tend to return the banks to their previous reserve position.

The effects on bank deposit expansion of those regular cash drains associated with the expansion process itself must be included in a consideration of the limits of that process. A drain of cash out of the banking system is likely to accompany an expansion in the volume of derivative demand deposits, since with a larger money stock the public is likely to want to hold at least part of the increment in the money supply in the form of currency. If the public finds it convenient to hold money in a ratio of one dollar of currency for every four dollars of demand deposits, it is reasonable to suppose that some part of the increment to the total money stock will be desired in the form of currency. If we assume a one to four ratio for the allocation of additions to the money stock between currency and demand deposits, for each additional five dollars of derivative deposits created by the banks one dollar will flow out of the banks as an external drain of currency into the hands of the public. This is a particularly interesting and important form of external drain since the loss of reserves is directly linked to the deposit expansion process. If we assume a consistent relationship between demand deposit expansion and the drain of currency into the hands of the public, this cash drain alone would limit the bank expansion process.

Another important regular drain sharply confines the expansion limits of an individual bank within a system of banks. Checks tend to be written on and received by banks roughly in proportion to the volume of demand deposits that their customers wish to hold with them (which is a crude measure of the economic importance of a bank's customers). If 10 per cent of all demand deposits are held in a particular bank by its customers, normally about 10 per cent of the dollar volume of checks will be written on that bank, about 10 per cent of the volume of checks drawn will be deposited in it by its customers, and it will tend to accumulate about 10 per cent of the cash reserves of the banking system. If a bank has an average daily inflow of checks roughly equal to the volume of checks written on it, the bank is in "clearing equilibrium." An internal cash drain is likely to affect any bank that disrupts the clearing equilibrium between it and other banks by expanding its earning assets more rapidly than the others (or failing to contract in step with the other banks).

Let us assume that all banks are in clearing equilibrium, that the minimum legal reserve ratio is 20 per cent, and that all banks are "loaned up" —i.e., they have expanded earning assets and deposit liabilities to a point where their excess reserves have been eliminated. Under these conditions, suppose that a bank which holds 10 per cent of the demand deposits of the banking system receives additional cash reserves of $1,000 as a result of a deposit of currency by one of its customers. If this bank decides to take advantage of this cash inflow by expanding its loans and deposits to the legal limit now possible, it can extend its loans and deposits by $4,000, since the $4,000 created by loan expansion plus the $1,000 primary deposit will give the bank additional deposits in a five to one ratio to its new reserves. However, if the borrowers of this newly created $4,000 write checks for this sum, and these checks are distributed through the system in proportion to the demand deposit holdings of banks, only one-tenth of the volume of checks, or $400, will be redeposited with the expanding bank, and the other $3,600 will be deposited in other banks. Since the original increment to cash for the expanding bank was only $1,000, this adverse clearing balance of $3,600 implies that the bank has suffered a net loss of cash of $2,600. This result is a consequence of the fact that the expansion of demand deposits by the bank disrupted the clearing equilibrium between it and other banks. It follows that, except under special circumstances,[4] a single bank within a system of banks cannot expand deposits by the amount that would be possible for a monopoly bank (or a banking system) that is not affected by an internal cash drain.

---

4. In particular this result rests on the assumption that only one bank within the system of banks is expanding. If *all* banks were expanding loans and deposits in proportion, the additional checks written on any single bank would be offset by added checks written on other banks, and no clearing deficit would emerge for any one bank.

EXPANSION LIMITS

Expansion Limits of a Monopoly Bank (or Banking System) with No External Drain

Having examined the three principal factors that set limits to bank deposit expansion, we are now in a position to look at their joint effects. Let us consider first the limits to money creation by commercial banks on the following assumptions:

1. That we are dealing with an economy that has a single commercial bank so that the individual bank and the banking system are one and the same. By means of this assumption, which will be relaxed later in this chapter, we eliminate the internal drain as a limiting factor in bank expansion since all clearings take place on the books of the monopoly bank. A banking system taken as a unit is also not subject to an internal drain so that the conclusions reached for our monopoly bank will be broadly applicable to a banking system composed of many banks.

2. That there is no external drain of cash as a consequence of the expansion of demand deposits.

3. That all deposit liabilities of this bank are in the form of demand deposits. This assumption permits us to disregard the effects on bank deposit expansion of movements between types of deposit with different reserve requirements.

4. That our monopoly bank always remains "loaned up"—that is, it always adjusts its earning assets and deposits so as to keep its legal reserves at an equality with its required reserves (or, it keeps its excess reserves at a zero level). This implies that loans and investments are available to it on terms that make full utilization desirable and that other factors (such as the desire for increased liquidity and safety) do not make excess legal reserves seem advantageous. We will return later to the limitations of this assumption as another qualification to our main argument.

In the analysis below the following symbols are taken to represent some commonly used terms:

D = the maximum dollar volume of demand deposits that a monopoly bank (or banking system) can maintain outstanding.
R = the dollar volume of cash reserves.
r = the minimum legal reserve ratio.

Given the above assumptions and symbols, each dollar of reserves can support $1/r$ dollars of deposits, so that with R dollars of reserves, the maximum amount of deposits that can be supported by the system may be indicated as

$$(1) \qquad\qquad D = R \cdot \left(\frac{1}{r}\right) \, , \quad \text{or} \quad D = \frac{R}{r}.$$

Thus, if we assume that R is \$5 billion and r is 20 per cent,

$$D = \$5 \text{ billion} \cdot \left(\frac{1}{0.20}\right) = \$25 \text{ billion}.$$

That is, with a minimum reserve ratio of 20 per cent, each dollar of the \$5 billion of legal reserves can support a volume of deposits five times as large, or \$5 billion of legal reserves can support \$25 billion in demand deposits.

Looking at the position of our monopoly bank from the standpoint of its balance sheet, it will be in equilibrium when it has expanded its earning assets and deposits to the point where the bank is "loaned up," or, in other words, where its reserves are in a one to five ratio to its deposit liabilities. These conditions would be met if the balance sheet of our monopoly bank were as follows:

Assets		Liabilities	
Cash	$ 5 billion	Demand deposits	$25 billion
Loans and investments	21 billion	Other liabilities	1 billion
Other assets	2 billion	Capital	2 billion
Total	$28 billion	Total	$28 billion

If we now assume an increment to legal reserves resulting from a primary deposit of say \$60 million, the new demand deposit limit may be computed either by adding \$60 million to our reserve total and recalculating D according to equation (1), or by using the expression

$$(2) \qquad\qquad \Delta D = \Delta R \cdot \left(\frac{1}{r}\right) \quad \text{or,} \quad \Delta D = \frac{\Delta R}{r}$$

where ΔD and ΔR refer to increments to or decrements from deposits and reserves. This expression permits us to deal directly with changes in reserves, and thus deposits, which we can then add to or subtract from our original totals. Thus, if $\Delta R = \$60$ million, then $\Delta D = \$300$ million, and D has grown to \$25,300 million. The addition to bank earning assets will be equal to the increment to demand deposits less the new primary deposit, or \$300 million $-$ \$60 million, or \$240 million.[5]

The balance sheet changes involved in this expansion may be described in two stages. First, the primary deposit increases the cash and demand deposits of the bank by \$60 million.

---

5. If the additional reserves had been obtained directly from the central bank by an exchange of bank-owned securities for cash, the addition to earning assets would have been identical with the increment to demand deposits.

Assets		*Liabilities*	
Cash	+$60 million	Demand deposits	+$60 million

Second, the bank increases its earning assets and deposits by $240 million, which brings it to its new expansion limit.

Assets		*Liabilities*	
Loans and investments	+$240 million	Demand deposits	+$240 million

If we momentarily relax our assumption barring any cash drain, and suppose a $3 million outflow of currency into the hands of the public, how would this affect bank deposits and earning assets? Since the monopoly bank is assumed to be loaned up, this outflow of cash will encroach on its required reserves and compel a multiple contraction of deposits and earning assets to bring reserves and deposits into a one to five ratio. If each dollar of reserves supports five dollars of deposits, from a loaned-up position each dollar of reserves lost requires a five-dollar contraction of demand deposits. Using our expansion formula applicable to increments (and decrements) of reserves, we can see that deposits must fall by $15 million as a consequence of the outflow of cash:

$$\Delta D = \Delta R \cdot \left(\frac{1}{r} \right)$$

$$= -\$3 \text{ million} \times \left(\frac{1}{.2} \right) = -\$3 \text{ million} \times 5$$

$$= -\$15 \text{ million.}$$

Since the initial outflow of cash was accompanied by a $3 million reduction in deposits, the bank must reduce its earning assets and deposits by another $12 million. The initial transaction affects the balance sheet in the following manner:

Assets		*Liabilities*	
Cash	−$3 million	Demand deposits	−$3 million

The transactions that bring about a final adjustment affect the balance sheet as follows:

Assets		*Liabilities*	
Loans and investments	−$12 million	Demand deposits	−$12 million

Expansion Limits of a Monopoly Bank (or Banking System)
with an External Drain

We have thus far examined the multiple expansion of demand deposits by a monopoly bank on the assumption that the cash reserves of the bank do not change in the process of deposit expansion or contraction. However, as we saw above in our discussion of the external drain, the expansion of demand deposits by commercial banks is likely to be accompanied by an outflow of cash into hand-to-hand circulation as the public attempts to maintain a desired balance in its holdings of currency and demand deposits. If this is so, the process of bank demand deposit expansion will bring with it a steady reduction in the size of bank reserves (R) that will cause the expansion process to come to a halt at a lower level of deposit expansion than otherwise.

Let us incorporate into our analysis a regular cash drain that causes currency to flow out of the banks and into the hands of the public at a fixed rate relative to the expansion of demand deposits. We will designate by the term c the rate at which the public converts demand deposits into currency (or vice versa) with the expansion (or contraction) of deposit money.[6] The actual outflow of cash will be equal to $(c \cdot \Delta D)$. If c is 5 per cent, for every $100 expansion of demand deposits the monopoly bank will lose $5 in hand-to-hand circulation as the public converts deposits into currency; if demand deposits contract by $100, $5 in currency will flow *into* the banks as the public finds that they are holding an excess of currency relative to deposit money.

We can readily bring c into our expansion formulas by recognizing that additional cash reserves (ΔR) will be distributed during the expansion process between cash drained out of the banking system $(c \cdot \Delta D)$ and cash absorbed in required reserves to support the newly created demand deposits $(r \cdot \Delta D)$. Thus,

$$\Delta R = r \cdot \Delta D + c \cdot \Delta D$$
$$\Delta R = \Delta D \cdot (r + c)$$

(3)
$$\Delta D = \Delta R \cdot \left(\frac{1}{r+c} \right), \quad \text{or} \quad \Delta D = \frac{\Delta R}{r+c}.$$

---

6. In the discussion that follows it will be assumed that the cash drain applies to changes in both derivative and primary deposits. This assumption seems entirely appropriate for changes in derivative deposits and for primary deposits that result from the creation of new money claims by the monetary authorities (e.g., through the purchase of securities on the open market by the Federal Reserve). If the increase in primary deposits resulted from a reduction in currency in circulation—reflecting a change in the public's desired holdings of currency relative to deposits, with the money supply unchanged—some doubts may be raised whether the cash drain would apply in the same degree. For simplicity this possible qualification is ignored in the text.

If we assume that the monopoly bank, starting from a loaned-up position, obtains excess cash reserves of $2 million directly from a central bank, and has a minimum legal reserve ratio of 25 per cent and a rate of cash drain (c) of 5 per cent, then

$$\Delta D = \$2 \text{ million} \cdot \left(\frac{1}{0.30}\right)$$
$$= \$2 \text{ million} \cdot (3.33)$$
$$= \$6.7 \text{ million.}$$

It will be noted that in the absence of the cash drain deposits would have expanded by $8 million, or four times the excess reserves; with the cash drain deposits can be expanded only by 3.33. The smaller increment to demand deposits is a consequence of the exodus from the banking system of $0.33 million in cash ($0.05 \cdot \$6.7$ million) during the expansion process. When the expansion process has been completed, however, the ratio of the net increment to reserves ($\Delta R - c \cdot \Delta D$) to the increment to demand deposits (ΔD) is equal to the value of r. That is, c is applicable as a factor affecting the final equilibrium position as we move from one deposit level to another, but the expression $D = R/r$ will describe the equilibrium relationship between these variables even if c is positive.

Let us consider this external drain in balance sheet terms, assuming that the monopoly bank obtains the additional $2 million of reserves as a result of a direct purchase of some of its portfolio securities by the central bank. The initial balance sheet changes would be as follows:

Assets		Liabilities
Cash	+$2 million	
Bonds	−$2 million	

The bank, now in possession of excess reserves of $2 million, will expand its loans, investments, and demand deposits. With a legal minimum reserve ratio of 25 per cent and no cash drain it could increase both its earning assets and demand deposits by $8 million. However, if the bank suffers an outflow of cash equal to 1/20 of the expansion of deposits, by the time demand deposits have grown by $6⅔ million, $⅓ million in cash will be lost and the limits of deposit expansion will have been reached. During the process of expansion the following balance sheet changes will have occurred:

Assets		Liabilities	
Cash	−$333,333	Demand deposits	+$7 million
Loans and invest-		Demand deposits	−$333,333
ments	+$7 million	Demand deposits (net)	+$6,666.667

These balance sheet changes indicate that there is a difference between the net expansion of bank demand deposits and the change in the *money supply* when bank expansion is affected by an external drain. In our example the monopoly bank has acquired $7 million of earning assets and has created the same volume of demand deposits, but $333,333 of deposits has been converted into currency, leaving a net addition to demand deposits of only $6.7 million. However, in calculating the effect of bank expansion on the money supply, we must take into account the extra $333,333 of currency in circulation, so that while demand deposits increased (net) by only $6.7 million in the expansion process, the money supply increased by $7 million. We may state this point in these terms: when there is an external drain the increase in the money supply is larger than the increase in demand deposits by the amount of the external drain $(c \cdot \Delta D)$.

Time Deposits, Financial Intermediaries, and Demand Deposit Expansion

Up to this point we have considered the limits of commercial bank deposit expansion on the assumption that commercial banks hold only demand deposit liabilities. We should therefore consider how these results might have to be modified by the existence of time deposits and liquid financial claims issued by other financial institutions. If the expansion of demand deposits causes the public to desire to hold a larger volume of time deposits or claims against other financial institutions, the growth of these liabilities may necessitate the holding of reserves that might otherwise have supported a larger volume of demand deposits.

Insofar as the public wishes to hold additional claims against non-bank financial institutions, they will present checks to intermediaries in exchange for near money claims (e.g., shares in savings and loan associations). The result is a shift of demand deposits from other members of the public to financial intermediaries, with no effect on total demand deposits or bank reserves. If the additional cash assets of these intermediaries take the form of demand deposits exclusively, there will be no effect on the expansion of demand deposits. If, however, the increase in the liabilities of financial intermediaries leads them to hold additional vault cash, there will be a corresponding reduction in the reserves of commercial banks. This is clearly only a special case of an external drain, similar to those described earlier.

If the expansion of demand deposits causes the public to increase their holdings of commercial bank time deposits, the effect on demand deposit growth is somewhat different from that just described. The commercial banks will have to set aside reserves against the added time deposits. These are subject to legal requirements which tend to be larger than the vault cash holdings of other financial institutions. The net pressure on reserves is therefore that much greater.

An illustration will show how, with initially given reserves, a shift from demand to time deposits limits the potential expansion of demand deposits. Assume that reserve requirements are 20 per cent for demand deposits and 5 per cent for time deposits, and that, with no excess reserves, depositors shift from holding $100,000 of demand deposits to time deposits. This is indicated below as transaction (1).

Assets	*Liabilities*
(2) Loans and Investments +$75,000	(1) Demand deposits −$100,000
	(1) Time deposits +$100,000
	(2) Demand deposits + $75,000

Total reserves are not affected but excess reserves rise by $15,000, since $20,000 are no longer required to support demand deposits while only $5,000 are absorbed as required reserves for time deposits. The banking system can now expand (assuming for simplicity no external drain) by $75,000. This is indicated as transaction (2) above.

It is clear that when the adjustment is complete the quantity of demand deposits is smaller than before because of what amounts to a "drain" of reserves from the commercial banking sector proper to a reserve for money substitutes. Assuming that an expansion of demand deposits leads to a regular and parallel expansion of time deposits, we may incorporate this fact in our expansion formula. Thus if a rise in demand deposits of $1.00 causes time deposits to rise by $0.50 (and reserves for time deposits therefore to rise by $0.025), the reduction of reserves available for supporting demand deposits is 2.5 per cent of each dollar increase in demand deposits. It is clear that this effect parallels that of the external drain previously incorporated in our expansion formula.

Actual versus Potential Deposits: The Role of Excess Reserves

Up to this point we have assumed that the equilibrium position of the monopoly bank is where it is "loaned up"—i.e., where its excess reserves are zero. We may view the existence of excess reserves as evidence of a difference between the actual level of deposits and the potential level which the bank could maintain—a difference between its achievement and its capability.

One reason for the existence of excess reserves at any time is that the acquisition of earning assets is not accomplished instantaneously, so that there is a necessary lag in bank adjustments to changes that tend to generate excess reserves (such as an inflow of gold from abroad or a net repayment of bank loans). Excess reserves existing for this reason imply a difference between the actual and the desired levels of deposits that tends to disappear in succeeding periods.

In addition, excess reserves may exist under particular circumstances where banks prefer excess reserves to additional holdings of any earning assets, given the terms on which they are available. Thus, in a period of economic disorder and uncertainty, bankers may desire excess reserves as a protection against potential cash drains. Also, in a period of declining business activity the demand for loans may fall and bank lending standards may tighten; if under these circumstances bankers do not find the securities market sufficiently attractive to absorb excess reserves, they may grow to impressive levels, as in the late 1930's.[7] Where excess reserves are held by banks for this reason we may say that the equilibrium level of deposits is less than the potential level set by legal minimum reserve requirements and the cash drain.

Expansion Limits of an Individual Bank within a System of Many Banks

Up to this point we have been discussing deposit creation in an economy with only one bank. While this is an obvious departure from reality, it is justified by the circumstance that the banking system as a whole is subject to limits similar to that of a monopoly bank.

The presence of other banks within the system, however, profoundly modifies the behavior of any individual bank. The individual bank within a system is subject to all of the constraints affecting a monopoly bank plus the internal (or clearing) drain, described above in the section on the cash drain. In order to focus attention on the distinctive features of deposit expansion by an individual bank within a banking system, let us neglect all factors which limit bank expansion except the minimum legal reserve ratio and the internal drain. We shall assume a banking system consisting of 100 banks of equal size, each initially loaned up and in clearing equilibrium, and each with a minimum legal reserve ratio of 20 per cent.

If one bank now receives additional reserves of $1 million as a result of a currency deposit of that amount by one of its customers, by how much can it expand its earning assets and deposits? A monopoly bank with a 20 per cent reserve requirement and no external drain could expand its earning assets and deposits by $4 million.[8] However, within a system of banks a single bank which expands its earning assets and deposits must contend with a potential adverse clearing balance, for the deposit expansion destroys the existing clearing equilibrium in its relations with other banks. Those who have obtained new deposit credits from the expanding bank are likely to write checks transferring these borrowed funds to others, and, since only a small fraction of system deposits (one-hundredth) is accounted for by the individual bank, only a small fraction of the dollar amount of checks written on the newly created deposits is likely to be redeposited with it. In the

---

7. See pp. 462-464.
8. The original $1 million primary deposit plus the $4 million expansion leads to a total increase in deposits of five times the $1 million increment of reserves.

clearing process, the checks on the newly created accounts which are deposited with other banks result in a corresponding loss of reserves to the expanding bank.

It follows that a single bank within a system can safely expand its earning assets and deposits on the basis of a given quantity of excess reserves by less than a monopoly bank (or system). If we assume as the most pessimistic possibility that all deposits created in the process of lending shortly thereafter will be drawn upon to their full amount, and that the probable volume of checks redeposited with the expanding bank will be so small as to be negligible, *the individual bank will be able to expand its lending safely by an amount equal to its excess reserves.*

Returning to our illustration of a multi-bank system in which a single bank has received additional currency of $1 million from a depositor under the conditions specified, it could legally expand its earning assets and deposits by $4 million; it does not do so, however, because its management knows that all or most of such newly created deposits will be shifted to other banks, with a resultant cash drain that the bank management must consider in its planning. If the bank expands its earning assets and deposits by the amount of its excess reserves, that is, by $800,000, it will be able to sustain the maximum induced adverse clearing balance without incurring deficient reserves. If Bank A operates in accordance with this rule, the acquisition of the new deposit and the expansion of earning assets equal in value to its additional excess reserves may be shown by the following changes in its balance sheet:

Bank A

Assets		*Liabilities*	
(1) Cash	+ $1 million	(1) Demand deposits	+ $1 million
(2) Loans and investments	+ $800,000	(2) Demand deposits	+ $800,000

If we assume that the entire $800,000 is drawn upon, and that (for simplicity) the checks involved are all deposited with Bank B, the balance sheets of A and B will change as follows:

Bank A		Bank B	
Assets	*Liabilities*	*Assets*	*Liabilities*
Cash − $800,000	Demand deposits − $800,000	Cash + $800,000	Demand deposits + $800,000

Bank A is now loaned up, but B has excess reserves of $640,000. If B now expands its earning assets and deposits by this amount, and the newly created deposits are checked away to Bank C, B and C will have undergone balance sheet changes as indicated by transactions (1)-(3) below:

Bank B

Assets		Liabilities	
(1) Cash	+ $800,000	(1) Demand deposits	+ $800,000
(2) Loans	+ 640,000	(2) Demand deposits	+ 640,000
(3) Cash	− 640,000	(3) Demand deposits	− 640,000

Bank C

Assets		Liabilities	
(3) Cash	+ $640,000	(3) Demand deposits	+ $640,000

Bank C is now in possession of excess reserves of $512,000, and it can expand its earning assets and demand deposits by that amount.

It may be noted that after Bank C expands its earning assets and deposits by $512,000, the original $1 million of additional reserves will be supporting deposits of $2.95 million ($1 million+$800,000+$640,000 | $512,000), and $590,400 of the $1 million of additional reserves will have become required reserves. This process can continue, with dwindling additions to deposits, until all $1 million of the reserve increment has been absorbed in the required category. When that point is reached, deposits which are supported by the new reserve money will total $5 million. That is to say, given our assumptions, individual banks alone may expand earning assets and deposits on the basis of increments to reserves by amounts equal to their excess reserves. But the aggregate of individual banks, each expanding by the amount of its excess reserves, gradually expands by a multiple of the excess reserves for the system. The balance sheet changes shown above for Banks A, B, and C are brought together and extended in Table 6-2.

TABLE 6-2. System Deposit Expansion as a Sum of the Expansions of Individual Banks

Bank	Added Deposits Received	Amount Lent	Additional Reserves Required for Deposits Retained
A	$1,000,000	$ 800,000	$ 200,000
B	800,000	640,000	160,000
C	640,000	512,000	128,000
D	512,000	409,600	102,400
E	409,600	327,680	81,920
F	327,680	262,144	65,536
G	262,144	209,715	52,429
H	209,715	167,772	41,943
I	167,772	134,218	33,554
J	134,218	107,374	26,844
Total for Banks A through J	$4,463,129	$3,570,503	$ 892,626
Additional banks	536,871	429,497	107,374
Grand total, all banks	$5,000,000	$4,000,000	$1,000,000

Source: Board of Governors of the Federal Reserve System, *The Federal Reserve System* (Washington: 1954), p. 23.

Qualifications Relating to the Expansion of the Individual Bank

We have made several major assumptions regarding the expansion of the individual bank that deserve brief comment. First, we have assumed that no net losses of reserves are attributable to checks written on the newly established primary deposit. This implies that checks drawn on such deposits are roughly offset by checks received by the relevant depositors, as is the case normally for the bulk of bank deposits. This is plausible if the initial deposit represents a more or less permanent addition to the bank's total deposits, reflecting a growth in the importance of the bank's customers. This does not imply that all primary deposits are of this character. Since the short-run relationship between additional primary deposits and the inflow of checks drawn on other banks is not entirely dependable, checks written on new primary deposits will sometimes be a source of a net drain of cash to other banks.

Second, we have assumed that funds created by the expanding bank on the basis of additional reserves are transferred in their entirety to other banks. Although a borrower who pays interest for bank credit may be expected to use it in some fashion, a part of these funds may be held as a liquidity cushion. Banks also commonly require borrowers to maintain deposit balances of some 10 to 20 per cent of loans granted as so-called compensating balances. This practice locks in a part of additional bank deposits and makes possible a somewhat greater expansion by the individual bank than might otherwise be possible.

Furthermore, some fraction of the checks written on newly created deposits will be redeposited in the expanding bank so that its adverse clearing balance is likely to be less than 100 per cent of the volume of checks written on these balances. In the short run the volume of redeposits may be considerably greater than the ratio of the deposits of the expanding bank to those of the system because the business associations of local borrowers tend to be local (rather than distributed randomly over the entire economy)— only gradually will the newly created deposits (and excess reserves) be redistributed over the entire system.

Although these qualifications are important from the standpoint of individual bank decision-making,[9] they need not affect the ultimate expansion of the banking system. If each bank adopts the safe rule of thumb of expanding by the amount of its excess reserves, and if this proves overly conservative, the signal for further expansion will appear as a greater amount of excess reserves than had been expected, leading to further expansion, until by a process of trial and error each bank and the banking system will have reached the limits described in our simplified explanation.

---

9. For example, the most profitable level of promotion expenditures designed to induce an expansion in deposits will depend, in part, on the volume of loans and investments that an individual bank feels it can safely acquire on the basis of a given increment to its reserves.

We have also assumed in our earlier discussion of individual bank expansion that newly created deposits will be checked away to one other bank, and that the deposits created by the second bank will be checked away to a third bank, and so on. This is useful for the purpose of illustrating the cumulation of individual bank extensions of credit to the system total. However, it is inaccurate and misleading in its implications regarding the process and pattern of redistribution of additional system reserve funds. It is more realistic to assume that checks on newly created deposits (and therefore additional reserve funds) will tend to be distributed among banks according to the economic importance of their customers, which will be roughly measured by their percentage of system deposits. If this is the basis of redistribution of new deposits and reserves, clearly it differs markedly from the process described in Table 6-2, but the system total arrived at will be the same.

SELECTED BIBLIOGRAPHY

ANGELL, J. W., and K. FICEK, "Expansion of Bank Credit," *Journal of Political Economy* (1933), pp. 1-32, 152-193.

Board of Governors of the Federal Reserve System, *The Federal Reserve System*. Washington: 1961, Chapters II and XIII.

CRICK, W. F., "The Genesis of Bank Deposits," *Economica* (1927), pp. 191-202. (Reprinted in American Economic Association, *Readings in Monetary Theory*.)

KEYNES, J. M., *A Treatise on Money*. New York: Harcourt Brace, 1930, Vol. II, Chapter 25.

PHILLIPS, C. A., *Bank Credit*. New York: Macmillan, 1921, Chapters I-IV.

SHAW, E. S., *Money, Income, and Monetary Policy*. Homewood, Ill.: Irwin, 1950, Chapters VI-X.

7

THE BANK AS A
BUSINESS ENTERPRISE

In the two preceding chapters we have looked at banks and their operations primarily from a collective point of view. In the present chapter banking is examined from the standpoint of operations at the level of the individual bank. Here we are concerned with the problems that confront the bankers themselves in the daily conduct of their business. Attention will be directed mainly to those aspects of banking which relate to the operations of commercial banks as lenders and deposit administrators. This necessitates omitting discussion of many of the specialized activities commonly carried on by banks which have earned them the title "department stores of finance."[1]

THE FUNDAMENTAL BANKING PROBLEM

We have seen that the business in which bankers are engaged may be described as that of "dealers in debts." In contrast to merchants and manufacturers, banks hold relatively few assets of a tangible sort. Their resources consist almost wholly of the debts of governments, businesses, and individuals. Insurance companies, whose assets like those of banks also consist mainly of claims, have liabilities which are so standardized as to be capable of actuarial determination. Other financial institutions have liabilities of a relatively deferred or determinable character. Commercial banks are unique in that they owe very large sums to the public in the form of time and demand

---

1. There will be no discussion, for example, of the operations of trust departments, safe-deposit departments, or of the many technical details which relate to the routine conduct of banking, the clearing and collection of checks, the extension and servicing of consumer loans, the maintenance of credit departments, and so on. For a discussion of the applied aspects of commercial banking, see R. A. Foulke and H. V. Prochnow, *Practical Bank Credit*, 2nd edition (Englewood Cliffs, N. J.: Prentice-Hall, 1950).

deposits. The demand deposits carry the unqualified obligation to pay currency or its equivalent whenever it is requested. For time deposits, a short period of grace is allowed by law but a bank would prefer not to invoke it and, in fact, very seldom does so. Thus the bulk of a bank's liabilities are fixed-dollar sums subject to payment on call, and it is essential that the resources of the bank be managed in such a way as to provide the means at all times for meeting demands for currency or other cash assets as they are made.

The obligation to pay cash upon demand constitutes the most immediate and compelling necessity faced by the management of a bank, since failure to remain in a position to meet all claims as they are presented leaves a bank with no alternative but to close its doors. A bank is *technically insolvent* the moment it fails to meet its obligations to convert its deposit liabilities into cash when requested to do so.

At the same time, commercial banks are profit-seeking enterprises, striving to increase net income and the present value of their net assets, taking account of both immediate and longer term considerations. In the long run the problem of the management of a bank, as of most other enterprises, is to provide satisfactory returns to stockholders.[2] This requires the holding of a sufficient volume of assets that prove to be both safe and productive of satisfactory yields.

Bankers must, therefore, maintain an adequate degree of liquidity (avoid technical insolvency) while at the same time pursuing the longer term problem of obtaining profits. What makes this task especially difficult is that the rate of return on assets tends to vary inversely with their degree of liquidity and safety. Thus the more suitable an asset to fulfil a bank's liquidity needs, the less likely it is to contribute much to bank earnings, and vice versa. If a bank were always to hold an amount of currency equal to its deposit liabilities, it would be assured of being able to meet all demands for withdrawal. It is clear, however, that such a bank would not be able to cover its current expenses, let alone show a profit. On the other hand, if it were to put all available cash into high yield and therefore relatively illiquid and risky credit instruments, it could perhaps count on a liberal income but might find itself in a position where it could not meet its promises to pay

---

2. In order to achieve this long-run objective it is also ordinarily necessary that a bank maintain *solvency*, i.e., that the realizable value of assets be kept at least equal to the value of non-owner liabilities. However, it is possible for a bank or banks to be insolvent for a shorter or longer period and still remain in business. There is a famous case of a Canadian bank, which was actually insolvent for a period of forty years but continued to remain open because it was able to meet the short-run problem of liquidity (i.e., it remained *technically solvent*). It is probable that upon more than one occasion many of our banks have been temporarily in a position where the current market value of their assets failed to cover liabilities. This could be the result of a sharp recession in business activity, as in 1920-1922, or of a drastic decline in security prices, such as occurred following the 1929 crash. By continuing in operation until recovery set in, the majority of banks were restored to full solvency.

cash when called upon to do so. Between these two extremes lies the path the successful banker has to follow.

In sum, the banker faces the dual problem of being able to meet all demands of depositors for currency (or its equivalent) and simultaneously earning sufficient income to stay in business. As one writer has said, "the problem of a bank is to tie up enough cash to earn a profit without tying up so much that it gets tied up itself." This dual problem must be attacked by the banker through appropriate management of his liabilities and assets. We turn now to a consideration of such policies.

MANAGEMENT OF BANK LIABILITIES

Liabilities to Stockholders

The capital structure of a bank includes three principal accounts, namely, capital, surplus, and undivided profits. The last-named account is an operating account which is increased through current earnings and reduced through payment of certain expenses, dividends, and occasionally by transfers to the surplus account. The other two accounts are relatively permanent. The capital account is established as part of starting the bank and may be added to out of surplus or by other means. A certain amount of surplus may be paid in at the time of subscription to the original capital of the bank,[3] and the surplus account is likely to be built up further out of earnings.[4] The former is frequently referred to as capital surplus; the latter as earned surplus. When losses have been incurred greater than can be charged against undivided profits, they may be absorbed by transfers out of the surplus account.

There are two principal ways in which the capital accounts are supposed to help in solving the fundamental banking problem. First, they represent the shareholders' stake in the business, and it is assumed that the management will pursue a careful policy in order to safeguard this stake. An important reason for attempts to limit deposits to a certain multiple of capital is so that the stockholders' stake in the success of the bank may be large enough to assure conservative lending and investing policies.

Second, and still more important, the capital accounts are expected to serve as a buffer to protect depositors. In case of loss or liquidation, the claims of depositors are satisfied before those of the stockholders. Until the middle 1930's it was customary for the safeguard afforded by capital to be reinforced by the double-liability provision. In case of failure, each stockholder

---

3. National banks are required by law to start out with a paid-in surplus equal to 20 per cent of their capital, which necessitates selling the initial issue of stock at the required premium over par value.

4. It is a legal requirement of the national and of many state banking systems that part of earnings be allocated to surplus until that account is as large as capital.

was liable for an assessment equal to the par value of the capital stock he owned. This provision failed to function satisfactorily and was generally abandoned, though it is still retained in some of the state banking laws.[5]

Although the desire to maintain a conservative ratio of capital to deposits helps to restrain the undue expansion of a bank's deposit liabilities, it is by no means an absolute limitation upon such expansion. Determination of the ratio depends on the policies of the banks and the banking and monetary authorities and rests upon custom rather than statute.[6] It is within the power of a bank's officers to change the ratio if they see fit, and for the country's banks as a whole very substantial changes in the ratio have, in fact, occurred. Furthermore, a wide range is to be observed in the ratios of capital to deposit liabilities maintained by different banks.

The ratio of capital accounts to combined bank-note and deposit liabilities declined greatly during the period from just before the Civil War to the end of World War II (see Table 7-1). The trend was particularly marked before the turn of the century and was greatly accelerated by World War II. The high ratio in earlier years was partially a reflection of the greater relative importance at that time of bank notes as compared with deposits. The great

TABLE 7-1. Capital Accounts, Bank Notes, and Deposits of Commercial Banks in the United States, 1860-1960 (values in millions of dollars)

	Capital Accounts	Bank Notes	Total Deposits	Ratio of Capital Accounts to Notes and Deposits
1860	422	207	309	81.8
1870	549	336	775	58.4
1880	825	318	2,222	32.1
1890	1,558	126	4,576	33.1
1900	1,907	265	8,513	21.7
1910	3,836	675	17,584	21.0
1920	5,954	688	41,725	14.0
1930	10,013	652	59,847	16.6
1940	8,325		71,153	11.7
1945	18,950		150,227	6.0
1950	11,590		155,265	7.5
1955	15,300		192,254	8.0
1960	20,986		229,843	9.1

Source: Comptroller of the Currency, *Annual Reports*, 1860-1940; *Federal Reserve Bulletin*, 1945-60.

5. Collections under double liability from 1865 to 1935 averaged exactly one-half the amount assessed on stock of failed national banks. The provision was evaded in various ways and was felt to operate as an undue penalty upon the more conscientious of a bank's stockholders. Its repeal was designed to render bank stock more attractive to investors at a time when bank capital was impaired and it was desired to facilitate the raising of additional capital. It was also argued that the introduction of the Federal Deposit Insurance Corporation had rendered the protection afforded by the double-liability provision less necessary than before.

6. At one time the FDIC sought, without great success, to establish the rule that deposits should not exceed ten times a bank's capital accounts including capital, surplus, and undivided profits.

expansion in deposits, which have never been restricted as rigidly as bank notes, was the governing factor in the decline in the ratio of capital accounts to liabilities. Capital accounts are comparatively stable in amount; consequently, whenever deposits change—as happened during the deposit contraction of the 1930's and the deposit expansion of the 1940's—a corresponding fluctuation occurs in the ratio of capital to deposits or to total assets.[7]

The capital accounts now provide less of a buffer for the protection of depositors than was once the case. No great significance is to be attached to this fact, however, inasmuch as many other factors have entered to offset the effect of this particular change. Among these other factors are changes in bank size, the diversification and character of earning assets, type of deposits,

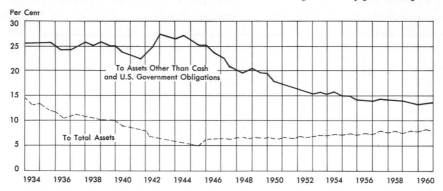

Figure 7-1.   Capital Ratios of Insured Commercial Banks, 1934-1960.

Source: Federal Deposit Insurance Corporation, *Annual Report.*

proportion of cash holdings, and the institutional setting including the Federal Deposit Insurance Corporation.

The function of the capital accounts in their role of buffer for the protection of depositors is to provide a margin of safety in case of a decline in the value of assets. The ratio that has significance, therefore, is not the ratio of capital to deposits or to total assets but rather the ratio of capital to "risk assets." These are usually defined as consisting of assets other than cash and obligations of the United States government. It has repeatedly happened that at times when the ratio of capital accounts to *total* assets was declining, the ratio to *risk* assets remained constant or even rose (cf. Figure 7-1). Nor is it to be supposed that the degree of risk contained in a given amount of risk assets is at all times the same; risk varies with credit conditions and business activity.

A good deal has been done in recent years to build up the capital of banks but it remains at a considerably lower percentage of total assets than pre-

7. The rise in the ratio of capital accounts to deposits during the early 1930's was because of the sharp contraction of deposits and not because of additions to capital.

vailed before World War II (cf. Figure 7-1). It would be a mistake to infer, however, that the lower ratio prevailing today is an indication that banks are less strong now then they were then.

Deposit Liabilities

A net withdrawal of deposits from an individual bank implies an equivalent internal or external drain of cash out of that bank. Actual or potential losses of reserves are of critical importance in bank administration, determining as they do the net cash demands that banks must be prepared to meet. Accordingly, deposit fluctuations, because they are the main source of changes in the reserves of individual banks, command the close attention of bank managers. Deposit fluctuations may result from a variety of factors: seasonal influences, the differential impact of cyclical fluctuations, competitive factors affecting the particular bank, secular changes in the economic position of the community served by the bank, chance, and other factors. Many of the influences affecting deposit behavior come to a focus in, and may be analyzed in terms of, the *types of deposits* that banks have outstanding and the *kinds of owners* who maintain these deposit accounts.

Commercial bank deposits are generally subdivided on the basis of differences in term to maturity into demand deposits and time and savings accounts. The former relate to deposits payable without delay; the latter are those whose withdrawal is, legally at least, subject to delay.[8] Ordinarily a depositor who plans to make frequent use of his deposit account maintains a demand deposit, while one who wishes to use a deposit as an investment medium maintains a time or savings account. The ratio of time and savings deposits to total deposits owned by the public reached a peak in the early 1930's, then fell until the early 1950's, rising somewhat thereafter in response to higher interest rates and savings, and a retardation in the growth of demand deposits. By the middle of 1962 time deposits constituted 45 percent of total commercial bank deposits held by the public.

On the whole, time and savings deposits are less active than demand deposits and involve the banks in less work and expense. Since they are

---

8. The term time deposit is sometimes used interchangeably with, or as a broader concept encompassing savings deposits, but in technical parlance they are distinct categories. Savings deposits are defined by the Board of Governors as those credited to individuals or non-profit organizations, evidenced by a passbook which must be presented for withdrawals, and subject to a withdrawal notice of not less than thirty days. Time deposits include those where business firms or individuals arrange special terms with banks under "time certificates of deposit," which govern the rate of interest paid and the particular date on which the covered funds may be withdrawn. Time deposits also include savings accounts of business firms and other deposits accumulated under special contracts and usually subject to thirty days notice if withdrawn prior to the maturing of the contract (e.g., Christmas and Vacation Club accounts).

For brevity time deposits will usually be employed to include savings accounts.

maintained primarily as a liquid form of investment rather than as working cash balances, they fluctuate less, generally speaking, than demand accounts. On the other hand, they draw interest and consequently involve an element of cost that banks do not incur in connection with demand deposits. Banks can afford to pay interest on time and savings accounts because they are so much less expensive to handle, because their reserve requirements are lower, and because their greater stability permits banks with relatively large holdings of time deposits to maintain a larger proportion of assets in the form of longer term securities.

The ownership distribution of deposits is also an important determinant of deposit behavior. Thus small personal deposits are relatively stable in terms of totals. Deposits and withdrawals tend to offset each other, and the fluctuations that do occur in totals are principally seasonal and therefore easily provided for. Large deposits, on the other hand, are much more unstable, and the nature and magnitude of variations differ widely with different types of depositors. By and large, the deposits owned by financial institutions such as insurance companies and mutual funds are subject to greater and more sudden changes than most other types of deposits. Similarly, substantial fluctuations may result from large single transactions such as payment by a railroad company for the purchase of rolling stock. Banks often arrange to have large corporate depositors notify them of impending withdrawals. The United States Treasury regularly gives advance notice of expected withdrawals.

Banks pay careful attention to the characteristics of the deposits they carry and to their probable behavior. In addition, they may follow such practices as having a particular officer notified whenever a large check is presented for payment. By such means they try to make sure that they will always have adequate ready cash and yet will not maintain greater liquidity than is required, which would tend to encroach upon earnings.

The fact that the total volume of earning assets which a bank can own is directly related to the total of deposit liabilities it has outstanding provides banks with a strong inducement to expand deposits. Banks attempt to attract and retain deposits mainly by various non-price methods of competing, such as the provision of free services, the appointment of influential businessmen to the bank's board of directors, advertising, and other promotional methods. Since the 1930's banks have been prohibited by law from paying interest on demand deposits, and ceilings on interest payments on time and savings deposits have been fixed by bank supervisory authorities. Price competition in the solicitation of deposits has necessarily been restricted by these limitations, although since World War II the pressures of increased interest rates paid on time and savings accounts by competitive financial institutions have tended to increase the importance of price as a factor in the competition for savings accounts. It should be noted that the total deposits of the banking system are not very responsive to changes in the rate of interest, with the result that competition for deposits, although advantageous to individual banks and bank customers, may tend to raise costs without producing any net benefits to the banks taken together.

In contrast to expansionist methods such as these, certain restrictive measures are also applied to deposit liabilities. One of the most familiar is service charges which, though relatively uncommon before the depression of the 1930's, have for many years accounted for over 5 per cent of the gross earnings of member banks. Charges typically are imposed on smaller deposits and are also usually related to the number of checks drawn and deposits made. The primary reason for imposing such charges is to insure that deposit accounts which are small or very active either pay their way or are driven away.

The expression "compensating balances" refers to the common arrangement whereby borrowers are expected to maintain certain minimum or average balances instead of being free to draw out the entire proceeds of a loan.[9] A borrower who pays 4 per cent on a loan of $10,000 but is required to maintain 20 per cent of that amount as a compensating balance, has, in effect, paid 5 per cent for the $8,000 which he is actually allowed to use. Since he presumably would have maintained some minimum balance in his deposit account in any case, the actual difference in rate is not so great as this example suggests. The practice of requiring compensating balances is sometimes defended on the ground that it provides the bank with a supplementary protection against loss. In case of default on a loan the bank is allowed to offset the entire amount of the customer's deposit balance against any part of the loan that remains unpaid.

Quantitative restrictions of a general character are also applied to deposits. The most important of these, of course, are the reserve requirements discussed in the preceding chapter, which contribute to a solution of the fundamental banking problem by helping to prevent an undue expansion of deposit liabilities. When the demand liabilities of banks took the form of circulating notes it was customary to limit the amount that could be outstanding to a prescribed percentage of the bank's capital. As was noted earlier, at one time the Federal Deposit Insurance Corporation sought to establish the rule that deposits should not exceed ten times a bank's capital accounts. Even now it is generally agreed that deposit liabilities should maintain a reasonable relationship to capital accounts, though what is reasonable is by no means clearly defined.

A final aspect of the management of bank liabilities, and thereby of a solution of the fundamental banking problem, involves methods of restricting the liquidity of liabilities.[10] Various devices have been employed at

---

9. Compensating balances are also frequently required in the granting of lines of credit (i.e., authorizations to borrow up to a specified amount).

10. By "liquidity of liabilities" we shall mean, in rough analogy with the liquidity of assets, the likelihood that depositors will exercise their rights in such degree as to cause

different times to restrict the demand on banks to redeem their liabilities. One of the simplest and crudest of these methods is simply to make it more difficult for depositors to draw currency out of the bank. This is a technique which has frequently been applied during runs. It has happened, for example, that banks impose obstacles to the payment of deposits at such times. All paying windows except one may be temporarily closed; excessive time may be consumed in counting out cash; or bank officials and others may issue reassuring statements to persuade depositors that it is unnecessary to attempt withdrawal. All these methods are designed to slow down the rate at which currency is called for.[11]

The establishment of the Federal Deposit Insurance Corporation in 1933 probably exerted an influence in the same direction. The assurance afforded by the knowledge that no loss will be incurred on deposits up to $10,000 should lessen the tendency of small depositors to demand cash during periods of uncertainty.[12] While the existence of the Federal Deposit Insurance Corporation is generally assumed to have reduced the danger of severe runs, its efficacy under crisis conditions has not been subjected to test. The fact that deposit insurance applies only up to $10,000 for each account signifies that depositors with balances in excess of that amount lack the full protection afforded other depositors. Larger depositors would still have reason to make sudden demands upon banks in case of serious danger to their solvency.

Deposits which are not covered by insurance because they are in excess of $10,000 constitute roughly 42 per cent of the dollar amount of all deposits in insured banks. Studies of bank failures show that it is precisely the larger deposits which are the first to be withdrawn in times of doubt as to the safety of banks. Withdrawals of the larger deposits have been the most important cause of sudden increases in the rate of conversion of liabilities. Thus the Federal Deposit Insurance Corporation fails to cover the very type of deposit which has chiefly contributed to difficulties in the past. The Corporation has probably reduced to some extent the danger of heavy withdrawals of cash, but it is too early to conclude that the problem has been solved. The most that can be said, on the basis of present evidence, is that the Federal Deposit Insurance Corporation is, among other things, a factor which should tend to reduce the liquidity of bank liabilities.

---

a net drain of cash from the bank. Where the expectation of a net cash loss to a bank is high, the bank's liabilities will be viewed as relatively "liquid"; where the probability of net cash withdrawals is deemed slight, the liabilites of the bank will be regarded as relatively illiquid.

11. A dramatic account of the use of these and other techniques during a run has been given by Marriner Eccles (a leading Western banker who, as Chairman of the Board of Governors of the Federal Reserve System, guided the System through some of its most critical and turbulent years). See *Beckoning Frontiers* (New York: Knopf, 1951), pp. 57-62. Also reproduced in Charles R. Whittlesey, *Readings in Money and Banking* (New York: Norton, 1952), pp. 40-43.

12. The Corporation is described more fully in Chapter 26.

MANAGEMENT OF BANK ASSETS

The Schedule of Priorities

The primary basis for management of bank assets is what Professor Robinson refers to as a "schedule of priorities."[13] This involves the estimation of prospective demands for cash and credit that may confront the bank and then the allocation of the bank's assets in such a way as to assure that these demands will be met in a manner most satisfactory and appropriate to the bank and its owners. Some sort of schedule of priorities, whether or not it is formulated in precise terms, serves to guide such an allocation of assets.

The schedule of priorities suggested by Professor Robinson consists of four parts:

1. The highest priority: *Primary reserves*. These consist of cash in the form of Federal Reserve deposits, vault cash, and balances with other banks.
2. The second priority: *Protective investment*. This category is synonymous with "secondary reserves." It comprises earning assets which can be readily converted into cash. The best example of such assets is short-term Treasury obligations, but other types of investments and even loans are not excluded. The purpose is to assure that currency or its equivalent will be available to meet any probable, and even more or less remotely possible, demands.
3. The third priority: *Customer credit demands*. Where the second category is designed to make the bank safe, the third looks toward the bank's serving its natural customers such as the businesses and individuals of its community.
4. The fourth priority: *Open market investment for income*. This category relates to the disposition of the bank's earning assets after the three higher priorities have been satisfied. While safety should be regarded as a paramount consideration (even more so than in the case of the third priority), the main purpose of this application of the bank's funds is to provide additional income.

The schedule of priorities shown here is intended to be general rather than precise, but the idea which it embodies is basic, namely, that bankers distribute cash assets and earning assets on the basis of anticipated requirements of differing degrees of urgency. To do so is implicit in any attempt to provide a rational solution of the fundamental banking problem.

Criteria of Portfolio Policy

One of the definitions of "portfolio" is "a list of the commercial paper and securities owned, especially by a bank." The expression "portfolio

13. Roland I. Robinson, *The Management of Bank Funds*, 2nd edition (New York: McGraw-Hill, 1962), pp. 13-18.

policy" refers primarily to the policy which a bank follows with respect to the character and maturity distribution of its earning assets. To some extent, cash assets are also involved. First, the amount of cash assets which a bank sees fit to maintain influences the volume of resources that can be held in the form of earning assets. Second, the lower the proportion of its cash assets the more liquid, presumably, should be its earning assets.

The criteria which a banker constantly must consider in the acquisition of earning assets are liquidity, safety, and profitability. The first of these is addressed, of course, primarily toward the short-run phase of the banking problem and othe others toward the long-run phase. The difficulty in applying these criteria arises out of the fact, noted earlier, that the attribute of profitability ordinarily varies inversely with the attributes of safety and liquidity. (Thus cash would be wholly liquid and safe but its profitability would be nil.)

The meaning of *profitability* is more or less obvious. Ordinarily, it is measured by the anticipated yield to maturity of the security, including any increase or decrease in the principal value of the asset between the time of purchase and the time of sale or redemption. In the case of discounted notes or Treasury bills, the receipt of interest takes the form, in fact, of the difference between the price at which they are bought and the price at which they are sold or redeemed. Considerations of profitability may dictate shifts from shorter to longer maturities in order to obtain higher yields, and to securities such as government bonds which involve a minimum of cost to administer.

Safety refers to the probability of full realization of all anticipated payments of interest and principal. The most important point to observe in connection with this attribute is that a security is not necessarily unsafe just because its market value may temporarily decline. If the promised payments of interest and principal are likely to be fully and faithfully made, the security is to be regarded as relatively safe. At various times the market value of Treasury bonds has declined substantially so that their liquidity was seriously impaired. Their safety, however, was never in doubt.

The quality of *liquidity* is rather more difficult to describe. While a great deal of refined analysis has been directed toward the question of liquidity in recent years, it is sufficient for present purposes to deal with liquidity in rather simplified and perhaps somewhat arbitrary terms. As noted in Chapter 1, the expressions liquid and liquidity are figures of speech. The important elements of the property of liquidity which this analogy suggests are the ease of transfer into other assets (*salability*) and the ability to make such transfers without sacrifice in capital values (*capital stability*, or *capital certainty*). Since money possesses this property to a degree beyond that of other types of assets, the liquidity of other assets may be ranked by their convertibility into money. A short-term government obligation ranks high on the liquidity scale because it is readily salable for cash without much risk of capital loss. On the other hand, a bank's premises are relatively illiquid because they probably could not be converted quickly into cash except at a substantial discount from the normal value of the property.

It is customary to distinguish between a number of different bases of liquidity, associated with the factors which permit assets to be converted into cash. First, an asset will be relatively liquid if it is bought and sold in well-developed and active secondary markets, as is the case with government securities or stocks of well-known companies sold on the New York Stock Exchange. Second, the liquidity of an asset will depend in part on the ease with which it can be borrowed upon. Liquidity based on salability and ease of use as collateral is said to depend upon "shiftability." Third, the liquidity of an asset will depend on its maturity date, which may influence both its salability and risk of fluctuation in market value. Thus a bond maturing ten years from now would be thought of as less liquid than the same bond on a date closer to maturity. If a bank acquires such bonds at a regular rate, it will, in the course of time, have bonds evenly distributed as to maturities from the present to a date ten years hence. The average maturity of the bonds is reduced by this process of "spacing" to five years. In this case, liquidity of the bond portfolio may be said to depend on a policy of spacing maturities.

Portfolio Policy Alternatives

In determining both the portfolio policy to be followed and its success, much will depend upon the skill of the management in calculating the particular needs of the bank and in judging general financial conditions. It will also depend to a great degree on the organization of the country's financial markets and institutions and the extent to which the Federal Reserve and the Treasury assist in their orderly functioning.

The ideal type of asset for a bank to hold would be a credit instrument which yields a high return, yet could always be converted into as much cash as was paid for it. Such an instrument obviously does not exist. The bank will, therefore, be obliged to effect some sort of compromise. It may hold a relatively large part of its assets in cash and another part in income-yielding credit instruments which are not always readily convertible into cash. It may hold less cash, but try to have its earning assets distributed in such a manner that a constant stream of money is flowing in which can be retained, if occasion warrants, and used to supplement customary reserves. It may try to divide its earning assets into one group which will yield a relatively high income but are not liquid and another which will yield less but will be readily convertible through sale or borrowing. Or it may employ a combination of such policies.

The distribution of a bank's resources among different types of assets including cash constitutes the bank's "asset mix." The composition of the asset mix will differ widely among banks because of differences in the judg-ments and preferences of the officials of the various banking institutions and because of different opportunities. For any particular bank, the asset mix is a reflection of that bank's "schedule of priorities" and asset alternatives.

Traditionally, commercial paper has been held in particularly high esteem as a bank asset. Of all forms of credit instruments it was looked on as coming closest to meeting the criteria of portfolio policy. Its yield was relatively high, and, because it was based on commercial transactions, the completion of which presumably would provide funds for discharging the obligation, it was regarded as safe. Even in the absence of facilities for disposing of it if cash was desired, the fact that it was of short maturity seemed to mean that simply by holding on to it, its liquidation could be counted upon within a short time. The feature of short maturity also signi-fied that the bank's assets were automatically subject to frequent check-up, thus increasing the probability that no serious deterioration in their quality would occur.

Although still regarded as a premium asset, commercial paper is no longer generally considered to be an important source of bank liquidity. This is so whether the perspective is that of the individual bank or the banking system. The experiences of the 1930's called painful attention to the limited contribution to be made by commercial loans in assuring the liquidity of the banking system as a whole. A single bank can improve its reserve position by contracting its earnings assets and deposits at a more rapid rate than other banks, but this is achieved mainly at the expense of other banks, which in that case undergo a net internal drain in favor of the contracting institution. If all banks are contracting at about the same rate, however, interbank clearings are roughly offsetting. In that case the only source of improvement in the reserve position of the commercial banks is the increase in excess reserves resulting from the net reduction in deposits. But this is a draconic method of increasing the liquidity of the banking system, since it involves a contraction of the money stock and a net reduction in the volume of credit extended to business and consumers. These deflationary developments tend to weaken the economic position of the many transactors who depend on the continued flow of spending based on bank credit. The result is to diminish their capacity to meet their debt obligations. Achieving liquidity by a reduction of deposits is therefore likely to be accompanied by secondary effects that impair the quality of bank assets and contribute further to a cumulative downswing.

Not only from the standpoint of the system as a whole, but also from that of the individual bank, loans have less liquidity than they might appear on the surface to have. Although a reduction in the volume of commercial loans of the individual bank would tend to improve its liquidity position by contracting deposits and increasing reserves (assuming other banks were not contracting as rapidly), this would be achieved by calling loans and

forcing customers to seek financing elsewhere. Since relationships with borrowers tend to be long-lived and profitable to the bank, this method of
improving liquidity is regarded by most bankers as a desperation expedient
rather than a normal procedure. Thus, with the exception of open-market
commercial paper, the portfolio policy of banks does not ordinarily include
customer loans as a source of liquidity.

Loans in general and short-term, self-liquidating commercial loans in
particular are of less relative importance than before the Great Depression.
Whereas bank assets at one time consisted predominantly of short-term
commercial loans, they are now largely in the form of investments and loans
other than short-term commercial loans. The change was partly the result
of an increase in the supply of these other types of obligations, but it is also
true that the amount of commercial paper is less than it once was relative
to the volume of transactions carried on. A rise in commercial and industrial
borrowing from banks occurred in the period of reconversion after World
War II, and such borrowing continued to expand with few interruptions
thereafter. Investments, which exceeded loans by a ratio of over three to
one at the end of World War II, fell in absolute as well as relative importance in bank portfolios as banks gradually reduced their holdings of
United States government obligations. The net result was that the dollar
volume of loans held by commercial banks came to exceed investments
by a substantial amount (see Figure 7-2).

It is important to bear in mind, however, that today the loan
category embraces a very different collection of obligations from the loans
of a predominantly short-term, commercial character that were formerly
the rule. Loans are now granted for longer terms than was customary in
the past. The so-called "term loan," which has become of increasing importance, is frequently extended for periods of five years or longer (to the
extent of roughly one-half by dollar volume in 1957). In addition, loans of
a non-commercial type have expanded considerably—among them real estate
loans and consumer loans (see Figure 7-3).

The holdings of longer-term claims has given rise to a number of distinctive problems and policies. A bank ordinarily plans on retaining until
maturity certain types of obligations, such as term loans and mortgages,
which have little or no marketability. In most cases it can safely plan on
doing so since even if all of its deposits were nominally payable on demand
it would never be called upon to redeem anything like all of them at any
one time. With an increase in longer term holdings, however, bank liquidity
has become dependent to an increasing degree on the shiftability of assets.
It is therefore of some consequence that a time when a particular bank wants
to sell is a time when other banks are also likely to want to sell, so that
liquidity is rapidly lessened. To a considerable extent, however, the increased dependence on shiftability has been offset by increases in bank
holdings of cash and highly liquid secondary assets, by deliberate and careful

policies of spacing maturities, and by the more explicit recognition of the role of the Federal Reserve as the ultimate guarantor of system liquidity in time of serious strain.

It should be noted that by no means all bank investments consist of long-term securities. At the end of 1960, 75 per cent of the investments of insured commercial banks consisted of United States government obligations. About 27 per cent of these securities had maturities under one year and 58 per cent had maturities under five years.

The resort to investment in long-term securities constitutes a long step

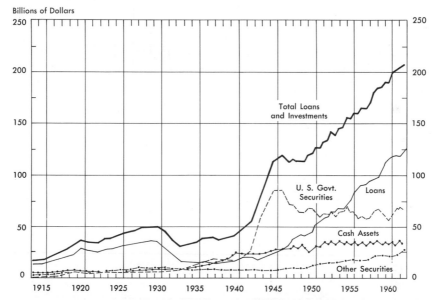

Figure 7-2.   Loans and Investments of All Commercial Banks, 1914-1962.

Source: Adapted from the *Federal Reserve Historical Chart Book.*

away from traditional methods of portfolio management. The certainty of ultimate payment may, of course, be as great for a long-term asset as for a short-term asset, but the element of a greater time period introduces an increased possibility that the market value may decline for varying periods. Such declines are not necessarily a threat to the technical solvency and profitability of banks provided that cash drains or pressures from supervisory authorities do not compel banks to contract total assets. Nevertheless, they may prove to be a disturbing influence and call for appropriate policies by the supervisory authorities.

From the standpoint of operations, the greatest advantage of investments is that the bank is not dependent on businessmen asking for loan accommodation. A bank with funds available for lending can take the initiative by buying securities in the open market. Thus the assumption of traditional banking theory referred to in Chapter 5 that banks are passive in their operations is a survival from the time when commercial paper was the principal asset of banks and does not apply with respect to investments.

Portfolio Policy in the Light of Changing Conditions

The policies actually employed in managing bank assets are greatly influenced by business conditions, as the preceding section may have

Billions of Dollars

* Revised to exclude loans
to   financial   institutions

Figure 7-3.   Principal Loans of Member Banks,
1952-1962.

Source: Adapted from the *Federal Reserve Chart Book.*

made clear. During the 1930's, for example, the practice grew up of holding a considerably larger proportion of cash to total assets than before that time. In part, the relative expansion of cash holdings constituted an offset to such lessening of the liquidity of banks as may have resulted from the shift to assets of longer maturities. Chiefly, however, it reflected the failure of banks to find an opportunity to lend on suitable credit or invest at satisfactory yields. It was probably not to any significant extent the result of increases in reserve requirements; these increases were the consequence rather than the cause of cash accumulation.

Ownership of relatively long-term investments exposes a bank to the risk of fluctuations in the market value of these securities. The possibility of loss carries with it also the possibility of gain if the market moves in the other direction. What is especially important to observe, however, is that the shift from loans to investments served not so much to increase the vulnerability of bank portfolios to market fluctuations as to expose them to a different type of market fluctuation. Investments are more likely to be jeopardized by a decline in bond prices, and loans are more likely to be jeopardized by a decline in commodity prices.

In the 1920-1922 depression, experience with commercial paper was less favorable than experience with investments. During the depression following 1929, just the opposite was true. The reason for the difference is primarily that the first period was distinguished by a sharp fall in commodity prices and the second by a serious drop in bond prices. It reflects the fact that in the earlier period, speculation was most active in commodity markets but in the later period it was most active in security markets. It would seem that *prevailing conditions may be as important as the particular type of asset* in determining the outcome of portfolio policy.

Particular Devices Affecting Bank Assets

It is a common practice for banks to grant their regular customers a "line of credit." The bank thereby agrees to extend loans up to a certain amount, subject, of course, to the meeting of specified conditions. The potential borrower then has the assurance that his business plans will not be interrupted by lack of funds. Borrowers sometimes pay a small interest charge amounting to perhaps ½ per cent per annum on the unused part of the line of credit. In Canada, Great Britain, and a few other countries, it is customary to grant customers an overdraft privilege. The bank agrees to honor drafts up to a specified amount and charges interest on such overdrafts until they are paid off. Both of these devices make it possible to obtain credit more or less automatically as it is desired.

Banks are prohibited from holding certain types of assets, aside from the limitations imposed by bank examiners on grounds of quality. The common and preferred stocks of corporations are ordinarily not held by banks except to the extent that they may have been acquired as a result of taking over the collateral on a loan previously made. Even then the bank is expected to sell the security as soon as can reasonably be done without undue sacrifice.

Banking laws customarily restrict the purchase of the securities of any private obligor to a specified percentage of the bank's capital and surplus. For banks which are members of the Federal Reserve System, the limit is set at 10 per cent, while the laws of some states allow a somewhat higher percentage. Government obligations, however, are exempt from this restriction. The purpose of the requirement is primarily to compel banks to diversify and thereby to spread the risk of depreciation of assets. It is probably a protection to banks in other ways. Very large advances to a single borrower would be likely to jeopardize the independence of a bank. A bank which had lent excessive amounts to a particular borrower might well find itself very much at the latter's mercy. One of the most extreme examples of the way in which it was possible to abuse the credit of a bank when no such rule obtained came to light many years ago:

> The Farmers' Exchange Bank, of Gloucester, Rhode Island, failed in 1809 with $86.50 in specie in its vaults, after having loaned $845,771 on the basis of $100,000 capital, on unendorsed notes reading: "I, Andrew Dexter Junr., do promise the President, Directors, and Co. of the Farmers' Exchange Bank, to pay them, or order,——dollars, in—— years from this date, with interest at two per cent. per annum; it being, however, understood that the said Dexter shall not be called upon to make payment until he thinks proper, he being the principal Stockholder and best knowing when it will be proper to pay the same."[14]

This illustration appropriately introduces a somewhat similar limitation, namely, the restriction on loans to bank officers. Member banks are prohibited from extending credit in excess of $2,500 to any of their own executive officers. A few states forbid any such loans, and all but two restrict them in one way or another.

Investment in mortgages may be restricted to a specified ratio of capital and surplus or of time deposits. As with the holding of common stocks or real estate itself, the restriction may be exceeded temporarily if this is necessary to avoid loss on other loans or investments. The proportion of restricted assets tends to be higher in depressions than in good times. For one thing, commercial and industrial loans decline more rapidly than other types of assets in a period of falling activity. For another, banks are more likely to acquire collateral as a result of default on loans granted earlier.

It would scarcely be possible to enumerate all the other methods employed to maintain the value of assets. A few of the more significant, however, may be briefly described. One of the most familiar is the practice of holding what are called "concealed assets." For example, it is quite common for banks to write down the book value of the bank's premises to a value which represents less than their actual worth in the market—sometimes as low as one dollar. This is ordinarily accomplished gradually by charges against the undivided profits account. In case the market value of earning assets declines, it is then possible to write down their book value and balance this by writing up the book value of the premises. The same end may also be

---

14. H. E. Miller, *Banking Theories in the United States before 1860* (Cambridge: Harvard University Press, 1922), p. 97.

accomplished by setting up contingency reserve accounts which, in case of need, can be used to adjust the book value of loans and investments to a decline in their realizable value.

Commercial banks have resorted increasingly to what is known as "valuation allowances."[15] Instead of setting up separate reserve accounts, the value at which assets are carried on the books of a bank are currently written down by charges against earnings, much the same as was described in the preceding paragraph. Even assets of the highest quality may be written down in this way, though at a slower rate than lower grade assets. The policy of making valuation allowances has been encouraged by examiners. It avoids disadvantages which attach to building up capital, surplus, or reserve accounts and assures that provision for losses will be made in good times as well as bad.

It might seem that such measures as the use of concealed assets or contingency reserve accounts would be of little importance except to change appearances. If the depreciation of assets is adjusted in the ways referred to, the true position of the bank is obviously not changed; all that has been done is to alter the way different values are entered on the books of the bank. While this criticism is valid, the practices described serve a useful purpose. An adjustment for decline in asset values could be effected, of course, through the undivided profits account without the indirectness involved in these other methods. But the intermediate step of writing down premises or setting up reserve accounts prevents the amount from entering the undivided profits account, and by so doing reduces the danger that it will be paid out in the form of unduly generous dividends. In that way it may help to retain values within the business and thus to maintain the total worth of assets; otherwise its contribution to satisfying the banking problem is formal rather than fundamental. It is worth noting that capital and surplus accounts cannot be reduced without the approval of the supervisory authorities. Thus if sums are transferred to surplus, they may not be sufficiently accessible; if they are left in the undivided profits account, they may be too accessible with the result that they are distributed in dividends. The use of concealed assets or reserve accounts helps to avoid these two difficulties.

A somewhat different type of device is what is known as "segregation of assets," which is provided for in one form or another in the laws of a dozen states. Segregation signifies the separation of assets held against time deposits from those held against demand deposits. Its purpose is to prevent the withdrawal of demand deposits from bringing about the liquidation of the best assets so that time deposits are left with only inferior securities behind them. Such a safeguard would presumably become important at a time when banks found it necessary to exercise the right to require notice of withdrawal of time deposits. Where there is segregation of assets, the assets against time

---

15. Also referred to as "unallocated charge-offs," "valuation reserves," "depreciation and amortization allowances," and "reserve accounting."

deposits are likely to be largely of the investment type while those held against demand deposits are more liquid.

PROFITS AND THE FUNDAMENTAL BANKING PROBLEM

One of the most familiar proposals for safeguarding the quality of banking assets has been to introduce measures, such as limiting the rate of interest paid on deposits, to enable banks to earn profits regarded as adequate. The defense of this proposal runs along the following lines. If banks have difficulty in earning reasonable profits, they may be tempted, in order to maintain their reputation as successful banks, to place their funds in securities yielding a high rate of return. These securities will presumably be less safe, and the danger will be greater of a subsequent decline in their value. On the other hand, if banks are enabled to earn satisfactory profits in other ways, they will be content to hold only safe assets. There will be little danger of such securities declining seriously in value.

Although this argument reflects widely held opinion, it is open to considerable qualification. The argument assumes that a bank must earn approximately as high a rate of profits as is normal for other comparable banks in order to be thought to be as "sound." But it would scarcely help matters to introduce measures that would enable one bank to earn higher profits if the result was also to increase the earnings of other banks and thereby to raise still further the level of profits the first bank considered essential to its standing in the community. The argument as it stands embodies a principle of "keeping up with the Joneses." Without suggesting that the argument was ever intended to be carried this far, it may be said that an attempt to justify *excessive* profits, whether for their own sake or in order to maintain appearances, is extremely dangerous. Moderation in the conception of what banks should earn is essential to conservative banking. Otherwise the way is always open to the acquisition of unsafe assets and the undue expansion of liabilities in a manner that would jeopardize a satisfactory solution of the fundamental banking problem.

If it were generally felt that the desire for higher profits than conditions warrant may lead bankers to acquire risky assets, support would be greatly strengthened for the direct regulation of bank assets. Action of this kind would be highly unpalatable to bankers. But it might seem to be more logical and certain, granted the apparent assumption that bankers would be willing to sacrifice safety to profitability, than a policy of indiscriminately facilitating the making of high earnings. The latter solution all too clearly resembles a policy of paying people to be good.

Whatever the merits of the case for high profits as a contribution to the safety of our banking system, it is a matter of record that in recent years official policy has supported the view that the assurance of comfortable earnings contributes to the safety of banks. Various measures, notably the prohibition of interest on demand deposits and the restriction of interest on time deposits, were introduced with the primary purpose of improving the earnings position of banks. The establishment of new banks was made more difficult, partly to protect the earnings of existing banks from the effects of competition. Other practices, such as the imposition of service charges by banks, were given the stamp of official approval even though no formal action was involved.

SELECTED BIBLIOGRAPHY

FOULKE, R. A., and H. V. PROCHNOW, *Practical Bank Credit*. Englewood Cliffs, N. J.: Prentice-Hall, 1950.

HODGMAN, DONALD R., "The Deposit Relationship and Commercial Bank Investment Behavior," *Review of Economics and Statistics* (August 1961), pp. 257-268.

LYON, ROGER A., *Investment Portfolio Management in the Commercial Bank*. New Brunswick: Rutgers University Press, 1960.

PARKS, ROBERT H., "Portfolio Operations of Commercial Banks in Treasury Securities," *Journal of Finance* (March 1957), pp. 52-66.

RITTER, L. S., (ed.), *Money and Economic Activity* (Readings in Money and Banking). Boston: Houghton Mifflin, 1961, Chapters III-IV.

ROBINSON, ROLAND I., *The Management of Bank Funds*. New York: McGraw-Hill, 1961.

SHAW, E. S., *Money, Income, and Monetary Policy*. Homewood, Ill.: Irwin, 1950, pp. 78-91.

WHITTLESEY, C. R., "The Stability of Demand Deposits," *American Economic Review* (December, 1949), pp. 1192-1203.

8

MONEY MARKETS AND
THE ADJUSTMENT OF
LIQUIDITY REQUIREMENTS

We have seen that the maintenance of adequate liquidity is a crucial problem in the administration of bank portfolios: a bank that falls short of the desired goal incurs the risk of technical insolvency; one that exceeds the desired goal sacrifices potential earnings.

For an individual banker the money market provides a place where changing liquidity requirements can be accommodated. But it is much more than that. It also serves the liquidity needs of an endless variety of individuals, businesses, and governmental units, foreign as well as domestic. It is an invaluable agency for promoting the flexibility, mobility, and full utilization of community resources. (At times, also, it may become the scene of financial crises.) And it is the principal point of contact for actions of the central bank designed to improve the operation of the economic system. The present chapter undertakes to describe this market and what goes on in it. But first it is well to identify the market within a broader framework.

THE MONEY MARKET IN RELATION TO OTHER
FINANCIAL MARKETS

Financial markets in general, like commodity markets and the real estate market, are part of the vast system of exchange and division of labor which goes to make up the modern economy. In the broadest sense, financial markets are to be regarded as embracing the exchange of all claims mediated by investment bankers, security dealers, and other financial institutions, and even dealings between individuals. The small saver who participates in a Christmas Club enters this market in exchanging his few dollars for a claim to money payable in December. The person who lends ten dollars to a friend constitutes, momentarily, a part of the market just as a person buying fruit from a farmer is a part of the commodity markets.

At the other extreme from this broad interpretation is the characterization of financial markets in terms of the particular type of financial instrument traded in it. One encounters such expressions, for example, as the "bond market," the "Federal funds market," the "bill market," the "commercial paper market." What these expressions refer to is not a formally organized exchange at a known location like the New York Stock Exchange or the Chicago Grain Market. They relate, rather, to a loose combination of enterprises, institutions, and practices which custom and to some extent legislation have built up to facilitate trade in the particular type of security specified. The markets to which they refer are likely to embrace a variety of dealers, including banks, as well as investment firms, brokers, and individuals who trade in credit instruments "over the counter." The dealers in New York and other major cities are in contact with dealers elsewhere in this country and even abroad.

Intermediate between financial markets in the broadest sense and specific kinds of such markets are the two classifications that are of most general concern, namely, the capital market and the money market. The "capital market" is concerned with transactions in bonds and stocks. Its function is primarily that of providing funds for relatively long-term use. The so-called "money market," on the other hand, is ordinarily thought of in relation to shorter term credit instruments. The traditional meaning of the expression, in fact, confined it to short-term obligations only. It is this narrower connotation that will concern us mainly in this chapter. It is not uncommon, however, for the expression "money market" to be extended to include medium-term securities and sometimes even long-term securities. Where the difference matters, the context will usually indicate what meaning is intended. It may be added that when people speak of "the" money market they are likely to have in mind not only the market in the narrow sense but also the money market as it exists in New York.

A final distinction, of a somewhat different and overlapping character, is that between the "new issues market" and the "secondary" market. The flotation of new issues is discussed in the following chapter in connection with investment banking. What is important to note here is that the secondary market makes it possible for buying and selling of securities to take place continuously regardless of the amount of new issues currently coming on the market. The market in outstanding issues places at the disposal of potential purchasers securities of the utmost variety with respect to maturity and obligor. It also provides assurance that holders of securities can dispose of them in case they wish to obtain cash or to switch to different securities.

The secondary market makes it possible to determine interest rates and yields over a wider range than would otherwise be possible. Because an active secondary market exists for Treasury bills, it is possible to obtain quotations on Treasury bills of less than three months' maturity (three months being the best that could be done on a new issue basis). The same holds true of other issues. It is worth observing that Treasury obligations of longer maturities, i.e., certificates, notes, and even bonds, become short-term securities as they approach the due date. They are then bought and sold in the secondary markets at interest rates comparable with Treasury bill rates.

DEVELOPMENT OF THE MONEY MARKET AND MONEY MARKET INSTRUMENTS

The first securities exchange in the United States was organized in 1791 by Robert Morris, Stephen Girard, and Nicholas Biddle, all Philadelphia capitalists. Early dealings both in Philadelphia and in New York about the same time were mainly in United States Government obligations and foreign exchange. Gradually additional stocks and bonds became available, and in 1817 the "New York Stock and Exchange Board" was established. Over the ensuing years types of securities traded proliferated, other exchanges were added, telegraphic and other communications developed, and New York grew into the undisputed financial center of the country.

An important stage in the development of a true money market was the rise of dealings in short-term commercial paper. This activity had assumed significant proportions by the middle of the nineteenth century. Buyers and sellers were widely distributed throughout the country but dealings were largely confined to New York. In the course of time ancillary services such as credit-rating agencies grew up, contributing to a further rounding out of the money market. For many years commercial paper was a major item in the market. Methods of business finance have changed, as have the portfolio policies of commercial banks. Since the 1930's commercial paper has occupied a relatively minor place in the money market.

Until—and notably at—the time of the stock market crash of 1929 call loans constituted an important feature of the New York money market. Their development was a product of the rising volume of security transactions and the tendency of out-of-town banks to place deposits with New York banks. Operations in the security markets were facilitated by the availability of funds. The banks, in turn, found that loans backed by collateral in the form of negotiable securities and payable on call met the need for liquidity. The subsequent decline in call loans was influenced by the low level of stock market activity in the 1930's, the imposition of various regulations and restrictions, and changes in methods of finance. The relatively small volume of call loans that remains is carried on directly by banks as a part of ordinary lending.

Today the stock in trade of the money market consists for the most part of commercial paper, bankers' acceptances, brokers' loans, Federal funds, and Treasury bills. The first three of these were described earlier and in any case are sufficiently identified by their names. It is the latter two types of financial assets that have now come to occupy a predominant position in the money market. Treasury bills constitute, moreover, the principal secondary reserves of commercial banks.

Federal funds are simply deposits at the Federal Reserve Banks. In a typical case a bank whose reserves are deficient obtains Federal funds by means of an overnight loan from a bank which has excess reserves. This is accomplished in a very simple manner. The lending bank gives the borrowing bank its check on the Reserve Bank and receives in return a cashier's check from the borrower. The first check is deposited on the same day, thus transferring reserves to the borrowing bank. The second check is collected the following day, thus returning them to the lending bank. The second check is larger than the first by the amount of interest for one day. In the case of inter-city transactions the same result is accomplished through the wire transfer facilities of the Federal Reserve.

For many years a single stock brokerage firm in New York acted as intermediary for Federal funds, doing so primarily as a method of building good will. It made no specific charge for the service of bringing together buyers and sellers of Federal funds but was compensated instead by other business given by the banks. In a few cases, the banks benefiting insisted upon paying a small fee. In the course of time the market for Federal funds has become broader and government security dealers are now fairly active participants in it. Still, however, the firm acting as intermediary typically makes no specific charge for its services.[1] The daily volume of transactions in Federal funds averages under a half billion dollars but has risen at times to close to 2 billion.

Because of their extreme liquidity and short maturity, the rate on Federal funds is regarded as the most sensitive barometer of conditions of tightness or ease prevailing in the money market. By its nature, however, the Federal funds rate reflects day-to-day conditions rather than long-run market influences.

Treasury bills are a promise of the Federal government to pay a specified sum of money (from $1000 to $1,000,000) and are ordinarily issued for a period of three months (actually, ninety to ninety-two days).[2] They are bought and sold on a discount basis; the difference between the price paid at time of issue and the face amount of the obligation, payable at maturity, represents interest. The rate of discount, and therefore the bill rate on new issues, is arrived at from the competitive bids submitted, mainly by large

1. For a detailed discussion of Federal funds, including a description of alternative techniques, see the authoritative Technical Paper, *The Federal Reserve Funds Market*, published by the Board of Governors, Washington, 1959.

2. In 1959 the Treasury began issuing bills of six-month and one-year maturity. The volume of such issues remains small, however, relative to the total of three-month bills.

banks and dealers in government securities, in advance of the weekly issues of bills by the Treasury. The bill rate, though not as volatile as the rate on Federal funds, is similarly an important barometer of money market conditions. It is commonly accepted as the basic rate on short-term funds.[3]

A final factor to be noted is the possibility of obtaining funds directly from the Federal Reserve. The fact that the central bank is always present as a lender of last resort provides an important continuing source of liquidity. The establishment of the Federal Reserve System in 1914 was largely inspired, in fact, by the hope of averting severe liquidity crises in the money market such as had occurred earlier. Two principal procedures are followed for obtaining funds from the Federal Reserve: borrowing in the case of member banks, and the purchase of securities by the Federal Reserve under a repurchase contract in the case of non-bank dealers in government securities.

In actual practice, a member bank can always count on obtaining cash at the discount window of its Federal Reserve Bank if the need becomes serious. The authorities are careful, however, to see that the borrowing privilege is not abused. Federal Reserve officials discourage banks from remaining chronically in debt or using the Reserve Banks as a convenient source of capital. Borrowing is viewed as "a safety valve, enabling individual banks to restore their reserves to the required levels when unforeseen losses of funds have created deficiencies."[4] The assurance thus afforded of being able to obtain funds in case of urgent necessity goes far to impart liquidity to the banking system and thereby to the money market as a whole. It serves likewise to overcome the possibly uneven impact of credit control measures. Accordingly, the central bank authorities can, if the need arises, pursue control policies more vigorously than they otherwise could. For they know that any bank which is pinched too hard can obtain relief at the discount window. In general, then, the borrowing privilege contributes to the smooth functioning of the money market mechanism.

Repurchase agreements were employed in the 1920's at a time when the Federal Reserve was trying to develop bankers' acceptances as a major money market instrument. The effort met with scant success and the repurchase device fell into relative disuse. It was employed to a limited extent for Government securities in the intervening years. After World War II it was used fairly extensively during periods of tight money.

The repurchase technique involves the purchase of securities from a government securities dealer by the Federal Reserve and upon its initiative, with the dealer entering into a contract to buy them back at the same price on or before a specified date. Repurchase contracts are made for a maximum

---

3. That is to say, it is regarded as an index of movements in short-term interest rates. In addition, certain classes of lenders place great emphasis on it in setting the rates which they charge borrowers.

4. Robert V. Roosa, *Federal Reserve Operations in the Money and Government Securities Markets* (New York: Federal Reserve Bank of New York, 1956), p. 24.

of fifteen days and the securities bought customarily have a maturity of not over fifteen months. A repurchase agreement may be terminated at the option of either party without advance notice. The Federal Reserve is paid interest at a stipulated rate for the length of time the securities were held by it. The rate is ordinarily the same as the discount rate. Thus dealers in government securities are provided with cash when needed, and possible stringencies in the money market are correspondingly ameliorated.

It may be asked why this rather circuitous procedure is followed. The answer is that the borrowing privilege is restricted, technically, to member banks. Accordingly, the authorities go through the form of making a purchase of securities and then selling them back again in order to provide funds where they are needed, without actually granting a loan.

Besides contributing to the preservation of liquidity in the money market, the repurchase technique serves a useful integrating purpose. Federal Reserve officials maintain close contacts with dealers as a means of ascertaining their probable needs for repurchase agreements. In this way the authorities are able to detect changing degrees of ease or pressure in the money market. The effect is to promote smooth and orderly market conditions, and at the same time to contribute to the carrying out of central bank objectives.

ORGANIZATION OF THE MONEY MARKET: MAJOR PARTICIPANTS

The existence of a money market implies two essential conditions. The first is a significant volume of highly liquid assets, i.e., assets which can be exchanged for cash quickly and without substantial loss. The second requirement is a relatively high degree of concentration, geographically speaking, in dealings in these assets. The market may, and ordinarily does, serve an extensive hinterland. And it is likely to have connections with other money markets. But the transactions themselves focus in a limited area. Otherwise it is not a money market in the accepted meaning of the term.

The more highly developed money markets are characterized by a wide variety of liquid assets, possessing different features and serving different purposes. A corresponding variety and degree of specialization is to be found among the organizations and affiliated businesses dealing in these assets. The result is likely to be a more efficient market, as indicated by services performed, economy of operation, and uniformity of charges. Major money markets such as New York, London, and Paris have close connections with one another as well as with local money markets within their respective countries. They are closely integrated also with their central banks which, as was noted earlier, tend to assume the role of ultimate guarantor of liquidity (lender of last resort).

We may look upon modern money markets, then, as centers where highly liquid assets are bought and sold. This observation gives the key to what they are and to the basic functions which they perform. It also provides the key to the institutional structure of the money market. The organization of the money market is most simply described in terms of three types of participants:

a. Suppliers and demanders of liquid assets.
b. Providers of ancillary services of a specialized character.
c. Suppliers of routine mechanical services.

Since only the first of these groups calls for extended explanation we may take them up in reverse order.

Among routine services are such things as telegraph, telephone, transfer, safekeeping, maintenance of records, and printing. Mechanical and routine though they are, these are factors that can contribute appreciably to the economy of a particular market. They also help to account for the concentration of money market activities in particular localities. For example, it has been estimated that monthly rental charges of $420 for telephone lines maintained by a particular firm in New York would come to $230,000 if (as is, of course, unlikely) the same services were maintained from Chicago and $640,000 if maintained from Los Angeles.[5] Economies of this kind not only result from concentration of money market activities but also tend to maintain and increase the degree of concentration.

Of a less mechanical nature are the services provided by such specialized agencies as credit-rating agencies, statistical bureaus, and security analysts. Many of these services are available to any subscriber and on a nationwide scale. Nevertheless, they also tend to be concentrated in New York; not infrequently there are advantages in the way of obtaining more detailed and possibly more current information by being on the spot.

The New York Clearing House, and to a less extent similar institutions in other cities, provide both mechanical services and information to the money markets of which they are a part. There were occasions, before the introduction of the Federal Reserve made it superfluous, when clearing houses provided emergency liquidity in periods of credit stringency by pooling resources and issuing highly negotiable certificates. (Sometimes these certificates circulated as currency.) Other financial institutions have also created central organizations to serve the interests of their particular groups.[6]

We turn now to the major category referred to above, the suppliers and demanders of liquid assets. The reason for combining the two aspects is simple but significant: the same participant may appear as supplier at one

---

5. Sidney M. Robbins and Nestor E. Terleckyj, *Money Metropolis* (Cambridge: Harvard University Press, 1960), p. 35.
6. *Ibid.*, p. 39.

time and as demander at another. There are exceptions to this statement, of course. Some groups are typically users and some are typically suppliers of liquid funds. Nevertheless, the institutional organization of the money market—as well as its role as a place where liquidity needs are constantly being adjusted with almost any degree of fineness—can best be seen by viewing the demand and supply aspects of the market structure in combination.

The chief institutional components of the money market are shown in Table 8-1. It will be observed that they are listed in systematic sequence for ease in remembering rather than by order of importance in terms of volume. Thus the federal government, which is listed toward the end, is by far the largest demander of short-term funds. It will be noted also that where possible an indication is given as to whether the particular agency or business is to be regarded as supplier, demander, or both.

TABLE 8-1. Major Suppliers and Demanders of Funds in the New York Money Market

	Supplier	Demander
Commercial Banks	xx	x
Dealers and brokers		xx
Other financial corporations		
Life insurance companies	x	
Finance companies		xx
Domestic business corporations	x	xx
Exporters and importers		xx
Foreign banks and others	xx	
Government		
Federal		xx
State and local	x	x
Federal Reserve Banks	xx	

    xx Major role
    x Minor role

Commercial banks are thought of primarily as suppliers of short-term credit. The so-called "money market banks" include the larger banks in New York City and a half dozen in Chicago, besides perhaps twenty-five scattered throughout the country. The exact number included in this category varies inasmuch as shifts in prevailing market conditions tend to make banks sometimes more and sometimes less money market conscious.[7] Thus the number may rise when credit continues tight for some time, and decline when it eases. By means of correspondent relations with the large city banks the temporarily idle funds of a great multitude of smaller banks scattered all over the country are brought within the orbit of the New York money market. By the same token funds may move away from New York to the more local money markets under the attraction of yield differentials.

---

7. Roosa, *op. cit.*, p. 27.

At the same time that some banks are supplying funds to the money market, others may be appearing there as demanders of cash. A bank requiring additional reserves may borrow Federal funds or sell Treasury bills. Or still other types of assets may be liquidated.

A second major group of participants in the money market comprises *dealers and brokers*. They often require substantial sums of money for the purpose of carrying inventories of securities during the period when these are being distributed to the general public. Or they may need funds for financing customers who have bought securities on margin. Such loans (so-called "brokers' loans") were of major importance during the 1920's. In recent years they have been of relatively minor proportions, especially in relation to stock market totals. Even so they were typically of a magnitude of three to four billion dollars in the early 1960's.[8]

Government securities dealers are specialists who "make a market" for government securities by continuously buying and selling all maturities. A few comparisons will indicate the scale of their operations and also the principal sources whereby they are financed. At a date in the early 1960's dealers in United States government securities held a total of approximately $3 billion, of which about 97 per cent were in maturities under one year. Roughly 44 per cent of the financing of this inventory was derived from commercial banks, with banks outside New York supplying a little over half of this amount. Nearly as much came from corporations other than banks and insurance companies, and the rest from all other sources.[9]

Of perhaps twenty important dealers engaged in this business, five are banks, three of them in New York and two in Chicago. Other banks are free to establish dealer departments but have not found it advantageous to do so. They may, of course, act as intermediaries in the purchase or sale of government securities for their customers, but they do so through the regular dealer market.

The role of dealers and brokers, then, is twofold: they are an important source of demand for short-term financing, and they themselves constitute a part of the market mechanism.

Life insurance companies are primarily suppliers of long-term funds and for that reason are more likely to participate in the capital market. It is not unusual, however, for them to find themselves with funds awaiting disposition on a more permanent basis. They may then offer funds for short-term use in the money market in order to keep them from remaining idle during the interim.

Finance companies employ large sums of money in connection with installment sales and personal loans. They find it necessary to supplement their own resources by borrowing in the money market. Finance company paper is offered in substantial amounts, making up to some extent for the reduced

8. See *Federal Reserve Bulletin* for current data.
9. *Federal Reserve Bulletin*, March 1962, p. 332.

importance of commercial paper of the traditional kind. In the early 1960's the volume outstanding was generally in excess of $3 billion.

Domestic business corporations are ordinarily regarded as demanders of short-term funds in the market. Since World War II, however, they have also become important suppliers of short-term funds. At the low rates that prevailed from the early 1930's to the early 1950's there was no great induce-ment for corporations to invest for short periods the balances that often accrue in advance of dividend and tax dates, as a consequence of longer term borrowing, or for other reasons. The sharp rise in rates at times when Federal Reserve authorities were pursuing tight money policies to combat inflation afforded a strong attraction for excess balances to move into the money market. Moreover, the pressure on profit margins provided a con-tinuing drive in the same direction. By the 1960's, financial officers of cor-porations had, in contrast to earlier times, become extraordinarily alert to putting temporarily idle funds to work in the money market.

Tax anticipation certificates issued by the Treasury are bought extensively by corporations as a means of earning income on funds accumulated to pay taxes. Holdings of Treasury bills by non-financial corporations are substan-tial, amounting to between $5 and $6 billion in the early 1960's. The more aggressively managed companies, however, have turned increasingly toward finance company paper and other commercial types of debt instruments be-cause of the higher yield.

Historically, *exporters and importers* were a leading source of com-mercial paper and therefore of demand for funds from the money market. They never assumed the importance in the United States money markets, however, that they once held in London. And the rise of other types of credit instruments decreased their relative importance still further. The trade acceptance, often sent along with a bill of lading, is a typical form used in foreign trade operations.

A notable feature of the period after World War II was the mounting volume of short-term funds invested in the New York money market by *foreign banks*, international institutions, and others. As may be seen from Figure 8-1, the total of short-term liabilities due to foreigners rose from under $9 billion to over $21 billion in the ten years ending in 1960. Most, though not all, of this sum entered the New York money market. An ap-preciable amount, it may be observed, was invested in short-term obligations of the United States Treasury. The rapid rise in the total amount of foreign short-term assets toward the end of the period is largely explained by an expansion in the resources of the International Monetary Fund, with a result-ing increase in their holdings in this country.[10]

By far the largest net demander of short-term funds in the money market is the *United States Government*. The importance of the Treasury bill as a

10. The precipitous rise shown in 1947 reflects the setting up of the Fund and World Bank in that year.

money market instrument has already been noted. The expansion in its use was particularly rapid in the late 1950's. At the end of 1954 the amount outstanding was $19.5 billion, not greatly in excess of the figure at the end of the war. Five years later it was $39.6 billion or more than double. Activity in the Treasury bill market involves a continuing "roll-over" of maturing bills and their replacement with a new series. Proportions of Treasury bills refinanced at the weekly intervals vary to some extent, mainly in response

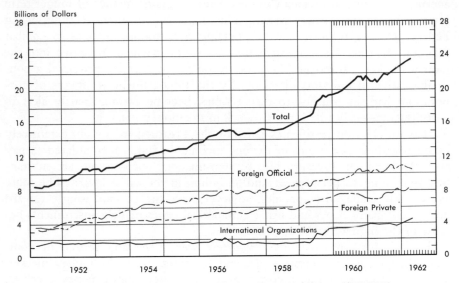

Figure 8-1.   Growth in External Short-Term Liabilities, 1951-1962.

Source: Adapted from the *Federal Reserve Historical Chart Book*.

to seasonal differences in anticipated receipts of tax revenues by the Treasury.

State and local governments similarly enter the money market from time to time to meet their requirements prior to the receipt of tax revenues. The instrument commonly used is the tax anticipation note, similar to the corresponding security issued by the Treasury. State and local governments may also, however, enter the money market as suppliers of short-term funds. Large sums of money are raised to finance municipal projects of various kinds. Since disbursements seldom coincide exactly with the receipt of funds, excess balances may be put to work in the money market. Another source is receipts from retirement and other trust funds administered by states and municipalities. These funds may be invested at short term pending long-term disposition or as a liquid secondary reserve.

The role of *Federal Reserve Banks* as the major current and contingent supplier of funds to the money market has already been noted. During and after World War II credit was supplied mainly through purchase of Treasury bills. There was a period just before the Treasury-Federal Reserve Accord of 1951, however, when they bought large amounts of bonds. Subsequently, there were times when they shifted into obligations of three- to twelve-month maturities or one- to five-year maturities. From 1951 to 1961 the total of all Governments held by the twelve Federal Reserve Banks ranged between $18 and $23 billion, though only a part of this sum represented funds supplied directly to the money market. The importance of Federal Reserve credit operations to the money market can hardly be exaggerated. More will be said in later chapters on these and other aspects of Federal Reserve actions.

INTEREST RATES IN THE MONEY MARKET

The money market, like any other market, is a place where prices are determined. The prices determined there are those of money market (that is, short-term credit) instruments. Determination of these prices establishes the level and structure of short-term interest rates.[11] Differences in interest rates reflect supply and demand. In other words, they will respond to differences in the collective advantages of each type of credit to borrowers and lenders of that particular type of credit, relative to all other types. And movements within the structure of rates will be sensitive to variations among these relative advantages.[12]

The first major point to bear in mind with respect to interest rates in the money market is the linkage that exists within the structure of rates. This means, first, that a major influence affecting one of the rates is likely to be felt all along the line. Second, it means that the entire complex of interest rates tends to move more or less together, though the degree of movement among particular rates may vary substantially, especially over short periods of time.

There are various reasons for the sympathetic movement of interest rates. For one thing, factors affecting one type of credit are likely to apply also to

---

11. See below, pp. 374-379.

12. A reminder may help the student to visualize the process that goes on in setting interest rates. The prices of securities change with supply and demand for the securities. And interest rates, which are calculated from the market prices of securities, vary inversely with these prices.

others. (This is particularly true within such broad categories as short rates and long rates. The degree of similarity of movement within these categories is therefore considerably greater than between the categories.) Another reason for the sympathetic movement of rates is that there is often a high degree of substitutability among different types of credit instruments. A bank ordinarily has the choice of getting funds by borrowing Federal funds, selling Treasury bills, or securing an advance at the Federal Reserve Bank. A corporation with excess cash on hand can probably put it into Treasury bills, bankers' acceptances, or finance company paper. Accordingly, any substantial distortion in the pattern of yields among the different types of credit may be expected to set forces in motion which will tend to correct the distortion.

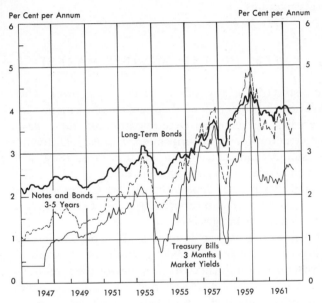

Figure 8-2.   Yields on U. S. Government Securities, 1946-1962.

Source: Adapted from the *Federal Reserve Historical Chart Book.*

The second major point to note with respect to rates in the money market is linkage of a spatial character, i.e., the connection that exists between rates in different parts of the country and among scattered money markets. Thus the New York money market is an important relay center, gathering to it available cash from any part of the country where rates are relatively low and releasing it to other areas where rates are relatively high. A similar service is performed by local markets throughout the country. There is a movement of funds among the local markets and between them and the New York market. Funds likewise flow between money markets in different countries, as we were forcibly reminded by the movement of short-term capital out of the United States in 1960-61, partly, presumably, in response to higher rates prevailing abroad.

Shifts such as these in short-term funds tend to bring about and sustain a certain geographical pattern of interest rates. Persistent rate differences in the different regions are presumably a reflection of fundamental supply and demand factors. As in the structural distortions among rates referred to above, any pronounced deviation in rate relationships among areas tends to set corrective forces in operation.

The level of advancement of a money market, whether this is defined in local or in the broadest national terms, is to be measured, more than anything else, in terms of the two linkages described above. In a developed

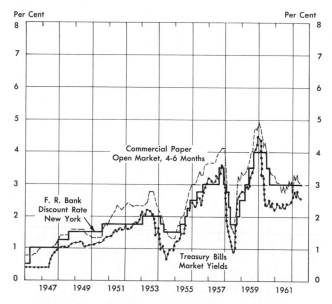

Figure 8-3.   Short-Term Interest Rates, 1946-1962.

Source: Board of Governors of the Federal Reserve System.

money market adjustments within the structure of rates and in the relationship of rates throughout the economy will, in fact, be constantly taking place. And they will take place speedily and smoothly. It is primarily on these grounds that we would say that the United States, England, and a number of Western European countries have mature money markets and that various other countries do not.

The foregoing is not to ignore the fact that even in the most highly developed markets some interest rates will be more sensitive than others. Some fluctuate from day to day or from hour to hour, as do those on Federal funds and Treasury bills. The rate on finance company paper is more sensitive than that on bankers' acceptances, and this is more sensitive than the prime rate on commercial paper. The discount rate, on the other hand, changes only when decided upon by the Federal Reserve authorities. And the rates paid on time deposits, notwithstanding the drastic changes initiated in 1962, are seldom altered at all.

Movements in interest rates for the period 1946 to 1962 are shown in Figures 8-2 and 8-3. The tendency for the general structure of rates to conform to similar trends is apparent both between short rates and long

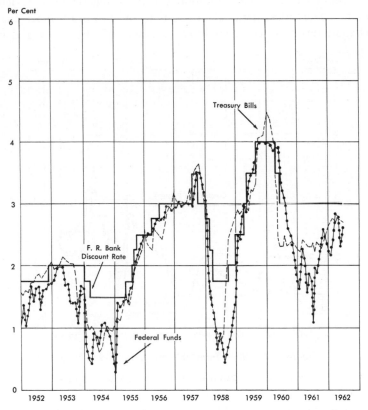

Figure 8-4. Rates on Federal Funds, Treasury Bills, and Federal Reserve Discounts, 1952-1962.

Source: *Federal Reserve Bulletin* and private sources.

(Figure 8-2) and among short rates (Figure 8-3). It is similarly seen that short rates fluctuated considerably more widely than long. For brief periods, as in 1956-57 and 1959-60, short rates even rose above long rates.[13] The close relation between the Treasury bill rate and the Federal funds rate is seen in Figure 8-4. A significant but less immediate relation is

13. This relationship, which has been very unusual in recent decades, was quite customary before World War I.

seen with the discount rate, which is, it will be remembered, the rate at which member banks can borrow at the Reserve Banks and at which re-purchase contracts are concluded.

Details as to the structure of money market rates are given in Table 8-2. The relative yields on different types of obligations disclose a familiar pattern. Thus Treasury bills tend to carry the lowest rate of those shown and others tend to vary upward according to the maturity and quality of the obligor.[14] Included in the table are weekly quotations covering, respectively, a period when the market was under pressure and rates were fluctuating widely and another period when the market was at ease and rate relationships were fairly stable. What stands out in this comparison of weekly quotations is the manner in which the structure of rates responds to differing market conditions. Both the tendency of rates to conform to a general pattern and the fact that, under differing conditions, substantial variations occur within that pattern are to be viewed as manifestations of the operation of a true market. These characteristics were lacking in the years before the Treasury-Federal Reserve Accord of 1951. The persistence in those years of wide spreads between yields and the relative absence of movement in rates were symptomatic of a market that was lacking in freedom and flexibility.

TABLE 8-2. Money Market Rates, 1952-1961 (Averages per cent per annum)

	Prime Commer- cial Paper 4 to 6 months	Finance Co. Paper Directly Placed 3 to 6 months	Prime Bankers' Accept- ances 90 days	3-month Bills	6-month Bills	United States Government 9- to 12- month Issues	3- to 5- year Issues
1952	2.33	2.16	1.75	1.72		1.81	2.13
1953	2.52	2.33	1.87	1.90		2.01	2.57
1954	1.58	1.41	1.35	.94		.92	1.82
1955	2.18	1.97	1.71	1.73		1.89	2.50
1956	3.31	3.06	2.64	2.62		2.83	3.12
1957	3.81	3.55	3.45	3.23		3.53	3.62
1958	2.46	2.12	2.04	1.78		2.09	2.90
1959	3.97	3.82	3.49	3.37	3.79	4.11	4.33
1960	3.85	3.54	3.51	2.87	3.20	3.41	3.99
1961	2.97	2.68	2.81	2.36	2.59	2.81	3.60

Source: *Federal Reserve Bulletin.*

Another manifestation of the improved functioning of money markets is to be seen in the narrowing of spreads between yields on short-term loans in New York, other northern and eastern cities, and cities in the South and West (Figure 8-5). The picture shown here is quite different from that which often prevailed in the past. In the 1920's and the 1930's, for example, the gap between rates in New York and outside was generally much greater than now (Figure 8-6). (An exception was during speculative excesses in the

---

14. The yield on Federal funds, of course, is usually the lowest of all.

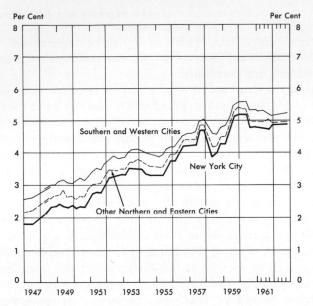

Figure 8-5. Regional Variation in Bank Rates on Short-Term Business
Loans, 1947-1962.

Source: Adapted from the *Federal Reserve Historical Chart Book.*

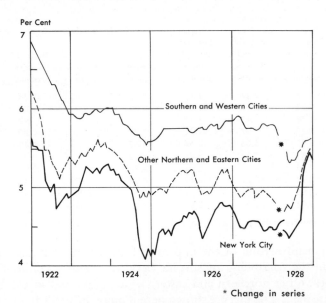

* Change in series

Figure 8-6. Bank Rates on Short-Term Business Loans,
1922-1928.

Source: Board of Governors of the Federal Reserve System.

late 1920's when short-term rates rose to extraordinary heights in New York.) The narrowness of the spread in recent years may partly reflect advances in the mechanical techniques of carrying out operations between regional money markets in the United States. To some extent it may indicate that the type of business done, particularly with respect to size of loan, has become more uniform. For the most part, however, it suggests that markets have become more truly national in scope and character, the mark of a mature, highly developed money market.

THE MONEY MARKET AND ADJUSTMENT OF LIQUIDITY NEEDS

Federal funds and Treasury bills provide nearly perfect media for adjusting the liquidity needs of commercial banks and, indeed, of the entire business community. Other securities, notably bankers' acceptances, commercial paper, and finance company paper contribute to the same end. It is partly because of this that the money market has been described as constituting the "haunts of liquidity." A bank or other holder of idle funds can turn to the money market and there find instant employment for them, possibly through sale as Federal funds or, for a longer period and higher return, through the purchase of Treasury bills. He can, that is, surrender some of his excess liquidity in return for income. Conversely, a bank in need of greater liquidity can obtain Federal funds at once by giving a check which will be collected on the next business day, or it may obtain the cash by selling Treasury bills. There are other means, such as the other credit instruments mentioned, and other places, e.g., borrowing from the Reserve Banks, whereby similar ends may be achieved. But it is the money market in the large sense that mainly performs the function of facilitating the adjustment of liquidity requirements. And the principal instruments for doing so are Federal funds and Treasury bills.

By enabling banks to pass around residual excesses or deficiencies of reserves the money market promotes a fuller utilization of financial resources. It facilitates the spacing of the maturities of earning assets in anticipation of variation in seasonal and other needs. (The credit or financial markets as broadly defined allow this process to be extended still further.) Allowance can be made for expected seasonal or other fluctuations in deposits and for reserve drains, whether internal or external. In case requirements are greater or less than was anticipated the mistaken judgment can be corrected by turning to the money market for or with ready funds.

Earnings are augmented in two ways. First, a higher ratio of earning assets can be maintained. It is not necessary to hold undesired idle balances until a credit-worthy borrower arrives on the scene. Through the money market it is ordinarily possible even on the shortest notice to find some disposition of available funds that will yield a return. Secondly, higher yield assets can be acquired. The money market gives to Treasury bills and to claims on Federal funds a liquidity barely short of that of excess reserves. The transfer of these assets assure banks and others of access to money in case of need. Lenders are therefore willing to place some proportion of their resources in less liquid, and higher yield, form than might otherwise be thought safe.

In short, the money market facilitates the management of earning assets. For the banking system it is a most important aid in solving the fundamental banking problem to which attention was directed earlier. In contributing to the liquidity of assets held by the banking system it helps to increase the amount of liquidity available to the entire economy. But it must not be overlooked that liquidity may at times become excessive. The money market then becomes, as will be seen in a later chapter, the locus of central bank policies for holding the condition of liquidity within the bounds of what the monetary authorities consider desirable.

SELECTED BIBLIOGRAPHY

BOARD OF GOVERNORS OF THE FEDERAL RESERVE SYSTEM, *The Federal Reserve System*. Washington: 1961, Chapters V-VI.
————, *The Federal Funds Market*. Washington: 1959.

FEDERAL RESERVE BANK OF NEW YORK, *Money Market Essays*. New York: 1952.
————, *Monthly Review*.

MADDEN, CARL H., *The Money Side of "The Street,"* New York: Federal Reserve Bank of New York, 1959.

MINSKY, HYMAN, "Central Banking and Money Market Changes," *Quarterly Journal of Economics* (May 1957), pp. 171-187.

RIEFLER, WINFIELD, *Money Rates and Money Markets in the United States*. New York: Harper, 1930, Chapters I-VII.

ROBBINS, SIDNEY M., and NESTOR E. TERLECKYJ, *Money Metropolis*. Cambridge: Harvard University Press, 1960, Chapters 1-5.

ROOSA, ROBERT V., *Federal Reserve Operations in the Money and Government Securities Markets*. New York: Federal Reserve Bank of New York, 1956.

WILSON, J. S. G., "The Structure of Money Markets," *Banca Nazionale de Lavoro Quarterly Review* (March 1961), pp. 51-75.

9

OTHER FINANCIAL
INSTITUTIONS

The purpose of this chapter is to outline the system of financial institutions and operations within which the activities of commercial banks and the Federal Reserve Banks are carried on. The end in view is to provide a basis for understanding money and banking, not to explain in detail the financial organization of the economy or give an adequate description of all the financial institutions which go to make it up. At the very least, such a detailed description would require a book—and books on the subject are already available. The interested reader may readily refer to them.[1]

THE GENERAL FUNCTIONS OF FINANCIAL INSTITUTIONS

Financial operations in general constitute, as do agriculture, mining, manufacturing, transportation, and merchandising, a particular phase of the specialization that exists among many different branches of economic activity. The process of division of labor within the field of finance has led to the creation of numerous specialized types of financial institutions. Financial specialization affords economies comparable with those resulting from specialization elsewhere. It thereby permits the more efficient discharge of financial functions by lenders and borrowers alike. But this is not all. It enables non-financial services to be carried on more economically since it relieves manufacturers, merchants, carriers, and farmers of the necessity of

1. Cf. Roland I. Robinson, ed., *Financial Institutions*, 3rd edition (Homewood, Ill.: Irwin, 1960), and Herbert V. Prochnow, *American Financial Institutions* (Englewood Cliffs, N. J.: Prentice-Hall, 1951). It should be noted that the present discussion relates to representative financial institutions and not just to financial intermediaries.

also being financiers. Without financial specialization there could not be as great specialization in other lines of endeavor as there now is.

The system of financial institutions embraces a wide range of public and private institutions, from a village post office selling money orders to a multi-billion dollar bank or insurance company. Despite the number and complexity of such institutions it is possible to distinguish three major functions which they perform.

The first major function of financial institutions is that of intermediary. The various savings institutions, for example, act as intermediaries between the individuals who accumulate money and the corporations and others who require money to expand factories or build homes. In general, financial intermediaries stand in the same relation to financial markets that retail merchants and wholesalers do to commodity markets. They are, in essence, part of the machinery for bringing together borrowers and lenders and accommodating their particular needs and preferences. They facilitate the allocation of resources. They may tend to specialize in large-scale or in small-scale operations, by type of credit, or in a variety of other ways, as will be noted presently in connection with the particular services furnished by financial institutions.

A second recognizable function is that of the reduction and sharing of risk. Risk may be reduced, in part, through maintaining fuller and more accurate information, thereby reducing that element of uncertainty which arises from lack of knowledge. In part, risk reduction may be accomplished by the acquisition of operational skills in the safeguarding of funds, the extension of credit, and the administration of credit after it has been granted. It may even involve measures to raise standards of operation: some large commercial banks and insurance companies, for example, utilize production and marketing experts not only to investigate the operating methods of borrowers and prospective borrowers but even to provide technical advice with a view to improving these methods. Lenders devote great effort to designing the terms of a loan contract so as to anticipate future contingencies and so minimize risk.

By operating on a large scale it is possible to distribute resources among a variety of assets, with the result that exposure to the risk of concentrated loss is less. Risk may be pooled in other ways, or outright insurance or guarantees may be obtained—in return, naturally, for payment of some kind of charge or premium.

Finally, financial institutions may provide liquidity. This is accomplished in different ways and in varying degrees. First, the particular financial institution is likely to be widely known and to have an established reputation. This alone ordinarily makes the promises which it gives more liquid than the promises which it takes in exchange. Second, the relatively large scale on which it operates enables it to provide for normal outflows of cash by utilizing the inflow of funds which can be counted on to take place at the same time. This feature is closely related, of course, to the intermediary role referred to above. Third, it is able, in case of special need, to tap supplementary sources of funds, by borrowing or liquidation of assets, that would not be so readily available to individuals or other businesses.

To the individual who entrusts his savings to a financial intermediary these savings appear virtually as liquid as the money which is in his pocket or held as demand deposits at a bank. They have a fixed-money value. He can ordinarily count on converting savings deposits, shares at a savings and loan association, and even the surrender value of life insurance policies into cash with little difficulty and at short notice.[2] For many purposes assets such as these are a satisfactory substitute for currency and demand deposits as a reserve of purchasing power, and consequently they tend to free cash for use in current transactions. The purchasing power which they provide can have an important effect on actual expenditures and presumably, therefore, on the course of business activity.

In substance, liquidity is increased in that individuals who turn their money over to savings intermediaries in exchange for claims on those institutions make this money available to manufacturers, builders, homeowners, and other borrowers while suffering little reduction in their own command over cash.

The three general functions of financial institutions just described are, of course, closely interrelated. The creation of a new savings and loan account or a savings bank deposit simultaneously results in a new liquid claim and therefore greater liquidity, intermediation, and, as compared with many uses to which the saver might have put his resources, a reduction in risk. It may also be noted that all of these functions are involved in the operations of perhaps every financial institution, though their relative importance varies, as will be seen below. Moreover, the intermediary relationship, risk amelioration, and liquidity all react to strengthen and re-enforce one another.

SPECIFIC SERVICES PERFORMED BY FINANCIAL INSTITUTIONS

Because of the tendency to combine more than one type of business within the same company the analysis of financial institutions is best approached in terms of the services which they perform. In this section, therefore, attention is directed primarily toward specific financial services and only secondarily toward the institutions which provide them. No attempt is

---

2. The same is true of savings bonds. The legal status of these various claims, of course, is not uniform. At certain times in the past, moreover, some of them proved less liquid than was anticipated. At the present time and for the foreseeable future, however, their liquidity, partly because of legal and administrative changes which have taken place, would seem certain to remain extremely high.

made to include all financial institutions or even to explain fully those institutions that are mentioned. Particular institutions are introduced primarily to identify or clarify the functions or services with which they are associated. A comparable treatment will be provided later for federally created financial institutions.

Provision of Circulating Medium

A major service afforded by financial institutions is that of providing circulating medium. It is included in the present discussion—which is primarily concerned with financial institutions other than those with money-creating powers—in order to permit a more complete listing of financial services. In the United States this function is performed chiefly by the Federal Reserve Banks and commercial banks.[3] The Reserve Banks issue currency in the form of Federal Reserve notes. The value of such notes is between five and six times that of all other kinds of currency combined. In addition, the Federal Reserve Banks help to provide circulating medium in the form of checking accounts for the United States Treasury. All important payments by the United States government are effected by means of checks drawn against deposits at the Federal Reserve Banks. Commercial banks, including a handful of private banking houses, create circulating medium in the form of demand deposits. The operations of commercial banks have been discussed above; those of the Reserve Banks will be examined later in full detail.

Providing Expert Management and Administration

While most, if not all, financial institutions are in one sense engaged in selling the services of their own trained experts, certain of the institutions have as their primary purpose the furnishing of financial management as such. This is especially true in the case of *trust companies* (and the trust departments of commercial banks, many of which have developed out of trust companies through merger or diversification of activities). The trust relationship is capable of being applied in a variety of ways. The essence of it is that something of value is "entrusted," as to a trust company, to be managed in particular ways and for particular purposes.

For the sake of illustration, let us assume that the head of a family wishes to provide for the future welfare of dependents. He may arrange that in the event of his death his estate will be turned over to the trust department of a bank to be administered at the discretion of its officers, subject to the limitations imposed by law or within terms laid down by him. The trust department will then assume the role of manager of the business affairs of

---

3. Coins and certain other types of currency are issued by the United States Treasury, which is not ordinarily thought of as a financial institution.

the estate. It will perform routine administrative functions, make decisions, dispose of property and income and, in general, conduct itself as the householder might have done if he had lived. It may collect rents, interest and dividends, supervise the care of real estate, shift investments, arrange for the schooling of minors, and distribute funds for living and other expenses.

Trust business may be carried on for others than the beneficiaries of some deceased person, as when funds or property are turned over to a trust company to be administered during the lifetime of the owner in order to relieve him of the care and responsibility of management and at the same time to secure the benefit of the expert technical knowledge of the trust officers.

All of the foregoing would be carried on in connection with personal trusts. It is also common for banks and trust companies to maintain what are known as corporate trust departments. Thus corporations may ask a trust company to invest and administer money which they have accumulated for particular purposes such as sinking funds, pensions, and retirement benefits, money which is awaiting use to replace or repair capital equipment, and undistributed profits. Trust companies may act as receivers, and very frequently they serve as agents in the distribution of interest and dividends to holders of bonds and stocks.

Trust business is chiefly carried on by banks. Approximately 1,450 national banks and more than half that many state banks are authorized to operate trust departments. The number of companies engaging exclusively in trust business is said to be between fifty and seventy-five. In addition, a substantial volume of personal trust business is in the hands of individuals, particularly lawyers and relatives.

Exact statistics are not available on the total market value of assets held in trust by banks and others. It appears, however, that instances are not rare in which the value of personal trusts placed with a large city bank exceeds one billion dollars. Trust departments may provide a significant proportion of the earnings of the bank of which they are a part. In the case of one bank with an important trust department, 30 per cent of gross earnings were contributed by the personal trust department and another 3 per cent by the corporate trust department. Together, approximately one-third of gross earnings were derived from the trust departments. This included payment for other services, yet to be described, which were also performed within the personal trust department.

Trust companies and the trust departments of banks are not the only suppliers of the services of financial management and administration. Among other organizations and institutions which devote a substantial part of their activities to providing expert financial management are investment counsel firms, insurance companies, savings banks, and investment companies.

Provision of Information and Advice

The great activity in the security markets during the 1920's led to the rise of a relatively new type of enterprise—the providing of investment information and advice, often with some degree of investment supervision. Further rapid expansion in this service occurred in the booming stock market conditions of the 1950's and 1960's. Under the terms of the Investment Company and Investment Advisers Acts of 1940, persons and firms offering investment counsel or supervision are required, subject to certain exemptions, to register with the Securities and Exchange Commission and to comply with various regulations.

Because banks which maintain trust departments were already equipped with staff and facilities for investment research and supervision, they were in a position to offer investment counseling at relatively little extra cost. Their high standing in the community and excellent contacts and associations were favorable to the expansion of such activities. Accordingly, investment management and advice are now offered by an increasing number of banks under a wide variety of descriptions.[4] The popularity of the service was undoubtedly aided by the prolonged rise in security prices. Some concern was expressed from time to time, however, over possible injurious effects on the public's attitude toward banks in case of an adverse trend in security markets.

Investment counseling services have developed into a profitable source of supplementary income to many banks, and their continued expansion seems assured. The fact that expenses of operation are shared with other parts of the banking and trust business permits important economies in providing such services. Activities connected with them are typically carried on by a division within an existing trust department, and charges are comparable with those exacted for other trust business.[5] The market for such services as these is not confined to individuals. Educational, philanthropic, and other non-profit institutions also make use of them. Management of investments may be supplemented by administration of other of their financial affairs.

---

4. One observer reported thirty-five different names for substantially the same service. Included were investment advisory service, investment counseling, investment management, custody accounts, etc.

5. The annual fee imposed by one well-known bank in the early 1960's was based on the market or appraised value of securities according to the following schedule:

On the first $100,000 $5 per $1,000 (1/2 per cent)
On the next $200,000 $4 per $1,000 (4/10 per cent)
On the next $300,000 $3 per $1,000 (3/10 per cent)
On the next $400,000 $2 per $1,000 (2/10 per cent)
On the excess over $1,000,000—subject to negotiation

The minimum charge was set at $200 and provision was made for independent determination of charges for administering other types of assets. Services included counseling, custody of assets, and supervision of investments. Lower charges were specified where not all of these services were desired.

Numerous businesses including individual proprietorships engage exclusively in providing investment information, advice, or supervison; many combine all three. Some of the services are designed for the general public, some for larger estates, and some—often elaborately statistical—for corporate and institutional investors. Many of these services are widely advertised in all types of media. It need hardly be added that the character and reliability of the services provided vary greatly. Nor is it to be supposed that those that cost the most necessarily have the best record.

By and large, this sort of dissemination of information on highly technical matters, no less than the administrative duties performed, may be assumed to contribute substantially to improving the functioning of financial markets.

Provision of Diversification

The element of diversification is present in the operations of most financial institutions. The owner of a savings deposit, for example, may be thought of as having a claim, in microscopic amounts, upon the entire range of assets which go to make up the portfolio of the savings bank. So also with the owner of a life insurance policy or of shares in a savings and loan association. But in cases such as these diversification is secondary to other purposes or is relatively limited in scope. There are, however, important financial institutions for which diversification of assets is the primary service provided.

A person with a large sum to invest can very easily obtain diversification through purchase of a considerable variety of securities. An individual having $1,000 to invest, on the other hand, could buy only a small number of different securities and so would be unable to obtain the protection that goes with spreading his investments over a list of diversified securities. By putting his money in the hands of an *investment company*,[6] along with the funds of many other small investors like himself, a sum can be accumulated which will be large enough to afford opportunity for wide diversification. The individual is given a share or stock certificate of the investment company or trust. He then has a participation, proportional to the contribution he has made to the total, in all securities owned by the company. Thus the investor's $1,000 gives him the same diversification that is obtained, for

6. Formerly more commonly called "investment trusts." The name "mutual fund" is usually applied to the so-called "open-end" companies which have become considerably more important in terms of volume of assets than the contrasting "closed-end" companies. These terms relate to important differences in the capital structure of the companies. The open-end companies are distinguished primarily by their standing offer to redeem outstanding shares at their current net asset value, and by their usual practice of offering new shares for sale on a continuous basis. The number of shares of a closed-end trust, on the other hand, remains unchanged for long periods of time. A person desiring to acquire shares in such a company would have to do so by obtaining them from previous holders. Cf. Prochnow, *op. cit.*, pp. 441-443.

example, by the entire $100,000,000, if that should be the total size of the investment company. In addition, an investment company can afford to employ the services of competent investment experts. Regardless of the relative size of his own investment, the holder of shares in such a company secures (at a cost) the full benefit of the investment skill of the officers.

Investment companies differ substantially in the degree of freedom and scope of their operations. Investments of a "fixed" trust are restricted to a prescribed list of securities, while those of a "management" trust are determined by the independent judgment of the officers. Other investment companies confine their acquisitions to the securities of companies in particular industries, such as electronics, public utilities, and so forth. Some, in turn, restrict their assets according to the characteristics of the industries in which they invest, as in the case of the so-called "growth funds," or by types of securities, as in the case of the "balanced funds" which undertake to maintain a suitable distribution of assets among bonds, preferred stocks, and common stocks. Even where the investments are restricted in some manner, the distinguishing feature of investment companies—that of affording the investor a greater degree of diversification than would otherwise be possible—is still present.

Investment trusts have had a long and distinguished history in England and more especially in Scotland. In the United States, investment companies, particularly management trusts of the open-end or mutual fund type,[7] came into their greatest popularity after World War II when the number and total assets of such companies increased spectacularly. The assets of open-end investment companies tripled between the end of the war and 1952, tripled again by 1958, and almost doubled between 1958 and 1962. Increases of as much as 30 per cent in the assets of individual funds within a single year were not uncommon.

In recent years, banks having trust departments have developed a technique of providing diversification which somewhat resembles that of investment companies. *Common trust funds* are a device whereby numerous small trust accounts are "commingled," i.e., combined into a single large fund. Each individual trust included in the fund is assigned shares indicating its right to participate in the combined total of assets held in the fund. The result is to facilitate diversification of investment operations and also greatly to simplify accounting and administrative tasks for the holder of the trusts. Thus common trust funds offer important advantages for bank as well as beneficiary.

Common trust funds owe their origin to the fact that the gradual increase in the number of small trust accounts had become a troublesome problem to banks and trust companies. It was expensive to operate each one of them on an independent basis as the common law restrictions on the

7. See footnote 6.

commingling of funds required. At the same time the trustee institutions were usually unable either to get rid of them or to charge enough to make them pay.[8] The beneficiaries suffered not so much because the impossibility of diversification exposed them to risk as because it led to the funds being held in cash or ultraconservative investments which yielded a low rate of return. In many instances, charges were gradually eating up the principal of the trust.

Obstacles to the organization of common trust funds were overcome by congressional action in 1936 and by subsequent state legislation. The number of such funds increased rapidly after World War II. Expansion in the size of individual funds was chiefly influenced by the action of the Federal Reserve authorities, under whom the funds are administered, in raising the size of the individual trusts eligible for inclusion in the common trust funds from $25,000 to $50,000 and then to $100,000. The liberalization of this provision was itself a testimony to the success of the earlier funds. Common trust funds have been established by groups of banks acting cooperatively in cases where the size of the individual banks is too small to permit the organization of independent funds.

Common trust funds are customarily set up within an existing trust department. Banks sometimes maintain both a "discretionary fund" where the officers have wide investment powers and a "legal fund" where investments are restricted to a so-called "legal list."[9] Income to participants is ordinarily somewhat higher for discretionary funds than for legal funds. On a recent date, one of the important companies in this field held common trust funds with assets worth over $122,000,000—about one-seventh in the legal fund and the remainder in the discretionary fund. Promotional advertisement of common trust funds is prohibited by law. Participation is limited to trusts already held by the institution maintaining the fund; investors must first establish a trust at a bank and then go through the formality of granting permission to have it included in the common trust fund.

Provision of Savings Facilities

A large group of financial institutions—large, that is, in total number, value of assets, variety, and size of some of the individual units[10]— are engaged in providing facilities for the safe handling of personal savings.

8. There are various reasons why a company might find itself in possession of such unprofitable trust accounts. In many cases they had been handed down from an earlier time when costs of operation were lower and banks less exact in their cost-accounting methods. Sometimes they were assigned to the bank by a court of law. Often they were assumed as part of settling an estate in which the bank served as executor or had other interests.

9. This means a list specified by the board of directors of the bank, not one laid down by governmental authorities.

10. Consider a single life insurance company with assets approaching 20 billion dollars in the early 1960's and growing at the rate of over three-quarters of a billion dollars a year.

Often this service is furnished along with others. Moreover, the motives which lead to funds being placed in their hands differ widely, as do the practices which they follow in finding outlets for these funds. The comparative size of the principal savings institutions as well as differences in relative rates of growth are indicated in Figure 9-1.

Life insurance companies represent by far the largest category of savings institutions in terms of assets, although the rapid growth of other savings intermediaries after World War II has appreciably reduced their lead. Two features tend to dominate the disposition made of their investible funds.

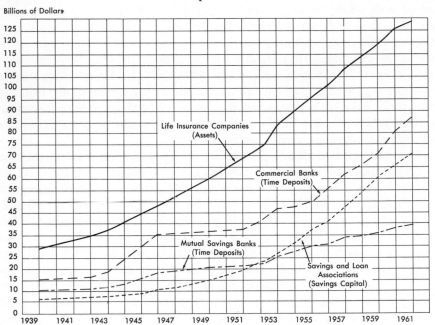

Figure 9-1.   Growth of Leading Savings Institutions, 1940-1961.
Source: Data from the *Federal Reserve Bulletin.*

First, because of the primary importance attached to safety, funds tend to be placed in highly conservative types of investment. Second, the fact that cash requirements are determinable with a high degree of actuarial probability combined with the fact that the inflow of funds is characteristically in excess of the outflow, makes it possible to invest on long term. (Liquidity is less of a problem for life insurance companies than for any other important type of enterprise.) Somewhat paradoxically, claims upon life insurance companies, as in the form of cash values of policies and matured claims, are among the most liquid non-cash assets available to the public. Thus we find that life insurance companies tend to hold safe but relatively illiquid assets and to issue obligations which are not only extremely safe but also highly liquid.

By far the largest proportion of time deposits (by value close to two-thirds of the total for the country) is held in the *savings departments of commercial banks.* Most of the remainder are held in *mutual savings banks,* a form of savings institution located predominantly in New England and the Middle Atlantic states. The fact that time deposits are likely to be left for long periods of time, and that advance notice of intention to withdraw can be demanded, makes it possible to place a large proportion of these funds also in long-term securities, but not to the same extent as is true of the insurance companies.

Before 1939 the volume of time deposits was in excess of demand deposits, but during World War II demand deposits increased much more rapidly than time deposits. After the war a recovery in the rate of growth of time deposits occurred. In the early 1960's time deposits in commercial banks and mutual savings banks combined were nearly equal to the total of adjusted demand deposits.

Pension funds, as the name indicates, administer savings which are set aside primarily for old age and retirement. The growth in such funds after World War II was rapid and continuous. The savings of consumers and non-profit organizations in privately operated pension funds rose from $6.7 billion to $49.9 billion between 1947 and 1960. The rise was slightly greater in dollar amount than the corresponding growth in private life insurance which increased from $44.4 billion to $84.3 billion. In relative terms, however, the increase was very much greater, 640 per cent against 90 per cent. A substantial but considerably smaller increase occurred at the same time in the savings held in government pension funds. At one time savings in government pension funds were considerably larger than in private funds, but by the 1960's the respective totals were approximately equal.

Savings and loan associations[11] combine the functions of a savings bank with those of an institution specializing in loans on residential mortgages. There are well over 6,000 such companies; for the most part they remain relatively small in size and local in character.

A typical association maintains what amount to ordinary savings accounts for its members, although formally what happens is that it sells its own shares to the public who are then shareholders rather than depositors.[12] These shares are non-assessable and have no fixed maturity date. In practice, however, they are usually redeemable on short notice. The association lends out the cash received from its shareholder-depositors for use in home financing. Repayments on loans granted by the association are made at a uniform monthly (or other period) rate which provides, in addition to interest, a steadily increasing amount to reduce principal. This form of

11. Formerly known under various names but most commonly as building and loan associations.

12. It may also hold savings in other forms, e.g., investment accounts and installment share accounts. The first are used for lump-sum deposits on which regular dividends are paid. The second are for persons who wish to save regularly in small amounts.

reducing or "amortized" loan has been widely copied by other types of lenders.

Prior to 1933 all savings and loan associations were state chartered. At the present time about one-fifth are chartered by the Federal Home Loan Bank Board. In addition to these federally chartered associations, a substantial proportion of the state-chartered associations are members of the Federal Home Loan Bank System, which is designed to provide for savings and loan associations somewhat the same services that the Federal Reserve System provides for member banks, and are entitled to borrow from the Federal Home Loan Banks. All members of the Federal Home Loan Bank system and a considerable number of state-chartered associations have their share accounts insured by the Federal Savings and Loan Insurance Corporation up to $10,000 each.

Savings and loan associations may be thought of as overlapping the activities of commercial banks in two principal ways. First, both share in the extension of loans on real estate. (For both commercial banks and savings and loan associations a substantial proportion of the real estate loans they make are guaranteed by the Federal Housing Administration or the Veterans Administration.) Second, there is considerable competition between them for the savings of persons of moderate incomes. Rates paid on share accounts in savings and loan associations are generally higher than those paid by commercial banks, but, as was noted above, their redemption rights are not as definite.

Trust companies, investment companies, and various other financial institutions also perform savings functions, but, as was noted previously, their other specialized functions, such as providing managerial services or diversification, constitute more distinctive features of their activities.

Acting as Intermediaries in Security Distribution

One of the most typical and important services performed by financial institutions is that of facilitating the marketing of securities, including a large variety of financial instruments ranging from short-term commercial paper to stocks and long-term bonds. The institutional organization involved in carrying out these activities is diverse and ramifies widely. Some companies engage in a wide variety of services, not all of them confined to dealing in securities. Others are narrowly specialized. Some have branches throughout the country and even abroad while others are purely local. The extent of interconnections is indicated by the fact that a person desiring to buy stocks may find himself dealing with his banker who places the order with a local broker who in turn has the order executed through a correspondent firm in a distant city. If the transaction is "over the counter," rather than through an organized security market, still other dealers may be involved.

Investment bankers and dealers are the principal intermediaries in the marketing and redistribution of securities. They serve public as well as private borrowers, i.e., the federal government and state and local governments as well as corporations. They customarily handle bonds and stocks and on occasion may deal in other obligations including commodity futures, term loans, and mortgages. Their operations fall into three main categories: the flotation of new issues, the marketing of blocks of outstanding securities that may have to be distributed more widely, and assisting in the ordinary day-to-day purchase and sale of securities already in the hands of the general public. Most of the larger investment houses regularly engage in all three types of transactions; smaller companies are likely to confine their activities primarily to the last.

In connection with primary distribution (new issues business), investment bankers perform services to the issuing organization which may be extremely valuable. They investigate the merits of the undertaking that gives rise to the need for the additional financing, often making use of the services of engineers and other specialists. They are likely to advise the borrower on conditions in the security market and to make recommendations about the terms, forms, and maturities of the securities to be offered. They may also attend to legal details and formalities, including compliance with requirements laid down by the Securities and Exchange Act. It is customary for them to support the market for new and outstanding issues in order to prevent prices of the securities from being depressed or unduly disturbed during the period of the flotation. Public acceptance of new issues is thereby facilitated, and the liquidity of outstanding issues is maintained.

In order for the borrower to be certain that the full amount of money desired will be realized from the sale of new securities, the investment banker customarily agrees to purchase the issue at a stipulated price. Because of the risk involved in such a commitment, an investment banker is likely to associate other investment bankers with him in the flotation of an issue of substantial size, foregoing a share of the return from the operation in order to reduce the contingent liability. This would constitute a "purchase group" or "underwriting syndicate."

The actual marketing of a corporate issue is ordinarily handled through a "selling group." This group is likely to contain most or all of the members of the purchase group along with others. Each member of this group ordinarily makes a formal commitment to purchase a certain amount which he undertakes to sell at the price stipulated for all members. The purchase group allows the sellers an "allowance" or "concession" from the price to the public out of which the seller is expected to cover costs and profit.

If buyers prove less receptive than was anticipated, the members of the purchase group may decide to hold a substantial part of the issue until conditions in the security market improve. They must then supply the borrower with the funds called for in the purchase agreement by drawing upon their own resources or by borrowing. Investment bankers often borrow substantial sums from commercial banks for this and other purposes. Similarly, members of the selling group may find themselves holding an inventory of securities which they have been unable to move successfully. In addition, investment houses often "maintain positions," i.e., hold inventories of particular issues in which they deal or which they regard as promising investments for their own funds.

Investment banks also engage in the "direct placement," sometimes called "private placement," of securities (especially bonds) which are not publicly marketed. This consists of placing the issue, usually in large blocks, by direct negotiation with insurance companies, educational institutions, pension funds, estates, or others having large sums to invest. One of the advantages of this method is that it avoids the expense and formalities of registering the securities with the Securities and Exchange Commission. A disadvantage is that marketability is thereby greatly impaired since the securities cannot then be sold publicly. Resort to direct placement has increased in recent years. In 1953 well over half of all corporate bond offerings took this form, compared with only a third in 1946. The proportion is believed to be even higher today. It is particularly important in the sale of securities to insurance companies and other large institutional lenders.

To a limited extent investment banking activities are carried on directly by commercial banks. Since 1933 banks have been prohibited from participating in the underwriting of corporate issues, but this restriction does not apply to obligations of the various governmental divisions. Some of the larger commercial banks take an active part in the flotation of state and municipal securities, in many cases actually organizing and heading the underwriting syndicate. A few are active as dealers in United States Treasury obligations.

Mortgage bankers, as the name indicates, are intermediaries in the handling of mortgages. Their main functions are essentially similar to those performed by investment bankers. Because of the nature of the business, however, operations involve chiefly the handling of newly issued mortgages and only to a small extent the resale of mortgages previously issued. That is to say, mortgages are not ordinarily resold in the way bonds and stocks often are. Builders and real estate dealers as demanders of mortgage funds maintain close relations with mortgage bankers. Large lenders such as insurance companies utilize the services of mortgage bankers in cities all over the country, thereby widening the market for their funds and at the same time securing broader diversification. Much of the business is of an agency or direct placement character.

The activities of mortgage bankers are likely to include other services related to real estate. Among these are the servicing of properties, collection of rents, and remittance of payments on interest and principal. They also include purchase and sale of real estate and the handling of fire and casualty insurance. These ancillary services are not directly those of a credit intermediary. Nevertheless, they influence the effectiveness as well as the economy with which the function of intermediary between borrowers and lenders of mortgage funds is performed.

Another type of intermediary financial institution, formerly of considerable importance, is the *commercial paper house*, which once did a substantial volume of business in buying and selling so-called "open-market commercial paper." This is short-term, self-liquidating paper of premium quality, sold by reputable issuers to an intermediary or directly to a clientele of commercial banks, investment companies, estates, and others desiring this type of high-grade liquid asset. The principal issuers of open-market commercial paper are the three large sales finance companies, General Motors Acceptance Corporation, Commercial Credit Company, and C.I.T. Financial Corporation, which normally account for well over half of the total volume of this type of instrument. These large sales finance companies usually sell their issues directly to banks and others without resorting to intermediaries.

The commercial paper houses are essentially dealer intermediaries who purchase paper at a discount, charging a commission of approximately ¼ of 1 per cent, and promptly resell it to banks and other investors. High credit standards are imposed by commercial paper dealers, who regularly investigate and pass upon the credit standing of the companies whose paper they handle. The volume of open-market commercial paper sold through dealer intermediaries is less today than in the past,[13] partly because of increased availability of other sources of short-term funds and greater reliance on internal resources. With this decline many of the commercial paper houses went out of business; others survived with the aid of reduced numbers and a diversification of activity.

Provision of Lending Facilities

The most basic service of financial institutions, to which most of the other services, in fact, are either peripheral or supplementary, is that of supplying credit to borrowers of every type and kind. Of the three major categories of lending to the private sector of the economy—business, mortgage, and consumer credit—the first two have a long and established history. The last is of relatively recent origin as a major organized service; it is a phenomenon closely related (as both cause and effect) to the growth since World War I of durable consumer goods and the concomitant spread of mass buying power.

Commercial banks are traditionally the principal suppliers of short-term business credit, with which they were at one time almost solely identified.

---

13. And the proportion of the total volume of open-market paper which is sold through dealers has declined from roughly four-fifths in the 1920's to one-fifth in the late 1950's.

They are still the major factor in this field. Today, however, they also provide a considerable volume of intermediate and some long-term business credit, not to mention mortgage and consumer credit. Lending activities of commercial banks were described in Chapter 7.

Life insurance companies constitute the largest source of long-term credit for business and also provide substantial amounts of intermediate credit. Mutual funds are important suppliers of long-term credit to business though much of their activities, as is also so with the other suppliers, is carried on indirectly through brokers and government securities dealers. Among other suppliers deserving mention are factors and the relatively new pension funds. Factors, which trace their origins to Roman times, are a specialized group presently concentrating in the financing of accounts receivable, especially in the textile trade.

By far the most rapidly growing source of mortgage credit is savings and loan associations. The relative growth of mortgage debt from 1941 to 1960 and the shares held by principal suppliers are shown in Table 9-1.

TABLE 9-1. Mortgage Credit Outstanding by Principal Suppliers, 1941 and 1960 (Billions of Dollars)

		1941		1960
Total		$37.6		$206.5
Federal Agencies (selected)		4.7		11.2
Individuals and Others		12.2		37.7
Financial Institutions		20.7		157.6
Commercial banks*	$4.9		$28.8	
Mutual savings banks	4.8		26.9	
Savings and loan associations	4.6		60.1	
Life insurance companies	6.4		41.8	

* Excludes trust departments of banks, which are included under "Individuals and Others."
Source: *Federal Reserve Bulletin*, June 1961, pp. 697-98.

At the end of this buoyant, and at times inflationary, period the total dollar volume of mortgage credit outstanding was almost five and a half times that at the start. As may be seen, the growth was unevenly distributed, the share of federal agencies[14] and individuals and others having grown more slowly and that of savings and loan associations very much more rapidly than the total. Both the base from which the start was made and the period itself were highly exceptional, factors which help to account for the exceptional rates of growth during these years. Data relating to current developments are reported regularly in the *Federal Reserve Bulletin*.

The third major category, consumer credit, is generally understood to include all credit extended to the private sector of the economy other than for business purposes and mortgages on real estate. Financial institutions which grant consumer credit engage chiefly in making personal loans and

_____
14. This does not include guarantees.

loans for the purchase of durable goods. Most of the loans are on an installment basis, calling for regular payments on account of interest and principal.

Consumer credit like real estate credit increased sharply after World War II. Table 9-2 indicates both totals and changes in the relative shares contributed by principal suppliers. The growth in non-installment credit—distributed fairly evenly among single payment loans, charge accounts, and service credit (e.g., unpaid doctors' bills)—was less rapid than in installment credit. It will be noted that the share of installment credit supplied by commercial banks rose more rapidly than that of any of the other sources except credit unions, whose share was very much smaller. At the end of the period commercial banks supplied close to two-fifths of installment credit, having surpassed sales finance companies which supplied slightly more than banks twenty years earlier. Banks also provided nearly a third of the non-installment credit, all of it in the form of single payment loans.

TABLE 9-2. Consumer Credit Outstanding, by Principal Suppliers, 1941 and 1960 (Billions of Dollars)

		1941		1960
Total		$9.2		$56.0
Non-installment Credit		3.1		12.8
Installment Credit		6.1		43.3
Commercial banks	$1.7		$16.4	
Sales finance companies	1.8		11.1	
Consumer finance companies	. . .*		4.2	
Credit unions	0.2		3.9	
Other financial institutions	0.8		1.9	
Retail outlets	1.6		5.8	

   * Included under "other financial institutions."
Source: *Federal Reserve Bulletin*, June 1961, p. 700.

Sales finance companies engage in financing the sale of durable consumer goods, chiefly automobiles, on the installment plan. Funds are obtained mainly by direct borrowing from banks and insurance companies and by sale on the open market of various types of secured or unsecured obligations of the finance company. Lending is of two types, wholesale and retail.

Wholesale financing consists of advancing funds to dealers, usually on the dealer's promissory note. The notes are ordinarily secured by warehouse or trust receipts covering, for example, the cars which are being financed. Much of this business is of a type customarily handled by commercial banks. Retail sales financing involves the financing of purchases made directly by consumers themselves. In addition to holding the promissory note of the buyer, the finance company is protected by documents allowing the article purchased, such as a car, to be attached in case of default in payment, as well as by insurance policies covering fire, theft, and accident. The practice is sometimes followed of asking the dealer to endorse the buyer's note as an added assurance that the dealer will exercise caution in selecting risks. In view of the protection afforded by these various devices, it is not surprising that the losses on this type of lending have been light.

Consumer finance companies came into prominence with the adoption by most states of the so-called uniform small-loan law. This law was sponsored by a distinguished philanthropic institution, the Russell Sage Foundation, in an effort to combat the loan-shark evil under which rates of 1,000 per cent a year or higher prevailed. It provided, typically, for loans to $300 at rates from 2 per cent to 3½ per cent a month on unpaid balances.[15] The reason for endorsing such a high rate (24 per cent to 42 per cent per annum) was that the costs were extremely high for this type of business. In order to attract legitimate lenders into the field, such rates must be authorized, and, if experience demonstrated that lower rates were justified, competition among lenders might be expected to force them down to a level that was reasonable.

Years of experience under drastic usury laws had proved that laws alone could not be relied on to prevent extortionate rates from being charged. The effect of stringent legislation was to drive necessitous borrowers into the arms of loan sharks whose rates were made the higher by the very laws which forbade high rates. Such lenders were able to charge these high rates because the effect of the laws was to limit competition to lenders who were willing to operate clandestinely. And they were inclined to charge higher rates than they otherwise might have done because of the added risk resulting from the fact that they were operating outside the law.

Credit unions are a form of financial cooperative, sometimes referred to as "self-help credit." They are small and ordinarily organized among groups in the same plant or occupation or among those having other interests in common. Small loans are made on the credit of the member, but for larger amounts collateral or the participation of a co-maker is generally required. Because of the unique advantages possessed by the union in the form of intimate knowledge of the creditworthiness of borrowers and, not less important, the moral compulsion that goes with the knowledge that one is borrowing from his fellows, the record of credit unions is extremely good. The rate customarily charged is 1 per cent a month on the unpaid balance. Since 1934, credit unions have been able to take out federal charters under the Farm Credit Administration. Well over half of all credit unions, however, are still under state charter. Total assets have been estimated at over four billion dollars, representing a membership of 10,500,000. While credit unions are allowed to borrow from banks and others, they seldom do so.

In general, the rates charged by commercial banks tend to be lower than those charged by other lenders of consumer credit. Certain officials of consumer finance companies have, in fact, maintained that commercial banks

15. In some states consumer loans of larger size are now common.

and consumer finance companies supplement one another rather than compete—the contention being that borrowers able to meet the high standards of the banks go to them and receive the benefit of lower rates while those whose credit qualifications are less good borrow from the finance companies. That each lender tends to have a somewhat distinctive clientele is probably correct, though the consumer credit market is by no means completely stratified.

In addition to complementing (and to some extent competing with) the other suppliers of consumer credit, commercial banks are also an important source from which these other lenders obtain the funds which they in turn lend out. Sales finance companies and consumer finance companies borrow heavily from commercial banks, generally on the most favorable terms. In this way, it may be noted, commercial banks regularly assist in financing their principal competitors in the supplying of consumer credit.

FINANCIAL SERVICES OF THE FEDERAL GOVERNMENT

This section is designed to indicate the manner in which the federal government has undertaken to furnish services and facilities of a financial character. As in the case of private financial institutions, the aim is to provide a background for understanding the financial organization of the economy, and not to describe in detail the vast array of credit activities in which the government is involved. The role of the Federal Reserve System, Federal Deposit Insurance Corporation, and Treasury will be examined later.[16]

The principal lending activities of the federal government have been in the fields of agricultural credit, housing and real estate credit, and foreign loans. It is to be expected that the credit operations of the government, in the future as in the past, will vary with domestic economic conditions (boom or depression), external demands (resulting from war, peacetime security needs, and our desire to extend aid to peoples less favored economically than ourselves), and changing public attitudes as to what services are essential and the adequacy of private institutions in providing them. We are concerned here with the reasons for the growth of such activities and their general dimensions and characteristics, rather than with cataloging all the agencies that have occupied this area.

Development of Lending Activities

Three principal influences dominated the extension of federal activities in the field of finance. The first was the belief that serious gaps

16. No attempt is made to consider the activities of state and local governments. It may be observed, however, that a number of states have established development corporations which provide credit and other inducements for such purposes as encouraging the establishment of new industries in blighted areas.

existed in our financial organization which would not be filled by private enterprise alone. This was responsible for the inauguration of the Postal Savings System in 1910. It was similarly the ground on which the first avowed entry of the federal government into actual lending operations was defended when the Federal Land Banks were established in 1917. Their purpose was to provide long-term credit for agriculture at lower rates and on more favorable terms than had been available in the past. It was maintained that private capital had been reluctant to enter this field in adequate volume and that farmers were therefore at a disadvantage compared with other producers. Similar considerations led to the establishment of the Federal Intermediate Credit Banks in 1923 to aid in furnishing intermediate and short-term credit for agriculture and for the marketing of agricultural products.

The second factor which led to federal participation in lending activities was the Great Depression. In 1932, near the end of the Hoover Administration, the Reconstruction Finance Corporation was organized along the lines of the War Finance Corporation which existed briefly in the period of World War I. This was followed in the early days of the New Deal by the establishment of a long list of credit institutions designed to relieve economic distress, promote recovery, and achieve other ends regarded as socially desirable. The names of some of these agencies give a general indication of the kind of thing attempted: Rural Electrification Administration, Bank for Cooperatives, Home Owners Loan Corporation, Export-Import Bank.

The third major influence contributing to the proliferation of federal lending agencies was World War II. A great many agencies were set up under the Reconstruction Finance Corporation or directly under the Treasury to provide financing regarded as essential to the prosecution of the war. They bore such names as Smaller War Plants Corporation, War Shipping Administration, and Rubber Development Corporation. At the same time there was extensive resort to the guarantee of private loans by the War Department, Navy Department, and Maritime Commission, with the Federal Reserve Banks acting as intermediary in arranging the guarantees.

After the war most of the emergency institutions were liquidated and their activities either discontinued or transferred to the Reconstruction Finance Corporation or other departments of the government. Some of the lending techniques, notably loan guarantees, were revived during the Korean war, though relatively little use was made of them. From time to time special purpose agencies were added, often with names indicative of their general purposes, e.g., the Urban Renewal Administration and the Community Facilities Administration (the latter being designed, among other things, to assist in financing the construction of college housing). What was most notable in the years after the war was the continued expansion in the aggregate amount of credit extended by the federal government.[17]

17. See Table 9-3, p. 177.

Major Services Provided

The credit activities of the federal government may be thought of as falling into two main categories. The first is encouragement of the flow of credit from private sources into desired channels and the second is the extension of credit directly by the government.[18] The latter category, however, must be subdivided to include loans which are genuine in the sense that repayment is fully intended and anticipated at the time the loan is made and those for which this is not so.

Facilitation of Private Lending. The extension of credit by private lenders may be fostered, in the first place, by governmentally sponsored guarantees. The most familiar example of this kind of assistance is the Federal Housing Administration which makes no loans but provides insurance against loss on mortgage loans and loans for the repair and modernization of houses. A premium of ½ per cent per annum is charged on the unpaid balance of the loan and appropriate loan requirements are specified. Somewhat similar insurance or guarantee (although it is considerably more liberal) is provided by the Veterans Administration. During both World War II and the Korean conflict the Federal Reserve banks guaranteed loans granted to private suppliers upon request of government agencies. The loans were actually made by private lenders and the guarantee applied only to amounts in excess of what the lenders were otherwise willing to grant.

Another device for encouraging the flow of credit from private sources is for the government to assist in setting up private lending institutions. While the government may provide some of the initial capital this is in order to get the organization going and not as a major source of funds. One example is the establishment of Small Business Investment Companies which was authorized by an act passed in 1958. These privately organized, state-chartered companies are eligible to obtain $150,000 each from the Small Business Administration in the form of subordinated credits, plus loans up to 50 per cent of paid-in capital and surplus. Mention may also be made of such institutions for extending different types of agricultural credit as National Farm Loan Associations, Intermediate Credit Banks, Production Credit Associations, and Banks for Cooperatives.

Finally, the governmental agency may encourage private lending by participating jointly in the extension of credit. This is a method long used by the Export-Import Bank and applied also by the Reconstruction Finance Corporation prior to its termination in 1954. Participation by the government involves not only a sharing of the risk but presumably also a supplementary check on the merits of the loan.

Direct Lending Operations. Further along on the scale of credit

---

18. As will be seen below, this distinction is not easily maintained in practice. The basis of the difference is whether the major financial burden is on private lenders or the Treasury.

operations by the government are those types of lending where the agency is regarded as the primary source of funds and not, as in the cases just described, as a facilitating agent or possible subsidiary source designed to stimulate the flow of capital from private lenders. Here again it is possible to distinguish three different types of lending. At one extreme is lending which is designed to close a purported "gap" in the coverage of existing lending institutions. Just as the Postal Savings System was viewed as closing a gap in the provision of facilities for small savings, so direct lending by the Small Business Administration has been defended as closing a gap in the provision of loan facilities for small business.[19]

A second type of lending by government rests on the contention that only a government body can operate on a scale large enough to accomplish the desired ends. The Federal National Mortgage Association, for example, has as its primary purpose the establishment of a "secondary" mortgage market, i.e., a market where outstanding mortgage loans can be bought and sold in much the same way as bonds and stocks. In its earlier years the Association was committed to a policy of buying mortgages at par and so became loaded down with a large volume of mortgages acquired at unrealistic prices. Since 1954 the FNMA has adjusted buying prices to market conditions. Time will tell to what extent these activities will eventually pay off and to what extent they may involve a net loss to the Treasury. The same is true of assistance granted by the Veterans Administration, the Rural Electrification Administration, the Farmers Home Administration, and others. In any case, the credit extended or underwritten was, nominally at least, asumed to be eventually self-liquidating and not a gift or grant.

Finally, there are "lending" operations in which the form of an ordinary loan or loan guarantee is maintained but with the understanding that the loan may not and probably will not be repaid. In essence, they are a type of subsidy. The leading example of this sort of activity is the Commodity Credit Corporation, created in 1933 and made permanent in 1948. The CCC is under the Department of Agriculture and has the primary function of supporting the price of farm products. A loan value corresponding to the support price is placed on each commodity. Loans are usually made by a local bank or lending agency subject to the promise of the CCC to take the note in case of non-payment. This is what happens when the price of the product falls below the support price. The CCC must, of course, absorb the loss.

The nature and extent of the government's lending activities are summarized in Table 9-3, which also shows the great increase which took place after World War II. As may be noted, the total of loans outstanding tripled

---

19. The existence of any such gap has been strenuously denied by lenders and others. Lending by the Federal Reserve Banks under the so-called Section 13-b provisions as well as some of the loans by the Reconstruction Finance Corporation were justified on similar grounds. One of the requirements for the extension of such loans was that they had previously been rejected by private lenders.

between 1945 and 1960, the greatest relative increase taking place in the first five-year period.[20] These are substantial increases even when allowance is made for the decline that occurred in the purchasing power of the dollar. It must be further borne in mind that these totals do not reflect the credit guarantees provided by government, to say nothing of credit supports of a more indirect character such as are provided by the Federal Reserve Banks.

TABLE 9-3. Loans of Governmental Agencies, by Purpose of Loans, 1945-1960 (Millions of Dollars)

	1945	1950	1955	1960
To aid agriculture	$2,878	$ 3,884	$ 6,715	$ 8,299
Federal intermediate credit banks	231	510	689	1,502
Rural Electrification Administration	407	1,543	2,348	3,287
Commodity Credit Corporation	99	898	2,621	1,877
Other	2,141	933	1,057	1,634
To aid home owners	896	1,528	3,205	8,032
Fed. Nat. Mortg. Assn.	7	1,347	2,651	6,342
Veterans Administration	. . .	35	480	1,498
Other	889	146	84	193
Industry	455	568	678	748
Financing institutions	267	824	1,419	2,027
States, territories, etc.	. . .	. . .	245	333
Foreign	526	6,078	7,988	10,394
Export-Import Bank	252	2,226	2,702	3,313
Treasury Department	. . .	3,750	3,519	3,320
International Cooperation Admin.	. . .	. . .	1,767	3,363
Other foreign	274	101	. . .	399
Other	707	531	256	1,003
Less: Reserves for losses	−438	−185	−268	−503
Net Total	$5,291	$13,228	$20,238	$30,333

Source: *Federal Reserve Bulletin.*

The concentration of lending in the three areas of foreign aid, agriculture, and housing is apparent from table 9-3. Equally noteworthy is the greater relative expansion of foreign lending in the period immediately after World War II and of aid to agriculture and home owners in the decade of the 1950's. The table strongly suggests that changes in both totals and distribution of federal lending activities reflect, as was true of their origin and early development, the main currents of domestic and foreign policy. These, in turn, are influenced by international political developments and by such internal factors as the movement of farm prices, the housing re-

---

20. The table is streamlined with a view to focusing upon major lending agencies only. A fuller breakdown is presented in current issues of the *Federal Reserve Bulletin*. A detailed classification is available in the monthly *Treasury Bulletin.*

quirements of veterans and others, and the apparent need to stimulate business activity.

It may be observed, finally, that most of the agencies, particularly those of a temporary or emergency character, have been financed by direct appropriations, and some have obtained funds from other government agencies or the Treasury. Others, however, obtain funds through the sale of their own securities, in the open market, some with and some without a guarantee by the federal government. Banks and other savings institutions have supplied a substantial proportion of the funds used by federal lending agencies. Obligations of the Federal Land Banks, Federal Intermediate Credit Banks, Federal Home Loan Banks, the Central Bank for Cooperatives, and FNMA are regularly quoted in bond lists along with Treasury obligations. The scale of operations is indicated by the fact that in a recent year these five agencies drew on the capital market for a net total of over $2 billion.

FLOW-OF-FUNDS ACCOUNTING

Finance, as was noted earlier, constitutes one phase, comparable with production and distribution, of division of labor in the modern economic society. This chapter and Chapter 8 have traced the institutional framework of finance. The postwar period witnessed the introduction of a new technique for summarizing the vast total of transactions that take place within this framework. This is known as flow-of-funds accounting.

Data showing the flow of funds through financial institutions and other channels are published currently in the *Federal Reserve Bulletin*.[21] Included in the summaries are all transactions in the economy which are effected by means of money or credit. The purpose of the Board of Governors in sponsoring and maintaining the series on flow of funds was to provide a tool for analyzing monetary and credit operations which would be comparable with the national income and product accounts for analyzing the flow of incomes and expenditures.[22] Flow-of-funds accounting is intended to do for our understanding of finance what national income accounting does for our knowledge of current production.

What the system of flow-of-funds accounts does is make it possible to show for particular periods of time the net change in the financial position ("sources and uses of funds") of a considerable number of "sectors."

21. The moving spirit in the intricate and laborious task of planning and preparing this system of accounts was Professor Morris A. Copeland of Cornell. Principal references are: M. A. Copeland, *A Study of Moneyflows in the United States* (New York: National Bureau of Economic Research, 1952); J. P. Powelson, *Economic Accounting* (New York: McGraw-Hill, 1955) and *National Income and Flow-of-Funds Analysis* (New York: McGraw-Hill, 1960); Board of Governors, *The Flow of Funds in the United States, 1939-1953* (Washington: 1955).

22. National income and product accounts are discussed in Chapter 16.

Sectors chosen for analysis may be organized in different ways. Those presented currently in the *Bulletin* are consumers and non-profit organizations, farm and non-corporate business, corporate non-financial business, federal government, state and local governments, and financial institutions.

A flow of funds may occur as a result of the transfer of existing assets as well as in the purchase and sale of current output. In contrast with national income data, therefore, these accounts reflect not only such items as the purchase and sale of *new* homes and *new* automobiles but also such items as exchanges of land, existing homes, and used cars. Shifts in cash balances and transactions in securities, trade credit, mortgages, and so on are similarly included.

Of particular interest are changes with respect to the net acquisition of financial assets and the net increase in liabilities, quantities which may, of course, sometimes be negative. The data are arranged to show the sectors raising funds and the sectors advancing them. (See Table 9-4.) Principal financial flows among the different sectors are also shown in terms of the expansion and contraction of particular types of financial assets. These include such items as demand deposits and currency, various types of fixed-value redeemable claims (e.g., time deposits and United States savings bonds), and credit and equity market instruments, including among others governmental and corporate obligations, corporate stocks, mortgages, consumer credit, and bank loans.

The flow-of-funds accounts closely resemble the balance-of-payments analysis used in connection with international transactions:[23]

> The flow-of-funds sector accounts can be visualized as a set of interlocking balance-of-payments statements, each of which, in major respects, is similar in format to balance-of-payments statements that have been developed to record the flow of international payments. Each flow-of-funds sector account records the sector's purchases and sales of commodities and services, its credit and capital outflows and inflows, and the changes in its monetary balances.[24]

The flow-of-funds accounts, then, record net changes in the asset-liability position of the different sectors regardless of whether these changes occur as a result of trade, current production, or the exchange of existing real and financial assets. The result is to provide a fairly complete picture of financial interrelationships among the different parts of the economy. They indicate the relative magnitude of different elements that enter into these relationships. In particular they call attention to the nature of net adjustments among the various sectors and the means of effecting them.

Two of the flow-of-funds categories, funds raised and funds advanced by sectors (involving transactions in credit and equity market instruments),

---

23. See Chapter 28.
24. Board of Governors, *Flow of Funds in the United States, 1939-1953*, p. 2.

are summarized in Table 9-4 to illustrate the kind of data currently available. (The *Bulletin* also publishes these data on a quarterly basis, along with various other combinations and breakdowns of the data.) As might be expected, the principal suppliers of funds were commercial banks, savings institutions, and insurance companies. This is usually the case, though the proportions may vary from year to year. It should be pointed out, however, that although consumers and non-profit organizations are shown on this table to have provided only 2.0 billion in 1961, this refers only to direct advances; commercial banks, savings banks, and insurance companies are to be regarded as largely indirect channels through which the personal savings of consumers are made available to borrowers. The principal users of funds were consumers and non-profit organizations and corporate non-financial businesses. This is also usually the case.

TABLE 9-4. Funds Raised and Advanced, by Sectors, 1961 (Billions of Dollars)

Raised		Advanced	
Consumer and nonprofit	15.7	Consumer and nonprofit	2.0
Farm business	1.6	Farm & noncorp. business	0.1
Noncorporate nonfinan. bus.	2.1	Corp. nonfinan. business	−0.1
Corporate nonfinan. business	12.7	Federal government	2.8
Federal government	6.7	State & local government	2.2
State & local government	5.4	Commercial banking system	17.4
Financial sectors	4.6	Savings institutions	12.0
Rest of the world	2.7	Insurance sector	10.7
		Finance n.e.c.	3.7
		Rest of the world	. . .
Total	51.6		51.6

Source: *Federal Reserve Bulletin,* September 1962, p. 1233.

SELECTED BIBLIOGRAPHY

BOARD OF GOVERNORS OF THE FEDERAL RESERVE SYSTEM, *Flow of Funds in the United States 1939-1953*. Washington: 1955.

Commission on Money and Credit, *Money and Credit*. Englewood Cliffs, N. J.: Prentice-Hall, 1961, Chapters 6-7.

COPELAND, M. A., *A Study of Moneyflows in the United States*. New York: National Bureau of Economic Research, 1952, especially Part I.

GOLDSMITH, R. W., *Financial Intermediaries in the United States Since 1900*. Princeton: Princeton University Press, 1958.

GURLEY, J. G., and E. S. SHAW, "Financial Aspects of Economic Development," *American Economic Review* (June 1955), pp. 515-538.

RITTER, L. S., (ed.), *Money and Economic Activity* (Readings in Money and Banking). Boston: Houghton Mifflin, 1961, Chapter XII.

ROBINSON, ROLAND I., (ed.), *Financial Institutions.* Homewood, Ill.: Irwin, 1960, Parts IV and V.

SMITH, W. L., "Financial Intermediaries and Monetary Controls," *Quarterly Journal of Economics* (November 1959), pp. 533-553.

PART THREE

Historical Background of Modern Monetary and Banking Developments

10

THE CURRENCY HISTORY
OF THE UNITED STATES
TO 1900

The next two chapters are primarily historical. The first deals with various problems relating to the development of monetary standards ◄ in the United States. The second is concerned with principal landmarks in the development of commercial banking and to a lesser extent with the beginnings of central banking. These chapters are a transition to later chapters which cover such subjects as the Federal Reserve System, recent financial history, and major problems of money and banking. They will illustrate and clarify the descriptive and theoretical material already presented and provide background for subsequent discussion.

This chapter is designed to do two things. It seeks to acquaint the student with a monetary principle which is of lasting importance. In addition, it undertakes to provide a brief survey of a significant period of American monetary history. This twofold objective involves a consideration of the interplay between economic principles and the unfolding of historical developments.

As will be seen, the difficulties encountered and the mistakes made were entirely the result of trying to fly in the face of fundamental monetary forces. When these were recognized and policies adapted to them the difficulties which had seemed so baffling and troublesome were quickly solved. A byproduct of the present discussion, therefore, should be a clear perception of the practicality of formulating public policy in accordance with valid economic principles.

GRESHAM'S LAW IN AMERICAN MONETARY HISTORY

The basis of an understanding of the monetary history of the United States lies in a recognition of the meaning and significance of Gresham's law.

This familiar but frequently misunderstood principle underlay the functioning of bimetallism while that was the legal standard of the country, but its importance was by no means confined to the period of legal bimetallism. Indeed, the history of money in the United States from 1792 to 1893 is largely the history of the operation of Gresham's law.

The usual statement of Gresham's law is that "bad money drives out good." This formulation of the principle possesses the qualities of epigram and paradox, but it is far from precise or clear and has probably led to more confusion than clarification. The disadvantages of this way of stating the principle are easily illustrated. For example, it fails to explain, except with the aid of a great deal of interpreting, why paper drives out gold and silver at one time and not at another, or why coins once driven out may later reappear in circulation. And it leaves unresolved such apparent contradictions of the law as the continued circulation of gold alongside of greenbacks in California during and after the War Between the States; or the flow of gold, dollars, and other "good" currencies into circulation in Germany in 1923 at a time when the mark was reaching the extremity of depreciation, i.e., of "badness." As will be seen, all these situations can be explained in terms of Gresham's law, but the familiar statement of the law is an obstacle rather than an aid to the explanation. The difficulty arises out of the highly arbitrary use of the words "good" and "bad." The connotation of these terms is relative and requires detailed explanation before the law, in this form, has any meaning.

Since we cannot very well dispense with the concept, and since the usual formulation is misleading and inadequate, the solution is to restate the law in a more exact form. In doing so the original epigrammatic brevity is lost, but this sacrifice is necessary in the interest of accuracy and precision. A correct statement of Gresham's law, and one which is applicable to all situations, is as follows: *Money that has value in a non-monetary use* (including use as money in another country) *will tend to move if it is free to do so, to the use* (monetary or non-monetary) *in which its value is the higher*. It need scarcely be added that if the value in the two uses is the same, there is no tendency for a shift to occur in either direction. Similarly, if it is already in use where its value is higher, it will stay there as long as the same relationship between monetary and non-monetary value continues.

This formulation of the principle is cumbersome but clear. In this form it provides an answer to the apparent inconsistencies noted above. The reason silver coins are not driven out by paper at the present time is simply that the silver in coins is more valuable as money than as metal. Again, silver coins reappeared in circulation in the 1870's, after having been driven out by the greenbacks, because a rise in the value of money and a fall in the value of silver bullion combined to make them more valuable as money than as a commodity.

The case of the continued use of gold in California throughout the period of greenback inflation calls for more extended explanation. The suggestion sometimes offered that it was because of the isolation of California and the amount of gold being produced there is entirely without validity. The spread between the price of gold and the price of greenbacks was sufficient to overcome any obstacles caused by factors such as these. Rather, it was that the people of California had become accustomed to the use of gold in current trade, even when it circulated other than in officially minted form, and after the introduction of greenbacks they continued to employ gold along with paper, paying and accepting gold *at a premium* corresponding to the current depreciation of the greenback. Because gold circulated at this higher money value it was able to remain in circulation along with the greenbacks. In terms of Gresham's law as formulated above, the premium on gold kept its money value as high as or higher than its bullion value. There was no economic inducement for gold to be driven out of the money use and consequently that did not happen. (In effect, there was a two-price system—one in terms of gold and one in terms of greenbacks.)

The use of dollars and other relatively strong currencies during the extreme stages of German inflation is accounted for on similar grounds. They entered into circulation in Germany because the premium offered when they were used for this purpose rose to such a point that they were more valuable as money in Germany than as money at home. The premium continued to rise in step with the depreciation of the reichsmark. Consequently, their value in the money use within Germany was maintained and there was no reason for them to be driven out of circulation.

It should be evident that Gresham's law is simply a particular expression of the well-known principle of substitution. This principle embodies the idea that an economic good will be applied to that use where its value is the highest. A good that can be obtained more cheaply will be substituted for a good which, because of its alternative use elsewhere, is more expensive.

Gresham's law is not to be thought of as an abstract principle of merely academic importance. Like other theoretical generalizations, its significance lies in the contribution it offers to an understanding of practical affairs. As the subsequent discussion will show, a knowledge of Gresham's law is essential to a clear comprehension of the monetary history of the United States. Moreover, a knowledge of the currency history of this country serves to strengthen one's understanding of the principle itself.

A SUMMARY OF THE CURRENCY HISTORY OF THE UNITED STATES

Before proceeding to a detailed account of the monetary history of the United States, and as a point of reference for later discussion, it will prove

TABLE 10-1. Changes in the Legal and Actual Monetary Standards of the United States

	Legal	Actual
1792	Bimetallism	Silver
1834	Bimetallism	Gold
1861	Bimetallism	Paper
1873	Gold	Paper
1879	Gold	Gold
1933	Paper	Paper
1934	Gold (Modified)	Gold (Modified)

helpful to examine Table 10-1. This summary shows that the legal standard of the United States was bimetallism from 1792 to 1873, gold from 1873 to 1933, then paper, and gold since 1934. The law of the land did not always determine, however, what was in fact the monetary standard. For the larger part of our history the effective monetary standard of the United States has been different from that which was provided for by law. This signifies that the operation of economic forces reflected in Gresham's law was often more powerful than legislation in determining the monetary standard. Where actual and legal standards were the same this was not because statutes overcame economic forces but because legislation worked with them rather than against them.

The form of presentation employed in Table 10-1 tends to exaggerate the sharpness of transitions and to obscure certain fairly important developments. These will be taken up below, but it may be noted in passing that silver was not instantaneously displaced by gold in 1834 as might be inferred from the table. On the contrary, the transition from silver to gold covered a period of ten or more years. During part of that time the two metals circulated alongside of one another on fairly even terms, giving the appearance of actual bimetallism. Nevertheless, the date of the change in ratio between gold and silver, 1834, marks the beginning of the shift from a silver to a gold basis. Similarly, on strict interpretation it could be denied that we were on the gold standard from 1917 to 1919 when there was an embargo on the export of gold or from 1934 onward when domestic circulation of gold was prohibited. In spite of these reservations, the table is helpful as indicating the major changes that occurred. Moreover, it emphasizes the important fact that throughout most of our history the question of standard was determined by more fundamental influences than legislation. These more fundamental influences are the forces summarized in Gresham's law.

THE FIRST PERIOD OF LEGAL BIMETALLISM, 1792-1834

A bimetallic currency system must be sharply distinguished from a "dual" or "parallel" standard. Under a dual system two metals are standard money, but no attempt is made to keep their values constant in terms of one another. This type of standard has been known since ancient times. There have also been instances where more than two metals were standard money, giving the country a "multiple" standard. The essential feature of bimetallism is the legal provision for a *fixed ratio between the two standard metals*. It is because of the introduction of this feature in our currency law of 1792 that the United States is generally credited with having originated legal bimetallism.

According to the Coinage Act of 1792, the dollar was defined as 371.25 grains of pure silver *or* 24.75 grains of fine gold, which established a "mint ratio" of 15 to 1 $\left(\dfrac{371.25}{24.75} = \dfrac{15}{1} \right)$. The Act provided, in other words, that "every fifteen pounds weight of pure silver shall be of equal value in all payments, with one pound weight of pure gold, and so on in proportion as to any greater or less quantities of the respective metals." A mint was organized under this legislation for the purpose of manufacturing gold, silver, and copper coins of specified denominations, mainly at the discretion of the public. Gold and silver bullion could be brought to the mint in unlimited quantities by any person, and there be coined without charge into legal tender money.[1] Apart from establishing a mint and fixing the mint ratio, the government took virtually no responsibility for the coinage of money and the management and operation of the monetary standard. Except for a small volume of minor copper coins issued on government account, there were no governmental currency issues outstanding in our early years.

Unfortunately, a serious blunder was made in connection with the mint ratio which was established in 1792. The ratio of 15:1 represented an overvaluation of silver as compared with the price prevailing in the market, a discrepancy which had increased still further by the end of the century. Under an effectively operating bimetallic standard a process of arbitrage would tend to shift the overvalued metal (in this case silver) from the market into monetary use, and the undervalued metal out of its money use into the commodity market, until market values adjusted to the mint ratio. For the process to work the flow of overvalued metal into the money use and of undervalued metal out of the money use would have to be of sufficient magnitude to dominate the supply of and demand for the two metals prevailing in the market. With many countries on the bimetallic standard at the same ratio, or perhaps even with a single very rich country on it, this requirement might be met. At that time it obviously was not. The United States was too small and weak to have any appreciable effect in bringing

---

1. To obtain immediate delivery of the desired coins payment of a charge equal to ½ per cent of the weight of the deposited metal was required.

the market ratio between the two metals into conformity with the legal ratio.[2]

A few years later the difficulties of our bimetallic standard were further compounded. In 1803 France adopted bimetallism at a ration of 15½:1. This was considerably closer to the market ratio than was our own 15:1 ratio. Since the monetary influence of France was so much greater at that time than that of the United States, the ratio set by France rather than the ratio provided in this country tended to dominate. The French ratio served, therefore, to strengthen the market ratio and to offset any tendency for it to conform to the American ratio. The result was to confirm and perpetuate the discrepancy between our legal ratio and the ratio prevailing in the market.

Since our official ratio overvalued silver and undervalued gold, the market value of gold tended to exceed its monetary value and relatively little gold was brought to the mint to be coined; on the other hand, silver was used as money since its monetary value tended to exceed its market value. At the same time and more surprisingly, new silver dollars gradually disappeared from circulation. While this was also a manifestation of Gresham's law, the reasons for it require special explanation. Since these dollars were accepted in the West Indies as the equivalent of Spanish dollars, they were sent there, exchanged for slightly heavier Spanish or Mexican dollars, and the silver from these coins was then shipped to the United States to be recoined into American money. It was largely as a result of this situation that Jefferson in 1806 directed the mint to cease coining silver dollars. From then on the principal coin minted was the silver half-dollar, but many of these were also exported and of the remainder a considerable part did not circulate but were held as bank reserves.

By a law of 1793 foreign coins were continued as legal money in the United States. In fact, it was not until 1857 that the last of the foreign coins were legally deprived of their status as circulating medium in this country. While the legal position of certain types of foreign coins during the intervening period was somewhat obscure, they were regarded by the public as legal tender and were so treated.

The supply of currency for minor transactions was extremely inadequate. The need was partially met by the circulation of clipped, lightweight foreign coins, most of them silver but some gold. The necessity of having at least some sort of money for small trade enabled these coins to continue in circulation despite their defective character. The exportation of full-weight American dollars and half-dollars, the importation of foreign silver as

2. Moreover, at the time of initiation of bimetallism in the United States there was little or no gold in circulation or in government held stocks to be shifted out of the monetary use into commodity markets. Furthermore, although silver was transferred into monetary use in some volume, the delays and inconveniences in minting, and the costs of transport to and from the mint, tended to diminish the effectiveness of the adjustment process.

bullion, and the importation of lightweight foreign coins to circulate here all illustrated the operation of Gresham's law. Lightweight foreign coins entered into circulation here because their value as money was above their bullion value. The exportation of full-weight American silver coins represented a movement of these coins into monetary use in the West Indies. There they displaced local coins which had the same money value but a higher commodity value, some of the displaced local coin being melted down and sold as bullion at the United States mint. Where this occurred, the money, in accordance with Gresham's law, moved into the commodity use because of its higher value as bullion than as money in the West Indies.

Thus the American monetary system was dominated in two principal ways by the operation of Gresham's law. First, the discrepancy between the mint ratio and the market ratio made it cheaper to use silver than gold for coinage purposes. Consequently, silver rather than gold was brought to the mint to be coined. Second, it was cheaper to use lightweight foreign coins than full-weight domestic coins. Consequently, the former were used extensively while the latter were not.

The net result of these developments was that during these years the United States was on a *de facto* silver standard with a monetary circulation made up of the following elements:

1. American fractional coins, especially fifty-cent pieces. Some of these were also driven out, though the trouble and expense involved in sending smaller coins abroad tended to keep them in circulation to a much greater extent than the American silver dollars.
2. Lightweight foreign coins.
3. Banknotes, often of dubious worth. These contributed to the expulsion of the heavier coins to the extent that their issue tended to raise the price level, so reducing the money value of the coins below their commodity value. Bank notes were commonly issued in fractional denominations, though this practice was later restricted by state laws.

THE SECOND PERIOD OF LEGAL BIMETALLISM, 1834-1873

It is apparent that bimetallism failed to operate in the United States during the period just discussed. It is equally clear that the basic trouble lay with the legal ratio, which had the effect of placing us on a monometallic silver basis. To remedy this situation the ratio was changed in 1834. This was accomplished by maintaining the content of the silver dollar unchanged, but reducing the metallic content of the gold dollar from 24.75 to 23.22 grains of pure gold. The result was to fix the ratio at 16:1. The ratio in France was still 15½:1 so that, where the previous ratio had overvalued silver, the new ratio simply reversed the situation by overvaluing gold.

Far from giving the United States actual bimetallism, the change in ratio principally resulted in the establishment of a *de facto* monometallic gold standard. Some time was required for the shift from silver to gold to be completed and in the intervening period, say to 1845, the mixture of gold and silver coins gave somewhat the outward appearance, and somewhat the actual character, of bimetallism.

The most serious consequence of the shift from a silver to a gold basis did not become fully apparent until about 1850. After the change in ratio and as a result of the premium this placed on silver, individuals suffered a slight loss in bringing silver to the mint for coinage. This disadvantage was partially offset, however, by improvements in minting procedure which greatly reduced delay and eliminated certain costs to which the public had been subject. Moreover, merchants and others were willing to suffer a small loss in order to secure newly minted small coins. Silver continued to be exported to Europe and the West Indies, but this was more than offset by the inflow of the metal consequent upon a great expansion in the output of silver in Mexico. As a result of all these factors, rather large quantities of small silver coins were issued during the decade following the change in ratio. While full-weight silver coins of large denomination were exported to a considerable extent, the expense connected with assembling and shipping small coins made it possible for them to remain in circulation.

Despite the unfortunate choice of a mint ratio, therefore, the coinage situation was on the whole considerably better after 1834 than it had been before. From 1844 on, the position with respect to silver became less favorable to the maintenance of silver coins in circulation. And it was rendered much worse by the opening up of new sources of gold production a little later. The effect of the great expansion in the output of gold in California and Australia was to depress the value of gold relative to that of silver. By 1851 the silver in coins having a monetary value of one dollar was worth $1.03½ in the market. The premium on silver was so large that the exportation of coins was greatly stimulated while at the same time the minting of new silver coins practically ceased. As a consequence, the problem of maintaining an adequate supply of small coins, which had been present all along, was seriously aggravated.

It is hard for us to realize the disordered state of the monetary circulation that existed during these years:

> Before the end of 1851 conditions in retail trade had become chaotic. Trade was being carried on with gold dollars, 3 cent pieces, underweight dimes and half-dimes, and badly worn Spanish reals and medios [nominally worth 12½¢ and 6¼¢]. The gold dollars were too small in size and too large in value. The dimes and half-dimes were the few survivors of a systematic culling out of good weight coins. The Spanish fractions were a motley collection of underweight coins. The adverse ratio had long since stopped the importation of Spanish coins of good condition, but badly worn pieces were still brought in. Sumner says that the whole world was ransacked

for Spanish coins that had been discarded as unfit for circulation. Ordinary business was hampered and retarded by the state of the currency. No United States or Spanish silver coin could circulate unless it was reduced by wear as much as 3 per cent. The average depreciation was much larger, possibly as great as 15 per cent. . . . The total fractional coin currency of all kinds was quite inadequate. . . . A Philadelphia paper refers derisively to shopkeepers scooping up 3 cent pieces with a ladle to make change for a $5 bank note.[3]

The basis of the difficulty with respect to small denomination currency lay in the prevailing attitude toward issuing coins of less than the legal metallic content. The view that a reduction of the metallic content of coins is debasement and a fraud upon the public is still widely held in relation to standard money. But at that time the same prejudice existed with respect to lowering the commodity value of fractional money, including halves, dimes, and even pennies, below their monetary value. In fact, it was primarily the attitude of insisting on full commodity value for *all* money that so long blocked efforts to find a rational solution for the problem of providing a decent circulating medium.

Since silver was undervalued it was not brought to the mint to be coined into fractional pieces, and even if it had been the coins would promptly have been withdrawn from use as money. Gold, the overvalued metal, was brought in for minting but it was obviously impossible to coin dimes and quarters, much less pennies, out of this metal. The net result was that, by demanding that each coin should be "good" in the narrow commodity sense, we made it inevitable that the coinage system as a whole should be exceedingly bad. The government was faced with the dilemma of either cheating itself or being thought to be cheating the public. If it had undertaken to coin full-weight fractional coins on its own initiative, it would have experienced a continuing financial loss, a sort of reverse seigniorage.[4] On the other hand, it hesitated to issue lightweight coins, such as we have today, because of the fear of being accused of debasing the currency.

The attitude just described played an important part in the history of silver as a monetary metal. Silver is particularly well adapted for use in full-weight coins of small denominations; gold coins would be too small and copper coins would be too large and heavy. As long as the view prevailed that fractional coins must be full weight, there was no practical alternative to the use of silver as a standard. The prestige enjoyed by silver as a monetary metal was to a considerable extent based on this fact. It contributed to the attempt to maintain bimetallism in this country and abroad and helps to

---

3. Neil Carothers, *Fractional Money* (New York: Wiley, 1930), pp. 110-111.
4. "Seigniorage" refers to a charge imposed or gain accruing for the services of coinage. It is over and above payment for costs of minting which is called "brassage." The value of newly minted coins is made up of cost of materials, plus brassage, plus seigniorage.

explain the survival of the silver standard in China and elsewhere down to recent years.

Perhaps the most interesting development during the period when small coins were such a problem in the United States was the use of postage stamps for small change. No one stopped to think how absurd it was to object to the issue of lightweight coins as being less than full bodied, while accepting the circulation of postage stamps which were wholly devoid of commodity value!

At last, after having endured the inconvenience of an unsatisfactory coinage system for years, a law was passed in 1853 authorizing the issue of lightweight coins on government account—on the same basis, that is, as small coins are issued today. The effect of this law was twofold. First, the government began the issue of small coins because it could do so without financial sacrifice. Second, the coins remained in circulation since they were more valuable as money than as metal.

Thus simply—by taking advantage of the operation of Gresham's law rather than opposing it—was the vexed question of fractional currency finally settled. A few lessons had to be learned about administering the law before it was discovered that the quantity of fractional money could be easily and automatically regulated through interconvertibility with higher denomination currency (i.e., dollars or multiples thereof). Nevertheless, the solution of the problem of subsidiary coins dates from the law of 1853. Thanks mainly to the advance made at that time, it was no longer necessary to depend upon foreign coins for small change. Accordingly, foreign coins were demonetized in 1857. Thus we achieved monetary independence, if the expression may be used, over eighty years after we declared our political independence and sixty-five years after the enactment of our original monetary law.

Notwithstanding the length of time it required and the simplicity of the final solution, this represents one of the major developments in the history of currency, at least so far as this country is concerned. It may be mentioned that England solved the same problem by similar means in 1816. Though we waited nearly forty years, we were still the second country to find the solution. Few discoveries have contributed as much to the successful functioning of the monetary mechanism. It is probably not too much to say that this discovery made possible the rise of the international gold standard by demonstrating that a satisfactory system of subsidiary currency was possible without depending upon either a silver or a bimetallic standard.

As has been seen, legal bimetallism in the United States passed through two stages; in the first the standard was actually silver and in the second it was gold. The period of legal bimetallism was to close with still a third stage, that of a paper standard.

Early in the War Between the States, the difficulties of war finance led to the issue of paper money, the so-called greenbacks. In 1862 redemption in gold was suspended and the actual monetary standard of the country became paper greenbacks.

Exaggerated ideas are held as to the extent of inflation that occurred during this period. The value of greenbacks fell at one time to 38¢ in terms of gold, but this does not measure the degree of inflation that took place. The price of 38¢ shows the decline in the value of the greenback in terms of the single commodity, gold.[5] For its depreciation in terms of goods and services generally one must look, as was explained in Chapter 1, to the reciprocal of changes in the general level of prices.

The maximum level of wholesale prices, reached in 1865, was approximately double that which prevailed when gold payments were suspended. Inflation at this time, that is, resulted in a 50¢ dollar measured by its purchasing power, a negligible degree of inflation compared with that which occurred in various countries after World Wars I and II. More surprising still, the inflation that occurred under the greenbacks was considerably less than existed in the United States in 1919 and 1920. In the latter year, the dollar was worth only about 40¢ as compared with 1914. Expressed in percentages of the base years, wholesale prices reached 200 in 1865 while in 1920 they rose above 240. It is also less than occurred during and after World War II. Between 1939 and 1951 (after the Korean inflation) the index of wholesale prices rose from 100 to 230, indicating a decline in the value of the dollar to 44¢ compared with one dollar in 1939.[6]

One consequence of the depreciation of the greenbacks was to bring to the fore again the problem of fractional money. Gold coins were almost immediately driven out of circulation except on the Pacific coast where, as has been noted, they circulated at a premium relative to paper. It was not long before the overissuance of greenbacks drove the money value of fractional coins below the commodity value of the metal they contained. As a result they were withdrawn from circulation, leaving a great dearth of small change. The obvious solution would have been to issue other coins of sufficiently low metallic content so that their money value would always have been more than their commodity value, but this was not done. The need was very inadequately met by the issue of "shinplasters," i.e., paper money of small denominations, and postage stamps.

An interesting sequel to the withdrawal of fractional coins was their reappearance in circulation, particularly in the year 1877. By that time the value of the dollar had risen fairly near to its old level. Changes in the supply of and demand for silver had led to a considerable lowering of its value. The point was reached where the commodity value of the silver in the fractional coins fell below its money value. To everyone's surprise, the

---

5. It meant that one dollar in paper money would purchase only 38 per cent of the gold in the official gold dollar.

6. It will be observed that in each case the comparison is with the level of prices at the start of the period. The 1939 base was above the 1914 base and the 1951 peak above the 1920 peak.

coins which had not been seen in circulation in this country for years again returned to use. Such a development should have been no cause for surprise. It was a normal manifestation of the operation of Gresham's law. The coins returned to their money use simply because they were more valuable as money than as a commodity. This reverse application of the more usual operation of Gresham's law was an equally clear illustration of the principle.

THE PERIOD OF THE LEGAL GOLD STANDARD

"The Crime of '73"

The period of the legal gold standard in the United States was ushered in by a law which attracted little attention at the time but which was to be the object of as prolonged and bitter an attack as has ever been directed against any law in our history.[7] The Coinage Act of 1873 included the gold dollar as legal money but omitted mention of the silver dollar. This omission seemed relatively unimportant at the time and aroused only moderate opposition. After all, neither gold nor silver was then current, and silver dollars had not been minted in appreciable quantities for many years. Some debate on the question was engendered but the passage of the bill was quite perfunctory.

The bill had hardly passed into law when the price of silver, which had been almost constant for centuries, began to decline relative to gold. The abandonment of bimetallism by a number of European countries and the adoption of a monometallic gold standard served to reduce the demand for silver and to increase the demand for gold. The supply of silver was expanded by the opening of rich deposits of the metal in the West, the most famous of them being the Comstock lode in Nevada. The result of these developments was to depress the value of silver and to raise the value of gold.

With the shift in the ratio of gold and silver, the silver mining interests suddenly realized that in closing the mints to the free coinage of silver the Act of 1873 had deprived them of a sure market which would have prevented a fall in the price of their product. They immediately attacked the law, alleging that it had been enacted by stealth and demanding that it be repealed. They were joined by the debtor classes, especially farmers, who were conscious of the burden of falling prices and desired the cheaper money unit which they believed silver would provide.

Thus was conjured up in the minds of disappointed miners and depressed debtors the idea of a "Crime of '73."

---

7. Not excluding the Volstead Act prohibiting the sale of alcoholic beverages.

The Curious Episode of the Trade Dollar

The Act of 1873 contained another provision whose consequences are of unusual monetary and political interest. This was the authorization of a silver dollar, to be known as the Trade Dollar, designed to be used in the Orient. For many years Spanish and Mexican dollars had enjoyed a wide circulation in the Far East; indeed, the "Dollar Mex" was the standard money of China until well into the present century. It was hoped that the new Trade Dollars would compete with these other dollars and provide beneficial advertising for the United States as well as create an outlet for American silver. To put this new dollar on a par with the Mexican dollar, it was given a silver content slightly greater than that of the old American dollar.

The Act provided that the Trade Dollar should have the right of free coinage and should be legal tender up to five dollars for payments in the United States. The first provision was a routine device to facilitate issue of the Trade Dollars; the second was expected to make the coin more acceptable abroad by giving it legal standing in this country. No one ever supposed that it would actually enter into domestic circulation. After all, the traditional silver dollar which was of lower silver content had been virtually unknown to the public since 1806. At the time, the *de facto* standard money of the country consisted of greenbacks.

By a curious coincidence, the passage of the law occurred during a period when developments were in process which were to upset these expectations. Factors already mentioned, the increased production of silver in this country and its demonetization abroad, resulted in a drop in its value relative to that of gold. Greenbacks, meanwhile, had risen much closer to a parity with gold. By 1876 a point had been reached where the Trade Dollars were worth more as money in the United States than as a commodity. To the extent that they circulated at all in the Orient, they did so at their commodity value. The result was that Trade Dollars were coined for use in this country and began to appear in circulation in increasing amounts. This also was a normal manifestation of the operation of Gresham's law: the coins were simply flowing into the use where their value was the highest.

Such a result was entirely contrary to the intentions of those responsible for the legislation. The legal tender provision was accordingly removed in 1876 and a little later, foreign demand for the Trade Dollar having proved disappointing, its issue was entirely discontinued. This action was taken without concerted opposition, and neither then nor since has it attracted any particular comment.

This is more remarkable since at the time strong pressure was already being brought to secure the remonetization of silver. The provisions relating to the Trade Dollar (free coinage and legal tender) were themselves tantamount to the monetization of silver. They were enough to make silver a standard money in the United States. If they had been continued we should shortly have been on either a straight silver standard or a bimetallic standard at a ratio of approximately 16⅓:1. The slightly higher ratio is a reflection of the fact that the Trade Dollar was a little heavier than the traditional silver dollar.

The net effect of the 1873 law, then, was to create for these few years a legal bimetallic standard at the ratio of 16⅓:1.[8] If these provisions had remained in force, the price of silver could never have fallen below $1.27 an ounce. While these ratios are slightly less favorable to silver than 16:1 and a price of $1.29 an ounce, they should be compared with market ratios and prices that have prevailed since, i.e., with ratios above 100:1 and prices for silver below 24¢ an ounce.

The absence of any serious effort to block the repeal of the Trade Dollar can hardly be explained on the ground that the prospect seemed bright for a still more advantageous ratio of silver to gold. It can only be that the silver interests failed to comprehend the implications of the law or to realize that legal bimetallism was already on the books. The action of 1876 repealing the legal tender provision was far more of a crime against silver, if one wishes to use the term, than that of 1873, for by that time it was open for all to see, as it had not been earlier, that the underlying position of silver had drastically altered. Whether events would have been different if its meaning had been grasped is impossible to say. Nevertheless, it would probably have been tactically easier to prevent the repeal of an existing law than to secure the passage of a new law.

The action taken in 1876 was doubtless a good thing, but nevertheless it is to be regarded as a monument to monetary illiteracy on the part of the silver interests. Nor is it likely that those who voted for repeal were fully aware of the true monetary significance of the Act. The actual importance of the Trade Dollar was very slight; it is chiefly significant as a reminder of the lack of economic understanding on the part of the silver interests.

The Resumption of Specie Payments

By the terms of the Specie Resumption Act of 1875, convertibility of currency into gold was restored on the first of January 1879. For years the greenback had been rising toward parity with gold. This was because the supply of circulating medium failed to increase as rapidly as the volume of business transacted. The country was "growing up to its money supply." As the resumption date approached, the premium on gold gradually disappeared, and the transition to gold parity was effected without incident. Thereafter gold coins were able to remain in circulation since they were as

---

8. While this statement is strictly correct, it has seemed best to adhere in Table 10-1 to the more generally recognized date of 1873 as the year when gold was adopted as the legal standard.

valuable in that use as they would have been in the commodity use. In essence, resumption was merely a matter of accommodation to the forces of Gresham's law.

It is worth mentioning in passing that the Specie Resumption Act of 1875 and the Coinage Act of 1853 represent two different, but equally logical, approaches to the problem of maintaining desired types of money in circulation. From Gresham's law it is clear that the one condition essential to a particular type of money remaining in circulation is that it should be more valuable, or at least not less valuable, as money than it is in any other use. The 1853 law brought this about for fractional coins by lowering their commodity value; the reduction in silver content of these coins rendered them less valuable in the commodity than in the monetary use. Accordingly, they remained in circulation. The Resumption Act, on the other hand, turned on the effectiveness of another factor in the relationship. It involved waiting for the money value of the dollar to rise to a point where a gold dollar was worth as much as money as it was as bullion. Thereafter gold coins were able to circulate.

The Silver Purchase Acts of 1878 and 1890

The Bland-Allison Act (1878) and the Sherman Silver Purchase Act (1890) were the tangible fruits of the silver agitation that followed 1873. They were designed to effect minor concessions to the friends of silver while avoiding more radical action such as was being demanded. The Bland-Allison Act, which was in force from 1878 until its repeal in 1890, required the Secretary of the Treasury to buy between 2 and 4 million dollars of silver bullion each month, to be coined and paid out by the Treasury as legal tender silver dollars. The Sherman Silver Purchase Act, which replaced the 1878 law, provided that the Secretary was to buy 4.5 million ounces of silver per month, to be paid for with Treasury notes that were given legal tender status. These notes were to be redeemable in either gold coin or in silver dollars coined from the acquired bullion.

There can be little doubt that the law of 1890 contributed to the Panic of 1893. The passage of the law seems to have hastened the withdrawal of foreign funds from this market with a resulting drain on gold reserves and further impairment of public confidence.[9] The Act was repealed in 1893.

The direct consequence of the laws of 1878 and 1890 was that the country acquired roughly 570 million silver dollars. From a monetary standpoint,

---

9. The most interesting feature of this episode is that the Sherman Silver Purchase Act was Republican legislation, supported by, among others, William McKinley. It helped to bring on the Panic of 1893 which broke, however, after a Democratic president had assumed office. It was partly responsible for establishing the view that the election of a Democrat makes for hard times, a belief which the Republican supporters of the silver legislation, it need hardly be said, did nothing to dispel.

the most interesting question is why the arbitrary addition of this sum of money failed either to raise prices or to drive existing standard money out of circulation in substantial amounts. The principal reason seems to be that expanding trade created a place for the new money as rapidly as it was introduced.[10]

The fact that, for the most part, gold was not directly driven out may be explained on the ground that expanding business tended to raise the value of money while the issues resulting from the silver acts tended to lower it. Since the first influence was fully as strong as the second, the money value of the gold coins did not fall below their commodity value, and there was thus no reason for them to be driven out. This also represents the functioning of Gresham's law, the chief difference being that the active factor was the volume of output rather than the volume of money.

The Gold Standard Act of 1900 specifically affirmed adherence by this country to the international gold standard and provided the Secretary of the Treasury with more adequate powers for maintaining convertibility between the dollar and gold. It is sometimes regarded as for the first time having established the United States firmly on the gold standard. It is chiefly important as marking the end of a long period of monetary controversy and political maneuvering over the issue of the standard.

CONCLUSION

The failure of bimetallism in the United States is often cited as proving that such a system is bound to break down. No such conclusion is justified by that experience. The ratio we chose was out of line with both the legal ratio established by France and the market ratio. The market ratio tended to conform to the mint ratio of the country with the stronger monetary demand and supply, namely, France. These two ratios did, in fact, stand in close agreement until France abandoned bimetallism at the time of the Franco-Prussian War. The failure of bimetallism in the United States is not to be regarded as conclusive proof of the impracticality of bimetallism.

---

10. During part of the period, also, the silver and silver-backed money took the place of national bank notes which had been retired. The amount of silver acquired by the Treasury under the Sherman Silver Purchase Act was only a little more than the amount of gold exported during the same years. This loss of gold was not so much because of the operation of Gresham's law as because of the psychological consequences of the legislation, particularly as these affected foreign holders of American securities. It weakened confidence in our financial policies and contributed to a liquidation of foreign investments in this country. The withdrawal of these funds was largely responsible for the export of gold, a movement which somewhat resembled the drain of gold that attracted attention in the early 1960's. In the absence of the silver purchase acts the money supply would probably have been increased, over the period as a whole, almost as much by the minting of additional gold as it was by the issue of silver dollars and silver certificates. One may think of the silver money as having largely displaced gold that would have been coined rather than gold already in the system.

The special conditions under which it was attempted in the United States foredoomed it to failure.

The feature that stands out most clearly in the discussion of American currency history is the extent to which the monetary difficulties of the nineteenth century sprang from the commodity aspect of our money. The problem of fractional coinage was quickly and easily solved by making it token in character, that is, by rendering the commodity of which the coins were made no longer a determinant of their value. While it might seem that the evil inflationary effects of the greenback issues show the dangers of token money, it must be remembered that the purchasing power of our currency declined even more during World War I, when the dollar remained convertible into gold. Still others of the monetary difficulties of the first hundred years of our history were also closely related to the commodity aspect of money. Looking backward, our struggle with subsidiary coins and with bimetallism seems largely unnecessary. Both the basis of the trouble and the solution now seem thoroughly obvious. Will the solution of present monetary problems seem as obvious a century from now?

SELECTED BIBLIOGRAPHY

CAROTHERS, NEIL, *Fractional Money*. New York: Wiley, 1930, Chapters VI-XIX

DEWEY, D. R., *Financial History of the United States*. New York: Longmans, Green, 1915, Chapters V, VII, XII-XX.

HEPBURN, A. B., *A History of Currency in the United States*. New York: Macmillan, 1915, Chapters V-XVI, XX-XXI.

MITCHELL, W. C., *A History of the Greenbacks*. Chicago: University of Chicago Press, 1903.

WHITE, HORACE, *Money and Banking*. Boston: Ginn, 1936, Chapters V-VII, IX-XI.

11

HISTORICAL BACKGROUND
OF THE AMERICAN
BANKING SYSTEM

The preceding chapter provided a brief summary of the early history of currency and monetary standards in the United States. The unifying thread that ran through that discussion was a fundamental monetary principle, Gresham's law. The present chapter is intended to provide the historical basis for a better understanding of commercial banks and of the Federal Reserve System which embodies the American version of a central bank. The theme that runs through this presentation is that the development of banking institutions in the United States has been an evolutionary process: most of the distinctive features of the banking organization which we have today are either derived from or show parallels with earlier banking forms and institutions which existed in this country.

The discussion that follows will furnish an introduction to the Federal Reserve System in other ways as well. Historical evidence indicates the great importance of having some kind of central financial institution by showing the improvement that followed the establishment of such institutions and the chaotic nature of monetary and banking conditions that developed when they were removed. It also shows something of the nature of the problems with which a central banking organization is confronted as well as some of the inadequate, *ad hoc* expedients that were improvised for dealing with them at a time when the country lacked a true central bank such as exists today.

BANKING DEVELOPMENTS BEFORE 1860

In the early history of this country, banking functions of a rudimentary character were performed by private money lenders, colonial governments, and groups of merchants who followed the practice of lending to one another at times when they had funds temporarily available. Out of such a pooling of resources developed the first bank established in this country, The Bank of North America founded in 1781.

The early banks that sprang up in centers along the Atlantic seaboard specialized in short-term, self-liquidating commercial paper. Among banks which were established farther to the interior, where economic activity was chiefly agricultural and the demand was more largely for longer term credit, commercial paper occupied a relatively less important place in bank portfolios. For all banks, however, the extension of bank credit took the form chiefly of circulating bank notes rather than deposits subject to check. It was not until after the middle of the nineteenth century that the volume of bank deposits reached an amount equal to that of bank notes. Accordingly, the principal banking problems of the day were those associated with the issue of bank notes, and this was the problem with which legislation was chiefly concerned.

The First Bank of the United States, 1791-1811

Acting on the recommendations of Alexander Hamilton, Congress chartered the Bank of the United States in 1791. The Bank was organized by the government and part of the capital was provided out of federal funds. Its operations, apart from acting as fiscal agent for the Treasury, were similar to those of the other banks of the country, from which it was distinguished chiefly by its greater size and larger number of branches. The Bank engaged in ordinary business lending and issued bank notes totaling on the average about 5 million dollars or approximately one-fifth of the entire bank note circulation of the country. In addition, the Bank followed the practice, partly for its own protection, of presenting promptly for redemption in specie the notes of state-chartered banks which came to it in the course of business. The effect of this policy was to compel these other banks to restrict the volume of their note issues and thus maintain the quality of their notes.

Both because it adhered to high standards itself and because it forced high standards upon other banks, the Bank of the United States was a very wholesome influence on banking affairs of the young country. But its methods, which involved competing with the state banks and forcing them to maintain redemption of notes, provoked bitter antagonism. Various other political and personal factors also contributed to the end result that when the Bank's charter expired at the end of twenty years it was not renewed.[1]

---

1. For a detailed discussion of these factors see Bray Hammond, *Banks and Politics in America* (Princeton: Princeton University Press, 1957), Chapter 8.

The Second Bank of the United States, 1816-1836

The demise of the first Bank of the United States was followed by an interim of five years during which the number of state-chartered banks increased rapidly, the volume of bank notes expanded, and depreciation of notes and bank failures became common. The financial difficulties of the times were undoubtedly aggravated by the War of 1812 and the low state of the Treasury's financial affairs. It was generally recognized, however, that they were made considerably worse by the absence of a strong banking institution such as the first Bank of the United States had been. Accordingly, in 1816 the second Bank of the United States was chartered. This bank was considerably larger than its predecessor, but in general pattern and policies it followed the lines already laid down.

Despite serious difficulties and charges of mismanagement in its early years, the second Bank of the United States helped to bring about a great improvement in banking conditions. Again the effect was to arouse the strenuous opposition of state banks, and the opposition was strengthened as a result of the restriction of credit which the Bank's methods caused in certain areas. In the course of time, the management of the bank became involved with President Jackson in the so-called "Bank War." This famous episode was one of the most violent financial engagements ever fought out in this country. Emotions were stirred to a high pitch and questionable methods were employed by both sides. The press of the day was strongly on the side of the Bank, a fact not wholly unrelated to the liberality of the Bank in extending substantial loans to publishers and paying rather generously for their services. At least two prominent senators, Clay and Webster, were on the payroll of the Bank at one time. During the heat of the struggle over renewal of the Bank's charter Daniel Webster wrote to Nicholas Biddle, its president:

> I believe my retainer has not been renewed or refreshed as usual. If it be wished that my relation to the Bank should be continued, it may be well to send me the usual retainer.[2]

Biddle is generally thought to have overestimated his own strength and underestimated the fighting qualities of his opponent. At any rate, the election of Jackson in 1832, partly on the basis of the stand he had taken against the Bank, sealed the fate of the institution and its charter was allowed to run out in 1836.[3] There followed an increase in the number of banks, an expan-

---

2. Alexander Fleisher, "Public Opinion and Practical Politics in 'The Bank War,'" *Economics and Business Bulletin*, Temple University, March 1952, p. 33. It may be added that in this instance Mr. Webster's request was refused.

3. Thereupon the Bank attempted to carry on under a state charter granted by Pennsylvania. It became heavily involved in investments in public improvements and in the cotton trade. Foreseeing that it would be compelled to suspend specie payments, officials of the Bank, by intricate financial manipulations, tried to force suspension upon New

sion of bank credit, and, during the financial panic of 1837, widespread suspension of redemption in specie and frequent failures. In many parts of the country, banking conditions continued in a more or less chaotic state until after the establishment of the National Banking System.

The usefulness of the second Bank of the United States is pretty clearly attested by the improvement in banking standards that followed its establishment and the prompt return to widespread conditions of banking disorder when it passed out of existence. The entire history of American banking might have been altered if the Bank—which conceivably would have developed into a true central bank—had been allowed to survive. It is unfortunate that in the end the fate of the Bank rested so little on the direct contributions which it had made to the financial life of the country and so largely on personalities, jealousies, and other irrelevancies which were capable of political exploitation.

The Suffolk Banking System, 1824

In the early decades of the nineteenth century some of the stronger banks in Boston found themselves—through the operation of Gresham's law—at a disadvantage because of the tendency for their notes to be driven out of circulation by the depreciated notes of outlying banks. Accordingly, a voluntary arrangement was introduced whereby the Suffolk Bank of Boston agreed to hold deposits of stipulated amounts for other banks, partcularly outlying country banks, and in return to redeem all notes of these banks at par. Banks which failed to participate were subject to the threat that the Suffolk Bank might accumulate their notes and present them for redemption in substantial volume. In substance, this amounted to bringing pressure on other banks by confronting them with the possibility of a sudden drain of reserves if they refused to cooperate in maintaining satisfactory banking standards. The system functioned with great success for many years, with the result that the notes of New England banks circulated generally at par value.

The Suffolk system shows interesting parallels with the Federal Reserve System which started operations just ninety years later. The Federal Reserve, as will be shown later, followed the same practice of requiring member institutions to maintain deposit balances with the Reserve Banks and in return undertook to honor at par the checks which were drawn on the member banks. At times it also employed the technique of presenting batches of checks drawn on non-member banks in an effort to induce them to abandon

York banks. This colorful story, which had as its sequel the failure of the Bank in 1841 and the undisputed "passing of financial primacy from Chestnut Street to Wall Street," is recounted in Sister M. Grace Madeleine, *Monetary and Banking Theories of Jacksonian Democracy* (Philadelphia: Dolphin Press, 1943), Chapter V, and Bray Hammond, "The Chestnut Street Raid on Wall Street," *Quarterly Journal of Economics*, August 1947, pp. 605-618.

the practice of redeeming at a discount checks that were drawn on themselves but presented for collection by out-of-town banks.

The New York Safety Fund System, 1829

The next notable, though somewhat less successful, banking development in the United States was the establishment of the Safety Fund System in the state of New York in 1829. This consisted of a guarantee fund, maintained by obligatory contributions from member banks, for the purpose of helping to meet the liabilities of banks that failed. Early experience with the Fund was far from successful, but the major defects were remedied by subsequent amendments. Thereafter, protection was confined to bank notes, and certain types of banks were excluded from membership. The Fund continued in existence for forty years and served as a model for a somewhat similar system in Canada. It is generally regarded as an early precursor of the Federal Deposit Insurance Corporation which introduced the guarantee of bank deposits in the United States on a national scale in 1933.

The Free Banking System, 1838

The New York Free Banking Act, passed in 1838, is a landmark in the banking history of the United States. It has been called America's most distinctive contribution to the development of banking organization. Up to that time, the organization of banks had been dependent on the grant of special charters by state legislatures. This practice savored of monopoly, was contrary to the democratic conception of a vigorous, expanding country, and lent itself to serious political abuse. Moreover, it erred in being too restrictive in the original establishment of banks and often too liberal in the powers exercised by banks once they had been created.

The Free Banking Act proceeded on a new principle. It sought to rely on continuing legislative requirements for the organization and operation of banks. It was assumed that by setting these requirements sufficiently high, banking could be safely made "a business open to all." The grant of a charter to engage in banking was made contingent upon compliance with certain legal stipulations which were open and uniform for everyone. The issue of notes was governed by the pledge of securities of specified types with the state comptroller. Securities held as collateral could be sold to redeem notes if a bank failed. The principal features of the Free Banking Act were later incorporated in the National Banking Act under which a large segment of our banks still operate.

The Free Banking System of New York was copied in the laws of a number of other states.[4] Experience under this legislation in the different

---

4. A similar law was adopted in Michigan a year earlier than in New York, but was actually based on the New York plan.

states varied from good to very bad, depending upon the provisions of the particular acts and the effectiveness of their administration. In most states the free banking laws suffered from two principal defects. First, they provided little or no protection to creditors and the public by means of reserve requirements. Even by the time of the passage of the National Banking Act in 1863, only two states, Louisiana and Massachusetts, had statutory reserve requirements applicable to both notes and deposits. The New York Act imposed a 12½ per cent specie reserve requirement on notes, which was eliminated in 1844, and no reserve requirement against deposits. In New York, as in most states at that time, the dubious assumption was made that adequate control over bank credit expansion could be achieved simply by requiring bank notes to be secured by an equivalent volume of bonds as collateral. "Rigidly limiting the issue of notes to the amount of bonds pledged to secure them seemed at the time to be a safeguard against inflation as well as a guaranty of individual note issues. But as such it amounted to nothing. It merely put a movable limit on the amount of notes each bank could issue—for the more bonds it bought the more notes it could put out and the more bonds it could buy . . ."[5]

The second major defect of the free banking laws of the pre-National Banking System period was the inadequacy and lack of enforcement of collateral requirements for note issues. This was especially so in the Western states, where free banking:

> degenerated into "wildcat" banking; banks were established in remote, inaccessible places where it was alleged that only wildcats throve and where there was little chance that circulating notes would find their way for redemption. Speculators and swindlers took advantage of frontier ignorance of investment securities and made it a regular practice to purchase bonds of little worth, pledge them in exchange for their face value in circulating notes, and vanish. There arose an intense opposition to banks, for which free banking abuses were . . . partly responsible.[6]

THE NATIONAL BANKING SYSTEM

Despite many expedients which were introduced to control banks, with the notable exception of a few states, banking conditions were far from satisfactory in the years between the demise of the second Bank of the United States and the passage of the National Banking Act. This was the day of the bank note reporter and counterfeit detector. These were periodicals issued at frequent intervals to provide information on the different kinds of money

---

5. Bray Hammond, *Banks and Politics in America*, p. 595.
6. Board of Governors of the Federal Reserve System, *Banking Studies* (Washington: 1941), p. 10.

in circulation, indicating what notes were to be accepted at par, what notes were worthless, and the rates of discount on others.

It is difficult for us to realize at the present day how chaotic the monetary circulation was in the middle of the last century. A single issue of one of these publications listed 5,400 separate descriptions of bank notes, all of them counterfeit, altered, or spurious. Included were thirty different counterfeits of the notes of a single bank.[7] At the outbreak of the War Between the States about 7,000 kinds of genuine bank notes, including the various denominations, were in circulation, in addition to 5,500 different kinds of fraudulent notes. The notes of three-quarters of the banks which issued bank notes had been altered or counterfeited.[8] It was against a background such as this that the National Banking Act was finally passed.

Origin of The National Banking System

From the start of the country the bank note circulation had not been really satisfactory, even though it was in the periods in which the influence of the first and second Banks of the United States was absent that conditions were the worst. There had been more or less active agitation for reform for a good many years, but the law establishing the National Banking System was not enacted until early in 1863. According to the Comptroller of the Currency in his Annual Report for the year 1875:

> The opportunity occasioned by a great war was seized upon, in the interest of the Government, to get rid of the burden of a circulation issued by authority of many different States, which had been, almost from the beginning of the Government, a grievous tax upon the business and the commerce of the country.

Two principal objectives were in the minds of those responsible for the passage of the law. First and most important was to provide—in place of the complex and multitudinous variety of notes, which ranged from par value to no value at all—a uniform bank note issue that would be of high quality. The second consideration, and the one that chiefly explains the introduction of the reform at this particular time, was to strengthen support for the government during the war. Increased demand for government bonds was to be assured by compelling the banks chartered under the new law to purchase them in substantial volume. In addition, it was expected, apparently on the principle that where one's treasure is there will his heart be also, that their investment in government bonds would increase the loyalty of northern financial interests to the Union cause.

Delay in getting the new system in operation prevented the expectations of the Treasury regarding the sale of bonds during the war from being

---

7. Horace White, *Money and Banking*, new edition (Boston: Ginn, 1936), p. 458.
8. C. W. Collins, *Rural Bank Reform* (New York: Macmillan, 1931), p. 16.

fully realized. At the conclusion of hostilities bonds held by national banks amounted to less than 4 per cent of total government issues outstanding.[9] By the 1880's the government was buying up Treasury bonds for the purpose of retiring them out of surplus revenues. The demand for government bonds by national banks was partly responsible for forcing up the price of government bonds at that time, with the result that the Treasury paid a premium of as much as 25 per cent on its own obligations. Thus the requirement that national banks should buy government bonds was of little help in the actual financing of the war, and in the long run may actually have added to the total monetary outlay.

Early Developments Under the National Banking Act

Partly because of flaws in the legislation, which made necessary a general revision of the law, it was some time before the system could be set in operation on any significant scale. The National Banking System, as we know it, may be said to date from the passage of the revised National Banking Act in 1864. Progress under this act was much more rapid than under the preceding, but even so was considerably less satisfactory than had been hoped. In many cases, it was still possible for state banks to issue their notes under less stringent requirements than those imposed upon the national banks. To meet this difficulty a law was passed the following year placing a tax of 10 per cent on all state bank notes paid out after July 1, 1866. It is of interest that as early as 1831 Gallatin, then Secretary of the Treasury, had recommended this means of driving the notes of state banks out of existence. He showed that Congress had the power to do so and that such action would be in conformity with:

> express provisions of the Constitution which vest in Congress exclusively the control over the monetary system of the United States, and more particularly those which imply the necessity of a uniform currency.[10]

The effectiveness of these measures was demonstrated by developments that followed. Since the issue of notes was a major feature of banking operations at that time, the vast majority of state banks promptly applied for national charters. State bank notes made their last appearance in the Treasury Reports on July 1, 1876, when the amount in circulation was given as $1,047,-335, but this figure probably represented notes that had been lost, destroyed, or were held in collections. State banks had ceased to issue notes after 1865. As the figures on the next page show, the number of national banks rose sharply and for some years the number of state banks declined.

With the rapid expansion of checking deposits after 1870, banks again

---

9. F. Cyril James, *The Economics of Money, Credit and Banking* (New York: Ronald Press, 1940), p. 193.

10. *Annual Report of the Comptroller of the Currency* for 1876, p. 34.

	National Banks	*State Banks and Trust Companies*
1863	66	1,466
1864	467	1,089
1865	1,294	349
1866	1,634	297
1867	1,636	272
1868	1,640	247
1869	1,619	259
1870	1,612	325
1871	1,723	452

found it profitable to take out state charters. From that time on the continued growth of the national banking system is to be explained not by a shift of banks from state to federal incorporation but by the growth of the country and the development of trade and production. By 1887 the number of state banks again exceeded the number of national banks. The total capitalization of banks in the national system, though not the total of deposits, remained greater than that of banks outside until the period of World War I. Since the early 1930's national banks have exceeded all other commercial banks by a considerable margin in assets, deposits, and capitalization, even though there are somewhat less than half as many of them.

Major Provisions of the National Banking Act

Organization. The National Banking Act created the office of Comptroller of the Currency under the Treasury Department. Following the general plan of the Free Banking System of New York, it was provided that five or more persons might organize an "association" and apply to the Comptroller for authority to engage in the banking business under conditions laid down in the Act. The Comptroller was required to satisfy himself that the purposes of the association were those stipulated in the law, but not that the individuals were qualified to engage in banking, or that the added banking facilities were needed, or that the bank was likely to succeed. The public interest with respect to these considerations was presumably to be safeguarded by the other requirements of the law and by the self-interest of those concerned.

Minimum capitalization of national banks was determined on the basis of the population of the cities where they were situated, as follows:

Not over 6,000	$ 50,000
From 6,000 to 50,000	100,000
Over 50,000	200,000

By a later amendment it was provided that in a town with a population of 3,000 or less a national bank might be chartered with a capital of only

$25,000, but this provision was repealed in 1933. Stock of national banks was subject to double liability, which means that in case of failure stockholders could be assessed up to the amount of the par value of stock owned. This provision also was removed by the 1933 legislation. The Comptroller of the Currency was placed in charge of administering these and other provisions of the Act, including examination of the banks at frequent intervals.

Note issue. Since the principal purpose of the National Banking Act was the reform of bank note circulation, particular importance is attached to the provisions governing the issue of circulating notes. The law authorized national banks to issue notes up to the lesser of 90 per cent of the face value, or the market value, of United States government bonds deposited with the Comptroller of the Currency. The amount of notes any bank might issue was limited to the total paid-in capital of the bank, and the bank was required to maintain a redemption fund of 5 per cent of its notes outstanding with the Comptroller.[11] National bank notes were backed by the Treasury bonds which had been deposited with the Comptroller of the Currency for use as collateral in case a bank failed. In addition, they were a first lien against the assets of the issuing banks. The notes were not legal tender (until 1933) but were receivable at par in payment of federal taxes.

Reserve requirements. Under the original act, the same reserves were required against both notes and deposits, but in 1874 notes were exempted from the reserve requirements. National banks in *central reserve cities* were required to hold reserves of 25 per cent in lawful money. Banks in *reserve cities* also had to keep reserves of 25 per cent, but half could be in the form of deposits with national banks in central reserve cities.[12] Other national banks, the so-called *country banks,* were required to keep reserves of 15 per cent, but three-fifths could be in the form of deposits with national banks in reserve and central reserve cities. At first New York was the only central reserve city, but later Chicago, and for a time St. Louis, assumed this status. The number of reserve cities, originally sixteen, was forty-nine in 1913.

These reserve provisions gave statutory recognition to the significant growth of the correspondent relationship which had taken place by the time of the Civil War. With the increase in use of demand deposits, and the steady expansion in the geographic scope of markets, outlying banks found it increasingly convenient and necessary to maintain balances with banks in financial centers, and city banks found such balances profitable. Correspondent balances were used by country banks to obtain currency, to pay for checks collected from distant points, for the purchase of securities, and for other money transfers desired by bank customers. The reserve pyramiding effect of the correspondent system was reinforced by the pro-

11. Funds held in the redemption fund could be counted as part of the reserves which banks were required to hold against deposits (see below).
12. For further discussion of this classification of banks, see Chapter 6, p. 99.

visions of the National Banking Act that permitted interbank deposits to serve as legal reserves of national banks.

Other provisions. At the inception of the National Banking System every national bank was required to purchase government bonds totalling one-third its capital stock unless this would amount to more than $50,000. The proportion was later reduced to one-fourth, but the figure of $50,000 as a maximum requirement was retained. Shortly after the entry of the United States into World War I, national banks were relieved of the necessity of holding government bonds except as backing for notes. National banks were prohibited from lending more than 10 per cent of capital (later capital and surplus) to any one borrower. Banks were subject to other restrictions of a rather exacting character, although some of these were relaxed by subsequent amendments. Many years later, for example, national banks were given permission to qualify for carrying on trust business and to grant a limited amount of real estate loans.

Some of the changes introduced were dictated by a desire to place national banks on a more even competitive footing with state banks. With a few notable exceptions, the requirements imposed by the National Banking Act as amended have been appreciably higher than those ordinarily imposed by state banking legislation.

Despite the enactment of sixty amendments between 1864 and 1913 the fundamental character of the National Banking System remained unaltered. The changes which were introduced dealt chiefly with details and for the most part merely served to patch up the existing system in those spots where it had demonstrated weakness.

Later History of the National Banking System

As was indicated above, the number of state banks grew more rapidly than that of national banks after about 1870, even though the number and capital of both were increasing at a rapid rate. The reason for the expansion of both groups of institutions is not hard to discover. The country was growing with phenomenal rapidity, and during the course of that development the use of checks and bank deposits came to replace the older form of hand-to-hand money as the typical means of effecting payment. Whereas in 1865 the deposits of national banks did not greatly exceed the amount of the note issue, by 1907 deposits were nine times the volume of notes. Bank deposits and bank notes constitute alternative forms of bank obligations. The ease with which deposits could be expanded rendered banking a very profitable enterprise during this period, even though banks could no longer freely issue their notes. It is quite possible that the expansion in the use of checking accounts would not have been as rapid at this time if the issue of bank notes had not been so restricted.

Throughout this period of rapid monetary change, the National Banking

System was concerned chiefly with questions regarding the regulation of note issue. Relatively little attention was paid to the regulation of deposits. This was a reflection of the failure of legislators, which has survived to a considerable extent to the present day, to understand the real nature and significance of demand deposits. In the case of the state banks, similarly, relatively little attention was given to regulation of demand deposits. Since state laws were generally more liberal than those of the federal government, many banks preferred to operate under state charters that hampered them less in performing whatever operations they desired to undertake.

The fact that demand deposits came to be by far the most important feature of the circulating medium of the country is of importance in forming any judgment as to the effectiveness of the National Banking Act in accomplishing a permanent reform of our banking system. It signifies that even if the Act had perfectly solved the problem of bank note issue—which, in fact, it did not—there would still have been room for the emergence of other serious banking problems, frequently of a character that could not have been foreseen at the time the National Banking System was created.

Accomplishments of the National Banking System

The foremost achievement of the National Banking System was to realize the principal object of its introduction, namely, the establishment of a safe and uniform bank note issue. From the time when the notes of state banks were driven out until 1914 when notes began to be issued under the authority of the Federal Reserve Act, the only bank notes circulating in this country were those issued by national banks. Various other types of money were, of course, issued during this period by the federal government.

The National Banking System also performed a service for American banking somewhat similar to that rendered by the first and second United States Banks: it set standards of banking requirements and practice which were generally higher than those in force elsewhere in the country. The effect of competition between the systems of national and state banks may at times have seemed to operate toward lowering the status of the former instead of raising that of the latter. But there can be no doubt that the National Banking Act served to improve banking conditions in the country as a whole and helped to maintain them on a higher plane than otherwise would have been likely. In general, the banks that remained outside the National Banking System were smaller than those with national charters. In 1913, for example, the average capitalization of national banks was over $140,000 while that of state banks and trust companies was about $56,000, and this was so in spite of the fact that some of the state banks were very large. The record of the national banks with respect to failures, while far from perfect, was considerably better than that of banks outside the system.

As it later turned out, one of the reasons for the introduction of the Federal Reserve System was to reduce the costs of transferring funds within the country. It is interesting to observe that a similar reduction had earlier been one of the accomplishments of the National Banking System. According to the Comptroller of the Currency:

> The cost to the people for domestic exchange between the commercial points and the remote districts was annually many times greater than the amount of interest now paid to the national banks upon the bonds deposited as security for their circulation, the average rate of exchange between the Eastern and Western States having been from six to twelve and sometimes twenty times the rates prevailing under the national system.[13]

The same source also informs us that the establishment of the system of national banks "was not advocated in the interest of any political party, and from its authorization to the present day it had been free from the control of partisan or sectional influence, its benefits being . . . open to all who may desire to organize banking institutions, subject only to the restrictions which are alike upon all."[14] It is well to add that the system maintained this record of remaining free from corruption and political entanglements. Such charges of favoritism as involved it were directed against the Secretary of the Treasury rather than against the system itself or those charged with its conduct.

Judged in the light of the banking conditions it was intended to improve, the National Banking System must be considered a pronounced success. It accomplished the purpose of providing both a safe and a uniform bank note issue, and it established a banking system subject to better standards of regulation and supervision than had existed theretofore.

The National Banking Act added little, it is true, to what was already commonly known. It consisted largely of piecing together the better features of other banking laws and practices. Indeed, the National Banking System has sometimes been referred to as a "synthesis of earlier banking systems." But this act of synthesis was itself no small accomplishment, and the National Banking Act must stand, along with the Federal Reserve Act and the Banking Act of 1935, as one of the three major legislative achievements in the history of banking in this country.

Major Defects

After the financial crises of 1893 and 1907 the public was considerably more mindful of the defects of the National Banking System than it was of its accomplishments, real as these undoubtedly had been. The

---

13. *Annual Report* for 1875, p. 36.
14. *Ibid.*

shortcomings of the National Banking System that loomed largest in the public mind were the following:

1. A system of reserves and reserve requirements that made for an inelastic supply of bank credit and a proneness to financial crises and panics.
2. An inelastic bank note issue.
3. An inefficient domestic exchange and transfer system.
4. Lack of any central coordination and control that would give unity and direction to monetary affairs.

1. Under the National Banking System the expansion of bank earning assets and deposits was limited by the volume of available bank reserves and the minimum reserve ratios fixed by law. When the banks had expanded to their lending limits, the volume of bank credit became almost completely inelastic since there was no administrative authority empowered to alter reserve requirements or increase the quantity of reserve money.[15] Furthermore, in the absence of any central institution that might supply them with additional reserves, the banks were readily placed in a difficult position by cash drains that pushed them below their reserve minima. This sensitivity to strain was aggravated by the pyramiding of bank reserves under the National Banking System, whereby a substantial part of the reserves of country banks was held in the form of deposits in the banks of reserve cities, and part of the reserves of reserve city banks were held in the banks of the central reserve cities, New York and Chicago. If external drains occurred when the banks were close to their lending limits, country banks attempted to convert their reserve city bank deposits into currency and the reserve city banks attempted to do the same with their central reserve city deposits. In effect, therefore, the currency reserves of reserve city and central reserve city banks supported the liabilities of their own customers plus those of their client banks that held deposit accounts with them. Since the central reserve city banks had nowhere to go to supplement their currency holdings, a small external drain could force the banks to suspend currency payments.[16] The pyramided structure of reserve holdings, with fixed reserve requirements and without any central institution capable of supplying additional reserve funds, seemed almost perfectly designed to generate financial crises.

The defects of the National Banking System were exhibited with the

---

15. Additional reserve money could conceivably be obtained by attracting hand-to-hand currency from the public or by importing gold from abroad. But these methods were either relatively ineffective (especially obtaining currency from the public) or unduly time consuming (importing gold, particularly in periods of tight money). Individual banks could on occasion borrow reserve funds from correspondent banks with surplus cash, but this method was not helpful when virtually all banks felt a shortage of reserves.

16. Moreover, since the precarious position of the banks was widely known, it tended to induce speculative activity in anticipation of bank redemption difficulties, which of course tended to worsen them.

greatest dramatic effect in the frequent financial crises that occurred between the Civil War and the establishment of the Federal Reserve System. Major panics occurred in 1873, 1884, 1893, and 1907, and minor crises also took their toll. These difficulties generally occurred during times when the banks were loaned up and were then for some reason subjected to an external drain of currency. If this drain became at all serious a widespread suspension of convertibility of bank deposits into currency tended to take place, with the banks grimly holding on to their vault cash, thereby aggravating the liquidity crisis. The tightness of credit at such times accounts for the fact, for example, that during crises such as those of 1893 and 1907 the interest rate on call loans in New York rose to 120 per cent a year or even higher. Loans were called or not renewed with the result that customers of banks as well as the banks themselves were subjected to strain. In brief, these crises involved a more or less complete breakdown of the financial machinery of society, which lasted from several days to several months, as in the 1907 crisis.

2. Inelasticity of bank note issue was largely the result of the provision for issuing notes only against the security of government bonds. This tended to cause their issuance to be related not to the volume of business to be transacted but to the movement of interest rates. If interest rates were high (bond prices low) this would tend to induce an expansion in the volume of notes irrespective of need, and the reverse was true in the case of low interest rates (high prices of bonds). It was generally believed that the result was not only to fail to bring about desired changes in note issue but also often to induce just the opposite changes with the result that a credit stringency or excess was aggravated instead of being relieved.

Over longer time periods, the quantity of outstanding national bank notes was influenced by fluctuations in the volume of eligible securities in existence. During the 1880's the stock of government securities available as collateral for national bank notes contracted sharply as budgetary surpluses were used to retire outstanding government obligations. This contributed to a 51 per cent decline in the total volume of national bank notes, from $345 million to $169 million, between 1880 and 1891. The contraction was more unfortunate because it occurred during a period of rapid expansion in population, industrial activity, wealth, and presumably public need for hand-to-hand money.

3. Today it is possible to remit funds by check to practically any place in the country with little or no expense and with a maximum of speed and efficiency. Under the National Banking System this was not so. Charges were made for the transfer of funds between different cities and parts of the country. Domestic exchange was quoted on payments to be made in Chicago from Philadelphia, for example, just as foreign exchange quotations now exist for payments abroad. Nor was this all. In order to minimize charges made by banks in collecting checks presented by other banks, a procedure

known as "routing" was followed. This consisted of sending checks for collection not by the most direct route but through correspondent banks which, because of the business connections they had with the sending bank, would not charge for collecting. Checks might travel a thousand miles in order to get to a point only a hundred miles away. Such a system was not only costly, but clumsy, inefficient, and time consuming.

4. A final major defect of the National Banking System was its failure to provide a central authority responsible for monetary management in the interests of the economy as a whole. As was already noted, the absence of a central banking institution able to create new reserve funds largely explains the inelasticity of the money supply and the recurrence of financial crises. In England and most other economically developed countries there was some central institution to keep an eye on economic and financial developments, to restrain the banks in times of excessive expansion, come to their aid in times of stress, and facilitate the flow of funds throughout the country, in these ways helping to create a unified financial entity. No such central institution was provided under the National Banking System, and consequently none of these functions was carried out effectively prior to the establishment of the Federal Reserve System. The consequences were that:

> During a period of rampant business activity, the volume of bank deposits was steadily expanded, under the pressure of competition, until a halt was called to the process by the reduction of reserve ratios to the legal minimum. When the crisis came, there was no source from which additional reserve funds could be obtained, so that a finanical panic usually supervened. Moreover, the extreme localization and independence of the various banks throughout the country, coupled with the defective exchange and transfer system, resulted in a situation in which funds might be scarce in one part of the country and plentiful in another. There was, therefore, a wide divergence of interest rates among the various geographical sections of the United States. Expressed briefly, there was never any possibility of coordinated and prearranged action on the part of the American banking system as a whole, no matter how strongly circumstances might demand such action. America was equally powerless in the face of a domestic credit crisis, or a foreign drain of gold.[17]

CENTRAL BANKING FUNCTIONS BEFORE THE FEDERAL RESERVE[18]

A central bank, as will be seen later in more detail, is an official or semi-official banking institution which helps to improve the operation of the banking and

---

17. F. Cyril James, *op. cit.*, pp. 208-9.
18. This section is based largely on Bray Hammond, "Historical Introduction," published in *Banking Studies*, pp. 17-25.

monetary system of the country. Its principal task is to promote economic stability. It assists in the administration of basic monetary reserves and creates or absorbs reserves in accordance with changes in community requirements for credit and currency. It provides services for banks roughly similar to those performed by banks for their customers, maintains banking standards, and acts as fiscal agent for the government.

No central bank existed in the United States until the establishment of the Federal Reserve System. This can be said because there was no institution directly charged with responsibility for essential central banking functions. Nevertheless, ways were found to accomplish some of the purposes of a central bank. Some of these substitutes were makeshift arrangements, and none of them succeeded in compensating for the absence of a genuine central bank. The most that can be said is that they helped to make the lack of a central bank somewhat less burdensome than it might otherwise have been.

Activities of the Secretary of the Treasury

One of the skirmishes in the famous Bank War with Jackson was the removal of Treasury deposits from the second Bank of the United States. In 1846 Congress, inspired in part by official distrust of and hostility toward the state banks of the day and in part by the desire to avoid the risk of political involvement with the banks, established the Independent Treasury System. This organization continued in existence until 1920 when its duties were transferred to the Federal Reserve Banks. The avowed purpose of the system, which consisted of subtreasuries distributed throughout the country, was to render the Treasury "independent of the banks."

It was inevitable from the beginning that the operations of the Treasury could not be divorced from the banks and the financial system as a whole. Merely taking in and paying out public funds had inevitable effects on the supply of money and bank reserves available in the market. Although policies varied widely with different administrations, under certain Secretaries of the Treasury these effects were employed deliberately to promote stable financial conditions.

The way in which the Treasury operations were used, after the manner of the open-market operations of the Federal Reserve, to check an overexpansion of credit was described in the annual report of the Secretary of the Treasury for 1856:

> The independent treasury, when overtrading takes place, gradually fills its vaults, withdraws the deposits, and, pressing the banks, the merchants and the dealers, exercises that temperate and timely control which serves to secure the fortunes of individuals and preserve the general prosperity.[19]

---

19. Quoted in *Banking Studies*, p. 23.

At other times the operations of the Treasury were used to expand bank reserves and promote easier banking conditions. Some Secretaries, in contrast, attempted to revert to the original spirit of the 1846 Act and divorce Treasury operations as far as possible from banking. However helpful the actions of the Secretary of the Treasury may have been upon occasion, the lack of consistency and continuity of policy greatly interfered with the exercise of central banking functions by the Treasury.

Banking Substitutes for Central Bank Functions

As was noted earlier, the first and second Banks of the United States acted in the capacity of fiscal agent for the government, helped to improve the quality of bank note circulation, and in general served to maintain banking standards at a relatively high level. In addition, the second Bank of the United States entered into an agreement with the state banks to discount for them when called upon to do so. The Suffolk Bank received from member banks deposits which formed part of their reserves, and by its activities helped to maintain banking standards in its area. In addition, it could lend to the member banks for the purpose of replenishing their balances, and it used its power of providing or refusing credit to promote stable and healthy credit conditions.

The first clearinghouse in the United States was established in New York in 1853. While the purpose of clearinghouses is primarily that of facilitating settlement between banks through the offsetting of balancing debits and credits, they have operated since as long ago as 1860 as a source of emergency funds in time of crises. In every major financial crisis until 1907, clearinghouses issued certificates which could be used to settle balances due the clearinghouse. Sometimes these certificates circulated as currency. Even though clearinghouse certificates were not reserves, their use, whether as currency or to settle balances with the clearinghouse, released legal reserve money for use other than in circulation.

A characteristic feature of American banking practice is the holding of deposits of correspondent banks. In the early 1960's there were 180 commercial banks with deposits due other banks of $10 million or more. Their aggregate correspondent deposits amounted to $14.4 billion, or 6.7 per cent of total bank deposits. In twenty of these banks, interbank deposits amounted to one-quarter or more of their total deposits. The number of correspondent accounts administered by these 180 banks frequently ran into the hundreds and in several cases, into the thousands; one large New York bank is reported to have nearly 4,000 correspondent accounts comprising deposits of banks in every state of the Union. For a considerable number of smaller banks also interbank deposits amounted to from one-fifth to one-fourth of all deposits. Formerly, as has been shown, national banks other than those in central reserve cities were allowed to count deposits with city correspondents as part of their legal reserves; some state banks are still permitted to do so. In holding the legal reserves of other banks and even more in lending to supplement these reserves when they became reduced, city correspondents assumed an important part of the role of a central bank.

From the standpoint of performing the functions of a central bank effectively, however, there was one great flaw in the correspondent relationship. Whenever, as at the harvest season, many banks drew on their reserve balances at the same time, the result was to place a heavy strain on city banks, particularly in New York. Such a situation interfered with their ability to provide for their regular customers and sometimes embarrassed them in meeting the demands of other country correspondents. In time of financial crisis, the situation was even more acute. Reserves became almost completely frozen as banks held on to them in a sometimes frenzied effort to prevent failure. Not only could additional reserves not be created at such a time but also even the reserves already in existence could not be effectively utilized.

It was this kind of situation in an aggravated form that produced a general paralysis of the banking system in 1907. The effect of that experience was to call attention anew to the urgent need for effective central banking machinery and the inadequacy of existing substitutes. The results were stopgap legislation in the form of the Aldrich-Vreeland Act passed in 1908, important investigations which culminated in the report of the National Monetary Commission in 1910, and, ultimately, the passage of the Federal Reserve Act in 1913.

SELECTED BIBLIOGRAPHY

Board of Governors of the Federal Reserve System, *Banking Studies.* Washington: 1941, Chapter 1.

HAMMOND, BRAY, *Banks and Politics in America From the Revolution to the Civil War.* Princeton: Princeton University Press, 1957.

SPRAGUE, O. M. W., *History of Crises Under the National Banking System.* S. Doc. No. 538, 61st Congress, 2nd Session. Washington: 1910.

SUMNER, W. G., *A History of Banking in the United States.* Chicago: Commerce Clearing House, 1896.

TAUS, E. R., *Central Banking Functions of the United States Treasury, 1789-1941.* New York: Columbia University Press, 1943, Chapters II-V.

WHITE, HORACE, *Money and Banking.* Boston: Ginn, 1936, Chapters XVIII-XXIII.

PART FOUR

The Federal Reserve System and Instruments of Monetary Management

12

STRUCTURE AND
FUNCTIONS OF THE
FEDERAL RESERVE SYSTEM

The Federal Reserve System was inaugurated in 1914 under the terms of an act passed the year before which was designed, according to the preamble: "To furnish an elastic currency, to afford means of rediscounting commercial paper, to establish a more effective supervision of banking in the United States, and for other purposes." It will be recognized from the terms of this preamble that the Act was aimed directly toward correcting three of the principal defects of the National Banking System referred to in the previous chapter.

The Federal Reserve Act may be said to have given the United States its first central bank, since earlier institutions in this country that undertook stabilization or regulatory functions, such as the first and second United States Banks and the United States Treasury, as was mentioned previously, lacked the authority and powers of true central banks. The Federal Reserve Act drew heavily on experience with central banking abroad, notably that of the Bank of England which had been since 1694 the leading exemplar of central banking. The Federal Reserve System embodied distinctive features of its own, however, and in its turn has been extensively copied in the organization of other central banks, particularly in Latin America.

The most conspicious contrast between the Federal Reserve System and earlier central banks is that it comprises not one but twelve separate central banking entities. Instead of establishing one bank with branches suitably located throughout the United States, the country was divided into twelve districts differing considerably in population, volume of business, and geographical extent (Figure 12-1). A Federal Reserve Bank, sometimes with and sometimes without branches, was placed at the head of each Federal Reserve District. This arrangement was partly the result of inability to agree on any single city as the headquarters of a central bank and of the desire to satisfy local pride by the establishment of a Reserve Bank in a number of

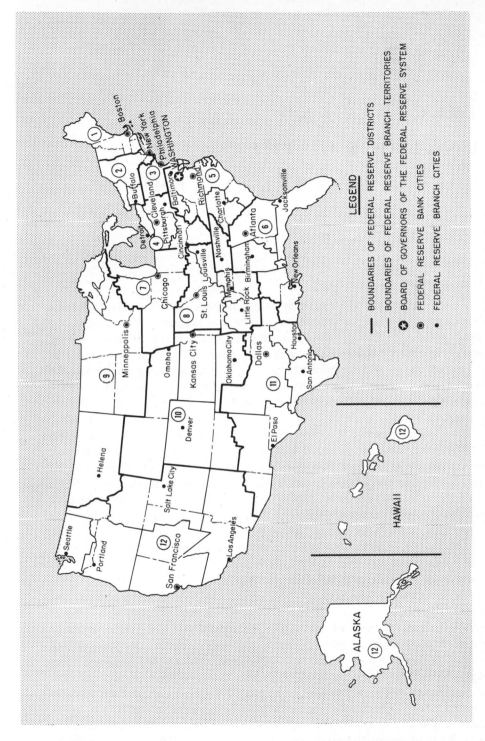

LEGEND

—— BOUNDARIES OF FEDERAL RESERVE DISTRICTS

---- BOUNDARIES OF FEDERAL RESERVE BRANCH TERRITORIES

✪ BOARD OF GOVERNORS OF THE FEDERAL RESERVE SYSTEM

● FEDERAL RESERVE BANK CITIES

• FEDERAL RESERVE BRANCH CITIES

Figure 12-1. Federal Reserve Districts and their Branch Territories.

Source: Federal Reserve Bulletin.

different cities. It was also influenced by the need to allay traditional Western fears of domination of monetary policy by Eastern financial interests.

At the time the Federal Reserve Act was under consideration it was also contended that a country with the size and regional variation of the United States ought to have a number of central banks so that monetary policy could be adapted to the widely varying needs of its different parts. This contention had little merit. The high degree of mobility of financial resources even in 1913 would have made it difficult to maintain regionally independent monetary policies, and any serious attempt at regional independence would certainly have prevented the development of a consistent and effective national monetary policy. Fortunately, because of the coordination worked out among the different Banks and the subsequent centralization of power in the Board of Governors in Washington, the multi-form structure of the Federal Reserve System, while it has served no really necessary purpose, has not constituted a serious handicap.

ORGANIZATION OF THE FEDERAL RESERVE SYSTEM

The organization of the Federal Reserve System consists of five main divisions: the Board of Governors, the twelve Federal Reserve Banks,[1] the Federal Open Market Committee, the Federal Advisory Council, and, finally, the thousands of banks which have taken out membership in the Federal Reserve System. Inclusion of the last as an integral part of the organization means that, in addition to being a central bank, the Federal Reserve also encompasses a system of commercial banks. These so-called "member banks" include not quite half of all commercial banks in the country, but they hold over five-sixths of all commercial banking assets. Each of the five major divisions of the Federal Reserve System will be described in detail.

Board of Governors

The highest administrative division of the Federal Reserve System is the Board of Governors. It consists of seven members, each appointed by the President of the United States for a term of fourteen years subject to confirmation by the Senate. The President designates one of the members to serve as Chairman and another as Vice-Chairman, each for a period of four years. The Chairman is the principal executive officer of the Board and at times has played a particularly dominant part in the affairs of the System. Compensation of members of the Board is $20,000 a year, with the exception of the Chairman, who receives $20,500, sums considerably below

1. Details concerning the Federal Reserve Banks, their branches if any, officers, directors, balance sheets, etc., are published regularly in the monthly *Federal Reserve Bulletin*.

those paid to presidents of the Federal Reserve Banks and of course far below what is paid to the presidents of some of the member banks. Expenses of the Board of Governors are defrayed out of semi-annual assessments levied on the various Federal Reserve Banks.

Appointments to the Board of Governors are spaced so that the term of one of the members expires every other year. A member who has served a full term is not eligible for reappointment. In the selection of members of the Board, the President may choose no more than one from a single Federal Reserve District. Originally it was provided that at least two members of the Board should be experienced in banking and finance but this requirement was abrogated in 1922. The law stipulates that in appointing members to the Board the President: "shall have due regard to a fair representation of the financial, agricultural, industrial and commercial interests and geographical divisions of the country." Presumably this general statement of qualifications was expected to assure that consideration would be given to diverse interest groups affected by the conduct of central banking.

It was further provided that no member may have any connection with a bank or trust company during his term of service, whether as employee, officer, director, or stockholder. If a member of the Board resigns before the expiration of his term, he shall not hold any position with a member bank within a period of two years from the date of his retirement.

The Board of Governors is the principal policy-making body of the System. The task of formulating monetary policy is shared, however, with officials of the Federal Reserve Banks and with the Federal Open Market Committee of which the members of the Board are a part *ex officio*. Various members of the Board participate in the activities of other groups and organizations which are concerned with financial problems, both nationally and internationally. The Chairman consults closely with the Secretary of the Treasury on matters affecting their mutual interests and responsibilities.

The specific powers of the Board of Governors extend to virtually all phases of the Federal Reserve System's activities. The Board is responsible for the issuance of general rules and regulations such as those for the control of margin requirements on credit used to purchase or carry securities. It is charged with supervision of the Reserve Banks, and it has power to suspend or remove any officer or director of a Federal Reserve Bank. It may permit or compel the establishment of Federal Reserve branches in the respective districts and may authorize branches, agencies, and correspondents of Reserve Banks abroad or in our insular possessions. Powers of the Board of Governors over member banks include the authorization of branches, removal of officers and directors for continued violations of the law or for unsafe banking practices, and regulation of interlocking relationships between member banks and non-member banks or security dealers.

The monetary powers of the Board of Governors are also extensive, including among others the following: (1) to review and determine the discount rates charged by the twelve Federal Reserve Banks; (2) along with other members of the Federal Open Market Committee, to control open-market purchases and sales by the Federal Reserve Banks; (3) to change the reserve requirements of member banks within certain limits fixed by law; (4) to suspend temporarily the reserve requirements of member banks and the Federal Reserve Banks; and (5) to regulate lending for the purpose of acquiring securities by fixing margin requirements on security purchases. These powers will be discussed at length in the following chapter.

The Federal Reserve Banks

Each Federal Reserve Bank holds a federal charter which was originally for twenty years but by later amendment was made of indefinite duration.

Capital accounts and distribution of earnings. Each member bank was required to subscribe to the capital of the Federal Reserve Bank of its district to an amount equal to 6 per cent of its own capital and surplus. Only 3 per cent, or half of the subscribed amount, was required to be paid in and it is doubtful that the member banks will ever be called upon to pay the remainder. As member banks expand their own capital and surplus, they must add proportionately to their stock in the Federal Reserve Banks and, similarly, the capital stock of the Reserve Banks is reduced when member banks withdraw from the Federal Reserve System or when their capital accounts are cut down. Member banks are allowed a 6 per cent cumulative dividend on paid-in stock. The largest part of earnings in excess of the 6 per cent dividend are turned over to the Treasury, with a much smaller amount being assigned to surplus.[2]

Paid-in capital of the twelve Federal Reserve Banks was approximately $100 million at the end of 1920, $170 million ten years later, and $139 million and $409 million at the end of 1940 and 1960, respectively. The surplus accounts of the Reserve Banks have continued to grow, with surplus in recent years consistently two or more times the amount of paid-in capital. The paid-in capital of the Federal Reserve Bank of New York represents more than a quarter of the total for all Federal Reserve Banks. Next in order are the Banks of Chicago, San Francisco, Cleveland, and Philadelphia. The smallest are St. Louis and Minneapolis.

Directors and officers. The board of directors of each Federal Reserve Bank consists of nine members comprising three groups known as A,

---

2. Close to a billion dollars has been paid to the Treasury in a single year. Over a period covering nearly a half century of operations the gross earnings of the Federal Reserve Banks were distributed as follows:

Current expenses	28 per cent
Dividends	5 per cent
Surplus	11 per cent
U. S. Treasury	56 per cent

B, and C directors. Each group is chosen on a basis designed to assure the desired breadth of representation and responsibility. Both A and B directors are elected by member banks, A directors from the ranks of bankers and B directors from non-banking pursuits such as industry, trade, and agriculture. In the election of directors, member banks are divided into categories of three sizes according to whether they are large, medium, or small, and each size group elects one A and one B director. Each bank has one vote, except that where more than one bank in the same Federal Reserve district is controlled by the same holding company, only one vote is allowed for the group of banks.

Just as A directors are chosen as representative of the banker interest and B directors as representative of the customer interest, so it was intended that the third category, the C directors, should be representative of the general public interest. They are appointed by the Board of Governors which also designates one of them as the chairman of the Board and Federal Reserve agent and another as deputy chairman. The chairman must be a man of "tested banking experience," but this requirement is interpreted somewhat freely. All directors serve for periods of three years, and their terms are so arranged that one director of each class is elected or appointed each year. For many years after the establishment of the Federal Reserve System, Class C directors were almost exclusively businessmen. In the 1930's it became increasingly common to appoint men from academic posts, but in the early 1960's over three-quarters of the C directors were still connected with business, with most of the remainder from academic circles.

At one time the chairman of the board of directors of each Federal Reserve Bank was required to devote full time to his duties as chairman and Federal Reserve agent. Today much of the work of the Federal Reserve agents is delegated to assistants appointed by the agents. While the chairman of the board and Federal Reserve agent is the official representative of the Board of Governors, the actual administration of the Bank's affairs is the responsibility of the president.

The presidents of the Federal Reserve Banks are appointed by the board of directors for a five-year term, subject to approval by the Board of Governors. The effect of the provisions governing the appointment of the president, which were instituted by the Banking Act of 1935, was to give the Board of Governors greater power over the top administrative personnel of the individual Reserve Banks; the names of the president and first vice-president (who is appointed on a similar basis) automatically come up for approval or disapproval by the Board of Governors every five years. Formerly the post of president was filled by men whose background was typically in business or the law. In recent years it has come to be occupied increasingly by economists. In the early 1960's half of the Federal Reserve Banks were headed by professional economists who had served within the

Federal Reserve System for many years before their appointment to the presidency.

   Conference of presidents. At least four times a year the presidents of the twelve Federal Reserve Banks meet together to discuss problems of mutual concern. Like the meetings which gave rise to the Open Market Committee, these conferences originated spontaneously out of the need for some means of sharing knowledge and coordinating policies. Unlike that committee, however, the conference of presidents has not been accorded formal status in law. While the conference has neither legal standing nor specific powers, it nevertheless enables the presidents to keep posted on what is happening in other parts of the System and to exchange ideas concerning the conduct of a central banking system. Plans and projects for improvement in operating procedures or future development are studied, and the work of carrying them forward may be assigned to subcommittees or to special groups made up of officers and employees of the various Banks. The meetings promote coordination of the work of the twelve Reserve Banks and at the same time facilitate the formulation of an informed and collective point of view in relations between the Federal Reserve Banks and the Board of Governors. The conferences of presidents, informal though they are, constitute an effective instrument for carrying out the work of the Federal Reserve at the highest administrative levels. More or less continuous contacts are maintained throughout the System by direct telephone connection.

The Federal Open Market Committee

   The Federal Open Market Committee was not part of the original plan of the Federal Reserve System. In the early years, purchases of securities in the open market were carried on locally by Federal Reserve Banks acting individually. They were resorted to as a means of acquiring earning assets at times when borrowing and discounting by members banks were insufficient to assure adequate earnings. More or less by accident it was discovered that operations in the open market were capable of having an important effect on the ease or tightness of credit conditions and therefore on business conditions generally. (The actual technique of these operations will be explained in the next chapter.)

   It was soon realized that in order to be sure of achieving desired results, as well as of avoiding undesirable effects, a greater degree of coordination of operations by the different banks in the open market was absolutely essential. Accordingly, a committee consisting of the heads of four (later five) of the Federal Reserve Banks was created in 1923 to effect purchases and sales in the open market in an orderly and systematic way. The initiative for this step came from the Treasury. Subsequently the Board brought the work of the Committee under its supervision and formulated principles for its guidance. Changes in the conduct and composition of the Committee, some of them designed to limit the dominant influence exerted by the Federal Reserve Bank of New York, were introduced from time to time. The Committee was given legal status by the emergency banking legislation of 1933, and in the Banking Act of 1935 assumed approximately its present form.

The Federal Open Market Committee consists of the seven members of the Board of Governors, plus five members chosen from the Reserve Banks. Of this group of five, one is from the Reserve Bank of New York, one from the Boston, Philadelphia, and Richmond Banks, one from the Atlanta, Dallas, and St. Louis Banks, one from the Chicago and Cleveland Banks, and one from the Banks of Minneapolis, Kansas City, and San Francisco. The Federal Reserve Bank of New York acts as the agent of the Committee and an officer of that Bank serves as Manager of the so-called "System Account" through which purchases and sales are conducted.

The Committee usually meets every three weeks in Washington, D. C., with all twelve Federal Reserve Bank presidents in attendance, although only five are members of the Open Market Committee and thus entitled to vote. The meetings have become a forum for the discussion of monetary issues among the leaders of the Federal Reserve System, and, since open market operations are the principal avenue through which monetary policy is implemented, they are the focal point of Federal Reserve policy-making. General directives are laid down to serve as a guide to the Manager of the System Account until the next meeting of the Committee. When necessary consultations are held among the members between scheduled meetings by long distance telephone. Meetings of the Federal Open Market Committee are attended by the Manager of the System Account and top members of the economics staff of the Banks and the Board.

Federal Advisory Council

The Federal Advisory Council consists of twelve members, one appointed by each of the Federal Reserve Banks. Members are usually leading bankers of the district from which they are chosen. They serve for one year but are customarily reappointed year after year. At least four meetings are held each year in Washington and additional meetings there or elsewhere may be called by the Board of Governors or by the Council itself. As its name suggests, the functions of the Council are only advisory and consultative. It is authorized to call for information and to present recommendations on matters relating to the operation of the Federal Reserve System, including particularly such questions as credit policy, gold transactions, note issues, and relations with foreign banks. The Council does not appear to have exerted a great deal of influence on the conduct of the Federal Reserve System, though the indirect and intangible effects of its activities are not easy to determine. The primary importance of the Council is that it enables the operating member bankers of the System to make their views known directly to the Board of Governors.

Member Banks

Composition of membership in the Federal Reserve System. The Federal Reserve Act required all national banks to join the Federal Reserve System. This was one of the means employed to assure that the Federal Reserve System would rest on a broad, strong base comprising a major segment of the commercial banks of the country. In addition, membership was made available to state banks which chose to enter the System and were able to meet the stipulated requirements. With the exception of the period of the depression when deposits of the Federal Reserve System shared the general shrinkage that affected practically all banks, total deposits in the Federal Reserve System have grown continuously with the passage of time.

Throughout its history the Federal Reserve System has comprised a minority of the banks of the country by number but has embraced a majority of banking assets. That is, on the average the banks which stayed out of the System were of smaller size than those in the System. The average size of s͏ te member banks, however, is larger than that of the national banks, since all national banks, large and small, are in the Federal Reserve System, while the state banks which joined were generally the larger ones. At the end of its first decade of existence, the Federal Reserve System embraced 34 per cent of all commercial banks of the United States and 72 per cent of total deposits in commercial banks; ten years later the proportions were 42 per cent and 83 per cent, respectively. In the early 1960's they were 46 per cent and 84 per cent.

The proportion of total banks and banking assets which are within the Federal Reserve System varies substantially from Federal Reserve district to district and from state to state. The relatively small size of many of the banks in the South and Middle West helps to account for the fact that the highest proportion of non-member banks are situated there. At one extreme are such states as Mississippi, Georgia, and Hawaii, with less than one-fifth of their commercial banks members of the Federal Reserve System, and at the other extreme are Massachusetts and New York, with over three-quarters of all commercial banks members of the system.

Member banks were long divided into the three categories of central reserve city banks, reserve city banks, and "country" banks, a classification which was taken from the national banking system. The first category included banks in the two central reserve cities of New York and Chicago. The second category of banks were situated in the reserve cities, which numbered between fifty and sixty. These two categories are now merged. The country banks include all others. The designation of banks is not determined solely by location; banks in outlying sections of large cities may be classified as country banks if they so desire and the character of their business justifies. They are then subject to the rules and requirements imposed upon that category of banks.

As might be expected, the size and character of operations vary appreciably for the different groups of banks. On a recent date sixteen of the member banks of New York City alone held one-sixth of all demand deposits in the system, and they together with thirty banks in Chicago held over one-fifth of the total. On the other hand, the two groups together held less than one-tenth of the system's time deposits. Country banks held a smaller amount of demand deposits than did reserve city banks but a somewhat larger amount of the time deposits. In other words, time deposits are of least importance for the large city banks and of greatest importance for country banks. Even for country banks, however, the volume of demand deposits is substantially greater than that of time deposits.

Conditions of membership in the Federal Reserve System. The standards established for membership in the Federal Reserve System are roughly similar to those of the national banking system. Minimum capital requirements subject to minor exceptions are set at $50,000, $100,000, and $200,000, according to the size of the community in which they are situated. Limitations imposed on types of loans and investments, on loans to individual borrowers and officers, and on the establishment of branches are somewhat more strict than those set by the laws of most states. In addition to requirements directed primarily toward the maintenance of a high level of banking standards, members are subject to certain provisions related to the operation of the Federal Reserve System. One of these is the obligation to subscribe to stock in the respective Federal Reserve Banks. Another requirement is that member banks hold all legal reserves behind their own deposits either as vault cash or in the form of deposits at the Federal Reserve Bank of the district in which the member bank is situated. A further important requirement is to redeem at par all checks properly drawn upon them and to clear at par checks which are processed through the System for collection.[3]

Privileges of membership in the Federal Reserve System. The advantages of membership in the Federal Reserve System are principally those implied in the characterization of the Reserve Banks as bankers' banks. Members enjoy the privileges that go with having their own bank, corresponding generally to the privileges an individual gains from being a customer in good standing of a commercial bank. Member banks are afforded the services of the Reserve Banks in facilitating the transfer of funds, collect-

---

3. "Par clearance" ordinarily refers to the payment in full of a check which is properly drawn on and presented to a bank, or is presented to one bank by another in the process of collection. It is entirely distinct from charges imposed on a customer of a bank for the service of collecting a check drawn on another bank. Charges of the latter sort are still allowed.

ing sums due them, obtaining information, and consulting with responsible experts on special and routine banking problems. They can turn to their respective Reserve Banks and obtain needed funds through borrowing or the discount of commercial paper. Through the relations of one Reserve Bank with another, a member bank, if necessary, can enlist indirectly the resources of the entire Federal Reserve System. And finally, the member bank is assured of a return of 6 per cent on its stock in the Reserve Bank, a rate of return which makes the stock one of its more profitable assets.

Some of the privileges afforded member banks are also available to banks outside the System. A non-member bank, if it maintains correspondent relationship with a member, is able to utilize indirectly most of the facilities of the Federal Reserve System. By depositing checks with a member bank, it can participate in the benefits of the same system of clearing and collection. By discounting paper with a correspondent bank which is a member, it may make use indirectly of the credit facilities of a Reserve Bank. Moreover, the participation of non-member banks in the operation of the Federal Reserve System has been formalized to the extent of creating a special category of institutions known as "clearing banks," which are given the right, upon compliance with certain regulations, to clear directly through the Federal Reserve System in the same way as member banks.

Deterrents to membership in Federal Reserve System. Banks tend to be kept from joining the Federal System by certain positive and negative considerations. One of the positive deterrents is the capital requirements, which are higher than for most state jurisdictions. Another is restrictions on lending practices, which are generally narrower than those imposed by state authorities. Again, state banks may be subject to lower reserve requirements and may be permitted to count as legal reserves deposits with correspondent banks and sometimes certain state and federal government securities. For a large group of banks, the most serious obstacle to membership in the Federal Reserve System is the par clearance provision, which prohibits a member bank from redeeming at a discount checks which are drawn against itself (as well as those received from other banks), even when they call for the payment of cash at some distant point. Redemption of checks at a discount was a long established practice and involved income to the banks running into many thousands of dollars. Consequently, many banks were unwilling to surrender the privilege.

By negative deterrents to membership is meant that many of the benefits of the Federal Reserve System are available to banks, as was noted in the preceding section, whether they join the System or not.

In summary, it may be said that the administrative organization of the Federal Reserve System discloses a significant blending of the characteristics of a private and a governmental institution. It is private in the sense that the underlying membership which constitutes the foundation of the whole system consists of private commercial banking institutions. It is also private in the sense that the Federal Reserve Banks are owned not by the government but by the member banks. Moreover, a majority of the directors of the twelve Reserve Banks are elected by the member banks, and the methods of election are framed to provide full assurance of broad representation and to prevent any group of members from gaining disproportionate power.

On the other hand, the semblance of private ownership is greatly modified by the fact that only limited dividends can be distributed to the stockholders while the bulk of the earnings accrue to the government. One reason for restricting profits in this manner was in order to free the Banks from any inducement to direct their activities toward earnings rather than toward economic stability. The public character is also apparent in the method of appointing the Board of Governors. Members of the central authority of the System are designated by the President of the United States subject to Senate approval. Election of the two top officers of the Reserve Banks must be approved by the Board, and, even though a minority of the directors of the Banks are appointed from Washington, the influence which that minority holds is very great. Finally, the Board has extensive powers over officials not only of the Reserve Banks but even of the member banks.

Attempts made from time to time by Congressional committees to determine the precise status of the Federal Reserve System have not been wholly successful. Apparently the Board of Governors is to be regarded as an "independent establishment" of the government. It is a creature of and subject to Congress but the Federal Reserve Act serves as its constitution with the intention that its operations should not be subject to undue interference by Congress.

The position of the Federal Reserve Banks is even harder to state precisely. They have been described generally as an "instrumentality" of the government. In a joint statement by the presidents of the twelve Federal Reserve Banks they were said to be "part of the private economy and . . . part of the functioning of the Government (although not technically a part of the Government)."[4] It was further stated that they were intended to be "allied to the Government but not . . . a part of the Government itself." Allan Sproul, formerly president of the New York Federal Reserve Bank, summed the matter up by saying that the Banks "should function somewhere between private enterprise and the Government."

4. The references in this paragraph are to Joint Committee on the Economic Report, *Monetary Policy and the Management of the Public Debt* (Washington: 1952), Part 2, p. 649.

FUNCTIONS OF THE FEDERAL RESERVE BANKS

Control of Credit and Stabilization of Business Conditions

The primary central banking function for which the Federal Reserve authorities are responsible is promoting the stability and growth of the national economy. This task is shared jointly by the Board of Governors and the Federal Reserve Banks. The principal "policy" actions of the Reserve Banks, as contrasted with the actions which do not require major policy decisions, fall chiefly under this heading. Non-policy or "service" functions will be described in the remainder of this chapter while a discussion of instruments and policies relevant to stabilizaton and growth will comprise the main content of the chapter that follows.

Bankers' Banks

A graphic but very incomplete description of the Federal Reserve Banks is that they are bankers' banks. This signifies that they provide for the thousands of individual banks which are members of the System the same kind of services that these banks provide for their customers. Member banks hold deposits with the Reserve Banks—deposits which constitute the major part of the legal reserves of member banks. Debits and credits to these deposit accounts are the means of transferring balances among banks, just as checking accounts permit funds to be transferred among individuals. The Reserve Banks provide facilities for conveniently clearing and collecting checks and other cash items.

Just as an individual would ordinarily go to his bank to obtain currency, so member banks typically meet their currency requirements by converting Federal Reserve deposits into Federal Reserve notes and Treasury currency. Federal Reserve notes we have seen to be the main type of paper money in the United States today; they are also the principal liability of the Federal Reserve Banks, usually comprising in excess of 50 per cent of the combined note and deposit liabilities of the twelve Banks.

Finally, where an individual might go to his bank to arrange a loan or to liquidate quick assets, so a member bank requiring additional cash may obtain it by borrowing from the Federal Reserve Bank of its district or through the sale of commercial paper to the Reserve Bank. In fact, in the latter part of the nineteenth century the Bank of England, partly as a result of the writings of the economist, Walter Bagehot, came to regard as its most important function that of acting as the "lender of last resort" to the commercial banks. Discharge of this function was integrated with the use of the discount rate, originally the most important instrument of central bank policy. It was generally accepted that in order to assure confidence and avoid financial panics the central bank should always stand ready to lend additional cash when needed, but at a price high enough to discourage less deserving borrowers.[5] Behind this conception of the duties of a central bank lay the belief that in time of crisis panic is generated by the fear of not being able to secure ready money. Observance of Bagehot's law, as the rule came to be known, was expected to assure that a deserving bank could always obtain additional money when it was needed.

Banks for the Government

The Federal Reserve Banks act as fiscal agents for the Treasury. In this capacity they carry on a multitude of duties involved in: the issue and retirement of public debt; the handling of current checking accounts; the supervision of currency, including the storage, issue, and withdrawal of coins and notes; and the transfer of funds between the United States government and other countries. The Reserve Banks are allowed compensation for some of the services they perform for the government, but the compensation received has seldom covered the cost in full; at times, especially during the war periods, the net cost to the Banks of their contribution to the fiscal operations of the Treasury has been particularly heavy, amounting to many millions of dollars.[6]

At different times, as during World War II and after the start of the Korean conflict, the Federal Reserve Banks have acted as intermediaries in arranging loans to contractors engaged in working for the government. Guarantees for repayment of sums borrowed were given by various branches of the government, but the funds were actually supplied by banks and other private lenders.

The Reserve Banks constitute an important but by no means the sole depository of cash balances of the United States Treasury. The proportion as well as the absolute amount of Treasury balances held with the Reserve Banks have varied widely. In June 1939, total deposits of the United States Treasury were $1,798 million, of which $1,022 million or 57 per cent was held with Federal Reserve Banks and the remainder with recognized depository banks throughout the country. In the period of heavy war financing, Treasury deposits reached extraordinary heights, ranging during 1944, for example, between $7,708 million and $21,596 million. The great bulk of the expanded Treasury deposits were held with depository banks. The peak of Treasury deposit holdings, over $25 billion, was reached in December 1945, at the end of the final war loan campaign. At that time only 6 per cent of

---

5. See Walter Bagehot, *Lombard Street* (New York: Scribner's, 1912), Chapter VII.
6. It may be noted, however, that, since the bulk of the net income of the Federal Reserve Banks ultimately finds its way to the Treasury, larger assessments against the Treasury would merely have increased the income of the Reserve Banks and thus Federal Reserve payments to the Treasury.

the deposits of the Treasury were with Federal Reserve Banks. In recent years Treasury deposit balances have generally fluctuated within a range of 4 to 8 billion dollars. The larger part of the total, often four-fifths or more, is held at the depository banks.

With minor exceptions deposits with the Federal Reserve Banks constitute the Treasury's only active checking accounts. For all practical purposes checks are drawn against deposits with other banks only when it is desired to transfer funds to the Reserve Banks. Disbursements to the public —for salaries, materials, supplies, payments on the national debt, and so on— are generally effected out of Treasury deposits with the Reserve Banks. Treasury deposits with banks other than the Reserve Banks are held in specially designated accounts. The name of War Loan Accounts, introduced during World War I, was employed throughout the entire interwar period to designate deposits of this type. During both wars deposits in War Loan Accounts were exempted from the usual legal reserve requirements. More recently Treasury depository accounts have been known as Tax and Loan Accounts.

Clearing and Collection

In addition to serving the usual purposes of bank reserves, the deposits of member banks with the Federal Reserve Banks provide the means whereby balances are settled between member banks. The bulk of checks drawn on banks within the same city are collected by means of an exchange of checks, carried out daily or more often at local clearinghouses. Net balances are settled by debits and credits on the books of the clearinghouse itself, some local bank, an outside correspondent bank, or the district Federal Reserve Bank. In a somewhat similar manner the Federal Reserve Banks and their branches constitute the center of a simple, efficient, and economical clearing mechanism for the member banks of their respective districts. A large proportion of checks drawn on out-of-town banks pass through the Federal Reserve Banks where they are credited and debited to the appropriate deposit accounts, with the result that the reserves of individual member banks rise or fall daily by the net balances of incoming and outgoing checks.

A non-member bank may collect checks indirectly by handling them through a correspondent bank which is a member, or directly by entering into special clearing arrangements with the Reserve Bank of the district in which it is situated and agreeing to maintain a deposit account with the Reserve Bank sufficient to permit direct debiting and crediting of checks. Not all checks on out-of-town banks are cleared in this way, since banks frequently find it more convenient to collect checks through a correspondent bank in the city where the paying bank is located. For banks located near the boundaries of different Federal Reserve Districts, considerable time and trouble may be saved by collecting checks directly instead of transmitting them by a more roundabout route through the respective Federal Reserve Banks.

The collection through Federal Reserve Banks of checks drawn on banks in another Federal Reserve district brings into play another feature of the Federal Reserve mechanism, namely, the Interdistrict Settlement Fund. Let us suppose that a check drawn on a Philadelphia member bank is deposited at a member bank in Sacramento. The Sacramento bank would send the check to the Federal Reserve Bank of San Francisco and would receive credit in its reserve account.[7] From the San Francisco Bank the check would be mailed to the Federal Reserve Bank of Philadelphia and from the Philadelphia Bank to the bank against which it was drawn, the Philadelphia Bank debiting that bank's reserve account for the amount of the check.

The operations just described would take care of the two member banks, but it is still necessary to explain how the Reserve Bank of San Francisco is reimbursed by the Reserve Bank of Philadelphia. This is accomplished through the Interdistrict Settlement Fund. At the conclusion of each day's business every Federal Reserve Bank communicates to the Board of Governors in Washington the amount that it owes to each of the other eleven Federal Reserve Banks because of that day's transactions. The Board of Governors computes the totals of all sums due to and due from the various Reserve Banks. Each Bank is then debited or credited in the Interdistrict Settlement Fund for the amount of its net balance for that day. The Fund itself is held in the vaults of the Treasury in Washington and comprises a substantial proportion of the legal reserves of the Federal Reserve Banks.[8] Thus the effect of transfers through the Interdistrict Settlement Fund is to raise or lower the reserves of the respective Reserve Banks. The shifting of balances in the Fund constitutes an "internal drain" of reserves among the Federal Reserve Banks.

As a result of the centralization of member bank reserves, the requirement of par collection of checks, and the operations of the Interdistrict Settlement Fund, the inefficiencies of earlier methods of clearing and collecting checks within the United States have been largely corrected.

Regulation and Supervision

The twelve Federal Reserve Banks are charged with supervision of the banks which hold membership in the Federal Reserve System, though part of the task of supervision, as was seen earlier, is shared with the Comp-

---

7. Credit for out-of-town checks is accorded on the basis of a time schedule, based originally on the time required to effect collection. The maximum delay in receiving credit is now two days.

8. On a recent date 30 per cent of the gold certificates constituting Federal Reserve Bank reserves were allocated to the Interdistrict Settlement Fund.

troller of the Currency. It is part of the responsibility of the Federal Reserve Banks to make certain that the requirements prescribed for membership in the Federal Reserve System are fully met. To this end each Federal Reserve Bank maintains a bank examination department staffed with expert auditors and accountants.

The role of the Reserve Banks, however, is by no means exclusively that of policeman and inspector; they serve also in the capacity of mentor and guide. Research departments in the various Banks and at the Board of Governors of the Federal Reserve System in Washington provide the most complete and reliable banking and monetary statistics available anywhere in the world. Officials of the Reserve Banks offer free consultation, which is directed not only toward perfecting the quality of banking operations but also toward keeping the bankers of their districts abreast of economic developments at home and abroad. As part of their bank relations program, they sponsor group discussions of significant problems and have gone so far as to inaugurate costly programs of recruiting and training future bank officers. These activities are carried through at Reserve Bank expense.

Miscellaneous

In the framing of the Federal Reserve Act, the Reserve Banks were carefully precluded from dealing directly with the general public. For one thing, such activities are not a necessary feature of central banks, even though they are a regular part of the operations of many foreign central banks. In addition, it was felt that the opposition of the banking community to the introduction of the Federal Reserve System would be much keener if the Reserve Banks appeared as probable competitors. While the tradition of not competing with private banking institutions has been carefully maintained, provisions were introduced during the depression for limited dealings with the public. As part of the recovery program, Reserve Banks were authorized under Section 13b of the Federal Reserve Act to make loans with maturities up to five years in cases where borrowers had been refused accommodation by other lending institutions. In addition, "commitments" could be made whereby, in return for a charge ranging from ½ per cent to 1¼ per cent per annum, the Reserve Bank agreed to lend up to a specified amount if called upon to do so. Both loans and commitments could be shared with other lending institutions.

The volume of these so-called "industrial loans" was never very large; the highest year-end total was $32,500,000 in 1935 for all twelve Federal Reserve Banks. Some expansion occurred after the start of fighting in Korea but for many years the total for the entire system was no more than a few million. The significance of these loans lay not in their absolute amount but in their extension of the original concept of the Federal Reserve System and in the precedent they established for possible use in future emergencies.

Authority for the Reserve Banks to make loans and commitments for industrial purposes was terminated in 1959.

The very nature of the Reserve Banks in the financial organization of the economy gives them a position of leadership in their respective districts. Moreover, they provide services too numerous and varied to permit classification. Some of these services extend far beyond the banks which hold membership in the System, ranging from consulting with the heads of great insurance companies on conditions in the financial markets or the probable course of government finance to assisting an educator in the preparation of a commencement address.

SELECTED BIBLIOGRAPHY

BACH, G. L., *Federal Reserve Policy-Making*, New York: Knopf, 1950, especially Chapters II, VIII, and XIV.

Board of Governors of the Federal Reserve System, *The Federal Reserve System*. Washington: 1961, Chapters I, IV, VIII-X, XIV.

———, *Banking Studies*. Washington: 1941.

———, *The Federal Reserve Act as Amended* (reissued periodically to incorporate changes resulting from revisions in the law).

Commission on Money and Credit, *Money and Credit*. Englewood Cliffs, N. J.: Prentice-Hall, 1961, pp. 81-93.

Joint Committee on the Economic Report, *Monetary Policy and the Management of the Public Debt*. S. Doc. No. 123, Part 1 (Washington: 1952), pp. 239-337.

WILLIS, H. PARKER, *The Federal Reserve System*. New York: Ronald, 1923, Chapters VII-XXI, XXIII-XXVI.

13

INSTRUMENTS OF
FEDERAL RESERVE
MONETARY MANAGEMENT

Valuable as are the service functions of the Federal Reserve System discussed in the preceding chapter, major interest and controversy centers in those which are directed toward promoting the stability and growth of the economic system. These may involve efforts to stimulate an expansion of total money expenditures at one time and to resist it at another. They may also involve attempts to direct financial resources into (or away from) channels regarded as particularly desirable (or undesirable) from the standpoint of the economy as a whole. This may be done by the application of controls that discriminate, for example, against lending for stock market speculation and in favor of the financing of industry and agriculture.

The responsibility for making decisions in the area of monetary control rests chiefly with the Board of Governors and with the officers and directors of the Federal Reserve Banks. Responsibility for carrying these decisions into effect is mainly in the hands of the Federal Open Market Committee and the officials of the twelve Federal Reserve Banks. In the present chapter we shall examine the instruments of Federal Reserve policy. In the succeeding chapter we consider briefly the monetary powers of the Treasury, which, although primarily a fiscal agency implementing expenditure and tax decisions made by Congress and the President, has such extensive dealings in money and securities as to exert significant monetary effects. In the next chapter we shall also extend our discussion beyond the instruments of monetary management to a review of the larger complex of factors influencing the volume of bank reserves.

The instruments for managing the money supply may be classified as general and selective. The general instruments are directed toward influencing the total quantity, availability, and cost of money, without special regard for the use to which it is put. The selective controls, on the other hand, single out ("select") certain areas of monetary expenditure and then attempt to stimulate or restrict the flow of funds to these particular sectors. Thus far in this country the selected areas have included stock market lending, consumer credit, and real estate credit.

THE GENERAL INSTRUMENTS OF MONETARY CONTROL

The general instruments of monetary control are designed to influence the quantity of money, primarily by altering the volume of "free reserves" available for expanding deposits.[1] They are indirect means of monetary control since their major focus is on the reserve position of banks rather than on deposits. The use of the general instruments of monetary control presumes that changes in commercial bank holdings of earning assets and deposits (and hence the size of the money supply) can be controlled by altering the net reserve position of the member banks.

The three instruments of general monetary control are the discount mechanism, open-market operations, and changes in reserve requirements. They relate to the different ways in which reserves can be made more or less available to commercial banks.

The Discount Mechanism

The only instrument for credit control which was embodied in the original Federal Reserve Act was the provision for discounting (or, alternatively, "rediscounting") commercial paper presented to the Reserve Banks by member banks. It was intended that a bank needing additional reserves would simply turn to its Federal Reserve Bank and sell (i.e., "discount") some of its assets—at prices governed by the discount rate—in exchange for the desired reserves. Each Reserve Bank would thus play the role of banker for the member banks of its district.

Discounts. To be eligible for discount at a Federal Reserve Bank, it was early established by the Federal Reserve Board that paper had to be in the form of promissory notes or bills of exchange which had been used to provide working capital for business or agriculture. Bills of exchange must have arisen out of the sale of goods and must have been drawn against the buyer, in the case of a trade acceptance, or against a bank, in the case of a bank acceptance. Paper used to provide fixed capital or funds for speculative purposes or to deal in other securities, such as stocks and bonds, was specifically excluded. Commercial and industrial paper was required to have a maturity at time of discount of not more than ninety days, except for

---

1. As noted earlier (Chapter 6) "free reserves" are defined as excess legal reserves of member banks less member bank borrowings from the Federal Reserve Banks. Where borrowings are larger than excess reserves the negative free reserves are commonly referred to as "net borrowed reserves."

certain types of paper which might run six months if secured by readily marketable staples. Agricultural paper had to have a maturity at time of discount of not more than nine months.

These *eligibility* requirements were designed to confine the discounting by member banks at the Federal Reserve Banks to self-liquidating commercial and agricultural paper. With an expansion in business activity, it was assumed that there would be an increase in the volume of paper brought to the banks for discounting. If the expansion in bank credit called for additional bank reserves, reserves could then be obtained by the member banks discounting at the Reserve Banks some of the eligible paper which they had received from their customers. With a contraction in the volume of business, a reduction in the volume of paper would bring about a contraction in outstanding Reserve Bank credit and, therefore, in the volume of member bank reserves. Thus changes in the volume of business activity were expected, through the discounting of eligible paper, to provide an automatic regulation of the volume of credit. The Federal Reserve authorities might influence adjustments by raising or lowering the discount rate, but even then the Federal Reserve was passive since the change in the discount rate would become effective only when member banks, on their own initiative, came to the Reserve Banks to discount eligible paper.

By 1923 the Federal Reserve Board had established the principle of *acceptability* by declaring that discounting by member banks was a privilege of membership and not a right. They announced that even though a member bank presented paper which fully met the tests of eligibility, it might be refused if the Reserve authorities found it in the public interest to do so. The reason for refusing was to be clearly indicated. The substitution of acceptability based on the will of the Reserve authorities for eligibility based on formal rules constituted a significant step in the retreat from the conception of an automatic banking system.

Advances. Another significant departure from the original idea of an automatic system occurred with the introduction of "advances" during World War I. According to a 1916 amendment to the Federal Reserve Act, member banks were permitted to obtain reserves from the Federal Reserve Banks by borrowing directly from the Banks on their own promissory notes (in contrast with the *sale* of eligible paper in the case of discounts). These advances had to be secured by Treasury obligations or paper eligible for discount, they ran for fifteen days with Treasury collateral and ninety days if collateral was in the form of eligible commercial paper, and they carried interest at the prevailing discount rates.

To Federal Reserve authorities, the difference between discounts and advances has been only a matter of form and not of substance. The effect on member bank reserves is the same in either case, and the cost is also ordinarily identical. The reason for extending Reserve lending power to the making of advances on the promissory notes of member banks was for the convenience of the banks,[2] and in recent years virtually all member bank borrowing from the Reserve Banks has been done on the basis of advances rather than discounts.

In the strained conditions that prevailed in the early 1930's banks found themselves with limited resources in the form of commercial paper eligible for discounting or Treasury obligations suitable as collateral for advances. Various temporary measures were introduced to broaden the base for granting advances. The Banking Act of 1935 granted permanent authority to the Federal Reserve Banks to make advances for periods to four months on promissory notes secured by any assets acceptable to the Reserve Bank. These advances must be at rates not less than ½ per cent above the current discount rate. Under this provision a member bank may be able to obtain credit, if the Reserve Bank is favorably disposed, on mortgages, bonds, and security loans, all of them types of assets which were excluded from the privilege of discounting by the terms of the original Federal Reserve Act. Thus the Amendment of 1935 greatly extended the power of the Reserve Banks to provide reserves for member banks. It was primarily intended, however, to enable the Reserve Banks to cope with the problem of bank liquidity in time of emergency. In the ordinary course of operations, advances to member banks have generally been made only against the pledge of Treasury obligations.

The rise and then the extension of advances had implications beyond the routine mechanics of credit operations. Although the initiative in borrowing by means of advances remained with the member bank, the extension of credit by the Reserve Banks was no longer based solely on self-liquidating commercial paper. It might rest on collateral in the form of Treasury obligations, whose volume could in no way be assumed to vary directly with the volume of business activity. The element of automatic regulation of the volume of credit was still further attenuated when the provision governing advances was extended to permit the pledging of any asset acceptable to the Federal Reserve authorities. The initiative still rested with the member banks, except to the extent that their willingness to borrow may have been influenced by changes in the discount rate. But the types of asset now eligible and the discretionary power placed in the hands of the Federal Reserve authorities meant that the basis of credit operations was utterly foreign to that of the traditional theory.

---

2. The preference for advances was influenced in part by the desire to retain commercial paper in the bank's portfolio because this was felt to contribute to good relations with the bank's customers. It was also a result of the flexibility with which collateral, especially government obligations, may be arranged to cover the loan. Banks frequently hold government securities for safekeeping at their local Federal Reserve Bank, so that instead of having to transport the collateral the borrowing bank can merely indicate which of its securities it wishes to use as collateral to cover its advance. For purposes of collateral for advances government securities are valued at par rather than market value.

The Role of the Discount Mechanism

The discount mechanism has served a dual role in the monetary structure of the United States: first, as one of the means whereby commercial banks have been able to replenish temporarily deficient reserve accounts,[3] and, second, as one of the weapons of monetary control used to restrain or stimulate economic activity.

It was noted earlier that accommodation of commercial banks by rediscounting commercial paper was an important central banking function envisaged in the Federal Reserve Act and in the widely accepted view of the central bank as a "lender of last resort." From this standpoint borrowing from the central bank may be regarded as a "part of the mechanism of *defensive* arrangements that can give each of the thousands of independent unit banks a supplemental source of temporary reserves to help meet the sudden and often unexpected reserve drains that may at any time strike any of them."[4] Such drains are particularly important because of the relatively decentralized banking system of this country, where a large proportion of clearings are *between* banks. "The flows between banking offices that create many of the individual bank reserve problems here are, in England [with its few branch systems], either balanced out within each of the branch systems or settled as net residuals through the money position adjustments made by their principal offices in London."[5] In our institutional environment the discount mechanism provides a supplementary source of reserves that cushions individual banks against the impact of unusual sources of reserve instability.

As an instrument of monetary control, the discount mechanism operates mainly through the impact of changes in the cost of accommodation on member bank borrowing, although variations in the intensity of administrative restrictions on borrowing could have monetary effects. The discount rate represents the price at which the Reserve Banks stand ready to sell or lend reserves to member banks in exchange for eligible paper or for a bank's promissory note backed by satisfactory collateral. A change in the discount rate means, in simplest terms, that the reserve authorities have raised or lowered the price at which they will sell or lend reserves to member banks. Assuming a given degree of administrative regulation and disregarding psychological influences, the effectiveness of this instrument of control will depend on the responsiveness of borrowing from the Federal Reserve Banks to changes in the discount rate. If bank borrowing is sensitive to the discount

---

3. They can also obtain reserves by selling Treasury bills or other readily marketable debt instruments in the open market, or by borrowing "Federal funds." These other devices do not involve an increase in the reserves of the banking system, as does borrowing from the Reserve Banks. But, except in periods of severe general liquidation, they present a satisfactory alternative to many individual banks.

4. Robert V. Roosa, *Federal Reserve Operations in the Money and Government Securities Markets* (New York: Federal Reserve Bank of New York, 1956), p. 15.

5. *Ibid.*

rate, a rise will restrict discounts, reserves, and ultimately earning assets and deposits. A lowering of the rate will tend to have the opposite effect.

There are several reasons for believing that bank borrowing is not likely to be strongly responsive to discount rate changes. For one thing, in the United States there is a "tradition against borrowing" by bankers that makes them reluctant to borrow from the Reserve Banks or to stay in debt for a long period (presumably to avoid giving the impression of weakness). This tradition antedates the Federal Reserve System but it was reinforced by the Federal Reserve authorities, who took the position that the discounting privilege is for meeting special or emergency needs, such as unexpected drains of cash or abnormally heavy loan demands. Where bank borrowing has been used continuously or for obviously profit-making purposes, the Reserve authorities have indicated disapproval. The result has been that administrative restrictions on access to the "discount window" at the Reserve Banks have tended to reinforce the tradition against borrowing in keeping the volume of member bank borrowing small, even though the discount rate has generally been at levels well below those charged their customers by member banks.

Following an all-time peak in member bank borrowing of $2.5 billion in the postwar boom of 1920 (a sum greater than total required reserves), borrowing remained relatively high in the 1920's, averaging about $600 million most of the time and between 25 and 40 per cent of the volume of required reserves. Excess reserves rose to substantial levels after 1932 and borrowing virtually disappeared (see Figure 6-1, p. 94). Borrowing revived somewhat during World War II, but then fell to about 100 to 200 million dollars until 1951. In the early 1950's an effort was made by the Federal Reserve authorities to moderate the hostility toward borrowing and make resort to advances more respectable among member banks. The reasoning was that if reserves had been obtained by borrowing, the necessity of paying off the loan would tend to reduce the amount of reserves thus created as soon as the need for them had passed. If reserves were provided by the purchase of Treasury obligations by the Reserve Banks, on the other hand, there would be no such automatic tendency toward subsequent contraction. Consequently, reserves might continue in existence and thereby contribute to building up inflationary pressures. At a time when inflation had come to be regarded as a continuing threat this difference loomed large in the minds of central bankers.

That some headway was made in overcoming the tradition against borrowing may be inferred from a sharp increase in the volume of discounts and advances after 1950. At times total borrowings rose above 1 billion dollars, and for most of the period after 1951 it was above $500 million. Even at these levels, however, it was considerably less important than before 1930. (During the 1920's the ratio of borrowings to required reserves never fell below 10 per cent; in the later period it never reached as high as 10 per cent.)

It should especially be noted that the increased resort to borrowing by member banks after 1950 was influenced not only by the attitude of the Reserve authorities but also by the great inducement to borrowing which resulted from the relatively low level of excess reserves and the strong demand for loans by the public.

Despite the influence of the tradition against borrowing, the profit factor as well as strictly emergency needs appears to affect the volume of member bank borrowing. Banks are regularly faced with decisions as to how they should alter their assets and liabilities so as to keep reserves at a desired level. They may adjust to the desired level by varying the volume of borrowing from the Reserve Banks, by borrowing Federal funds, or by buying or selling assets in the open market (usually Treasury bills). If banks require more reserves they will consider whether to sell Treasury bills or borrow. With the discount rate high relative to the rate on Treasury bills, banks tend to sell bills in the open market. If the discount rate is raised, the inducement is so much the greater for a reduction in borrowing and an increase in sales of open-market obligations. We should therefore expect changes in the discount rate to have some effect on the volume and distribution of bank reserves.

If, however, the bulk of member bank borrowing is confined to meeting emergency requirements, which appears to be the case, the volume of discounts is not likely to be very sensitive to moderate changes in the discount rate. Furthermore, if the discount window is kept open to accommodate abnormal needs of banks, it may sometimes enable the banks to offset (as well as cushion individual banks against) the effects of other instruments of monetary management. If open-market sales by the Federal Reserve to put pressure on bank reserves were to induce borrowing from the Reserve Banks, the impact of such sales would be dissipated to that extent. This possibility is no doubt limited, but borrowing does afford some means of escape from pressures generated by other instruments.

Finally, the possibility of effects of discount rate changes on expectations must be considered. The standard view is that rate increases will depress expectations, make bank lending more cautious, and thus reinforce tight money. But it is also possible that they might stimulate borrowing in anticipation of further rises. It is also possible that a rise in the discount rate may be interpreted as confirming bullish, or even inflationary, forecasts and therefore serve to accelerate business expansion plans instead of retarding them.

On the whole, the most widely held view is that the effects of discount rate changes are likely to be in the right direction but weak. Thus the main function of the discount mechanism has been to aid banks in meeting temporary strains on their reserve position. It enables the Federal Reserve Banks to function as the lender of last resort but it is not a major control device. In recent years the volume of borrowing by member banks has not been large nor has the number of banks making use of the facility been high.

Open-Market Operations

Open-market operations have come to be regarded as the most important of all the instruments of monetary management. As was mentioned previously, the Federal Reserve Act gave the Reserve Banks the power to buy and sell certain types of securities in the open market. The original expectation was that this power would be used merely to enable the Reserve Banks to acquire sufficient earning assets to pay their necessary expenses at times when there was little discounting by member banks. As a result of buying operations carried on in the early 1920's, it was observed that the effect of these purchases of securities in the open market was to increase member bank reserves and the money supply and thereby ease credit conditions. The authorities soon realized that such operations could be used not just as a means of obtaining earning assets but for purposes of monetary control.

The way in which open-market operations can be used to control credit may be seen by observing their balance sheet effects. When the Reserve Banks, through the Federal Open Market Committee, purchase securities in the open market, payment is made in the form of checks drawn on the Reserve Banks.[6] If the seller of the securities is a member bank, the check it receives as payment is deposited at its Reserve Bank and the legal reserves of the member bank are thereby immediately increased. The accounts of the Reserve Bank and the commercial bank will have changed as follows:

RESERVE BANK		COMMERCIAL BANK	
Assets	*Liabilities*	*Assets*	*Liabilities*
+Securities	+Member bank reserve deposits	−Securities +Reserve with Federal Reserve Bank	

If the seller is a corporation or individual, the check which is received in payment is almost certain to be deposited within a short time at the seller's

6. All open-market purchases and sales are made through established government securities dealers, several of which are commercial banks with government securities departments. Simple but effective means exist for carrying out the mechanical details of the transactions. A large New York bank, the Manufacturers Trust Company, serves as a clearing agent. Actual delivery of government securities purchased or sold are effected through a cage which it maintains at the Federal Reserve Bank of New York. The Federal Reserve Bank credits or debits the account of the Trust Company which, of course, makes the appropriate entries in the deposit accounts maintained with it by the government securities dealers. In the case of transactions with one of the commercial banks, debits or credits may be made directly to the respective bank's reserve account with the Federal Reserve Bank.

bank. The bank, in turn, deposits this check to its account at its Federal Reserve Bank, and, in this case also, the bank's legal reserves are immediately increased by the amount of the open-market purchase. In addition, in this instance the volume of demand deposits also increases immediately by the amount of the security purchase.[7] The changes in the relevant accounts are as follows:

RESERVE BANK		COMMERCIAL BANK	
Assets	*Liabilities*	*Assets*	*Liabilities*
+Securities	+Member bank reserve deposits	+Reserve with Federal Reserve Bank	+Demand deposits

The opposite occurs when the Reserve Banks sell securities in the open market. If the buyer is a commercial bank, the bank acquires securities and loses reserves of the same amount, as in the following balance sheets:

RESERVE BANK		COMMERCIAL BANK	
Assets	*Liabilities*	*Assets*	*Liabilities*
−Securities	−Member bank reserve deposits	+Securities −Reserve with Federal Reserve Bank	

If the buyer is an individual or non-bank business concern, checks drawn to pay for the securities will be given to the Reserve Banks. This will result in a reduction in member bank deposits at the Reserve Bank and the buyer's deposit at the member bank by the amount of securities bought and sold. The transactions involved are described in the following balance sheets:

RESERVE BANK		COMMERCIAL BANK	
Assets	*Liabilities*	*Assets*	*Liabilities*
−Securities	−Member bank reserve deposits	−Reserve with Federal Reserve Bank	−Demand deposits

In both cases the reserves of the member banks are reduced by the amount of securities sold by the Federal Reserve authorities. The direct effect on the money supply differs in the two cases, but the potential monetary effect is

7. In both of these cases the potential deposit expansion is identical. In this instance, however, the transaction having increased demand deposits of the bank by the amount of the security sale, excess reserves are less than in the previous case, where the full expansion potential remains to be realized.

identical. In general, open-market operations may be said to expand or contract the reserves of member banks and by this means to extend or restrict the power of member banks to increase earning assets and demand deposits.

The adoption of measures which allowed the Federal Reserve authorities to take the initiative was an acknowledgment that in order to make monetary control effective, a central bank must be able to act positively and without delay. While the element of monetary management is present even in the case of discounts and advances, it is carried to much greater lengths by the use of open-market operations. More especially, in contrast to control by means of discount policy, all semblance of an automatic system of adjustment in reserves disappears.

One of the lessons in the conduct of open-market operations which was learned fairly early was the importance of coordinating them with discount policy. The problem of coordination between open-market operations and discount policy manifests itself in two ways. First, if member banks are in debt to the Reserve Banks, the proceeds of open-market purchases may merely lead to a reduction of indebtedness with no net increase in bank reserves. Such improvement in liquidity as results takes the form of a reduction in banks' indebtedness, not of an increase in reserves. Second, the question of coordination arises in the use of open-market operations to prepare the way for changes in the discount rate. Sales of securities in the open market were sometimes used to tighten credit and put the banks in a position where they had to borrow and thereby face the penalty of the higher discount rate then in effect. This was often referred to as using open-market operations as a means of "making the discount rate effective."

Open-market operations are considered in this chapter primarily in relation to their effect on member bank reserves. It is important to recognize, however, that their use has not been confined to this purpose alone. In the early years of the Federal Reserve it was desired to increase the popularity of bankers' acceptances. These were drafts drawn usually by a seller against a buyer which were "accepted" by a bank in order to make them more readily marketable. It was thought that their development would help to provide the kind of ready discount market that was lacking under the National Banking System. The Federal Reserve undertook to buy such paper at a rate of discount more favorable than the official discount rate. Such purchases were very important in the 1920's but have been small in recent years.

Another example of the use of open-market operations not solely for purposes of providing reserves occurred in the later 1930's when the Federal Reserve bought government securities, at a time when excess reserves were already burdensome, for the purpose of maintaining orderly conditions in the security markets. In its annual report for 1938 the Board of Governors justified the action as helping to steady the entire capital market and to safeguard member bank portfolios from undue fluctuations in bond prices.

Later the Federal Reserve found itself using open-market operations to maintain a relatively fixed pattern of interest rates on Treasury securities, a problem which will be discussed later.

Open-market operations, then, have shown a lengthy and somewhat involved development. Operations have been directed toward a wide variety of instruments including bankers' acceptances, Treasury bills, and many other types of Treasury obligations. For many years open-market operations have been limited almost exclusively to United States government securities. And for a considerable period after World War II the attempt was made to confine open-market operations to Treasury bills, the so-called "bills-only policy." Purposes have varied from the obvious goal of changing the volume of member bank reserves to providing earning assets for the Reserve Banks and maintaining orderly, or even "pegged," conditions in the security markets. One of the great virtues of open-market operations is their adaptability and versatility. It is one of the reasons for believing that they will continue to occupy a major place in Federal Reserve policy.

Changes in Reserve Requirements

As early as 1916 the Federal Reserve Board suggested that it be given power to raise the reserve requirements of member banks, on the ground that this would enable the Federal Reserve to "check any tendency toward . . . undue extension of credit." It was not until 1933, however, that the provision for changing reserve requirements was finally enacted into law. It was given permanent instead of emergency status by the Banking Act of 1935. The period when this law was passed was characterized by a large volume of excess reserves and a heavy movement of gold to this country, conditions closely resembling those that had given rise many years before to the original suggestion for changing reserve requirements. By the Act of 1935 the Board of Governors was authorized, on the affirmative vote of four members, to raise or lower reserve requirements of member banks within the range of from one to two times the percentages required at the time of the enactment of the law. Requirements could be altered for all member banks or for any of the three categories of banks separately.

The original limits and rules of procedure have been changed only slightly over the years. In the early 1960's the difference between the reserve requirement limits of reserve city and central reserve city banks was eliminated in anticipation of the merger of the latter classification into that of reserve city. With this change the limits in effect were 7 per cent minimum and 14 per cent maximum on net demand deposits for country banks and 10 and 22 per cent limits for all others. On time deposits the limits were 3 and 6 per cent for all member banks.[8]

---

8. Provisions initiated in 1959 authorizing the inclusion of vault cash in legal reserves were equivalent to a minor reduction in the effective limits of reserve requirements.

Discount policy and open-market operations are designed to alter the total quantity of reserves and thereby the amount of free reserves. A change in reserve requirements, on the other hand, alters the volume of free reserves directly. While total reserves remain unchanged, the quantity available for deposit expansion or other purposes is increased or decreased by the simple expedient of declaring that a smaller or larger share of the total must be counted as required reserves. The effect of such a change extends beyond the volume of reserves thereby impounded or made available: it also governs the amount of deposits that can be created on the basis of each dollar of new reserves.

For example, with a reserve requirement of 25 per cent, $25 million of reserves would be required to support $100 million of deposits, as in the balance sheet below:

COMMERCIAL BANKS

Assets		*Liabilities*	
Reserves	$25 million	Deposits	$100 million
⎡ Required $25 million ⎤			
⎣ Excess 0 ⎦			

But a reduction in the legal requirement to 20 per cent would reduce the volume of reserves tied up in the required category by $5 million, releasing these reserves for use in the creation of additional bank deposits. This is shown in the following balance sheet:

COMMERCIAL BANKS

Assets		*Liabilities*	
Reserves	$25 million	Deposits	$100 million
⎡ Required $20 million ⎤			
⎣ Excess 5 million ⎦			

Similarly, an increase in reserve requirements increases the amount of required reserves at the expense of the excess category. Thus an increase in the reserve requirement from 20 to 25 per cent will reabsorb the $5 million of excess reserves in the required category. With an increase in reserve requirements when the banks have no excess reserves, they would be forced to liquidate assets until deposits fell to a level in line with the existing volume of reserves.

Viewing the general instruments of credit control historically, open-market operations are seen to have been of the greatest continuing importance. Of the four periods of substantial and rapid expansion in Federal Reserve credit, discounts were the most important vehicle from 1918 to

1921, and United States government securities of various denominations in the other three periods—the 1930's, the period of our participation in World War II, and the years of the Korean conflict (1950-1952). The discount mechanism has been of distinctly subordinate importance since the 1920's. Reserve requirement changes have been used only sporadically, chiefly as a means of effecting major adjustments in the volume of excess reserves.

Limits to Federal Reserve Credit Expansion

In order to carry out monetary management functions by means of the general instruments of control the Federal Reserve authorities must be able to increase and decrease the free reserves of member banks. This can be accomplished either by lowering reserve requirements or by expanding the volume of Federal Reserve credit outstanding (by increasing advances or acquiring securities in the open market). The basic factor limiting the ability of the Reserve Banks to create member bank reserves is the same as that limiting the ability of member banks to create deposits, namely, the reserves each is required to hold against its deposit liabilities. As in the case of member banks, the maximum amount of deposit credit, i.e., member bank reserves, that can be created on the basis of a given amount of Reserve Bank reserves is governed by the reciprocal of the reserve ratio which the Reserve Banks are required to maintain.[9]

The Federal Reserve Banks are subject to a minimum reserve requirement fixed by law at 25 per cent of their note and deposit liabilities. This requirement may be met solely by gold·certificates, which therefore constitute the legal reserves of the Federal Reserve Banks. With a 25 per cent legal reserve requirement, it follows that the total of note and deposit liabilities must not exceed four times the amount of gold certificates owned by the Federal Reserve Banks. Neither the legal reserve requirement of the Banks nor their holdings of gold certificates are subject to control by the Federal Reserve authorities: the former is fixed by act of Congress, while the volume of gold certificates owned by the Banks depends on the size of the monetary gold stock of the Treasury.[10]

If we assume a 20 per cent legal minimum reserve requirement for commercial banks, and no external drain, the banks would be able to expand deposits by five times the amount of any additional reserves. This means that potentially a dollar of Federal Reserve Bank reserves (gold certificates) can support twenty dollars of commercial bank deposits: it can support directly four dollars of Federal Reserve Bank deposit and note liabilities,

---

9. The law permits some flexibility in these requirements at times of emergency.

10. In accordance with policies followed since before World War II, all gold that enters (or leaves) the monetary system results in an equivalent addition to (or subtraction from) the volume of gold certificates held by the Reserve Banks. See p. 272.

which can in turn, if held as member bank legal reserves, support five times that amount of deposits.

It is of course extremely important to recognize that the central bank is subject to a different set of motivations and pressures from commercial banks, and as a consequence its expansion potential has a different significance from that of the commercial banks viewed in isolation. Commercial banks are private businesses, and a strong impulse toward realizing their potential deposit limits may be regarded as a likely consequence of the profit motive. The Federal Reserve Banks, on the other hand, are not significantly influenced in their monetary actions by probable effects on their income. Moreover, a substantial volume of excess central bank reserves is essential for flexibility of action. Ordinarily the Federal Reserve Banks maintain a liberal stock of the basic ammunition necessary for central bank action—a supply of government securities that can be sold in the open market to contract bank reserves and excess central bank legal reserves that permit an expansion of Federal Reserve credit.[11]

THE SELECTIVE INSTRUMENTS OF CREDIT CONTROL

The selective instruments of credit control are distinguishable from other tools of monetary management by the fact that they are directed toward particular uses of credit and not merely the total volume outstanding. It is because of this specific, particularized application that they are called "selective" controls.

Selective controls operate by tightening or relaxing the terms applicable to a particular class of loans. This involves a change in the required down payments or the length of maturities (affecting the amount of repayment per period) or both. The result is to alter the flow of funds destined for particular purposes without influencing bank reserve positions or the availability of bank credit in general.

In the United States, as was noted earlier, selective instruments of credit control have been directed toward stock market credit, consumer credit, and real estate credit. Of these, only the regulation of stock market credit is a continuing power of the Board of Governors. The other methods were introduced to meet particular emergencies. When the emergency was past

---

11. In 1962, for example, after several years of substantial net reductions of gold and gold certificate holdings, the Federal Reserve Banks had excess gold certificate reserves of over $4.5 billion, which could have sustained an expansion of Federal Reserve credit of more than $18 billion. It may also be noted that when Federal Reserve Bank excess reserves declined to low levels during World War II as a consequence of the wartime expansion of Federal Reserve credit, Congress quickly reduced the legal reserve requirement of the Banks from 40 per cent on notes and 35 per cent on deposits to the present 25 per cent level for both. This experience suggests that the minimum legal reserve requirement is not likely to present a serious barrier to the expansion of Federal Reserve liabilities.

the control was removed and Congress did not see fit to give the Federal Reserve standby authorization to impose the controls anew if they should decide that this was desirable. This does not preclude the possibility that Congress will again grant such authorization if a new emergency should arise. Even though the Board does not have the power to employ all the instruments of selective control, an understanding of the various methods is nevertheless important as showing what has been attempted by these means and as indicating what may possibly be attempted in the future.

The selective instruments of credit control operate by means of official regulations and prohibitions issued and enforced by the Board of Governors. These are much more direct in their incidence than the general controls which rely upon pressure resulting from the stringency or ease of member bank reserves. They are frequently felt, therefore, to involve a greater degree of interference with free-market forces and, for this and other reasons, have aroused more strenuous opposition than the general controls. On the other hand, their capacity for dealing with special sectoral maladjustments without necessitating drastic shifts in overall monetary and fiscal policies gives them a flexibility that has taken on increasing importance in an environment of conflicting objectives. We shall return to this issue in Chapters 23-25.

Margin Requirements (Regulations T and U)[12]

The Securities Exchange Act of 1934 gave the Board of Governors the power to prescribe the margin which must be required on loans for purchasing or carrying securities. It now applies to all margin transactions (short sales included) in securities registered on security exchanges, and to bank loans for the purpose of trading or carrying stocks regardless of whether they are registered on such exchanges. At one time the margin requirement was set at 100 per cent which was equivalent to prohibiting the use of credit in transactions of this character. A requirement of 75 per cent means that 25 per cent of the value of the collateral security can be borrowed, 60 per cent that 40 per cent can be borrowed, and so on.

The Board of Governors has given a clear description of the way in which margin requirements affect borrowing.

Before the regulation was authorized, a person having, say, $1,000 to put in the market could arrange with a broker, if the broker was willing to accept the risk, for the purchase of 100 shares of stock at $100 a share—that is, $10,000 worth—the stock being held by the broker as collateral for the

---

12. The distinction between Regulation T and Regulation U relates to certain differences in their application to non-bank and bank lenders respectively. The differences are technical and not significant for present purposes. The term "margin" refers to a spread between the market value of securities accepted as collateral for a loan and the face amount of the loan granted. It may be thought of both as the initial equity of the investor in securities and as a margin of safety to protect the lender in case of a decline in the market value of the securities posted as collateral.

$9,000 he was lending and giving him a margin of 10 percent. If the stock rose or fell $5 a share, the borrower would have a profit or loss of $500. Customary margins in pre-regulation days ranged from 10 to 25 percent. Under a requirement of a 75 percent margin, the buyer could arrange to purchase only about 13 shares at $100 each, and a rise or fall of $5 a share would bring him a profit or loss of only $65.[13]

Since security prices have sometimes continued to rise even in the face of increases in margin requirements, considerable dispute has arisen as to the effectiveness of this particular device. The uncertainty of the course security prices would have followed in the absence of the measures taken renders final conclusions impossible. The underlying rationale in the use of this instrument, of course, is that the restriction of the use of credit for stock market purposes will serve to reduce demand at a time of rising security prices, and also (something that is often overlooked) that it will lessen the probability of a dumping of securities in a situation where falling security prices encroach on established margins. Since banks are presumably able to safeguard themselves by the margins they are willing to accept, the purpose of the provision is not to protect the banks except in the sense that the preservation of healthy, stable conditions in the security markets is also in the best interests of banks.

An indication that changes in margin requirements may have a rather strong influence on stock market borrowing is afforded by comparing changes in margin requirements with changes in the volume of customers' debit balances (a form of stock market borrowing) of firms which are members of the New York Stock Exchange. This comparison is presented for the period 1948-1961 in Figure 13-1. It will be observed that time after time a change in margin requirements was followed shortly thereafter by an opposite change in the volume of customer indebtedness. While the evidence is not conclusive it provides, over an extended period of time, a strong *prima facie* indication of the effectiveness of margin requirements in regulating the volume of stock market credit. (This does not imply that it is equally successful in influencing stock market *prices!*)

Control of Consumer Credit (Regulation W)

Shortly before the entry of the United States into World War II, the Board of Governors was authorized by an Executive Order of the President to restrict the use of credit for consumer purchases. They did so by prescribing, first, the minimum size of down payments and, second, the maximum time to maturity of sales contracts made on the installment plan. The primary purpose of the measure was to reduce the inflationary danger, especially during the war, by restricting the demand for consumer goods. It was also argued that the action would help to maintain consumer

---

13. *The Federal Reserve System* (Washington: 1954), p. 41.

purchases in the event of a postwar slump in business by postponing demand for consumer goods to that later time.

The power to control credit terms was subsequently extended to cover charge accounts and personal loans to consumers. The Board of Governors was able to make the credit restrictions more or less severe by changing the list of items to which they applied and varying the size of the down payment and the period of time the loans might run. Flexibility in the administration of the controls was further introduced by providing different terms for different commodities. The disadvantage, unfortunately, was that this tended to invite the criticism from those directly affected that the controls were being employed in an arbitrary and unfair manner.

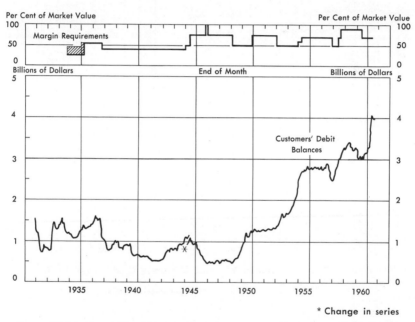

Figure 13-1.   Margin Requirements and Customers' Debit Balances, 1934-1961.
Source: Adapted from the *Federal Reserve Historical Chart Book.*

The precise effect of the introduction of Regulation W in 1941 is obscured by changes resulting from the war. While the volume of consumer credit declined substantially after the introduction of Regulation W it is impossible to say how much of the contraction was the result of the restrictions imposed under its terms and how much to the unavailability of types of durable consumer goods for which this form of credit had been used. The vigor with which a continuance of the controls was opposed by many retail sales organizations indicates that these groups at least evidently believed that the device was capable of having an appreciable effect on consumer purchases.

The relationship between changes in consumer credit and the imposition of Regulation W is shown by Figure 13-2 covering the period 1946-1953. As in the previous chart, evidence such as this seems to provide support for the view that selective instruments of credit control are genuinely effective in accomplishing the restriction in the flow of credit to the selected area.[14] It cannot, of course, be accepted as conclusive proof inasmuch as the period was relatively short in terms of the life of central banking and because many other forces were at work. In addition, some would maintain that even if it is effective it may nevertheless be objectionable on other

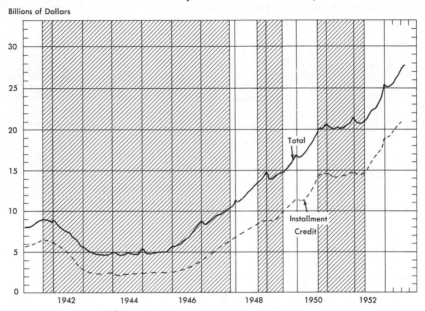

Figure 13-2. "Regulation W" and Consumer Credit, 1946-1953.

Source: Data from the *Federal Reserve Bulletin*.

grounds, especially that it interferes unduly with free markets and discriminates unfairly both against producers of certain types of goods and against consumers whose limited means make it necessary for them to purchase with the aid of installment credit.

Control of Real Estate Credit (Regulation X)

Restriction of real estate credit was first imposed in October 1950 as part of the program to check inflation after the start of fighting

14. This leaves open the question of the effect of the selective instruments on total spending. If monetary conditions are generally tight, it is possible that a reduction of the flow in one direction simply makes credit more readily available in others.

in Korea. It was largely inspired by the apparent effectiveness of the control of consumer credit and in general followed the pattern laid down by Regulation W. It prescribed maximum loan values for the construction of one- and two-family houses, maximum maturities, and minimum amortization terms. Terms were made less restrictive for lower priced than for higher priced property and also less restrictive for loans to veterans than for loans to others. Subsequently the coverage was extended to additional types of real estate construction including certain commercial properties. Regulations relating to the control of credit for residential purposes were issued in cooperation with the Housing and Home Finance Administrator, the Federal Housing Administration, and the Veterans Administration.

The bases of the restrictive effects of Regulations X and W are similar. First, the requirement of a larger down payment limits the use of credit to those who are able and willing to put up the higher initial payment. Second, the shortening of the time to maturity means that each monthly (or other) payment must be larger than it would be with a longer time to run. Individuals who cannot arrange to budget so large a monthly charge are accordingly prevented from borrowing. Others may also be deterred by the size of the current installments, even though the total cost is thereby reduced since the total interest cost is less because the maturity is shorter.

The operation of Regulation X was considerably less successful than that of Regulation W. Part of the difficulty, however, arose out of faulty timing in the way it was introduced. The occasion for its introduction was an unprecedented expansion of real estate credit, combined with other inflationary pressures associated with the crisis in Korea. Not only was there delay in securing authority to restrict real estate credit but even after Congress had taken steps to grant authorization more than a month elapsed before controls were actually introduced.

Because of commitments already entered into, Regulation X had relatively little restrictive effect for a considerable period of time. According to banker testimony, "builders and contractors were tipped off and secured commitments" which were enough to last them for several years.[15] In addition, the regulation of real estate credit was enmeshed with such delicate political questions as the adequacy of low-cost housing and aid to veterans.

Both Regulation W and Regulation X are particularly difficult to administer, a fact which helps to explain the notable lack of enthusiasm with which officials of the Federal Reserve System customarily view them. The opposition of influential groups is likely to be particularly strong, and this has been expressed in interference by Senators, Congressmen, and even, upon occasion, by the President of the United States. Evasion can take place in ways hard to prove, such as granting excessive trade-in allowances as a means of circumventing higher down payments or agreeing to excessive real

---

15. *Monetary Policy and Management of the Public Debt,* Part 2, p. 1203.

estate valuations as a means of getting a larger mortgage than would otherwise be possible with the prescribed margin requirement. To cope with the administrative problems, a considerable staff is required and this gives rise to the familiar difficulties of an expanded bureaucracy.

Three conclusions emerge from our discussion of the operation of the principal selective instruments of credit control. First, it seems clear that under certain circumstances the selective credit controls may be highly effective in limiting the expansion of credit in the fields subject to control. Second, the resistance to maintenance of such controls, especially Regulations W and X, is ordinarily very strong. Finally, administrative problems are particularly difficult. This follows partly from the preceding point. At the same time, the administration was perhaps not always as well handled as seems, with the advantage of hindsight, to have been possible.

PSYCHOLOGICAL MEANS OF CONTROLLING CREDIT

The principal means whereby the Federal Reserve Authorities undertake to exercise credit control have been described and their operation summarized. There remains to be considered a final category of methods, the so-called "psychological" means of controlling credit.

Moral Suasion

In certain foreign countries, notably England and the Scandinavian countries, great reliance has been placed on the use of direct discussion between commercial bankers and the central banking authorities to bring about desired changes in credit conditions. Such measures are facilitated there by the great prestige of their central banks and the small number of banking institutions with which they have to deal. Eleven branch banking systems, for example, hold over 90 per cent of the total assets of all banks in England and Wales. One advantage of such direct and personal methods is that they can be directed toward investment bankers, institutional investors such as life insurance companies, and even beyond.

In the United States what is generally referred to as "moral suasion" has often been exercised by Federal Reserve officials to induce member banks to follow desired courses of action. While the Federal Reserve Board has the power to expel members from the System, it is seldom if ever necessary to threaten reprisals of any sort. Appeals to patriotism, banker responsibility, and simple reason, or the realization that unfavorable publicity might result from persisting in practices of which the Reserve authorities disapprove, may be sufficient.

Extensive use was made of direct appeals after World War II when the Federal Reserve, in compliance with Treasury wishes, was supporting the price of government bonds. Representatives of the System met with dealers and officials of principal lending institutions to persuade them to avoid actions which would tend to depress the market. Appeals were issued in the form of speeches, articles, and public statements. These practices were carried so far that feature writers and others began to speak of them as the Federal Reserve's "open mouth policy." The Federal Reserve authorities were perhaps not unaffected by the feeling that they were being mildly ridiculed. More especially, the experience convinced them that moral suasion was "not a particularly effective means of limiting open-market operations over an extended period of time."[16] In addition, they feared that the use of persuasion would be interpreted by some of the investors and dealers as committing the Federal Reserve to the indefinite continuance of the support policy. To the extent that some individuals refused to cooperate, other and more conscientious business men would be placed at a competitive disadvantage. Because of these and similar considerations the authorities declared that:

> It is the desire of the Federal Open Market Committee to conduct all of its open-market operations on a completely impersonal basis and without resort to moral suasion.[17]

A milder form of influencing credit conditions results from the fact that the psychological effects of Federal Reserve policy may be a factor in the credit operations of member banks. The mere fact that the Federal Reserve authorities saw fit to raise the discount rate or take other steps to restrict credit has at times been interpreted as an indication, from a particularly well-informed source, that business conditions had reached a point where banks would be wise to exercise increased caution in their lending activities. In addition, it is to be supposed that the various means whereby the Board of Governors and the Federal Reserve Banks keep the banking community and others informed of current economic developments will have some effect on the policies and practices which they follow.

Moral suasion has proved least effective in periods of great confidence and great pessimism. Naturally enough, central bankers in this country prefer to place their trust in methods of a more positive character. Nevertheless, its accomplishments abroad have been significant and at times it has proved useful in this country.

The Voluntary Credit Restraint Program

The most ambitious effort of the Federal Reserve authorities to control by persuasion was the Voluntary Credit Restraint Program, which was part of the attempt to stem the post-Korean inflationary boom. After

---

16. *Monetary Policy and Management of the Public Debt*, Part 1, p. 631.
17. *Ibid.*, p. 630.

consulting with other branches of the government to make sure that the program would not violate antitrust legislation, the Board of Governors created an organization whose task it was to bring about a voluntary reduction in lending. The organization comprised national and regional committees composed of representatives of leading lending institutions including commercial banks, life insurance companies, investment bankers, mutual savings banks, and savings and loan associations. The modesty of its aims is indicated by the fact that the program was described in terms of "restraint" and not of "control."

Standards and classifications were drawn up to differentiate between loans that should be encouraged and those that should be discouraged under conditions currently prevailing. The program was voluntary in character with respect to membership on the committees and to adherence to the recommendations laid down. Cooperation was excellent; the representatives on the committees were men who commanded respect; and the program was held by business men and officials alike to have accomplished significant results. Not the least of these results was to inform the business public more widely concerning the credit problems facing the country. It was felt also that for the first time the operations of other important lenders such as life insurance companies had been brought within the scope of some degree of credit control.

Fears were expressed from time to time that the Voluntary Credit Restraint Program might serve to cloak collusive or otherwise monopolistic practices among lenders. It was said that the program was inconsistent with a belief in the virtues of competition and free markets. While there is little indication that the fears were borne out by experience, it is hardly to be expected that such a program would work effectively except under short-run emergency conditions.

SELECTED BIBLIOGRAPHY

BAGEHOT, WALTER, *Lombard Street*. New York: Scribner, Armstrong, 1873, Chapters VII, XII and XIII.

BOARD OF GOVERNORS OF THE FEDERAL RESERVE SYSTEM, *Annual Reports*.

———, *The Federal Reserve System*. Washington: 1961, Chapter III.

FOUSEK, PETER G., *Foreign Central Banking: The Instrument of Monetary Policy*. Federal Reserve Bank of New York, 1957.

GOLDENWEISER, E. A., *Monetary Management*. New York: McGraw-Hill, 1949, Chapters I-II and VII.

JOINT COMMITTEE ON THE ECONOMICS REPORT, *Monetary Policy and Management of the Public Debt.* S. Doc. No. 123, Part 1 (1952), Chapters II-III.

ROOSA, ROBERT V., *Federal Reserve Operations in the Money and Government Securities Markets.* New York: Federal Reserve Bank of New York, 1956.

SAYERS, R. S., *Central Banking After Bagehot.* London: Oxford University Press, 1957, Chapters 1-2, 5-9.

————, *Modern Banking.* London: Oxford University Press, 1960, Chapters 4-5.

SMITHIES, ARTHUR, "Uses of Selective Credit Controls." In American Assembly, *United States Monetary Policy.* New York: 1958, Chapter 3.

YOUNG, RALPH A., "Tools and Processes of Monetary Policy." In American Assembly, *United States Monetary Policy.* New York: 1958, Chapter 1.

14

TREASURY AND
OTHER INFLUENCES ON
BANK RESERVES:
THE RESERVE EQUATION

The preceding chapter showed that the volume of commercial bank reserves is greatly influenced by actions of the Federal Reserve authorities designed to achieve broad policy objectives. Bank reserves are influenced by a variety of other factors which are summarized in the "reserve equation." In the main, these other factors constitute part of the environment within which monetary policy operates and not, as in the case of Federal Reserve actions, monetary policies themselves. Reserves are also affected by the Treasury's handling of its cash balances, the size and distribution of which are influenced by various characteristics of the revenues, expenditures, and debt of the federal government. The actions of the Treasury are a part of the control apparatus of the economy, and their effects on bank reserves and the money supply are ordinarily brought about with due regard to their impact on the economy.

The present chapter is devoted to examining the manner in which certain major Treasury and other non-Federal Reserve influences affect the volume of commercial bank reserves. In order to facilitate the use of bank balance sheets as a tool of analysis, and to contribute to an understanding of the forces making for changes in bank reserves and the money supply, a summary of the effects of the major classes of monetary transactions on the balance sheets of the commercial banks and Federal Reserve Banks is presented in an appendix to the present chapter.

TREASURY INSTRUMENTS OF MONETARY MANAGEMENT

From the standpoint of both powers and responsibilities, the United States Treasury is secondary to the Federal Reserve authorities in the sphere of monetary management. The Treasury has potentially important monetary powers that derive from its position as a money issuer, as a major buyer and seller of gold and silver, as the manager of the large federal debt, and as administrator of the substantial cash balances built up and depleted in the process of implementing the tax and expenditure decisions of the United States government. Its area of primary concern, however, is the fiscal affairs of the government. In spite of its possession of significant monetary powers, therefore, efficient division of labor between the Treasury and Federal Reserve and the Treasury's preoccupation with its main responsibilities have resulted in relatively little use being made of Treasury instruments for purposes of direct monetary control. Nevertheless, the Treasury's activities deserve close attention since they have potentially important effects on bank reserves and the money supply.

The following discussion of Treasury instruments of monetary control deals with the Treasury's powers and responsibilities as a money issuer and as a manager of cash balances. Debt management is reserved for discussion in Chapter 22.

Treasury Currency Issues

It has already been noted that the United States Treasury is an important money issuer, accounting for all metallic coins outstanding and a significant fraction of our paper money. By increasing or decreasing its money issues in accordance with changing economic conditions the Treasury conceivably could contribute to economic stabilization. If in a period of declining economic activity the Treasury printed new currency and spent it directly or (more likely) indirectly in the form of deposits at the Federal Reserve or commercial banks obtained in exchange for the new issues, the expenditure of this newly created money would increase bank reserves and the money supply. In contrast, a tax-financed outlay would have no direct effect on the money supply or bank reserves. Conversely, in a period of inflation the Treasury might retire currency issues that make their way to the Federal Reserve Banks, thereby reducing Treasury deposits at the Federal Reserve by the same amount. In order to restore the previous level of deposits at the Federal Reserve, the Treasury would have to transfer deposits from its accounts at commercial banks or sell securities, both of which would reduce bank reserves.

Actually, however, the Treasury is subject to the constraint of various legal restrictions and traditional procedures in connection with its money-issuing activities. These render the issuance and destruction of Treasury currency of relatively minor importance as an instrument of discretionary monetary policy. In the handling of metallic coins the Treasury operates entirely as a passive agent. When the public chooses to hold more coins relative to other kinds of money, or to alter the composition of its holdings, the coin holdings of the banks are immediately affected. The effects are transmitted from the banks to the mints, ordinarily through the Federal Reserve Banks. An increased demand for coins automatically elicits a larger stock of the desired items, and a redundancy evidenced by an unusually large inflow of coins to the banks tends to increase Treasury holdings of currency (referred to as "Treasury cash").

The only substantial currency issue of the Treasury, in addition to coins, is silver certificates. Silver certificates are issued in connection with silver purchases by the Treasury, and some slight margin of discretion exists in expanding and contracting their issue. In the early 1960's the Treasury was required to purchase all domestically mined silver offered to it at 90.5 cents per fine ounce and could buy foreign silver in amounts and at prices decided upon by the Treasury. If it buys silver bullion the Treasury may issue silver certificates at the rate of $1.29 in silver certificates for each ounce of silver acquired, although since 1934 the Treasury has issued certificates only to the value of the acquired bullion rather than the $1.29 limit. Thus the Treasury has had some discretionary powers in foreign silver purchases, and some margin of flexibility afforded by the excess reserve of bullion that could provide the basis for additions to Treasury currency. By and large, however, the discretionary element in silver policy has been of small importance. In the period before 1958, when the market price of silver tended to fall below the domestic buying price (90.5 cents per ounce), the Treasury was essentially a passive buyer of silver, issuing new currency in relatively small amounts that were equal to the value of acquired bullion. In the late 1950's and early 1960's a rise in the market price of silver halted sales to the Treasury and made it possible for the Treasury to dispose of a substantial part of its free silver held in reserve. These net sales of silver by the Treasury were brought to a halt by presidential order late in 1961.

When the Treasury buys silver, payment is made by checks drawn on the Treasury's accounts with the Federal Reserve Banks. When these checks are deposited in the commercial banks and cleared, both demand deposits and bank reserves increase by the amounts of the checks. The Treasury then replenishes its account at the Federal Reserve Banks by issuing silver certificates to the amount of the purchased bullion and depositing them in the Reserve Banks, thereby increasing the cash assets of the Reserve Banks in the form of the silver certificates and demand liabilities to the account of the Treasury. The net result of these transactions is an increase in the money supply and bank reserves by the amount of the acquired bullion and an increase in Treasury stocks of silver bullion. The Treasury exercises no discretion in this expansionary operation, except in refraining from issuing silver certificates to their full legal limit.

Treasury Management of Its Cash Balances

The Treasury's policies in handling its cash balances have the most significant monetary effects of any of its discretionary powers. It was noted earlier that prior to the organization of the Federal Reserve System the Treasury sometimes engaged in stabilization efforts, carried out by regional shifts in its cash balances or by transferring its holdings between the commercial banks and the Independent Treasuries.[1] After the establishment of the Federal Reserve System, the Treasury declined in importance as an agency for monetary stabilization, but the growth in the absolute and relative economic importance of Treasury expenditures, receipts, and debt transactions since 1914, and especially since 1940, has tended nonetheless to increase the significance of Treasury monetary operations. This has necessitated increased attention to the monetary effects of Treasury cash balance policies, for the minimal purpose of preventing their having major undesired effects on the banks and money market.

The proceeds of Treasury tax collections and security sales are channeled initially into either Treasury Tax and Loan Accounts at almost 12,000 commercial bank depositories or into the Treasury's accounts at the Federal Reserve Banks. With minor exceptions Treasury disbursements are made by checks drawn on Federal Reserve Bank deposits so that virtually all Treasury receipts flow eventually through the Federal Reserve Banks. When the Treasury increases its Federal Reserve accounts, either by directly placing there the checks received as a result of tax collections or security sales, or by shifting deposits from its Tax and Loan accounts to the Federal Reserve Banks, member bank reserves are reduced accordingly, and when the Treasury writes checks on its Federal Reserve accounts and these are cleared, member bank reserves are increased by the amount of the checks drawn. With Treasury cash receipts and outlays each in excess of $100 billion per annum in the early 1960's, and with tax collections subject to seasonal fluctuations while outlays are made more or less continuously, not only can the Treasury deliberately influence the money market by its method of handling its cash balances, but it also may require very judicious management to avoid unplanned and unwanted money market effects.

In order to avoid major disturbances of the banks and the money market, the Treasury has for a number of years followed the policy of holding most of its cash balance in commercial bank accounts, with only a relatively small active account maintained at the Federal Reserve Banks (in the order of $500 million, which has been a rough target). Periodically, "calls" are made on the Treasury Tax and Loan accounts at the commercial banks, instructing the relevant banks that at a certain date in the near future the Treasury intends to transfer some fraction of the deposits held in these banks to the Treasury Accounts at the Federal Reserve Banks.[2] These transfers

---

1. See below, p. 279.
2. The frequency of calls on banks and the amount of notice given prior to withdrawals depends on the size of the bank and the volume of Tax and Loan Accounts maintained there by the Treasury. Group A banks, which include all those with Tax and Loan Accounts of less than $150,000 on some base date, are subject to call once or twice a month. Withdrawals from the accounts of Group A banks, which are by far the most numerous, are usually made upon advance notice of one week. Group B banks,

reduce bank reserves, but the Treasury outlays which necessitated the calls increase bank reserves. If the Treasury accounts with the Federal Reserve Banks are successfully maintained at a constant level, the reserve reducing effects of the transfers are exactly offset by the reserve increasing effects of Treasury outlays.

If the Treasury wished to bring about a tightening of credit conditions it could contribute to this end by raising its average Federal Reserve balance through transfers from its Tax and Loan Accounts at the commercial banks to its Federal Reserve accounts of larger sums than are needed to offset expenditures. If, for example, it increased its Federal Reserve balance from a normal $500 million to $1 billion, this would tend to depress bank reserves by $500 million. If, on the other hand, the Treasury wished to contribute to an easing of credit conditions, it could attempt to reduce the average size of its Federal Reserve balance. This would be less easy than the tightening process, since in the interests of minimizing disruptions resulting from Treasury cash flows through the Reserve Banks, the Treasury has tended to fix a target balance at as low a level as is feasible. Substantial reductions in the Federal Reserve accounts of the Treasury below this level might result in some inconvenience and inflexibility in Treasury operations.

Although it constitutes a means for influencing bank reserves, the Treasury has rarely used "cash-balance management" as a monetary weapon. This has been due primarily to the fact that monetary control is the specialized province of the Federal Reserve authorities. Treasury policy in managing its cash balances has been directed primarily toward minimizing its influence on the banks and money market.

OTHER MAJOR FACTORS AFFECTING BANK RESERVES

Gold Purchases and Sales

Under the modified gold bullion standard which has been in force in the United States since 1933, the Treasury is always ready to buy unlimited amounts of gold at $35 an ounce and to sell gold to foreign central banks at the same price. When the Treasury buys gold the money supply, bank reserves, and central bank reserves increase by the amount of the purchase, and when it sells gold there is a reverse effect.

A gold acquisition by the Treasury is paid for by a check written by the

---

which comprise those with Tax and Loan Accounts of over $150,000 but which have total deposits of less than $500 million, are regularly subject to call once or twice a week with notice of transfer four to seven days later. Group C banks, with total deposits of $500 million or more, are subject to the regular weekly calls applicable to Group B banks, but they are also subject to calls for transfer on shorter notice, including the same day as the call, if Treasury balances at the Reserve Banks are tending to fall significantly below the target level.

Treasury on its Reserve Bank account. When this check is deposited in a commercial bank and cleared, the resultant balance sheet adjustments are as follows:

FEDERAL RESERVE BANKS		COMMERCIAL BANKS	
Assets	*Liabilities*	*Assets*	*Liabilities*
	+Member bank deposits	+Deposits at	+Demand
	−Treasury deposits	Federal Reserve	deposits

In order to replenish its account with the Federal Reserve Banks, the Treasury is authorized to issue gold certificates and transfer them to the Federal Reserve Banks in exchange for an addition to its deposit account. This transaction increases Federal Reserve Bank assets in the form of gold certificates (which are legal reserves of the Reserve Banks) and liabilities in the form of a corresponding addition to Treasury deposits with the Reserve Banks. This gold certificate transaction is regularly and normally carried out in a gold purchase. Thus the acquisition of gold by the Treasury automatically increases the money supply, bank reserves, and central bank reserves. It also increases the potential expansion limits of the monetary system, an indirect effect which may or may not be realized.

Neither the Federal Reserve nor the Treasury authorities have any substantial discretionary control over gold flows, although they may (and often do) attempt to offset the monetary effects of such flows if these are felt to be undesirable in the context of existing domestic economic conditions. Gold flows are related mainly to factors affecting the balance of payments, present and anticipated, interest rate differentials between countries, speculative considerations, and other matters discussed in Part VII. The monetary effects of an outflow of gold such as was suffered by the United States in the late 1950's and early 1960's are of course highly deflationary and would have had serious domestic economic consequences if they had not been offset in large part by deliberate Federal Reserve action.

Currency in Circulation

Another important factor that may affect the volume of bank reserves is the decision of the public as to the distribution of its money holdings between demand deposits and currency. If the public decides to hold a larger proportion of its money in the form of currency, as it may do at certain seasons of the year, such as Christmas, when retail expenditures are unusually large, this will reduce bank reserves by the amount of the currency withdrawals. These withdrawals are effected by a conversion of publicly owned demand deposits into currency, so that demand deposits decline by the same amount as the currency withdrawn.

A loss of currency into circulation reduces the vault cash held by the affected banks. If such losses are substantial the banks will take measures to replenish their currency holdings; for member banks this will be done by converting a part of their Federal Reserve deposits into currency. It should be noted that just as the public is free to determine the proportion of its holdings in the form of currency and demand deposits, so member banks are free to fix the proportion of their cash assets held in the form of deposits at the Federal Reserve Banks and currency.

The Federal Reserve authorities have no way of controlling or influencing the proportion of currency to demand deposits in the total money supply; but, as in the case of gold flows, the monetary authority is free to carry out offsetting actions even though it cannot directly control this source of reserve change. This is, in fact, what the Federal Reserve authorities regularly do: as the seasonal outflow of currency commences during the Christmas season, the Federal Reserve carries out actions that provide bank reserves roughly equal to the amount of currency lost by the banks.

SOURCES AND USES OF RESERVE FUNDS

The principal factors affecting the volume of bank reserves have been discussed separately in the preceding pages. It may be useful at this point to draw them together, along with several other minor items influencing bank reserves, in an equation that summarizes the entire complex of factors that directly determine their volume.

The Reserve Equation

The reserve equation shows that member bank reserve holdings at any moment of time are dependent on the magnitude of certain factors determining the stock of potential reserve funds, *less* the amounts of these funds which have been absorbed in uses other than as member bank reserves. The factors determining the stock of potential reserves are grouped together under the heading "Sources"; the factors (other than member bank reserves) tending to absorb some part of these potential reserve funds are placed under the heading "Competing Uses."[3]

---

3. It will be noted that the reserve equation focuses on *member bank* reserves rather than on *total commercial bank* reserves. This formulation was developed largely because the Federal Reserve authorities, in carrying out their regulatory activities, collect and publish excellent and detailed statistics relating to member banks.

The emphasis on member bank reserves affects other terms in the reserve equation. Thus vault cash holdings of non-member banks are here included along with the currency holdings of the public under the heading "Currency in circulation." Also, the small volume of deposits maintained by non-members at the Federal Reserve banks are segregated from member bank deposits and included under "Other deposits" at the Federal Reserve.

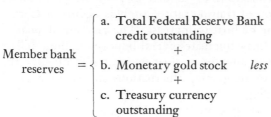

Sources   *Competing Uses*

Member bank reserves = {
a. Total Federal Reserve Bank credit outstanding
+
b. Monetary gold stock
+
c. Treasury currency outstanding
}
less
{
d. Currency in circulation
+
e. Treasury deposits at Federal Reserve Banks
+
f. Treasury cash
+
g. Other deposits and Federal Reserve accounts
}

This equation indicates that, other things given, the volume of member bank reserves changes directly with changes in the sources of potential reserve money and inversely with changes in the volume of money absorbed in competing uses. That is to say, if Federal Reserve Bank credit, or the size of the monetary gold stock, or Treasury currency outstanding increase by one dollar, member bank reserves will increase by one dollar, assuming no change in the volume of funds absorbed in competing uses. If currency in circulation, Treasury cash or deposits held with the Federal Reserve Banks, or other Federal Reserve Bank deposits increase by one dollar, member bank reserves will *decrease* by one dollar, barring any change in the volume of potential reserve money. It should be obvious that *reductions* on the sources side will reduce bank reserves, other things being constant, and reductions in holdings of funds in competing uses will increase bank reserves.

We examined earlier the three factors that constitute the sources of member bank reserves. It was seen that only the first, Federal Reserve Bank credit, is subject to substantial discretionary control, and, in fact, that its changes reflect the operations of two of the principal instruments of general credit control, open-market operations and discount policy. The other two sources of potential bank reserves, the monetary gold stock and Treasury currency outstanding, are not subject to important direct discretionary action; by and large they reflect the operation of factors external to the monetary machinery and may require offsetting changes in Federal Reserve credit in the interests of a consistent and effective stabilization policy.

It should be pointed out that one source of change in Federal Reserve credit lies outside of the immediate control of the Federal Reserve authorities. This is the phenomenon known as "float." It was noted earlier that the Federal Reserve Banks grant credit for items in process of collection within a period of two business days. (A check drawn on a Seattle bank deposited in Philadelphia on a Friday would be credited the following Tuesday; if deposited on Tuesday, it would be credited on Thursday.) It often happens that credit is given before collection is completed. Then the Federal Reserve Bank has, in effect, given a non-interest-bearing loan to the sending bank. That is what is meant by "float." It arises as a result of the time allowed by the availability schedule established by the Federal Reserve Banks being less than the actual time of collection. A sudden increase in the number of checks drawn or a congestion of transportation, such as occurs at Christmas time, will cause the volume of float to increase. The amount of float as reported by the Reserve Banks may fluctuate several hundred million dollars in a single week. Changes in the amount of float are not infrequently the principal factor contributing to temporary fluctuations in the volume of Federal Reserve credit outstanding.

Of the "competing uses" of potential bank reserves, the first two, currency in circulation and Treasury deposits at the Federal Reserve Banks, were discussed earlier in this chapter. The competing use shown in the reserve equation as "Treasury cash" refers to the coins and paper money held by the Treasury in its own vaults. These include Treasury coin and paper money issues, Federal Reserve notes, and stocks of gold which are not held against gold certificates (i.e., "free" gold).[4] The category "other deposits and Federal Reserve accounts" consists mainly of deposit accounts maintained by the Reserve Banks for others besides the member banks and the United States Treasury. These include: non-member commercial banks which have arranged with the Reserve Banks to hold deposits there for convenience in clearing checks (the so-called "clearing banks"); federal government agencies and corporations, such as the Export-Import Bank; deposits of international organizations, such as the International Monetary Fund; and foreign deposits, owned largely by foreign central banks. When any of these "other" deposits with the Reserve Banks increase with no offsetting change in any other sources or competing uses of reserve funds, member bank reserves decline correspondingly. Thus an increase in non-member bank deposits with the Reserve Banks resulting from transfers from member bank correspondent balances to the Reserve Banks would reduce member bank reserves by an amount just equal to the increase in non-member clearing deposits.

In addition to these other deposits maintained by the Federal Reserve Banks, "other accounts" includes minor liabilities and the capital accounts of the Federal Reserve Banks. As in the case of other deposits, an increase in the size of these accounts also decreases member bank reserves. The effect of changes in Reserve Bank capital accounts on member bank reserves, for

---

4. For years the Treasury has issued and retired gold certificates, dollar for dollar, in accordance with acquisitions and sales of gold, and if such policy had been followed invariably it is obvious that the Treasury would hold no stock of "free" gold. However, the Treasury is not compelled to issue and retire gold certificates in response to changes in the value of its gold holdings, and on occasion it has not done so. In particular, in 1934 when the price of gold in the United States was increased from $20.67 to $35 per ounce, with a resultant increase in the value of the Treasury's gold stock of close to $3 billion, the so-called "revaluation profits" were not used as a basis of an increase in gold certificates. This large volume of free gold was reduced in various ways after 1934. In the early 1960's the Treasury's holdings of free gold amounted to approximately $100 million.

example, may be illustrated by tracing the effects of an additional purchase of Federal Reserve Bank stock by a member bank (which will have to make such purchase if it increases the size of its own capital and surplus). In this case the reserve deposit of the member bank is reduced and the capital stock of the Reserve Bank is increased by an equal amount.

Determination of the Volume of Member Bank Reserves

In Table 14-1 the sources and uses of potential reserve funds are shown for weeks ending April 26, 1961 and April 25, 1962. It will be observed that Federal Reserve credit and the monetary gold stock are the major sources of potential reserve supplies and that currency in circulation is the most important competing use for potential reserve money. Ordinarily these three factors are also the principal source of *changes* in bank reserves.

TABLE 14-1. Factors Affecting Member Bank Reserves, Week Ending April 26, 1961 and April 25, 1962 (Averages of daily figures in millions of dollars)

	Week Ending		Effect of Change on Member Bank Reserves
	April 26, 1961	April 25, 1962	
Sources			
a. Federal reserve credit	27,755*	30,722**	+ 2,967
(1) U.S. Government securities	(26,389)	(29,033)	
(2) Discounts and advances	(42)	(150)	
(3) Float	(1,279)	(1,500)	
b. Monetary gold stock	17,390	16,523	− 867
c. Treasury currency outstanding	5,417	5,586	+ 169
Total Sources	50,562	52,831	+ 2,269
Competing Uses			
d. Currency in circulation	29,300	30,481	− 1,181
e. Treasury deposits at Federal Reserve Banks	374	518	− 144
f. Treasury cash	414	428	− 14
g. Other deposits and Federal Reserve accounts	1,455	1,526	− 71
Total Competing Uses	31,543	32,953	− 1,410
Total Member Bank Reserves	19,019	19,878	+ 859

* Total Federal Reserve credit includes $45 million in industrial loans and acceptances.
** Total Federal Reserve credit includes $39 million in industrial loans and acceptances.
Source: Data taken from *Federal Reserve Bulletin.*

The net change in member bank reserves between any two periods may be calculated readily by computing the net change in each factor between the two dates, aggregating the net changes in sources and competing uses, and subtracting the latter from the former to arrive at the change in reserves. In Table 14-1 it may be seen that the net increase in sources $(a+b+c)$ between the two dates expanded potential reserves by $2,269 million. Lower down on the table it may be seen that the net change in competing uses

$(d+e+f+g)$ reduced potential reserves by \$1,410 million, resulting in a net increase in member bank reserves of \$859 million. It should be noted that the reserve reducing effect of the decline in the monetary gold stock was more than offset by the increase in Federal Reserve holdings of United States government securities.

The *free* reserves of member banks tend to be affected in the same direction as total reserves by the factors listed above. In addition, however, free reserves are inversely affected by changes in the amount of *required* reserves. A rise in the volume of required reserves, as through an increase in the volume of deposits, or the raising of the reserve ratio required, tends to reduce excess reserves, and a decline in required reserves to increase excess reserves.

There is no guarantee, of course, that the reserves of any individual member bank will vary in accordance with the reserves of member banks as a whole, though the tendency would be in that direction. It will often happen, as a result of an uneven flow of clearings between banks, that some banks will find themselves deficient in reserves at a time when other banks may have a considerable excess. It is not unusual, under such circumstances, for a bank which is short of reserves to borrow Federal funds from a bank having an excess. This is accomplished by a loan between banks, the loan being effected by a draft against deposits at the Federal Reserve Bank. In substance, such an operation amounts to creating an internal drain of reserves from the bank where reserves are in excess to the other where they are deficient.

APPENDIX:

A SUMMARY OF

FINANCIAL MECHANICS[5]

This appendix provides a review of financial mechanics by tracing the effects of changes in major elements of the reserve equation on the balance sheets of the Federal Reserve Banks and the commercial banks. The twelve Federal Reserve Banks are consolidated into one account, identified as "Federal Reserve Banks"; all commercial banks are consolidated into a second account, "Commercial Banks." For simplicity all banks are assumed to be member banks. Balance sheet changes are examined which result from four classes of transactions: (1) the expansion or contraction of Federal Reserve credit, (2) gold flows, (3) currency flows, and (4) various Treasury transactions.

The purpose of this summary is not to describe actual accounting practice, but to lay the foundation for analysis. This technique may be extended usefully to a wide range of transactions, of which those presented here constitute a significant sample. Only the immediate or direct changes accompanying each transaction are presented here. The more interesting indirect effects of these transactions are treated elsewhere in connection with commercial bank expansion (Chapter 6), monetary management (Chapters 13-14), and monetary and fiscal theory and their applications (Parts V and VI).

In each of the following it is assumed that the amount of the transaction is $100.

---

5. This summary draws on a pamphlet issued by the Federal Reserve Bank of Philadelphia, "Exercises in the Debits and Credits of Bank Reserves." A useful similar treatment with somewhat different emphasis and coverage may be found in *Modern Money Mechanics, A Workbook on Deposits, Currency and Bank Reserves*, published by the Federal Reserve Bank of Chicago.

I. Federal Reserve Credit

A. The Federal Reserve purchases securities from the public in the open market.

    (1) The Federal Reserve buys securities from a dealer in exchange for a check on itself, the dealer depositing the check in his bank.

    (2) The bank collects by sending the check to the Federal Reserve, which increases the bank's reserve deposit.

FEDERAL RESERVE BANKS		COMMERCIAL BANKS	
Assets	*Liabilities*	*Assets*	*Liabilities*
(1) Government securities + 100	(1) Cashier's checks outstanding + $100	(1) Cash items + $100	(1) Deposits + $100
	(2) Cashier's checks outstanding − $100	(2) Cash items − $100	
	(2) Member bank reserve deposit + $100	(2) Reserve with Federal Reserve Bank + $100	

B. The Federal Reserve purchases securities from a member bank.

    (1) The Federal Reserve acquires the securities in exchange for a check on itself.

    (2) The bank collects by sending the check to the Federal Reserve, receiving in exchange an equivalent increase in its reserve deposit account.

FEDERAL RESERVE BANKS		COMMERCIAL BANKS	
Assets	*Liabilities*	*Assets*	*Liabilities*
(1) Government securities + $100	(1) Cashier's check + $100	(1) Government securities − $100	
	(2) Cashier's check − $100	(1) Cash items + $100	
	(2) Member bank deposit + $100	(2) Cash items − $100	
		(2) Reserve with Federal Reserve Bank + $100	

C. The Federal Reserve lends to a member bank.

    The Federal Reserve receives the bank's note and in exchange credits the bank's reserve deposit.

FEDERAL RESERVE BANKS		COMMERCIAL BANKS	
Assets	*Liabilities*	*Assets*	*Liabilities*
Discounts and advances + $100	Member bank reserve deposit + $100	Reserve with Federal Reserve Bank + $100	Notes payable + $100

II. Gold Flows

A. The Treasury purchases gold from a domestic producer or gold importer.

   (1) Treasury pays for the gold by drawing a check on its account at the Federal Reserve; the seller deposits the check in his bank.[6]

   (2) The bank collects by sending the check to the Federal Reserve, resulting in an addition to its reserve deposit and a deduction from the deposit of the Treasury.

   (3) The Treasury rebuilds its deposit by issuing gold certificates to the Federal Reserve.[7]

FEDERAL RESERVE BANKS		COMMERCIAL BANKS	
Assets	*Liabilities*	*Assets*	*Liabilities*
(3) Gold certificates + $100	(2) Member bank reserve deposit + $100 (2) Treasury deposit − $100 (3) Treasury deposit + $100	(1) Cash items + $100 (2) Cash items − $100 (2) Reserve with Federal Reserve Bank + $100	(1) Deposits + $100

B. The Treasury sells gold.

   (1) The buyer pays for the gold by writing a check on a commercial bank;[8] the Treasury deposits the check in the Federal Reserve.

   (2) The Federal Reserve collects by reducing the commercial bank's

---

6. If the seller is a foreign central bank, the check may be deposited in a Federal Reserve Bank, thereby shifting deposits from the Treasury to "other deposits" at the Federal Reserve. When these accounts are drawn on to pay American sellers of goods or securities, the result is as indicated here.

7. If the Treasury wished to offset the effects of (or "sterilize") the inflow of gold, it could rebuild its account instead by means of an equivalent amount of bond sales or additional taxes as traced below in Treasury operations.

8. This assumes a purchase by a licensed domestic user of gold. If the purchase were by a foreign central bank, the check would be drawn on a Federal Reserve Bank. In this case if we include a preceding transaction in which the central bank account at the Federal Reserve is acquired by selling securities in the American money market, or by depositing checks drawn against the commercial bank accounts of American importers, the result would be identical with that indicated here.

reserve deposit; it then sends the check to the bank, which reduces the depositor's account.

(3) The Treasury draws on its Federal Reserve balance to retire an equivalent amount of gold certificates.

FEDERAL RESERVE BANKS		COMMERCIAL BANKS	
Assets	*Liabilities*	*Assets*	*Liabilities*
(1) Cash items + $100	(1) Treasury deposit + $100	(2) Reserves with Federal Reserve Bank − $100	(2) Deposits − $100
(2) Cash items − $100	(3) Treasury deposit − $100		
(3) Gold certificates − $100	(2) Member bank reserve deposit − $100		

III. Currency Flows

A. Currency flows into circulation.
 (1) A depositor cashes a check, exchanging deposit money for pocket money.
 (2) The bank may replenish its vault cash by drawing down deposits at the Federal Reserve. In exchange the Federal Reserve issues Federal Reserve notes or provides Treasury currency. (We assume here equal amounts of each.)

FEDERAL RESERVE BANKS		COMMERCIAL BANKS	
Assets	*Liabilities*	*Assets*	*Liabilities*
(2) Treasury currency − $50	(2) Member bank reserve deposit − $100	(1) Vault cash − $100	(1) Deposits − $100
	(2) Federal Reserve notes + $50	(2) Reserve with Federal Reserve Bank − $100	
		(2) Vault cash + $100	

B. Currency returns from circulation.
 (1) Depositors exchange pocket money for deposit money.
 (2) The bank may send the currency to the Federal Reserve in exchange for a credit to its reserve account. The Federal Reserve retires its notes or increases its holdings of Treasury currency. (We assume here equal amounts of each.)

FEDERAL RESERVE BANKS		COMMERCIAL BANKS	
Assets	*Liabilities*	*Assets*	*Liabilities*
(2) Treasury currency + $50	(2) Member bank reserve deposit + $100	(1) Vault cash + $100	(1) Deposits + $100
	(2) Federal Reserve notes − $50	(2) Vault cash − $100	
		(2) Reserves at Federal Reserve Bank + $100	

IV. Treasury Transactions

A. The Treasury collects taxes from the public.
   (1) The Treasury deposits checks received from the public in Tax and Loan accounts at banks.
   (2) The Treasury transfers its deposits from member banks to the Federal Reserve.

FEDERAL RESERVE BANKS		COMMERCIAL BANKS	
Assets	*Liabilities*	*Assets*	*Liabilities*
	(2) Treasury deposit + $100	(2) Reserves at Federal Reserve Bank − $100	(1) Private deposits − $100
	(2) Member bank reserve deposit − $100		(1) Treasury deposit + $100
			(2) Treasury deposit − $100

B. The Treasury sells securities to the non-banking public. (The effects are the same as in IV A above.)
C. The Treasury sells securities to member banks.
   (1) The member bank pays the Treasury by a credit to the Treasury's account.
   (2) The Treasury eventually transfers its deposit from the member bank to the Federal Reserve.

FEDERAL RESERVE BANKS		COMMERCIAL BANKS	
Assets	*Liabilities*	*Assets*	*Liabilities*
	(2) Treasury deposit + $100	(1) Government securities + $100	(1) Treasury deposit + $100
	(2) Member bank reserve deposit − $100	(2) Reserves at Federal Reserve Bank − $100	(2) Treasury deposit − $100

D. The Treasury sells securities to the Federal Reserve Banks.

The Treasury issues the securities to the Federal Reserve in exchange for an increase in the Treasury's deposit.

FEDERAL RESERVE BANKS		COMMERCIAL BANKS	
Assets	*Liabilities*	*Assets*	*Liabilities*
Government securities + $100	Treasury deposit + $100	(Not affected)	

E. The Treasury purchases goods and services from the public.
   (1) The Treasury writes a check on its deposit at the Federal Reserve; the recipient of the check transfers it to his bank.
   (2) The member bank collects by sending the check to the Federal Reserve.

FEDERAL RESERVE BANKS		COMMERCIAL BANKS	
Assets	*Liabilities*	*Assets*	*Liabilities*
	(2) Treasury deposit − $100	(1) Cash items + $100	(1) Deposits + $100
	(2) Member bank reserve deposit + $100	(2) Cash items − $100 (2) Reserves at Federal Reserve Bank + $100	

F. The Treasury retires government bonds held by the non-banking public. (The effects on the Federal Reserve and commercial bank accounts are the same as in IV E above.) Note that this transaction and the two following relate only to the *retirement* of federal debt out of *given* Treasury balances, and not to the process by which such balances were established.

G. The Treasury retires government debt held by member banks.
   (1) The Treasury writes a check on its deposit at the Federal Reserve and sends it to a bank to pay for maturing securities.
   (2) The member bank collects by sending the check to the Federal Reserve.

FEDERAL RESERVE BANKS		COMMERCIAL BANKS	
Assets	*Liabilities*	*Assets*	*Liabilities*
	(2) Treasury deposits — $100	(1) Government securities — $100	
	(2) Member bank reserve deposits + $100	(1) Cash items + $100	
		(2) Cash items — $100	
		(2) Reserves at Federal Reserve Bank + $100	

H. The Treasury retires government debt held by the Federal Reserve Banks.

(1) The Treasury issues a check in exchange for the securities and the Federal Reserve reduces the Treasury's deposit at the Federal Reserve.

FEDERAL RESERVE BANKS		COMMERCIAL BANKS	
Assets	*Liabilities*	*Assets*	*Liabilities*
(1) Government securities — $100	(1) Treasury deposit — $100	(Not affected)	

The effects of any combination of these transactions can be obtained by consolidation. For example, if additional taxes are used by the Treasury to retire debt held by the Federal Reserve, the net effects are derived by consolidating IV A and IV H. If the Treasury sells securities to banks and spends the proceeds on goods and services, the net effects are derived by consolidating IV C and IV E.

SELECTED BIBLIOGRAPHY

FEDERAL RESERVE BANK OF CHICAGO, *Modern Money Mechanics*, A Workbook on Deposits, Currency and Bank Reserves. Chicago: 1961.

FEDERAL RESERVE BANK OF NEW YORK, *Bank Reserves: Some Major Factors Affecting Them*. New York: 1951.

———, *The Treasury and the Money Market*. New York: 1954.

Joint Economic Committee, *The Federal Budget as an Economic Document*, 87th Congress, 2nd Session. Washington: 1962, Chapters II and III.

SHAW, E. S., *Money, Income, and Monetary Policy*. Homewood, Ill.: Irwin, 1950, Chapters III and XI.

PART FIVE

An Introduction to Monetary and Fiscal Analysis

15

MONEY AND PRICES:
THE QUANTITY THEORIES

At this point we turn from description of monetary institutions, processes of monetary creation, and instruments of monetary control to interpretation and explanation—that is, to monetary theory. The primary aim of what follows is to relate changes originating on the side of money —changes in monetary supply or demand—to the behavior of the economy. Monetary analysis is concerned with the processes by which monetary change affects such variables as the flow of aggregate spending, the level and structure of prices, the level and structure of interest rates or security prices, the volume of employment and output, and the rate of growth of real assets.

The analysis should provide further insight into the role of financial institutions, especially commercial banks and the Federal Reserve System. Above all, it will furnish an introduction to a number of the vital economic issues of our time: the causes of inflation and deflation, the effectiveness of policies for stabilizing income and employment, the respective roles of monetary and fiscal policy, the efficacy of "tight money," the virtues and burdens of public debt, and the adequacy of existing instruments of monetary control.

In the present century three approaches to monetary analysis have dominated economic discussion. They may be called:

1. The quantity-velocity approach.
2. The cash-balances approach.
3. The income-expenditure approach.

The quantity-velocity and cash-balances approaches, usually grouped together as the quantity theories of money, were overshadowed during and after the Great Depression of the 1930's by the rise of the so-called income-expenditure approach. The quantity theories never, however, approached extinction; not only have they always commanded distinguished (as well as superficial) support, but they have also experienced a significant contemporary revival. A review of these more traditional perspectives will permit us to appraise monetary questions from several points of view and will help to establish the conceptual framework for understanding much of past and current monetary debate.

The quantity theories tended to divorce real from monetary influences. In interpreting swings of the price level (or the value of money) they centered on the assumption, for the most part implicit, that the structure of relative prices, rates of interest, levels of employment and output, and rate of economic growth would be controlled in the long run by non-monetary ("real") forces. In this system the theories of value and distribution explained how forces of supply and demand, exclusive of money, determine the relative values of goods and productive services. Money was viewed as simply allowing these relative values to be expressed in terms of a common unit or measure. It was the real factors which were stressed as crucial for economic welfare; money, though recognized as highly useful, was cast in a subordinate role.

With the development of the income-expenditure approach, on the other hand, the scope of monetary analysis was significantly broadened to include explicit consideration of the processes of short-run adjustment and the effects of monetary change on real income and employment. In the process the traditional separation of real from monetary economics was broken down.

Since the quantity theories were concerned primarily with the factors influencing the value of money, we may commence our discussion with a brief review of concepts relating to, and problems involved in measuring, the value of money. The remainder of this chapter is devoted mainly to an analysis of the traditional approaches to monetary theory. The subsequent chapters of this section outline at considerably greater length the income-expenditure approach to monetary analysis.

MEANINGS OF THE VALUE OF MONEY

The value of anything, in the specialized language of economists, is its command over other things in exchange: the value of a $20,000 house may be 10,000 second-hand books or ten compact cars. While more abstract meanings are sometimes attached to the word "value" in general discourse, power in exchange is its dominant economic usage, and it is in this sense that we ordinarily speak of the value of money.

The value of money is customarily measured by what money will buy. Since money is used to purchase an endless variety of goods and services, it is common to measure changes in the value of money by suitable indexes of prices, such as are published regularly by the Bureau of Labor Statistics of the Department of Labor. The value of money is said to vary inversely with the price index; a rise in the index signifies that a given amount of money will command fewer goods and services than before, while a fall in the index signifies that it will command more. Interest has tended to shift from the concept of the value of money with respect to things in general, as measured by a sample of prices from all possible exchanges, to the value of money in particular uses, as in the purchase of consumer goods or commodities in wholesale trade, or in calculating the national product as a whole.

From our definition of the value of money it is clear that whenever the appropriate price level doubles, this means that the value of money in this use has fallen to half. It would be incorrect to think of either the price level or the value of money changing *because* of a change in the other; whatever causes are effective operate reciprocally on both. Changes in the price level and the value of money are simply alternative ways of describing identical events. Whenever convenient, therefore, we may elaborate the theory of the value of money alternatively as a theory of price levels, and this focus on price levels characterizes the theories discussed below.

Purchasing power over goods and services is not, however, the only possible meaning that may be attached to the expression "value of money." Some of the other meanings are familiar and quite unobjectionable. The main reason for calling attention to them here is to distinguish them clearly from the purchasing-power use of the expression which will be our main concern.

First, the value of money may refer to its value in terms of some recognized standard money substance. The "mint parity" that exists under the gold standard is the official price or value of a currency in terms of the specific commodity gold. Somewhat similar value relationships have existed among other commodities used as money, including cattle, cowrie shells, and many other substances. Second, the value of money may relate to the value of one domestic money in terms of another, as in the case of some state bank notes which were valued at a discount in terms of gold, silver coins, or par currency (currency accepted at its face value) in the period before the introduction of national bank notes. Third, value of money may relate to the price of the monetary unit of one country in terms of the monetary unit of another country. This is what we mean by the foreign exchange rate, as when we say that the pound is worth $2.80 or the dollar is worth 4.9 French francs.

Interest is also sometimes referred to as "the price of money," but this usage is open to the objection that interest is paid not for money itself but for its *use* for a period of time. This "price" is analogous, therefore, to ordinary rent which is the return for the *use* of real property for a period of time.[1] Other usages relate the term "value of money" to the marginal

1. Consideration of the interest *rate* as the "price" of money, as in some usages, is objectionable on other grounds. The interest rate literally is not a price at all in the

utility of money to the individual or to its social usefulness to the community viewed collectively.

Of these various connotations of the value of money other than purchasing power in terms of economic goods, we shall be concerned with the exchange rate and the interest rate. In no case, however, is confusion with the customary purchasing-power usage likely to arise.

MEASURES OF PRICE LEVEL CHANGE

While it is unnecessary for our purposes to go into the technicalities of the design of index numbers, a brief review is warranted by their increased significance in recent years. Measures of changes in the level of prices have become the basis for important public and private decisions. This is true of monetary or fiscal policies aimed at price stabilization, for wages linked to the "cost of living" by a given index, and for many business contracts with escalator clauses related to a specific price index. Moreover, the behavior of an index in the past may influence expectations and thereby affect present behavior. The nature and limitations of the major indexes have become, therefore, a matter of important public concern.

We examine below the three general price indexes which measure price movements in broad sectors of the economy: the Consumer Price Index, the Wholesale Price Index, and the Gross National Product Implicit Price Deflator.

The Consumer Price Index

The best known and most widely used of all price indexes is the Bureau of Labor Statistics Consumer Price Index. In recent years it has been based on a sample of about 300 items collected monthly or quarterly in the larger cities throughout the country. These prices are averaged, using weights reflecting the expenditure patterns of moderate income urban families. Over time the weights have been changed only infrequently. In effect, therefore, the Consumers Price Index measures relative changes in the prices of a market basket of commodities and services fixed by the weighting system then in vogue.

Based as it is on sample data, the index implies an imputation from retail prices in covered lines to similar lines uncovered, with the implication that the selected prices are representative of retail prices as a whole. The observations are normally carefully made and the representativeness of the sample

---

usual sense of a certain number of dollars per unit of commodity. Rather than a number of dollars the interest rate is a percentage indicating by how much a number of dollars promised in the future must be discounted per period, usually a year, in exchange for present money.

is periodically tested. But the fixed-commodity-basket approach to measuring prices has several well-known deficiencies—all difficult to remedy in principle, even as measures of changes in the values of the moderate-income urban dwellers' dollar.

The first, and perhaps most important, of these shortcomings stems from changes in quality. The index measures changes in the prices of given commodities and services—a tire, a medical consultation, a washing machine. But in the course of time goods may become more durable, or more versatile, or more reliable, or more or less pleasing in style. Thus a current tire may be stronger and provide increased mileage as compared with one of five years ago; a unit of medical service—say an office visit—may provide more effective diagnosis and treatment. Quality may deteriorate, of course, as well as improve over time. But if improved quality predominates, as apparently tends to be the case, the nominally unchanged market basket of goods conceals an actual increase in potential contribution to well-being. The failure to give recognition to quality changes thus implies an upward bias in the Consumers' Price Index.

A second deficiency also arises from the use of fixed weights over an extended interval. When new products are introduced which are lower cost substitutes for items included in the official market basket, the index will not necessarily reflect this deflationary influence on the cost of living. An important example was the trend to the smaller automobile. So long as the retreat from elephantine proportions was fashionable, the consumer found acceptable means of transportation at lower cost.

Finally, there is the effect of shifts in patterns of expenditure which are independent of new products or changes in tastes. As some elements in the price structure fall more, or rise less, than others over time, consumers are likely to shift their expenditures to items falling relatively in price. A rise in the price of the official market basket thus overstates the rise in price of the changed market basket of goods actually purchased. For this reason, recent or current weights used in deriving a price index tend to provide a slower rise in average prices than weights reflecting expenditure patterns of the past.

The Wholesale Price Index

The Wholesale Price Index of the Bureau of Labor Statistics averages prices for some 2,000 items drawn from various levels in the productive process and is constructed with a technique similar to that of the consumer price index. It uses a fixed pattern of weights, revised about every five years. In general, the influence of quality changes, introduction of new products, and shifts in the composition of expenditures over time may be expected to lead to qualifications similar to those already noted.

The Gross National Product Implicit Price Deflator

This cumbrously titled index (which, for brevity, we shall term the GNP price index) was developed by the Department of Commerce to deflate (that is, to eliminate the effects of price changes on) the gross national product, i.e., all final goods and services purchased in the national economy. It represents, therefore, the most comprehensive measure of changes in prices of current output as a whole. It may be described as a weighted average of the individual indexes of the changing collection of several hundred categories of the national output. With weights changed annually it tends to reflect promptly current spending patterns.

The price components of the GNP price index come in large part from the Consumers' Price Index and the Wholesale Price Index, and to this extent they reflect the upward bias noted earlier. But the GNP price index also provides representation to areas not covered in either previously discussed index, such as prices of governmental services, and a number of products largely custom-built, such as ships, aircraft, and construction. In all these areas, either because the product is not provided for sale, as with government services, or because of the lack of a definable and consistent product over time, as in the construction industry, the measure of price movements is essentially a measure of changes in costs of inputs. The result is that these elements of the combined index do not reflect adequately the effects of increases in productivity and therefore tend to overstate the increase in cost per unit of output.

Our discussion suggests that index numbers should be interpreted with caution and restraint. Price observations that go into them are normally carefully made and combined, so that the established averages may be expected to be reasonably representative within the range of activities covered. They are infinitely more dependable than the impressions of the casual observer. But in a dynamic environment of changing preferences, products, and qualities, there are inherent limitations on the precision of even the most refined index numbers. The sophisticate will treat indexes with respect as a useful tool of measurement, but with skepticism as to the significance of the final digit.

RELATION OF COMMODITY CONTENT TO THE VALUE OF MONEY

Before examining the quantity theories of money it is necessary to touch upon a long standing source of confusion to students of money. This is the question of the connection between the commodity content of money and its purchasing power or value. In light of the extended history of commodity moneys and standards it is not at all surprising that value as a commodity was long looked upon as governing the value of money. Changes in the value of money were then attributed to the variety of forces influencing the value of the quantity of gold (or other commodities) into which all other forms of money were convertible, or with which equality of value was maintained.[2] The value of the token constituents of the money supply—currency and demand deposits—were regarded as reflecting the value of the underlying standard money. The value of depreciated money not currently convertible into gold was explained in terms of estimates as to the probability and terms of its future redemption in gold.

As long as convertibility is maintained between one ounce of gold and $35, whatever influences the exchange value (purchasing power) of gold must necessarily influence the value of dollars in equal degree. But the reverse is equally true: with the price of gold fixed, changes in the price level (i.e., in the value of money in general) imply changes in the purchasing power of gold and vice versa. In this sense what we have is a truism: under a commodity standard the value of money is determined by the same complex of forces that govern the value of the standard commodity.

A more substantive, though also more questionable, contention is that the value of gold is determined by *commodity* demand and supply as in the case of any other metal, and that this value is then transmitted to the monetary unit such as the dollar through interconvertibility. The basic flaw in this argument is that gold (or any other money commodity) is not like just any other metal. The fact that gold has monetary uses leads to the accumulation of gold as monetary reserves (and formerly as circulating medium), in a much greater volume, actually, than the amount taken for commercial use such as dentistry and the manufacture of jewelry. Thus the demand for and the value of gold, as distinguished, say, from tin, depends in large part on the fact that it is used as money.

Two implications of the existence of a monetary demand for gold are to be noted: (1) an increase in the level of economic activity would give rise to an increase in the transactions demand for money and hence would lead to an increase in demand for, and value of, gold. This rise in the value of gold (or fall in price levels) would occur even with unchanged costs of gold production and demand for gold as a commodity. (2) An increase in demand deposits or paper currency in circulation would increase the supply of substitutes for gold in its use as a medium of exchange. Applying a familiar theorem of price analysis, we would expect an increase in the supply of substitutes for gold to lead to a decrease in the demand for, and value of,

---

2. We should recall that the *value* of a prescribed weight of gold refers to its command over other goods in exchange, so that under a gold standard a rise in the value of gold implies a fall in the prices of goods in general. The *price* of gold, however, is its rate of exchange in terms of dollars. It follows that so long as the standard remains unchanged, the price of gold remains constant (say at $35 per ounce), but its value may change significantly, reflecting a rise or fall of prices in general.

gold (a rise in price levels), again despite unchanged costs and commodity demand for gold. In short, to treat gold like any other commodity must seriously falsify our estimate of the forces influencing its value since the demand for gold is not dominated by its use as a commodity.

These considerations also suggest limitations of the more general commodity emphasis noted above, which does not exclude monetary demand for gold as an influence on its value. For we are forced to treat the effects of changes in the amounts of bank credit, paper money, and level of activity on prices via their effects on the value of gold, and from changes in the value of gold to changes in the reflected value of money in general, i.e., the price level. Even under conditions of full convertibility this approach is indirect and cumbersome. Under modern conditions with convertibility circumscribed everywhere, it maintains only remote touch with the essential forces influencing monetary values.

As long as commodity money was in general use as the standard, it was understandable that the general public should continue to associate the value of money with the valuable commodity into which the circulating medium was exchangeable. In the decade of the 1930's the limitations of such an explanation became glaringly evident. Year after year, most of the world continued to employ money which had no commodity value, was convertible into no money commodity, and had no apparent prospect of future convertibility into a valuable money commodity. Yet in many countries the money continued to maintain its value as successfully as when it was attached to some commodity base.

Even before this worldwide object lesson many special situations had arisen which tended to discredit the view that commodity value and money value are closely related. One such instance was the famous case of the Bank of Amsterdam whose notes continued to circulate at the same high value as before, even after the Bank's gold reserves had been dissipated as a result of fraudulent activities of the Bank's officers. While this instance was often treated as an exception, since the loss was not publicly known, it was disproof of the idea that the actual existence of a commodity backing was an essential of monetary value. There was also the instance in the early history of this country of money continuing to circulate even though it was known to be counterfeit, its monetary value sustained by the fact that circulating medium was so scarce that people preferred to accept counterfeit money rather than try to get along without money.

In Sweden during World War I and in Switzerland after World War II, convertibility of the local currency into gold was suspended, and the money, far from depreciating, went to a premium in terms of the gold into which it had theretofore been convertible. In the decade of the 1950's the non-convertible Canadian dollar went to a substantial premium over the United States dollar, which maintained its official convertibility into gold. In all these cases the appreciation relative to gold was unrelated to any prospect that a new and higher rate of convertibility between currency and gold would be established.

In the early days of the New Deal the view that the commodity value of money governs price levels was put to practical test. A rise in commodity prices in the United States was then urgently desired. Accordingly, over a period of several months in 1933-34 the price of gold was gradually raised from $20.67 to $35 an ounce on the assurance of the sponsors of the plan that this would produce a corresponding rise in commodity prices.[3] Assuming that the value of gold was fixed, the devaluation of the dollar in the approximate ratio of 21/35 should have reduced the value (i.e., purchasing power) of each dollar correspondingly, raising prices to 35/21 of their former level—an increase of about 70 per cent. In fact, however, the price level effects proved to be negligible. Gold had been called in prior to the devaluation and the change in the price of gold had no influence on the market behavior of the public. They had the same number of dollars,[4] and they continued, sensibly, to plan expenditures and calculate costs just as they had done before the change.

Thus the commodity-value fallacy indicated by logic is further demonstrated by experience. Nevertheless, it embodies perhaps the most tenacious of popular misconceptions concerning money, namely, that some kind of commodity "backing" is necessary if money is to retain its value, and that the value of monetary reserves uniquely determines the value of the monetary unit.

THE QUANTITY-VELOCITY APPROACH

Much more relevant to current issues of monetary policy are those approaches which explain changes in monetary expenditures and prices in terms of variations in the quantity and rate of turnover of, or demand for, money. As was noted earlier, these are usually described as quantity theories of the value of money.

The Equation of Exchange: Transactions-Velocity Formulation

By the time of World War I it had become customary in the United States to link the quantity of money to prices by means of a formula popularized by Professor Irving Fisher.[5] This is the equation of exchange. In its most familiar form it is usually written:

$$MV = PT.$$

3. This was the so-called Warren Gold-Purchase Plan. See p. 461.
4. Except for those who sold currently produced gold to the Treasury at higher prices.
5. Irving Fisher, *Purchasing Power of Money* (New York: Macmillan, 1911).

This formula is derived from a very simple and self-evident fact, namely, that what is given in payment for anything in a given period is equal in value to what is sold. Stated somewhat more fully, the quantity of money (M), multiplied by the average number of times each unit of money is used during a given period (V), is equal to the sum total of goods and claims traded (T), during the period, multiplied by their average price (P).

It is important to remember that *the equation of exchange is not the quantity theory of money*. The equation itself is a simple statement of identity. This means that it organizes a system of definitions so framed that the left-hand member equals the right-hand member necessarily, because they are in fact identical except for different names. The identity lies in the fact that since for every monetary payment there must be a monetary receipt (payment and receipt being really two names for the same transaction), the sum of all monetary payments (MV) must be identical to the sum of all receipts (PT).

One implication of the definitional nature of the equation is that it can never be proved false by facts. Thus, if we should find independent empirical measures of the four terms and in combining them should find an inequality between MV and PT, we should be led, not to reject the equation as contrary to experience, but to conclude that we had made a mistake in measurement. The equation is not a theory, provides no basis for prediction, and is open to no dispute as to its "truth" or "falsity." The only issue posed by this set of definitions, as by any other, is the usefulness of the categories as a framework for analysis.

The Equation of Exchange: Income-Velocity Formulation

The transactions formula relates to total money transactions, i.e., all exchanges involving payment in money. It includes transfers of securities, real estate, wage payments, intermediate products, and so on. A variant of the equation restricts transactions to those involving real income (y). The price level corresponding to this aggregate may be designated P_y (to distinguish it from P which relates to total transactions), so that $P_y y$ represents total money income payments or receipts. If we divide total money income by M, we have the average number of times each dollar enters into income in the given period, or the *income velocity* of money (V_y). The corresponding equation then becomes

$$MV_y = P_y y.$$

Framing the approach in this manner provides the advantage of greater measurability, for it makes it possible to call upon the rich supply of national income data now available. Moreover, because the price level of current output (P_y) is linked directly to productive activity, it is more significant than P as an objective of control. Modern writers in the quantity-velocity tradition, therefore, have tended to stress the income-velocity formulation. The formal properties of both versions, however, are similar. While the following discussion emphasizes the traditional transactions account, the conclusions are applicable to the income-velocity approach, with only minor amendments.

The Quantity Theory in Transactions-Velocity Terms

Basic assumptions. The equation of exchange, as we have seen, is essentially a truism. It is only when certain assertions are made concerning the various terms in the equation of exchange that it is conjured into a theory, and then it ceases to be a truism or, possibly, even true. The most extreme set of assertions regarding the different factors in the equation were those advanced in arriving at the so-called "rigid" quantity theory. This is substantially the form in which it achieved its early popularity in this country, though the following statement has been made somewhat extreme for the sake of simplicity in explaining it. The assumptions or contentions underlying the rigid quantity theory are as follows:

1. *The constancy of V and T.* It was maintained that ordinarily the velocity or turnover of money is determined by custom, habits, and payment patterns—all of which were expected to change slowly and independently of changes in M. The volume of transactions, it was maintained, is limited by physical considerations and similarly can change only gradually as technology advances, population grows, and trading areas expand.
2. *The passivity of P.* Price was held to be a dependent variable, initiating no changes in other factors in the equation, but completely responsive to the changes occurring in those factors.
3. *The proportionality of P to M.* The conclusion that P is proportional to M necessarily follows if the two preceding assumptions are valid. It represents an abbreviated statement of the extreme or "rigid" quantity theory of money, to wit, that *the value of money changes inversely with and as a result of changes in the quantity of money.*

Modified versions of the quantity theory consisted of gradations between one extreme which is represented by the rigid quantity theory and the other extreme which is represented by the equation of exchange. The nearer the formulation approached the latter extreme, the less debatable it became, but at the same time the closer it approximated a degree of generality that deprived it of any practical usefulness as an instrument of policy. Qualifications were attached to the theory in its rigid form, such as "in the long run," "except during periods of transition," "at similar stages of the business cycle," etc. Or the theory was restated as *the value of money changes inversely with changes in the quantity* (M) *and velocity* (V) *of money and directly with changes in the volume of trade* (T), in all cases P being result rather than cause. This is the "loose" quantity theory. It amounts to little more than a restatement of the equation of exchange, except that the assumption is still retained that P is passive, i.e., that it is the resultant of changes in the other factors, M, V, and T, rather than also a possible cause of changes in them.

To summarize, to the question of what determines price-level changes the answer given by the rigid quantity theory is that they are governed simply by the quantity of money. The loose quantity theory, on the other hand, suggests that changes in price levels are determined by a combination of three factors consisting of the quantity of money, the rate at which it is used, and the volume of transactions.

LIMITATIONS OF THE TRANSACTIONS-VELOCITY FORM OF THE QUANTITY THEORY

At one time criticism of the transactions form of the quantity theory was directed almost exclusively to attacking its reliability as an economic generalization. It consisted principally of challenging the basic assumptions underlying the theory, particularly in its more rigid form. At the present time, however, the tendency is more to criticize the approach on the score of *usefulness*. There is a widespread feeling that in a form sufficiently loose to be logically tenable the quantity theory is not particularly helpful either as an analytical tool or as a guide to policy.

The reliability of the rigid formulation of the theory is attacked on the score of all the basic assumptions indicated above. It is now generally accepted, for example, that neither the volume of transactions nor the velocity of money is as stable as was once believed. The volume of transactions is obviously subject to large even though gradual changes over longer periods of time. Moreover, the "miracle of production" in this country from 1942 to 1944 and the rapid expansion of output in other special situations of emergency or recovery demonstrated that a considerable change in transactions may occur even during a relatively short period.

The assumption that velocity may be regarded as more or less constant has led to particularly vigorous dissent. It is maintained that, on the contrary, changes in the velocity of money are of great importance—often, in fact, of greater importance than changes in the quantity of money. According to the estimates of Professor Graham, the German reichsmark in 1923 attained a rate of turnover twenty-six times normal. (Substantial as this was, it was negligible, of course, alongside the increase amounting to many billionfold in the volume of marks in circulation.) The rate of turnover of demand deposits of all commercial banks in the United States was nearly fifty-four times a year in 1929 and less than nineteen times in 1940. Between 1952 and the early 1960's the increase in turnover of demand deposits in centers outside New York City was three times as great as the increase in money supply (currency and adjusted demand deposits). Inclusion of New York would make the disparity even greater.

It is now recognized that because of changes associated with different stages of the business cycle, the velocity of money may be a more important factor than quantity in accounting for short-run variations in the level of prices. Some writers on money have consequently tended to make the theory of money more a velocity theory than a quantity theory as originally understood.

In criticizing the validity of the transactions theory in either its loose or rigid formulations, it is also maintained that *P*, far from being entirely passive, may contribute to changes in other factors. To illustrate, a rise in the level of prices may lead people to try to get rid of their money for fear its purchasing power may decline further, with the result that velocity of circulation is increased. Furthermore, the considerations that justify trying to get rid of money if prices are expected to rise also justify trying to hold on to goods under the same circumstances. Thus it is maintained that rising prices tend to reduce transactions as well as increase velocity, both of these tendencies helping to accelerate the rise in prices.

It is also pointed out that under gold-standard conditions a change in the level of prices influences the production of gold. Thus falling prices tend to reduce the costs of producing gold and thereby to stimulate current output of gold. A rising level of prices has the opposite effect on gold production. On this ground it is contended that instead of being entirely passive the level of prices (*P*), through its effect on gold production, plays an active role in determining what the quantity of money will be at some future time. Although this introduces a considerable time factor, it is still, the critics maintain, a matter of importance. In these various ways, it is said, prices (*P*), far from remaining passive, may be a positive causal factor influencing velocity (*V*), transactions (*T*), and the quantity of money (*M*).

Perhaps the principal objection to the loose formulation is that it merely accounts for changes in the value of money rather than providing a causal explanation of them. It calls attention to quantitative elements which would tend—if they were to change—to cause a change in prices. But it does not suggest why, in fact, they do change. Upon occasion even this may, of course, be a useful reminder to have—as Germany learned to her sorrow during the period of inflation after World War I when the importance of the quantity of money was largely disregarded. But for the most part the quantitative elements have to be assumed; the theory fails to show what causes the quantities *M*, *V*, and *T* to change.

The rigid quantity theory, if it could be accepted as valid, would constitute an invaluable guide to policy. All that would be necessary in order to establish a desired level of prices or to check an inflationary or deflationary trend of prices would be to effect appropriate adjustments in the volume of circulating medium. Such changes in the quantity of money are by no means impossible to bring about.

In its loose form, on the other hand, the quantity theory ceases to be any such exact guide to policy. When the velocity of money (*V*) and the volume of transactions (T) as well as the quantity of circulating medium (M) are all regarded as important factors influencing the general level of prices, the task of monetary control becomes extremely complicated. It is then a matter of regulating all three of these factors instead of just the one. The difficulty of effectively balancing the three variables is very great, especially since certain of them—V in particular—are not easy to control. Furthermore, action to control any one of them is impeded by the thought that such an attempt might be complicated by a perverse change in one or both of the others.

Despite a certain rehabilitation after World War II, the popularity of the transactions formulation of the quantity theory of money has declined considerably since the period of its greatest vogue in the 1920's. Its reputation undoubtedly suffered from the tendency of its proponents to apply it in altogether too rigid and mechanical a manner. Nevertheless, when limited to broad movements over relatively long periods, the transaction theory provides a simple first approximation which may be useful as a rough indicator of monetary forces. Moreover, many current discussions of Federal Reserve policy are couched in quantity theory terms, and the equation of exchange retains widespread use as a simple expository device.

THE CASH-BALANCES APPROACH

As we have seen, the quantity-velocity approach envisions average price as determined by a *flow* of money expenditures over relevant periods meeting an opposing flow of salable entities.[6] The effects of a changing money supply are analyzed in terms of its direct influence on the flow of monetary expenditures. An alternative approach which originated in Cambridge, England, also places emphasis on the quantity of money and until recent years was as widely used there as the velocity version is in this country.

The Cambridge cash-balance approach frames the demand for money as the demand to hold a stock of liquid balances, confronted by the stock of money balances which is made available by the banking system and monetary authorities. All money which exists must be held by someone, and no more can be held than is currently available. But the demand to hold balances may be inconsistent with the available supply. The cash-balances approach focuses on the conditions necessary for all money to find willing holders and on the consequences if these conditions are not met. With some over-

---

6. In some accounts, MV, the flow of expenditures, is referred to as the "supply of money," and T, the aggregate of items offered in exchange, as the "demand for money," with P emerging to equilibrate the two. Clearly, however, it would be inconsistent with the quantity theory to take MV or T as *depending* on P, as supply and demand *schedules*, for this would violate the required independence of MV and T, and the passivity of P. Thus with P emerging as a simple ratio of MV to T, there is no advantage in using supply and demand concepts.

simplification it may be said that where the velocity approach looks at money in movement as a flow of expenditures or money "on the wing," the Cambridge approach looks at money "sitting" and investigates why it has not yet been spent.

The Cash-balances Identity

As in the quantity-velocity formulation, the cash-balance approach may be formulated either as an identity or as a theory of the determinants of the value of money. Let us look at the identity first.

Where, as in the income-velocity equation, M is the stock of money, y is the annual real national income, and P_y is the related price level, so that yP_y is aggregate money national income, let

$$K = \frac{M}{yP_y}.$$

Thus K is simply the proportion of aggregate annual income represented by the aggregate stock of money, or the proportion of real income held in monetary form. Rearranging terms we have

$$M = KyP_y$$

which is the usual form of the cash-balances equation.

An increase in M might be accompanied by an increase in K, thus increasing money balances and real balances, and increasing the proportion of annual income held in the form of money balances; or by an increase in y, thus increasing money and real balances, but not increasing their proportion to national income; or by an increase in P_y, thus increasing money balances but not real balances, and maintaining constant the ratio of money balances to income; or by a combination of all of these.

The Quantity Theory in Cash-balances Terms

When certain restrictions are placed on y and K (for example, if we assume or prove that y tends to be maintained at the full-employment level, and that K is based on relatively stable customs and practices), the cash-balances identity is converted into a theory of the price level. For Ky now represents a demand for a given real command over income in the form of money balances. How many dollars are demanded depends on the prevailing level of prices. The demand for dollars to hold is thus KyP_y. If the number of dollars supplied (M) is equal to the number demanded (KyP_y), there will be no attempt to change the rate of monetary expenditures so as to increase or decrease the real command over income held in the form of money balances; prices will remain constant and in equilibrium with the supply of money.

If, now, the money supply were increased, people's actual holdings of cash balances would exceed their desired holdings. In the attempted adjust-ment to reduce the excess the level of expenditures would increase, indi-viduals passing money balances on to others and increasing general mone-tary demand for output. With the expansion of demand prices would rise, lowering the real value of cash balances until the augumented money supply would bear the desired (constant) relationship to the money value of output. Assuming a given real demand for money, the change in prices would be in proportion to the change in M.

In similar fashion the theory may be applied to show the effects of changes in the real demand for money (a change in Ky). Suppose that everyone decided to hold a smaller proportion of his real annual income in cash (a decline in K). The decrease in demand for money would not decrease the supply of money in existence—the total amount would have to be held by someone—but the increase in spending resulting from the efforts of individuals to reduce balances would force up prices. This would continue until the real value of money balances (M/P_y) was sufficiently reduced to correspond to the desired new and lower value of Ky. By this process the public, while not controlling the number of dollars available, is able to con-trol the aggregate real value which the existing supply of dollars commands.

Relationship between the Velocity and Cash-balances Approaches

In terms of the income-velocity form of the equation of exchange, the adjustment just noted could be described as an increase in the income velocity of money accompanied by an increase in P_y. The relationship be-tween K and V_y follows from their definitions. Letting Y represent aggre-gate money income (i.e., yP_y), and recalling that K is defined as M/Y and V_y as Y/M, it is clear that they are reciprocals; that is, $K=1/V_y$ and $V_y=1/K$. Thus it is possible to substitute either in a statement containing the other.[7]

7. This conclusion embodies perhaps the standard view, but to maintain it requires rather special definitions of M, K, and P_y, which were somewhat glossed over in the text. in the income version of the equation of exchange, since V_y is defined as Y divided by the *average* amount of money in circulation during the period, M, P_y, and V_y all are averages for the period. If M is similarly defined in the cash-balances approach, then K is the *average* ratio of M to Y (of several possibly different values at various points in time within the period), and P_y is the *average* of price levels of output over the period, as in the velocity approach. In this case the identity discussed in the text holds.

But if M in the Cambridge formulation is taken as the amount of money existing at a *moment* in time, say a point at the beginning of a period, and K is defined as the desired proportion of prospective income to be held in cash balances at that moment, then P_y is the appropriate momentary price, not the average over the period. It is true that while K would equal $1/V_y$ even in this case if equilibrium prevailed over time so that all the variables were constant, they are not identical, and their values would differ during a period of disequilibrium—that is, when prices were in process of changing. It follows that the cash-balances and income-velocity approaches, while necessarily closely related, are not identical.

It may be noted in passing that K is not to be confused with $1/V$ of the transactions

It is sometimes maintained that the cash-balances approach is preferable in that it gives more immediate emphasis to human choices in comparison with the rather mechanical implications of V. Changes in public psychology —particularly the public's disposition to hold on to money or to spend it more freely—are given equal emphasis in the cash-balances approach along with the quantity of money. The distinction was perhaps more important at one time than it is now, since users of the velocity formula today, in short-run analysis, are accustomed to place considerable emphasis on changes in velocity as well.

In general the strengths and weaknesses of the quantity-velocity and the cash-balances approaches are much the same. It may be noted, for example, that the assumption that society will hold a constant fraction (K) of its real income in the form of money is no less extreme than the assumption that velocity (V or V_y) is a constant. Choice between the two formulations is very much a matter of personal preference. The student will probably find that in some situations reference to the cash-balances formulation seems more helpful and in other situations reference to the velocity formulation is preferred.

The Cambridge Approach and the Transition to Later Monetary Analysis

As we have seen, the cash-balances approach brought to monetary analysis an emphasis on the demand for money as well as supply and analyzed that demand by an application of familiar principles of weighing benefits at the margin. These were important contributions to monetary economics. Some brief comments on remaining limitations of the approach may provide a useful introduction to the monetary analysis of the following chapters.

First, money was still viewed almost exclusively as a medium of exchange rather than jointly as a medium of exchange and store of value—that is, as an asset. Thus the basic motive for holding money balances was related to the amounts, timing, and degree of synchronization of receipts and expenditures, which Keynes later called the "transactions motive." Money was viewed as being held temporarily in anticipation of expenditures for goods and services (or prospective financial payments). Thus an increase in M resulting in an excess of money holdings was expected to lead directly to an increase in expenditures on output. There was little suggestion of another frontier—between money and securities—across which an increase in the supply of money might lead to an increase in, say, the demand for bonds, with possibly indirect, diverse, and complex effects on the demand for output.

Second, the approach did not deal at all adequately with the role of

---

form of the equation of exchange since this V concerns the turnover of money in relation to all transactions and not just those involving real income.

uncertainty in influencing the holding and disposition of balances. In particular there was no systematic attempt to link the holding of balances to expectations and the rate of interest. In part this may have been due to the general long-run orientation of the quantity theories, in which it was believed that monetary forces would have little continuing influence on interest rates, but these habits of thought persisted when applying the framework of analysis to problems associated with the business cycle. Nevertheless, emerging out of the Cambridge demand-for-money concept was the Keynesian liquidity-preference formulation (to be examined later), which is a significant part of modern analysis.

Third, the analysis of prices presented in the quantity theories went little beyond the determination of general averages, passing over influences on price structures and the effects of price dispersion on the process of change as well as ultimate levels of prices. Questions of the speed and channels of inflation, for example—that is, the mechanism of the inflationary process—were not easily handled.

Finally, the theory provided no adequate explanation of the level of output or income as a whole, or of the interaction between income, the money supply, the value of money, and the demand for money balances. The following chapters constitute an introduction to this broader conception of monetary analysis.

SELECTED BIBLIOGRAPHY

CASSEL, GUSTAV, *Theory of Social Economy*. New York: Harcourt, Brace, 1932, Chapter XI.

FISHER, IRVING, *The Making of Index Numbers*. Boston: Houghton Mifflin, 1922.

———, *The Purchasing Power of Money*. (Revised edition) New York: Macmillan, 1926.

FRIEDMAN, MILTON, "The Quantity Theory of Money—A Restatement." In *Studies in the Quantity Theory of Money*. Milton Friedman (ed.): University of Chicago Press, 1956.

Joint Economic Committee, *Government Price Statistics*. Hearings before the Subcommittee on Economic Statistics, 87th Congress, 1st Session, Washington: 1961.

HANSEN, ALVIN H., *Monetary Theory and Fiscal Policy*. New York: McGraw-Hill, 1949, Chapters 1 and 3.

ROBERTSON, D. H., *Money*. London: Nisbet, 1948, Chapter 2.

16

THE NATIONAL INCOME

The theories described in the preceding chapter were primarily directed toward explaining the value of money, or, what comes to the same thing, the level of prices. The income-expenditure approach which constitutes the subject of the next four chapters is concerned with the determination of the level of output, i.e., real national income, as well as prices. Instead of relating aggregate monetary expenditures to the stock of money, as in the quantity approaches, the present analysis relates the flow of expenditures to *sources* of monetary outlay. The income version of Fisher's identity, $P_y y = M V_y$, expresses aggregate income ($P_y y$ or Y) as equal to the total money supply multiplied by the number of times it is spent to produce income. The Keynesian identity, on the other hand, views aggregate income as equal to sums spent on output by four groups or sectors, namely, households, business firms, government, and the rest of the world. Upon this classification is erected a theoretical system which seeks to explain these components of expenditure as well as their aggregate. This approach is known variously as income or income-expenditure analysis, macro-economic analysis, or aggregative economics.

The present chapter provides an introduction to income analysis by means of a summary and review of the national income accounts. In recent years these accounts have found significant applications in many different areas. They are important as measures of aggregate performance, depicting cyclical instability as well as longer term growth; as a basis for appraisal, in comparisons between countries and regions, as well as over time; as a foundation for policy, as in wartime planning, or in prescribing monetary or fiscal controls; and as a framework for forecasting overall and sectoral business activity. In addition, the national income accounts contribute to monetary analysis by providing a structure of definitions and a rich body of data to suggest and test theoretical propositions.[1]

1. For more extended description of the national income concepts and economic and statistical issues underlying their definition, see the Department of Commerce, *National*

THE CIRCULAR FLOW IN A SIMPLE ECONOMY

The national product or income in any period may be considered from three points of view: (1) as a *spending total*, the aggregate of money expenditures on output; (2) as an *output* total, the aggregate money values of final products and services ensuing from productive activity; and (3) as an *earnings* total, the aggregate of claims against output generated in the process of production. Properly conceived, these three concepts of total performance must provide the same measured result. In the language of the preceding chapter, they are identities, i.e., they are necessarily equal because of consistent definitions. The main purpose of this chapter is to establish the definitional framework and to demonstrate these identities for economies or circumstances of various complexity.

The basic concepts may be clarified by examining first a simple economy. Assume a closed system (and therefore no international transactions) and the absence of government (hence no government purchases of goods and. services, taxes, or governmental transfers, subsidies, and interest payments). Of the four sectors listed above we have left but two: households and business firms.

In this scheme we conceive of households as seeking satisfaction via consumption and the accumulation of assets, and we assume production to be centered exclusively in firms and guided by prospective profits.[2] In addition all firms will be considered proprietorships (or if corporations, we assume they pay out all earnings) so that we need make no distinction between earnings of the firm and of its owners. Hence, we need not distinguish between earned and "disposable" income. In this discussion we also treat the transactions of each sector on a consolidated basis; that is, we ignore intrasectoral transactions (between firms, or between households), just as we may ignore transactions within the family in setting up the family accounts.

We are prepared now to note the relations between sectors as described in Figure 16-1. In this purely private economy all resources are owned ultimately by households. Thus all assets of our consolidated firm are obtained from households as creditors or owners, and all labor services are obtained from households as well. This flow of productive services from households to firms is indicated by the lower arc at the top of the figure. In exchange, households receive a stream of money payments which, from the standpoint of the firms, are "costs" (including profits) and, from the standpoint of

---

Income, a Supplement to the *Survey of Current Business,* 1954, and *U. S. Income and Output,* a Supplement to the *Survey of Current Business,* 1959.

2. The assumption that all production takes place in firms implies that individual sellers of services, such as maids, gardeners, television repairmen, and dentists, are considered, for the purposes of this account, to be firms.

households, are incomes. This is shown as the clockwise flow of the upper-most arc.

The productive services are combined in the firm sector to produce outputs, which in turn flow to consumers (the inner arc of the lower section). In exchange, the firms receive consumers' expenditures, which in turn provide the funds from which aggregate money incomes, shown at the top, are paid. In this diagram we see economic activity depicted as two opposing circular flows, one real and the other monetary. There is a real flow of productive services from households to firms and of real outputs from

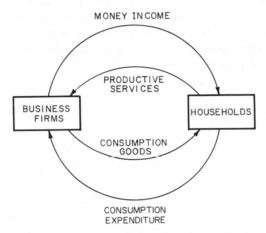

MONEY INCOME

PRODUCTIVE SERVICES

BUSINESS FIRMS

HOUSEHOLDS

CONSUMPTION GOODS

CONSUMPTION EXPENDITURE

Figure 16-1.   The Circular Flow in a Simple Economy.

firms to households. And there is a flow of money incomes from firms to households and of money expenditures from households to firms.

Figure 16-1 may be seen to embody two assumptions in addition to the elimination of government and foreign trade. First, it implies that households spend all of their incomes on consumption; there is no saving. Second, the net outputs of firms consist solely of consumption goods sold to households; there is no addition to the stock of capital goods—no accumulation or net investment.

Because of our definitions and assumptions, the money values embodied in all four loops must be identical for any period. For example, if consumption expenditures were $100 billion, the money value of output would aggregate $100 billion (for the value of anything, we have seen, is what it can command in exchange).[3] And since, in a purely private economy, the

3. We have said that consumption expenditures equal the corresponding money value of *output*, when it might be argued plausibly that consumption expenditures measure only the money value of *goods sold* to households, which might be more or less than output in the period. But if, for example, goods sold were less than output produced, accumulation or net investment would have occurred, which we have

values of output must accrue to households, total claims or incomes (the upper loop) must equal $100 billion, which may be taken also as the money value of productive services rendered to business firms.[4] Thus we can measure the total flow of the economy of Figure 16-1 either in the upper sector as aggregate incomes earned (we shall disregard the counterflow of services), or in the lower sector as total expenditures for or values of output.

The conceptual equality of these three aggregates provides more than a useful check on alternative measurements, for the three approaches yield different useful breakdowns. *Expenditures* may normally be classified by sources, depending on the number of sectors envisioned in the accounts. Values of *output* may be traced to the industrial sectors in which outputs originate, as values produced in manufacturing, agriculture, mining, service industries, etc. And earned *incomes* may be classified as wages and salaries, rents, interest, and profits.

NATIONAL INCOME FLOWS

The description of basic economic processes in terms of circular flows leads naturally into an explanation of the national income accounts. In substance, the analysis of national income, in all its complex refinements, represents nothing more than an elaboration of the simple scheme of circular flows outlined above.

---

ruled out by assumption. Moreover, it would imply that households, having received income from the production of output which remained unsold, must have spent less than their earned incomes on consumption—they must have saved—which we have also ruled out.

In the more generalized treatment below in which these assumptions are relaxed, when production exceeds sales and accumulation occurs, we shall count this as a separate category of expenditure for output by firms—investment expenditure—so that the general statement that total expenditures on output equal the money values of output will still hold.

4. We may fortify our understanding of these identities by the following example. Suppose, with income at $100 billion, as in the text example, an extra $10 billion is injected into the expenditure stream from any source. (To take one possibility, it may be newly created money borrowed by households from banks.) Then the money value of output must be marked up to $110 billion. If physical output were constant, prices must have risen 10 per cent; if prices were constant, output must have risen 10 per cent; or the result might embody a combination of both. At the same time the $110 billion now accrues to someone as income. If business contractual payments to factors remain constant (which would be true if rents were controlled by the terms of long-term leases; wages, by collective bargaining agreements; and interest, by long-term debt contracts), the increment in earnings would appear exclusively as profits. If productive service prices are flexible, competition among firms may bid up prices of scarce resources, so that some or all of the $10 billion appears as incomes other than profits. But the aggregate increase in incomes including profits, however distributed, must be $10 billion.

Income and Transfer Payments

In arriving at national income as a sum of earnings (the third of the three aggregates mentioned above), the main requirement is to distinguish between receipts which are earnings—and hence a constituent of national income—and those which are not. The test essentially is this: *any payment in exchange for a contribution to output in the current period is classified as an income payment, and counted in national income.* Other money receipts are called transfers. Included in transfers are such receipts as the proceeds from the sale of a share of stock, a used car, or an existing house; pension and annuity payments, gifts, and allowances; and, where government is included, relief payments, unemployment allowances, and interest on government debt.[5] Including financial transfers and expenditures for intermediate products (described in the next section), total payments in any period are likely to be much larger than income payments.[6]

National Product as the Sum of Values Added

In seeking to build up national income from the values of product turned out by an economy in a given period, we must beware of taking the sum of all business sales as our measure, for this would involve multiple counting. The value of coke would be included in the value of steel and included again together with the value of steel in the values of automobiles, appliances, and other products using steel. The key concept to be applied here is that of *value added*. The value added by any firm or industry is the excess of the value of sales over purchases of goods and services from other firms which contribute to the value of goods sold in the current period.[7]

---

5. The last is a debatable case. Interest on private debt is counted as earned income on the presumption that it represents payment for the contributions to production of resources over which command was transferred by creditors to debtors. On the balance sheets of business firms, therefore, the liabilities to households are matched by capital goods, or items of wealth, on the asset side. In the case of government, expansion of its debt also can be used to increase the capital of society—e.g., construction of TVA's, road systems, airports, etc. But in fact the bulk of the federal debt was accumulated during wartime, leaving no heritage of an expanded capital base to enhance subsequent production. Accordingly, the national income statistician treats this process as a massive orgy of collective consumption, rather than as investment. Rather than attempting to make the difficult judgments as to what part of government debt is "productive" and what part of the (homogeneous) annual interest charges on the debt are "income," they are all counted arbitrarily as transfers.

6. Just as, in the previous chapter, V, the transactions velocity of money, was much larger than V_y, the income velocity of money.

7. If Firm A has sales of $100,000, and goods and services bought from other firms (such as raw materials, gasoline, stationery, and electric power) total $40,000, the value added at this stage must be $60,000. In our simple model the $60,000 in turn must accrue to private factors contributing to output in Firm A; it is equal to claims in the form of wages, interest, rents, and profits. The $40,000, on the other hand, represents value added in other firms, which similarly can be resolved into its income components.

This recognizes, as noted above, that the national income accounts treat the business sector as a vast consolidated enterprise. Therefore, we must eliminate from gross sales of business all sales (purchases) between firms which are included in sales at a subsequent stage. The result is net sales to other sectors (in this case the household sector), or the aggregate value of final outputs. The fact that at each stage the value added is allocated as earnings to productive services provides another demonstration of the identity of the sum of values added and the sum of household earnings.

Saving and Investment

As noted above, Figure 16-1 represents households as spending all their incomes on consumption and depicts firms as producing only consumption goods. This implies that both saving and investment are zero. We shall now drop this restriction to consider other than zero rates of saving and investment.

Household *saving* may be defined as the difference between income available to households and expenditures on consumption. This makes saving turn on what is included in consumption expenditures. The national income statistician includes in consumption expenditures purchases not only of services and non-durable goods, about which there is little question, but also durable goods. But he treats the purchase of residential housing as investment. In part this is because of the large capital sum involved; in part because of the great durability of houses, so that purchase and use are widely separated in time; in part because of the fact that people do invest in houses and there is a rental market, so that pragmatically the rental values of houses can be approximated. Since the capital outlay for new housing is treated as investment, owners are regarded as renting their houses to themselves. Thus the rental value of owner-occupied housing, along with rentals paid by tenants, is included in consumption spending.

It is to be noted that *saving is simply income which is not spent on consumption*. In particular, saving has no necessary relationship to decisions to add to holdings of cash balances, sometimes ambiguously called "hoarding." Decisions about adding to cash holdings relate to the administration of households' accumulated assets. Saving, on the other hand, implies an increase in households' net worth—an increase in the difference between assets and obligations to others. The increase in net worth made possible by saving may take a variety of forms: an increase in assets such as money, securities, or real wealth; or the reduction of liabilities by repayment of debt, as in retirement of part of the principal of a real estate loan. Thus it is possible for an increase in saving to accompany a decline in household cash balances, or just the opposite.

Investment as treated in national income analysis consists of the increase in the stock of capital goods in any period. It is obvious that current productive activity of business firms may be directed not only to supplying households with consumer goods but also to increasing the stock of productive wealth in such forms as buildings, machine tools, and inventories of materials. The goods which compose the stock of productive wealth are termed investment goods or capital goods (in turn the firms in which they originate may be referred to as the investment or capital goods industries).[8] *Investment expenditure is expenditure for newly produced output which is added to the stock of productive wealth.*

Investment expenditure so defined occupies a strategic position in modern monetary analysis, and this usage, when unqualified, will be intended throughout this book. We must emphasize the distinction between this use of the term and its use popularly to encompass the purchase of stocks, bonds, or other claims. We may, if we wish, think of the purchase of a bond as *financial* investment to the individual, but then we must classify the same transaction as financial *disinvestment* to the seller of the instrument so that the net effect of considering both participants in the transaction is zero investment. The purchase and sale of claims involve transfer payments and have no direct effect on output and income. Only the purchase of newly created investment goods can add to the non-monetary assets of purchasers without decreasing the non-monetary assets or increasing the liabilities of others. Thus only expenditures which induce the creation of new investment goods can add directly to the wealth of the community as a whole.

Investment may be classified in various ways. In the national income accounts private domestic investment is classified as:

1. Fixed investment
   a. Residential non-farm construction
   b. Other construction
   c. Producers' durable equipment
2. Change in business inventories

Gross and Net Investment

If we were to add the total quantity of final fixed investment goods produced in any period and any change in business inventories, this would overstate the net growth in productive wealth by an amount equal to the decrease in the stock of wealth existing at the beginning of the period which is used up in current production. From total current production of investment goods, which is termed *gross investment*, we must therefore deduct capital consumption allowances (largely depreciation and accidental

---

8. This usage is clearly inexact. Since the output of any industry producing a storable product may be accumulated and thus may contribute to the stock of productive wealth, the boundaries of investment goods industries can not be neatly specified.

damage to capital goods) to find the net growth of the capital stock, or *net investment*.

Saving and Investment in the Circular Flow

We have found that households may dispose of income (Y) in two ways: they may spend it for consumption goods (C), or not spend it, which we have called saving (S). This is indicated in the modified circular flow diagram of Figure 16-2, where household income is shown devoted partly to C, which becomes a receipt stream of business firms, and partly to S, which does not. But there is now a new component of expenditure for output, which is shown at the left of the diagram as investment ex-

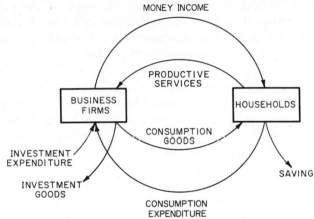

Figure 16-2. The Circular Flow with Saving and Investment.

penditure (I). At the same time the output of firms no longer consists exclusively of consumers' goods, but also includes a flow of investment goods in exchange for the flow of investment expenditure. Our fundamental identities may be stated now as follows:

Total expenditure on output $(C+I)$
    = value of consumption goods produced
    + value of investment goods produced
    = total earnings of factors $(C+S)$

As we have seen, we may view this stream as gross or net, depending on whether we adjust investment for capital consumption allowances or not. The gross output aggregate is termed Gross National Product (GNP) and the net output flow is called Net National Product (NNP), but it would be equally appropriate to consider these totals as measuring gross or net incomes accruing to productive factors. For the moment, let us look at the stream as net. For any completed period, expenditures on (and value of) output are equal to $C+I$. This sum is also equal to total earnings in the period, of which an amount C has been spent on consumption and has contributed to current income. It follows that the amount of income not spent on consumption, S, must have been exactly equal to the non-consumption expenditures on output in the period, I.

Thus, if C is 80 and I is 20, total earnings must be 100, of which 80 is disposed of as C, leaving 20 as S. For any completed period, both S and I, having been defined as equivalent to the unconsumed output of the period (i.e., $Y-C$), must be equal to each other. We shall call the accomplished or measurable saving or investment of a completed period *actual* S or I. We conclude that *actual* S and I are always identical.[9]

NATIONAL INCOME CONCEPTS IN A COMPLEX ECONOMY

We shall now expand our two-sector world of households and business firms to include government and international transactions as well, and we shall abandon the assumption that all business income becomes available to households by recognizing the existence of corporations and the reality of retained business earnings, i.e., business saving. Whereas under our simple scheme we could get along with but two concepts of income—gross national product and net national product—we now are obliged to use five: the two of our previous system plus national income, personal income, and disposable income. We shall explain these concepts briefly, emphasizing the main elements of Department of Commerce definitions.

Gross National Product

From the expenditure view the total flow directed to the purchase of final products includes not only $C+I$, with which we are already familiar, but expenditures on goods and services by government (G) and net expenditures directed toward domestic output resulting from international trade, i.e., net exports of goods and services (E). Gross national product (GNP) may then be defined as:

$$C+I+G+E=GNP.$$

In the G component we must be careful to include only expenditures for output during the period. This is less than total governmental expenditures by the amount of governmental transfers, which, as we have seen, include such elements as pension payments, agricultural subsidies, relief payments,

9. But not necessarily *planned* S and I. We shall find below that relations between planned values of S and I help explain changes in total expenditures and economic activity, but relations between actual S and I, since they are always equal by definition, are useless for explaining changes in any variables.

unemployment benefits, veterans' benefits, and interest on governmental debt. In part, government expenditures on goods and services are directed to the purchase of outputs of private firms (such as typewriters, military aircraft, and construction materials, which are included as value added in the private sphere) and, in part, to the purchase of services from households (such as those of schoolteachers, policemen, senators, and clerks). The value of the services bought directly by the government measure "value added" by government; this valuation at cost is resorted to since the product is not sold in the market.[10]

The remaining component of total expenditures for output, E, results from the flow of goods and services across international boundaries. Insofar as Americans spend part of their incomes on imports, total expenditures on domestic output are reduced, but insofar as foreigners spend part of their incomes on American exports, total expenditures on domestic output are increased. The net effect of international transactions on expenditures on domestic output is the difference between the values of imports and exports. To the extent that exports exceed imports, E will be positive, and GNP will be increased. To the extent that imports exceed exports, E becomes negative, and GNP will be correspondingly reduced.[11] In practice net ex-

---

10. The failure to recognize that in our mixed economy governmental units administer resources and turn out a product sometimes leads to distorted and captious criticism of the effects of public finance. For example, under circumstances where total taxes absorb some 25 per cent of total income, we sometimes hear that "we work one day out of four for the government," or "the government's take must come out of that which is first produced by private industry." Our study of national income accounts should show that neither of these points is well taken. While it may be true that we contribute one-fourth of our incomes to government, there is also a corresponding output, and this statistic alone tells us nothing about the effects of the exchange on our welfare. For in the same sense it may be argued that we work, say, one day out of four for farmers and distributors of food, and one day out of five for producers of automobiles and associated services, etc. The real issue is the complex one of judging the relative desirability of providing certain kinds of outputs by governmental or private administration. But we are not likely to arrive at a reasonably sound judgment by assuming in advance that the resources turned over to the government have no output at all.

11. The concept of net exports of goods and services or E must be distinguished from the concept of net foreign investment which appears in the balance of payments. E is designed to reflect net *product* flows to or from the international sector and the corresponding expenditure effects on GNP, while foreign investment is a *financial* concept, reflecting the change in international indebtedness. If American exports exceed imports, the excess, E, may be financed either by making gifts to or by acquiring claims against the rest of the world. An increase in American claims against others is termed foreign investment, since, like other investment, it reflects an increase in wealth of the American economy. If imports exceed exports, and E becomes negative, gifts must be received from others, American claims against foreign citizens be reduced, or foreign claims against Americans be increased. A net reduction in American claims against the rest of the world would constitute a decrease in net national wealth and may be termed foreign disinvestment.

As actually computed after 1959, the component E included exports of goods and services financed by *cash* grants of the federal government in various international assistance programs. These governmental expenditures, therefore, were not counted as part of government purchases of goods and services, G. But grants of international assistance in *kind* were included in G rather than in E. As a matter of expediency, private gifts and grants are counted as consumption expenditures rather than as a component in E.

ports of goods and services are rarely large for the United States (see Table 16-1 on page 318). Hence, for simplicity, most of our subsequent national income analysis will be carried out under the assumption of a closed economy. International transactions are reserved for special consideration in Chapters 28-30.

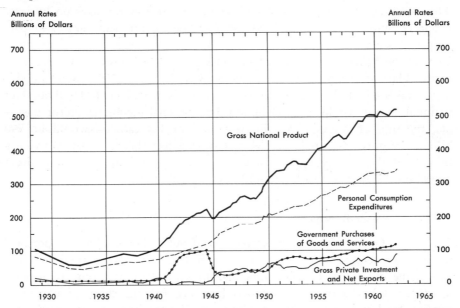

Figure 16-3. Gross National Product and its Major Components, 1929-1962. (Annually from 1929 to 1938 and quarterly from 1939 to 1962. Quarterly figures adjusted for seasonal variation.)

Source: Department of Commerce Estimates. Adapted from the *Federal Reserve Historical Chart Book.*

Movements of United States gross national product and its components over the last thirty years are presented in Figure 16-3 (*E* being combined with *I*).

Net National Product

Starting with gross national product and deducting capital consumption allowances, we arrive at net national product. The net national product represents the aggregate of outputs, valued at market prices, which potentially could be consumed in a given year and leave the community exactly as well endowed with wealth at the end as at the beginning. In principle, therefore, *NNP* may provide a better measure than *GNP* of the efficiency of aggregate economic performance. It suffers the defect, however, that while *GNP* is based on estimates of market values of final outputs, which in principle are objectively ascertainable, capital consumption allowances, whose estimated magnitude must depend on arbitrary assumptions, can be made with much less confidence.

National Income at Factor Cost

In the simple model given above the market value of output was equal to incomes earned by households, so that net national product was equal to national income measured in terms of the cost of private factors. The existence of indirect taxes, such as excises, real estate taxes on business property, etc., destroys this identity. For the government now also participates as a claimant against part of the market values of total product. Part of the business outlays and incomes generated accrue to the government. Thus, if the market values of net output were $100 billion and indirect taxes $10 billion, earnings of households would be $90 billion. Net national output would be $100 billion, but national income at factor cost— i.e., the sum of wages, rents, interest, and profits earned—would be $90 billion.[12] Figure 16-2 could be elaborated to reflect this result by showing a branch of the money income stream in the upper loop, labeled indirect taxes, and leading not to households but to government.

Personal Income

To find the amount actually paid out to households, i.e., personal income, we need to make two types of adjustments in total earned incomes: (1) Some incomes are included in earnings but not paid out to persons. These must be subtracted. Included here are (a) the share of corporate profits owed as taxes on corporate income, (b) the part of corporate earnings retained by the firm, called retained earnings or undistributed profits, and (c) that part of the category "wages, salaries, and supplements" which are paid to the government as contributions to social insurance. (2) Some incomes are received by households, but not earned; that is, they are not included in national income but nevertheless are part of the income of persons. These must be added. The major item here is governmental transfers, including social security benefits and interest on government debt.[13]

---

12. This result is approximate. In Commerce Department adjustments between net national product and national income, four minor items also will be found: (1) The surplus of governmental enterprises selling a marketed product, since it enters into market values of outputs, but does not accrue as private earned income, must be subtracted. (2) Any governmental subsidies to producers, since they add to earned incomes, but not market values of output, must be added. (3) Private transfer payments must be subtracted. These are such items as business gifts, charitable contributions, and losses on bad debts. Although included in the market values of output, they do not accrue to anyone as *earned* income; hence, we must reduce earned income accordingly. Though not earned, they become part of personal and disposable income as we shall see below. (4) Since net national product is computed on a product or expenditure basis and national income is computed independently as a sum of earnings, there is always a small statistical discrepancy, plus or minus, reflecting errors or omissions in either or both series. This appears as an adjusting item in reconciling the two aggregates.

13. A minor addition, mentioned in n. 12 above, is business transfers.

Disposable Income

This magnitude represents what households have available for disposal as consumption expenditures and saving. It equals personal income less personal taxes.

It is approximately true that starting with net national product, we can obtain disposable income by subtracting retained earnings of corporations and all taxes, and adding governmental transfers. We shall find this relationship useful later.

THE PURCHASE AND DISPOSAL OF THE GROSS NATIONAL PRODUCT

The value of gross national product provides a measure not only of outputs but of values available for disposal by the various sectors of the economy. As we have seen, these are households, business firms, and government. Figure 16-4 indicates the allocation of the *GNP* among those having disposition of it and provides a review and summary of the major elements of the national income accounts.

Starting from the left, *GNP* is shown as equal to the sum of consumption expenditure, gross private investment expenditure, and governmental expenditure on output. By means of the indicated adjustments the successive columns representing *NNP*, *NI*, *PI*, and *DI* are obtained. Grouping the same items to reflect the disposition of the *GNP*, we may start at the right with that part disposable by households, or disposable income. *DI* is allocated in part to consumption (*C*) and in part to *personal* saving, which is a component of gross private saving. The remainder of gross private saving is made up of the disposable income of business units or gross *business* saving. This consists of two elements: the part of corporate profits after taxes retained by firms (net business saving), and capital consumption allowances.[14]

Combining personal taxes, corporate profits taxes, social security contributions, and indirect taxes we arrive at gross tax receipts. But this overstates the government's disposable income, since the government, acting as an intermediary, returns a significant part of its gross receipts to the public as transfer payments and interest, where they are accounted for in personal income, disposable income, and thus in *C* and S_p. We shall count the gov-

---

14. Capital consumption allowances are part of gross business saving because they represent a part of the gross income of the economy retained by firms and not spent on consumption. They are included in the sale values of final product, but, though classed as costs and thus subtracted to arrive at net profits, they do not accrue to any household as income. Thus the disposition of these funds is retained by firms as in the case of retained net earnings.

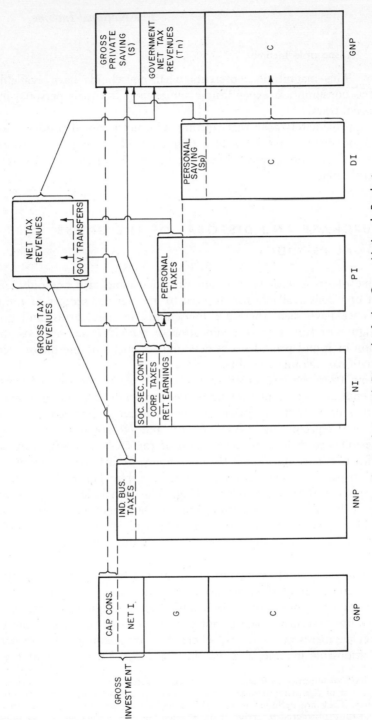

Figure 16-4. The Purchase and Disposal of the Gross National Product.

ernment's disposable income as gross taxes minus transfers; this equals net taxes (T_n).

As indicated,

$$C+I+G=C+S+T_n.$$

The total spending on output of the three sectors is equal to the values of gross incomes (i.e., *GNP*) devoted to consumption, private saving, and net governmental tax receipts.

If we subtract C from both sides, we establish a relationship corresponding to the saving-investment identity of our simple model:

$$I+G=S+T_n$$

This indicates that for a completed period the total withdrawals (sometimes called "leakages") from the expenditure stream in the form of saving and taxes must equal the amount of non-consumption spending (sometimes called "offsets" to saving) in the form of private investment and government expenditures.[15]

With these definitions and relationships before us, we can proceed to an explanation of changes in national income and related variables.

Data for the national accounts for selected recent years, indicating relationships among the concepts, are presented in Table 16-1.

SELECTED BIBLIOGRAPHY

DEPARTMENT OF COMMERCE, *National Income*, a Supplement to the *Survey of Current Business*. Washington: 1954.

————, *U. S. Income and Output*, a Supplement to the *Survey of Current Business*. Washington: 1959.

15. The basic relationship may be rearranged in a variety of ways. If tax receipts are less than governmental expenditures, $G-T_n$ is positive, and in some accounts is called government "investment." By transferring T_n to the left member we then have:
$$I+(G-T_n)=S.$$
The equation may now be interpreted as stating that the sum of private investment plus government investment is equal to saving. On the other hand, where T_n exceeds G, the excess is then referred to as government "saving." Rewritten in the form
$$I=S+(T_n-G),$$
the equation may be interpreted as indicating that gross private investment is equal to the sum of private plus governmental saving. This indicates that by suitable manipulation it is possible to affirm that saving is identical to investment, despite the existence of taxes and governmental expenditures. But since little is gained by bringing these activities so dissimilar in motive, nature, and possible effects under a common verbal umbrella, in this book we shall maintain the terminology indicated in the text. In the analytical sections we shall analyze separately the forces influencing I, G, S, and T (or T_n).

TABLE 16-1. The National Income Accounts for Selected Years (In billions of dollars)

		1929	1933	1941	1950	1955	1956	1957	1958	1959	1960	1961
Add:	Personal Consumption Expenditure	79.0	46.4	81.9	195.0	256.9	269.9	285.2	293.2	314.0	328.9	339.0
	Private Domestic Investment	16.2	1.4	18.0	50.0	63.8	67.4	66.1	56.6	72.4	72.4	69.6
	Government Purchases of Goods and Services	8.5	8.0	24.8	39.0	75.6	79.0	86.5	93.5	97.1	100.1	108.7
	Net Exports of Goods and Services	0.8	0.2	1.1	0.6	1.1	2.9	4.9	1.2	−0.7	3.0	4.0
Equals:	Gross National Product	104.4	56.0	125.8	284.6	397.5	419.2	442.8	444.5	482.8	504.4	521.3
Less:	Capital consumption allowances	8.6	7.2	9.0	19.1	32.0	34.4	37.4	38.6	40.8	43.1	45.2
Equals:	Net National Product	95.8	48.8	116.8	265.5	365.5	384.8	405.3	405.9	442.0	461.3	476.1
Less:	Indirect business taxes	7.0	7.1	11.3	23.7	32.9	35.7	38.2	39.3	42.7	45.6	47.1
	Business transfer payments	0.6	0.7	0.5	0.8	1.5	1.6	1.8	1.8	1.8	1.8	1.8
	Statistical discrepancy	0.3	0.9	0.4	−0.7	1.0	−2.4	−0.6	−1.5	−1.7	−2.6	−1.5
Plus:	Subsidies minus surplus of gov't enterprises	−0.1	0.0	0.1	0.2	0.0	0.9	1.0	1.1	0.4	0.5	1.4
Equals:	National Income	87.8	40.2	104.7	241.9	330.2	350.8	366.9	367.4	399.6	417.1	430.2
Plus:	Government transfers and interest	1.9	2.6	3.9	19.1	21.4	22.9	26.3	30.7	32.5	35.1	38.3
	Business transfer payments	0.6	0.7	0.5	0.8	1.5	1.6	1.8	1.8	1.8	1.8	1.8
Less:	Undistributed Profits*	2.9	−4.6	2.4	8.6	10.1	8.6	8.2	6.2	9.9	8.7	8.8
	Contributions for social insurance	0.2	0.3	2.8	6.9	11.0	12.6	14.5	14.8	17.6	20.7	21.9
	Corporate profits taxes	1.4	0.5	7.6	17.9	21.8	21.2	20.9	18.6	23.1	22.3	22.8
Equals:	Personal Income	85.8	47.2	96.3	228.5	310.2	332.9	351.4	360.3	383.3	402.2	416.7
Less:	Personal taxes	2.6	1.5	3.3	20.8	35.7	40.0	42.6	42.3	46.0	50.4	51.8
Equals:	Disposable Income	83.1	45.7	93.0	207.7	274.4	292.9	308.8	317.9	337.3	351.8	364.9
Less:	Personal consumption expenditures	79.0	46.4	81.9	195.0	256.9	269.9	285.2	293.2	314.0	328.9	339.0
Equals:	Personal Saving	4.2	−0.6	11.1	12.6	17.5	23.0	23.6	24.7	23.4	22.9	25.8

* Adjusted for inventory valuation.

Source: Derived from Department of Commerce estimates, reported in the *Federal Reserve Bulletin*, July, 1962.

HICKS, J. R., A. G. HART, and J. W. FORD, *The Social Framework of the American Economy* (2nd edition). New York: Oxford University Press, 1955, Parts IV and V.

KUZNETS, S. S., "National Income," *Encyclopaedia of the Social Sciences.* New York: Macmillan, 1933. (Reprinted in American Economic Association. *Readings in the Theory of Income Distribution.*)

17

THE DETERMINATION OF INCOME (I): THE CONSUMPTION FUNCTION AND THE MULTIPLIER

In the traditional quantity theories of money, as we have seen, monetary discussion was directed toward an explanation of aggregate monetary expenditures as influenced primarily by the stock of money. Implicit in this explanation of aggregate demand was a theory of aggregate supply which assumed that output would automatically adjust to the level necessary to employ all available factors of production, i.e., the theory assumed "full employment." With real output determined independently of the level of monetary demand, variation of total monetary expenditures (MV_y) would influence the price level, and of course aggregate money income, but not real output and employment.

Modern monetary analysis has recast both components of the traditional approach. Instead of focusing on the money stock, it attempts to explain monetary demand in terms of the sectoral sources of expenditure on national income as noted in the last chapter, i.e., C, I, and G. And, of particular significance, the income-expenditure approach drops the assumption that output is determined independently of monetary demand. It is assumed instead that changes in monetary expenditures may affect *either* output or prices, depending on prevailing circumstances. In this way the analysis becomes more general, while still encompassing the traditional results as a special case.

In this chapter and the next attention is confined to aggregate demand. Provisionally, we shall assume that prices are constant, so that changes in aggregate *money* income and *real* income, or output, are proportional. In effect, this implies a perfectly elastic supply curve at the current price level, with the result that output is determined by demand.

Our analysis is also primarily short run. In the economics of an individual firm or industry a short-run analysis implies a period too short for full adaptation of capacity to change. So also, characterizing an aggregative analysis as "short run" implies a period sufficiently short so that current additions to the stock of capital are negligible. Accordingly, we treat the aggregate stock of capital as constant. With the stock of capital constant, the sole variable factor in the economy is labor, and changes in output and changes in employment must therefore be closely related.[1] The employment-output relation—sometimes called the production function—implies that each level of output (or real income) requires a specific quantity of employment and each quantity of employment will produce a specific aggregate output. The level of output associated with a fully employed labor force may be called the full-employment level of output or income.[2] The assumption introduced above of a highly elastic aggregate supply curve means, therefore, that we are first examining income determination under conditions of less-than-full employment. In Chapter 20 our investigation will be extended to full-employment conditions where we allow for changing price levels.

We may begin by considering a purely private economy populated exclusively by households and business firms, as in the two-sector system of the previous chapter. Total expenditures on output in this system consist of consumption expenditures (C) and investment expenditures (I). As we have seen, values equivalent to $C+I$ accrue to owners of factors as income, which, in turn, may be spent on output (C), or used to add to household net worth in the form of money or other claims, which we have defined as saving (S). Our discussion of national income also demonstrated that for any past period saving and investment must have been identical since both are but different names for the unconsumed output of the period. But the *planned* magnitudes of C, I, or S need not be the same as their *actual* magnitudes; in this event changes in expenditures and income will occur, leading to revision of plans, further changes in expenditures, etc., until consistency is achieved between realized and planned values and equilibrium exists.

The behavior plans which we need to consider, then, are the investment

---

1. But the relationship need not be proportional. Inasmuch as more labor is associated with a fixed stock of capital, the principle of diminishing returns implies that beyond a certain point output will increase less rapidly than employment: beyond that point, for example, an increase in man hours of 5 per cent would be accompanied by an increase in output of less than 5 per cent.

2. If we conceive of a relationship between quantities of man hours which workers are willing to supply and various possible real wage rates (presumably a positive sloping curve over most of its range), we may describe any quantity of employment to the left of this supply curve of labor as involving involuntary unemployment. This implies excess supply in the labor market. In other words, more qualified man-hours are offered at the going real wage than employers are willing to purchase. Full employment (absence of involuntary unemployment) is compatible with unemployment by those who for various reasons are not employable, and with temporary unemployment of those who are shifting jobs.

plans of firms and the consumption and saving plans of households. Although household plans and business plans are being undertaken by different sectors, impelled by largely independent motives, an equilibrium relationship requires that they be consistent. The central problem to be examined, therefore, is specification of conditions under which the plans and reactions of the various sectors of the economy will or will not be consistent and therefore will not or will lead to change in the level of income.

In this chapter we shall assume that investment plans are determined by forces outside the scope of our analysis.[3] This enables us to focus attention on factors influencing consumption-saving plans, and on the relationship of such consumption plans, a given level of investment, and income.

THE CONSUMPTION FUNCTION

The consumption function, also called the propensity to consume, describes the relationship between aggregate real consumption and aggregate real income.[4] In Figure 17-1 levels of income are measured horizontally and levels of consumption, as well as income, are measured vertically. The C-curve indicates the quantities of consumption expenditures households would intend ("plan") to make for each level of income measured on the horizontal axis. If households always planned[5] to spend all their incomes on consumption, the consumption function would lie along the line OFA, which is drawn at a 45-degree angle with the horizontal base line. The 45-degree line provides a vertical indication of any income level measured horizontally; thus $AY_2 = OY_2$, $DY_1 = OY_1$, and $FY_0 = OY_0$. Since the vertical distance of the 45-degree line from the base measures income (and inasmuch as $Y = C + S$), the difference between that line and the C-curve measures planned savings at each level of income. Thus at income AY_2, consumption equals BY_2, and saving equals AB. Similarly, saving is zero at DY_1, and negative (consumption exceeds income by EF) at income FY_0.

The Marginal Propensities to Consume and Save

As we have drawn the C-curve, it is clear that as income increases, consumption also increases, but not by as much as income. A measure of the relationship between the change in consumption (ΔC) and the

---

3. This is the simplest investment assumption involving independent household and business plans; it permits, therefore, an outline of income analysis in simplest form. In the following chapter, determinants of investment are considered explicitly.

4. We recall that in the simple economy considered, net national product, national income, and disposable income are identical. Influences other than income on consumption are considered below.

5. It will be recognized that the term "planned" (or "intended") as used in aggregative analysis is a specialized terminology comparable to that used in conventional price

change in income to which it is related (ΔY) is called the marginal propensity to consume (*MPC*). Thus the *MPC* is defined as $\Delta C / \Delta Y$.[6] As the ratio of the upward movement to the horizontal movement along the curve, it measures the slope of the curve. Where, as in this case, a given curve is shown as a straight line, the slope is, of course, constant throughout. This signifies that the *MPC* is constant for all levels of income.[7]

The marginal propensity to save (*MPS*) is similarly defined as $\Delta S / \Delta Y$. Since in our two-sector system that part of income which is not spent on consumption is necessarily saved, it must be true that that part of additions to income not added to consumption must be added to saving. Thus it must be true that $MPS = 1 - MPC$. If the $MPC = 0.7$, the *MPS* must be 0.3, etc.

The slope of the consumption function shown in Figure 17-1 is less than

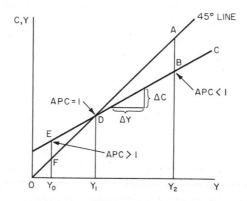

Figure 17-1. The Consumption Function.

1 throughout. Alternatively we may say that the *MPS* is positive. The doctrine that as income increases consumption will increase, but by less than the increase in income, was termed by Keynes a "fundamental psychological law." This characteristic of the consumption function is so basic to the analysis of income that we should note grounds for believing it to be true.

First, a variety of empirical studies have yielded data consistent with this conclusion. The Bureau of Labor Statistics household budget studies undertaken at intervals for establishing the weighting system of the Con-

---

analysis. Here the relationship between consumption and income is analogous to the familiar demand and supply schedules relating prices and quantities "planned" for purchase or sale. None of these relationships necessarily implies a closely calculated weighing of alternatives.

6. If a change of income from 100 to 110 ($\Delta Y = 10$) was associated with a rise in C from 90 to 98 ($\Delta C = 8$), the *MPC* would equal 0.8. If a rise in income from 110 to 120 ($\Delta Y = 10$) involved a rise in C from 98 to 105 ($\Delta C = 7$), the *MPC* would equal 0.7.

7. Where the C-curve is not a straight line, its slope, and the *MPC*, will vary throughout, in accordance with the relationships indicated by $\Delta C / \Delta Y$.

sumers Price Index have shown values of the *MPC* in the indicated range as between families with different incomes, and studies of aggregate data over time have been similarly consistent with it.

Second, the conclusion seems plausible as an extension of the general theory of consumers' choice. In general, we may think of saving as the allocation of a part of income to the building up of assets, in place of devoting it to consumption. Why, then, should a household seek to accumulate assets? First, in an uncertain world, wealth provides a hedge against unforeseen contingencies which may reduce future income, or the means for its acquisition or enjoyment (e.g., illness); in brief, it contributes to security. In addition, assets are a means of providing for specific future wants, as for education, a house, or retirement. Asset accumulation may provide a degree of freedom from the consequences of other peoples' decisions—hence a greater independence. Moreover, additional wealth may provide greater power to maneuver, an ability to respond to opportunities and to execute one's own ideas. Clearly, as income expands, we should expect some part of the addition to be used to accumulate money, other claims, or real assets, rather than to be allocated entirely to consumption goods.

Finally, we may judge the plausibility of the fundamental psychological law by its consequences. To anticipate a conclusion whose proof will be provided later in this chapter, we may assert that if the *MPC* were not less than one, our economic world would be more unstable than in fact it is. A slight increase in the rates of investment or government spending would tend toward cumulative increases in income without limit, and slight declines in these same variables would tend to force income cumulatively downward. Despite the observable instability of economic life, it would be far more unstable if the fundamental psychological law were not valid.

The Average Propensities to Consume and Save

In addition to the measure of the sensitivity of consumption to changes in income which the *marginal* propensity to consume provides, we may be concerned with another ratio, that of total consumption to total income of society or of particular individuals and groups. This ratio is known as the *average* propensity to consume (*APC*), and the particular applications to which it is put will be examined later. We may similarly define the average propensity to save (*APS*) as the ratio of aggregate saving to aggregate income. In the simplified economy which we have assumed, the sum of the two average propensities must be equal to one since that portion of earnings which is not consumed must obviously have been saved. It follows that either propensity may be determined from a knowledge of the other.

With the consumption curve shown in Figure 17-1 the average propensity to consume varies at different levels of income. At income OY_2, the APC is BY_2/AY_2, or less than one. It is equal to one at income OY_1, and greater than one at income OY_0. Since the marginal propensity to consume of this consumption function is constant throughout while the average propensity to consume varies with the income level, it is clear that the two measures need not be equal.

If we express the consumption function of Figure 17-1 in the explicit form

$$C = 20 + 4/5 \ Y,$$

we may calculate the values of C appropriate to various values of Y. From the relation $C + S = Y$, we may also deduce the related values of S. The various values of C and S, and the related average and marginal quantities, are set forth in Table 17-1.

TABLE 17-1 Consumption, Saving, Income Relationships

(C=20+4/5Y)

Y	C	S	MPC	MPS	APC	APS
70	76	−6			1.09	−0.09
80	84	−4	0.8	0.2	1.05	−0.05
90	92	−2	0.8	0.2	1.02	−0.02
100	100	0	0.8	0.2	1.00	0.00
110	108	2	0.8	0.2	0.98	0.02
120	116	4	0.8	0.2	0.97	0.03
130	124	6	0.8	0.2	0.95	0.05

Other Influences on Consumption

When we represent consumption as related to income we do not mean to imply that there are not other variables which may also influence consumption, but rather that the consumption-income relation is particularly strategic, and that it may be expected to remain stable if other influences are reasonably constant (or change in a dependable way with changes in income). Just as the familiar demand schedule, relating quantities of a good demanded with a range of possible prices, may be expected to shift with changes in such other variables as incomes, other prices, and preference patterns, so also changes in variables other than aggregate income may be interpreted as shifting the consumption-income schedule.

It may be well to note explicitly the variables which may cause a shifting of the consumption curve. This knowledge will be of value in adapting the framework of income analysis to the interpretation of events, for it will indicate the circumstances under which the consumption function may be reasonably stable, or may shift in a predictable way. In addition, recognition of these factors may have implications for policy by providing clues as to means by which consumption spending may be influenced in desired directions.

Among the important factors other than income that influence consumption are the following:

1. *The distribution of family income.* Insofar as the marginal propensities to consume differ between families, any redistribution of a constant total income would affect the aggregate consumption related to that income level. While casual observation suggests wide variations in *average* propensities to consume of households with different incomes, budgetary survey evidence suggests much less variation in relevant *marginal* propensities, so that the effects of income redistribution on aggregate expenditure are likely to be modest.

2. *Size of population.* Budget studies generally reveal significant differences in families' average propensities to consume, with values in excess of one for those with the lowest incomes and declining significantly for those with higher incomes. In addition, consumption out of a given family income tends to vary directly with the size of the family. The greater the population, therefore, among which a given national income must be distributed, the greater will tend to be the volume of consumption, for implied are lower family incomes, or larger families with given incomes, or both. Because of this consideration, consumption studies over significant periods of time are usually adjusted to a per capita basis.

3. *Changes in standards of living.* The consumption function illustrated above may be interpreted as relating to a system where consumption habits are oriented to given conventional standards with respect to form and size of consumer outlays. As real incomes rise over time, conceptions of adequate levels of consumption may rise more or less in proportion, reflecting a corresponding growth in standards of decency and respectability. This would imply an upward shift of the short-period function. Then if income falls, the influence of the current standard would be expected to lead to a movement back along our short-period curve, with saving sacrificed in greater proportion than consumption, rather than to levels of consumption achieved at these same lower income levels when standards were also lower. The influence of shifting standards makes longer period consumption-income relationships essentially irreversible.

4. *The interest rate and credit terms.* The interest rate may be viewed as the pecuniary reward for holding accumulated savings in the form of claims. Most writers formerly laid emphasis on the interest rate as a regulator of saving, generally assuming a positive relationship between interest and saving out of a given income. Modern writers, stressing such motivations as those noted above, have been skeptical of the strength and even the direction of the interest-saving relation. Nevertheless, easier credit terms together with increased availability of credit are likely to encourage increased consumption or dissaving on the part of some, even without necessarily discouraging saving by others, so that *aggregate* saving is decreased, in response to a decline in the interest rate.

5. *Taxes or transfers.* These variables lead beyond the purely private system we are now considering, but will be examined later. In brief, we may note that both taxes and transfers may shift the level of disposable income related to a given level of earned income and thus influence the amount of consumption associated with it.

6. *The price level.* The consumption function is considered to be a relationship between *real* consumption and *real* income. While we measure both variables in money terms in this chapter, this is valid only because we are assuming prices constant, so that real and money measures change in equal degree. If prices and money incomes increased while real incomes remained constant, the consumption function measured in money terms would shift upward.

The logic of this price influence may be seen from the following example. If the real consumption-income relation is $C = 20 + \frac{4}{5} Y$, then, as we have seen, when Y is 100, C would also equal 100. If money income were to double at constant prices (implying a doubling of real income), we would expect consumption to rise to 180. But if all prices and money incomes were to double (leaving real income constant), then at the new money national income of 200, we would expect consumption to rise to 200, maintaining the same real relation to income as before the change. *In money terms* the consumption function must be depicted as having remained constant in the first case, but having risen in the second. We shall find use for this effect in the analysis of inflation in Chapter 20.

7. *The stock of assets (or wealth effect).* If we consider households as seeking to accumulate a desired quantity of private assets, or wealth, the greater the present stock of assets and the smaller the difference between desired and actual accumulation, the weaker is the motive for saving out of a given income. With a given aggregate income, we should expect an inverse saving-asset relation, and a direct consumption-asset relation. It may be noted in passing that, since a lower interest rate implies a higher capital value for fixed-income claims, manipulation of interest rates may be thought of as accomplishing its effects, in part at least, by altering the market value of financial assets.

Another variant of the asset effect emphasizes changes in real values of fixed-dollar obligations, such as money and bonds, with changes in price levels. A halving of the price level should double the real value of private claims against the government in such forms as money and government bonds and thus increase the real "wealth" of the private community. If the wealth-consumption effect is positive, this should result in a rise in the real consumption function.

Having looked briefly at factors other than income affecting consumption, we can turn to an analysis of the implications of the simple consumption function. The factors noted, it will be observed, are excluded from the present discussion: in the short run we should expect the distribution of family incomes, population, standards of living, and the stock of assets to be virtually constant; we have temporarily assumed prices and interest rates (in effect) constant; and we have deferred consideration of taxes and transfers.

THE DETERMINATION OF EQUILIBRIUM INCOME

Given the consumption function, we cannot tell what consumption expenditures will be, for consumption depends on income, and income depends partly on consumption and partly on investment. But given the level of investment, which we are assuming is determined outside of our system, we have enough information to determine the values of C and Y which are consistent with the given relationships.

We can see this intuitively within the framework of the circular flow diagram of Figure 16-2 of the previous chapter. In that context suppose I is 10, and consumers always seek to spend $\frac{4}{5}$ of their earned income. If income to begin with were 100, it could not be maintained because consumers would spend 80 and business firms would spend 10, so that earnings would fall to 90, which would lead to a reduction in C, and so on. Income, in this case, will fall until consumption, which is $\frac{4}{5}$ of income, plus 10 provided by investment, is equal to the level of income. By inspection, or by trial and error, we find that this condition is satisfied by an income level of 50.

Alternatively, we may frame the discussion in terms of relationships between plans of households to save and plans of businessmen to invest. Attempts to save may be considered a "leakage," tending to reduce the circular flow of income. If the income level is to be maintained in equilibrium—neither rising nor falling over time—the leakages in the form of saving must be offset precisely by the expansionary influence of investment. Again, suppose as above that I is maintained at 10 and consumers attempt always to spend $\frac{4}{5}$ of their earned income. The latter condition implies that households try to save $\frac{1}{5}$ of their income. Beginning with income of 100, planned saving (20) would exceed planned investment (10), and the difference would measure the amount by which total planned spending on output would fall short of actual earnings (100). Thus actual income would tend to fall, leading to a reduction in planned saving, until income fell to a level at which planned saving equalled the level of investment. Again we find this condition is satisfied by an income level of 50.

In general, therefore, the condition necessary for income to remain constant over time—frequently termed the equilibrium condition—may be stated as either

$$C + I = Y, \text{ or}$$
$$S = I.$$

The first represents equilibrium as requiring that planned expenditures for consumption and investment equal the level of income which generates the expenditures, while the second indicates equilibrium as requiring an equality between planned saving leakages and planned investment offsets.[8] It is clear that either condition implies the other, and that choice between them depends solely on relative convenience for the purpose at hand. Chief emphasis in most of the following is placed on the expenditure formulation, $C+I=Y$, but on occasion the $S=I$ version also will be found useful.

An Arithmetic Approach to Income Determination

Let us formalize this analysis, starting with slightly altered conditions. Suppose that with investment given at 20, consumers' behavior may be described by the equation of Table 17-1. Then our system is:

$$
\begin{align}
(1) & \quad C = 20 + \tfrac{4}{5}Y \\
(2) & \quad I = 20 \\
(3) & \quad C + I = Y
\end{align}
$$

The solution of this system proceeds by substituting equations (1) and (2) in (3). We then have

$$20 + \tfrac{4}{5}Y + 20 = Y, \text{ or}$$
$$\tfrac{1}{5}Y = 40, \text{ and}$$
$$Y = 200.$$

Substituting this value of Y in (1), we find the equilibrium value of C which is 180. As a check on the consistency of the solution we note that when $Y=200$, planned C as determined by (1) plus I ($=20$) is equal to the level of income out of which planned consumption emerges.[9]

---

8. It is well to note the distinction between these equations expressing equilibrium conditions and the definitional identities related to the national income accounts of Chapter 16 which appear similar. Here the variables C, I, and S denote *planned* magnitudes; there they referred to *actual* or measured magnitudes. There it was shown that *actual C* + *actual I* must equal *actual* income, also that *actual* investment always must be identical to *actual* saving. Here, $C + I$ as *planned* values may not equal Y, or planned S may not equal planned I. Either inequality implies an inconsistency between plans and actualities, and a change in actual behavior in the direction of the appropriate plans. Attempts to achieve the relevant planned values change actual income and react on plans to spend as noted above. Only if planned C equals actual C (which implies that planned S equals actual S) and planned I equals actual I is there no tendency for the level of expenditure or income to change. This in turn implies the equilibrium conditions $C + I = Y$ or $S = I$ as given in the text above.
9. In more general terms, let

$$
\begin{align}
(1a) & \quad C = a + bY \\
(2a) & \quad I = \bar{I} \\
(3a) & \quad C + I = Y
\end{align}
$$

In equation (1a), a is the height of the C-curve at the point of intersection with the

A Graphic Approach to Income Determination

It will be helpful to depict this same system graphically. In Figure 17-2 (*a*), we add vertically to the consumption function of Figure 17-1 the given amount of investment, so that the curve *C+I* indicates the planned level of expenditures, measured vertically, associated with each level of earned income, measured horizontally. Since the 45-degree line shows all points in the plane of the diagram at which planned expenditures equal earned income, the intersection of this line with *C+I* at *E* indicates the

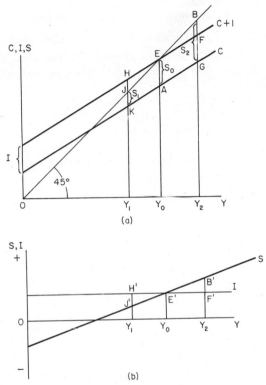

Figure 17-2.   Determination of the Equilibrium Level
of Income.

vertical axis (corresponding to a value of $Y = 0$), and b is the marginal propensity to consume. Equation (2*a*) depicts I as some *given* magnitude.

In the solution, (1*a*) and (2*a*) are substituted in (3*a*) to yield $a+bY+\bar{I}=Y$. Subtracting bY from both sides,

$$a + \bar{I} = Y - bY = Y(1 - b).$$

Dividing both sides by $(1 - b)$ and transposing,

$$Y = a/(1 - b) + \bar{I}/(1 - b).$$

This expression indicates how the equilibrium value of Y depends on the given "constants" a and b of the consumption function, and the level of $\bar{I}$.

equilibrium income. When earnings are OY_0, expenditures forthcoming are the equal amount EY_0. At this level of income, the equilibrium level of consumption is AY_0.

Income OY_0 may be termed the equilibrium income for the reason that any departure from this level cannot persist, given the conditions specified for the system. If, for example, employment consistent with income OY_1 were provided, consumption would tend toward KY_1, and, with the given level of investment, total expenditures would tend toward HY_1, in excess of OY_1 by the amount HJ. The expansion of expenditures would increase income, in turn increasing $C+I$, until E was reached.

In the other direction, if businessmen provided a level of output and income equal to OY_2, again this level could not be maintained. For aggregate expenditures on output would now move to the level FY_2, which would fall short of earned income by the amount BF. Earnings would thus decline, inducing a further decline in C and $C+I$, until level OY_0 was reached.

The same information may be presented and the same conclusions derived by means of saving and investment curves as in Figure 17-2 (b). Here investment is shown as a horizontal line at an appropriate distance above the zero line, while the S curve portrays directly the distance between the C curve and the 45-degree line of Figure 17-2 (a). As we have seen, income OY_2 is unattainable in terms of the upper chart because planned spending FY_2 falls short of the required level by BF; so also it is unattainable below because S exceeds I by the same amount $B'F'$. And as income OY_1 $(=JY_1)$ above is too small because planned expenditures HY_1 exceeds this level of income by HJ, so also below I exceeds S by the identical amount $H'J'$. We see also that equilibrium income level OY_0 which is equal to $C+I$ in Figure 17-2 (a) is identical to the level of income in Figure 17-2 (b) at which $S=I$.

The statement that income tends toward the level of OY_0, or that income OY_0 is the equilibrium level, should not be interpreted to mean that OY_0 is a *desirable* level of income. For if OY_0 is associated with substantial unemployment, income OY_2 may be preferable. But income OY_2 is unattainable under the conditions postulated. For, as we have seen, at income OY_2, planned spending falls short of earnings, or alternatively the "leakage" from the income stream represented by saving exceeds the investment "offsets" by the same amount, leading to contraction as described. Thus the distance between the 45-degree line and the C-curve or the amount of saving associated with each level of income indicates how much investment expenditure must be forthcoming in order that each level of income may be maintained.

The Investment Multiplier

The theory of income determination just described indicates that the equilibrium level of income depends on (1) the characteristics of the consumption (or saving) function and (2) the level of investment. It follows that *changes* in the level of income can be traced either to changes in the rate of I, or shifts in the consumption function. If we wish to know how much income will change as a result of a change in I or the consumption function, we could substitute the changed values into our system and find by how much equilibrium income is displaced by the assumed change.

In the graphical presentation of this system in Figure 17-3, given the consumption curve, C_0, and the rate of investment, I_0, the equilibrium income would be OY_0. If investment now rose by an amount ΔI to I_1, this would be shown in Figure 17-3 as an upward shift in the planned expenditures curve

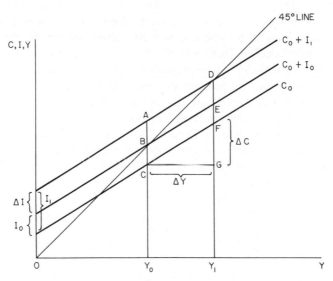

Figure 17-3.   Effect of an Increase in the Rate of Investment on Income: The Investment Multiplier.

to $C_0 + I_1$. Planned expenditures on output, AY_0, now exceed the former equilibrium level of income OY_0 (equal to BY_0) by AB (which is the amount by which planned investment I_1, or AC, exceeds planned saving, BC). Thus income expands ultimately to OY_1, bringing about a new equilibrium between planned expenditures and current income.

From Figure 17-3 we can see that the rise in income from OY_0 to OY_1, or ΔY, will be greater than ΔI because the rise in income resulting from the rise in I also induces a rise in consumption spending (the marginal propensity to consume always being assumed to be positive). The difference between income levels OY_1 and OY_0 is equal to the change in investment, DE, plus the change in consumption, FG, induced by the change in investment.

Just as the effect of a change in the rate of investment resulted from a shift in the total expenditure curve by the amount AB, any shift of the consumption curve by an equal amount should bring identical aggregate effects. We recognize that in actual practice consumption, particularly its durable goods component, cannot be regarded simply as passively responding (as the simplified explanation assumes) to prior changes in income. Nevertheless the special volatility of investment fully justifies placing primary emphasis on changes in the rate of investment as the main source of instability in the rate of overall expenditures.

Given a change in one of the variables influencing the national income, we may deduce the effects on the new equilibrium by an analysis of the system as a whole under the changed circumstances, as we have suggested in our diagrammatic technique above. Alternatively, we may seek a direct expression linking changes in income to changes in investment or other possible independent determinants. These short-cut expressions are called "multipliers."[10] The investment multiplier, K_1, indicates by what amount we must multiply a given change in investment to derive the induced change in equilibrium income. In symbols, $K_I \cdot \Delta I = \Delta Y$, or

$$K_I = \frac{\Delta Y}{\Delta I}.$$

In Figure 17-3 the investment multiplier (indicated by the ratio of the change in income, ΔY, to the change in investment, ΔI) is greater than one. This is due, as noted above, to the circumstance that ΔY is composed of ΔI, the cause of the change, plus ΔC, induced by the change in income. Intuitively, we should expect the multiplier to be higher the more sensitive is consumption to changes in income—that is, the higher is the marginal propensity to consume (the more steeply sloped is the C-curve)—for the larger then will be the ΔC-component of the new level of equilibrium income. This is borne out by the equation for the multiplier, which is

$$K_I = \frac{1}{1 - MPC}.\text{[11]}$$

---

10. Later we shall examine the effects on income of changes in government expenditures, taxes, or transfers. These also might be linked to income changes by "multipliers." In the present framework as well as in an expanded system a shift in the consumption function—i.e., a change in the average propensity to consume—would shift the total expenditures curve and lead to an augmented change in income in degree identical with that of an equal shift of the total expenditure curve caused by a change in investment.

11. We may derive this result as follows: by definition, $K_I = \Delta Y / \Delta I$. But as seen in Figure 17-3, the change in income, ΔY is equal to $\Delta I + \Delta C$. Thus $\Delta I = \Delta Y - \Delta C$. Substituting this expression for ΔI in the definition implies

$$K_I = \frac{\Delta Y}{\Delta Y - \Delta C}.$$

Dividing numerator and denominator by ΔY yields:

This implies that if consumers seek to spend $\frac{4}{5}$ of any increase in income on additional consumption, the multiplier would be 5. If the *MPC* were $\frac{2}{3}$, the multiplier would be 3.[12]

The Adjustment Process

So far our discussion of the multiplier has been confined to equilibrium relationships. We have seen that a given change in the rate of investment will lead eventually to a new equilibrium level of income that will continue higher or lower than the original level by K_I times the change in *I*. But our discussion has not specified the step-by-step time sequence in the movement of income from one level to another—the dynamics of the process. As we noted above, a study of the adjustment processes of a system is more complicated than a study of destinations (equilibria) toward which adjustment may tend. Even with a given aggregate consumption function linking *C* to various stable levels of income, a large number of different processes of adjustment to change could occur, depending on the exact timing of reactions of consumers to variation in their incomes, and the timing and degree of response of businessmen to changes in the demand for their products.

To illustrate the process of adjusting to a change in the rate of investment, let us assume that time may be divided into periods such that the

---

$$K_I = \frac{1}{1 - \dfrac{\Delta C}{\Delta Y}}.$$

Since $\Delta C/\Delta Y$, the slope of the consumption curve, or FG/CG in Figure 17-3, is the marginal propensity to consume, we obtain

$$K_I = \frac{1}{1 - MPC}$$

In the solution of the algebraic system described above, we found that $Y = \dfrac{a}{1 - b} + \dfrac{I}{1 - b}$ where a and b are the constants of the consumption function, $C = a + bY$. By inspection of this solution we observe that as I increases, Y increases by $\dfrac{1}{1 - b} \cdot I$; that is, $\Delta Y = \dfrac{1}{1 - b}\Delta I$, or $\Delta Y/\Delta I = \dfrac{1}{1 - b}$. The investment multiplier is, therefore, $\dfrac{1}{1 - b}$, and, since b in the consumption function is the rate of change of C with respect to Y, or the *MPC*, this expression is the same as that given in the text above.

12. Since the marginal propensity to save (*MPS*) in this simplified system is $1 - MPC$, we may also express the multiplier in this case as the reciprocal of *MPS*—that is, as $1/MPS$. But since this reciprocal relationship does not hold in more complicated systems, such as those which include leakages from the spending stream in the form of taxes or imports, it is advantageous to adhere to the more generally valid statement of the multiplier formula which utilizes *MPC*.

planned consumption of any period depends on the income earned in the previous period; thus, if we number periods starting from some base date, consumption in period 1 will depend on income earned in period 0, and consumption in period 2 will depend on income earned in period 1, etc.

In addition, in order to eliminate the complexities of unintended disinvestment, and possibly accelerated restocking following an unanticipated increase in sales, we shall assume that producers anticipate correctly any change in C, so that no lag occurs between changes in consumption and changes in output or earned income. Given these conditions, the period-to-period working out of the multiplier process may be represented as in Figure 17-4, where intervals of time are measured from left to right, and

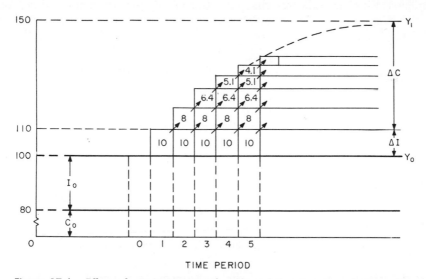

TIME PERIOD

Figure 17-4. Effect of an Increase in the Rate of Investment on Income: The Adjustment Process.

quantities of expenditure vertically. During early periods at the left the system is in equilibrium, with income constant from period to period at the rate of 100, consisting of 20 investment and 80 consumption. We shall assume that households will consume $\frac{4}{5}$ of any *additional* income as well.

Let us suppose now an increase in the rate of investment from 20 to 30, beginning in period 1 and maintained indefinitely. In period 1 total expenditure on output will rise to 110. This will consist of I of 30 plus C of 80, C being unchanged from previous levels, since C in period 1 is assumed to depend on the level of income in period 0. The rise in income over the base income of 100 is shown by the height of blocks originating at the 100 level. The arrows show the origins of the changes for each period. In period 2 the rise in income over that of the base period consists of a rise in I of 10, supplemented now by a rise in C of 8, resulting from the rise in income in period 1 by 10. Income in period 2 is thus 118. In period 3, ΔI again contributes 10 to expenditures, supplemented by a rise in C of 8 because of the augmented investment of the previous period, and a further rise in C of 6.4, traceable in turn to the rise in C of 8 in period 2. Income thus rises to 124.4. Continuing this process, we would expect the rise in income in each subsequent period to be equal to ⅘ of the rise in each preceding period, forming a geometric progression whose limit approaches the income level of 150. At this new equilibrium level the rise of income of 50 consists of the rise in the rate of investment of 10, plus the induced rise in consumption of 40.

Our illustration points up a number of considerations which deserve emphasis. First, it indicates that adjustments to change require time, and

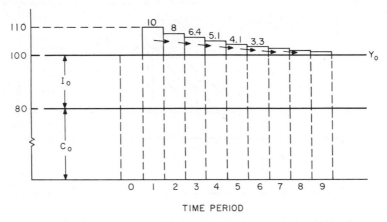

Figure 17-5.   Effect of a Single Investment Injection on Income.

that the nature and duration of the adjustment period will depend on the nature and timing of reactions of economic participants. Only one lagged reaction is included here—that between spending and earning income, assumed to be one period.

Second, in analyzing how changes in investment (or other variables) affect income, we are interested in the influence of a sustained change in the level of these variables on the sustained level of income. The related flows per period are measured vertically in Figure 17-4. Our concern is not with the sum of the horizontally measured effects of an isolated expenditure at one time. In Figure 17-4 if we trace repercussions of the specific increment to investment in period 1, we see that it leads to a rise in C of 8 in period 2, of 6.4 in period 3, of 5.1 in period 4, etc. This sequence is isolated in Figure 17-5 which depicts the assumed single dose of added investment in period 1, after which investment recedes to its previous level. We see that this single item leaves a lingering, but diminishing, influence on succeeding levels of income. In all, incomes rise by five times the original expenditure, but in the end the equilibrium level of income remains unchanged at 100. (We could view this process as a rise in the *rate* of investment by 10 in period 1, followed by a fall in the *rate* of investment by 10 in period 2. Our equilibrium analysis above would give us the correct conclusion: there would be a possible temporary effect during the process of adjustment, but the new equilibrium level of income would be unchanged.) When we refer to an increase in the *rate* of investment, we mean an increase in the flow per period of additions to the stock of capital. Given this *continuing* flow at a higher level, we are interested in the eventual augmented but constant flow of income, once full adjustment has been made to the change.

Finally, we may note that although our discussion of the multiplier has focused mainly on positive changes in investment, the multiplier also operates in the opposite direction. With a multiplier of 5, we should expect to find in the new equilibrium a reduction of 4 dollars of consumption and 5 dollars of income for each dollar by which the rate of investment is reduced.

The multiplier analysis suggests a number of direct applications. If there are cyclical fluctuations in investment, other things the same, we should expect fluctuations in national income which are some multiple of those in investment. This provides a clue that has been found helpful for explaining the business cycle. The multiplier also aids in assessing the requirements of policy. Assuming a multiplier of three, if the current level of income is $30 billion less than that consistent with the desired level of employment, the size of the multiplier indicates that to attain that goal the total expenditure curve must be raised not by $30 billion but by $10 billion.

SELECTED BIBLIOGRAPHY

ACKLEY, GARDNER, *Macroeconomic Theory*. New York: Macmillan, 1961, Chapters 10-13.

HANSEN, ALVIN H., *A Guide to Keynes*. New York: McGraw-Hill, 1953, Chapters 3, 4.

KEYNES, J. M., *The General Theory of Employment, Interest and Money*. New York: Harcourt, Brace, 1936, Chapters 8-10.

KLEIN, L. R., *The Keynesian Revolution*. New York: Macmillan, 1947, Chapter 3, pp. 56-79 and Chapter 4.

SAMUELSON, PAUL, "The Simple Mathematics of Income Determination." In *Income, Employment, and Public Policy: Essays in Honor of Alvin Hansen*. New York: McGraw-Hill, 1948.

18

THE DETERMINATION OF INCOME (II): INVESTMENT, THE ACCELERATOR, AND FISCAL EFFECTS

The present chapter extends the discussion of income determination in two directions. First, the provisional assumption used in the preceding chapter that investment is a given magnitude is relaxed and the factors determining the rate of investment expenditure are examined. The main objective of this investigation is to establish an investment demand schedule relating investment to the rate of interest. In addition the influence of changes in output on investment—the "acceleration effect"—is considered in relation to its effects on both equilibrium income levels and cyclical adjustment patterns.

Second, the analysis is extended from a concern with a purely private economy to one including government as well. This involves consideration of the effects of changes in government expenditures, taxes, and transfer payments on the level of income.

THE DETERMINATION OF THE RATE OF INVESTMENT

Investment depends on a vast number of subjective and objective influences. The aim of this section is to present a framework which will permit this complex array of facts and tendencies to be so organized as to clarify their probable effects on investment activity.

The "Efficiency" of an Asset

Just as the purchaser of a financial instrument such as a bond may expect a certain rate of return or "yield" on his money—which will depend on the prospective payments to be received and the purchase price—

so also the investor in a newly produced real asset will expect some rate of return on funds invested. This rate of return may be called the *efficiency* of the asset. To estimate it we shall need to know (1) the amounts and timing of the series of prospective money receipts which may be expected from possession of the asset, and (2) its current cost of production.

The stream of money receipts may be called the *prospective return* of the asset. (This is not the same as its "efficiency.") It includes the sale value of the series of outputs which an additional unit of equipment makes possible over its useful life, minus the cost of cooperating factors such as labor, materials, power, and taxes. It is a series of net returns. But since we do not deduct depreciation or interest costs of financing, it is a stream of net money receipts, rather than a net income stream.

Assume that the series of annual returns to which an asset entitles its owner is represented by R_1 at the end of the first year, R_2 at the end of the second year, through R_{10} at the end of the tenth year, after which the asset becomes useless and its returns zero. Assume that its cost of production is C. If we discount each element of this stream of returns at the rate r, so that the present value[1] of this series of returns is equal to C, we have

$$(1) \qquad C = \frac{R_1}{1+r} + \frac{R_2}{(1+r)^2} + \frac{R_3}{(1+r)^3} + \cdots + \frac{R_{10}}{(1+r)^{10}}$$

In this equation we know C, the present cost of the capital good, and estimates of the prospective R's. The value of r which makes both sides equal is the "efficiency" of this asset.

Let us illustrate this relationship by substituting numbers in equation (1). Suppose we anticipate net returns of $1,000 at the end of each of the ten years of the life of the capital good. Then the rate of return on an investment in this field will depend on the cost of the capital good. If it costs $10,000, we shall expect only to recoup our initial outlay over the ten years, and the yield would be zero. But if the cost were less than $10,000, we

---

1. We mean by the present value of, say, A dollars in the future, the number of dollars in the present, which if invested at the rate of r, compounded annually, would grow into A dollars in the specified period. Thus the present value of $104 due in one year, discounted at 4 per cent, is $100; for $100 + 0.04 ($100) = $104 [or $100 (1 + 0.04) = $104].

Moreover, if we accumulate $104 at the end of one year to the end of year 2 at 4 per cent, we have the amount $104 + $104 (0.04), or $104 (1 + 0.04), or $100 (1.04) (1.04), or $100 (1.04)² —all of which equal $108.16.

Thus we may write: $100 (1.04)^2 = $108.16, or, dividing both terms by $(1.04)^2$, $100 = \dfrac{\$108.16}{(1.04)^2}$. The last expression indicates that $108.16, discounted at the rate (0.04) for two periods, is equal to $100. Generalizing, $P (1 + r)^3 = A$, indicates that P dollars, accumulated over three periods at the rate r is equal to A dollars; or $P = \dfrac{A}{(1 + r)^3}$; which indicates that the present value of A dollars three years from now, discounted at the rate r, is equal to P dollars.

would anticipate a positive return, and, the lower the cost, the greater would be the expected rate of return. In Table 18-1, the implicit rates of yield, or "efficiencies," are presented for various alternative values of C.

TABLE 18-1. Efficiences (r) Related to Various Costs (C) of an Asset Expected to Return $1000 Per Year for Ten Years

C	r
$10,000	0.0
8,982.59	0.02
8,110.90	0.04
7,360.09	0.06
6,710.08	0.08

In general, we may say that anything that increases the prospective R's, assuming a constant C, or anything that reduces C, if expectations as to prospective returns are constant, will raise the efficiency (r) of the asset in question.

The Marginal Efficiency of Capital

At any given time there will be an array of possible efficiencies relating to the production of additional units of various assets. But there is only one most efficient way of utilizing a small addition to the stock of capital of society. The highest of the potential rates of return from adding one more unit of capital is called the *marginal efficiency of capital* (*MEC*).

The marginal efficiency of capital will depend, in part, on the amount of capital already accumulated. In Figure 18-1(a), rates of return as well as interest rates are measured on the vertical axis, and quantities of accumulated capital goods or the stock of capital in value terms, on the horizontal axis. (For the present, Figure 18-1 (b) should be disregarded.) If the stock of capital is K_0, valued, say, at $1,000 billion, the marginal efficiency of that stock is r_0. If the capital stock were larger, we should expect the marginal efficiency to fall, for in accordance with the principle of diminishing returns each additional unit of capital would be expected to add less to the increase in output than preceding increments and thus lead to a reduction of the R's of our formula, and so also the r's. With other forces constant— in particular, population, knowledge, and the state of expectations—the various rates of return appropriate to the alternative stocks of capital (K_0, K_1, K_2 etc.) trace out the marginal efficiency of capital curve (MEC_0).

If the capital stock is K_0 (or $1,000 billion) and the interest rate is i_0, the excess of the marginal efficiency of capital (r_0) over i_0 should encourage net investment in capital instruments. For a firm may borrow at the rate i_0, and by investing at the expected return on real assets r_0, it will expect to increase the flow of profits of the firm, which in turn will increase the present value of the firm by the capitalized value of the increase in prospective income.

Alternately, if we discount the prospective returns of capital assets by the market rate of interest (i_0), we find the *market value* of the capital goods as investments. This tells us what investors could afford to pay for the capital instruments in order to earn a rate of return equivalent to that on bonds. So long as the market rate of interest is less than the marginal efficiency of capital, the market values of the capital goods will be greater than their costs, and this provides the incentive for their production.[2]

Given the schedule of marginal efficiencies (MEC_0) and the interest

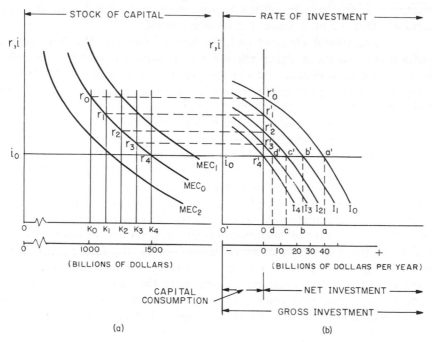

Figure 18-1. The Rate of Return on Capital and the Demand for Investment.

rate r_0, Figure 18-1 (a) indicates that capital will tend to accumulate to K_4 ($\$1,500$ billion) at which level the marginal efficiency of capital (r_4) would equal i_0.

2. We may illustrate this result by reference to Table 18-1. Suppose that r_0, the *MEC*, is 8 per cent. This implies that the cost of production of a capital good whose prospective returns are estimated at $\$1,000$ a year for ten years is $\$6,710$. If the market rate of interest (i_0) were 4 per cent, such a prospective returns stream would have a market value as an investment of $\$8,110$. By borrowing funds at 4 per cent and investing in real assets, the firm can increase its market value by the difference between $\$8,110$ and $\$6,710$, or $\$1,400$.

This suggests that we may think of firms as arbitragers between the capital markets and capital goods markets, strategically placed to improve their position by simultaneous purchase and sale whenever the yields in these related markets differ.

The Investment Demand Schedule

But Figure 18-1(a) does not indicate the *rate* of investment, which will depend on how rapidly the difference between K_4 and K_0 is eliminated. If the gap is $500 billion and is closed in one year, the indicated annual rate of investment is $500 billion; if closed in 10 years, the annual rate averages $50 billion; if the desired accumulation is spread over 50 years, the indicated rate averages $10 billion. These considerations emphasize that investment, like consumption, saving, income, and production, is a flow and must be measured always with a time dimension as so much per period. Investment is the growth of the capital stock per period, and it is this magnitude that we must know for income analysis.

Investment Demand and the Rate of Interest. We have seen in equation (1) that the marginal efficiency of resources devoted to increasing the stock of capital depends on (1) the prospective returns (R's) related to newly produced capital goods, and (2) the costs of production of these or similar capital goods. But further consideration indicates that neither of these factors is independent of the rate of accumulation. On the side of cost, to look at this aspect first, the explanation is straightforward: as the output of investment goods increases beyond some point, we may expect their marginal costs of production to increase. This factor alone should tend to reduce the rate of return on investment, particularly when the rise in rate of accumulation reaches the high tempo characteristic of boom periods.

In addition, considerations of uncertainty lead to a significant relationship between the rate of accumulation and prospective returns on capital investment. Because of the existence of uncertainty, the future returns from investment goods constitute a range of probable values rather than single values expected with assurance. In estimating the rate of return on such assets, the investing firm must give weight not only to some average returns expected for each period in the future, but also to the probability of less favorable as well as more favorable outcomes. As a firm gives up a current asset or creates a liability against itself to acquire an additional capital good, it will increase its profits if its expectation of a favorable outcome is realized. But in the event of an adverse contingency, the firm will lose. The acquisition of the real asset thus increases the firm's profit opportunities, but also places it in a more risky position. In general, the higher the rate of real investment per period and the greater the growth of financial commitments in relation to original equities, the more vulnerable are firms and their managers to unfavorable contingencies. Losses that might be of minor concern with relatively modest commitments may be disastrous when undertaken on a large scale. When increased risk is on balance considered to outweigh the prospect of higher profits, we may treat the increasing risk attending increasing investment commitments as a factor reducing prospective yields of capital goods.

Thus, both determinants of the efficiency of capital assets in equation (1) are adversely affected by an increase in the rate of capital investment per period: marginal costs are increased, and expected (risk-adjusted) returns are reduced.

Given the stock of capital, we should expect increasing amounts of investment per period to involve declining rates of return; this relationship we may term the *marginal efficiency of investment* schedule or curve. For each rate of interest there would be some appropriate rate of investment at which the marginal efficiency of investment (*MEI*) would equal the rate of interest. Investment thus becomes a function of the rate of interest, and the *MEI* schedule which describes the amount of investment which would occur at various interest rates may be termed the *investment-demand schedule*.

Investment Demand and the Marginal Efficiency of Capital. The relationship of the investment demand curve and the marginal efficiency of capital curve may be illustrated by turning from Figure 18-1(*a*) to the related Figure 18-1(*b*) which depicts hypothetical investment-demand schedules. The horizontal axis now measures, not accumulated stocks of capital, but rates of change in the current stock, such as *x*-dollars worth per period.[3] To the right of the O-axis we measure net positive investment, while the distance O'O indicates the rate of capital consumption appropriate to the current stock of capital, so that distances to the right of the O'-axis provide a measure of gross investment. An investment rate lying between O' and O would constitute positive gross, but negative net, investment.[4]

Given the stock of capital K_0 in Figure 18-1(*a*), the marginal efficiency of capital (*MEC*), r_0, corresponds to the marginal efficiency (*MEI*) of a rate of production of capital goods of O'O in Figure 18-1 (*b*), or zero net investment.[5] This provides one point, r'_0, on the related investment demand curve. For greater quantities of investment per period, the marginal efficien-

3. Note also the change of scale. An interval which on the horizontal scale of Figure 18-1(*b*) measures $40 billion per period measures $500 billion on the scale of Figure 18-1(*a*).

4. For simplicity, capital consumption is represented as constant in Figure 18-1(*b*). If, more realistically, we wish to take account of the likely growth of capital consumption as capital accumulates, we can visualize the axis O' in the chart being moved to the left in proportion to the growth of capital consumption. This would permit measurement of *net* investment, as before, from the axis O to the right.

5. We have seen that the rate of return on investment activity depends not only on the stock of capital, but also on the rate of increase in that stock. We must, therefore, specify the rate of production of capital goods to which any rate of return corresponds. This leads to a more precise definition of the marginal efficiency of capital than that given above. The marginal efficiency of a given stock of capital may be defined as the highest of the potential rates of return corresponding to a rate of investment activity which would just suffice to maintain the stock of capital constant. In brief, it is the rate of return on the most profitable marginal investment *while just maintaining a given capital stock.*

cies will fall, because of increasing risk and cost, tracing out the *MEI*-curve, I_0. (The I_0-curve is drawn concave to the origin to reflect the tendency of both risks and costs to increase at increasing rates in response to increases in investment.) Moving along the I_0-curve, the marginal efficiency of investment becomes equal to the interest rate at a', leading to a rate of net investment of Oa, or $40 billion per year. With interest rates higher or lower than i_0, the corresponding amount of investment is indicated by the appropriate points on the I_0-curve. The I_0-curve may thus be taken as an investment demand schedule, and its shape, not that of MEC_0, determines the sensitivity of investment—at any given moment—to interest rate changes.

As Figure 18-1(b) is drawn, investment takes place at Oa per period and the stock of capital gradually shifts to the right so that the marginal efficiency, moving along MEC_0, falls. When the stock of capital reaches K_1, its marginal efficiency is r_1, reducing the gap between the yield on assets and bonds and shifting the related investment demand curve to I_1. At the prevailing interest rate i_0, the rate of investment falls to Ob. With continued accumulation, the investment demand curve shifts to the left as the marginal efficiency of capital falls, slowing the rate of investment until the quantity of capital reaches K_4 and its marginal efficiency falls to r_4; at this rate the appropriate investment curve shifts to I_4, intersecting the interest rate line at the point r'_4, corresponding to zero net investment.

The point illustrated is that capital accumulation tends to shift the investment demand curve to the left, weakening the inducement to invest. In part this may be offset by a reduction in the rate of interest. But, as our diagram indicates, where the investment demand curves are not highly interest elastic, not much may be hoped for in this direction. In that case, the main force leading to a recovery of investment must take the form of a shift of the investment demand curve to the right. This implies an upward shift of the *MEC*-curve in Figure 18-1(a). Thus during a period in which the capital stock increased from K_0 to K_2, which would lead to a shift of the *I*-curve from I_0 to I_2 and (at the given rate of interest) to a decline in investment from Oa to Oc, the decline in investment could be avoided by a sufficient shift in the *MEC*-curve, say to MEC_1. At this higher level, as our chart indicates, the investment curve and rate of investment would be maintained, despite the greater stock of capital. Similarly, a greater upward movement of the *MEC*-curve would tend to push the *I*-curve farther to the right and expand investment, while a fall in the *MEC*-curve, as to MEC_2, would tend to depress investment.

What forces tend to shift the *MEC*-curve? In general terms, the answer is any factor which reduces the costs of capital goods or raises expected returns, without an offsetting change in the other. But what are the factors which have these effects? Broadly speaking, the underlying causes of such shifts in costs and expectations are associated with the forces of change in the economy. The growth of new technical knowledge and its applications tend to reduce the cost of producing familiar goods and render previous technologies obsolete, leading to their replacement with more up-to-date methods. The development of new products and services is also a powerful force stimulating the production of entirely new types of capacity. As new knowledge provides incentive for additional capital growth, we may expect it to increase the amount of capital utilized per unit of output, i.e., to result in a *deepening* of capital.

Another major source of increase in prospective returns is associated with the growth in absolute size of the economy. Thus the expansion of population and geographic area may necessitate more capital goods of accustomed types to produce greater outputs, without a change in the capital-output ratio. This growth in capital utilization is called a *widening* of capital.

Finally, we must stress that the returns influenced by the elements of growth and change are *expected* returns. Applying as they do to an uncertain future, the individual investor can never feel entirely confident that he has correctly evaluated all possible events which might bear on his investment decision. The estimates of the future on which investment depends are particularly precarious, subject to considerable shifts with changes in the news, or confidence, or the climate of opinion. Thus psychological forces contribute to the observed volatility of investment, but, at the same time, we may not doubt that, however distorted it may be by our imperfect vision of the future, investment activity is also firmly rooted in the real factors which were discussed above.

INTERRELATIONS BETWEEN INVESTMENT AND CONSUMPTION

Widening and deepening of capital have very different influences on the process whereby the economy adjusts to changed conditions. The basis of the difference lies in the distinction between induced and autonomous investment. *Induced investment* refers to the growth in size of capital stock caused by the growth of output. It is to be distinguished from investment which is caused by shifts in the marginal efficiency schedule resulting from external changes such as advances in scientific knowledge. This is termed *autonomous investment*.

The Accelerator

The existence of induced investment (and the related "accelerator" together with the multiplier) provides the basis for some of the best-known explanations of the business cycle. Aside from the light which it sheds on cyclical behavior, a consideration of induced investment is also of interest because it brings out the difference between the analysis of a self-generating process, frequently termed "dynamics," and the analysis of equilibrium with which this book is mainly concerned.

Let us assume a given state of knowledge and given interest rates so that the quantity of capital equipment required to produce a unit of output of some good is constant. Then an increase in output (taken for the moment as given) would require a proportionate increase in capital, and induced investment would be positive. If output were constant, the desired capital stock would also be constant and induced investment zero. And if output declined, the required capital stock would fall, and induced investment would be negative. It is clear that the induced investment in a given period depends on (1) the amount of capital required per unit of output (the capital-output ratio), and (2) the change in output during the period.

These relationships may be clarified by an example. Suppose that a plant producing 100,000 pairs of shoes per period requires 100 shoe machines, that the life of each machine is 10 years, and that the timing of purchases in the past results in 10 machines wearing out every year. Then the demand for shoes, the demand for machines for replacement, and the net induced demand for machines would be as shown in the entries in Table 18-2.

TABLE 18-2. Demand for Shoe Machines as Derived from the Demand for Shoes

Period (1)	Demand for Shoes (2)	Required Number of Machines (3)	Replacement Demand for Machines (4)	Additional Net Demand for Machines (5)	Total Demand for Machines (6)
0	100,000	100	10	0	10
1	100,000	100	10	0	10
2	110,000	110	10	10	20
3	120,000	120	10	10	20
4	125,000	125	10	5	15
5	125,000	125	10	0	10
6	120,000	120	10	−5	5

In period 0 production of the 100,000 pairs of shoes requires 100 machines. To maintain this stock in the period requires a replacement demand of 10; since no net increment to capacity is called for, the total demand for shoe machines also is 10. If the output of shoes remains constant at 100,000, as in period 1, the result is a constant number of machines required, a constant rate of replacement, and a constant total demand for shoe machines. If now in period 2 the demand for shoes increased to 110,000, 110 machines would be needed, and the replacement demand for machines would be augmented by a demand for 10 additional machines, increasing the total demand for machines to 20. (An increase of 10 per cent in consumption demand by inducing a rise in net investment, brings about a 100 per cent increase in total investment demand.) If output in period 3 rose to 120,000, the stock of machines required would increase to 120, again supplementing the replacement demand of 10 by an incremental demand of

10, and so maintaining total demand for machines at 20. We see here that in order to maintain the incremental demand (or induced net investment) for machines constant (column 5) the shoe output must increase by a constant amount per period.

In period 4 if demand increases to 125,000, i.e., by less than 10,000, 125 machines are needed. Replacement demand remains at 10, but induced net investment falls to 5, and total demand for machines falls to 15. If now demand for shoes were to level off at the new plateau of 125,000, as assumed for period 5, induced investment would disappear, and the demand for machines would revert to the replacement level necessary to maintain the stock of machines constant at 125.[6]

Finally, if the demand for shoes now fell to 120,000, as in period 6, the reduction in the required stock of machines to 120 (inducing net investment of −5) would lead to a reduction in the total demand for machines to 5. If final demand now levels off, net investment will rise to 0, total demand for machines depending exclusively on replacement requirements. On the other hand, if final demand declines further, induced investment may continue as a negative quantity, and total demand for machines may be correspondingly reduced.

In general, Table 18-2 suggests that the *level* of induced investment in machines in column 5 depends on the *change* in demand for shoes in column 2. For each increase in demand for shoes of 1,000, induced machine investment is 1; for each decrease in final demand of 1,000, induced investment is −1; a constant final demand for shoes is associated with induced investment of zero. If we now translate these physical units into dollar values, we might get the following. If 1,000 pairs sold for $5,000, and the price of a machine was $10,000, for each $1 increase in final sales, induced investment would be $2; for each $1 decrease in final sales, induced investment would be −$2. The level of induced investment would be 2 times the change (plus or minus) in final sales value of shoes. This constant, linking the level of induced dollar investment with the change in demand for final products in dollars (2 in our example) is termed the *accelerator*.

The accelerator and induced investment are relevant whenever there is a relatively fixed relation between the stock of capital and the flow of production to which it contributes. Supplementing the shoe illustration, which relates to the use of fixed capital goods in manufacturing, the principle might be applied to increments in inventories (inventory investment) as induced by changes in sales, apartment building (construction investment) as related to changes in demand for housing, and expansion in the stock of railroad cars (equipment investment) as induced by an increase in demand for passenger or freight service. For the economy as a whole we

---

6. At this point replacement demand is 10 but ultimately the enlarged stock of machines necessary for producing shoe output at the new higher level will require a rise of replacement to 12.5 per period.

could relate aggregate induced investment to changes in the aggregate value of consumption goods, or even more generally, to changes in the value of total final output.

Interaction of Accelerator and Multiplier

It may be useful now to examine how the process of income adjustment is affected by the introduction of the accelerator. But first a word of recapitulation is in order.

In Chapter 17 we traced the period-to-period adjustments in income caused by a rise in planned investment. It was assumed that the rate of investment would be maintained constant at the new level. As a result, income rose from period to period not only because the rise in investment increased income directly, but also because this initial rise in income induced a rise in consumption which in turn induced a further rise in income, and so on, period after period. Successive rounds tapered off and in the end a new equilibrium level of income was attained. This new level was higher than the old by the change in autonomous investment times the multiplier. The substance of the multiplier analysis was to show the effect on consumption and income of a given change in *investment*.

The explanation of the accelerator presented in the previous section reverses the argument. Instead of starting with a change in investment we start with a change in consumption. The accelerator concept helps us to trace the effects on investment, and therefore on income and output, of an assumed change in *consumption*. We may now proceed to combine the accelerator effect with the multiplier effect.[7] It will be seen that the resulting period-to-period adjustments may be dramatically different from the changes indicated by either the multiplier or accelerator when viewed in isolation.

Let us assume once more that autonomous investment rises to a new level thereby inducing, in accordance with the multiplier, a rise in consumption. The accelerator concept tells us that the rise in consumption now calls for an expansion in capital goods to produce the larger stream of consumption goods. This induced investment increases income further, thus leading to further repercussions on consumption and induced investment in mutual interaction, period after period.

We see that the rise in income over the initial equilibrium level consists of three elements: (1) the rise in autonomous investment, assumed to be constant at the new level, (2) the induced rise in consumption, and (3) induced investment. Consumption will rise if income rises, the amount depending on the marginal propensity to consume. Induced investment, in

7. The pioneering statement of these interrelations is in Paul Samuelson, "Interactions between the Multiplier Analysis and the Principle of Acceleration," *The Review of Economic Statistics*, XXI (May 1939), pp. 75-78 (reprinted in AEA, *Readings in Business Cycle Theory*, pp. 261-69).

turn, depends on the rate of change of consumption and the accelerator: induced investment may either rise or fall, depending on whether the *rate of change* of consumption is increasing or decreasing. In the end, assuming that equilibrium is attained, it will be at the level determined by the change in autonomous investment and the multiplier. At that point the accelerator will no longer exert any influence since in equilibrium the rate of change

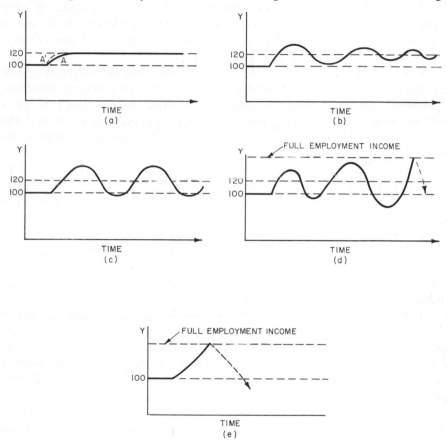

Figure 18-2.   Interactions Between the Investment Multiplier and the Accelerator.

of consumption is zero and induced investment is therefore also zero. But while the accelerator may have no influence on the equilibrium toward which income may tend, it will affect the process whereby equilibrium is reached. Indeed, it may possibly determine whether or not an equilibrium position can ever be reached.

The pattern of income adjustment depends on two factors: (1) the marginal propensity to consume (or the multiplier), and (2) the accelerator. The interrelation of these two factors is not easily summarized, but the possibilities and general directions may be suggested by a further example. Suppose an initial equilibrium income of 100, a marginal propensity to consume of ½, and a permanent rise in the rate of autonomous investment of 10. Neglecting the accelerator (or assuming it to be zero) income would rise smoothly over time to a new equilibrium level of 120, as shown by the solid line A in Figure 18-2(a).

If induced investment is now introduced but the accelerator is very small, income again will rise directly to the new equilibrium level, but it will do so somewhat more rapidly. This path of adjustment over time is shown as the dotted line A' in Figure 18-2(a).

If the accelerator is now made larger, income will no longer approach equilibrium directly, but will tend to overshoot the mark, reverse direction, overshoot again, and reverse, tracing out a cyclical pattern. But the cycles will be damped; they will gradually subside, approaching eventually the same stable equilibrium of 120 described above. This income pattern is depicted in Figure 18-2(b).

As the accelerator is increased to a certain critical value (in this case to 2), cycles in income of constant amplitude are generated, as in Figure 18-2(c). For these particular values of the accelerator and multiplier, once income is disturbed it continues to fluctuate indefinitely without ever attaining a stable value.

If the accelerator is increased somewhat more, cycles of increasing amplitude are generated, as in Figure 18-2(d). Clearly this pattern of instability cannot continue indefinitely. For widening cycles brought about by large induced-investment effects are limited in the upper direction by full-employment output, and in the lower direction by the fact that negative induced investment is limited by the amount of potential capital consumption of the period. Thus income can go no lower than the level associated with zero *gross* investment, reaching a floor at a level corresponding to expenditure on consumption alone. And at the top the growth of consumption goods output is restrained by the limit to total production at full employment.

It is important to note that under the given assumptions the decline in the *rate of increase* leads to a decline in induced investment and consequent decline in income, a further decline in consumption, and thus on to a continued downward swing of income. Ultimately this leads to negative induced investment. But negative induced investment is limited as noted above; hence income is also limited in the downward direction. Eventually, negative investment will run its course as the capital stock is reduced to a level which requires a renewal of replacement investment to service the continuing level of consumption demand. At this point a rise in income, initiated by the renewed investment demand, will set in motion a new cyclical response of rising amplitude, repeating the pattern just described.

Finally, it may be assumed that the accelerator has an even higher value so that there is no cyclical response but, instead, income rises at an increasing rate, as in Figure 18-2 (*e*). Should such a situation develop, full employment would set an upper limit to the expansion. As in the previous case, induced investment would then fall, leading to a fall in income, reduced consumption, and negative investment. Eventual recovery would lead to a cumulative rise again to the upper limit, and hence a reverse and decline to the lower limit, and so on through time.

Qualifications of the Multiplier-Accelerator Analysis

The foregoing sketch of interactions between the multiplier and accelerator has treated them as if they were virtual constants. This is helpful in a preliminary view of the mechanism of adjustment but is altogether too mechanical: decisions as to the proper quantity of capital relative to output, and the desired level of consumption relative to income, are economic. They may be influenced by physical environment and technique but there is room also for human elements, e.g., for uncertainty, changes in expectations of the future, habit, and personal adjustments.

Our analysis of the accelerator has been based on the assumption of a fixed capital-output ratio, which rests in part upon two rigid premises. The first is the absence of excess capacity in the consumption goods industries, and the second, a pattern of expectations in which any change in level of demand for consumer goods is expected to be permanent. At the same time, the model implies excess capacity in the investment goods industries so that an increase in demand for investment goods in the consumer goods section can be met immediately by induced investment. But if excess investment goods capacity did not exist, an increase in consumer goods output would result not in induced investment but in (1) a lengthening of the backlog of orders on the books of producers of investment goods or (2) a tendency to higher prices of investment goods, or both. Similarly, a decline in the rate of growth of consumer demand might (1) decrease the new order backlog or (2) tend to decrease prices.

Considerations such as these call for a relaxation of the strict form in which our description of the accelerator-multiplier relationship was cast. Thus we may interpret the changes in the new order backlog as suggesting lags and a more sluggish response than was indicated in our simplified account. On the upswing a leveling off of consumption goods output at full employment would tend to retard induced investment. But with a backlog of orders the decrease in investment goods output would be delayed by a period depending on the length of the order backlog; thus income might be maintained for some time at the full-employment ceiling.

Similar qualifications could be made for other stages of the business cycle, for the effects of price changes on the desired capital-output ratios, and for the effect of expectations.

It is unnecessary to carry these refinements further. The general implication of the interactions which have been described is that cyclical instability in income and employment, far from being a matter of simple maladjustment in a normally smooth operating mechanism, is inherent in the mechanism itself. The view of the business cycle as an interaction between external impulses and induced responses is thus significant both for understanding the workings of a market economy and for public policy. Alvin Hansen states the policy implications of this view as follows:

> The suggestion is frequently encountered nowadays that the business cycle reveals a pathological condition in the economy which can readily be cured if certain structural adjustments are made. If a wage-price balance is found, if labor-management relations are improved, if the tax structure is reformed, et cetera, the economy will be in a sufficiently healthy state, it is said, to resist any tendency to fluctuate violently. This is, however, a dangerous illusion. Structural balance in the economy is indeed important for the healthy functioning of the economy. But the tendency to fluctuate is not a pathological disease. It is an inherent characteristic of the private enterprise, market economy. To stabilize it requires something more than structural adjustments; it requires a deliberate and positive anti-cyclical program.[8]

For the most part in this book, the business cycle and dynamic analysis are deliberately set aside in favor of the much simpler analysis of equilibrium conditions. It is well to note again that when equilibrium is attained, and rates of consumption, income, and investment are all constant over time, induced investment is necessarily zero. The gross investment component of the stable GNP then consists exclusively of replacement investment, based on the stock of capital, and autonomous investment, which is largely independent of output. This implies that where we are concerned with effects on equilibrium we may ignore the accelerator. Thus in the interaction of the multiplier and accelerator, it is the accelerator which plays such tricks as bringing about a cyclical adjustment process, but it is the multiplier which dominates after the adjustment is completed, and we stand back to appraise what has been accomplished.

GOVERNMENTAL FISCAL EFFECTS

So far we have been concerned with the interrelation of but two sectors in the economy—households and business firms. While still deferring explicit consideration of money and interest rates, we shall now introduce and examine the effects of the governmental sector on the level of aggregate demand. Although virtually all activities of government have some relevance in this connection—including, for example, the enforcement of the antitrust

---

8. Alvin H. Hansen, *Business Cycles and National Income* (New York: Norton, 1951), p. 4.

laws, the negotiation of trade treaties, and the regulation of security issues—we shall limit our analysis to the fiscal or budgetary actions of government. From this viewpoint we consider government as (1) spending money on goods and services, (2) collecting taxes, and (3) reallocating as transfer expenditures some part of the funds collected. In this section our purpose is to analyze the potential effects of variations of each of these elements.

It is important to note that each of the components may be varied independently. Thus an increase in expenditures need not be accompanied by an increase in taxes; it may instead be financed by an increase in government money issues, or security issues (a rise in government debt), or a decrease in the government's cash balances. Each of these alternatives implies an increase in the government's deficit or a reduction in its surplus.[9] Similarly, an increase in tax receipts need not be accompanied by a rise in expenditures: the additional proceeds may be devoted to retirement of money or debt (or reduction in their expansion) or to increasing cash balances (or reduction in their decrease). Each of these alternatives implies an increase in any budget surplus or a decline in any deficit.

The following analysis traces the effects of changes in each budgetary element, assuming other components of receipts and expenditures to remain constant. We may call this fiscal *analysis*. We reserve for later consideration how a knowledge of these potential fiscal effects in a context of desired goals may lead to alternative courses of action, or fiscal *policy*.[10]

The Effects of Government Expenditures

Analysis of the effects of governmental expenditures on aggregate demand requires only minor amendment of the framework with which we have already become familiar. In Figure 18-3, with a given C-curve and a constant I, the total expenditure curve, $C+I$, establishes an equilibrium level of income OY_0, equal to BY_0. Suppose now the government spends an additional amount per period on output, equal to AB, leading to an excess of planned expenditures over existing income by an equal amount. The increase in expenditures leads directly, as we have seen before, to an increase in income, in turn inducing a rise in consumption expenditures, which in turn induce further rises in C, until total income rises to the level OY_1, or EY_1. At income OY_1, total planned expenditures as given by the curve $C+I+G$ are equal to the actual level of income. At this level of income the sum of $I+G$ equals S, the difference between income and C, or EG.

The changes in aggregate income induced by a rise in G are formally

---

9. An excess of expenditures over tax receipts in a given period is termed a budget "deficit," an excess of tax receipts over expenditures a budget "surplus," and equality between the two streams a "balanced budget."

10. Activities classified primarily as fiscal may induce substantial monetary effects as well. These will be discussed in Chapters 21 and 22.

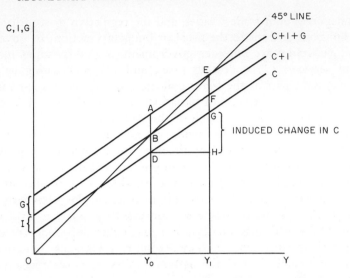

Figure 18-3. Effect of an Increase in Government Expenditures on Income.

identical to those arising from an equivalent rise in *I*. If the marginal propensity to consume is ⅔, the "government-expenditure multiplier" would be 3.[11] If the rise in *G* (taken as *AB* in the chart) is $10 billion, the rise in income would be $30 billion. In Figure 18-3, income EY_1 exceeds BY_0 by the amount *EF* (the rise in *G*) plus *GH* (the rise in *C*). In the specific conditions assumed here, the rise in value of output of $30 billion consists of 10 billions of governmentally acquired or produced output (*EF*) plus 20 billions of consumption goods (*GH*).

We see, therefore, that government spending for output may supplement private investment in providing offsets to saving and thus make possible a level of income in excess of that related to a given rate of private investment alone. It is this effect which makes the control of *G* a potential instrument for influencing aggregate demand in an overall stabilization program.

---

11. We may demonstrate this by expanding the algebraic system we have previously examined. Let us add the variable *G* (government spending for goods and services), so that the system becomes:

$$(1) \quad C = a + bY$$
$$(2) \quad I = I_0$$
$$(3) \quad G = G_0$$
$$(4) \quad C + I + G = Y$$

Solving for *Y*, as previously, by substituting equations (1), (2), and (3) in (4), yields the relation:

$$Y = \frac{a}{1-b} + \frac{1}{1-b} I_0 + \frac{1}{1-b} G_0.$$

This implies that the influence of *G* on *Y* is formally identical to that of *I*. And just as the investment multiplier (K_I) is $1/(1-b)$, the government expenditure multiplier (K_G) is also $1/(1-b)$. Since *b* is the *MPC*, we may write $K_G = 1/(1 - MPC)$.

The Effects of Taxes

While taking account of government spending requires but minimum modification of our explanation of income determination, introduction of taxes brings with it somewhat greater complication. In particular, the existence of taxes requires us to distinguish between earned and disposable income. For if consumption is assumed to be related to disposable income, for any given level of *national* income, disposable income will be reduced by an increase in taxes, and this will serve to reduce the level of consumption spending associated with each level of national income. In a graph showing the relationship of consumption to national income or net national product, we should expect that an increase in taxes would shift the consumption curve downward and thus depress the total spending curve.

Before formulating this argument in detail, we must distinguish between two kinds of taxes. First, there are those which are independent of changes in income, such as head taxes, or real estate taxes. These we shall term *fixed* taxes. Second, there are those which vary in response to changes in income, such as income or sales taxes. These we shall classify as *variable* taxes. While variable taxes are more important, their analysis is somewhat more complex because of the interaction between the amount of taxes and the level of income. We shall begin, therefore, with the simpler but still instructive problem of the effect on aggregate demand of a change in the level of a tax which is independent of changes in income.

Let us assume a per capita tax designed to raise, say, $10 billion in an otherwise purely private economy. The problem is illustrated in Figure 18-4. In using this diagram we must recall that the OY axis measures total earnings derived from expenditures on output, or net national product, which must be distinguished from disposable income whenever taxes are introduced. The C-curve then represents the relationship of consumption to net national product where no taxes exist. Given the amount of investment, the level of income is maintained at OY_0 ($=EY_0$). The introduction now of $10 billion in fixed taxes will reduce the level of disposable income associated with each level of NNP by $10 billion and thus lower the corresponding amount of consumption for each level of NNP by the $MPC \times \$10$ billion. This reduction of the C-curve to C' is indicated in Figure 18-4 by the distance AB. If the MPC is $\frac{2}{3}$, the shift in consumption function, AB, will be $\$6\frac{2}{3}$ billion.[12] The total spending curve would shift by an equal amount, to $C'+I$, leading to a new equilibrium level of income of OY_1 ($=E'Y_1$).

We should expect the reduction in income, $\triangle Y$, to be greater than AB

---

12. This result assumes that the MPC of the new taxpayers is the same as that of income-receivers in general. But it is easy to allow for the effects of taxes levied on groups whose MPC is different. The impact of taxes levied on those with a lower MPC would shift the C-curve less, and those levied on groups with a higher MPC would shift the C-curve more.

because the impact of the taxes on consumption and income on the first round is reinforced by a further reduction in consumption induced by the decline in income, as implied in the multiplier process described above. On the basis of our assumption of an *MPC* of ⅔, we should expect that additional taxes of $10 billion would lead to a decline in the consumption curve of $6⅔ billion, and, with a multiplier of 3, to a decline in *NNP* of $20 billion. Of this decline of $20 billion—which in our diagram is represented by the difference between EY_0 and $E'Y_1$—*AB*, or $6⅔ billion, is due to the *shift* in the *C*-curve as a result of the tax, and *BC*, or $13⅓ billion, is the further induced decline in consumption as a result of the decline in income.

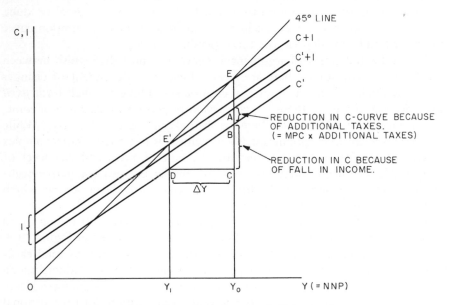

Figure 18-4.   Effect of an Increase in Taxes on Income.

If taxes had been *decreased* by $10 billion under similar conditions, we would have expected the consumption curve to *rise* by $6⅔ billion, leading to a rise in the equilibrium level of income by $20 billion.

From this example we infer that a change in the amount of taxes tends to change income in the opposite direction and by more than the change in taxes. If we represent taxes by T, we may say that the "tax multiplier," K_T, expressed by the ratio $\triangle Y/\triangle T$, is negative, but numerically greater than 1. In general we would except the numerical value of the tax multiplier to be less than that of the investment or government-expenditure multiplier $(1/[1-MPC])$ because, as we have seen, a change in taxes tends to shift the total expenditure curve, not by the amount of the change in taxes, but by this amount times *MPC*, which normally is less than one. An increase in taxes is paid, in effect, partly out of reduced consumption and partly out of foregone saving. Since the shift in the total expenditure curve induced by a change in taxes is a fraction (the marginal propensity to spend out of taxes) of an equal change in G or I, the tax multiplier is smaller in the same proportion. We thus conclude that

$$K_T = -(MPC \cdot \frac{1}{1-MPC}) = -\frac{MPC}{1-MPC} \text{ .}^{[13]}$$

This implies that a cut in taxes of \$10 billion would have less expansionary effect than an increase in government spending on output (or additional investment spending) of equal amount, because an increase in I or G increases the value of output and earnings in the first round by the amount of the increased expenditures, while the decrease in taxes increases *disposable income* in equal degree, but augments consumption spending on the first round by the $MPC \cdot \$10$ billion. Thus the initial effect on spending is less in this case by the change in planned saving induced by the change in disposable income—that is, by the marginal propensity to save times the change in disposable income.

Balanced Budget Effects

The analysis above suggests that if government expenditures and taxes are increased by equal amounts—that is, if the changes maintain any given state of balance in the budget—the result is not likely to be neutral. For the rise in G increases the demand for output by G, while a rise in T reduces disposable income by this same amount. But the change in expenditures in the latter case is affected by what taxpayers would have done with the taxed income. If, in accordance with the expected consumption-income relation, part would have been saved and part consumed, the decline in consumption resulting directly from the additional taxes would be less than the rise in G, and total expenditures on output would rise. Thus, a larger but still balanced budget would tend, other things the same, to be expansionary.

These forces may be illustrated by combining the effects of government expenditures shown in Figure 18-3 with the effects of taxes shown in Figure

---

13. We have seen that the shift of the C-curve will be $-(\Delta T \cdot MPC)$, and that this change in the total expenditure curve will change income by $\frac{1}{1-MPC}$ times the shift. In symbols, the change in income resulting from a change in taxes, ΔT, is

$$\Delta Y = -\left(\Delta T \cdot MPC \frac{1}{1-MPC} \right).$$

Dividing both sides by ΔT,

$$\frac{\Delta Y}{\Delta T} = -\frac{MPC}{1-MPC},$$

which is the tax multiplier. Thus, if the MPC is ⅔, the investment multiplier would be 3, and the tax multiplier would be -2; if the MPC is ⅘, the investment multiplier would be 5, and the tax multiplier would be -4.

18-4, as in Figure 18-5. Given the consumption function and level of investment, shown as $C+I$, the initial equilibrium income level EY_0 is established by the intersection of the $C+I$ curve and the 45-degree line.

If both T and G are now each increased by the amount DF, the consumption function would fall by an amount equal to EF, i.e., the MPC times the new taxes, leading to a decline in the total expenditure curve from $C+I$ to $C'+I$. Adding the constant G, equal to DF, raises the total expenditure curve to $C'+I+G$. At income level OY_0, total planned expenditures now exceed their former level by DE, the excess of the rise in G over the decline in the C-curve. The effect is similar to that of an equivalent rise in I or G, leading, as we have seen, to a rise in income to OY_1 ($=E'Y_1$), a rise equal to DE times the investment (or government-expenditure) multiplier.

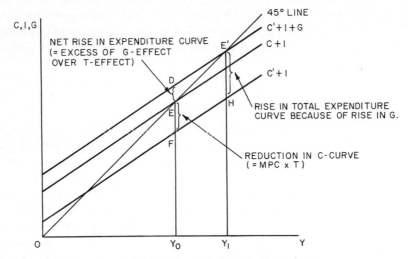

Figure 18-5.   The Balanced Budget Effect.

It may be helpful to illustrate this result by substituting values already used in the examples above. Suppose the MPC is $\frac{2}{3}$ and the increases in T and G are $10 billion. Then the private expenditures curve will fall by $6\frac{2}{3}$ billion ($=EF$) to $C'+I$ as a result of the influence of taxes on consumption, but total planned expenditures $C'+I+G$ will be greater at all levels of income by $10 billion ($=DF$), leading to a net rise in planned expenditures of $3\frac{1}{3}$ billion ($=DE$). Since the expenditure multiplier in this example is 3, we expect the rise in income to OY_1 to be $10 billion. Again, suppose MPC equals $\frac{4}{5}$, with the same budgetary change. Then the fall in private expenditures to $C'+I$ would equal 8, more than offset by a rise in G of 10, leading to a total rise in planned expenditures of 2. Since the multiplier is now 5, we conclude that in this case also the total effect on income will be 10.

In both cases the change in equilibrium level of income is equal to the change in the size of the balanced budget. This relationship is sometimes expressed by saying that the "balanced-budget multiplier" is equal to one.[14]

While the implication is clear that an increasing balanced budget may be expansionary, the degree of influence of such a budget is uncertain for the following reasons. First, the result noted above assumes that the *MPC*'s of new taxpayers and the general public are identical. The wide variety of taxes, many with significantly different rate structures and incidence, means that such identity can only be accidental.[15]

Second, there is an implicit assumption in what has been said that the level of investment is completely independent of changes in *G* or *Y*. Clearly, however, if each extra $1 billion of government spending so disturbed business confidence as to frighten off $2 billion in private investment, the net effect would be negative. (Indeed, in this event, if the "confidence effect" were dependable, the correct fiscal measure for expanding income would be a *reduction* in government expenditures!) But empirical laws of confidence are noticeably transient. Levels of government budgets which are frightening at one time may be accepted with equanimity later. And conceivably businessmen may be more likely to increase investment provided government purchases help to decrease excess capacity.

Finally, we must make allowances for other simplifications which were introduced. We have excluded monetary forces and interest rates. When these factors are included, as in the following chapter, we find it likely that rising levels of income will be accompanied by higher interest rates, or "tighter" money. This indirect consequence of a budgetary change may tend to reduce the level of investment otherwise planned. In short, changes in investment will depend on the relative strength of opposing forces: the possible expansionary effect of a rise in income because of the balanced budget effect, the uncertain effect of changes in confidence, and the possible effect of tighter conditions in the money markets.

---

14. This follows if we combine the effects of the government expenditures and tax multipliers already discussed. By summing their effects the total change in income may be indicated as

$$\Delta Y = \Delta G\left(\frac{1}{1-MPC}\right) + \Delta T\left(-\frac{MPC}{1-MPC}\right).$$

But since ΔG equals ΔT in the balanced budget case,

$$\Delta Y = \Delta T\left(\frac{1}{1-MPC} - \frac{MPC}{1-MPC}\right) = \Delta T\left(\frac{1-MPC}{1-MPC}\right) = \Delta T.$$

15. In the controversy attending prospective changes in income tax rates or the choice between regressive and progressive taxes a major issue typically is the extent to which the alternatives would influence additional spending. Where the circumstances call for anti-inflationary measures, the issue focuses on the relative inhibiting effects of various tax increases. Where stabilization policy calls for expansion the same issue takes the form of the extent to which various tax cuts are likely to be spent. The implicit assumption in both cases is that the marginal propensities to consume of different groups of taxpayers are significantly different.

The Effects of Government Transfers

With taxes and government expenditures on output constant, the impact of an increase of transfers such as pensions, unemployment benefits, and direct subsidies would appear first as a rise in the level of disposable income relative to the current level of national income. As a consequence, we would expect an increase in the level of consumption by *MPC* times the increase in transfers. This would imply an increase in the consumption-national income curve by the same amount. Thus, if transfers were expanded by $10 billion, we should expect, with an *MPC* of ⅔, a rise in the consumption curve by $6⅔ billion, and, via multiplier effects, a total rise in equilibrium income of $20 billion.

Formally, therefore, transfers may be handled simply as negative taxes, that is, they have effects identical in magnitude, but opposite in sign. From the viewpoint of aggregate demand, an increase in transfers is equivalent to a cut in taxes, and vice versa. And just as a reduction in taxes is likely to prove less expansionary than an equivalent dollar rise in *G*, a rise in transfers of the same amount is also likely to prove less potent, for the same reasons.

Variable Taxes as Built-in Stabilizers

Any component of the government budget may be considered an automatic stabilizer if it responds so as to oppose or diminish the influence of forces leading to changes in income and in this way tends to damp the effect of other causes of instability. Thus unemployment benefits, a transfer component, may expand during periods of decline and contract during periods of expansion. Government purchases of output also could react automatically in a countercyclical manner. This might be true of agricultural purchases under a support program. Variable taxes also have important stabilizing effects. While a full account of these tax influences would introduce complexities beyond our immediate requirements, we may indicate briefly how a variable tax might reduce fluctuations in aggregate demand.

If we assume that the *MPC* of households with respect to disposable income is ¾ and that the marginal tax rate (that is, the rate of tax applicable to extra earned income) is ⅕, under circumstances in which earned income rises or falls by 10, disposable income would rise or fall by 8, and consumption would change by 6. In this example the existence of a variable tax makes for a weaker response of consumption to changes in income because part of an increase in income results in increased tax liability and part of a fall in income is offset by reduced tax liability.

In the absence of variable taxes, with conditions otherwise as above, the multiplier would be 4; a rise or fall of $10 billion of private investment would tend to change income by $40 billion. With the variable tax rate assumed, the change in consumption would always be 0.6 of the change in income.

We may call this the marginal propensity to consume out of national product, or MPC'. Applying our usual investment multiplier formula, with MPC' substituted for MPC, we have

$$K_I = \frac{1}{1-MPC'} = \frac{1}{1-0.6} = \frac{1}{0.4} = 2.5. \quad ^{16}$$

In this case a rise or fall of investment by $10 billion would induce a variation in national income of $40 billion without the variable tax but with the tax would cause a fluctuation of only $25 billion. Because it reduces the responsiveness of the system to outside sources of instability, a variable tax qualifies as an automatic stabilizer.

SELECTED BIBLIOGRAPHY

ACKLEY, GARDNER, *Macroeconomic Theory.* New York: Macmillan, 1961, Chapter 17.

BAUMOL, W. J., *Economic Dynamics.* New York: Macmillan, 1951, Chapters 4, 10, 12.

COLM, GERHARD, "The Theory of Public Expenditures." In *Essays in Public Finance and Fiscal Policy.* New York: Oxford University Press, 1955, pp. 27-43.

HANSEN, ALVIN H., *A Guide to Keynes.* New York: McGraw-Hill, 1953, Chapter 5.

KEYNES, J. M., *General Theory of Employment, Interest and Money.* New York: Harcourt, Brace, 1936, Chapters 11, 12.

LERNER, A. P., *The Economics of Control.* New York: Macmillan, 1944, Chapter 25.

SAMUELSON, PAUL, "Interactions Between the Multiplier Analysis and the Principle of Acceleration," *Review of Economic Statistics* (1939). (Reprinted in the American Economic Association, *Readings in Business Cycle Theory.*)

---

16. In general, where b represents the marginal propensity to consume with respect to disposable income, and t represents the marginal tax rate, the investment multiplier may be indicated as

$$K_I = \frac{1}{1-b+bt}.$$

This implies that the higher is t, the lower is the multiplier. Where $t=0$, this expression reduces to the same formula as with fixed taxes.

19

MONEY, INTEREST,
AND INCOME

I n order that investment, saving, consumption, government fiscal operations, and income could be related without excessive complexity, no explicit consideration has been given to the influence of money in the discussion of income determination. The money supply was assumed to have adapted passively to whatever income level was established by other factors. In particular, no attention was paid to the influence of money on interest rates and the possible reactions of interest rate changes on investment (with the further repercussions which this would have on income).

The purpose of this chapter is to bring money into the analysis as an active factor. The ideas of the preceding two chapters are combined with an analysis of money and interest into an integrated theory of money and business activity. First, the determination of the level of interest rates in the market for claims and money is examined, assuming income given. Second, the forces in the money market are integrated with those of income determination, in order to show the interaction of monetary and real factors. Third, brief consideration is given to factors influencing the structure of interest rates.[1]

The preceding chapter indicated the kinds of factors which bear on the investment demand schedule and how, given that schedule, the rate of investment depends on the rate of interest. We turn now to consider the forces determining this significant economic variable.

As in other sections, we shall resort here to severe simplification, in order that fundamental forces may be described more clearly. In particular, references to "the" interest rate, as in the previous chapter and in traditional writings in this field, abstract from the variety of interest rates which in fact

---

1. In the main the discussion of this chapter views interest as determined by the demand for and the supply of *stocks* of assets, including money. A widely used alternative approach which considers interest rates as determined by the demand for and the supply of a *flow* of loanable funds is presented briefly in an appendix.

exist. We have referred in previous chapters to the great variety of credit instruments, differing with respect to issuer, risk of default, and maturity, as well as in certain other minor ways. This implies, as was noted earlier, that there exists at any time, not a single rate, but a structure or pattern of rates or yields, reflecting the diversity of instruments to which they apply.

But despite the diversity in yields, there is also a degree of consensus in their movements. If, for example, the yields of a particular class of securities were to increase, say yields on long-term governments, this would influence the desirability of holding other securities. In a competitive market with reasonably adequate knowledge of alternatives, there would be incentives for investors to shift from close substitutes for governments to governments themselves, leading to a rise in yields (or fall in price) of the substitutes, and a fall in yield (a rise in price) of governments, until normal relationships had been re-established. In this way, economic forces which have an initial impact on particular yields may be expected to induce repercussions throughout the yield structure. When discussing "the" interest rate, therefore, we may be understood as referring to an abstract rate of interest which reflects the common forces which lead to a rise or fall in interest rates in general.

In the first part of this chapter we shall simplify even further. We shall assume that business firms and governments issue only a single, homogeneous debt instrument in the form of a perpetual bond, and that households hold their accumulated assets other than household goods only in the form of money or these homogeneous bonds.[2] We have already noted that the wealth-holding choices of people require two different sets of decisions. The first relates to the rate of growth of household net worth and concerns the proportion of current income to be devoted to asset accumulation or debt retirement as opposed to immediate satisfaction. In other words, it relates to consumption-saving plans. The second is an asset decision. It relates to the form in which past as well as current accumulated asset values are held.

A proper appraisal of the forces influencing interest rates as well as the effects of a change in the money supply requires us to keep these two types of decisions distinct.[3] Our discussion of the interest rate focuses on the

---

2. By confining these issues to perpetual bonds, we not only simplify capital value calculations—capital value and yield for any instrument will move in simple inverse fashion—but we insure that our bonds remain homogeneous as new issues appear over time.

With this single type of credit instrument available, anyone wishing to lend for six months must purchase a perpetuity and plan to sell it at the end of that period, and a firm wishing to borrow for three months must issue perpetuities, planning to repurchase them at the end of three months. There are, of course, special risks in this procedure to both borrowers and lenders, which in reality lead to the design of shorter maturities.

3. We may illustrate this point by assuming an open-market purchase of bonds from the public by the Federal Reserve. Clearly this reduces the bonds held by the public in exchange for an equal increase in money holdings and thus affects the composition of the assets of the public. But it leaves the total assets and incomes of households unaffected. It is superficially inviting to conclude that the increase in the money in the hands of the public should lead to an increase in consumption spending. But if

second of these decisions—on the asset market—in which we analyze how the demand of the public for money and bonds, interacting with the quantities of both available, determines the equilibrium rate of interest.

THE DEMAND FOR MONEY

In the early 1960's the public held approximately $150 billion in the form of money. If, instead, equivalent values had been held in the form of non-money claims or real assets, pecuniary returns could have been obtained in the form of interest, dividends, profits, or rents. Even at so conservative a return as 4 per cent, people were voluntarily relinquishing about $6 billion in annual income by holding money instead of earning assets.[4]

Why should people wish to hold this volume of non-earning assets? In Chapter 1 the motives for holding cash balances were classified as transactions, precautionary, and speculative motives.

The Transactions Motive

We have seen that the transactions motive is based largely on the convenience of holding cash balances in a society where payments and receipts of money by households and firms are not perfectly synchronized. While it might conceivably be possible for a transactor to invest in financial assets at the moment of receipt of money and then to disinvest just before making a payment—for example, to cash a bond before going to lunch—and thus insure no loss of interest within the income period, clearly the costs and inconveniences of such a procedure make it more economic to hold cash balances.

We should note that this reason for holding cash balances does not depend on the existence of uncertainty either of the timing and amounts of receipts and expenditures or of future interest rates, but only on discontinuities in receipts and expenditures and the costs and inconveniences of financial transfers. Such balances, held as a means of financing a planned level of expenditures in the income period, presumably depend on the aggregate of

we recall that both aggregate income and aggregate assets of the public, the principal determinants of consumption, remain unchanged by the open-market purchase, we may be inclined to doubt this direct result. Instead of affecting consumption spending or saving out of given incomes, the changed composition of assets is likely to exert its most immediate influence on asset prices. We shall investigate below how the changed proportion of money and bonds may affect the price of bonds and the effects of changed bond prices (and therefore interest rates) in turn on aggregate demand for output.

4. Since all money in circulation must be held by someone, how do we know that the money people in fact hold is held *voluntarily*? The clue is that if they did not wish to hold dollars currently available, the attempt to exchange them for other assets would lead to rising asset prices. But if asset prices are reasonably stable we must conclude that people who hold upwards of $150 billion of assets yielding no pecuniary return do so willingly.

payments to be made. We shall consider them here to be roughly proportional to national income.

The Precautionary Motive

The precautionary demand for money depends largely on uncertainty of future receipts and expenditures. Thus a reserve of assets is desired, above the level indicated by transactions requirements, in order to meet unexpected expenditures or to withstand an unexpected decline in receipts. In the absence of uncertainty as to future rates of interest, contingency requirements might be covered largely by holding earning assets. But with interest rates uncertain, this course would involve the risk that requirements for funds might coincide with periods in which the capital value of bonds was low. Thus, where a given command over resources or a given debt-

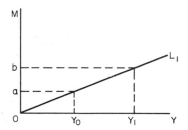

Figure 19-1. The L_1 Demand for Money.

paying capability is viewed as important, some significant proportion of contingency requirements will be held in the form of money. The demand for money for precautionary purposes may be expected to depend on: (1) the total level of money payments, or national income; (2) the degree of uncertainty—so that this source of demand would increase during a financial crisis, for example, at the inception of a war; and (3) to some extent on the rate of interest, which provides a measure of the cost of holding assets as money rather than bonds.

We may combine a substantial portion of the precautionary demand for money with the demand for transactions balances on the grounds that both are mainly a function of income. We shall call this component of the demand for money the L_1 demand, which we may indicate as $L_1 = L_1(Y)$. A proportional form of this relationship is indicated in Figure 19-1.[5] This diagram

5. It is likely that an increase in income and expenditures permits greater efficiency in the administration of active balances so that transactions requirements of money increase less than in proportion to income. Then the L_1 curve, instead of being a straight line, would be a curve rising at a decreasing rate. This is a refinement of minor importance, and by ignoring it the general character of the succeeding discussion is not significantly affected.

assumes that transactors will wish to hold a constant proportion, say one-third, of annual income in the form of L_1 balances. Thus, when income is OY_0, desired L_1 balances would be Oa, and if income were to double to OY_1, desired L_1 balances would also double to attain the level Ob.

The Speculative Motive

The speculative demand for money balances, referred to above, is particularly strategic in our analysis of interest. It is the demand for money balances that reflects the belief that money itself is the best asset to hold under the circumstances. This component of monetary demand, together perhaps with some part of precautionary balances, may be termed the L_2 demand and taken as a function of the interest rate. In symbols we may indicate this relation as $L_2 = L_2(i)$.

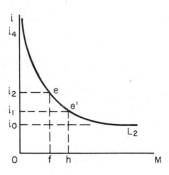

Figure 19-2. The L_2 Demand
for Money.

The L_1 demand, since it is related to the level of prospective income payments, is sometimes called a demand for *active* balances, and the L_2 demand, which is motivated by views of money as an asset, is termed a demand for *idle* balances. The balances held in response to these demands may be designated, then, active and idle balances, respectively.

The relationship between L_2 and interest is shown in Figure 19-2. The L_2-curve indicates that the lower the interest rate (measured on the vertical axis), the greater will be the quantity of assets which people will wish to hold in the form of money (measured from left to right). This inverse relationship between the demand for idle balances and the rate of interest depends on three considerations:

1. Holding bonds as opposed to money in an uncertain world implies the willingness to endure uncertainty as to the capital value of our assets during future periods of ownership when the interest rate may be higher or lower than at present. Thus we may view the current interest rate as the reward obtainable by giving up capital certainty in the form of money in

exchange for the capital uncertainty which accompanies the holding of bonds. We may also consider the cost of holding any given number of dollars —the cost of the liquidity they may provide us—as consisting of the interest income which we give up by not holding bonds. Given these preliminaries, we see that the higher the interest rate, the greater is the reward for assuming any given degree of uncertainty attached to holding bonds and the greater is the cost of holding money. At high rates, therefore, we should find bonds relatively more attractive, and money less so. As interest rates reach lower levels and the reward for assuming the risks of holding bonds declines, the cost of holding money balances is correspondingly reduced; we should then expect the public to hold a smaller proportion of their assets in the form of bonds and a larger proportion in the form of money.

2. Given the amount of money and bonds in the possession of households, the aggregate value of these holdings varies with the rate of interest. As the rate of interest falls, the market value of bonds rises, increasing the total value of investors' assets. As the total value of assets rises we should expect some part of the increase to be held in monetary form.

3. The third factor contributing to an inverse relationship between interest and speculative money demand results from the development of conventional views of an average, or "normal," level of rates. If, as a result of experience, the norm is believed to be 4 per cent, when market rates move upward to 4½ or 5 per cent, the probability of a fall in the future will be considered greater than that of a further rise. But a fall in the interest rate means an increase in capital values. Thus, at higher rates, not only is there a greater reward for assuming the capital uncertainty of holding bonds (point 1, above), but also the chance of loss is believed to be less and the probability of a capital gain greater. Thus the enhancement of the attractiveness of bonds because of a higher yield is reinforced by a simultaneous greater likelihood of capital appreciation on securities bought now and sold in the future.

In the other direction, the lower the rate, the greater the chance of a rise rather than a fall and the greater the chance of capital loss rather than gain. These considerations, together with the lower reward implicit in the lower yield, induce a greater holding of money at the expense of bonds.

Figure 19-2 is drawn to suggest also that at some rate which is sufficiently high, such as i_4, the demand for L_2 balances may be reduced to zero. At this rate no one would prefer idle balances to bonds. At the other extreme, the figure suggests that there is some rate above zero, such as i_0, at which the L_2-curve becomes perfectly elastic. This reflects the belief of money holders that below some rate, with low rewards and a high probability of capital losses, the holding of bonds becomes unduly perilous. At such a rate, any new money provided by the monetary authorities would simply be added to idle balances, rather than utilized to bid up further the price of bonds.

DETERMINATION OF THE MARKET RATE OF INTEREST

On the basis of this analysis of the demand for money, the manner in which the interest rate is determined at any moment may be stated briefly. If the demand for active balances (L_1) depends on money income (Y), and the demand for idle balances (L_2) depends on the rate of interest (i), the total demand for money balances (L) depends on both Y and i, or $L = L_1(Y) + L_2$ (i). Given the amount of money and the current level of income, the interest rate must adjust to whatever level is necessary to make the demand for money equal to the supply.

These forces are represented in Figure 19-3, where quantities of money demanded and supplied are depicted on one axis, and the rate of interest on the other. If the prevailing level of income is, say, OY_0, as in Figure 19-1,

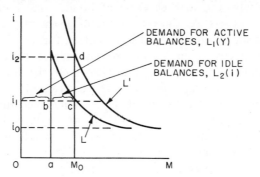

Figure 19-3.   Determination of the Market Rate
of Interest.

the demand for L_1 balances would be Oa. The same demand for L_1 balances is indicated also in Figure 19-3 by the distance Oa. The L_1 demand, being dependent only on income, is shown as inelastic with respect to the rate of interest. We now add horizontally the demand for L_2 balances, which is sensitive to interest, to form the total demand curve for money, L. If the stock of money made available by monetary institutions is M_0, demand and supply would be equilibrated at c, and the equilibrium interest rate would be i_1. At this rate, out of the total quantity of money OM_0, the quantity i_1b is devoted to L_1 balances, and the quantity bc to idle, or L_2 balances.

Under the conditions depicted in Figure 19-3, the demand for money could shift either because of a change in income, which would affect the L_1 component, or because of a shift in expectations, which would affect L_2. Suppose that for either reason, demand shifted to the right to L'. Then the demand for money would exceed the supply at the current rate i_1, inducing transactors to attempt to sell bonds on net balance and leading in turn to a reduction in their price, i.e., to a rise in the rate of interest. Our diagram indicates that, assuming an unchanged quantity of money, people will be content to hold precisely the quantity of money OM_0 only when the new rate has risen to i_2. Similarly, it may be seen that an increase in the quantity of money would tend to lower the interest rate and a decrease to raise it.

While we have concentrated on monetary demand and supply, it is well to remind ourselves that, in fact, the determination of the interest rate takes place in the market for assets in general. In the two-asset market of money and bonds assumed above, there is but one exchange rate to be established between the two, which may be viewed either as the rate of interest or as the price of bonds. Whenever there is an excess of demand over supply of money, there must be an equal excess of supply over demand for bonds. For to say that there is excess demand for money means that at the current price of bonds we are willing to offer additional bonds for money.

In short, the price of bonds (or rate of interest) which equates the demand and supply of money must likewise equate the demand and supply of bonds. This means that the rate of interest can be affected not only by changes in monetary demand and supply, but also by the supply of bonds. We have been able to work with an analysis like that of Figure 19-3 only on the implicit assumption that the quantity of bonds was constant.

Consistency between desired and actual holdings of bonds and money can be achieved rapidly in financial markets, since only exchanges of existing assets are involved. For this reason the speed of attainment of market equilibrium in asset holdings is much greater than adjustments involving changes in production and income, as described in the discussion of the multiplier process. Therefore, in looking at the re-establishment of equilibrium in financial markets after some disruption of equality between demand and supply, we may disregard changes induced in income in estimating what will happen to interest rates today, or in any short interval.

In time, changes in interest rates may be expected to affect investment, which in turn will influence income, and this will absorb or release balances from active use, which will react back on the rate of interest. It is apparent that a deeper understanding of the relationship between money, interest rates, and income requires an integration of the workings of the asset market, which we have just examined, with the influences affecting income, which were discussed in the preceding chapters. This is the aim of the following section.

THE INTEGRATION OF MONEY, INTEREST, AND INCOME

A Graphic Approach

We may integrate monetary and interest elements into a system of income determination by means of Figure 19-4. This four-quadrant diagram actually presents nothing that is entirely new; it merely brings within a single structure elements which we have heretofore considered in isolation.[6] In Figure 19-4 quantities are measured primarily from the origin: investment and saving to the right, quantities of money to the left, interest from the origin up, and income from the origin down.

Let us turn first to the money market, which is dealt with in quadrant IV. We shall assume a given quantity of money, measured by the distance

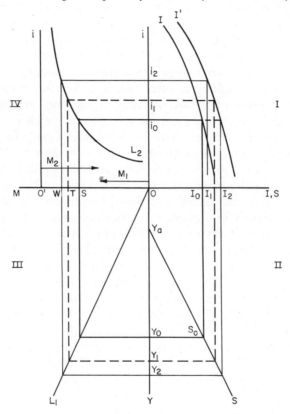

Figure 19-4. The Integration of Money, Interest, and
Income.

OO'; and at O' we erect a secondary axis. We now measure active balances required by the income level from the O-origin to the left, and the supply of idle balances from the O'-axis to the right. Thus, if OO' is the total amount of money supplied, and OS is absorbed in active balances, the supply of idle balances must be $O'S$. Similarly, if active balances absorb the quantity OT,

6. A similar exposition appears in Ira O. Scott, Jr., "An Exposition of the Keynesian System," *Review of Economic Studies*, 19 (1951), pp. 12-18. A variant also may be found in A. G. Hart and Peter B. Kenen, *Money, Debt, and Economic Activity* (Englewood Cliffs, N. J.: Prentice-Hall, 1961), Chapter 13.

the supply of idle balances must be $O'T$. We now show the demand for idle balances (L_2) as a function of the rate of interest, measuring quantities of money demanded from the O' axis.

We can now determine the rate of interest which would provide equilibrium in the money market. Assuming provisionally that income is at a level which will absorb OS of the money supply in active balances, the supply of idle balances becomes $O'S$. The L_2-curve tells us that people will be willing to hold this quantity of idle balances when the interest rate is i_0. This is, therefore, the equilibrium rate of interest consistent with the given money supply and the assumed level of income.

We turn now to quadrant I, with axes measuring interest and investment. With the demand for investment given by the I-curve, the rate of interest i_0 elicits the rate of investment OI_0.

We now move to quadrant II, to learn what level of income is consistent with the level of investment OI_0. For this purpose we construct a curve in quadrant II relating saving, measured to the right, to income, measured from the origin downward. It may be seen that saving is zero at income level Y_a (which is the same level of income at which consumption crosses the 45-degree line on a consumption-income diagram) and that as income increases saving grows at a rate given by the marginal propensity to save. From our previous analysis of the process by which planned saving is brought into equality with planned investment by appropriate changes in income, we may interpret the saving curve as indicating the equilibrium levels of income consistent with various possible rates of investment. When the rate of investment is OI_0, the level of income bringing about an equal flow of planned saving (Y_0S_0), is Y_0.

We now turn to quadrant III. Represented here is the demand for active balances as a function of income, which was described in Figure 19-1. Given the L_1-demand schedule, and the level of income Y_0, the required active balances are OS, which in this illustration are equal to the level of active balances assumed originally in arriving at equilibrium in the money market in quadrant IV.

The diagram illustrates how the dependent variables of the economy are related to given quantities and behavioral relationships of the system. The given factors are (1) the quantity of money, (2) the L_2-curve, (3) the L_1-curve, (4) the I-curve, and (5) the saving function. The variables determined are (1) the interest rate (i_0), (2) the rate of investment (I_0), (3) the level of income (Y_0), (4) the amount of money allocated to active balances (OS), and (5) the amount of money held in idle balances $(O'S)$.

Changes in Underlying Factors

Let us now suppose that the level of active balances indicated by the L_1-curve and the level of income do not equal OS, the quantity assumed at the beginning. This would be a symptom of disequilibrium, an indication that all the variables were subject to further adjustments in order to achieve a consistent relationship; it would be equivalent in effect to a shift in an underlying determinant starting from a position of equilibrium. (The equilibrium of the system may be disturbed by autonomous changes in any of the given factors listed above, and a primary purpose of aggregative analysis is to indicate, at least qualitatively, what effects may be expected from a shift in each of them.)

A change in the inducement to invest. Beginning with the equilibrium of Figure 19-4 described above, we may assume an improvement in the inducement to invest, so that the I-curve shifts to the position I'. Assuming provisionally that i_0 is unchanged, investment would increase to I_2, requiring an increase in income to Y_2, an increase in transactions balances to OW, a decline in idle balances to $O'W$, and a rise in the rate of interest to i_2. We see that the higher interest rate would require a movement back along the new investment curve, cutting back investment, income, transactions balances, etc. While it is not suggested that the economic system adjusts to change by solving equations or diagrams, our graph effectively describes the nature of the mutual adjustments by which the system tends to establish equilibrium values I_1, Y_1, and i_1, with OT of the money supply in active balances, and $O'T$ in idle balances. We conclude that the effect of a rise in investment demand is to increase investment and income, and to raise the rate of interest.[7]

We may note that the rise in income in response to a rise in the inducement to invest comes about despite an assumed constancy in the money supply. What is implied, therefore (in the terminology of the equation of exchange), is an increase in the income velocity of money. The mechanism bringing about a more effective use of the money supply works through the increase in the interest rate, which, by reducing the willingness of the public to hold idle balances, provides a larger supply to mediate income payments. This effect suggests why the relationship between the total money supply and aggregate expenditures is variable, rather than fixed as in simple versions of the quantity theory. The analysis also suggests limitations of a policy which seeks to restrain an expansion of expenditures in a period of inflation by restricting the growth of the money supply. Within appreciable limits the interest mechanism provides an automatic means whereby the economy tends to substitute for more money a more effective utilization of its existing supply.

An increase in thriftiness. In order to investigate an additional change, let us assume that people become more thrifty (the average propensity to save at all levels of income increases). This is described in Figure

7. Unless interest is so low, and idle balances so large, as to provide an effective rate within the horizontal segment of the L_2-curve.

19-5. The impact appears first in quadrant II as a shift in the saving curve to the right to S'. At the previous equilibrium level of income Y_0, planned savings Y_0S_4 would exceed planned investment OI_0, so that income would fall, tending to reduce active balance requirements and the interest rate. Moving directly now to the new equilibrium relationships, income would fall to Y_3, and interest to i_3, while investment would expand slightly to I_3, because of the interest effect. Other changes may be analyzed in similar fashion.[8]

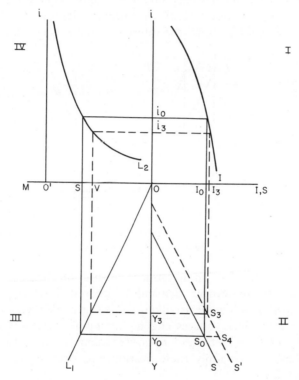

Figure 19-5. Effects of an Increase in the Propensity to Save.

An increase in the money supply. A change in the money supply, however, requires some slight elaboration. For this purpose we have reproduced quadrant IV in Figure 19-6. We may assume an increase in the money supply by $O'O''$, so that the secondary axis now shifts leftward by this distance. And since we are measuring the demand and supply of idle

---

8. We shall leave it as a student exercise to analyze the effects of a rise in the use of credit cards for ordinary purchases, or a vertical integration of firms, or a reduction in the income-payment interval—all of which would tend to shift the L_1-demand schedule, or the effects of a newly developed general expectation that interest rates are likely to be higher (or lower) in the future, which would affect the L_2-curve.

balances from this axis, we must shift the L_2-curve to the left also by the amount $O'O''$. This is indicated as the L'_2-curve. With unchanged demand for idle balances, the increase in supply from $O'S$ to $O''S$ causes a reduction in the rate of interest to i_3, which may affect investment, income, and transactions balances, with reactions again on the rate of interest.

The last example indicates how we may use our analysis to shed light on the degree of leverage which a monetary change may have on aggregate demand. An increase in the money supply will tend to reduce interest by an amount dependent on the elasticity of the L_2-curve. Where the demand for idle balances is highly interest elastic, as during a depression when both income and interest rates are low, the interest effect will be slight. Given the

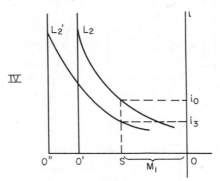

Figure 19-6. Effects of an Increase in the Money Supply.

change in interest, the effect on investment depends on the interest sensitivity of the I-curve. If investment demand is interest inelastic, again direct monetary influences on income are likely to be slight. We see, therefore, that highly interest-inelastic L_2-curves and highly interest-elastic I-curves make for strong monetary effects, and opposite characteristics make for weak effects. We shall seek to apply these relationships later in our consideration of monetary policy.

THE STRUCTURE OF INTEREST RATES

So far this discussion has proceeded under the assumption of a single rate of interest, related to a single homogeneous credit instrument. But the financial world presents securities in great variety which provide in turn a corresponding variety of interest rates. The different yields existing at any time constitute the structure of interest rates. In this section we shall consider briefly factors influencing, not the general level of rates, but the interest structure and its changes.

General influences on the interest rate structure already have been noted. As indicated, the yields relating to various credit instruments may differ because of:

1. Differences in risk of default, frequently termed "credit risk."
2. Differences in the costs of credit investigation and other administrative costs associated with different loans.
3. Differences in the applicability of taxes to different securities.
4. Differences in maturity, or term.

The first three of these considerations influence rate structures in ways which are largely self-evident. Discussion of them here will be confined, therefore, to an indication of their nature. The last element, resulting in yield differences which make up the "term structure" of interest rates, requires somewhat greater attention.

Default Risk, Tax Effects, and Administrative Costs

Where the lender of funds is not sure that payments specified in the loan agreement will be made, either because of incapacity or irresolution of the borrower, a higher yield must be provided to induce him to give up the greater safety of alternative investments. Thus United States government securities, with full assurance of payment, other terms being equal, would be expected to command the lowest yield. Corporate bonds of the most successful firms, or those secured amply by first mortgages on choice real property, would command yields lower than those secured by second mortgages, or unsecured bonds of less well-known firms, or those having a past record of default. Differences in "risk premium" are as extensive as differences in the credit ratings and collateral offerings of the various issuers of debt instruments.

If the creditor is to appraise the degree of credit risk which a given loan entails, some trouble and expense is normally necessary. This may vary from virtually nothing for some governments to detailed study of financial statements and physical inspection and appraisal of property in the case of many private loans. Varying costs of investigation account for the differences in "gross yields" of certain claims. Costs of investigation may be expected to bulk relatively larger on small loans than on large, and on short-term loans than on long-term loans. Administrative costs, such as those involved in installment and certain collateral loans that require continuous work and close attention by the lender, also influence gross yields on loans. In general, gross yields would be expected to be larger in proportion to the relative importance of investigative and administrative costs.

The exemption of state and local government securities from federal income taxation increases their after-tax yield in proportion to the tax bracket of the investor. To an investor subject to a marginal tax of 50 per cent, a municipal security yielding 4 per cent is as attractive as an equally safe taxable security yielding 8 per cent. These issues may be expected to sell at a premium in comparison with taxable issues of equal standing. This is the explanation of yields on municipal issues being lower than on those of the federal government.

The Term Structure of Interest Rates

Even in the absence of differences in risk of default, tax treatment, or costs, yields on securities may differ because of differences in maturity. This effect is illustrated by the differences in yields on various maturities of United States government issues, in which differences other than maturity are negligible. Table 19-1 presents yields on governments of various

TABLE 19-1. Market Yields on U.S. Government Securities for Selected Months

Maturity	June 1958	December 1959	May 1961	December 1961
Three Months	.83	4.49	2.29	2.60
9-12 Months	.98	4.99	2.72	2.97
3-5 Years	2.25	4.95	3.28	3.82
10 Years or over	3.19	4.27	3.72	4.06

Source: *Federal Reserve Bulletin.*

maturities during four months chosen to reveal changes in level and structure. The months selected correspond to periods in which interest rates were at their lowest level in the business cycle trough of 1958, at the succeeding high in December of 1959, and at the lowest and highest levels in 1961.

The term structure of table 19-1 is shown more clearly in Figure 19-7, where yields are measured vertically and maturities horizontally. For each month, points are located describing the combination of yield and maturity for each of the four classes of securities taken as a sample. A free-hand line is then drawn in for each month to provide an approximation of yields for maturities not given in the table, and to provide an indication of the general term structure.

From this information some generalizations may be drawn. It is clear that short rates may be either above or below long. It is also evident that yields of various maturities tend to rise or fall together, but that short rates are more volatile. Their change is greater than that of longs both in absolute and relative terms.

To facilitate analysis of these movements we shall simplify by supposing there are but two debt instruments—short-term bills and long-term bonds. Asset-holders would then have a choice of bills, bonds, or money. And borrowers could issue either bills or bonds.

If there were no uncertainty as to future interest rates, the yield on bonds would tend to equal the average of expected bill yields over the term of the bonds. For example, the yield on a ten-year bond would equal the average of the yields on the successive forty three-month bills over the ten years. For if the bond yield were less than this average, bond holders would shift from bonds to bills, reducing the price of bonds and raising that of bills, until the indicated relationship was established. (We are neglecting here costs of transactions.) If borrowers were also free to shift, since costs of long-term borrowing would be less than on bills successively renewed, they would issue more bonds to retire outstanding bills, thus further facilitating the adjustment.

Suppose now, more realistically, that interest rates were expected to vary in the future in a manner which cannot be predicted in detail in the present. This uncertainty of future interest rates implies very different characteristics for bills and bonds. For bonds, the contractual coupon pay-

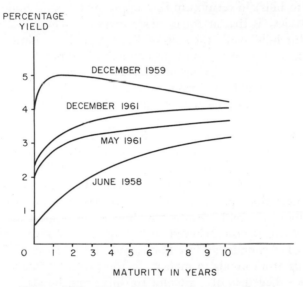

Figure 19-7. Term Structure of Interest Rates.

ments are assured over the life of the instruments, but their market values are subject to fluctuations in accordance with fluctuations in market yields. Bonds acquire the characteristic of "capital uncertainty." Bills, on the other hand, being very short term, suffer minor fluctuations in capital value over time. But at maturity the capital values must be reinvested at the then prevailing rate of interest. If it has changed, the earnings of the bill-holder over the succeeding period will change accordingly. Bills are relatively free of capital uncertainty, but possess a high degree of "income uncertainty."

Given these characteristics of bills and bonds, we may ask two questions: (1) what determines the average relationship between the yields on bills and bonds over time? and (2) what factors may account for a departure from this average relationship? We shall deal with these questions briefly in turn.

The average relationship of bill and bond yields. At times interest rates may be expected to rise, at other times to fall. Over an extended period the effects of these differing expectations on the relationship of short- and long-term rates may be expected to be offsetting. The average relationship of short and long rates may be clarified by supposing that future rates on the average are not expected to differ significantly from those of the present. But to maintain the central element of uncertainty, let us assume that no one knows with assurance what future rates will be at any particular time. What will be the relation of short to long rates under these conditions?

The answer depends on the distribution of total assets between those having a high aversion to capital uncertainty (and hence a higher preference for bills) and those with a high preference for income certainty (and hence an aversion to bills) in relation to the supply of bills and bonds available. A widely held view is that at equal yields investors would express a decided preference for bills, while the role of fixed capital in industrial production would induce borrowers to issue a preponderance of bonds. The result would be that starting from a position of equality the yield on bonds would rise and that on bills would fall until no further shifts occurred. This implies an average relationship in which the bond yield lies somewhere above that on bills.

The role of expectations. Given the average relationship described above, we may now look at the effects on bill and bond yields of a shift in expectations. Let us start from a position in which the dominant expectation is that the average of future long rates will equal the current long rate. Suppose that expectations generally shift so that a rise in rates in the future is considered more probable than a fall. Bonds will appear less attractive to lenders, for there is now believed to be a greater chance of future capital loss. In a market containing only bonds and money, asset-holders would attempt to shift from bonds to money. In the present context they have another choice—they may also attempt to shift from bonds to bills, and thus not give up earning assets altogether. The result is to reduce the yield on bills and raise the yield on bonds. This effect is reinforced by the activities of borrowers, who, with similar expectations, would seek to issue more bonds and retire bills.

If, on the other hand, the prevailing view shifted to a belief that future rates were more likely to fall than rise, both asset-holders and issuers would attempt to shift in the other direction. A bond-holder would expect to benefit not only from the receipt of higher current interest, but also from a capital gain when yields fell. As shifting by asset-holders occurred, the yield on bills would have to rise enough in relation to bond yields to compensate bill-holders for foregoing this prospective capital gain. Again these movements would be reinforced by activities of borrowers who would postpone the offering or hasten the retirement of bonds in favor of the sale of bills. The bill rate would rise in relation to the bond yield and could rise above it.

With the aid of this analysis we may interpret Table 19-1 and Figure 19-7 as indicating that during periods of rising business activity in which income rises faster than the money supply, interest rates rise. But short rates rise more than long, reflecting the expectation of a lessened probability of a future rise in rates and a greater probability of a future fall. Similarly, during periods of recession and easy money the greater fall of short rates in relation to long reflects the view that the reduced rates are not considered permanent. Their very fall invokes expectations of a greater chance of a future rise.

APPENDIX:

THE LOANABLE FUNDS APPROACH

Because the concept of loanable funds is widely used in the financial world as well as in more formal writings in the field, a brief account of the loanable funds approach to interest is in order.

Stock versus Flow Analysis

The chief characteristic of the loanable funds approach is that it places emphasis on *flows* of money and securities over time. In this respect it differs from the explanation of interest developed in the main body of this chapter, which was framed in terms of *stocks* of money and other claims.

In its simplest form the stock approach views the interest rate as bringing into consistency the quantities of money and bonds which exist with the quantities which participants in the market willingly hold. In this view, if at a given interest rate people wished to hold more bonds (and, therefore, less money), they would offer more money for bonds, resulting in a rise in the price of bonds. As a result, the relative attractiveness of bonds would be reduced and that of money increased until there was no further incentive to shift from one to the other. In the equilibrium toward which the market tends, the plans of all participants to hold assets would correspond exactly to the assets which they actually hold. No one would have any incentive to buy or sell bonds.

If stocks of money or bonds were to change, or if expectations were to shift, plans to hold assets would be inconsistent with actual stocks. New transactions would occur and the price of bonds would change until a new stock equilibrium was achieved. If we consider the period between the original equilibrium and the new, some people would have offered and given up money, and others would have demanded and acquired money. There would have been a flow of "loanable funds" from lenders (buyers of securities) to borrowers (sellers of securities). If all parties were content with their holdings at the end, the same rate of interest which established stock equilibrium at the end of the period may be described as providing equality between the supply of and the demand for loanable funds during the period.

The loanable funds approach thus views the market in which interest rates are determined as analogous to that relating flows of ordinary commodities. Suppliers determine at what rate funds flow onto the market. Users determine at what rate funds are taken off the market. And flows on and off the market are regulated and made consistent by the "price" (i.e., the interest rate).

It remains to identify the sources of the funds flowing onto the market in any given period, and the purposes for which such funds are demanded. For simplicity, it is assumed that the economy is purely private.

Components of the Supply and Demand of Loanable Funds

Sources of the supply of loanable funds may be classified as follows:

1. Gross savings by households (total saving by households without subtracting any household dissaving).
2. Gross business savings (retained earnings, depreciation accruals, and liquidations of working capital).
3. Dishoarding during the period (decreases in "idle" balances by lenders).
4. Net change in the supply of money.

The demand for loanable funds includes the following:

5. Net investment by business firms.
6. Replacement of fixed, and reinvestment in working, capital.
7. Consumption expenditures by some households in excess of income (i.e., dissaving).
8. Increases in idle balances by borrowers.[9]

These items may be consolidated in various ways. It is, in general, arbitrary whether an item is included as an addition to demand, or as a reduction in supply. Thus items 6 and 7 may be subtracted from 1 and 2 to give net aggregate saving during the period, and 8 deducted from 3 to give net hoarding or dishoarding during the period. The variables are then reduced to four: net saving, net investment, changes in net hoarding, and changes in

9. Governmental operations could be included in this framework in the following manner. Where government loan-financed expenditures occur, they may be treated as social investment and added to the gross investment component of the demand for loanable funds, or treated as social consumption, thus reducing savings on the supply side, or added to demand as a separate component. Similarly, where a government surplus occurs, it may be added to savings on the supply side either as an increase in aggregate social saving or as a separate component. It is obvious that changes in the government's cash balance may also supply or absorb funds in a given period.

the money supply. Generally, the first three are considered sensitive in some degree to the rate of interest. They may be combined, therefore, to form supply and demand schedules as functions of the rate of interest.

Net saving plus additions (or less reductions) to the active money supply may be taken as the supply of loanable funds, and net investment plus net hoarding (or less dishoarding) may be taken as the demand for loanable funds. In this framework the rate of interest adjusts so as to equate demand and supply for the defined interval.

Graphic Illustration

Figure 19-8 illustrates the essential elements of the approach.[10]

In this figure, the rate of interest is measured on the vertical axis, and the quantities of loanable funds on the horizontal axis. The S-curve represents

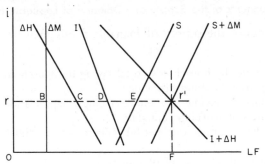

Figure 19-8. The Interest Rate as Determined in the Market for Loanable Funds.

net saving during the period as related positively to the rate of interest. The *I*-curve represents the demand for funds for investment as a negative function of the rate of interest. The change in the stock of money during the period, ΔM, is shown here as positive and insensitive to interest. If changes in bank credit were considered related to interest, ΔM might be positively sloping, or, if the change in money supply were negative, ΔM would appear to the left of O, and would then reduce the supply of loanable funds. The curve ΔH represents the public's net desire to add to hoards during the period. Changes in hoards are taken as negatively related to interest rates and as positive amounts for the range of rates shown. If dishoarding were to occur for some rates, the ΔH-curve would lie to the left of the vertical axis for part of its length, and the amount of dishoarding could be considered as a decrease in demand for, or addition to the supply of, loanable funds. (The positions of the ΔM- and ΔH-curves in the diagram are given as positive, but

10. The figure is adapted from A. P. Lerner, "Alternative Formulations of the Theory of Interest," *Economic Journal*, XLVIII (1938), p. 215; and G. Haberler, *Prosperity and Depression*, 3rd Edition; (Lake Success, N. Y.: United Nations, 1946), pp. 184-186.

this is a matter of convenience, and does not affect the substance of the argument.)

The total demand for loanable funds is derived by adding the investment demand and the demand for additional hoards horizontally at all relevant rates. This summation is shown as the curve $(I+\Delta H)$. In similar fashion the total supply of loanable funds is derived by adding funds provided from net saving and new money, to give the curve $(S+\Delta M)$. The equilibrium rate of interest for the period emerges, then, as Or $(=Fr')$. Following general supply and demand technique, any rise in interest can be traced to an increase in demand or decrease in supply (or some suitable combination), and any decrease in interest can be explained by a decrease in demand or increase in supply (or suitable combination).

Concluding Note

A major difficulty with the loanable funds analysis is that it requires too much of a simple supply-and-demand framework. There are too many interrelated variables to be handled conveniently in this fashion. For example, in Figure 19-8 the total supply is made equal to total demand at interest rate Or, but at this rate saving exceeds investment (and correspondingly additions to idle balances exceed the additions to the money supply). This implies that income will fall in subsequent periods. But since saving depends on income, the S-curve will shift leftward, and, if we include accelerator effects, the I-curve will shift as well. This leaves the interest rate to be determined not only by information given by the current supply and demand curves, but also by additional factors not included. In general it is apparent that the curves are not independent. A shift in either demand or supply will be accompanied by a shift in the other as well. These shifts may be more important than movements along the (temporarily) given supply and demand curves in influencing i.

The analysis thus describes conditions existing during a slice of time in which income may be in disequilibrium and thus subject to change. The loanable funds approach requires supplementing by an additional body of analysis to shed light on the interactions between interest rates and income. It is one of the virtues of the approach used in the main body of the text that it provides a framework in which interest rates and income are mutually determined.

SELECTED BIBLIOGRAPHY

ACKLEY, GARDNER, *Macroeconomic Theory*. New York: Macmillan, 1961, pp. 201-207.

CONARD, JOSEPH W., *An Introduction to the Theory of Interest*. Berkeley and Los Angeles: University of California Press, 1959, Chapters IX, XII, XIV–XVII.

HANSEN, ALVIN H., *A Guide to Keynes*. New York: McGraw-Hill, 1953, Chapters 6, 7.

HICKS, J. R., "Mr. Keynes and the 'Classics': A Suggested Interpretation," *Econometrica* (April 1937). (Reprinted in the American Economic Association, *Readings in the Theory of Income Determination*.)

KEYNES, J. M., *General Theory of Employment, Interest and Money*. New York: Harcourt, Brace, 1936, Chapters 13, 15.

LUTZ, F. A., "The Structure of Interest Rates," *Quarterly Journal of Economics* (1940-1941). (Reprinted in the American Economic Association, *Readings in the Theory of Income Distribution*.)

ROBINSON, JOAN, "The Rate of Interest." In *The Rate of Interest and Other Essays*. London: Macmillan, 1953.

20

INFLATION

Up to this point in the analysis of income determination we have assumed provisionally that price levels are constant, so that levels of aggregate money income and real income change in concert with no need to distinguish between them. This chapter eliminates this simplification and brings general price movements as well as real income effects within the scope of our discussion. It is intended to shed light on the forces leading to changes in price levels, particularly in the recent past, and to provide a framework for evaluating alternative instruments of control and policies as discussed in subsequent chapters.

In general, because of the focus of public concern in the postwar years, our analysis will center on inflation. But since prices are more flexible upward than downward, inflationary and deflationary forces do not lead simply to symmetrically opposite effects. For this reason deflation will be dealt with briefly where the analogy with inflation provides incomplete guidance.

THE MEANING OF INFLATION

In this discussion, the term *inflation* will relate to any general increase in the level of prices. The degree of inflation may be measured therefore by the movements of one of the general price indexes described earlier. This definition has the virtue of simplicity, of consistency with the aggregative analysis presented above, and of reasonable accord with common usage. But because differences in definition have led to apparent differences in diagnosis as well as prescription in this field, two familiar variants deserve brief attention.

First, confusion frequently has arisen through an extension of the term "inflation" to include several related terms. Thus one encounters the expressions *monetary* inflation, *credit* inflation, *profit* inflation, *wage* inflation, *cost-push* inflation, *rent* inflation, and the like. But it is clear that the term "inflation" does not connote the same thing in each of these examples. Some of them relate primarily to causes of price rises, while others may be looked upon as particular types or manifestations of price inflation, while still others may be both. Confusion will be minimized in what follows by confining the term "inflation" to general price movements. In other connections different expressions are to be preferred, e.g., expansion of money or credit, an abnormal rise in profits or rents, and so forth.

Second, some definitions make inflation turn on considerations of degree or duration, as a "significant" increase, or "sustained" increase of prices. The intent in these usages is to link the term inflation to phenomena which have important policy implications. It is true that not all price rises are of equal significance. However, use of the term inflation to refer to any price level increase regardless of degree can be qualified by suitable adjectives—as "creeping" inflation, or "galloping" inflation, or "sporadic" inflation. The significance of each type may then be appraised in relation to circumstances and objectives relevant at the time.

INFLATION IN THE TOTAL EXPENDITURES FRAMEWORK

We shall first consider the inflationary process in terms of the total expenditures approach. In doing so we simply extend the application of a framework used earlier in the analysis of income determination. There it was applied under the simplifying assumptions of substantial unemployment, a perfectly elastic supply of output in response to expenditure changes, and, consequently, a constant price level. But under conditions in which the supply of output is less than perfectly elastic, but still responsive to changes in expenditure, an increase in expenditures would increase both output *and* prices. At the other extreme, where plant and equipment and the labor force are so fully utilized that output is no longer expansible in the short run, an increase in expenditures will be reflected entirely in a rise in prices.[1] This condition is referred to as *pure inflation*.

Pure Inflation

Let us assume, as in Figure 20-1, that total planned expenditures, as represented by the curve $(C+I+G)$, provides an equilibrium aggregate income of Y_0 which also corresponds to a condition of full employment

---

1. Whether an increase in aggregate expenditure results in a change in output alone, a combined output-price response, or a purely inflationary effect depends on the factors influencing the aggregate supply curve of the economy. These are discussed in a later section of this chapter.

without inflation. Suppose Y_0 is 100 and the marginal propensity to consume is ⅔. Now assume a rise in planned total expenditures by 10 per cent of the real and money income level represented by Y_0, so that the total expenditures curve now goes through point a, and aY_0 exceeds bY_0 by 10. (It is not important for our purposes to specify which component of planned expenditures has shifted, but to make our succeeding discussion explicit, assume that the shift is in G.) The quantity represented by ab is sometimes referred to as an *inflationary gap*. It is the excess of planned expenditures over the full-employment value of national income at current prices. The significance of the term is that it indicates the degree to which planned expenditures must

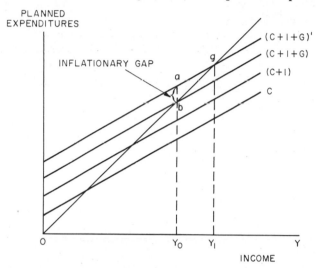

Figure 20-1. Total Expenditures and the Inflationary Gap.

be reduced by monetary and fiscal controls in order to eliminate inflationary pressures from the side of demand.

We might expect the newly established equilibrium level of income to be Y_1, which would exceed the previous level, Y_0, by the change in G times the multiplier, or by $10 \times 3 = 30$. This expectation would be unwarranted. For since Y_0 is full-employment income, any rise in money income beyond Y_0 must be due entirely to a rise in the prices at which the unchanged aggregate real income is valued. Our discussion of the consumption function stressed the relationship of real consumption to *real* income, not money income. And to specify the slope of the real consumption-income relation, or the marginal propensity to consume, as ⅔, implies an increase in *real* consumption of ⅔ of any increase in *real* income. But since Y_0 is full-employment income, there is no increase in real income beyond Y_0. It follows that we cannot simply extend the four expenditure curves of Figure 20-1 beyond aY_0. We must revise the expenditure curves to reflect the change in prices.

The way this may be done is indicated in Figure 20-2. The consumption curve CC is drawn on the assumption of constant prices. It represents, therefore, a *real* consumption-income relation. But if increases in income beyond Y_0 result exclusively from price rises, to maintain real consumption in consistent relation to real income as described by the real consumption function, consumption expenditures must expand in proportion to the rise in income. If, for example, consumption constitutes 80 per cent of income when income is Y_0, consumption must also constitute 80 per cent of the higher incomes—rising in step with prices. This means that beyond income Y_0, consumption expenditures follow the constant-proportion line OdC'.

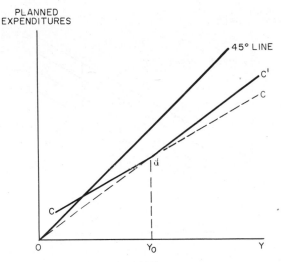

Figure 20-2.   The Consumption Function as Influenced by Rising
Prices.

Thus if the price level is constant as income increase from O to Y_0 and rises in proportion to money income beyond Y_0, the consumption curve has a kink at d. The appropriate relationship of C to Y is Cd to the left of Y_0, where real and money values are changing in concert, and dC' to the right of Y_0, where only money values change. In the range dC', the MPC and APC of the dollar consumption curve are identical.

In Figure 20-3 the effect of price increases on planned expenditures is shown for other components of the expenditure stream. The curves (C), $(C+I)$, $(C+I+G)$, and $(C+I+G')$ are shown in solid lines to the left of Y_0, simply reproducing that same portion of Figure 20-1. Beyond Y_0 they are continued as broken lines, suggesting the levels of expenditure that would, in each case, occur at higher incomes and constant prices. But since prices will rise beyond Y_0, these portions of the curves are no longer relevant. Instead, we must substitute new expenditure curves expressing the response of real expenditure plans to higher prices.

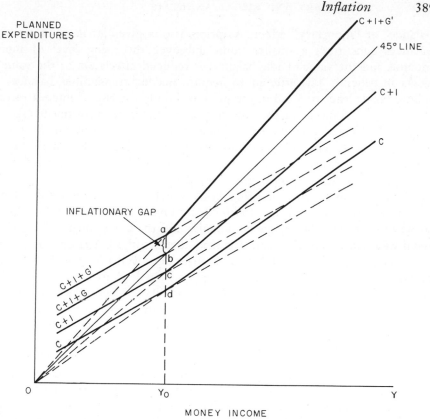

Figure 20-3. Cumulative Excess-Demand Inflation.

Assuming as in the case of consumption above, that real investment and governmental expenditure plans are maintained in the face of rising prices, monetary expenditures in each case would also rise in proportion to rising income, tracing out the solid portions of the respective curves beyond aY_0. This implies an indefinite continuation of the condition of fundamental disequilibrium with the community bidding continuously for more than the available output.

Price increases are a symptom of this fundamental disequilibrium. To end the disequilibrium requires either that full-employment output be expanded, which is a vain hope in the short period, or that buyers be induced or required to adjust their real demands to the available output. This brings us to the question of what factors may reduce the inflationary gap and slow down or end the rise in prices.

Limits to Inflation: The Price Level and the Real Demand for Output

If the money supply is not increased, rising prices will bring about a reduction in the real value of the money supply. This is termed the "real balance" or "monetary" effect. As prices rise, a given stock of transactions balances constitutes a smaller command over the rising level of money income, and the value of idle balances is reduced in relation to the value of assets in general. The attempt to acquire needed transactions balances by selling bonds leads to a fall in the price of bonds (or rise of interest rates in general).[2] At some point the rise in costs of financing investment expenditures will affect the ability or willingness of firms to maintain the rate of real investment. Thus the inflationary gap may be closed in part through the effect of a rising interest rate on the rate of investment, provided that increases in the money supply are restrained.

Another consequence of rising prices, operating through a reduction in private wealth, is termed the *wealth effect*. This is a result of a redistribution of wealth between the private community and the government. The government as a debtor on net balance is made better off by a rise in prices, and the private sector, as a net lender, is made less well off. The reduction in real net worth of the private community may lead to an increase in the saving function (a reduction in the propensity to consume) in order to redress the loss in private wealth. In this manner the wealth effect may influence the demand for output in the right direction; there is little empirical indication, however, that the effect is very substantial.

Another potentially restraining factor derives from the influence of taxes. If there is an effective progressive income tax structure, taxes will rise faster than money incomes. Although money incomes tend to rise in step with prices, the increments to income become subject to higher marginal rates of taxation. Consequently, disposable income in dollars rises more slowly, leading to a decline in disposable real income. The familiar consumption-income relation suggests a resultant decline in real consumption. Thus with rising prices the tax system imposes a special kind of redistribution, reducing the real disposable income of taxpayers in general and increasing the disposable income of the government. How this will affect aggregate demand depends on the relative marginal propensities to consume of taxpayers and the government. Inasmuch as the real level of expenditures of the government is determined mainly on the basis of social, political, and military objectives, we would ordinarily expect the government to have a relatively low marginal propensity to consume out of additional tax receipts. The rising real tax income of government will provide the opportunity for reducing its deficit or expanding its surplus (applied possibly to a reduction of its debt). If the government takes advantage of this opportunity, which it may be more inclined to do if it wishes to combat inflation, the decline in planned real consumption expenditures of households leads to a net decline in

---

2. These effects may be reinforced if holders of financial assets become convinced that the rise in prices constitutes a trend rather than a completed change in level. They then tend to shift away from fixed-dollar obligations such as bonds to equities; this further depresses the prices of debt instruments, that is, it raises interest rates.

the total quantity of output demanded, reducing the gap between demand and supply of output as a whole. If, on the other hand, the government uses its increased real income to cut taxes or expand outlays that were held back by political constraints, the tax effect would be weakened or eliminated.

Finally, we may note the influence of international transactions. As will be stressed in a later chapter, a rise in prices will tend to encourage imports and discourage exports, and in this way bring about a net reduction in the demand for domestic output. (But this equilibrating effect will be weakened insofar as inflation is also occurring abroad, or imports are restricted by controls, or the reduction in purchasing power of dollars at home is matched by a depreciation of dollars in terms of foreign currencies, so that the dollar price of, say, pounds sterling rises as fast as domestic prices.)

These considerations indicate the nature of the forces which may lead to a slowing down or ending of an inflation growing out of a rise in the total expenditures curve. The chief requirements are a restriction on increases in the money supply, the maintenance of the effectiveness of the tax system, and (where prices abroad are rising less rapidly) freedom for goods to move in international trade. Where these conditions are met the inflationary gap of Figure 20-3 would tend to be eliminated by the convergence of the total expenditures curve with the 45-degree line as prices and money incomes rise.

Inflation without Limit: "Hyper-inflation"

The existence of forces tending to retard the process of inflation does not, of course, rule out the possibility of a hyper-inflation in which prices rise rapidly without limit. Such a process ends only with an astronomical depreciation of the currency and eventual breakdown of the monetary system. Such a development implies a continuous reopening of the excess expenditures gap by the emergence of profitable opportunities for investment, spontaneous shifts in the consumption curve, and—crucially important in this case—autonomous shifts in government expenditures.

Hyper-inflations have been rare but spectacular episodes in monetary history, extremely disruptive and costly to the societies involved. Generally they have been a product of wars, revolutions, and their aftermaths, in which productivity has been impaired by physical destruction and dislocation. Lengthy deprivation and depressed standards of living, along with a high degree of liquidity, have made the public's demand for goods and services urgent. The public's faith in the preservation of the value of the monetary unit—the "money illusion"—has been undermined, leading to a flight from money and debt instruments into goods and equities. The government has had to finance large military outlays, reparations, and reconstruction, and the tax system has broken down. Under these circumstances, when the government has resorted to creating new money to finance its deficit this has aggravated an already inflationary situation.

It should be noted that neither of the main conditions for limiting the in-flationary process described in the previous section is fulfilled under hyper-inflation: the money supply is not contained and the tax structure does not function effectively. Hyper-inflation has typically been a product of serious social and economic breakdown. The unusual conditions that have resulted in hyper-inflation suggest that the fear frequently encountered of "galloping inflation" emerging inevitably out of "creeping inflation" is a gross over-simplification.

PRICE LEVELS AS DETERMINED BY AGGREGATE DEMAND AND SUPPLY

The total expenditures approach described above provided a number of useful insights into the inflationary process, but supply factors were left largely in the background. To bring supply forces explicitly into the analysis we may borrow and adapt the demand and supply framework familiar in explaining prices and outputs of individual industries. For pur-poses of explanation economists use the terms demand and supply in a specialized and precise sense, not to relate to quantities of goods purchased or sold, but to describe plans of potential buyers and sellers as influenced by price. They are, therefore, *schedules* or, in graphical form, curves, rather than single quantities. For our purpose we may thus conceive of an aggregate demand schedule or curve depicting planned aggregate real purchases of output as related to various alternative price levels, and of an aggregate supply curve describing quantities of real output planned per period in relation to alternative price levels. As in the case of the individual firm, the price level in this analysis tends toward an equilibrium level in which planned purchases are consistent with planned output. Similarly, movements in price levels and aggregate outputs may be explained in terms of *shifts* in supply and demand schedules, the particular outcomes depending on the extent and direction of shifts and the sensitivity to prices (price elasticities) of both curves. The chief problem in adapting this technique of analysis to the explanation of price level changes lies in identifying the forces which influence the shape and movements of aggregate demand and supply schedules.

The Aggregate Supply Schedule

In the analysis of national income determination presented in previous chapters use was made of the concept of a total expenditure curve, such as $(C+I+G)_0$ in Figure 20-4. In this diagram the OY-axis measures money values of output (or output times the price level), and the vertical axis measures planned monetary expenditures on output. The crucial assumption was made that the price level was constant. This implies that a rise in equilibrium money income, as from OY_0 to OY_1, as a result of the rise in the total expenditure curve from $(C+I+G)_0$ to $(C+I+G)_1$, results in a proportional rise in real output produced and demanded. As we move in this manner along the 45-degree line, the increase in expenditures must be interpreted as a *shift* to the right of an aggregate *demand* curve. Our assumption of constant prices, therefore, implies that we are moving along a horizontal (or perfectly elastic) segment of an aggregate *supply* curve. These relationships are shown by D_0, D_1, D_2 in Figure 20-5.

In this presentation we measure aggregate real output (and income) to the right, and the price level vertically. When aggregate income, as depicted in Figure 20-4, is in equilibrium at OY_0, this implies a position of the aggregate demand curve at D_0 in Figure 20-5, so that output Oy_0 times the price level P_0 equals income OY_0. When income is in equilibrium in Figure 20-4 at OY_1, this implies that aggregate demand has shifted to the right to D_1 in Figure 20-5, so that output Oy_1 times price P_0 now equals income OY_1. A similar construction relates a rise of income to OY_2 and the demand curve D_2.

Where the economy is operating along a perfectly elastic aggregate supply schedule, the price level is clearly determined by the supply schedule, while aggregate output is determined by the strength of aggregate demand.

Changes in the level of output can respond significantly to increases in demand only when substantial unemployment of labor and other economic resources exists. Thus the horizontal section of the supply curve (to the left of output y_f) implies the existence of less than full employment.[3] The horizontal character of the supply curve of Figure 20-5 in this region also conforms reasonably well to a widely noted price-output behavior characteristic of modern industrial economies, namely that when unemployed men and excess capacity exist, changes in demand, especially for manufactures, lead primarily to changes in output rather than to changes in prices.

As demand increases from D_1 to D_2 to D_3, we may expect costs and prices to rise. The rise in costs associated with increased output in the neighborhood of full employment comes about as a result of two sets of forces. The first is reflected in the shape of the supply curve, while the second accounts for an upward shift in the curve itself. With respect to the structure of the curve, as output increases some industrial sectors exhaust their excess capacity before others, leading to diminishing returns in those "bottleneck" areas before full employment is achieved generally. This element in rising unit costs is due, therefore, to unequal rates of utilization

3. Because of conceptual difficulties relating to the size of the work force, the extent of frictional or transitional unemployment, and structural unemployment as well, "full employment" should be considered not a point, but a range depending on circumstances. The reference to output y_f in Figure 20-5 as corresponding to the level of full employment, therefore, is solely for convenience.

of capacity in different sectors of the economy. This effect is indicated in Figure 20-5 by the rise in slope of the supply curve for levels of output in excess of y_2.

The second factor inducing rising costs as full employment is approached is the tendency for wages to rise as a result of the increasing scarcity of labor, rising business profits associated with fuller utilization of capacity, and the

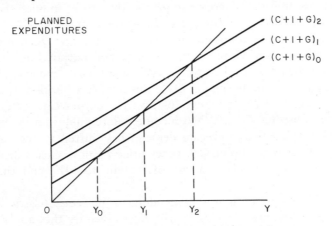

Figure 20-4.   Total Expenditures and National Income.

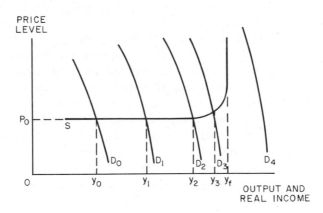

Figure 20-5.   Shifts of Demand and the Aggregate Supply
Curve.

resultant improved bargaining power of labor unions. We treat the effect of an increase in wages as an upward shift of the supply curve. For both of these reasons an expansion of demand in the full employment zone is reflected increasingly in a rise in prices. At the limit, depicted as y_f, the supply curve associated with a given wage level becomes completely inelastic, and in the event of rising demand this is reinforced in its effects on the price level by rising wages as well.

Before turning to the aggregate demand curve we may note briefly the forces tending to cause the supply curve to shift. Other things given, an *increase in productivity*, by reducing cost per unit and bringing forth a larger output with a fully employed labor force, will shift the supply curve down and to the right. A decrease in productivity will shift the curve upward and to the left. Similarly, a *rise in wages* will shift the curve upward and a fall in wages will shift it downward. The qualification "other things given" is important. For rising wages do not necessarily increase costs per unit under circumstances in which productivity is rising in equal or greater proportion. The impact of wages on costs, therefore, must be considered in relation to changes in productivity.

The Aggregate Demand Schedule

In Figure 20-6, as in Figure 20-5, real output is measured to the right and the price level upwards. The shape of the aggregate demand schedule, i.e., how changes in the price level influence the quantity of real output people wish to buy and thus total expenditure (price times quantity), is determined by the very factors which were considered in the earlier discussion of influences on total expenditures.[4] Assuming a given money supply and tax structure, as prices rise the combined effects of the reduced value of real balances, the reduction in private net worth, the contraction of private real disposable income, and the reduction in net exports—all serve to lower the amount of output demanded. It is these forces which underlie the slope downward from left to right of the aggregate demand curve as drawn in Figures 20-5 and 20-6. The more powerful the self-limiting forces discussed above, the more elastic is the aggregate demand curve.

By use of this apparatus, let us consider the same inflationary gap whose effects were discussed above in reference to Figure 20-3. We assume first (cf. Figure 20-6) a position of full employment at output y_1 and price level P_1, resulting from the intersection of the aggregate demand curve D_1 with the aggregate supply curve S_1. Suppose now that some component of demand increases autonomously—say government demand, financed by means which do not reduce private demand—so that aggregate demand shifts to D_2, and AB represents the excess of demand over supply at the current price level P_1.[5] The excess of demand over supply leads to a rise in prices. If the government seeks to maintain its real command over output by expenditures which increase in proportion to prices, and if private real demand for consumption and investment goods is maintained by proportionate increases in expenditures as well, the demand schedule would be perfectly inelastic, as at D_2', and prices would tend to rise indefinitely.

4. Cf. pp. 389-391.

5. *AB*, or real excess demand, multiplied by the price level P_1 equals the inflationary gap of Figure 20-3.

But as was indicated, under normal conditions, with a constant or slowly changing money supply, a progressive tax structure, etc., the appropriate demand curve has some elasticity, as, say D_2, so that as the price level rises the real quantity of output which the public is willing or able to purchase declines, until at price level P_2 demand is brought into equilibrium with supply. The extent of increase in the price level necessary to achieve equilibrium depends on the elasticity of the D_2 curve.[6]

We may now ask what forces may shift the demand schedule to the right, open up a new inflationary gap, and so initiate a new inflationary process? The answer to this question involves nothing that we have not previously investigated. In general, the forces shifting the demand schedule to the right are identical with those elevating the total expenditure curve. They may

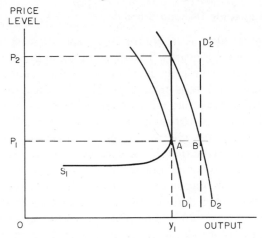

Figure 20-6.   The Aggregate Demand Curve and
the Price Level.

include among others: (1) an increase in government demand for output; (2) an autonomous increase in investment demand; (3) a reduction in tax rates; (4) an increase in the supply of money; (5) a rise in the consumption function; and (6) an increase in prices of imported goods.

THE MECHANISMS OF INFLATION

Excess-demand Inflation

Traditional explanations of inflation generally have been excess-demand or demand-oriented theories, in which price level increases are

---

6. In other words, on the rate at which price level increases bring about a reduction in the quantities of real output which people are willing to buy.

brought about by factors causing demand to exceed supply at current prices. Indeed, there are some who would deny that any other basic mechanism can exist. We have already discussed demand-oriented inflation in several versions. In the income-expenditure approach described above, we saw that inflation may be initiated by a shift in the aggregate demand schedule which brings about an excess of planned expenditures over the full-employment level of income.

This emphasis on demand as the underlying source of inflation is also characteristic of the various forms of the quantity theory, but the explanation of initiation, the process of expansion, and ending differs significantly between the two approaches. The income-expenditure approach traces the expansion of demand to such decision-making units, as firms, households, and the government and seeks to explain levels and interrelations between demand for consumption goods, investment goods, and government outlays. The money supply is not deemed unimportant in this view, but its influence is accounted for through its effects on the main elements of the flow of expenditures $(C+I+G)$. In this view, a rise in prices, even when initiated by demand, may be accompanied by a rise in the money supply of lesser degree, or, indeed, by none at all since existing money may simply be induced to work harder.

In traditional statements of the quantity theory there was a tendency to deny that a higher price level could be maintained without an increase in the quantity of money. How does modern monetary analysis explain the mechanism for making money do more work, thereby supporting a higher level of income without a proportionate increase in the money supply? The answer lies in the interest elasticity of the demand for idle balances. Any autonomous but sustained increase in the demand for output raises money incomes directly and induces a further rise via multiplier and price effects, as we have seen. The rise in incomes requires a corresponding increase in transactions balances, which reduces the supply of idle balances, leading to a rise in the rate of interest. The interest rate rises to a level sufficient to induce holders of idle balances to release the exact amount required for active circulation. Thus it is the rise in the rate of interest which puts into effect a mechanism for economizing on money balances, thereby increasing the effectiveness of a given stock of money. But it was noted above in reference to the real balance effect that there are limits to this process. After a certain point, the restrictions of a given money supply will impose increasingly burdensome terms on borrowers which will progressively restrict expenditures, and so tend to limit the expansion of money income.

Thus, while an expansion of money is not necessary for a rise in prices, a continuing rise undoubtedly cannot be sustained unless the quantity of money rises as well. For this reason we find no significant inflation in history which has not been accompanied by a substantial expansion of money. But are all increases in the stock of money inflationary? Unless we slip into the semantic confusion of defining an increase in money as inflation, the answer must be no. For if substantial unemployment exists (so that aggregate demand intersects the supply schedule of Figure 20-6 in its horizontal segment), although an increase in money may shift the aggregate demand schedule somewhat to the right,[7] the effect may well be a rise in output rather than of the price level.

Supply Induced Inflation

In the years following the Korean conflict the coexistence of rising prices and wages together with substantial excess capacity and relative ease in labor markets provided a phenomenon difficult to reconcile with the excess aggregate demand theory described above.[8] As awareness of the "new inflation" developed, several hypotheses were put forward to explain inflation without excess demand. All of these depend on the presence of imperfectly competitive labor or product markets—the presence of monopoly power—in one form or other, and operate initially via a shift in supply rather than demand. Within this group the "wage-push" hypothesis has been most popular, but a markup inflation hypothesis, including as variants an "overhead-cost push" and "profits push," has also received attention. As a hybrid of supply-and-demand forces the "structural inflation" hypothesis is worthy of note.

The Wage-push Mechanism. Let us assume, as represented in Figure 20-7, that aggregate demand is D_0, supply is S_0, and the level of income, y_0, is consistent with reasonably full employment. Through the process of collective bargaining workers are assumed to obtain wage increases in excess of increases in productivity. This raises costs and the supply curve to S_1, and employers either mark up prices directly in administered price industries, or the reduction in supply induces a price rise in competitive markets. Thus where the demand curve is sensitive to prices, the price level rises to P_1 and output is reduced to y_1. The process need not stop at this point, for another round of wage increases could raise the supply curve another notch, increasing prices and reducing output and employment still further.

The wage push alone would appear to be self-limiting, for the rising level of unemployment and reduction in output undoubtedly could not fail at some point to moderate labor's demands, or the willingness of employers to meet them. But if, in the interest of fuller employment, expansionary monetary and fiscal policies were invoked, shifting aggregate demand to

7. The degree to which aggregate demand may be shifted by a change in the money supply will be discussed in greater detail in relation to considerations of monetary policy in the succeeding chapter.

8. This is on the ground that substantial excess capacity and unemployment are ordinarily regarded as *prima facie* evidence of an absence of excess aggregate demand.

D_1, this would induce a rise in prices to P_2, as a result of moving along the current supply schedule S_1, and beyond this could encourage a renewal of wage demands in excess of productivity, and so inaugurate a further round of price increases. In this fashion the combination of monopoly power in labor markets, together with an attempt of a responsive democratic government to maintain full employment, provides the possibility of a continuously creeping inflation.

We shall not attempt an evaluation of the wage-push thesis here, but a few cautions are in order. Its popularity stems from a period of rapid change in output and price levels following the upheavals of war. But whatever contribution the wage-push hypothesis may make to an understanding of the immediate postwar inflation (and by itself it is by no means a satisfactory explanation of that inflation), its longer term significance depends on its

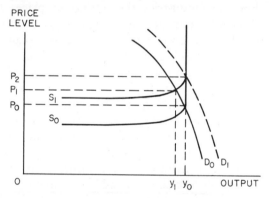

Figure 20-7.   The Price Level as Influenced by Shifts in Demand and Supply.

applicability to developments in a (hopefully) more normal future. It is significant that the hypothesis is based largely on assertions as to tendencies which, whether valid or not during the disturbances noted in the period of their genesis, cannot be accepted with great confidence as holding true under all other conditions. Among other things, the wage-push hypothesis implies certain specific long-run wage goals of labor unions, their ability to implement their demands in face of a labor force two-thirds of which is unorganized, and their effects on prospective changes of wage rates in relation to changes in productivity. The bases for these conclusions have not been demonstrated in convincing fashion.

Markup Inflation. Markup is the percentage by which selling price exceeds variable costs. It includes charges for overhead costs and profits. The markup acts as a supply-oriented inflationary force when it is increased to cover higher overhead costs or to provide a larger profit margin. It is sometimes argued that the overhead-cost push or profit push implied here cannot be significant except on the assumption of entrepreneurial irrationality. If firms seek to maximize their profits, their equilibrium position would be determined by demand and cost considerations and prices would already be set at this point. Beyond this point, a spontaneous change in profit margins could not benefit them. If demand increased, prices might, of course, be raised, but then the price increase would have to be classified as demand-oriented, as explained earlier. A deliberate or even inadvertent expansion of overhead costs, leading to an administered increase in prices, again seems inconsistent with profit-maximizing behavior. What is left would appear to be spontaneous, erratic, non-profit-maximizing price increases.

These doubts are plausible for purely competitive and, perhaps, completely monopolized industries. But they are less compelling for the numerous and important industries characterized by a few dominant sellers, where the intent to maximize profits is conditioned by the sharing of significant market power. For such industries the setting of prices may depend on conventions, loose tacit agreements, price leadership, or traditional markups over agreed-on standards of costs. Consequently, there can develop a mushrooming growth in overhead costs as a reflection of various non-price mechanisms of rivalry.[9] These may take such forms as selling, promotional, and advertising expenses, research and development costs, and costs of styling changes and product variation. Assuming price leadership or some other type of concerted behavior, growth in overhead expenses can lead to a rise in prices in the absence of an increase in demand. This may be particularly true where the explicit goal for pricing is a pre-established or "target" rate of return on invested capital, rather than profit maximization as such.[10] The profit-push mechanism would then operate by an autonomous increase in the target rate. To affect the aggregate supply curve significantly, of course, markups must be increased over a substantial portion of the economy, affect industries important in the price index, or affect industries whose products are of widespread importance as inputs.

The mechanics of markup inflation are similar to those outlined for the wage-push thesis. A rise in markup leads to a rise in the aggregate supply curve, a rise in price, and, with a given demand, to a reduction in output. This output effect may be expected to weaken the tendency toward autonomous markups. Thus a sustained inflation is likely to emerge from this cause only if the higher price level is, in a sense, validated by an increase in demand induced by measures of public policy.

In addition to the mechanisms already noted, the downward inflexibility of wage rates and other costs and the inflexibility of administered prices

---

9. See, for example, Chapter 4, "Nonprice Competition," in the *Study of Administered Prices in the Automobile Industry*, Report of the Subcommittee on Antitrust and Monopoly of the Committee on the Judiciary, U. S. Senate, 85th Congress, 2nd Session (Washington: 1958).

10. For evidence bearing on the profit objectives of the automobile industry see *ibid.*, Chapter 5.

under pressures of decreased demand suggest another mechanism which could lead to a general long-period upward bias in price level movements. If demand fluctuates in response to the business cycle, sometimes being deficient and sometimes in excess, the downward inflexibility of wages and prices could act as a ratchet to prevent prices from falling but not from rising. Returning again to Figure 20-7, assume that we start with equilibrium at income y_0, demand curve D_0, and supply curve S_0, as before. But now demand increases to D_1, providing an inflationary gap, and in response prices rise to P_2, and costs are bid up, so that the new supply curve is now S_1. If demand now shifts back to D_0 providing a *deflationary gap*, the price level will fall, because of the inflexibility of some prices, not to P_0 but to P_1. And unemployment will tend to increase, in correspondence with the fall in output from y_0 to y_1. This indicates the essential irreversibility of the supply curve. That is to say, the response to a rise in demand is different from that of a fall. For example, if demand later on should shift to the right in Figure 20-7 beyond D_1, prices would rise again, raising the supply curve and establishing the ratchet at a new and higher level.

Structural Inflation

So far our analysis of the inflationary process has treated supply and demand solely as aggregates. The structural inflation thesis looks beneath these global quantities at the various components of supply and demand. It emphasizes the possibility that even where there is no excess aggregate demand and no autonomous decrease in supply, price levels may rise because of *shifts* in demand between sectors of the economy.[11] The result is excess demand in some sectors, and a deficiency of demand, unemployment, and excess capacity in others.

Although no overall excess demand is in evidence, prices may rise in some sectors where there is excess demand. The downward wage and price inflexibilities noted above would keep prices from falling in sectors of deficient demand. The result, therefore, is a net rise in the price level. Moreover, wage rates are likely to rise, as we have noted, in the sectors to which demand has shifted, and thereby establish new wage patterns for emulation in wage bargaining elsewhere. In addition, the prices of the industries with rising prices may enter as rising costs into the cost calculations of industries with deficient demand, tending to shift up the aggregate supply curve, and to reduce output further. If demand is now supported to maintain full employment, the stage is set for a new shift of the demand curve to the right which would initiate a further round of price level increases.

---

11. See Charles L. Schultze, *Recent Inflation in the United States*, Study Paper No. 1, Joint Economic Committee, 86th Congress, 1st Session (Washington: 1958).

THE EFFECTS OF INFLATION

The most important economic effects of inflation are those associated with contracts, business activity, and liquid assets. These divisions of the problem are far from exclusive, since the various effects are closely interrelated, but the breakdown makes for clarity and helps to emphasize significant differences.

Contractual Relationships

Perhaps the most widely recognized consequence of inflation is its effect on contractual relationships stated in monetary terms. As a class, debtors gain during periods of inflation and creditors lose. The longer the period of time to which the contractual commitment applies, the greater is the exposure to loss or gain. Holders of long-term bonds and owners of life insurance policies are among the most vulnerable groups in the economy; landlords dependent on fixed rentals and recipients of salaried income are somewhat less vulnerable; debtors and persons dependent on profits may actually benefit from inflation. Formerly it was customary to assume a substantial lag in wage income during periods of rising prices, but this is less true than it once was—partly, no doubt, because of the increased power of trade unions. Experience in the German inflation after World War I indicated that while certain wages lagged behind prices, the lag was less in the lowest income wage brackets than in higher brackets. For one reason, such wages are likely to be on the shortest term basis and, for another, workers in the lowest categories are nearest to a minimum level of subsistence and hence the resistance to a reduction in their real income is strongest.

The changes just described relate to the effects of inflation in causing an alteration in the distribution of current income among the different factors of production. Largely because of the contractual element, income in the form of interest and rent is likely to show the greatest relative decline, and profits—which are in the nature of a "residual" share—the greatest relative increase in time of inflation. But this is by no means the only way in which inflation affects contracts. Inflation also leads to a redistribution of capital values.

The way in which inflation tends to cause a shifting of capital values may be illustrated by assuming a farm worth $10,000 on which there is a mortgage of $5,000. Before inflation the respective interests are:

Mortgagee's interest	$5,000
Owner's equity	5,000
Total value of farm	$10,000

Let us suppose that an inflation raises the price of farm products and that this in turn leads to a doubling of the market value of the farm property. The mortgage, because it is a contract fixed in money terms, remains the same as before. The respective interests are therefore as follows:

Mortgagee's interest	$5,000
Owner's equity	15,000
Total value of farm	$20,000

The effect of inflation has been to deprive the mortgagee of half the relative interest he had, even though the nominal value of the mortgage remains unchanged. The owner has gained as a result of inflation and the mortgagee has lost. Inflation has arbitrarily altered the respective shares of mortgagee and owner in the property from a 1 to 1 ratio to a 1 to 3 ratio. Just the opposite, of course, would tend to happen with falling price levels.

The same type of redistribution is likely to occur between bondholders and stockholders of a corporation. Assume a company with gross sales of $1,000,000 a year which yield a net return (before payment of interest on bonds) of $100,000. Assume further that of this sum $50,000 is used to pay fixed interest charges on the bonds outstanding and the remaining $50,000 accrues to holders of common stock. Assume that as a result of a doubling of the general price level and with no change in physical volume of output, sales rise to $2,000,000 and return after expenses becomes $200,000. The share going to bondholders remains fixed, of course, at $50,000, and the remaining $150,000 accrues to stockholders. Thus a doubling of return caused by inflation results in a tripling of the dollar income of stockholders while the dollar income of bondholders stays the same. Since the dollar buys only half as much as before, the real income of bondholders (what the dollar income will buy) is reduced by 50 per cent and that of stockholders is increased by 50 per cent. With a capital structure consisting of common stock only, this would not occur; under the circumstances assumed, the doubling of dollar volume of return would lead merely to a doubling of the stockholders' monetary income with no change in real income.

Business Activity

The chief effect of inflation on business activity is to alter the pattern of production. At one time it was generally believed that the tendency of profits to expand relative to other shares during inflation would serve to stimulate total output. It has now come to be widely accepted that inflation can occur only in a state of approximately full employment, and therefore cannot be expected to produce a significant expansion of output.

The change in character of production as a result of inflation is a natural consequence of the distortion of price relationships and of the redistribution of wealth and income described in the preceding section. For one thing, consumption and investment will presumably be different after the arbitrary alteration in the distribution of income caused by inflation from what it was before—it is not to be expected that those who gained as a result of inflation will have the same pattern of expenditure as those who lost.

Furthermore, the uneven expansion in profits in different industries brought about by the change in price relationships and the altered pattern of expenditures, would both provide an inducement and afford a necessary means to bring about a shift in the pattern of production. Thus enterprises which had earned more than the prevailing average of profits would appear more attractive and at the same time would be in a position to bid labor and materials away from enterprises which had earned less than the average.

The changed character of production—resting as it does on abnormal causes—is hardly likely to contribute most effectively to satisfying the long-run wants of the community. The situation which developed during the German inflation came to be known as "misinvestment." In the end it entailed a vast amount of lost effort and wasted materials. The distortion of the pattern of industrial production that occurs in a period of inflation may also contribute to the post-inflation deflation and depression.

Other Effects

Inflation may have an important bearing on the level and structure of interest rates. Certain of the effects of inflation, as in the encouragement afforded speculation and other types of public behavior, may, at the same time, be part of the processes of inflation. Psychological effects—as the experience of Germany between the wars clearly demonstrated—can be both devastating and enduring. The German experience also disclosed how inflation, by sapping the strength of the middle class, may alter the entire social fabric of a country and contribute importantly to the course of subsequent political events.

POLICY IMPLICATIONS

If inflation were invariably caused by excess demand, the problem of controlling inflation would imply simply a sufficient use of monetary and fiscal controls to restrict demand to a level consistent with stable prices. The effectiveness of existing instruments for controlling demand would, of course, remain an open question.[12] But that we should wish to restrain demand would not be open to doubt.

Where the sources of inflation are supply oriented, however, applica-

---

12. We shall discuss this question in the following chapters.

tion of classical inflationary remedies in the form of restraints on demand carries with it the undesirable effects of underutilization and unemployment. Restrictive monetary and fiscal policies might eventually stabilize prices by reducing the incentives for the exercise of autonomous market power, but this could require levels of underutilization which are considered intolerable. The market-power hypotheses appear to cast doubt on the consistency of full employment and more rapid growth on the one hand, and price stability on the other.

If controlling inflation by means of restricting demand appears too costly where inflation stems from the exercise of market power, the main alternatives would seem to be a reduction in monopoly power or increased social control over its use. This would require action in fields far removed from traditional monetary and fiscal controls. Among the possibilities that have been considered are: (1) direct price and wage controls in the non-competitive sectors of the economy; (2) a fragmenting of oligopolistic industrial structures; (3) breaking up of labor unions, or a banning of industry-wide bargaining; (4) greater reliance on selective controls to inhibit price instabilities arising from structural imbalance as a consequence of shifts in demand; and (5) more active governmental provision of information, use of exhortation and persuasion, and encouragement of voluntary restraints. As a final possibility, society may decide that a moderate degree of inflation is less objectionable than effective remedies. We shall return to these issues in their recent historical context in Chapter 25.

SELECTED BIBLIOGRAPHY

BOWEN, W. G., *The Wage-Price Issue: A Theoretical Analysis.* Princeton: Princeton University Press, 1960.

BRESCIANI-TURRONI, C., *The Economics of Inflation.* London: George Allen and Unwin, 1931, Chapters II-V, VIII.

DAY, A. C. L., AND STERIE T. BEZA, *Money and Income.* New York: Oxford, 1960, Chapters 19-22.

HABERLER, GOTTFRIED, *Inflation, Its Causes and Cures.* Washington: American Enterprise Association, 1961.

HARRIS, SEYMOUR E., *The Incidence of Inflation: or Who Gets Hurt.* Study Paper No. 7, Joint Economic Committee, 86th Congress, 1st Session. Washington: 1959.

KEYNES, J. M., *How to Pay for the War*. New York: Harcourt, Brace, 1940.

———, *Monetary Reform*. New York: Harcourt, Brace, 1924, Chapter I.

SCHULTZE, CHARLES L., *Recent Inflation in the United States*. Study Paper No. 1, Joint Economic Committee, 86th Congress 1st Session. Washington: 1959.

PART SIX

Financial Policies
in Operation

21

STABILIZATION POLICY

At this point we turn to a consideration of policy questions. In the present chapter attention is directed to general issues such as the objectives of stabilization policy, the means and channels through which stabilization policies are effected, issues concerning the different characteristics of policy weapons, and strategies of choice in selecting among alternative goals and instruments.

OBJECTIVES OF STABILIZATION POLICY

Conceptions vary greatly as to what guidance should be given to the economy and what actions the authorities should take in varying circumstances. And this, of course, is greatly affected by what people think it is possible for governments and central banks to accomplish. Here we are dealing partly in intangibles where social, political, and economic philosophies are likely to be influential.

Evolution of Major Aims

Prior to the decade of the 1930's the main objectives of stabilization policy, ranged in historical rather than logical sequence, would have been given as:

1. Preservation of convertibility of the monetary unit with gold.
2. Exchange rate stability.
3. Stability of purchasing power.

A listing of stabilization objectives for the United States in the 1960's would be:

409

1. Stability of purchasing power.
2. Balance-of-payments equilibrium.
3. Full employment.
4. Maximum sustainable growth.

The most important contrast between these two lists lies in the direction of stabilization policy which is implicit in them. It is to be noted that all three objectives in the first list relate to the value of the monetary unit: in terms, respectively, of gold, foreign currencies, and commodities. The last two objectives in the second list, on the other hand, relate to the performance of the economy as a whole. The two reflect, therefore, a shift in the focus of stabilization policy from the value of the monetary unit to the level of business activity. From controlling the money unit, stabilization policy has extended to controlling the economy as a whole.

Conflict and Compatibility

All of the objectives on both lists are desirable in themselves. But it is no less apparent that they may be seriously in conflict with one another. If, for example, one country devalues its currency, other countries must choose between maintaining exchange rate stability in relation to the devaluing country and stability in terms of gold. If gold changes in purchasing power, as has been more often the rule than the exception, stability of currency in terms of both gold and the price level becomes impossible. The conflict of objectives also appears at closer range. Under conditions of recent years the pursuit of price stability in the United States apparently tended to jeopardize full employment.

At one time the likelihood of conflict among monetary objectives was not clearly recognized, or it was assumed that adherence to gold would provide the closest approach to the other goals. Experience after World War II led to greater recognition of the existence of a considerable degree of conflict among the objectives of stabilization policy and of the need for resourcefulness in shaping instruments of policy to facilitate the achievement of multiple ends.

THE MEANS OF STABILIZATION POLICY

Stabilization policy in the developed countries of the Atlantic community has been implemented in recent years by four types of instruments: monetary, fiscal, debt management, and direct controls. The emphasis given the different measures varies among countries and within countries over time. Moreover, the importance attached to particular types of instrument is not a simple progression but varies with changes in the political and economic environment (witness, e.g., the drastic increase in the importance of direct controls under the pressure of war).

Monetary controls, which were discussed at length in Chapter 13, are those which operate through influencing the quantity and use of money, and thus the availability of credit and the level and structure of interest rates. This is mainly the province of the Federal Reserve authorities, but we have also seen that the Treasury has powers to influence the money supply.

Fiscal controls, which were considered in Chapter 18, are those which operate through changes in government spending and taxation (i.e., budgetary changes). They affect the level of income by directly altering the disposable income of the public (in the case of taxes) and total expenditures (in the case of government spending). Moreover, in contrast to general monetary instruments or debt management controls, which primarily affect the structure rather than the total of private assets, fiscal instruments are also likely to affect the total assets of the public, as well as its disposable income. Fiscal controls are implemented by the Treasury under authorization granted by Congress.

Debt management as an instrument of stabilization policy refers mainly to actions to influence aggregate demand through changes in the composition or structure of government debt. Such actions may be taken by either the Treasury or Federal Reserve authorities. Debt management, together with other issues relating to government debt, is reserved for discussion in the following chapter.

Direct controls are those which operate by means of explicit instructions as to what can or cannot be done and the terms on which transactions may be effected. Direct controls are essentially negative. They establish prohibitions, or limitations on activities permitted, or terms which cannot be exceeded. Price and wage ceilings as used during World War II, together with devices for rationing products in short supply, are well known examples. Minimum wage laws and maximum interest charges under small loan laws are other examples. Selective credit controls, which are usually classed as monetary instruments, may be regarded as direct controls since they operate through orders by the Board of Governors as to minimum terms in the contracts subject to control. Direct controls may be administered by a pre-existing control body such as the Board of Governors, or by *ad hoc* agencies formed for the purpose (as in the case of the OPA during World War II).

THE OPERATION OF MONETARY POLICY

In our earlier analysis of monetary effects on the economy in Chapter 19, the interest rate was mentioned as the channel linking changes in the supply of money to changes in spending on output. A tight money policy was shown to affect the stock of idle balances, and thus the interest rate and via the interest rate the level of investment spending. The restrictive effects of a given degree of monetary restraint would depend, according to this analysis, on the interest elasticities of two curves, the liquidity preference curve and the investment demand curve. If the liquidity preference curve is highly elastic, any slight rise in the interest rate will tend to induce substantial shifts from idle balances to bonds; a decrease in the money supply would therefore raise the interest rate only slightly. On the other hand, if the liquidity preference curve is less elastic, the same restriction on the supply of money would lead to a larger rise in the interest rate.

Similarly, if the investment demand curve is sensitive to interest so that a slight rise in the interest rate leads to a significant downward revision in plans for investment expenditures, the interest rate may exercise significant leverage on aggregate demand. The contrary is the case where the interest elasticity of investment demand is low.

This analysis implies that monetary policy has maximum effect where the demand for money balances is relatively inelastic (thus maximizing the interest effect of a given monetary change) and where the investment demand curve is relatively elastic (thus maximizing the expenditure effect of any given change in interest). On the other hand, monetary effects are likely to be weak where the demand for money balances is highly elastic (minimizing the effect on interest of a given monetary change) and where the investment demand curve is relatively inelastic (minimizing the effect on investment of a given change in interest).

These conclusions were reached within a framework which was severely simplified. In particular, it was assumed that there were but two financial assets, money and homogeneous bonds, and thus a single rate of interest; that the consumption and saving functions were relatively insensitive to interest changes; that competitive markets prevailed so that price was the effective regulator to bring about equality between offers of and demands for funds; and (in the analysis of equilibrium) that given expectations were maintained by both financial and real investors. In examining the role of monetary changes in the more complex real environment, we must consider the other channels through which monetary policy may influence the aggregate level of expenditures.

Effects on Expectations

Monetary policy may alter the expectations of financial investors as regards future interest rates and thus shift the demand curve for cash balances. (We shall take up this aspect of the monetary mechanism below.) It may also influence expectations of businessmen regarding the future incomes to be derived from present possession of real assets. Where prices are expected to rise in the future, the higher prospective returns on present or newly acquired equipment will tend to raise the rate of return on (or efficiency of) capital goods. If a tight money policy is expected to restrain aggregate expenditures and restrict the upward movement of prices, businessmen may revise downward their estimate of the stream of proceeds from capital goods, and the marginal efficiency of a given stock of capital goods will fall. Thus, it is argued that monetary policy may affect investment expenditure not only through a change in the rate of interest, a movement along a *given* investment demand curve, but by an appropriate *shift* in the investment demand curve. In this way, tight money may have appreciable effects, even though interest changes are relatively small or investment demand is highly insensitive to the rate of interest.

The forces affecting expectations are complex, and dependable predictions of the effects of policy changes on expectations are difficult. It is even possible that the effect on expectations may be of a "boomerang" type. Suppose, for example, that in the early stages of recovery the business community is still uncertain as to the stage of the business cycle, and particularly as to the time and speed of revival ultimately expected. Assume that under these circumstances the Chairman of the Board of Governors makes a speech indicating that the Board is concerned with an imminent revival of inflationary pressures and is determined to protect the soundness of the dollar. Suppose also that this announcement is implemented by an increase in the discount rate. What may be the effect on expectations?

If businessmen are impressed with the determination of the Board to maintain a tight rein on the money supply and if they are confident it will restrain inflation effectively, investment demand may well be depressed below levels which would otherwise have ruled. On the other hand, businessmen may take the Chairman's expression as a clear indication from an authoritative source that the economy has turned the corner and that a renewed threat of inflation is indeed imminent. But having more regard for the Board's powers of foresight than for the effectiveness of its controls, businessmen may then interpret the message as a signal to shift from dollars or fixed-dollar obligations, to goods or shares, and thus beat the gun. The marginal efficiency of capital will rise.[1]

Effects on "Availability"

With a given demand for funds for investment, any increase in the interest rate must be due to a decrease in the supply of funds (in the schedule sense), and the rise in interest rates must be sufficient to restrain

---

1. In this connection it is of interest that Chairman Martin in a speech in July 1958, some three or four months after what was later established as the trough of the recession of 1957-58, indicated renewed concern for inflation, and the determination of the Board to utilize its powers to combat the danger. The judgment of those in the stock market was revealed by an immediate rise in share prices.

enough borrowers (moving along the demand curve) to restrict demand to the reduced supply forthcoming. This assumes a relatively perfect market in which price (the interest rate) bears the major burden of allocating limited supplies among alternative uses. With demand relatively inelastic, interest rate increases will have to be substantial to bring about a significant restriction.

In the postwar years the "availability" doctrine was developed to prove that monetary restriction could be effective even with a relatively inelastic investment demand and moderate interest rate changes. Stressing the fact that financial markets are imperfectly competitive, it was argued that under conditions of tight money limitations on bank lending would work not so much by way of the interest rate on bank loans (though interest rates would be expected to harden after a time) as through informal rationing by lenders of the limited funds available for loans. This might operate by means of closer scrutiny of loan applications, the imposition of higher standards of risk and profitability on borrowers, and by reducing effective lines of credit of existing customers.

As disappointed borrowers shift to other sources of accommodation and as banks try to gain additional funds for lending by shifting part of their investment portfolio to others, the excess of demand over supply is transmitted broadly throughout the money and capital markets. The forces of restraint will operate through a generalization of rationing by lenders in these other areas. Thus a restrictive policy, instead of restraining the borrower exclusively by a rise in the rate of interest, may affect nonprice terms of lending. In short, there may be a reduction in the "availability" of funds at the going rate of interest.

In this form the argument appears to be essentially short run: with the lapse of time lenders would presumably be more inclined to meet excess demand for funds by raising the price of funds, with results more in accord with competitive analysis.

Effects of a Decline in Asset Values

With a tight money policy in effect, bond prices would be depressed as a result of security sales by the Federal Reserve, the impact of induced portfolio liquidation by banks, and portfolio shifts by traders. Consequently, holders of fixed income-bearing assets would suffer varying degrees of decline in capital value. This impoverishment of asset-holders may influence aggregate spending on output through channels other than the cost of borrowing. Among other channels suggested have been the "locking-in" of securities in the hands of existing holders, the effects on the liquidity of the economy as a whole, and the "wealth effect" on aggregate consumption spending. We shall discuss these briefly in turn.

The "locked-in" effect. It has been argued that in a period of buoyant expectations financial institutions such as insurance companies and savings banks as well as commercial banks normally would sell securities to acquire funds to lend to prospective borrowers, thus increasing the level of aggregate demand for output. These funds must be attracted from holders of idle balances. Thus the process envisages that holders of idle balances relinquish them in exchange for securities formerly held by financial institutions, and the funds so released are lent to finance current expenditures. The result is a transfer of part of the existing money supply from idle to active balances.

The "locked-in" effect involves the blocking of this source of funds as a result of the impact of tight money on security prices. Institutional investors, it is said, will be reluctant to sell securities at reduced prices since this would involve taking a realized loss. It is this reluctance that "locks in" some or all of the securities of these potential lenders. Thus the intermediary function of financial institutions is restricted and the availability of loan funds reduced. To the extent that the locked-in effect is operative it tends to reduce the velocity of circulation of money and, other things equal, to reduce total expenditures.

Both analysis and experience cast grave doubt on the significance of the locked-in effect. In periods of tight money and high interest rates, when the locked-in effect is presumably operating to reduce velocity, the velocity of circulation of money typically increases, and in periods of easy money and lower rates velocity is usually relatively low. Thus the degree to which a tight money policy may restrict expenditures by this means must be slight and more than offset by factors operating in the other direction.

It is important to realize that the "locked-in" effect depends largely on the irrationality of lenders.[2] If the best use of a given sum of money, in the judgment of a lender, is the granting of additional business loans, the best use of an equally valued holding of securities is their sale and conversion into similar loans. The price at which the securities were bought originally is clearly irrelevant. To continue to hold securities because their sale involves a capital loss in a situation where an equivalent amount of cash would be allocated to loans is irrational because it is inconsistent with maximizing the net return on assets. It is doubtful whether much confidence can be placed in an effect which depends on persistent behavior by institutional investors which is contrary to their best pecuniary interests. Even where some "locking-in" does, in fact, occur, the record of financial transactions indicates that this force is not dominant, but must be viewed at most as lessening the tendency to shift freely from bonds to loans as noted above.

---

2. To be locked in by a fall in security prices may be largely, but not entirely, irrational. It may be admitted that the saving of "face" by not realizing a loss may have some advantage among business associates; again, it may permit the payment of dividends which might be prevented by a realized loss.

Liquidity effects. In addition to the "locked-in" effect, tight money may also restrict the availability of funds by reducing the liquidity of potential lenders. In some quarters this mechanism is made to bear the main burden of monetary restriction.[3] A reduction in liquidity may be accomplished in a variety of ways. In the first place, the reduction in security values which attends a tight money policy may be considered primarily a reduction in the nominal wealth of holders of financial claims, but, inasmuch as the reduction occurs in financial assets on which some reliance is placed for liquidity, total liquidity is thereby reduced. In addition, effective monetary restraints may induce caution by lenders because of increased uncertainty of the borrowers' ability to service the loan. The reduction in the liquidity of potential lenders thus tends to encourage a preference for relatively liquid assets, including cash, and further reduces their willingness to lend.

Tight money and consumption spending. Tight money may affect not only investment but consumption spending as well. A restriction of consumption (or increase of saving) might occur, first, because higher interest rates increase the rewards for saving and lending; a given sacrifice of consumption now will command more consumption later. Second, it might occur because the decline in capital values which accompanies a tight money policy makes the public feel poorer. They may be led to compensate for their decline in nominal wealth by saving more out of given incomes in an attempt to redress the deficit.

Both of these channels imply that consumption depends not only on aggregate income but also on interest rate incentives and aggregate nominal wealth. Empirically, however, there is little to indicate that the interest and wealth influences are of great importance.

FISCAL POLICY

In Chapter 18 it was shown how government purchases of goods and services may increase the value of national output and income directly by the amount of the purchases, and indirectly through the secondary effects of income changes. Changes in tax or transfer payments affect disposable income and induce responses by those whose disposable income has been altered.

Types of Fiscal Policies

Discretionary fiscal policies are those such as increases in tax rates or expenditures on public works, that are the result of deliberate adminis-

---

3. See the *Report of the Committee on the Working of the Monetary System* (the "Radcliffe Report"), London, 1959.

trative or legislative decision. They involve the exercise of power by men in authority, and in this respect are similar to the exercise of monetary control by the Board of Governors. There is little question as to the potency of fiscal instruments in their effect on aggregate income. The extent of their use, however, has been limited by political constraints, by conventional ideas as to the proper role of the budget, and by certain technical difficulties in their application.

Discretionary fiscal policies, while helpful at times in the postwar period were unstabilizing at others. When stabilizing, their contribution appeared to be largely fortuitous. It was a byproduct of other objectives, such as the overhauling of the tax structure, an increase in defense expenditures in response to external events, or meeting the challenge of space exploration.

Any factor which spontaneously serves to restrict the response of the economy to outside disturbances may be considered an *automatic* stabilizer. It acts like a gyroscope or a shock absorber by applying a counter force to any source of movement, thus restraining the amplitude of oscillations. The two most important fiscal stabilizers are variable taxes and unemployment compensation.[4]

By variable taxes are meant such taxes as those on personal income, corporate income, or sales, where the amount of the tax (not necessarily the rate, as in progressive taxes) increases and decreases with changes in national income. As *GNP* expands, disposable income, because of variable taxes, expands by less than it otherwise would, so restraining the rise in consumption. As *GNP* contracts, disposable income falls less than it otherwise would, thereby restraining the fall in consumption. The result is that national income which, in the absence of such stabilizers, would have moved in response to disturbing forces as indicated by curve *A* in Figure 21-1, now traces out the pattern indicated by *B*.

The strength of automatic tax stabilizers depends on how rapidly taxes increase in response to increases in the tax base,[5] and how sensitive the tax base is to swings in economic activity. Taxes increase or decrease in response to increases in output by less than 100 per cent (and unemployment insurance provides compensation for lost income by less than 100 per cent). For this reason, automatic fiscal stabilizers reduce the amplitude of fluctuations but do not eliminate them.

In the postwar period automatic fiscal stabilizers were undoubtedly the major fiscal factor contributing to economic stability. Estimates differ as to the actual strength of automatic stabilizers in these years. The available evidence indicates, however, that offsets to rises and declines in *GNP* were on the order of 30 to 40 per cent. These amounts are far larger than in the prewar period. They were not the result of a deliberate reconstruction of

---

4. The gold standard might be considered to be an automatic monetary stabilizer. As we shall see in the next chapter, national debt also operates as an automatic stabilizer.

5. Progression, of course, increases the sensitivity of taxes to changes in the tax base.

the economy to achieve increased stability; they more largely reflect the expansion in the federal budget (hence high tax rates) and the attempt to relieve social distress occasioned by unemployment.

In deeper economic recessions or stronger booms, the damping brought about by built-in stabilizers might be inadequate. Stronger measures might be needed. For this purpose various quasi-automatic or *formula* plans have been suggested. They provide for a change in tax rates, and thus act like discretionary measures. But the changes in rates are linked to some objective signal, such as the percentage of unemployment. They are thus able to combine a variation in strength with the concurrent response of the automatic stabilizers. The response again might be entirely by rule, or it might

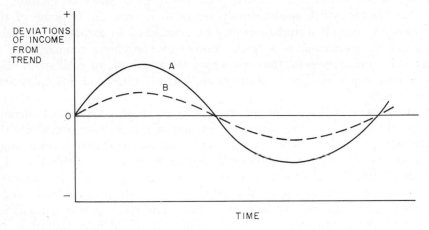

Figure 21-1.   Effect of Automatic Stabilizers on Income Fluctuations.

be subject to executive decision with authority granted by Congress for discretionary changes within predetermined limits in response to established signals. Formula flexibility tied to changes in the first-bracket rate of the personal income tax was strongly recommended by the Commission on Money and Credit.[6]

The Allocative Effects of Alternative Fiscal Policies

Governments have a potentially wide choice of monetary, fiscal, debt management, and direct techniques for influencing total expenditures. Within each of these categories the range of choice is further diversified. Among fiscal instruments we have discussed expenditure, tax, and transfer components. In principle, any desired degree of expansion or contraction

---

6. See Commission on Money and Credit, *Money and Credit* (Englewood Cliffs, N. J.: Prentice-Hall, 1961), Chapter 5.

could be accomplished by any one of them if it were carried through with sufficient resolution. But this does not fully describe the extent of choice or the diversity of weapons in the art of fiscal policy. There remain such questions as the kind of expenditures, the type of taxes, and the particular transfer payments which should be increased or decreased. Consequently, policy decisions must be concerned with much more than a few sector totals. To illustrate the differing effects on the allocation, or composition of outputs, we may direct attention to the choice between taxes and expenditures, with only incidental comment on other details.[7]

Let us assume an equilibrium level of national income of $100 billion with a given government budget containing only fixed taxes, a marginal propensity to consume of ⅔, and given private investment. Suppose also that the level of income desired is $130 billion. A number of alternative budget policies could be suggested. Each would have the immediate objective of raising the total expenditure curve by 10; secondary effects (summarized as the multiplier) would lead to an increase in income of 30. Let us look at the following possible programs:

1. *An increase in expenditures.* An increase in government expenditures by $10 billion would raise the total spending curve directly by this amount and lead to a secondary movement upward along the consumption function, resulting finally in a total increase in income of $30 billion. Of the additional $30 billion of output, $10 billion would consist of collective consumption or collective investment goods, and $20 billion of private consumption goods.

2. *A decrease in taxes.* To accomplish the upward shift of $10 billion in the total expenditures curve would require a $15 billion tax cut ($5 billion would leak into non-consumption uses). The rise of the consumption curve by $10 billion would lead also to a movement along the new curve, again raising total income and output by $30 billion. In this case, all of the increased output would consist of consumption goods.

3. *An equal increase in expenditures and taxes.* Under conditions in which the balanced budget multiplier was unity (see pp. 357-9), the budget would have to be increased by $30 billion. The increase in the level of government expenditures by this amount would be offset by a reduction of the consumption curve by $20 billion as a result of the added taxes; the result would be a net upward shift of $10 billion in the total expenditures curve. As a result of the induced expansion, consumption would increase by $20 billion as a result of movement along the new consumption curve, arriving again at a level of income increased by $30 billion. In this case, all of the $30 billion would consist of collective consumption or collective investment goods.

These results are brought together in Table 21-1.

---

7. A review of pp. 352-361 is desirable in connection with the ensuing discussion.

TABLE 21-1. Effects on the Allocation of Output of Alternative Expansionary Fiscal Policies

				Changes in	
	Government Expenditures	Taxes	Output	Private Consumption Goods Output	Collective Consumption and Investment Output
1. Increase in Spending	+10	0	+30	+20	+10
2. Decrease in Taxes	0	−15	+30	+30	0
3. Increase in Balanced Budget	+30	+30	+30	0	+30

The last two columns indicate how different the allocative effects may be for programs whose aggregate output effects are identical. They emphasize a significant issue accompanying an expansionary program during recession, namely, how much of the increment in output should be devoted to schools, roads, or other public works, and how much to output devoted to private use.

Again, given an inflationary gap, different alternatives have different allocation implications, which are suggested by a simple reversal of the example above. Reducing the gap by personal tax increases puts major pressure on private consumption spending. Cutting taxes *and* expenditures sufficiently puts the major burden on the collective component of total expenditures. Cutting expenditures reduces both collectively and privately acquired outputs.

This example suggests the allocative implications of actual fiscal decisions. The fact that fiscal variables affect particular sectors (as recipients of benefits or bearers of new burdens) not only complicates fiscal strategy but raises practical difficulties in administration as well. What is true of allocative differences within the category of fiscal instruments applies also in comparisons among general categories. These we consider below in notes on general strategies of choice.

The Case for Federal Fiscal Policy

Assuming that a private economy does not automatically generate the right amount of aggregate expenditures, why should compensatory finance become a federal function? Why should not state and local authorities assume this function and thereby preserve a greater diffusion of governmental power?

First, federal taxing power is greater than that of state and local governments. It is hardly conceivable that by independent action the states could achieve or maintain a 52 per cent corporate income tax, or the present average level and steep rates of progression in the personal income tax. If the states were to attempt such rates, any one state might gain a differential advantage in attracting individuals and businesses by offering somewhat more favorable treatment. As a result competition among states could easily reduce average tax rates generally to levels not far from those with the lowest rates.[8]

Second, the power to borrow and run deficits is greater for the federal government than for the sum of the states and local authorities. This stems partly from the greater taxing power already noted and also from the power to create money which is a monopoly of the central government.

Finally, and above all, only the central government is in position to take account of costs and benefits for the economy as a whole. Suppose, for example, that an optimum rate of expenditure required a $5 billion government deficit. If the result were an increase in overall well-being, why could not the local governments cooperate to bring about an equivalent expansion of demand? (We pass over the problem of coordination of efforts, and allocating the shares of the individual governments.) Each community would bear its share of the costs, and could expect to receive even greater benefits. But if it did not cooperate on costs while other communities did, it would still shares the benefits derived from the expenditures of others.

If a community carried through its program in good faith but others did not, a significant proportion of the expansionary effects would occur outside its boundaries. Thus, while the costs of the program would be borne by a particular group, the benefits would largely accrue to others. Local leaders could be expected to find compelling reasons for curbing their enthusiasm to contribute to the costs of fiscal endeavor.

THE CHOICE OF POLICY INSTRUMENTS

Differences in Stabilization Instruments

Policy instruments differ with respect to timing, flexibility, potency, and allocation or composition effects.

Timing refers to the speed with which changes in a control variable may be imposed once the need for change becomes apparent, and the period required before a significant impact on the economy occurs. Two lags are involved. One relates to implementation; it depends largely on whether the decision is administrative or legislative. The other is economic, depending on how much "play" the system provides in circumventing a given change,

---

8. The same principle holds in other fields as well. Standards for granting corporate charters are set by states establishing the least onerous terms. Similarly for standards relating to divorce and gambling: Nevada finds an important resource in the more rigorous standards set by other states.

or how directly it affects factors having an impact on income and output.

An instrument is *flexible* if it may be varied in degree of application or changed from plus to minus with ease. It is inflexible if a certain continuity is required for reasons of efficiency, so that once imposed it can not be reversed without loss.

Potency refers to the strength or leverage exercised by an instrument. A potent instrument accomplishes great quantitative output effects by relatively small and otherwise non-disturbing changes in the control variable.

Allocation effects of fiscal instruments were examined above. They refer to effects on the composition of demand, and hence allocation of resources and outputs within the total output.

Monetary policy obviously excels in flexibility. Open-market operations, its pre-eminent technique, can be varied in fine degree or reversed in short periods. Adjustments may be initiated with little delay once their need is apparent. For these reasons monetary policy may act tentatively in response to an emerging situation, standing ready to strengthen or reverse pressures once underlying trends become clearer. But while monetary instruments may be invoked without delay, their effects may be subject to uncertain delays. Some effects, such as those on expectations and on the availability of bank credit, may occur quickly. Short-term interest rate changes occur fairly promptly but long-rate changes, as we have seen, are more sluggish. After changes in the financial markets become apparent, there is a further interval before changes in plans affect actual spending. The financial system, because it sometimes compensates for changes in the money supply by changes in its efficiency of use (changes in V), also introduces a looseness in the linkage between the use of the instrument and the result intended. Monetary controls are commonly regarded as being weaker in overcoming depression than in restraining a boom. This follows from the fact that the reduction in interest rates that can be accomplished is limited and the further fact that the leftward shift of investment demand more than offsets the effect of monetary ease. In boom, the restrictions of tight money bear most heavily on capital formation, particularly construction and undertakings offering relatively poorer credit risks.

Discretionary fiscal controls are normally less flexible and slower in implementation than monetary controls. Lags result from the legislative process and the practice of annual budgets. Some of the delays could be reduced by administrative action to speed up or delay existing programs, by special legislative enactments, and, of course, by adoption of some sort of formula plan. Expenditure programs for such projects as highways, even though undertaken by stages which sometimes could be halted without excessive waste, would often need to be carried to conclusion. In that event they might provide significant expenditures in a succeeding phase of the cycle when a fiscal stimulus was objectionable rather than desirable. Tax changes, especially on incomes, could be imposed more flexibly with relatively prompt impact on expenditures.[9]

Fiscal controls acting directly on incomes are undoubtedly the heavy artillery of the stabilization arsenal. It is possible, of course, for offsets to appear, as by perverse effects on private spending. But such limitations are not likely to continue if the measures are applied, and maintained, with determination.

The allocation effects of fiscal controls depend on the choice of measures. Personal income tax changes, as we have seen, are likely to have an immediate impact on consumption. Corporate income tax changes, by affecting the supply of internal funds as well as profits after taxes, may alter investment while exercising a weak effect on consumption. Changes in expenditures are likely to affect the construction and durable goods industries.

Direct controls (assuming an established administrative machinery) can be put into effect rapidly and flexibly. The interval between initiation and effect, as well as strength depends on the form of control. Changes in margin requirements, having a remote relationship to spending decisions, are likely to be weak and uncertain. Varying the terms on insured mortgage lending, however, is more potent and can affect spending without undue delay. Allocative effects may be made highly selective and depend, of course, on the particular measures. The supplanting of market forces by administrative decisions constitutes at once the major virtue of as well as chief source of opposition to direct controls.

Allocation Issues in the Choice of Controls

It is clear that in attaining any predetermined level of aggregate demand a choice of alternative instruments is available. But each will bring a different composition to total demand and induce a different structure of output. These structural differences may be sufficiently compelling to overcome such other considerations at timing and flexibility in the choice of instruments.

In an inflationary period, for example, the use of tight money as a major weapon means that restrictive pressures will be applied to capital formation. As an alternative, taxes could be employed to restrain consumption and permit higher rates of investment without increasing aggregate demand. Thus an easier monetary policy and lower rates of interest could be maintained. Such a combination of policies would tend to transfer re-

---

9. Use of tax rate changes as a cyclical stabilizer implies that any change is to be considered temporary. Questions have been raised as to whether a temporary tax cut would have the same expansionary influence on spending as an equal increase in disposable income which was considered permanent. This has led to the suggestion that during a recession we should invoke a *permanent* tax cut, designed to be replaced, if desired, by a permanent increase after one year!

sources from the production of consumption goods to investment goods, so contributing to economic growth.

Should major reliance be placed on tax cuts or on increases in government expenditures to combat recession? Elements of timing, flexibility, and possibly expediency might well favor tax reductions. But proponents of expenditure increases could argue that a tax cut would increase output mainly in consumption goods. Against this might be ranged the claims of other sectors. For a growing economy, expansion of social capital—schools, roads, hospitals—becomes pressing. When should such facilities be built? Instead of waiting until their construction can no longer be delayed it might be better to use some part of the unemployed resources for this purpose immediately. This implies that a part of the increase in output would occur as public investment along with an induced rise in consumption expenditures and output. The argument turns once again on allocation effects.

A further example relates to conditions during the recession of 1960-61 when anti-recession policy was subject to a balance-of-payments constraint. Under ordinary conditions of recession conventional policy might have implied an easing of monetary measures including a reduction of interest rates, particularly on short-term issues. A large volume of short-term instruments, however, was in the hands of foreign holders. Lower rates in this sector would have made a shift into similar obligations abroad more profitable. In the process the drain on United States monetary reserves would have been aggravated. In the choice of policy instruments, one objective related to the structure of interest rates: to raise short-term rates while bearing down on long.[10] Another possibility was greater use of fiscal policies for expansion, thereby reducing the need for reliance on monetary ease and lower interest rates in general.

In comparing fiscal and monetary methods it may be argued that long-term rates are easier to manipulate up than down. Therefore, where monetary policy is actively employed to compensate for cyclical swings, the *average* level of long-term rates will be higher than if fiscal devices were used. It would follow that a greater use of fiscal weapons might make for a higher average rate of investment and a higher rate of growth.

The Choice between Discretionary and Automatic Stabilizers

In practice, automatic stabilizers have dominated fiscal operations and discretionary controls have been the rule in the use of monetary means. The issue of whether controls should be discretionary or automatic has centered mainly on fiscal controls, although the issue is general and applies to other means of control as well.

---

10. This is discussed on pp. 514 and 597.

It is clear that the use of instruments for influencing total expenditures may be unstabilizing as well as stabilizing and may deter as well as encourage economic growth. Because of lags between the application of a policy and its effects, the conditions with which a given policy must deal are not those of the period in which it is imposed, but those of a later period—in some instances considerably later. Forecasts rather than current measurements must be relied upon. Views on the relative desirability of discretionary and automatic controls may differ, therefore, because of differences in confidence in the art of forecasting.

Differences may also stem from different views as to the weights that should be given to price stability and full employment as objectives of policy. Where these are competing objectives, the use of discretionary controls permits a result closer to one or the other of them. Those who believe that political expediency will cause undue weight to be given to the employment objective will prefer automatic stabilizers.

SELECTED BIBLIOGRAPHY

AMERICAN ECONOMIC ASSOCIATION, "The Problem of Economic Stability," *American Economic Review* (September 1950), pp. 501-538.

BEVERIDGE, WILLIAM, *Full Employment in a Free Society*. New York: Norton, 1945, Parts I, II, III (Sections 1 and 2), VII, and Appendix C (by Nicholas Kaldor).

CHASE, SAMUEL B., JR., "The Lock-in Effect: Bank Reactions to Securities Losses," *Monthly Review*, Federal Reserve Bank of Kansas City (June 1960), pp. 9-16. [Reprinted in Ritter (ed.), *Money and Economic Activity*.]

COMMISSION ON MONEY AND CREDIT, *Money and Credit*. Englewood Cliffs, N. J.: Prentice-Hall, 1961, Chapters 2-3, 5.

FRIEDMAN, MILTON, *A Program for Monetary Stability*. New York: Fordham University Press, 1960.

MUSGRAVE, R. A., "Credit Controls, Interest Rates, and Management of the Public Debt." In *Income, Employment and Public Policy: Essays in Honor of Alvin Hansen*. New York: Norton, 1948, pp. 221-234.

ROSA, R. V., "Interest Rates and the Central Bank." In *Money, Trade, and Economic Growth: Essays in Honor of John H. Williams*. New York: Macmillan, 1951, pp. 270-295.

SIMONS, H. C., "Rules Versus Authorities in Monetary Policy," *Journal of Political Economy* (1936), pp. 1-30. (Reprinted in Simons, *Economic Policy for a Free Society*, and American Economic Association, *Readings in Monetary Theory*.)

WHITTLESEY, C. R., *Lectures on Monetary Management*. Bombay: Vora, 1960.

22

THE NATIONAL DEBT
AND DEBT MANAGEMENT

One of the major financial developments of the present century has been the growth of the national debt. From a position of negligible importance before World War I the national debt has grown to a point where it overshadows any other single element in the credit structure. For a time during and after World War II it represented a larger total than all other types of debt combined. Its growth alone would be enough to render it of prime significance to the student of finance.

What makes the growth in national debt of chief interest in the present context, however, is that it impinges on money, banking, and stabilization policy at almost every point. It has raised important issues concerning the proper objectives of monetary policy, and it brought into sharp focus the problem of possible conflicts between Treasury and Federal Reserve objectives and policies. The fears of the burden of a large national debt have provided an important popular argument against (and obstacle to) the use of fiscal policy for stabilization purposes.[1] Commercial banking has also been greatly affected by the vast increase in volume of Treasury obligations, which now occupy a prominent place in bank portfolios. The rise in national debt has given to the art of debt management a new and expanded importance which reaches far beyond the banking system. This art, which has its private as well as its public applications, has already developed a substantial body of principles and practices.

---

1. In this view it is easy enough to run deficits during periods of recession, but during periods of recovery and boom political expediency will permit little beyond a bare balance in the current budget. With deficits in the troughs of successive cycles and mere balanced budgets in stages of boom, a fluctuating economy will generate a persistently increasing national debt. If a rising absolute debt is viewed as sufficiently serious, it may prevent the use of fiscal stabilizers, not because of doubt as to their efficacy, but because of fears for the burden of debt that will follow from their use. One general objective of this chapter is to provide perspectives on the significance or "burden" of a growing national debt.

427

QUANTITATIVE ASPECTS OF FEDERAL DEBT

The growth in the absolute amount of national debt is primarily significant when related to concurrent changes in the economy, such as those involving the amount of private debt, the level of prices, and the national income. And the importance of interest cost of the debt is also a relative matter, depending on the relationship between these payments and the national income.

The Federal Debt in Relation to Total Debt

At the start of World War I the federal debt was an insignificant proportion, only 1 or 2 per cent, of the combined total of public and private debt oustanding. By 1919 it had risen to over 20 per cent of the total. In 1930 it stood at 8 per cent and in 1940 at nearly 21 per cent, or about where it was in 1919. The heavy borrowing resulting from World War II raised the proportion to a peak of 66 per cent at the end of 1945.

Between the end of 1945 and 1961 the debt of the federal government changed only slightly, while the debts of state and local governments increased about fourfold and private debt increased somewhat more than four times. As a result the proportion of federal debt to total debt declined from about two-thirds at the end of World War II to approximately one-fourth in the early 1960's (cf. Figure 22-1).

The Debt in Current and Constant Dollars

Comparisons of the size of debt expressed in dollar amounts imply a stability in the value of the monetary unit which is illusory. It occasionally happened in the period between the wars that the equivalent of the national debt in real terms, i.e., the total adjusted for changes in the purchasing power of the dollar, changed in exactly the opposite manner from the stated amount of the debt. This meant that the change in the purchasing power of the dollar more than offset the change in the magnitude of the debt.

An extreme illustration of the effect of changes in the purchasing power of money on the real value of the national debt occurred between 1920 and 1932. Between these dates the dollar amount of the debt was reduced by approximately one-fifth. As a result of the decline in prices, however, its size at the end of the period, measured in terms of wholesale commodities, was nearly double what it was at the start. In other words, our efforts to reduce the debt by taxing to build up budgetary surpluses were frustrated by the change in the value of the dollar. In real terms—i.e., in terms of what the debt represented in goods and services—we were more deeply in debt at the end of the period than we had been at the beginning.

The rise in prices after 1932, on the other hand, had the effect of holding down the real value of the debt. The growth of national debt during the 1930's, and particularly after the start of heavy borrowing for war purposes, was partly offset by the decline in the purchasing power of the dollar. At the end of 1961 the dollar amount of the national debt was

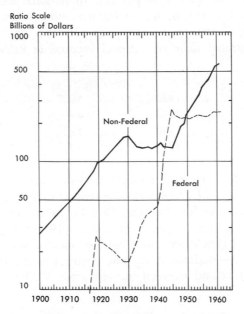

Figure 22-1.   Federal and Non-Federal Debt,
1900-1961.

Source: Adapted from the Federal Reserve Historical Chart Book.

almost twelve times higher than in December 1932. In terms of what the debt represented in commodities at wholesale, however, it was only about four times higher.

The National Debt and National Income

In an economy in which the incomes of the Treasury and the public are increasing, a constant debt (assuming a fairly stable rate of interest) represents a relatively declining obligation of the Treasury to pay and a relatively declining right of the public to receive. A debt which grows as fast as aggregate income may be considered to maintain its *relative* magnitude, and, from this standpoint, only a debt which grows faster than income becomes *relatively* greater. We may therefore appraise the relative importance of the debt by comparing changes in its total with changes in the national income.

In June 1920 the federal debt represented about 35 per cent of the national income for that year. By 1929, as a result of paying off the debt and of the rise in income, the proportion had fallen to under 20 per cent. By 1932, however, national income had declined to less than half of the 1929 level and the debt had begun to rise, with the result that in that year the national debt was equal to 50 per cent of national income. The proportion remained close to this figure for the next nine years, as the rate of rise in national income kept approximate pace with that of the growth in debt. The ratio of national debt to national income at selected dates was as follows:

1932	50%
1937	54%
1940	57%
1941	52%

Thereafter, despite a great increase in national income, the ratio of debt to income rose rapidly. In June 1946 the federal debt was over 150 per cent of the national income for the year. Because of the continued rise in national income thereafter, national income by 1951 was again higher than the national debt. In the early 1960's national income was approximately half again as large as the national debt. The changes in the relative magnitudes of the internal debt and national income after 1929 are shown in Figure 22-2.

Interest on the Debt and the Level of Income

The total public debt indicates the gross liability of the government but it fails to show the payments which the Treasury has to meet currently because of the debt. Assuming the debt is not retired but refunded —that is, that new obligations are issued to raise the funds for those that mature—then the financial load imposed on the federal budget is measured by the annual interest payments required. If we take these interest payments as a percentage of national income, this budgetary burden becomes more meaningful. Assuming that taxes are imposed on the public to pay the annual interest charges, the ratio of interest to national income provides a simple index of the level of tax rates required. (Specifically, it indicates what flat rate on total earned income would be necessary to raise the required funds.)

The amount of interest actually paid by the government is governed by the size of the debt and the average rate of interest on it. The average interest cost of Treasury borrowing declined from nearly 4¼ per cent in

1920 to well under 2 per cent in 1944. This drastic reduction was the result of three factors, a fall in the general level of interest rates, a shift in the pattern of rates whereby short-term rates declined much more than long-term, and a policy on the part of the Treasury of borrowing a larger proportion on short term. These factors were reversed after the war, and especially after the Treasury-Federal Reserve Accord of 1951. Interest payments consequently rose. At the end of fiscal 1961, a national debt some

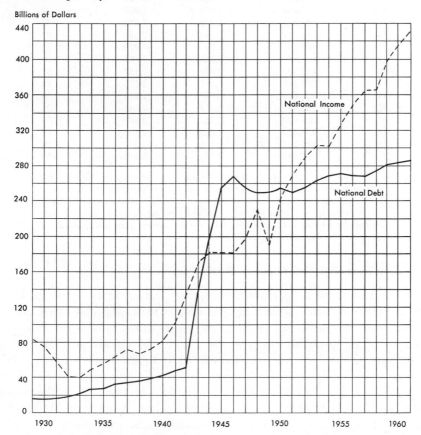

Figure 22-2. National Income and National Debt, 1929-1961.

Source: *Federal Reserve Bulletin; Secretary of the Treasury, Annual Reports.*

7 per cent larger than that of 1946 required annual interest outlays that were $3.4 billion dollars (over 63 per cent) higher than 15 years before (cf. Table 22-1). This was largely a reflection of a rise in the average interest cost of the debt from approximately 2 per cent to 3 per cent. Nevertheless, despite the 7 per cent increase in the size of the debt and the 50 per cent increase in average interest cost, the ratio of interest payments to national income declined substantially between 1946 and 1961 (from approximately 3 per cent to 2 per cent).

TABLE 22-1. National Debt and Interest Payments As Related to National Income, 1920-1961 (totals in millions)

June 30	Interest bearing debt	Annual interest	Average interest rate	Interest as a % of national income
1920	$ 24,061	$1,017	4.225%	1.54
1925	20,211	830	4.105	1.14
1930	15,922	606	3.807	.77
1940	42,376	1,095	2.583	1.48
1942	71,968	1,644	2.285	1.51
1944	199,543	3,849	1.929	2.45
1946	268,111	5,351	1.996	3.07
1948	250,063	5,455	2.182	2.59
1950	255,209	5,613	2.200	2.44
1952	256,863	5,981	2.329	2.10
1954	268,910	6,298	2.342	2.07
1956	269,883	6,950	2.576	2.04
1958	274,698	7,245	2.638	1.97
1960	283,241	9,316	3.297	2.30
1961	285,672	8,761	3.072	2.07

Sources: Data relating to debt and interest are from Secretary of the Treasury, *Annual Report.* Data relating to national income are from National Bureau of Economic Research estimates for 1920 and 1925 and Department of Commerce estimates for 1930 to 1961. National income for fiscal years is calculated by adding one-half of the total for the current year and one-half of the total for the preceding year.

Ownership and Maturity Distribution

The federal debt consists of three major parts—marketable securities, non-marketable securities, and special issues. Special issues are securities made available to government trust funds, often on relatively generous terms, to enable them to earn a rate of return provided for in earlier legislation. They may constitute an indirect means of granting a subsidy. At the end of 1945, these special issues amounted to $20 billion, compared with less than $5 billion in the middle of 1940. From the middle 1950's on they maintained a fairly stable total within a range of $42 and $46 billion. Non-marketable securities represented a little over one-fifth of outstanding federal debt at the end of war financing, the bulk consisting of United States savings bonds, with Series E—which were sold widely to small individual lenders—the most important type. By the 1960's they were about one-sixth of the total or not much larger than the special issues.

The remainder of the public debt at the end of 1945 was in the form of marketable securities, comprising 71 per cent of the total. Of this amount, over one-third was scheduled to mature within one year.[2] Over half, 53

2. Treasury bills, which amounted to $17 billion, usually run three months and, therefore, could have been regarded as maturing four times during the year. If each series were considered separately, the total of all securities maturing during the year would have amounted to about $120 billion.

per cent, was due or callable in five years or less, and only 13 per cent had a maturity of over twenty years. In June 1919, by contrast, Treasury obligations maturing within five years amounted to only 30 per cent of the total, while 26 per cent were of over twenty years maturity.

In terms of volume, commercial banks constituted the largest single class of owners of government securities at the end of the war, holding over 32 per cent of the total (cf. Table 22-2). Insurance companies with 9 per cent and mutual savings banks with 4 per cent brought the holdings of these three major types of institutional investor to 45 per cent of the total. Other corporations and other investors (mainly individuals) together held over 34 per cent of the outstanding debt. The Federal Reserve Banks and United States government agencies and trust funds held approximately 18 per cent of the federal debt at the end of the war.

A considerable redistribution of ownership of Treasury obligations took place in the years after the war. The principal reductions between 1945 and

TABLE 22-2. Ownership of Treasury Securities, 1945 and 1961 (end of year; par value, in billions)

	1945	1961
Federal Reserve Banks	24.3	28.9
Commercial Banks	96.8	67.2
Mutual savings banks	10.7	6.1
Insurance companies	24.0	11.4
Other corporations and associations	22.2	19.6
State and local governments	6.5	18.3
U.S. government agencies and trust funds	27.0	54.5
Other investors	73.2	90.4
Total	278.7	296.5

Source: *Federal Reserve Bulletin.*

1961 were in holdings by commercial banks and insurance companies, especially life insurance companies. The principal increases were in holdings by United States government agencies and trust funds, other investors (including savings and loan associations, pension funds, and dealers and brokers, as well as individuals), and state and local governments. As a result of these shifts, the proportion of debt held by commercial banks fell from almost one-third to under 23 per cent. The share of the three major institutional investors was down from 45 to about 29 per cent and that of state and local governments was up from under 3 to over 6 per cent. The holdings of the Federal Reserve Banks and United States government agencies and trust funds amounted to $84.4 billion, or 28 per cent of the outstanding interest-bearing debt of the Treasury.

A distinction is sometimes drawn between the gross federal debt and the net, or publicly held, debt outstanding, the latter being defined as the gross debt less the federal debt held by the Federal Reserve Banks and

United States government agencies and trust funds. This distinction is based on the fact that Federal Reserve and government agency holdings are internal to the government; hence they involve no debt management problems for the Treasury.[3] It is worth noting that while the gross federal debt increased from $278.7 billion to $296.5 billion between 1945 and 1961, the net or publicly held debt of the Treasury actually declined during this period from $227.4 billion to $213.1 billion.

As is to be expected, the types of securities held by the different ownership groups differ widely. The holdings of marketable Treasury debt by non-financial corporations are heavily concentrated (about 85 per cent) in maturities under one year. Holdings by the Federal Reserve Banks are not quite so liquid. At a date in the 1960's about a third of the holdings of commercial banks were in maturities under a year and more than half in maturities of one to five years. Formerly life insurance companies tended to concentrate in longer term issues. By the 1960's not only was the absolute amount of government securities held by insurance companies substantially lower than ten years before but a much higher proportion was in medium-range maturities. The distribution of the holdings of mutual savings banks was roughly similar to that of insurance companies.

The composition of the holdings of different investor groups is largely governed by the nature of their business. Life insurance companies and mutual savings banks have comparatively little need for liquidity and consequently are not averse to holding long-term debt. Commercial banks and fire and casualty insurance companies, requiring more liquidity, hold a larger proportion of short-term securities. In addition, custom may play a considerable role in determining the composition of portfolios of government securities.

As was mentioned previously, Treasury financing in the period of World War II was characterized by the high proportion of short-term borrowing. The relative shortness of the national debt, instead of being overcome in the years after the war, became more and more aggravated, as may be seen in Figure 22-3. The further shortening of the average maturity of the national debt was the result of two factors. First, maturing securities were frequently replaced by an issue of shorter term securities. This occurred under both Democratic and Republican administrations. Second, the mere passage of time served to shorten the time to maturity of all securities still outstanding. Of the two factors, the latter was the more important. The volume of marketable Treasury obligations maturing in one year, which declined to a postwar low of $42 billion in 1950, rose to nearly $100 billion in 1962.

---

3. The internal character of this sector of the debt is reflected in the fact that in the case of debt held by the Reserve Banks, a substantial part of Treasury interest payments are subsequently returned to the Treasury.

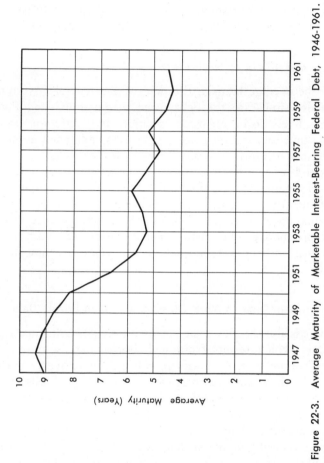

Figure 22-3. Average Maturity of Marketable Interest-Bearing Federal Debt, 1946-1961.

Source: Secretary of the Treasury, Annual Reports.

WAYS OF VIEWING THE NATIONAL DEBT

Four main points of view on the subject of national debt are encountered in current discussions of the subject. Not all of these views are mutually exclusive, and the same individual may share more than one of them—sometimes consciously and sometimes, no doubt, without fully realizing it. Each of the lines of thought contains elements of validity, with its respective merit turning on questions of degree, timing, and circumstance.

Government Debt as Similar to Private Debt

To the average layman, the debt of the federal government appears substantially similar to the debt owed by an individual. Public and private debt are likely to be regarded as simply two different examples of the same thing, and easy reliance upon either is condemned as being contrary to established canons of sound finance. In both public and private finance, resort to borrowing is recognized as sometimes justifiable, but only as exceptions to a generally accepted rule. The usual exceptions are in the case of borrowing for emergencies and for making productive investments. For governments, the typical emergencies are wars and severe business depressions, and productive investments include enterprises, such as building the Panama Canal and highway improvement, which are not suitable for private capital.

Government Debt as More Objectionable than Private Debt

There is also the view that borrowing by governments, and consequently the debt which results from such borrowing, is more dangerous than its private counterpart. As a way to cultivate favor with the electorate through tax reductions and extravagance with federal funds, borrowing is unquestionably capable of political abuse—though the extent to which voters are likely to be hoodwinked by such obvious tactics can be exaggerated. The necessity of making fixed annual payments on the national debt is said to impose a dead-weight burden on the budget and to introduce an element of rigidity into the administration of government finance. Although it is advanced as an objection to public debt, the problem of rigidity applies to any fixed-income obligation, whether public or private. It is a serious consideration only if the magnitude of the burden is out of proportion to the ability to carry it.

Government Debt as Beneficial

The conception that public debt may be not only preferable to private debt but intrinsically beneficial did not originate with the New

Deal Administration and its much criticized "new philosophy of public debt."[4] It dates, surprisingly enough, from the parent of so much that is conservative in American economic and political thought, Alexander Hamilton. In his famous report on the public debt, Hamilton argued that the existence of a certain amount of public debt serves a useful economic function by affording savers a safe place into which to put their funds, whether temporarily or more or less permanently.

Later a certain amount of debt owed by the government came to be regarded as a cushion which would facilitate the orderly administration of Treasury finance. A surplus of receipts over expenditures could be applied to reducing outstanding debt until the budget was brought into closer balance. In the absence of a debt, the government might be under pressure to dispose of funds unwisely during periods when there was a surplus.

It has frequently been said that the large volume of Treasury obligations is essential to the continued existence of our financial institutions. Whether or not one regards that as an adequate justification for perpetuating a public debt, the importance of the debt to commercial banks, pension funds, insurance companies, mutual savings banks, and others cannot be denied. To say that our economy would find it extremely difficult to function without a substantial volume of Treasury securities does not, of course, mean that a federal debt of the present proportions is necessary.

Government Debt as an Instrument of Policy

The national debt may be used as an instrument of policy, but changes in its size are usually a reflection of fiscal policies rather than an application of debt policy per se. Acceptance of the use of fiscal policy to bring about a desired level of spending implies that the government budget should be judged by its overall economic effects, not by its state of balance or imbalance. Thus when business activity requires a fiscal stimulant, the national debt should presumably be allowed to grow. When circumstances warrant fiscal restraints, the debt should be reduced. The growth and decline in the total debt is thus a reflection of budgetary policies that fix levels of spending and taxation.[5]

In addition to changes in total debt, which depend on fiscal decisions, control over the kinds and maturities of debt instruments within any given total provides a means of influencing the level of business activity. While the strength of stabilizing action that may be achieved by managing a debt of given size is much less than that of fiscal or monetary policy, the growth in the size of the debt has increased the possibility of debt manage-

---

4. Cf. H. G. Moulton, *New Philosophy of Public Debt* (Washington: Brookings Institution, 1943).

5. Of course the government could, by expanding the money supply, spend without taxing or issuing securities. As we have seen, increasing the stock of money (as opposed to bonds) in the hands of the public would make for lower interest rates and easier credit.

ment for policy purposes. This type of action is discussed in the concluding section of this chapter.

THE BURDEN OF NATIONAL DEBT

A debt may be said to impose a burden on society if it adversely affects economic welfare in any of its dimensions. This includes potential effects on incentives to provide the efforts and sacrifices related to production, on the efficiency of use of productive resources, and on equity in the distribution of income. By and large it may be assumed that any burden of debt will be reflected in a reduction or undesirable redistribution of the real income of society.

The Burden of an Existing Debt

It is universally recognized by economists—even by those who fear that unwarranted conclusions may be drawn from the observation—that an internal debt is essentially different from a debt held abroad. The basis of the difference is as simple as double entry bookkeeping—since debits equal credits, it follows that where debtors and creditors are citizens of the same country the *net* obligation of the community as a whole is nil.

Just as there cannot be more sales than there are purchases, so likewise there cannot be more debt than there is credit. Debt and credit are opposite ways of viewing the same thing..The one must, therefore, be equal to the other. In the case of an internally held debt, it is absolutely correct to say that "we owe it to ourselves." The amount *owed by* the taxpayers is exactly equal to the amount *owed to* the bondholders. In the case of an internally held debt, there is literally no net debt. It is, therefore, not true that the *existence* of a national debt reduces the net assets (total assets less total liabilities) of the American people. But it by no means follows—and this is apparently the reason why so many people resist accepting this view —that the existence of a huge national debt is of no importance. It only means that the real signficance of the debt lies elsewhere.

The most significant potential burden of a national debt lies in the possibility that the service charges on the debt might entail so large a redistribution of the national income, through taxation of individuals and business, as to prove a deterrent to economic endeavor. The degree of burden would depend not only on the magnitude of the service charges in relation to taxable incomes, but also on the character of the tax structure and the way in which the distribution of tax burden influences investment, consumption, and effort. A large federal debt also requires administration, and administration involves cost. It follows that a domestic debt does impose a financial burden on society, even though no net debt can be said to exist. The magnitude of the administrative burden, however, is ordinarily not large relative to the total debt or even to the annual service on the debt. And certainly this is hardly what is in the minds of those who speak most critically concerning "the burden of national debt."

Granting that the principal burden of the debt relates to the taxes made necessary by the service charges on the debt, it follows that the relative burden is influenced by the relationship between service charges and national income. If interest rates were to remain more or less the same so that service charges are roughly proportional to the debt, the relative burden would decline even with a growing debt, provided income grew at a more rapid rate.

Transferring the Burden to Future Generations

In addition to pointing to the burden of an existing debt, critics of a rising federal debt have argued that debt passes on to future generations part of the burden of current expenditures, so that future generations are charged for the follies and extravagances of the present.

Again the argument takes certain forms which are clearly fallacious, but also more subtle forms which have an element of validity but whose significance is open to question. One of the fallacious arguments is that the ultimate repayment of the debt places a burden on future generations since the taxes required to finance the debt reduction will reduce total real incomes. It is true, as we have seen in the analysis of fiscal policies, that a surplus used to retire existing debt tends to depress national income. But this merely implies that debt retirement is consistent with full employment only when aggregate expenditures would otherwise be excessive. In this case the decline in income is not due to the inherited debt, but to the deliberate budget surplus undertaken to reduce it. Any depressing effect on the level of real income could be avoided by reducing the debt only in times of excess demand or by not reducing the debt at all, but simply refunding all maturing issues. (It should be reiterated here that in a growing economy this would be consistent with a declining burden of debt, measured by the ratio of service charges to national income.) Any burden involved is simply that related to an existing debt, which was discussed above.

A more substantial argument for the transfer of some burden to future generations as a result of present debt-financed expenditure centers on the interaction of fiscal operations, monetary policy, and interest rates. Assuming that aggregate demand for output is being restricted in the interest of economic stabilization, then loan-financed expenditure by the government would require a tighter monetary policy to limit demand than tax-financed expenditure. Thus the two programs involve different resource allocations at the time of the expenditure. Financing government expenditures by taxes is likely to shift resources from the production of consumption goods to collective consumption (or investment), while financing the same expenditures via bonds, requiring higher interest rates to prevent inflation, may shift the resources in some degree from investment. This restrains economic growth, and provides future generations with a smaller endowment of capital goods, a smaller productive capacity, and hence a smaller full-employment income. In effect, by saving and investing less the present generation can consume more, with the result that future generations will have a smaller total income to allocate.

If this is considered a transfer of debt burden, charges of transfer of burden are valid. But in this general form many other actions not commonly considered in this context must be charged with burdening future generations as well. This would include the use of monetary policy to fight inflation (as opposed to fiscal policy), the use of advertising to encourage consumption expenditures, and the promotion of consumer credit for the same purpose.

National Debt and Economic Growth

From time immemorial dire consequences have been predicted from actual or impending increases in the size of the public debt. The prevailing sentiments regarding the disastrous effects of the growth in the debt of the British government before and during the Napoleonic wars was described eloquently by Lord Macaulay more than a century ago as follows:

> At every stage in the growth of that debt it has been seriously asserted by wise men that bankruptcy and ruin were at hand. . . . When the great contest with Lewis the Fourteenth was finally terminated by the Peace of Utrecht the nation owed about fifty millions [pounds]; and that debt was considered, not merely by the rude multitude . . . but by acute and profound thinkers, as an incumbrance which would permanently cripple the body politic. Nevertheless trade flourished: wealth increased: the nation became richer and richer. Then came the war of the Austrian Succession; and the debt rose to eighty millions. Pamphleteers, historians, and orators pronounced that now, at all events, our case was desperate. . . . Soon war again broke forth; and under the energetic and prodigal administration of the first William Pitt, the debt rapidly swelled to a hundred and forty millions. As soon as the first intoxication of victory was over, men of theory and men of business almost unanimously pronounced that the fatal day had now really arrived. . . . The attempt to lay a portion of the load on the American colonies produced another war. That war left us with an additional hundred millions of debt, and without the colonies whose help had been represented as indispensable. Again England was given over; and again the strange patient persisted in becoming stronger and more blooming . . . As she had been visibly more prosperous with a debt of one hundred and forty millions than with a debt of fifty millions, so she was visibly more prosperous with a debt of two hundred and forty

millions than with a debt of one hundred and forty millions. Soon however the wars which sprang from the French Revolution . . . tasked the powers of public credit to the utmost. When the world was again at rest the funded debt of England amounted to eight hundred millions. . . . It was in truth a gigantic, a fabulous, debt; and we can hardly wonder that the cry of despair should have been louder than ever. But again that cry was found to have been as unreasonable as ever. After a few years of exhaustion, England recovered herself. Yet like Addison's valetudinarian, who continued to whimper that he was dying of consumption till he became so fat that he was shamed into silence, she went on complaining that she was sunk in poverty till her wealth showed itself by tokens which made her complaints ridiculous. The beggared, the bankrupt, society not only proved able to meet all its obligations, but, while meeting these obligations, grew richer and richer so fast that the growth could almost be discerned by the eye.[6]

During the 125-year period extending from 1690 to the end of the Napoleonic Wars in 1815, the rise in the national debt of Great Britain was persistent and substantial. Yet during these years the industrial revolution was successfully nurtured in Great Britain. The British national debt at the close of the Napoleonic wars was about twice the level of national income of Britain at that time—as compared with a peak ratio for the United States of about one and one-half to one at the close of World War II. In spite of the burden of this large debt the British economy was preeminent in the world's economy during the nineteenth century. It is also relevant that the lesser but still relatively large burden of debt imposed upon the economy of the United States during and after World War II did not prevent a rapid and unusually long sustained expansion of output in the succeeding decade and a half. It would seem reasonable to conclude that the burden of a large public debt is not a decisive obstacle to economic growth.

The Bogey of National Bankruptcy

The statement is encountered again and again that continued expansion of the public debt would plunge the country into national bankruptcy. Even though we have passed more than once the point at which the danger was said to be critical, the bogey of national bankruptcy refuses to down. It is important to recognize that bankruptcy is strictly a juridical concept; and the nation cannot be sued against its will or thrown into legal bankruptcy. It follows that the term is not to be taken literally when applied to a nation. In 1922-1923 Germany passed through one of the most extreme inflation experiences in history but was never technically chargeable with default on its bonds. The contractual obligation to pay was legally met—

6. *The Works of Lord Macaulay,* Edinburgh Edition (New York: Longmans, Green, 1900), Vol. III, pp. 617-19.

even though payment was effected in marks which were practically worthless.

The expression "national bankruptcy," then, is a figure of speech. While it is often employed recklessly, the meaning which it is intended to convey is not hard to define. It refers to a set of economic and fiscal conditions where the government loses control of its finances and the public suffers severe disturbances as a consequence. There can be no doubt that German finance reached such a state in 1922-1923, and the same could be said of a good many other countries before and since. In the decade of the 1930's, on the other hand, the United States consistently failed to balance the budget, but borrowing remained orderly and the disturbances and dislocations imposed upon the public could not—at least in comparison with the conditions like those in Germany—be called severe.

The essence of fiscal exigency, then, is a scale of expenditures which the Treasury can no longer succeed in covering by taxation and orderly methods of borrowing. To the extent that the public debt contributes to the emergence of such a state of affairs, it presumably does so primarily by the magnitude of the service charges arising out of the debt and, secondarily, by its effect on the country's credit standing and ability to borrow through desired channels.

DEBT MANAGEMENT

In the postwar period increased attention has come to be focused upon management of the public debt. Debt management is to be regarded, in fact, as the latest recruit to the array of techniques for controlling and directing the course of economic activity and the level of prices. Just as the use of fiscal policy as a stabilizing device was an outgrowth of the greatly expanded scale of fiscal operations, so the increasing importance of debt management reflects the rise in the size of the national debt.

The Nature of Debt Management

Debt management refers, first, to actions affecting the structure or composition of the publicly held debt where the purpose is to influence the rate or direction of spending by the public. It may include, in addition, policies operating through changes in the composition of the debt which are designed to influence the security markets directly, as for the purpose of holding down the cost of borrowing or otherwise facilitating Treasury operations. "Structure or composition" refers to the types of security by maturity and intended holder. The "actions" relate chiefly to setting the terms on new issues, the refunding of old issues, and open-market sales and purchases.

The intent that lies back of changes in the structure of debt must also be considered. Routine adjustments to meet normal operating procedures where there is no effort to influence expenditures or conditions in the market are no more to be dignified as debt management than adjustments by number and types of currency to meet seasonal fluctuations in demand are to be construed as monetary management.[7] In the primary sense referred to above, debt management implies the pursuit of ends similar to those of monetary policy and fiscal policy by means, not of changes in the money supply or revenues and expenditures, but of changes in composition of the federal debt. It is another technique for influencing economic activity.

It should be noted that where the public debt is increasing in size this reflects not debt management but a *fiscal policy* decision to spend more than is received in taxes, and a contraction of debt reflects a fiscal policy decision to spend less than the amount of taxes collected. (This is not to preclude the possibility that with a given increase or decrease in total a decision as to the method or form of the change in debt may constitute debt management.)

Just as monetary management is primarily the province of the central bank and fiscal policy the province of the Treasury, so debt management is the responsibility of both. The Treasury is concerned mainly with deciding on the types of securities issued and the terms on which they will be offered. The Federal Reserve conducts purchases and sales of government securities in the open market. Close relations are maintained between the two bodies with a view to sharing ideas and coordinating activities.[8]

The Objectives of Debt Management

The principal objectives of debt management have been the minimization of the interest cost of the debt, the facilitating of Treasury debt operations, and influencing the level of aggregate demand for contracyclical stabilization purposes.

Economy in interest cost has always been an objective of debt management policy, but its ranking among the various objectives has rarely been high. For many years the Treasury urged the necessity of maintaining conditions which would facilitate orderly financing of government requirements.

---

7. Routine procedures could better be embraced under the general concept of debt (or monetary) *administration*. If, as may sometimes happen, debt management is employed in this general sense it is to be sharply distinguished from the specialized usage followed in the present discussion.

8. This brief description is suggestive only. A great variety of specific techniques are or have been employed. During and after World War I, for example, the government followed an elaborate and rather costly program of stabilizing the market for outstanding Treasury issues. At times since World War II purchases and sales by Treasury trust funds have been carried out with a view to influencing conditions in the security markets.

Federal Reserve operations between 1942 and 1951 gave substantial weight to the objective of Treasury convenience, providing full assurance of orderly conditions in government securities markets. After the Accord the objective of Treasury convenience was given a low weight by the Federal Reserve authorities, who committed themselves only to correct disorderly conditions and to maintain a policy of neutrality at times when the Treasury was in the market seeking funds.

The objective of using debt management for stabilization purposes is relatively new and its mechanics require some explanation. The balance of this discussion will therefore be devoted mainly to a consideration of the uses of debt management for stabilization.

Debt Management as an Instrument for Influencing Aggregate Demand

Changing the maturity distribution of the debt may influence aggregate demand by affecting the structure of interest rates and liquidity. Let us look first at effects via the structure of rates. By replacing maturing short-term obligations with long-term issues the Treasury can exert a downward pressure on the prices of long-term securities (raising their yields), and at the same time contribute to a rise in the price of short-term instruments. If aggregate spending is more sensitive to changes in the long-term rate of interest than to short-term rates, the lengthening of the debt may serve to reduce spending. However, although it is usually assumed that changes in the long-term rate have a stronger impact on spending, this is far from certain. Furthermore, since spending appears to be relatively insensitive to the general level of rates of interest, the leverage of debt management, involving only changes in interest structure within a given level, is even more open to question.[9]

Changes in the structure of the debt may also affect total spending by altering the liquidity position of wealth holders. If we assume a lengthening of the debt by replacing maturing bills with twenty-year bonds, close money substitutes have been replaced by instruments that fluctuate more widely in price and are less satisfactory substitutes for money in asset port-folios. Insofar as total spending is influenced by the liquidity of private wealth, this shift would tend to reduce private outlays. It should be noted, however, that these liquidity effects are brought about by changes in the maturity of some (usually small) fraction of a given stock of wealth; the total stock of assets is not changed, and debt management does not ordinarily involve an immediate transformation of the maturity of the entire debt. Furthermore, the shift in maturities does not displace a wholly liquid asset with one that is completely illiquid; it is a substitution of a less liquid asset type for one that is more liquid. The net effect on liquidity will depend

9. See Warren L. Smith, *Debt Management in the United States*, Study Paper No. 19, Joint Economic Committee, 86th Congress, 2nd Session (Washington: 1960), p. 8.

on the differences in liquidity of two relatively liquid assets. All this suggests that the leverage of such maturity shifts is not likely to be large.

The Debt as an Automatic Stabilizer

Although marginal changes in the maturity distribution of the public debt would appear to provide a rather ineffectual means of influencing aggregate spending, the total maturity structure of debt may have a significant impact on the stability of the system. If, for example, the debt were comprised entirely of bills, spending units would have greater leeway in enlarging expenditures in periods of expansion, as they could move from bills to cash quickly and with little capital loss. On the other hand, a debt comprised entirely of long-term bonds would tend to fluctuate more in price, so that greater capital losses would have to be realized to move to cash. These liquidity plus wealth effects make existing bonds function as an automatic stabilizer. Consequently, although marginal changes in the maturity structure of the debt would appear to have only a slight effect on the flow of spending, cumulative changes in the maturity structure may be of considerably greater significance from the standpoint of stabilization.

As noted earlier, after the end of World War II the average maturity of the publicly held debt fell steadily. This tended to reduce the automatic stabilization properties of the debt. It also increased the frequency with which the Treasury engaged in refunding operations, which in turn increases the Treasury's sensitivity to money market conditions and hampers the Federal Reserve's monetary policy. This suggests that a longer average maturity of the debt would have substantial advantages from the standpoint of stabilization policy.

The gradual shortening of the maturity structure of the debt has been due to the passage of time, the relative decline in the market position of government obligations, and the adherence to what might be called the "orthodox" theory of debt management—that long-term bonds ought to be issued in periods of overexpansion to exercise a restraining influence on economic activity, and that short-term issues are appropriate to periods of recession. The passage of time is clearly inescapable, and its shortening effects can be offset only by including long-term issues in Treasury refunding operations. The loss in favor of Treasury obligations has been due mainly to prosperity and the growth in availability of competitive private instruments (some, incidentally, made competitive by guarantees of the government). This can be compensated for by a sufficient rise in yields on Treasury obligations, or by an abandonment of the orthodox theory and a more vigorous sale of Treasury bonds in periods of recession. The sale of bonds in recessions would have the advantages of reducing Treasury interest costs and contributing to the reversal of the process of shortening of the maturity structure of the debt. It would have the disadvantage, however, of abandoning short-run debt management as a stabilization device. We have seen that the stabilization contribution of marginal changes in the structure of debt are not likely to be great. And over the last decade the Treasury has found it extremely difficult to sell long-term bonds in periods of vigorous expansion and tight money. Under the circumstances, there would appear to be a strong case for abandoning attempts at contracyclical maturity changes in favor of attempting a significant lengthening in the maturity structure of the public debt whenever this is practicable. By confining its role to that of automatic stabilizer debt management assumes a more modest posture, but one better measured to its capabilities.

SELECTED BIBLIOGRAPHY

COMMISSION ON MONEY AND CREDIT, *Money and Credit*. Englewood Cliffs, N.J.: Prentice-Hall, 1961, Chapter 4.

DOMAR, E. D., "Public Debt and the National Income." In Board of Governors of the Federal Reserve System, *Public Finance and Full Employment*, Postwar Economic Studies No. 3, Washington: 1945, pp. 53-68.

HANSEN, ALVIN H., *Fiscal Policy and Business Cycles*. New York: Norton, 1941, Chapter IX.

LERNER, A. P., "Functional Finance and the Federal Debt," *Social Research* (1943), pp. 38-51. (Reprinted in American Economic Association, *Readings in Fiscal Policy*.)

———, "The Burden of Debt," *Review of Economics and Statistics* (May 1961), pp. 139-141.

RATCHFORD, B. U. "The Burden of a Domestic Debt," *American Economic Review* (1942), pp. 451-467. (Reprinted in American Economic Association, *Readings in Fiscal Policy*.)

SMITH, WARREN L., *Debt Management in the United States*. Study Paper No. 19, Joint Economic Committee, 86th Congress, 2nd Session. Washington: 1960.

23

MONETARY AND FISCAL
POLICIES, 1914-1939

When war broke out in 1914 the institutional framework of finance in the United States was relatively undeveloped. The Federal Reserve was new, inexperienced, and the object of considerable hostility in this particularly critical period of its history.[1]

During the war, and largely because of it, the new central banking organization quickly achieved size, power, and prestige, but the American banking system as a whole retained much of its original character. It comprised many thousands of small unit banks, the majority of them subject only to the widely varying standards set by state banking laws. The Federal Land Bank System and the War Finance Corporation, precursor of the Reconstruction Finance Corporation, were instituted in 1917. But the elaborate collection of governmentally initiated financial institutions which featured the period of World War II was entirely absent.

Underlying and largely governing the financial policies of the period was a general adherence to the traditional, conservative peacetime rules of "sound" finance, strongly influenced by a laissez faire philosophy. Governmental controls were relatively unimportant. Central bank policies were in their infancy, and commercial banking was thought of in terms of lending on the basis of short-term, self-liquidating commercial paper. The principles of federal finance were not sharply differentiated from those of private finance, and the interest rate was assumed to be a satisfactory, or at least a necessary, regulator of credit in war as in peace.

---

1. Not long before, the American Bankers Association had passed a resolution opposing the establishment of the proposed Federal Reserve System on the ground that it was socialistic.

FINANCIAL POLICIES DURING AND IMMEDIATELY AFTER WORLD WAR I

The pace of American involvement in World War I was, to say the least, unhurried. In the two years prior to our declaration of war in April 1917, Treasury disbursements on the military establishment, far from being expanded, were actually reduced. Two months before our entry into the war, Congress was still debating whether or not to undertake military preparations, and it was another month before taxes to pay for preparedness were actually voted. Federal outlays began to exceed revenue about the time we entered the war, but deficits remained relatively moderate for another year. The peak of spending for military purposes was not reached until after the signing of the armistice. This helps to explain why some of the more extreme effects of war finance occurred during the year and a half after the conclusion of hostilities.

Monetary Standards and Exchange Rates

The leading belligerents abandoned convertibility into gold at the start of hostilities, and the United States placed an embargo on gold exports soon after our entry into the war. Even though convertibility between the dollar and gold was maintained within the United States, the restrictions on the export of gold constituted abandonment of the international gold standard. Exchange rates between the dollar and the pound sterling and the French franc were kept at a fixed level, a little below the old parity, by a policy known as "pegging." The dollar fell to a considerable discount, however, in terms of a number of currencies—including the Spanish peso, Swiss franc, Japanese yen, and some of the currencies of Latin America—which fully retained their position relative to gold.

A drain of gold from the United States resulted from the repatriation of foreign capital at the start of the war, but a little later the expansion of exports of food and war materials to the belligerent countries led to a heavy flow of gold to this country. This movement virtually ceased after our entry into the war (cf. Table 23-1). Early in 1919, the United States lifted its embargo on gold, placing the dollar again back on the international gold standard. A considerable exportation of gold ensued, but it was not long before the movement was reversed and the dollar commanded a premium over some of the foreign currencies in terms of which it had previously been at a discount.

Financing World War I

The constitutional amendment legalizing the federal income tax was enacted in 1913, just in time to permit the use of this form of taxation

TABLE 23-1. Gold Stocks and Gold Movements, 1914-1922 (in millions of dollars)

Year	Gold Stock (end of year)	Increase or decrease (−)	Domestic gold production	Net gold import or export (−)
1914	1,526	−100.2	93.4	−165.2
1915	2,025	499.1	99.7	420.5
1916	2,556	530.7	91.1	530.2
1917	2,868	312.2	82.3	180.6
1918	2,873	4.9	67.4	21.0
1919	2,707	−165.8	59.5	−291.7
1920	2,639	− 68.4	49.9	95.0
1921	3,373	734.6	48.8	667.4
1922	3,642	268.5	47.3	238.3

Source: Banking and Monetary Statistics.

in financing the war. Federal expenditures rose from $734 million in the fiscal year ending June 1916 to $18,515 million three years later. While spending fell far short of the heights reached in 1942-45, the growth relative to the scale of expenditures at the start of the period was much greater. About 28 per cent of federal expenditures in the fiscal year 1918-1919 were covered by taxation (see Table 23-2).

TABLE 23-2. Treasury Finances, 1916-1922 (millions of dollars)

Fiscal Year Ending June	Net Revenues	Total Expenditures	Net Revenues as % of Expenditures	Increases or Decreases (−) in Public Debt	Total Public Debt
1916	783	734	106.7	34	1,225.1
1917	1,124	1,978	56.8	1,751	2,975.6
1918	3,665	12,697	28.9	9,480	12,455.2
1919	5,152	18,515	27.8	13,029	25,484.5
1920	6,695	6,403	104.6	− 1,185	24,299.3
1921	5,630	5,116	110.0	− 322	23,977.5
1922	4,109	3,373	121.8	− 1,014	22,963.4

Source: Secretary of Treasury, Annual Report for 1960.

Thus, notwithstanding a sevenfold increase in tax receipts between 1916 and 1920, World War I was financed chiefly by borrowing. Most of the money borrowed came directly from individual investors but indirectly from the banks. The public was encouraged to pay for bonds by loans from banks, pledging the bonds thus acquired as security for the loans. Loans of this type were popularized under the slogan "Borrow and Buy." The rates charged by banks were customarily the same as the rates paid by the government on the bonds serving as collateral. Since the loans were repaid either currently or out of deposits which had been accumulated gradually, the effect was similar to the purchase of bonds on the installment plan. While these loans were technically of a non-bank character, their effect was to make bank credit indirectly available to the government. This was, of course, a highly inflationary means of financing.

Also worthy of note is the fact that the Treasury raised the rates of interest and offered tax-exemption privileges in an effort to make bonds attractive. Machinery was introduced for supporting the price of outstanding issues, and in 1918 the Treasury asked for and obtained an increase in the level of income taxes, chiefly for the purpose of strengthening the market price of tax-exempt obligations.[2] The practice of allowing interest rates to rise, far from making it easier for the Treasury to borrow, seemed to make it more difficult. For one thing, lenders tended to hold off in anticipation of being able to invest at higher rates a little later. Frequently, too, bonds were sold before a new issue was about to come out as a means of obtaining funds to reinvest at the higher yields. The decline in market price and rise in yields of outstanding issues—which accompanied such selling—acted as a deterrent to buyers of the new issues. It suggested all too realistically the possibility of depreciation on the issue currently offered.

During most of the period, higher rates were paid on short-term than on long-term issues. Partly for this reason but chiefly because of the anticipated dangers of a large floating debt, short-term issues—which amounted to something over 14 per cent of the total debt in 1918 and 1919—were largely refunded in longer term issues. After the completion of the Victory Loan, little attention was given to supporting the price of government bonds and by 1920 certain issues had fallen more than 18 per cent below par value.

Federal Reserve Monetary Policy to 1921

Experience in this country and abroad shows that wars produce consequences of great significance to central banks. The magnitude of the central bank's tasks as fiscal agent, custodian of reserves, and controller of credit is enormously increased. At the same time, the central bank must accommodate its activities more closely than in peace to policies of the Treasury and other branches of the government. War underscores the importance of central banks and strengthens their standing and prestige, but, for a time at least, it drastically reduces their independence.

The prime objective of Federal Reserve policy during World War I was to assure adequate funds for the Treasury. The Federal Reserve authorities encouraged the sale of government bonds to the non-banking public, but at the same time they established a low and preferential discount rate on loans secured by government obligations (i.e., "advances") so that banks would "feel free to assist would-be bond buyers, knowing that they could protect themselves if necessary by rediscounting the paper with the Reserve Bank." This easy money policy provided the reserves that enabled the commercial banks to lend heavily to business, to finance individual purchases of securities under the Borrow and Buy program, and to acquire (by

2. The average rate of interest paid on government obligations was between 4 per cent and 4½ per cent per annum. At the time, Treasury rates were regarded as low.

June 30, 1919) some $4 billion of government securities for their own account.[3]

Immediately after the Armistice a slight recession in industrial production set in and lasted until early in 1919. From March onward a speculative and inflationary situation developed which grew steadily more pronounced. At the same time, the substantial floating debt was in process of being refunded by the Treasury into longer term issues. The Federal Reserve authorities were thus involved in their first major policy dilemma: considerations of cost and convenience to the Treasury called for continuation of relatively easy money to facilitate refunding operations at low cost, but the developing speculative and inflationary situation pointed to the need for credit restraint.

The Reserve authorities attempted to resolve this dilemma by a compromise that gave primary weight to the interests of Treasury financing. Discount rates were kept at low levels in recognition of the Treasury's "unwieldy floating debt," and an attempt was made to control inflationary extensions of bank credit by means of moral suasion. Banks and investment houses were urged to restrict loans and investments to those needed by government and essential industries. Although this effort had some momentary impact on lending by individual banks, it was largely ineffective, and speculation and inflation reached new heights in 1919 and the first half of 1920.

Toward the end of 1919 the Board decided that Treasury refunding operations had reached a point where Reserve support was no longer indispensable and that the time had come to bring credit under effective control. Accordingly, in January 1920 the New York Federal Reserve Bank raised its discount rate from 4¾ to 6 per cent, and in May to 7 per cent. Almost simultaneously with the last increase one of the most severe deflations in our history began. The collapse of the postwar speculative boom was undoubtedly accelerated by the tight money policy, but the boom had already approached its peak and could not have been sustained much longer.

The recession of 1920-1921 was regarded with equanimity by the Board as a necessary episode in a return to normality. The Reserve authorities maintained the high discount rates of the spring of 1920 well into 1921, in the face of a sharp deflation and periodic illiquidity crises that assumed almost panic proportions. They intensified their efforts to force member banks to reduce their borrowings from the Reserve Banks and carried out a stricter examination policy. Federal Reserve credit fell precipitously, as may be seen in Figure 23-1. The maintenance and even intensification of tight money through a period of severe deflation was based on the view

---

3. The importance of member bank borrowing from the Reserve Banks during the war is indicated by the fact that for a considerable period of time the volume of member bank indebtedness was greater than total legal reserves. This suggests that the member banks as a whole were operating entirely on borrowed reserves.

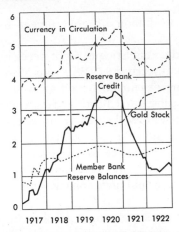

Figure 23-1.   Reserve Bank Credit
and Related Items, 1917-1922.

Source: Adapted from the Federal
Reserve Historical Chart Book

that the economy had not yet been completely purged of speculative elements, and that this was essential to a sound recovery. This neglect of the real income costs of a deflationary policy as well as the potentially damaging effect of tight money on expectations was not too serious in the early 1920's because of favorable underlying demand. In the early 1930's, however, when demand was depressed, similar attitudes contributed to the inadequacy of monetary policy.

PROSPERITY AND BOOM, 1922-29

Financial developments of the interwar years fall into three clearly defined periods—the first terminated by the stock market collapse in 1929, the second by the inauguration of the Roosevelt Administration, and the third by the start of the war in Europe.

General Characteristics of the Period, 1922-1929

The years from the end of the First World War to the stock market crash were dominated by a surge of investment activity sufficiently strong to overcome the deflation of 1920-1921 and minor inventory recessions in 1924 and 1927. The investment boom had run its course by 1929, so that no offsetting wave of investment was forthcoming to counteract the deflationary effects of the stock market shock. The high tempo of investment during the 1920's was based on the pent-up demands accumulated during World War I, the high level of exports (heavily financed by frequently unwise American lending), the coincidence of a general economic upswing with the expansion phase of the building cycle, and the great impetus to investment resulting from the rapid spread of the automobile and the growth of the electric power and other industries. A sharp decline in construction activity after 1928, rather than the stock market crash, signaled the incipient ending of this great investment boom.

Economic policy in the 1920's was conservative and orthodox. The dominant view held that laissez faire was appropriate (except, of course, for the tariff) and that government activity should be sharply restricted; the budget should be kept in balance and governmental debt eliminated as promptly as possible. In short, fiscal policy and debt management were not viewed as instruments of stabilization policy. (In fact, the reduction of federal debt out of tax revenues was continued tenaciously in the early 1930's, despite its deflationary effects.) The prevalent position was that instability was a problem of the price level and could be controlled by a judicious use of general monetary weapons. This view was reinforced by the stability of prices and the apparent success of minor open-market operations in the mild recessions of 1924 and 1927. However, as Professor Hansen has said,

> The apparent success of these measures distracted attention away from the deeper causes of the sustained prosperity of the twenties—the powerful upsurge of investment activity in building and in a half-dozen growing industries especially related to the automobile and electrical industries. Like Rostand's Chantecler (with his faith in the causal connection between his morning crowing and the rising sun), monetary enthusiasts watched with satisfaction the apparently favorable results of monetary policy.[4]

The Attempt to Stabilize Prices

The early 1920's witnessed the start of an ambitious attempt to achieve stability of commodity prices. Popular acceptance of the quantity theory of money had given rise to a widespread belief in the feasibility of price level stabilization. Confidence in the powers of the Federal Reserve to control money and credit—and in the effectiveness of price level stabilization in promoting stable economic activity generally—combined to encourage the introduction of such a policy. The policy coincided from 1922 to 1929 with a period of stable prices, as measured by indexes of wholesale prices. This was the heyday of Federal Reserve credit control policy and marks the peak of confidence inside and outside the System in the powers of the Federal Reserve authorities.

A number of significant lessons emerged from the experience of these years. First, it was shown that stabilization of the wholesale price level was

4. Alvin H. Hansen, *Fiscal Policy and Business Cycles* (New York: Norton, 1941), p. 75.

no guarantee of the long run stabilization of the economy as a whole. Second, it became clear that stable wholesale prices could exist alongside great instability of other price series; the period also featured dramatic increases in the prices of real estate and securities. Indeed, the later 1920's are marked *chiefly* by the extraordinary stock market boom and collapse. In short, the general price level (which corresponds to P in the equation of exchange and is therefore related to *all* transactions) is by no means homogeneous. It is composed instead of many different prices and classes of prices which may behave in varying fashion.

During the 1920's technological advance and the introduction of mass production methods increased output per man-hour and, in the absence of an equal increase in wage rates, brought about a reduction in unit costs of production. Stability of the general level of selling prices at a time when increases in productivity outran the rise in wages tended to widen the spread between costs and selling prices and thereby contributed to swollen profits and the distortions in production normally associated with inflation.

Development of Federal Reserve Policies

The period of the 1920's is noteworthy in the annals of the Federal Reserve for the origin and development of open-market policy. After discovering more or less by chance the usefulness of operations in the open market for controlling credit, the Reserve authorities used the new technique frequently (cf. Figure 23-2). Purchases of over one-half billion dollars of government securities between the end of 1923 and the late summer of 1924 were followed by sufficient recovery of business and of commodity and security prices so that the Federal Reserve turned to selling in the open market in late 1924 and early 1925. Restrictive measures continued until early 1926 and by April there was a sufficient slowing down to lead the Reserve authorities to resort once again to expansionist credit policies. In these and other cases the apparent success of open-market policies, especially when used in conjunction with changes in the discount rate, was so great as to build up the feeling referred to earlier of extraordinary confidence in monetary policy among both bankers and Federal Reserve officials. Unfortunately, all was not quite as well as appeared on the surface.

During this period monetary policy was based less on gold movements, which had been the traditional guide for central bank policy, and more on the considerably less definite goal of maintaining "sound credit conditions." But the various measures of the soundness of credit conditions were frequently found to conflict with one another. Moreover, gold movements continued to be a complicating factor. The action of the Federal Reserve Banks in holding down the discount rate in order to avoid draining gold reserves from abroad is believed to have contributed to the speculative boom in Wall Street. To the extent that funds were thereby attracted to this country (and into the stock market), the action of the Reserve Banks—which had been designed to facilitate the restoration and maintenance of the international gold standard—may have had the opposite effect from what was intended.

The Federal Reserve authorities became increasingly concerned over the development of speculative activity in the stock market. Starting early in 1928 they endeavored to curb further increases in loans on securities by raising the discount rate and selling securities in the open market. In 1929 they resorted to direct pressure on member banks ("moral suasion") to induce them to avoid further expansion of security loans.

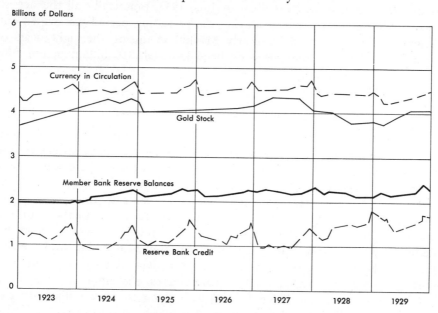

Figure 23-2.   Reserve Bank Credit and Related Items, 1923-1929.

Source: Adapted from the Federal Reserve Historical Chart Book.

With general economic conditions showing signs of serious weakness, the Reserve authorities found themselves confronted by the difficult problem of desiring to curb an unduly buoyant stock market while fearing to impose curbs which might place a damper on business elsewhere. Conflict of opinion within the circle of Federal Reserve officials and strenuous protests from outside the System impeded the pursuit of a more vigorous policy in combating the speculative boom. Policy changes were made so frequently as to indicate confusion among the monetary authorities. Finally, the discount rate in New York was raised to 6 per cent in August 1929—but the stock market boom proceeded headlong into its final stages with no apparent regard for central bankers or anyone else.

The frustrations of the later 1920's bore fruit in some of the reforms introduced later, one of them being the introduction of Regulations T and U for the control of margin requirements on security loans. Doubtless the experience, disillusioning as it was, gave the Federal Reserve authorities and the public generally a somewhat more realistic conception of the magnitude of the tasks of economic stabilization and of the limitations of monetary policies for dealing with them.

FINANCIAL POLICIES IN MOUNTING DEPRESSION, 1929-1933

In the four years from June 1929 to June 1933, practically all the deposit expansion which had occurred during the preceding period was wiped out. Where deposits had risen by nearly $17 billion during the eight years of expansion and boom, they now declined by over $16 billion in but four years of the depression.

Efforts of the Federal Reserve to Stem the Deflation

The immediate effect of the break in the stock market in October 1929 was to cause a heavy withdrawal of funds by panic-stricken, non-banking lenders of money on a call basis. Consequently, there was a sharp increase in the demand for bank credit by brokers to replace the credit withdrawn. Member banks in New York City came to the rescue of the brokers by taking over a large amount of brokers' loans. In the course of one week, October 23 to October 30, the loans and investments of reporting member banks in New York City increased from $7.6 billion to $9 billion. This increase was possible only because the Federal Reserve Bank of New York provided the necessary additional reserves, the amount of reporting member banks' reserves rising from $739 million to $982 million. In two critical days following the stock market crash, open-market purchases amounted to $120 million. Nowhere outside New York City was there a substantial advance in bank credit during the week of the crisis, though minor increases occurred in Chicago, Boston, and St. Louis. The Federal Reserve discount rate was quickly dropped from 6 per cent to 2 per cent in New York, and smaller reductions were made by the other Reserve Banks.

Despite assistance afforded by the Federal Reserve Banks in providing liquidity at other times of heavy strain, on balance Federal Reserve policy during the crucial early years of the depression was timorous and ineffectual. The extent of the boom in 1928 and 1929 was influenced by overconfidence in the ability of the Federal Reserve System to prevent crisis. It was an easy decent from this state of undue confidence in the Federal Reserve to a state of excessive disillusionment. In this prevailing hopelessness, the Federal Reserve authorities—as their limited efforts to expand credit by lower discount rates and open-market purchases proved unavailing—came generally to share.

Federal Reserve policy to ease credit in the early 1930's had the effect principally of enabling member banks to reduce their indebtedness to the Reserve Banks. But the hope that the banks, influenced by the "tradition against borrowing," would begin to lend freely when their debts to the central bank were smaller proved vain. Gold losses and an increase in currency in circulation provided additional offsets to open market purchases, with the combined result that total Federal Reserve credit declined in the first few years of the depression (see Figure 23-3). It was not until 1932

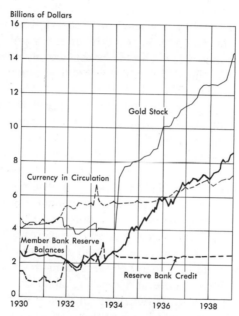

Figure 23-3. Reserve Bank Credit and Related Items, 1930-1938.

Source: Adapted from the Federal Reserve Historical Chart Book.

that open-market buying was carried out with vigor, but by then monetary means were powerless to overcome the ravages which deflation had wrought on the financial system and on expectations.

The hesitancy of Federal Reserve policy during this period resulted in part from the unfamiliarity of the authorities with a serious deflation and from their failure to realize the aggressiveness and scale of operations that were necessary to cope with it. The minor adjustments that had seemed to suffice in 1923 and 1927 had no noticeable effect on the course of deflation. Rather than embark on a sustained anti-deflationary effort the Federal Reserve tended to take refuge in traditional principles and rules of laissez faire.

Federal Reserve policy in the early years of depression also suffered from the view held by some policy-makers that a liquidation of speculative excesses was healthy and should not be interrupted by monetary intervention. This attitude, based on a superficial organic analogy, was not harmful in 1921 when expansionary forces were strong, but it was injurious in the later deflationary period when the cumulative downward process could have been slowed only by determined action.

Another factor which appears to have contributed to the caution of Federal Reserve policies during this period was the legal restriction on collateral applicable to Federal Reserve notes. Before the passage of the Glass-Steagall Act in 1932 the issuance of Federal Reserve notes required backing of 40 per cent gold and 60 per cent in either gold or eligible commercial paper. At a time when eligible paper was in short supply it was necessary to make up the deficiency by holding amounts of gold over and above the 40 per cent. To relieve the situation, the Glass-Steagall Act was passed early in 1932 giving the Federal Reserve Banks the power to use United States government securities as collateral against Federal Reserve notes. The effect of authorizing the use of government bonds as collateral was to increase the amount of available gold reserves by well over a billion dollars. In addition, by authorizing the Reserve Banks under special conditions to accept previously ineligible paper as collateral for advances, the Glass-Steagall Act also made it possible to extend assistance to member banks that lacked adequate amounts of eligible paper.

Notwithstanding these measures of relief, the increase in Federal Reserve notes in circulation and the decrease in gold holdings that occurred early in 1933 reduced the ratio of Federal Reserve Bank reserves by March 3 to 45.3 per cent of combined note and deposit liabilities. The required ratio on that date was 38 per cent. Anticipating an even greater need for Federal Reserve credit, the Board found it advisable to suspend the reserve requirements to which the Reserve Banks were subject for a period of thirty days from March 3, with a tax on the amount by which reserves were deficient. With the improvement in conditions after the reopening of the banks, little use was made of this suspension, and it was not renewed at the end of the thirty-day period. It is well to observe that the powers of the Federal Reserve Banks to extend further credit and to supply additional gold were far from exhausted when a general Banking Holiday was declared by the incoming Roosevelt Administration.

Suspension of the Gold Standard

In the six weeks following Britain's abandonment of the gold standard in the autumn of 1931, the United States lost nearly three-quarters of a billion dollars of gold. A second sharp outflow of gold occurred in May and June of 1932. The net loss of gold in these two movements amounted to approximately $1.1 billion. In the second half of 1932, the flow was reversed and by the end of the year the country's gold stock had gained about $600 million from the low point. The banking system was able to withstand the pressure caused by the flow of gold abroad and the expansion of currency in 1931 and 1932, mainly because the Federal Reserve Banks were able to extend credit to member banks. At the beginning of 1933, however, gold reserves began to decline again, and this time the movement continued until it was stopped—and the pressure on banks relieved—by the closing of the banks and an embargo on the export of gold. These measures were the first major official acts of President Roosevelt after his inauguration.

Abandonment of the gold standard in this country and abroad was the manifestation in considerable part of a sharp reversal of public opinion. Prior to the onset of the depression, the general public in this country had been inflation-conscious. This attitude had been greatly strengthened by the examples of extreme inflation during and after World War I. As a result of the prolonged deflation starting in 1929, the public, here and abroad, became just as strongly deflation-conscious and deflation came to be popularly associated with the gold standard. This preoccupation with the evils of deflation, amounting at times to an obsession, not only helps to account for our own action with respect to gold but also served to color monetary policies throughout the ensuing years.

FINANCIAL DEVELOPMENTS, 1933-1939

Never before in our history was there such a concentrated period of legislative activity affecting money and banking as in the early years of the Roosevelt Administration. The principal laws enacted from 1933 to 1935 were:

> Emergency Banking Act of 1933 (March 1933)
> Thomas Amendment to the Agricultural Adjustment Act (April 1933)
> Banking Act of 1933 (June 1933)
> Gold Reserve Act of 1934 (January 1934)
> Silver Purchase Act (June 1934)
> Banking Act of 1935 (August 1935)

In addition, there was a succession of other laws, resolutions, rulings, executive orders, and messages and statements of policy by the President. Many of the provisions dealt with matters narrowly related to the immediate emergency, or were of a temporary character. Other parts of the legislation—such as the provisions of the Thomas Amendment, which authorized the issue of 3 billion dollars of greenbacks and the establishment of bimetallism at the discretion of the President—were not exercised and were subsequently repealed.

Many of the steps taken at this time were condemned as bad economics and some, notably the Congressional resolution abrogating the gold clause in existing contracts, as bad morals. Few would deny that the measures adopted were hasty, often ill-conceived, and sometimes conflicting. It is probable, however, that the show of vigorous leadership and the tactics of shock, particularly in the first days after the closing of the banks, helped to arouse the financial community from the fear and paralysis which had oppressed it for so long. At any rate, it cannot be denied that from the opening of the banks after the Banking Holiday the banking system moved forward in strength and prosperity.

Monetary Objectives

The hectic early days of the Roosevelt Administration allowed little time for working out a considered and consistent monetary program. Coupled with this fact was a strong determination on the part of the Administration to adopt positive action of some sort at a time when the customary sources of monetary action, namely bankers and the Federal Reserve authorities, had little that was definite and decisive to offer. Under the circumstances, it is far from easy to trace clear lines of monetary thought and action. Nevertheless, it appears that the financial policies of the Roosevelt Administration were influenced, consciously or unconsciously, by a desire to achieve the following major objectives:

1. Restoration of commodity prices and thereafter the maintenance of "a continuing purchasing power which does not vary greatly in terms of commodities" (to use the words of the message sent to the London Economic Conference by President Roosevelt in July 1933).
2. Insulation of the bases of credit, and of the monetary system generally, from external influences.
3. Encouragement of investment and industrial expansion.
4. Prevention of a speculative boom in Wall Street.

These potentially conflicting objectives help to explain the distinctive monetary and banking policies which characterized the period—the departure from gold, the gold purchase program, and the sterilization and subsequent desterilization of gold; easy money policies; introduction of new instruments of credit control such as the provision for changing margin requirements; and the verbal attacks on so-called "economic royalists" and "money-changers."

Dollar Devaluation and the Gold Policies

The major monetary action of the period was the abandonment of the gold standard and the subsequent devaluation of the dollar in terms of gold to 59.06 per cent of the former parity. This represented an increase in the dollar price of gold from $20.67 to $35 an ounce. At the same time, changes were introduced in the provisions governing the operation of the gold standard which had the effect of giving us a gold bullion standard with restricted convertibility. Approximately $2.8 billion was immediately realized as profit from writing up the value of the monetary gold stocks to their new dollar equivalent. Of this amount, two billion was set aside to provide an Exchange Stabilization Fund.

The rise in the price of gold was designed to raise the price level, i.e. "reflate." The leading exponent of the view that the price of gold and the level of prices were directly correlated was Professor George F. Warren of Cornell, a leading expert on farm administration who became, for a short time, one of President Roosevelt's advisers on monetary policy. The argument was based on long-run, historical evidence from a period when gold was a major component and determinant of the money supply. The shallowness of the reasoning is indicated by its failure to recognize that increasing the price of gold in the circumstances of the Thirties merely gave the Treasury a paper profit without directly affecting the amount of money in the hands of the public. When commodity prices failed to respond as readily as had been hoped, the policy was abandoned and the price of gold stabilized at the new rate of $35 an ounce. For about sixteen months from 1936 to 1938 the Treasury pursued a gold sterilization policy, whereby the effect of gold imports on bank reserves was largely offset through the sale of Treasury obligations in the open market. Of the monetary improvisations introduced in these years the most significant was the Exchange Stabilization Fund, whose name indicates its purpose.

The Silver Purchase Act of 1934

The silver legislation of the Roosevelt Administration was of the same general character as earlier silver purchase acts, with the principal difference that it involved far larger sums and was not repealed. That is to say, it was a production subsidy in the guise of monetary legislation. It called for purchases of silver by the Treasury until the price of silver reached $1.29 an ounce or the value of Treasury stocks of silver, computed at $1.29 an ounce, reached one-third the value of our gold stocks. Payment was to be made by the issue of silver certificates in amounts sufficient to cover the cost of the bullion acquired. The Treasury was authorized to pay a higher price for domestically mined silver than for foreign silver.

The arguments on which the passage of the law was based were almost wholly specious. The claim that it would increase the monetary reserves of the country disregarded the fact that silver does not constitute legal reserves and could be counted as monetary reserve only if we were to adopt a silver or bimetallic standard. Moreover, our gold reserves were already adequate at the time—and were destined shortly to expand enormously. The argument that the law would increase the purchasing power of the Orient and so promote our export trade overlooked the fact that silver was not used as a means of paying for imports by the oriental countries and that our exports to China, the principal country in question, were being considerably better maintained than our exports to countries which had been on the gold standard. The most that can be said in defense of the silver legislation is that it may possibly have forestalled even more unwise proposals which were then current.

Heavy purchases of silver were made in the early years of the law, but after 1941 no serious effort was made to purchase foreign silver. The Secretary of the Treasury was required, under subsequent legislation, to purchase all newly mined domestic silver offered at the official price. Total net purchases under the Act amounted to about $1.4 billion up to the end of 1961. Despite strong criticism of the law by Treasury and Federal Reserve officials, bankers, and economists, efforts to secure its repeal were unavailing. The chief benefit from the silver policy was derived by foreign and domestic producers of the metal. The most significant consequences of the Silver Purchase Act were the abandonment of the silver standard by China, which for years had been the greatest source of demand for silver in the world, and a reduction in the use of silver as circulating medium in many countries, including India and the United Kingdom. As a result of these moves, supplies of silver bullion were poured into world markets by these countries.

Growth of Excess Member Bank Reserves

The existence of excess commercial bank reserves was not unknown before the early 1930's, but they had never continued long enough to be considered a serious problem. Lord Keynes once explained just why it was that banks could not be expected to hold excess reserves. He laid it down as a fact, demonstrable by both reason and experience, that "banks use their reserves up to the hilt . . . and seldom or never maintain idle reserves. . . . Indeed, why should they?"[5] In support of this conclusion, Keynes argued that to allow reserves to fall below the accepted figure would reflect discredit on the banks (suggesting "weakness or weakmindedness"), while to allow them to rise above would be to forego unnecessarily a source of profit. He admitted that this reasoning assumed the availability of liquid income-yielding assets, but quite properly concluded that in England and in the United States this condition was certain to be met.[6]

These views were presented in 1930. It is a minor irony that beginning almost immediately thereafter excess reserves in the United States rose into the billions, and strict economy in the use of reserves seemed to have little significance as a banking objective (cf. Table 23-3).

---

5. J. M. Keynes, *A Treatise on Money* (London: Macmillan, 1930), Vol. II, p. 53.
6. *Ibid.*, p. 54.

A number of different factors contributed to the growth in both total and excess member bank reserves. From 1929 to 1934 operations of the Federal Reserve Banks designed to promote recovery (particularly the purchase of securities in the open market) added to the supply of reserve funds. For part of the period, as we have seen, this increase was offset by a return of funds by member banks to reduce their borrowing at the Reserve Banks. On the other hand, a decline in the volume of deposits—from $33 billion at the end of 1929 to under $27 billion in June 1934—helped to cause excess reserves to rise, even at times when the absolute amount of reserves was decreasing.

TABLE 23-3. Legal Reserves of Member Banks, 1929-1943 (year-end figures in billions)

Year	Required Reserves	Excess Reserves	Total Reserves	Ratio of Total Reserves to Deposits Requiring Reserves
1929	$ 2.4	$−0.05	$ 2.4	7.4%
1930	2.4	0.1	2.5	7.3
1932	1.9	0.6	2.5	7.5
1934	2.3	1.8	4.1	14.2
1936	4.6	2.0	6.6	18.0
1938	5.5	3.2	8.7	22.4
1940	7.4	6.6	14.0	29.4
1941	9.4	3.1	12.5	23.8
1942	11.1	1.9	13.1	19.2
1943	11.6	1.2	12.8	17.5

Source: Member Bank Call Reports.

By far the most important factor contributing to the rise of total member bank reserves from 1934 on was the growth of the gold stocks of the United States. Between the end of 1933 and the end of 1940, gold stocks increased by $15 billion. A large part of this increase entailed an expansion in the reserve balances of member banks (see Figure 23-3 above). A further factor operating in the same direction was the purchase of silver by the United States Treasury under the terms of the Silver Purchase Act of 1934. Although the gold and silver was added to Treasury stocks rather than remaining in the banks, the effect of payment for the metals by the Treasury was to increase the reserves of member banks.

Even with a very rapid growth in total reserves, it remains to be considered why banks did not put them to use more expeditiously. One factor was the increased desire for liquidity on the part of the banking community, which had so recently suffered from bank runs and other uncertainties. A second factor was the extent of decline in economic activity and the sluggishness of recovery, which retarded the expansion in demand for bank loans. A third factor was the reluctance of the banks to buy government securities at prevailing low yields (under $\frac{1}{10}$ per cent a year on three-months bills). This reluctance was reinforced by the growing threat of war in the late 1930's and recollections of the favorable effects of war on interest rates.

Excess reserves reached their maximum, nearly $7 billion, in October 1940. From that point they declined even more rapidly than they had grown. At the end of the war, excess reserves were not much larger than they were in 1932. This was largely a result of the great expansion in deposits and currency, which was so rapid as to compel the Federal Reserve to supply additional reserve funds soon after our entry into the war.

Fiscal Policy under the Roosevelt Administration

The spending policies of the New Deal Administration are often cited as an example of the use of fiscal policy to promote full employment. Actually, however, they provide a very imperfect testing of the theory. Deficit spending in the 1930's was an innovation to which the business community had not yet become adjusted (as it has to a considerable degree by now), so that secondary adverse effects on business expectations may have been relatively substantial. Furthermore, even more than in the case of monetary policy, deficit spending was introduced belatedly, after deflation had been permitted to wreak such havoc on public confidence and on the institutional structure as to make recovery a far more difficult task. It would be a mistake to identify the New Deal policies too closely with the theory of fiscal policy as an instrument of economic stabilization[7], whether the purpose of the identification is to praise or to condemn.

The inauguration of the deliberate use of fiscal measures to influence the level of business activity may be said to have begun in 1934. Deficits incurred before that time, including the substantial deficits in the last two years of the Republican administration, were the result not of intention but of the shrinkage of revenue which resulted from the decline in business activity and national income. The start of increased spending by the government in 1934 was accompanied by a rise in business activity. When the payment of a bonus to veterans was added to this spending, a mild boom ensued in 1936-1937.

In 1937 net deficit financing may be said to have come to an end. In August of that year the net receipts from social security were equal to the net deficit in the federal administrative budget. Consequently the national accounts comprising the cash-consolidated budget were in balance. There followed a sharp recession in business activity. A revival of deficit spending

---

7. It may be noted that these policies were initiated before the publication of Keynes' momentous book, and, while they may have been influenced by the ideas contained in the book, it is more likely that the book was used to justify an improvised program which had been adopted on a rather opportunistic basis with no thoroughgoing foundation in theory.

in 1938 was followed by an increase in business activity. From 1939 to 1945 the great expansion in deficit financing caused by preparation for war and then the war itself was accompanied by an enormous rise in business activity. It is possible to find in the sequence of deficit spending and rising business activity during these years some support for the theory of fiscal policy, even though the goal of full employment was not attained until the war period.

Later, the huge war deficits produced the inflationary pressures that found their expression in the upward movement of prices after the removal of many of the wartime controls in 1946. The inflationary experience during World War II was not as bad as in other wars before the theory of fiscal policy had been developed. It may be observed that exponents of the theory were among the strongest advocates of heavier taxation during the war. If the fiscal policies advocated by these economists had been adopted at the time, later difficulties might have been much less severe.

It is clear that the timing of fiscal policies in relation to private expenditures is of utmost importance. In the period of the 1930's, apparently, excessive lags in introducing substantial deficits, and their premature removal, seriously reduced their effectiveness. In the war years restrictive fiscal policies were not applied with the full vigor which the theory would have called for.

THE DECLINE OF AUTOMATISM

The original Federal Reserve Act embodied a plan for the automatic functioning of the Reserve System which rested on two bases, the gold standard and the use of self-liquidating commercial paper. The discounting of commercial paper by member banks and its rediscount by the Reserve Bank was expected to control the volume of bank credit, and the operation of the international gold standard was expected to control the volume of basic central bank reserves. The result was to be a system operating almost automatically, with the Reserve Banks playing a passive role.

During the period between the two world wars there was a general weakening and then the more or less complete abandonment of the regulation of the money supply in accordance with gold flows. In the United States this was reflected in the accumulation of idle gold reserves by the Federal Reserve Banks. This was sometimes referred to in the 1920's and 1930's as the sterilization or partial sterilization of gold. The motive for such action was thoroughly laudable—namely, to avoid the tendency believed to be present toward overexpansion of the circulating medium. But the action involved a departure from a fixed relationship between reserves and the money stock, which is the essential condition of a purely automatic monetary system.

So long as commercial paper constituted a substantial part of bank port-folios an important element of an automatic system[8] still remained. The subordination of short-term, self-liquidating commercial paper and the rise of other types of loans and of investments in the portfolios of commercial banks was a development covering many years, even though the magnitude and rapidity of the shift which took place after 1929 and particularly during the war years were exceptional. As early as 1934 the volume of investments had come to exceed the volume of loans and discounts. It was not until the first half of 1943, however, with the dollar value of investments approxi-mately double the dollar value of loans and discounts, that the income from investments surpassed the income from loans and discounts, a situation that prevailed until 1947. The end of the war brought a reversal of the movement into government securities.

At one time it was customary to think of bank loans—not altogether accurately, perhaps—as consisting entirely of commercial loans. For many years they have included substantial amounts of collateral, real estate, term, and consumer loans. They have very largely ceased to be commercial in origin or self-liquidating in character. Even with the great recovery of loans since 1945, therefore, little of the traditional basis for the automatic regula-tion of the money supply can be said to remain.

Along with a decline in the importance of gold and commercial paper as the bases of an automatic monetary and banking system has gone an in-creased resort to monetary management in the form of central bank policies and Treasury operations. Adoption of such methods, even when they are as mild as open-market operations and discount policy, is clearly a deviation from strict principles of an automatic monetary system. Although such measures may have been employed at first, less to resist automatic forces than to hasten and facilitate adjustments that would have taken place any-way, they still represented a departure from automatism.

In summary, then, the ideal of an automatic system cannot be said to have been achieved at any time, but with the passage of time the reality be-came progressively more removed from the ideal. The international gold standard, which had not been allowed to control reserves even in the 1920's, ceased to exist in anything like the traditional form in the 1930's. Commer-cial paper gave way to Treasury obligations and other types of credit instru-ments as the principal basis of the credit operations of both member banks and Reserve Banks. Methods of credit control which rest on the initiative of the Federal Reserve authorities assumed increasing importance. With these changes, even the semblance of an automatic monetary and banking system had largely disappeared.

---

8. As presented, for example, in Gustav Cassel, *Theory of Social Economy*, revised edition (New York: Harcourt Brace, 1932), Section 46.

SELECTED BIBLIOGRAPHY

BOPP, KARL R., "Three Decades of Federal Reserve Policy." In Board of Governors of the Federal Reserve System, *Federal Reserve Policy*, Postwar Economic Studies No. 8. Washington: 1947, pp. 1-29.

CHANDLER, L. V., *Benjamin Strong*. Washington: Brookings Institution, 1958, Chapters III-VII.

ECCLES, MARRINER S., *Beckoning Frontiers*. New York: Knopf, 1951, Parts III-IV.

GALBRAITH, J. K., *The Great Crash*. Boston: Houghton Mifflin, 1955.

GOLDENWEISER, E. A., *American Monetary Policy*. New York: McGraw-Hill, 1951, Chapters VII-IX.

GORDON, R. A., *Business Fluctuations*. New York: Harper, 1961, Chapter 14.

HANSEN, ALVIN H., *Fiscal Policy and Business Cycles*. New York: Norton, 1941, Chapters I-IV.

NURKSE, R., *International Currency Experience*. League of Nations, 1944.

SCHUMPETER, J. A., "The Decade of the Twenties," *American Economic Review* (May 1946), pp. 1-10. (Reprinted in A. H. Hansen and R. V. Clemence, *Readings in Business Cycles and National Income*.)

SMITHIES, ARTHUR, "The American Economy in the Thirties," *American Economic Review* (May 1946), pp. 11-27. (Reprinted in Hansen and Clemence, *op. cit.*)

24

MONETARY AND FISCAL
POLICIES, 1940-1951

At the outbreak of war in 1939, there was tremendous slack in the American economy, notwithstanding the stimulus already afforded by the imminent prospect that there would be a war. This situation of slack was evidenced by about 9 million unemployed and an abundance of idle productive capacity. We had grown accustomed to a high degree of governmental participation in economic affairs and we were equipped with an extensive array of governmental agencies capable of adaptation to the guidance or conduct of wartime economic activity. The Federal Reserve System was in possession of various instruments of policy and had a wealth of knowledge and experience to draw upon.

The total federal debt amounted to nearly $41 billion at the end of August 1939, compared with less than $1 billion at the outbreak of war in 1914. At the start of heavy war financing the national debt was double what it was at the end of financing World War I. The altered fiscal position of the Treasury was not without its practical advantages: after nine years of continuous deficit, the Treasury was thoroughly familiar with large-scale borrowing operations, and banks and private investors with the technique of lending to the government.

In short, economic and ideological conditions at the start of World War II were strikingly different from those at the start of World War I. The differences help to explain why the financial history of the two periods, notwithstanding numerous similarities, presents so many significant contrasts.

MONETARY AND FISCAL DEVELOPMENTS DURING WORLD WAR II

The International Monetary Situation

August 1939 found the world without any such common international monetary system as the gold standard had provided twenty-five years earlier. Instead, there was a wide diversity of monetary practice. At one extreme stood the United States, holding to a modified gold standard—which could not, because of the lack of adherence by other major countries, be called international. At the other extreme were Germany and a number of other countries, maintaining arbitrary quotations for their currencies by policies which entailed stringent control of all transactions involving foreign exchange. In between were many countries, including Great Britain, France, and numerous satellites, which exercised more moderate control over exchange operations than that prevailing in Germany.

The start of war in Europe was the signal for a stiffening of the control of exchange dealings by both belligerent and non-belligerent countries. Gold stocks had already been pretty well concentrated in the hands of treasuries and central banks, but now other types of assets, particularly stocks and bonds of foreign corporations, were brought under governmental supervision and in many instances compulsorily transferred to the government.

Financial Markets

The fact that the New York security markets were spared the sudden shock which led to their being closed from August to December 1914 was partly because the war merely brought about an extension of governmental controls already in existence at home and abroad and, therefore, more or less familiar. Security and exchange markets could not be demoralized by a rupture of the international gold standard because of the simple fact that, as a consequence of the events of the 1930's, there was no longer an international gold standard to break down. Exchange rates could not fluctuate as they once had done because there was nowhere a free market for foreign exchange.

While there was never any apparent question of the security markets being closed, the immediate effect of the declaration of war in 1939 was a sharp decline in bond prices. The prices of common stocks, on the other hand, rose almost as sharply as bond prices fell. Security markets were again upset by the events of December 1941, but with certain conspicuous differences. The decline in Treasury bond prices was considerably less than in 1939, but common stocks which previously had risen about 10 per cent within a period of three weeks declined more than 10 per cent in the same length of time following Pearl Harbor.

In both periods the break in security prices was largely influenced by the recollection of past effects of war on interest rates and security prices, and in both instances the temporary weakness was met by prompt action on the part of Federal Reserve officials. In the two weeks ending September 13, 1939, the Federal Reserve Banks increased their holdings of Treasury securities by $400 million. During the ensuing weeks, there was a gradual recovery in the bond market and by the end of the year security prices, yields, and the volume of Federal Reserve holdings of Treasury issues were not far from what they had been shortly before the outbreak of war. Following Pearl Harbor, the security market was again supported by Federal Reserve purchases, but this time the assistance required to assure orderly conditions was much less than it had been in 1939.

Gold and International Capital Movements

From the start of 1934, there was a heavy flow of gold to the United States. With the growing prospect and then the fact of large-scale war, the movement of gold to this country approached the proportions of an avalanche.

So heavy a movement of gold was bound to come to an early end, if for no other reason than that there was simply not enough gold in the world to allow it to continue. The inauguration of Lend-Lease early in 1941 furnished the allied powers with an alternative method of acquiring war materials and so removed the main reason for shipping gold to the United States. After our entry into the war, the heavy importation of raw materials into the United States and restrictions on the export of commodities in exchange gave rise to large dollar balances in favor of many countries in Latin America and elsewhere. Part of these dollar balances were converted into gold either to be held under earmark in this country or to be exported. As a consequence, monetary stocks of gold in the United States declined from $22.7 billion at the end of June 1942 to about $20 billion at the end of 1945 (see Figure 24-1).

Fiscal Policies

World War I was regarded at the time as an enormously costly undertaking, yet the entire cost of that war through final demobilization, $37 billions, was barely one-tenth of the expenditures of World War II through the end of the fiscal year 1946, $375 billions. Since price levels were considerably lower during World War II than World War I, the difference cannot be attributed to a change in the purchasing power of the dollar.

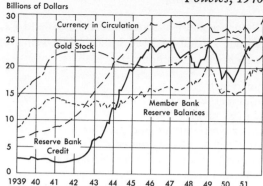

Figure 24-1.   Reserve Bank Credit and Related Items,
1939-1951.

Source: Adapted from the Federal Reserve Historical Chart
Book.

In the three fiscal years 1943 to 1945, close to one-half (46, 49, and 49 per cent) of the gross national product was devoted to federal expenditures, compared with about a quarter at the peak of the previous war. The volume of federal expenditures reached about two-thirds of total national income. In 1944 and 1945, they were larger in dollar amount than the total national income of the United States in any year of our history prior to 1942.

TABLE 24-1. Treasury Finances, 1940-1946 (billions of dollars)

Fiscal Year Ending June	Net Revenues	Total Expenditures	Net Revenues as % of Expenditures	Increase or Decrease (—) in Public Debt	Total Public Debt
1940	5.1	9.0	55.6	2.5	43.0
1941	7.1	12.7	55.9	6.0	49.0
1942	12.6	32.4	38.9	23.5	72.4
1943	22.0	78.2	28.1	64.3	139.7
1944	43.6	93.7	46.5	64.3	201.0
1945	44.5	100.4	44.3	57.7	258.7
1946	39.8	65.0	61.2	10.7	269.4

Source: Secretary of the Treasury, *Annual Report for 1960.*

For the fiscal years 1941 to 1945, 41 per cent of total expenditures were financed out of taxation, the highest ratio being in the fiscal year 1945 with 46 per cent. Net receipts from taxes in 1945 were nine times their total in 1940 (Table 24-1). The most important source of revenue consisted of income and profits taxes which provided over 75 per cent of total revenue in 1945. Income from this source increased sixteenfold from 1940 to 1945, from $2.1 billion to $35.2 billion. The rise in tax income is attributable in part to the great increase in national income and in part to a drastic increase in rates.

Of the total interest-bearing federal debt of $257 billion at the end of

June 1945, $84 billion was held by commercial banks and $22 billion by the Federal Reserve Banks, a total of $106 billion. The remaining $151 billion was distributed as follows (in billions):[1]

Individuals	$58.6
Insurance companies	22.7
Mutual savings banks	9.6
Other corporations and associations	30.3
State and local governments	4.9
United States Government agencies and Trust Funds	24.0

A distinctive feature of borrowing in World War II was the extensive resort to short-term securities. Of the increase in federal debt between April 1, 1939 and March 31, 1945, 43 per cent was in securities maturing in one year or less, 40 per cent in from one to ten years and only 17 per cent in over ten years.[2] The large volume of floating debt (as much as $65 billion falling due within a single year) represented a break with traditional policies of Treasury financing. It was adopted deliberately on two principal grounds, namely, that short-term securities were more suitable for certain types of purchasers, notably banks and corporations anticipating heavy tax liabilities, and that the Treasury could borrow on short term at a lower rate of interest.

The success of the policy as a means of holding down the cost of war financing is attested by the fact that the computed average interest rate on federal debt outstanding fell almost continuously throughout the war. At the end of June 1940, the rate was 2.5 per cent per annum; five years later it was a little over 1.9 per cent. Since the rate on identical maturities remained unchanged, the decline in average rate was largely the result of issuing a great proportion of relatively short-term, low-yield obligations. During World War I, the computed average interest rate rose from 2.4 per cent in June 1916 to over 4.2 per cent four years later. In that period the interest rate on particular maturities was allowed to rise and the rate on short-term securities was generally as high as on long, if not higher.

Another feature of Treasury policy, and one somewhat contradictory to the preceding, was the emphasis placed on borrowing from individuals. The rate paid on War Savings Bonds, Series E, was 2.9 per cent if held to maturity. This rate was far above that paid on other issues and at the same time the securities were more costly to place and more trouble to administer. Nevertheless, greater effort was devoted to their sale than to the sale of all other issues combined. The explanation of maintaining such a policy lies almost wholly in the anticipated indirect effects of this type of borrowing; it was expected, first, to exert a strongly anti-inflationary influence at the time of borrowing and, second, to provide a reserve of individual sav-

---

1. *Treasury Bulletin*, October 1945, p. 48.
2. *Op. cit.*, p. 11.

ings which would contribute to the maintenance of consumer demand in the years after the war.

Federal Reserve Policy During World War II

On the morning after the attack on Pearl Harbor, the Board of Governors announced as the major objectives of Federal Reserve policy:

> To assure that an ample supply of funds is available at all times for financing the war effort and to exert its influence toward maintaining conditions in the United States Government security market that are satisfactory from the standpoint of the Government's requirements.[3]

The two most distinctive measures put into force following this announcement provided for the purchase and sale of Treasury bills at a guaranteed rate and for the establishment of a fixed pattern of interest rates on government obligations.

Treasury Bill Policy. Excess member bank reserves, whose magnitude had caused serious concern for a number of years, were reduced by the middle of 1942 to a point where it became necessary, in order to assure the success of the Treasury's program of war financing, to make additional reserve funds available. The total of Federal Reserve Bank liabilities, which had stood in the neighborhood of two and one-half billion dollars for a decade, increased by over $21 billion between 1942 and 1945, reaching a total at the year's end of more than $24 billion. Part of the increase was required to provide reserves for the increased volume of member bank deposits, but the bulk of the increase served simply to offset the external drain of currency into the hands of the public (see Figure 24-1).

The distinctive method introduced to supply additional Reserve Bank credit was through the purchase of Treasury bills under a standing offer of the Reserve Banks to buy Treasury bills at a rate to yield ⅜ per cent and to sell them back again on the same basis if desired. Methods formerly used to create Reserve Bank credit were either relatively unavailable or in disfavor. In particular, the supply of discountable paper was limited and member banks were unwilling to relinquish such desirable assets. Resort to advances was hindered by the strong tradition which had grown up against borrowing by member banks. Changes in reserve requirements were viewed with general disapproval, influenced partly by a lack of familiarity with the device and partly by a belief that maintenance of relatively high requirements would facilitate the control of credit in the postwar period. Thus, the Treasury bill policy was adopted as a way out of the difficulty caused by the failure, real or anticipated, of the other methods of making reserves available.

Open-Market Operations. Federal Reserve open-market opera-

---

3. *Federal Reserve Bulletin*, January 1942, p. 2.

tions before the war, as we have seen, had been directed toward three principal objectives. Their wartime use added a fourth. Originally, purchases in the open market were made for the purpose of obtaining earning assets for the Reserve Banks.[4] In their second and most familiar phase, open-market operations were and are directed toward influencing the volume of member bank reserves in order to control credit. The third phase began in 1937 when purchases were made to preserve "orderly conditions" in the security market. The Reserve authorities indicated the principal aims of this policy in explaining why they undertook to stabilize security prices at the outbreak of war in 1939. The first reason given was the desire to exert a steadying influence on the entire capital market, and the second was the feeling that the Federal Reserve system "has a measure of responsibility for safeguarding the large United States Government portfolio of the member banks from unnecessarily wide and violent fluctuations in price."[5]

The fourth phase of open market operations, initiated in May 1942, involved their use to maintain a fixed pattern of interest rates on Treasury obligations. In substance, this policy amounted to placing a floor under the entire structure of Treasury obligations. The structure of rates agreed upon in 1942 was approximately that in effect at the time, ranging from ⅜ per cent on 90-day Treasury bills through ⅞ per cent on Treasury certificates, to 2½ per cent on the longest term Treasury bonds. While the second and third phases of open-market policy were of some importance during the war, their origin antedated the war. The fourth phase was entirely the product of the war and it constituted a central feature of the entire program of war financing.

The policy of preserving a stable pattern of interest rates rendered Treasury obligations virtually as liquid as cash. In view of the large amount of such securities held by banks, this meant that there could scarcely be any question of the adequacy of liquid banking assets. Moreover, with a guaranteed pattern of rates on marketable government securities the liquidity of all issues became virtually the same. But with different yields still maintained on securities of different maturity, but of substantially equivalent liquidity, market shifts were encouraged that tended to reduce rate differentials.

This phase of open-market policy was initiated with the dual purpose of enabling the Treasury to finance the war at a low cost and of weakening the speculative expectation, based on past experiences in wartime, that interest rates would gradually be increased. (The appeal to patriotism in the selling of bonds is likely to be more effective currently if the investor does not come to expect that delay in demonstrating his patriotism will be rewarded by a higher yield.) These main purposes were achieved to a remarkable degree. For the first time in history a major war was financed at a declining average

---

4. Open-market purchases were also employed to broaden the market for certain types of securities such as bankers' bills and United States certificates of indebtedness.

5. *Annual Report* for 1939, p. 5.

rate of interest. This was due in part to the effectiveness with which the adoption of a policy of maintaining a fixed pattern of rates persuaded investors of the advantage of current over deferred purchase.

Yet, in spite of this success, the wartime policies of the Reserve authorities proved exceedingly troublesome when continued into the postwar period. The logical consequence of providing a guaranteed market for Treasury bills and of establishing a fixed pattern of rates on other Treasury securities was to take away the power of the Federal Reserve authorities to control the volume of member bank reserves. Thus an important prerequisite for the effective use of the general credit controls was lost. This became increasingly burdensome to the Federal Reserve authorities in the period of strong inflationary tendencies that followed World War II. The consequences and conflicts growing out of these policies are discussed below.

Direct Controls and the "Disequilibrium System"

An important feature of public policy during World War II was the extensive reliance on direct controls for purposes of stabilization and resource allocation. Economists in general favored the vigorous use of monetary and fiscal measures to prevent private incomes and expenditures from growing much faster than the limited supply of goods left for private use after the drain of resources into war use. This would have limited the emergence of an inflationary gap by a better adjustment of private spending to the resources available for the private sector. This method of attack would have dealt with the problem of inflation at its source.

It was soon obvious that an adequate level of taxes was not politically feasible. For this and other reasons, commencing in the spring of 1942 heavy reliance was placed on direct controls over prices, wages, and the allocation of materials and final products. A general price freeze was ordered in April 1942. The Office of Price Administration (OPA) administered, and gave some elasticity to, this regulated price structure. A system of priorities and direct allocation of raw materials was effected, and rationing was used to accomplish for consumers goods what allocation did for raw materials.

Labor unions accepted a no-strike agreement and a "wage freeze" in exchange for the stabilization of rents, the price of clothing, most foods, and many other consumer goods. The business community accepted price controls, materials allocations, and a tax on excess profits in exchange for the concessions made by organized labor. Farmers finally accepted controls over food supplies and prices after farm prices had reached a satisfactory level in 1943. Direct controls thus rested on a temporary compromise among the principal interest groups in the economy, influenced to an important degree by war and the force of patriotic sentiment.

With full or overfull employment and with the Treasury incurring a cash deficit at the height of the war of $50 billion or more per year, the economy was characterized by a substantial inflationary gap for most of World War II. The size of the gap was reduced somewhat by patriotic appeals to save, particularly in the form of purchases of government securities, and by the sheer unavailability of many durable goods, along with an expectation that they would again be available before too many years and at prices not far different from those that had prevailed earlier. The great excess of money demand over the supply of goods and services available at existing prices did not cause serious inflation during the war largely because of the extensive system of direct controls over prices and access to economic resources. This overall structure of relationships with excess aggregate demand at current prices held in check by a system of direct controls, has been characterized by J. K. Galbraith as the "Disequilibrium System."[6] During the relatively brief period of World War II and under the special conditions which then prevailed, it provided a surprisingly effective alternative to exclusive reliance on free markets.

MAJOR FINANCIAL INFLUENCES IN THE POSTWAR PERIOD

The years after World War II were characterized by prolonged prosperity which contrasted sharply with the conditions of depression that preceded the war. In place of chronic underemployment there now seemed to be a hardly less persistent tendency toward overemployment and inflation. In large part, the contrast in economic conditions was traceable to the emergence during and after the war of a number of significant financial pressures. The first and one of the most important was the rise of financial liquidity.

Conditions of Relative Liquidity

The net result of policies adopted during World War II—more specifically, of the extent of government borrowing from commercial banks, the great expansion of demand deposits and other financial claims, and the control of prices—was a condition of unprecedented liquidity in the economic system. This state of financial ease was one of the key factors underlying the continuing inflationary pressure which characterized the period of reconversion to peacetime production and of cold war that followed. At the same time, it was an important factor in the maintenance of the high level of demand which enabled the transition to peacetime production to be effected without the masses of unemployed which were generally anticipated as the war drew to an end.

The unprecedented increase in liquidity was not a usual consequence of a wartime increase in the money supply. Other periods in history had witnessed instances of greater expansion in the circulating medium. In every

6. J. K. Galbraith, "The Disequilibrium System," *American Economic Review*, June 1947, pp. 287-302. A condition in which the usual manifestations of inflation are held in check by direct controls is sometimes also referred to as "repressed inflation."

other case, however, there was a more pronounced rise in prices. What was unique about the monetary experience of 1939-1946 was not the increase in the money supply but the absence of a somewhat similar increase in the general price level. The contrast between the period of World War II and that of World War I is clearly shown in Figure 24-2. In World War I the increase in wholesale prices was considerably greater than the increase in circulating medium. Precisely the opposite relationship existed in World War II, the rise in prices being much less than the increase in circulating medium. The unique combination of monetary expansion unaccompanied by a corresponding elevation of prices helped to bring about an exceptional state of liquidity in the economy.

A number of factors serve to explain why the growth in circulating

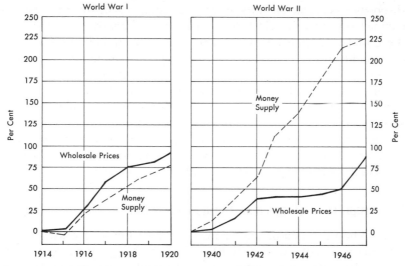

Figure 24-2. Increase in Wholesale Prices and the Money Supply During the First and Second World Wars (Cumulated Annual Percentage Increases).

Source: Adapted from C. R. Whittlesey, *The Effect of the War on Currency and Deposits,* New York, National Bureau of Economic Research, 1943.

medium failed to bring about as great a rise in prices as was to be expected in the light of the experience of other war periods. First, the existence of a large amount of unemployed capacity at the start of the war facilitated a rapid expansion of output. This increase in activity resulted in the absorption of some part of the increase in the money stock in transactions balances. Second, as we have seen, during World War II a system of price controls directly limited increases in prices. Third, there was a sharp increase in the rate of saving during the war. Finally, the rates of taxation of individuals and business firms were stepped up sharply during the war, thus reducing disposable incomes of individuals and the net savings of business firms.

The mechanics of the rise in financial liquidity that took place in this period is easily explained. The gigantic government outlays for war goods were financed in large part by an expansion of the public debt amounting to some $225 billion between 1942 and 1946. A large portion of this debt was acquired by the commercial banks and the Federal Reserve Banks, and in the process the money stock was greatly increased. Another segment of the debt was acquired by the public, whose high rate of saving resulted in the vast public accumulation of government securities, money, and other financial assets built up during the war. The growing stock of money and other liquid assets did not have its usual effects on spending, output, and prices during the war because of price controls, priorities, allocations, the unavailability of consumer goods, and patriotic appeals and pressures. In terms of relationships with which we are already familiar, the investment and consumption functions were sharply reduced by the wartime framework of controls and patriotic sentiments. Under conditions in which profits and disposable personal incomes were increasing markedly, the result was the accumulation of privately held, liquid financial assets.

There are two principal ways in which the resultant condition of extreme liquidity could be overcome. The former degree of liquidity might be restored through the volume of transactions increasing to a level corresponding to the expanded volume of circulating medium—what was once called "growing up to the money supply." Or, with the existing volume of goods and services, liquidity could diminish through a rise in prices which would reduce the purchasing power of existing liquid assets. It is apparent that the rise in prices starting in 1946 had the effect of neutralizing in this way part of the liquidity left over from the period of war financing.

High Level of Spending by the Government

The most conspicuous consequence of the long drawn out cold war was the maintenance of a high level of spending by the government. In the five years after the wartime peak of spending reached in 1865, total federal expenditure had been reduced by three-fourths. After World War I the total was reduced by five-sixths within a period of six years. A corresponding reduction after World War II would have lowered federal expenditures to between $17 and $25 billion rather than to the actual low of $38 billion, which represented a reduction of about three-fifths from the maximum. The chief factor in the continued heavy spending by the government was expenditure on the military establishment. After both the earlier wars expenditure for the War and Navy Departments dropped within a few years to approximately double the last prewar year. The lowest comparable figure reached after World War II was ten times the total for 1939 and a little later the developments in Korea and elsewhere had brought the figure back up to forty times the prewar level.

Other expenditures by the government were also related to past or prospective wars. These included interest on the national debt, payments by the Veterans Administration, and foreign aid. In addition to the direct effects of such spending on the economy was the fact that it imposed a corresponding burden on the fiscal authorities. The swollen federal budget together with an expanded national debt made it considerably more difficult to return to the methods of finance and the relatively free financial markets which had been customary after earlier wars.

Private Investment and Consumer Outlays

Toward the end of World War II there were widespread forebodings of serious transitional unemployment and even of a return to the stagnation of the 1930's, because of the expected drop in government expenditures immediately after the war. These fears were confounded, in part, because of the immense backlogs of consumer and business investment requirements, the high incomes, the large stock of liquid assets, and the ready credit available to implement current demand in the immediate postwar years.

Producers' plant and equipment had deteriorated as a consequence of inadequate maintenance during the war years and, even before that, in the depressed 1930's. Inventories in many fields had run far down. Meanwhile, new technologies had been developed and products such as television and air-conditioners had become commercially feasible. A surge in population and family formations, along with the general economic growth of the country, combined to create a strong demand for residential construction. Similar shortages prevailed with respect to consumer goods. Many types of consumer durables were unavailable during the war or available only in greatly reduced amounts. From 1942 to 1945, for example, production of automobiles for consumer use was at a standstill. Even many types of nondurables had been in short supply for years, such things as cigarets, nylon stockings, shoes.

Given these backlogs, the high incomes, and the exceptional degree of liquidity discussed above, a continuance of high levels of consumer, business, and government demands appeared to be in the offing. The prospects for business investment looked, and turned out to be, favorable indeed. Expenditures for producers' plant and equipment increased from $9.3 billion in 1945 to $23.3 billion in 1948. In the early postwar years expenditures on residential construction increased from $1.1 billion in 1945 to $4.8 billion in 1946, and to $10.1 billion in 1948. Outlays for other consumers goods and services were also at a high level in the years immediately after World War II.

Our entry into World War II had led to a substantial reduction in the volume of consumer credit outstanding. Durable goods such as automobiles, refrigerators, radios, and the like, for which consumer credit is particularly important, became less available. Restrictions were imposed on the expansion of consumer credit through the introduction of Regulation W. Finally, the rise in consumer incomes made it easier for consumers to purchase for cash. The first two of these reasons for the decline in consumer credit were probably the most important.

The combined effect of the absolute reduction in consumer credit and the growth in national income during those years was a sharp decline in the percentage relationship of consumer credit to national income. In 1939 and 1940 consumer credit outstanding had been close to 10 per cent of disposable personal income; by 1944 and 1945 it was little more than 3 per cent. In the years after the war the factors mentioned above as contributing to the war-time decline in consumer credit operated to a smaller extent or not at all. Except during the periods when Regulation W was in force, the volume of consumer credit rose steadily. By 1952 the ratio of outstanding consumer credit to disposable personal income was back at 10 per cent and by 1962 it was 14 per cent.

INFLATION AND RECESSION: 1946-1951

The extreme liquidity of the economy, the high level of government spending, and the heavy demands of consumers and business firms for goods and materials maintained a substantial inflationary gap immediately after the war. A sizable gap had, of course, existed during the war without serious inflation. But this we have seen to have been due to controls, taxes, patriotism, and a wage freeze and excess profits tax compromise that together produced a temporarily stable "disequilibrium system."

The disequilibrium system broke down rather rapidly after World War II. Food rationing was dropped in the fall of 1945, and the excess profits tax was repealed in the same year, thus opening the gates to "adjustments" for organized labor and farmers. The decline in patriotic inducements to compliance, powerful opposition from the business community, and a refusal of Congress to maintain effective price controls spelled the end of OPA in the summer of 1946.[7]

Between early 1946 and the end of 1948, after the ending of price controls and the breakdown of the wage-profits compromise of World War II, the consumer price index rose by approximately one-third. This was the most drastic upswing of prices in the entire war and postwar period. Although it was a period of rising money wages and labor unrest there seems little doubt that the main impetus was from demand. This inflationary surge ended with the moderate inventory recession of late 1948 and 1949, which was followed in turn by a renewed outburst of inflation coming with the onset of the Korean conflict in 1950.

7. Consumers are still awaiting, however, the lower prices which, according to predictions by the National Association of Manufacturers were to follow the ending of price controls, after a slight time lag.

Federal Reserve Policy from World War II to the Korean Conflict

The history of the Federal Reserve System in the first years after the end of World War II is chiefly a record of attempts of the Federal Reserve authorities to throw off existing limitations on their power to control credit. These limitations were themselves largely a consequence of policies introduced during the war. The inevitable consequence of providing a guaranteed market for Treasury bills and of establishing a fixed pattern of rates on other Treasury securities was to make it impossible, as we have seen, for the Federal Reserve authorities to refuse to furnish reserves. The initiative in determining the volume of reserves had therefore passed from the central bank to the member banks or other holders of Treasury obligations.

It should be noted that at the end of the war very few people questioned the desirability of continuing the system of price supports for government securities. This was due to a variety of considerations—the expectation of substantial and perhaps chronic unemployment and thus a need for expansionary policies which would not be seriously obstructed by the support policy; uncertainty concerning the firmness with which the unprecedently large public debt was held by investors, and fear of disaster in case of large-scale dumping; unwillingness to accept substantial increases in the interest costs on government securities; and pessimism regarding the probable effectiveness of monetary policy, in any case.

The Federal Reserve authorities were among those who shared some or all of these views, and they did not advocate a removal of price supports immediately after the war. However, they became increasingly restive during the inflationary periods 1946-1948 and 1950-1951 because of their inability to use the general instruments to stem the tide of inflation. Gradually they sought to free themselves from the support commitment as well as to find other means of meeting their broader policy responsibilities.

During the inflationary surge of 1946-1948, Federal Reserve efforts to develop a policy of restraint were ineffective. The Reserve authorities raised discount rates and reserve requirements, but these actions had little impact in the face of continued adherence to the bond support price policy. Consumer credit controls were utilized to advantage up to the time of their removal in November 1947; they were imposed again under Congressional authorization in August 1948, to be abolished once more in 1949.

During the first phase of inflation the Reserve authorities succeeded in removing the preferential discount rate on member bank loans secured by government securities (in 1946), and in 1947 the exceptionally low rates on Treasury bills and certificates were permitted to increase somewhat. The Federal Reserve also supported (without success) a security reserve proposal that would have required banks to hold a certain amount of short-term government securities, subject to variation by the authorities, as a special reserve. It was thought that this might help to reduce the flow of short-term government securities into the Federal Reserve Banks in exchange for reserve money and give some play to general monetary controls without giving up bond price supports in general.

It should be noted that while the money supply did increase substantially in 1946, it grew by only about 1.4 per cent between the end of 1946 and the end of 1948; the inflation of this period was sustained largely by an 18 per cent increase in income velocity. Thus, although the Reserve authorities were unable to take vigorous steps to combat inflation during this period, they managed to avoid being active contributors to it. Effective anti-inflationary policy in the first phase of the postwar inflation was restricted almost exclusively to the application of fiscal measures; the Treasury had cash surpluses in 1947 and 1948 totaling $13.7 billion, which were used to retire public debt.

The recession beginning in the second half of 1948 reduced the pressure on the Reserve authorities to find some means of rejuvenating general monetary controls for restrictive purposes. But the resurgence of inflation accompanying the outbreak of the Korean conflict in 1950 once more called sharp attention to the limitations on monetary policy that were implicit in the bond support program still adhered to by the Federal Reserve authorities (increasingly because of pressures from the Treasury).

Federal Reserve Policy in the Korean War Inflation

The immediate effect of the start of fighting in Korea was to touch off an outburst of buying by consumers and business firms throughout the country. The seasonally adjusted index of department store sales jumped from 298 in June to 362 in July, and the same reaction was experienced in other branches of retail trade. Scare buying by consumers had its counterpart in the actions of buyers for retail establishments. Outstanding orders as reported for a group of department stores jumped from $360 million in June to $755 million at the end of August. In the same months of the preceding year the rise was only half as great.

The sudden stimulation of purchases at all levels was reflected in the sharp increase in rate of turnover of demand deposits. The expansion of consumer spending was financed partly by a further rise in consumer credit. In addition there were heavy drafts on accumulated assets—net redemptions of War Savings Bonds increased and there was an even greater drain on time deposits at commercial banks. Deposits in the Postal Savings System also declined.

That the wave of buying was dominated by recollections of experience in World War II was indicated by the direction of consumer purchasing. Between the second and third quarters of 1950 spending on durables increased by over 25 per cent but spending on non-durables increased by only a little over 5 per cent. With the favorable turn of military events in Korea during the early autumn there was a relaxation of the inflationary spending. Department store sales reverted to a normal level, the wholesale index dipped slightly, and the prices of food at retail leveled off. Abnormally heavy buying was again resumed, however, after the intervention in the war by the Chinese, and again prices moved sharply upward.

Federal Reserve officials were fully aware of the seriousness of the inflationary danger. Speeches, letters, and public statements reiterated the threat to the country. In the course of the ensuing months all available methods of restraint were put to use. Bankers were called upon to exercise voluntary restraint. The discount rate was increased from 1½ per cent to 1¾ per cent. Reserve requirements were raised. After some delays Regulation W was reinstated and a newly authorized Regulation X was imposed to restrict mortgage credit. Somewhat belatedly, margin requirements were raised.

Chief responsibility for the delay in restricting consumer and mortgage credit rests not with the Reserve authorities, however, but with Congress. Some twelve months earlier Congress had refused, despite strong urging by Federal Reserve officials and academic economists to provide the Federal Reserve with stand-by power to control consumer credit. It was only under the pressure of events following Korea that the power was restored. Similarly, the Board of Governors was obliged to wait for authorization from Congress before it could restrict mortgage credit. It is conceivable that prices might have followed a very different course if these powers had been at hand when the war began and had been applied decisively and at once.

Federal Reserve policy was further weakened, and even rendered perverse, by the continuation, in the face of strong Federal Reserve protests, of the bond support program. The speculative boom of 1950-1951 was sustained largely by an increase in velocity, rather than by an increase in the money supply. Nevertheless, the Federal Reserve was unable to engage in a restrictive monetary policy by the use of its general instruments of control; in fact, substantial Federal Reserve purchases under the peg permitted member bank reserves to increase by $2.9 billion between June 1950 and March 1951.

TREASURY-FEDERAL RESERVE RELATIONS: THE ACCORD OF 1951

Development of Treasury-Federal Reserve Relations

In view of the widespread feeling that in the years after World War II the Federal Reserve was subjected to undue domination by the executive branch of the government in general and the Treasury in particular, it is worth observing that this was not a new occurrence in the annals of central banking. We are told that at different times Napoleon ordered the Bank of France to lower the discount rate following notable military achievements: "Napoleon viewed the Bank rate as a political tool; reductions following victories might dull recollections of their cost in lives."[8] It is a commonplace that central bank policies are subservient to Treasury policies in time of war. It is hardly surprising that something of the same relationship should tend to prevail in the milder version of such conditions that exists during a cold war.

The problem of satisfactory relations between Treasury and Federal Reserve was recognized from the start of the System. The attempt to solve the problem by making two Treasury officials, the Secretary and the Comptroller of the Currency, ex officio members of the Board of Governors came to be looked upon as unsatisfactory and was abandoned by the 1935 legislation. One of the reasons for dissatisfaction with the arrangement was the belief that the Secretary, by reason of the importance of his office, tended to overshadow the other members of the Board and to hold, potentially at least, too dominant a position in their councils.

As was shown above, the bond support policy developed naturally out of war financing and the policy initiated in 1937 of maintaining orderly conditions in the security market. No one stated more positively or explained more persuasively the desirability of maintaining the price of government bonds after World War II than officials of the Federal Reserve System. Successive chairmen of the Board of Governors made such statements as:

> The market for government debt securities must be one where investors can deal at all times with confidence. . . . For the foreseeable future the support program must be continued. This conviction is shared by all members of the Board of Governors, the Open Market Committee, and the Treasury.[9]

In its *Annual Report* issued in the middle of 1949 the Board of Governors declared:

> In earlier periods . . . Federal Reserve policies could be . . . directed . . . toward reserves. . . . With a large Government debt which is likely to be a dominant part of the debt structure for many years, the Federal Reserve has to cope with the dual problem of maintaining an orderly Government security market and exercising control over the volume of bank reserves.[10]

As noted earlier, some relaxation of the support policy was gradually introduced, beginning in 1947, particularly in the form of allowing rates to rise on shorter term issues. The Reserve authorities suggested that they be

8. Karl R. Bopp, "Bank of France Policy," *American Journal of Economics and Sociology*, April 1952, p. 229.
9. Thomas B. McCabe in a speech at Philadelphia during 1949.
10. Page 4.

given additional powers which would help to compensate for the impairment of open-market powers consequent upon support of Treasury obligations. When no such powers were forthcoming and in the face of continuing inflationary pressure, the Federal Reserve became increasingly restive under the confinements of the support program. Open hostility between Treasury and the Federal Reserve was aired in Congress and the press, a conflict which was not without its political overtones. Pertinent issues were explored in two major Congressional investigations under the chairmanship of Senator Paul Douglas and Representative Wright Patman, respectively. An agreement was reached in March 1951, the so-called "Accord," which, without resolving clearly all questions of policy, at least permitted the rigid support to be abandoned, brought an end to open conflict between the two bodies, and allowed financial policies at the topmost levels to move forward in a spirit of mutual harmony. In essence, the Accord provided that the Federal Reserve should be free to carry out monetary policy in the interests of economic stability and that the Treasury should adapt itself to the level and structure of interest rates established by the Reserve authorities.

Principal Issues in the Conflict between the Treasury and the Federal Reserve

In any discussion of the issues between the Treasury and the Federal Reserve due allowance must be made for the distortions and exaggerations that always accompany so heated a controversy.

The independence of the Federal Reserve from Treasury domination became a rallying cry for the more extreme supporters of the Federal Reserve and for sundry critics of the party in power. It was voiced most noisily by the very persons and politicians who a little earlier had been least willing to allow the Federal Reserve to apply its selective instruments of control or to grant additional powers to carry out the duties with which it had been charged.

Legally, of course, the Federal Reserve is a creature of Congress and accountable to Congress. It is administratively distinct from and independent of the executive arm of the government of which the Treasury is a part. The Federal Reserve Act, which has been described as the "Constitution of the Federal Reserve System," is a safeguard against undue interference in Federal Reserve operations even by Congress. On these points there is no real dispute.

On the broader issue, however, the simple truth is that there can be no such thing as the literal independence of the Federal Reserve from the Treasury, or, for that matter, of the Treasury from the Federal Reserve. Each is a prisoner of the other. The actions of either are bound inevitably to enter into the discharge of the other's responsibilities. The problem is not one of independence but one of coordination.

It is clear from the quotations given above that at least as late as 1949 the Reserve officials appeared to place a high valuation on the stabilization of the market for government securities. The Treasury, for its part, continued to insist that it was sincerely concerned over the avoidance of inflation. Nevertheless, it seems that the differences in suggested means reflected a serious disagreement on the scaling of policy ends. The Treasury has budgetary and debt management problems and responsibilities that are greatly facilitated by a Federal Reserve policy of maintaining low and stable interest rates. Treasury officials tended to question the effectiveness of general monetary controls (mainly on the grounds of the insensitivity of spending to the rate of interest) and urged the appropriateness of fiscal policy and selective monetary controls for dealing with the postwar inflation. It may be conjectured, of course, that these views as to appropriate means, whatever their validity, were shaped in some measure by the interest of Treasury officials in keeping down the cost of the debt and minimizing the difficulties in its administration.

The Federal Reserve authorities, on the other hand, are less intimately involved in administration of the public debt and are more directly responsible for the maintenance of overall economic stability. In pursuing this objective, the Reserve authorities took the position in the period just before the Accord that abandonment of the peg on government bonds would contribute enough to countering inflation to offset its disadvantages to the Treasury. Considerable stress was laid by spokesmen for a more vigorous monetary policy on the importance of Federal Reserve control over the "availability" as well as the price of bank credit. Again, it is difficult to dissociate the policies and instruments advocated from the apparently higher priority given the problem of price stability by the Reserve authorities.

After the fact, it appears that a more flexible use of general monetary weapons would have somewhat mitigated but by no means eliminated the inflationary developments that preceded the Accord. It may also be safely stated that the Accord enabled the Federal Reserve to escape to some extent from a position of subordination carried over from the period of World War II. And it made it possible for Reserve authorities to carry greater weight in the shaping of financial policies, thereafter jointly worked out by the Treasury and the Federal Reserve.

SELECTED BIBLIOGRAPHY

CHANDLER, L. V., *Inflation in the United States, 1940-1948*. New York: Harper, 1951.

ECCLES, MARRINER S., *Beckoning Frontiers*. New York: Knopf, 1951, Parts VI-VII.

GALBRAITH, J. K., "The Disequilibrium System," American Economic Review (June 1947), pp. 287-302.

GOLDENWEISER, E. A., *American Monetary Policy*. New York: McGraw-Hill, 1951, Chapters X-XII.

HICKMAN, BERT G., *Growth and Stability of the Postwar Economy*. Washington: Brookings Institution, 1960.

Joint Committee on the Economic Report, *Monetary, Credit, and Fiscal Policies*. Report of the Subcommittee on Monetary, Credit, and Fiscal Policies, Sen. Doc. No. 129, 81st Congress, 2nd Session. Washington: 1950, pp. 1-32.

SPROUL, ALLAN, "Changing Concepts of Central Banking." In *Money, Trade, and Economic Growth:* Essays in Honor of John H. Williams. New York: Macmillan, 1951, pp. 296-325.

25

MONETARY AND FISCAL POLICIES AFTER THE "ACCORD"

The Treasury-Federal Reserve Accord was reached early in March 1951. The ensuing decade witnessed a substantial rise in output, one which was interrupted, however, by a succession of business recessions (see Figure 16-3). None of the three cyclical declines was much more than a momentary pause in the general upward trend, but they came more frequently and the succeeding recoveries tended to be less buoyant as the period proceeded. Toward the end of the decade idle men and idle capacity became matters of continuing national concern (see Figure 25-1). The economy seemed to have lost much of its vigor and appeared unable to grow at a rate sufficient to absorb the current increment in the work force.

The post-Accord decade witnessed not only an expansion of real output but an appreciable rise in prices. As may be seen from Figures 25-2 and 25-3 this price rise was somewhat uneven, with a sharper rise between 1955 and 1958. During the ten years following the Accord, consumer prices rose on the average about 1 per cent a year, wholesale prices about 0.5 per cent, and the prices of aggregate output (more heavily weighted by construction costs and costs of government) rose over 2 per cent a year. This price rise, which came to be designated the "new inflation," was noteworthy because of its persistence in periods of fairly substantial unemployment, recession, and unusually restrictive monetary policy. An increasing price level under such circumstances aroused serious doubts concerning the adequacy of general monetary controls to deal with inflation and the compatibility of the various objectives of stabilization policy.

The post-Accord decade saw a return to monetary orthodoxy. The distinguishing features of Federal Reserve policies during the period were: increased reliance on general controls, limitation of open-market operations to "bills-only" in an attempt to minimize interference with the interest rate structure, vigorous use of "tight money" for anti-inflationary purposes, and

Figure 25-1. Unemployment as a Percentage of the Civilian Labor Force, 1952-1962 (seasonally adjusted).

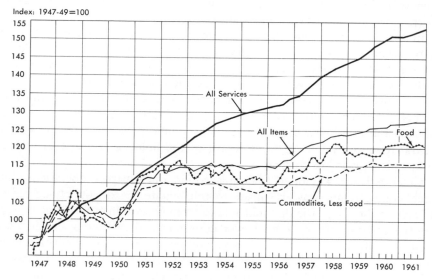

Figure 25-2. Consumer Prices, 1947-1961.

Source: Department of Labor

an almost complete abandonment of earlier policies of supporting the Treasury's financing activities. An attempt was also made by the Treasury to use debt management as an instrument of stabilization. These developments are discussed later in this chapter.

Finally, mention must be made of the balance of payments difficulties and consequent outflow of gold encountered by the United States toward the end of the decade. This development, which had some impact on monetary and fiscal policies, is referred to below, and discussed more fully in Chapter 30.

THE RETURN TO ORTHODOXY: 1951-1954

Initial Developments

The Treasury-Federal Accord of March 1951 was a notable event in the history of the Federal Reserve System. On the whole, however, it represented not so much a new departure as a reaction from attitudes and policies inherited from the Great Depression and particularly from the war period. During the war, as we have seen, the Federal Reserve had accepted responsibility for maintaining a floor under the government bond market. This commitment was willingly assumed and even after the war continued to be strongly defended by Federal Reserve officials. Gradually, however, it came to be recognized both inside and outside the System as a serious obstacle to monetary policy. The Accord is noteworthy for making it possible once again to make use of the general instruments of credit control. It was, in effect, a major step in the dismantling of wartime controls.

In the face of considerable uncertainty as to the effect which flexible interest rates would have on the behavior of government security holders, Federal Reserve policy following the Accord was distinctly cautious. For the first time in many years, however, the interest rate on long-term bonds was permitted to rise above 2½ per cent. And, as the Reserve authorities observed, "discontinuation of rigid pegging of Government security prices removed the possibility of monetizing the public debt through sale to the Federal Reserve System at the initiative of the holders, nonbank as well as bank, and without loss to them."[1]

Chief reliance was once again placed on open-market operations, but a deliberate attempt was also made to rehabilitate the discount mechanism and restore the use of the discount rate as an important instrument of policy. Selective instruments of control over consumer and real estate credit were taken away from the Federal Reserve authorities by Congressional action, primarily on the ground that they interfered with freedom in the market. Federal Reserve controls over margin requirements were retained, and were used periodically to curb or ease activity in the stock market. In general, the Federal Reserve followed standard central bank procedures to maintain the degree of ease or pressure on reserves that seemed best suited, in accordance with orthodox principles, to promote stable prices and reasonably stable business activity.

The course of economic progress following the Accord was generally favorable. Expansion continued into 1953, after which a sharp reaction set in. Recovery from the recession of 1953-54 was rapid, however, and by the summer of 1955 the seasonally adjusted figure for industrial pro-

---

1. *United States Monetary Policy: Recent Thinking and Experience*, Hearings before the Sub-Committee on Economic Stabilization of the Joint Committee on the Economic Report (Washington: 1954), p. 6.

duction was well above the previous peak. Much the same story is told by unemployment figures. Unemployment remained low after the Accord, reaching a low point of 1,162,000 in 1953. A rapid increase in the unemployed then occurred which carried unemployment totals to 3,725,000 early in 1954. Subsquent improvement was substantial but left the total of unemployed a million or so above the figure that had prevailed before the recession.

Developments after the Accord, particularly the abatement of inflationary pressures and the mildness of the downturn in 1953-1954, were regarded in some circles as demonstrating the effectiveness of orthodox central bank policies. Actually, however, the inflationary surge caused by the Korean conflict appears to have run its full course by the time of the Accord: rising production, easing of the fears of global war, and swollen inventories had already brought the price spurt to a halt.

The mildness of the 1953-1954 recession was undoubtedly influenced by a vigorous application of monetary policy. It should be noted, however, that recovery was also aided by tax reductions and other fiscal measures. Moreover, the vigor of the policy of monetary ease at the onset of recession in 1953 was largely attributable to the fact that tight money early in the year had caused serious disturbance in the money and capital markets. It has been argued that the downturn in business may have been influenced by the undue restrictiveness of Federal Reserve policies and that the promptness of recovery measures was partly to correct a disruption which was largely of their own making.

The Bills-Only Policy

The most distinctive measure adopted by the Federal Reserve after the Accord was the so-called "bills-only policy." It is also one of the most controversial measures ever pursued by the Federal Reserve. Maintained for nearly eight years, from 1953 to 1961, it provided for confining open-market operations to Treasury bills to the exclusion of longer term governments, except for possible intervention to correct market conditions which had become disorderly.

The bills-only policy was introduced in order to provide for a free, "self-reliant" market which would, it was maintained, possess the desired qualities of "depth, breadth, and resiliency." It was also defended on the grounds of the mechanical superiority of Treasury bills as the medium for open-market operations. Open-market purchases and sales not only alter the volume of bank reserves but also tend to raise or lower the price of the securities bought and sold. Since short-term securities are inherently subject to smaller changes in market price than longer term, and are traded in a more active market, the least market disturbance will result by confining operations to the shortest term securities, namely, Treasury bills. The change in volume of reserves and the supply of funds available has its impact on prices in the short end of the market. Shifts of traders and investors will generalize the change in security prices all along the line. But the structure of security prices and interest rates will reflect the preferences of individuals and not the decisions of officials in Washington and New York.

Among the objections raised to the bills-only policy were, first, that a free market is not necessarily an ideal market. This is recognized by the adoption in many places of orderly marketing procedures to prevent or restrain self-inflammatory tendencies. Insistence upon freedom under all conditions would preclude any form whatever of open-market operations— or even the central bank itself.[2]

Second, it was argued that a central bank should occupy the role of banker for the government. Borrowers, public or private, need the services of an underwriter during periods of new borrowng or of restructuring existing debt, as through the lengthening of maturities. Only the Federal Reserve has the financial strength to provide this service for the government. It is a legitimate function for the central bank to perform and in no way implies either undue credit creation by the central bank or establishment of significantly artificial conditions in the market.

The main argument against the bills-only policy was that operations in longer maturities are desirable because they are more effective in attaining modern-day goals. To achieve cyclical stability and rapid economic growth it is capital spending plans which are strategic, and they are affected by changes in the cost and availability of longer term credit. Since long-term rates are more rapidly and strongly affected by direct purchase and sales of longer maturities, the achievement of those objectives would appear to call for operations in the long-term market.

Despite some apparent conflict within the Federal Reserve system and the almost unanimous opposition of monetary economists, the Federal Reserve adhered closely to the bills-only policy. On the few occasions, 1955 and 1958, when it departed from the policy it did so in order to rescue Treasury borrowing operations that were running into difficulties. In the presidential campaign of 1960 the bills-only policy was one of the principal targets of Democratic critics of the policies of the Eisenhower Administration. In the autumn of that year the outflow of gold led the Federal Reserve to relax the bills-only policy in the hope that higher short-term rates (in-

---

2. The ideal that the structure of interest rates, in the present era of large government debt, may still be conceived of as emerging from the free play of market forces must surely be viewed as an expression of financial nostalgia. So long as managers of the federal debt influence the term structure of debt outstanding, and thereby the supply of various maturities, they inevitably influence the structure of interest rates. To prescribe Federal Reserve operations in other than the shortest securities in order to eliminate other than free-market forces would seem to imply likewise a ban on discretionary debt management. To carry the argument to its logical conclusion, exponents of complete free-market determination of the structure of interest rates should also espouse a conversion of the entire outstanding federal debt into bills only.

duced by selling bills and buying long-term obligations), by reducing the disparity between rates in this country and abroad, would check the gold drain. A few months later formal announcement was made of what amounted to abandonment of the bills-only policy.

In retrospect it would seem that any hard and fast rule such as the bills-only policy embodied should be regarded as an undesirable limitation on the freedom of the central bank. Freedom of the market was in conflict with the freedom of the Federal Reserve to carry out normal central banking functions. To be committed never (or almost never) to intervene in the longer term market could be as rigid and stultifying as to be obliged to intervene to maintain a fixed pattern of rates. It was merely rigidity at the opposite pole.

Perhaps the most surprising feature of the whole episode was the assumption that the possibility of buying and selling by the Federal Reserve could be expected to have an unsettling effect on securities markets. What is doubly surprising is that Reserve authorities themselves should have propagated this view. Any such assumption is as unrealistic as it is uncomplimentary, notwithstanding that it had Federal Reserve endorsement. The only reasonable assumption, surely, is that the central bank would intervene only if the market was moving out of line with what they, better than any other observers, were able to recognize as normal and desirable. And no less surely the induced expectations would tend to be of a stabilizing rather than a destabilizing character so far as their effect on other market participants was concerned.

EXPANSION, INFLATION, AND TIGHT MONEY, 1955-1957

The boom extending from late in 1954 to the latter part of 1957 holds a unique place in American financial history. The period witnessed an extended effort, by the application of general monetary controls, to contain inflationary pressures apparently arising from causes other than excess aggregate demand. The "New Inflation" was variously explained as resulting from wage and administered price increases, sectoral instability in expenditures combined with downward inflexibilities of prices and wages, lagged effects of past demand-oriented inflation, the increased relative importance of the service sector of the economy, a slackening of the rate of economic growth, and other factors and combinations of factors.

Growth of Output and Sectoral Fluctuations

By late 1954 the economy had moved into a period of recovery from the mild recession of 1953-1954. Inventory liquidation had been succeeded by net accumulation, and purchases of consumers' durables had turned upwards. The ensuing expansion and boom continued until the third quarter of 1957. During this three-year period GNP in current prices increased by 21 per cent, though only by 11 per cent in constant prices.

The increase in real output during this period was confined largely to the early phase; the annual rate of growth in 1955 was 8.4 per cent, whereas between the last quarter of 1955 and the third quarter of 1957 it was a mere 1.3 per cent. Productivity per man-hour remained virtually unchanged after 1955. A substantial part of the increase in real output in 1955 resulted from the fall in unemployment, which declined from an average of 5.4 per cent of the labor force in the last quarter of 1954 to 4.2 per cent in the final quarter of 1955. It may be seen from Figure 25-2 that despite the drop in unemployment in 1955, average rates of unemployment tended to be higher in the boom of 1955-1957 than in earlier postwar periods of prosperity. In short, the boom tapered off before it had reduced unemployment below levels exceeding 4 per cent of the working force.

The rapid growth immediately following the 1953-54 recession was influenced by boom conditions in two important sectors, residential construction and passenger automobiles. Private non-farm housing starts increased from 1,068,000 in 1953 to 1,202,000 units in 1954 and 1,310,000 units in 1955. Although the increase in number of houses between 1954 and 1955 was only 9 per cent, there was a 21 per cent rise in expenditures on residential construction. The difference reflects the increased average size, quality, and price of houses.

Easier credit contributed to the expansion of home purchases. Loans without any down payments grew from 11 per cent of the total in 1953 to 48 per cent in 1955 and long-term loans of 30 years from 5 to 44 per cent. The increased availability of credit for lending in residential construction was a result of two sets of forces. First, the recession decline in demand for funds plus the easy money policy of 1953 and 1954 had combined to push down open-market interest rates. Second, the maximum permissible interest rates on FHA-insured and VA-guaranteed mortgages were increased from 4¼ and 4 per cent, respectively, to 4½ per cent in May 1953. Most of the increase in housing starts between 1953 and 1955 was accounted for by VA financing. Thus the housing boom showed the combined effects of governmentally fixed ceilings on mortgage rates and flexible interest rates on competitive investments.

It should be noted that when open-market rates of interest fall as they do in periods of recession, or mortgage rate ceilings are increased, or both occur at the same time, the increased differential tends to attract funds into the residential mortgage market. The opposite developments, occurring in boom conditions, tend to dry up the flow of funds into mortgage lending. In the period under consideration this helpful anticyclical pattern rested on governmental insurance and guarantee programs, in conjunction with the inflexible rate ceilings imposed in connection with FHA and VA financing. Subsequently a decline in the relative importance of VA guarantees and an increase in conventional financing weakened the effectiveness of this anti-cyclical mechanism.

Early in 1955 it became apparent that the boom in residential, business, and public construction was pushing up construction costs. Restrictive measures were soon imposed to bring this sectoral overexpansion under control. Terms on VA-guaranteed and FHA-insured loans were tightened; and the increasingly restrictive monetary policy of the Federal Reserve authorities began to take effect. It is highly significant that during the 1955-1957 period of tight money and rising interest rates residential construction was the only major expenditure category that showed a decline (amounting to roughly 8 per cent between early 1955 and the third quarter of 1957).

The automobile industry experienced a record year in 1955, with factory sales of vehicles up from 6.6 million in 1954 to 9.2 million (an increase of 39 per cent) and consumer outlays on automobiles and parts up by one-third. Despite a general tightening of credit, the uneven impact of tight money was reflected in the ready availability of credit in the sale of automobiles. This was an important factor in the automobile boom of 1955, although the style appeal of the 1955 models also appears to have induced some purchases that otherwise would have been spread over subsequent years.

The rapid growth of consumer credit in 1955 caused concern among economists and public officials. Question was raised whether consumer credit fluctuations were not an important source of instability, and whether general credit controls were adequate to deal with the sectoral fluctuations then under way. In his Economic Report to Congress in January 1956, President Eisenhower indicated that it might be desirable to re-establish standby controls over consumer credit. Accordingly, the Board of Governors sponsored a large-scale study of selective controls, which was published in 1957. Although the consensus was that consumer credit contributes to fluctuations in the demand for durable goods and that general credit controls do not have a strong impact on consumer credit, the Board took the position that the re-establishment of standby consumer credit controls was not warranted.

Despite substantial declines in residential construction and automobile production after 1955, a sharp rise in business expenditures for plant and equipment (sparked in part by the 1955 expansion in durable goods sales) helped to maintain a high level of business activity in the succeeding two years. The very considerable expansion was heavily concentrated in the construction and machinery sectors, both of which were subject to pressures on materials and capacity that resulted in substantial price increases. Fluctuations in plant and equipment expenditures are shown in Figure 25-3.

A large part of the capital goods expansion of the period was financed internally, but new corporate security issues increased steadily from $9.4 billion in 1954 to $12.7 billion in 1957, an increase of 35 per cent. The growth in external financing and the boom in capital expenditures contributed to, and were carried out in the face of, a 41 per cent increase in yields on

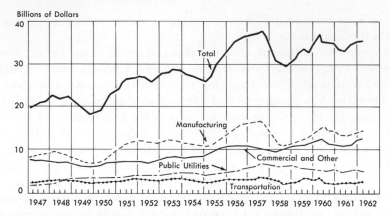

Figure 25-3. Expenditures for New Plant and Equipment, 1947-1962 (quarterly data, seasonally adjusted).

Source: Data from the Securities and Exchange Commission and the Department of Commerce.

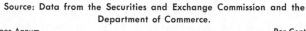

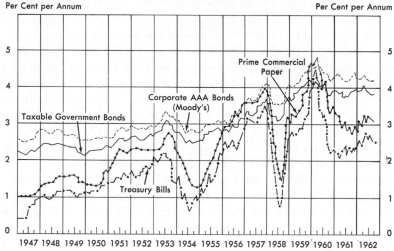

Figure 25-4. Bond Yields and Interest Rates, 1955-1962.

Source: Data from Moody's Investor's Service, The Board of Governors of the Federal Reserve System, and the Treasury Department.

outstanding issues of high grade (Aaa) corporate bonds between early 1955 and September 1957. Interest rate changes may be seen in Figure 25-4.

The simultaneous increase in investment outlays and interest rates does not, of course, demonstrate the absence of restrictive effects of tight money inasmuch as marginal efficiency and investment demand curves were shifting rapidly to the right during this period. It is likely that easier credit would have contributed to even larger expenditures. Nevertheless, it is clear that the exceptional degree of tightness of credit which characterized a good part of this period was not sufficient by itself to prevent a sharp increase in business investment. This positive correlation of tight money and increasing business capital outlays tends to support the view that aggregate investment is relatively insensitive to the rate of interest. The experience also indicates that deliberate attempts to reduce the availability of credit may be aborted by a more efficient mobilization of funds within the private economy (see below, pp. 501-503).

The Renewal of Inflation

We have already seen that postwar price movements, while generally upward, were far from regular. The GNP price index from 1947 to 1961 (see Figure 25-5) suggests the following phases: (1) a rapid rise

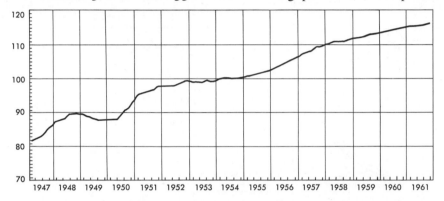

Figure 25.5   GNP Price Index, 1947-1961. (Seasonally adjusted.1954=100.)

Sources: *U. S. Income and Output* and *Survey of Current Business,* July 1959 and July 1962.

in prices in 1947-48, followed by a slight decline in 1949; (2) a rapid rise from 1950 to 1952; (3) relative stability from 1952 through 1954; and (4) a renewal of moderately rising prices in 1955, with a slower rate of increase after 1957.

In terms of the classification of inflationary forces as demand-pull or supply-push,[3] it seems reasonable to account for the first two inflationary movements as induced primarily by demand-oriented forces, though influences of market power cannot be excluded entirely. The backlogs of demand stemming from the Great Depression and wartime shortages, supported by high money incomes and adequate financial reserves, provided the main demand elements for the 1947-48 increase. And the rise in demand associated with the Korean conflict was the underlying impetus for the movement of 1950-52. Further evidence of the demand orientation of in-

3. The reader will do well to review the analysis of inflationary forces presented in Chapter 20.

flation in these periods is found in the relatively rapid increase in output and relatively tight labor markets, as indicated by low rates of unemployment.

The price increases after 1955, however, illustrate the difficulty of a simple classification of inflations as either demand-induced or supply-induced, and the corresponding complexities in the choice of remedies. In general, the slow rate of increase in output together with the somewhat higher rate of unemployment and general lack of tightness in labor markets suggest that supply of output as a whole was not inelastic in relation to demand. (This was even more true, of course, in the recession of 1957-58, when output *declined*, even though prices continued to rise.) On the other hand, there is a considerable body of evidence relating to the 1955-57 price increase which is not easily reconciled with simple wage-push or markup explanations.

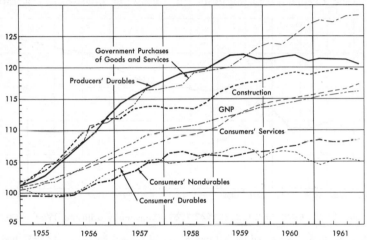

Figure 25-6.   GNP Price Index and Main Subgroups, 1955-1961.
(Seasonally adjusted; 1954=100.)

Sources: *U. S. Income and Output* and *Survey of Current Business,*
July 1959 and July 1962.

In part, difficulties of identification stem from the fact that it is possible for the exercise of market power and demand forces to contribute simultaneously to rising prices in an industry. And for the economy as a whole, supply-induced inflation may be present in some industries while demand-induced inflation is present in others. This suggests that it may be useful to look into the behavior of the components of the average price level for clues to the sources of the "creeping" inflation characteristic of the period after 1955. The variety of behavior of the prices of the main groups of products and services making up the GNP can be seen in Figure 25-6. It may be observed that post-1955 price increases are largely concentrated in producers' durables, in related raw materials, such as steel, in construction, and in the service industries (governmental and consumers').

The rapid recovery from the 1953-54 recession, which centered at first in the automobile and residential construction industries, spread into the steel, rubber, and building materials fields, leading to a substantial capital goods boom affecting the machinery and non-residential construction industries. The rise in producers' durables and construction prices, therefore, may well have been dominated by rising demand, even while slack remained in other sectors of the economy. In the case of machinery, the lengthening of un-filled orders and a large rise in profit margins suggest the pressure of demand on limited capacity. For steel, however, price increases appear to reflect market power in the product market and labor markets, conditioned by favorable demand conditions.[4] Similarly, the rise in construction prices despite a contracyclical decline in the residential component reflects buoyant demand for non-residential construction, together with the exercise of market power by strong building trades unions.

The rise in prices of government-purchased goods and services resulted partly from higher prices of producers' durables, and partly from a rise in wages of government employees, influenced by the rise in wages in manufac-turing. The rise in consumers' service prices reflects a number of divergent forces. In medical services, rising demand has pressed against a lagging supply of trained practitioners. In the unskilled services groups, rising prices reflected a rise in wages which was less than in manufacturing, but was combined with a low rate of increase in productivity. Rents, influenced by growing housing demand and the fact that controls had held them down earlier, rose throughout the postwar period. In the consumer durable goods sector prices tended to respond to wage increases in such key in-dustries as steel and automobiles, and to the rising cost of materials and machinery. For manufacturing industries generally price performance was mixed. Prices rose most in industries with greater output increases and high degrees of concentration of production; they rose least (or fell) where output rose least and concentration ratios were lowest.

We see, thus, a mixed pattern of forces operating on prices. Neither the demand-pull nor the market-power hypothesis alone is adequate. An im-portant study of the forces of this period emphasizes what we have called previously "structural inflation."[5] Although there was no clear excess de-mand in the aggregate, there was excess demand in particular markets, particularly in industries associated with automobiles and durable invest-ment goods. This led directly to rising prices and wages in these industries, or permitted wage- or profits-push to be sustained, and, because of down-ward price inflexibility elsewhere, average prices to rise. Long-term key wage bargains in automobiles and steel, originated under the buoyant con-

---

4. See O. Eckstein and G. Fromm, *Steel and the Postwar Inflation*, Study Paper No. 2, Joint Economic Committee, 86th Congress, 1st Session (Washington: 1959).

5. See Charles L. Schultze, *Recent Inflation in the United States*, Study Paper No. 1, *ibid.*

ditions of 1955 and 1956, influenced wage rates elsewhere, tending toward generalization of cost-push and automatic wage increases carrying into the recession of 1957-58.

Federal Reserve Monetary Policy, 1955-1957

The Federal Reserve authorities began to be seriously concerned with overexpansion and inflation early in 1955. The previous policy of monetary ease was brought to a halt and a restrictive policy introduced which was progressively increased in intensity until late in 1957. The tight money policy was carried out almost exclusively by general instruments of credit control. The first restrictive move, however, was an increase in margin requirements from 50 to 60 per cent in January 1955. The stock market had undergone a major boom between September 1953 and early 1955, and there was increasing evidence of speculative activity in the latter part of 1954. In April 1955 the Board raised margin requirements again, from 60 to 70 per cent. A significant drop in the rate of increase of stock market credit followed.

Of the general instruments of control, reliance was placed entirely on open-market operations and the operation of discount policy.[6] Open-market sales in the first half of 1955 were somewhat larger than necessary for off-setting seasonal increases in bank-held currency and declines in deposits. Thereafter, open-market operations were not used on any significant scale to reduce bank reserves, but they may be said to have contributed to restraint in the sense that failure to provide normal additions to bank reserves in a growing economy has a tightening effect.

The discount rate, which had been lowered to 1½ per cent in April 1954, was raised to 1¾ per cent a year later. This was the first of seven increases, the last of which raised the discount rate to 3½ per cent in August 1957.

Thus the progressive tightening of credit by the Federal Reserve authorities was accomplished by providing less than normal increases in bank reserves and increasing the cost of member banks borrowing from the Reserve Banks. (The former tended to make reserves and money increasingly scarce in an expanding economy; the latter made it increasingly costly to compensate for this stringency by the use the discount mechanism.) In 1955 the money supply increased by 2.8 per cent, which was close to the 3 per cent level of the previous year. In 1956 the money stock grew only 1.1 per cent and in 1957 the money supply actually declined almost 1 per cent. The free reserves of member banks, which had begun to decline late in 1954, continued to fall in 1955. They became negative in amount (i.e., member bank borrowing exceeded excess reserves) in August 1955 and remained a

---

6. Reserve requirements were not raised at all during this period or, indeed, during the entire period 1951-1960. There were however, reductions.

negative quantity throughout 1956 and 1957, reaching minus $500 million and beyond in mid-1957 (see Figure 6-2 above, p. 95).

Under the joint impact of increasing private expenditures and a restrictive monetary policy, interest rates rose slowly in 1955 and then at an accelerating pace. By late 1957 they were higher than at any time since the early 1930's.

Limitations of General Monetary Policies

Although recovery following the recession of 1953-1954 was vigorous, the performance of the economy and the accomplishments of general monetary controls during the succeeding boom were disappointing. In this section we examine briefly some of the main difficulties encountered in the application of general monetary controls during the boom of 1955-1957 and in subsequent years.

As we have seen, the beginning of business recovery in 1954 led to a restrictive monetary policy that limited the rise in the money supply to 3.5 per cent from the end of 1954 to the end of 1956, and actually induced a decline in 1957. From mid-1954 to the end of 1957, the gross national product rose about 25 per cent while the money supply rose only about 6 per cent (most of the rise occurring in 1954). Under conditions of increasing demand for final output, the economic system somehow compensated for the failure of the money supply to rise proportionately by utilizing the existing money supply more intensively. In terms of the income velocity of money (GNP divided by the stock of money), we may say that income velocity, V_y, rose throughout the expansion. Specifically, V_y rose from 2.84 in the second quarter of 1954 to 3.33 in the third quarter of 1957, or 17.3 per cent. If velocity had not risen in the period, the level of income attained would have required a $22 billion greater increase in the stock of money, or almost four times that which actually occurred.[7] Throughout the postwar period velocity tended to increase during periods of tight money and decrease during periods of easy money; almost invariably the changes in velocity were larger than changes in the quantity of money. This implies an uncertain connection between the money supply and total expenditures and a corresponding lack of precision in the effect of general monetary instruments. Insofar as the offsets to changes in the quantity of money are systematic (that is, are automatically induced, so that tight money leads to more efficient monetary use and easy money to less efficient use), the leverage of monetary changes is reduced. Consequently, moderate changes in bank reserves have relatively weak effects on aggregate spending. Moreover, as we shall see below, the attempt to compensate for the weakness of monetary controls by more intensive application may create other dif-

---

7. See Warren L. Smith, "Monetary Policy and Debt Management," *Staff Report on Employment, Growth, and Price Levels*, prepared for the Joint Economic Committee, 86th Congress, 1st Session (Washington: 1959), Table 9-7, p. 345.

ficulties. We shall review first how changes in velocity may be induced systematically by changes in the money supply.

Where the demand for money balances has increased more than supply, the rate of interest is bid up. This induces the holders of idle balances to shift from cash balances to securities, thus providing more money for active circulation (implying a rise in V_y). The condition necessary for this reaction to be important is a fairly elastic liquidity preference curve, so that moderate increases in the interest rate lead to a substantial shift from cash balances to bonds.

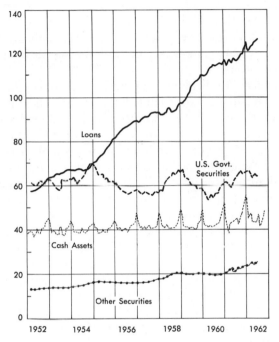

Figure 25-7. Principal Assets of Commercial Banks, 1952-1962 (billions of dollars).

Source: Board of Governors of the Federal Reserve System.

In the complex financial system this effect is achieved by the operations of institutions and individuals in a variety of interrelated markets. Most important is the role of banks. As economic activity and the resulting demand for credit expand, banks tend (assuming lack of excess reserves because of monetary restraint) to sell bonds to the public (which destroys deposits but not reserves) and expand loans (reestablishing the deposits and therefore the money supply). Figure 25-7 indicates that in the period 1955-57 there was a sharp decline in governments in bank portfolios and an opposite movement in loans. This was followed by a restocking of governments in the succeeding recession, a shift away from governments into loans in the expansion of 1959-

1960, and a recovery of holdings of governments in 1960-61, all in systematic cyclical pattern.[8] As long as the Federal Reserve does not purchase the securities which the banks wish to sell, the increase in offers to sell tends to depress their price and raise their yield, causing a shift of otherwise idle balances to the banks. In effect, banks transfer the idle balances to borrowers, and by this means the balances are injected into the active circulation. On this reasoning we should expect interest rates to rise in periods of economic expansion and decline during recession. This expectation is borne out in the record of the yields on governments of various maturities as shown in Figure 25-5.

A second important mechanism that served to activate idle balances resulted from the efforts of non-financial corporations to adapt their liquid asset holdings according to conditions prevailing in the money market. With increasingly tight money and higher yields corporate treasurers made strenuous efforts to economize in the use of cash and to meet liquidity needs as much as possible by holding treasury bills and other liquid securities. The shifting of corporate money balances into bills helped to channel idle balances into active circulation.

Financial intermediaries such as savings banks, savings and loan associations, life insurance companies, and pension funds, all of which grew rapidly after World War II, also tended to shift their portfolios in the same fashion as commercial banks, and with similar effects. By selling bonds, savings banks, for example, may attract idle balances in exchange, and, in lending for the purpose of, say, new home construction, they put the same balances into active circulation. Thus total expenditures may increase without an increase in the money supply. In addition, if saving institutions were able to induce holders of demand deposits to shift to holding claims on them, these intermediaries could lend a substantial proportion of the previously idle demand deposits to active users. This would expand the expenditures stream with the given volume of money.[9] While evidence indicates that this may have occurred to some degree in the period under review, the role of intermediaries appears small relative to that of non-financial corporations and commercial banks.

So far we have focused primarily on describing how the financial system responded to a restrictive policy by marshalling the existing money supply more effectively, thus moderating the intended restraints. These reactions apparently dilute monetary controls and make them less precise. But why cannot the weakness of the medicine be offset by a larger dose? The first

---

8. In Figure 25-7 the loan category does not show equally large fluctuations upward and downward, but rather retarded rates of growth during recessions and more rapid rates of growth during expansions. This is due to the upward trend in total loans and investments over the period.

9. Because of the difference in legal reserve requirements, an expansion of bank lending could similarly occur as a result of the reserves freed by the transfer of deposits from demand to time categories within commercial banks.

difficulty arises from possible disturbance of financial markets. A widely emphasized virtue of monetary policy is that it can be sensitive and flexible, adjusting quickly and with a response sufficiently powerful to contend with the changed conditions. This is no doubt feasible where necessary effects on financial markets are moderate, and would nonetheless be effective provided the leverage associated with moderate changes in interest rates were high. But with leverage low, the massive action required could seriously disrupt the financial markets. This is not the kind of action responsible Federal Reserve officials could be expected to undertake.

A second difficulty is that resort to firm restraints would tend to reinforce the uneven impact of general monetary controls on different sectors of the economy. For while tight money may have had somewhat mild effects on aggregate expenditures, it may have had important effects in particular sectors. House building, for example, showed great sensitivity to monetary policy.[10] There is, in addition, some evidence that tight money tends to curtail state and local government expenditures and has greater impact on small firms than larger firms (presumably because of the greater reliance of small firms on external financing). Insofar as a differential effect by the size of firms prevails, general monetary instruments would appear to exert a bias toward increased industrial concentration.

Furthermore, tight money appears to have been weak in precisely those areas which figured most prominently in the instabilities of the post-Accord period. Thus plant and equipment expenditures, influenced by expectations generated by high profits and financed largely out of retained earnings, showed little response to high interest rates; inventory investments showed little effect; and consumer installment credit appeared insensitive, expanding in periods of tight money and contracting somewhat during recession and monetary ease.[11]

There is evidence that in this period the inflationary forces did not stem from *general* excess demand. Rather, there were areas of demand-pull, some of which were characterized by market power in both the labor and product markets, and other areas of deficient demand or excess supply. The main sources of instability and inflationary pressure were thus relatively immune to moderate general monetary restraints. Critics argued that the attempt to maintain price stability by restricting aggregate demand could only result in reducing output and employment, without mitigating the upward pressure on prices, unless underutilization was carried to a point clearly unacceptable. As an alternative it was suggested that general monetary controls should be supplemented by selective restraints capable of dealing with instability in particular areas. In the expansion of 1955-57, for example, the automobile boom might have been reached by a revival of installment

---

10. See above, pp. 494-495.

11. An excellent documenting of these sectoral effects may be found in Smith, *op. cit.*, pp. 362-94.

credit controls, thus preventing the sharp increase in output in 1955 and the depressed levels thereafter. By checking automobile output somewhat, the derived demand for investment goods might have been limited in related industries, and so a more stable rate of growth maintained.

Fiscal Policy and Debt Management, 1955-1957

On balance, discretionary fiscal policy seems to have made little if any contribution to economic stability during this period. This was due in part to the preoccupation with monetary as opposed to fiscal measures of stabilization. It was also a result of the apparent political inexpediency of altering tax rates for anticyclical purposes. Such stabilization effects of fiscal policy as existed resulted mainly from the "automatic" effects of a relatively fixed structure of progressive tax rates, slowly changing government outlays, and cyclical variations in income.

In 1955 the federal government had a cash deficit of $700 million, while in the two succeeding years it had cash surpluses of $5.5 and $1.2 billion, respectively. These surpluses probably had a moderate restraining effect. Since the increase in aggregate demand does not appear, however, to have been excessive in 1956 and 1957, fiscal as well as general monetary controls were not well adapted to deal with the problems of that period. Furthermore, the pattern of federal expenditures tended to be destabilizing: defense orders for hard goods rose sharply (from $7.9 billion in 1955 to $18.5 billion in 1956) thereby increasing federal government demands at the height of the private investment boom and doing so in the very sectors which were already subject to strong upward demand pressures.

Moderate budgetary surpluses lowered the public debt from $278.8 billion to $275 billion between the close of 1954 and 1957. This eased the burden on the Treasury, which could concern itself with refunding maturing debt without the additional complication of large new cash issues. Nonetheless this was not a happy period for Treasury debt management.

The high hopes entertained after the Accord that Treasury debt management could make a substantial contribution to stabilization policy, were disappointed. The experience of the post-Accord decade indicated that at times when, from the standpoint of orthodox debt management principles, the issuance of long-term securities would be considered desirable it would be painfully expensive and possibly disruptive of financial markets; and at times when it would be cheap and easy to issue long-term obligations, orthodox doctrine rejects such action as tending to aggravate deflationary conditions.[12] In the period under discussion, weakness in the bond market together with reluctance to compete with home builders and other borrowers impelled the Treasury to concentrate its refundings very heavily in short-term securities. After July, 1955 no effort was made to sell long-

12. Cf. Chapter 22, pp. 444-446.

term securities until October of 1957, when a modest amount of 12-year bonds were marketed. The volume of Treasury obligations maturing in one year increased from $43.3 billion at the close of 1954 to $51.7 billion at the end of 1957.

RECESSION AND RECOVERY, 1957-1958

Economic Characteristics of the Decline and Recovery

The recession that brought the boom of the mid 1950's to a close began in the summer of 1957, reached its trough in April or May of 1958, and was succeeded by a period of rapid but incomplete recovery during the remainder of 1958. The decline was characterized by a substantial drop in both inventory and fixed capital expenditures.

A noteworthy feature of the period was the fact that personal consumption expenditures remained approximately constant between the third quarter of 1957 and the first quarter of 1958 and rose in succeeding quarters. Similar stability characterized the recessions of 1949-1950 and 1953-1954, reflecting the impact of automatic stabilizers and the ability of consumers to maintain consumption by reducing their rate of saving and by borrowing or disposing of previously accumulated wealth. The stability of consumer expenditures in the face of recession was an important factor in the maintenance of high levels of effective demand after World War II.

The rate of decline of economic activity in the recession of 1957-1958 was sharper than that of the two preceding recessions, but it also took a shorter time to reach bottom. As measured by the rate of unemployment, the 1957-1958 recession reached a slightly lower level than the recession of 1949-1950 and a substantially lower level than that of 1953-1954. Furthermore, although the lower turning point was reached relatively quickly, high rates of unemployment persisted for an exceptionally long period. The annual averages for 1959 and 1960 (5.5 and 5.6 per cent) approximated that of the recession year 1954 (5.6 per cent) and substantially exceeded unemployment rates for 1955 and 1956 (4.4 and 4.2 per cent), which were themselves high in comparison with earlier postwar prosperity years. In the decade following the Accord, each of the three periods of prosperity was characterized by a higher average rate of unemployment than its predecessor.

Another notable feature of the 1957-1958 recession was the behavior of the price level. Between July 1957 and July 1958 the CPI, WPI, and GNP price indexes rose 2.6 per cent, 0.8 per cent, and 1.5 per cent, respectively. This phenomenon was widely pointed to as confirming the view that the United States had entered a phase of continuous, creeping inflation. It was also important in influencing the actions of the Federal Reserve authorities in dealing with the recession and subsequent recovery (to which we return shortly). It is interesting to note that in the 1953-1954 recession the CPI and WPI remained roughly constant, or fell very slightly, while the GNP price index increased over 1 per cent. In the recession of 1949-1950 all three price indices pointed to a definite though modest decline. Thus the trend appears to have been away from a tendency for the price level to fall under the impact of a moderate decline in effective demand. This may be accounted for in part by the greater stability of consumer outlays; the increasing importance of services the prices of which appear to be insensitive to fluctuations in overall demand; the greater effect of wage-push and markup factors; and special factors such as sectoral instability with its consequent effects on machinery and raw material costs and long-term wage contracts.

Monetary Policy in Recession and Recovery

Although the recession of 1957-1958 is considered to have begun in the summer of 1957, the Federal Reserve authorities did not relax their tight money policy until late October. In fact, although it was generally recognized at the time that business was at best manifesting a "sidewise" movement, the Board approved an increase in the discount rate from 3 to 3½ per cent in August. And in the face of growing criticism in September and October, monetary policy continued to be one of tight money to restrain inflationary influences. In late October the Open Market Committee still insisted that "there was no immediate occasion to reverse its policy of restraint in credit expansion," but it nevertheless agreed to a slight easing. It was not until November 12 that the Federal Reserve authorities finally decided that a recession was definitely under way and changed their policy directive to "fostering sustainable growth in the economy without inflation, by moderating the pressures on bank reserves." Shortly thereafter the Board approved reductions in the discount rate to 3 per cent.

A more vigorous monetary attack on recession was decided upon in December and there was a considerable step-up of Federal Reserve action in early 1958. The discount rate was reduced three times in the first quarter of 1958, and finally to 1¾ per cent in April 1958. The volume of net borrowed reserves (reflecting the continuation of tight money) declined during the last three months of 1957, and free reserves emerged in January 1958, and increased to $500 million in March, at which level they were stabilized until July 1958. Reserve requirements were lowered in three stages between February and April 1958, releasing about $1.4 billion in reserves, some of which were subsequently reabsorbed by open-market sales.

Interest rates fell sharply in late 1957 and early 1958, under the impact of the easier money policy and the decline in demand for money associated with recession. The most pronounced interest rate effects were on short term issues. The lag in decline of long-terms was due largely to the maintenance of demand for long-term funds by corporations and state and local governments which came into the market with borrowing which had been deferred earlier because of exceptionally high rates. The easier money policy had its most notable effect on residential construction, which (owing to lags between mortgage commitments and housing starts) had fallen to a low of 915,000 units by February 1958. Thereafter residential construction started upward, reaching an annual rate of 1,432,00 units in December. The housing expansion was also assisted by liberalization of interest rate requirements on FHA-insured and VA-guaranteed mortgages in 1957 and 1958.

Easy money policy also had a stimulating effect on speculation in government securities markets, especially in connection with new issues of long-term securities. With interest rates falling (bond prices rising) and the business outlook uncertain, a speculative upsurge developed in long-term governments financed on the basis of very small margins. But an improved economic outlook, a military threat in the Middle East, and prospects of a much larger federal deficit led to a sharp change in expectations regarding Federal Reserve policy and interest rates. The resulting rise in interest rates caused large (and frequently forced) sales of government securities as falling bond prices eliminated the thin speculative margins. As sales mounted and government securities prices continued to fall, the Federal Open Market Committee concluded that the market situation had become "disorderly," thereby justifying departure from the bills-only policy. Between July 18 and 23 the Federal Reserve absorbed over $1.2 billion in securities, most of them outside the short-term category. Although the market disruption was relatively short-lived, its severity and speculative character were striking. The episode was a blow to advocates of the "bills-only" policy which was supposed to improve the workings of the government securities market.

The Federal Reserve began to temper its easy money policy in the summer of 1958, in view of the spread of what Chairman Martin described as an "inflationary and speculative psychology." Open-market operations carried out during the summer were less than called for to meet rising credit demands, and the discount rate was raised in August from 1¾ per cent to 2 per cent, and again in mid-autumn to 2½ per cent. This tightening policy was instituted and continued even though (in the words of Mr. Martin) "unemployment remained disquietingly high." Real output had reached its pre-recession level by the fall of 1958, but with the increase in productivity this was insufficient to restore earlier employment rates.

The lag in Federal Reserve response to growing evidence of a downturn in the summer and fall of 1957 and the prompt renewal of credit restraint in the summer of 1958, despite high levels of unemployment, caused considerable controversy as to the compatibility of the general objectives of monetary management and the relative importance attached to the various aims by the Federal Reserve authorities. The Federal Reserve claimed adherence to three broad objectives of monetary policy: full employment, price level stability, and maximum sustainable rates of economic growth. Formerly it was not unreasonable to suppose that policies to achieve one objective would be consistent with the achievement of other goals. In the period after the Accord, and especially in the recession of 1957-1958, it appeared that vigorous action in the interest of full employment and rapid economic growth tended to accelerate the upward movement of a price level that was already creeping up. Conversely, determined pursuit of price stability appeared to conflict with the effort to achieve the other two objectives.

The Federal Reserve authorities have expressed deep attachment to all three of the basic objectives noted above. The evidence suggests, however, that they have given especial weight to the objective of price level stability. This is indicated by the emphasis placed on inflation in Federal Reserve pronouncements of the mid and late 1950's, as well as by policy actions. The indecisiveness of late 1957 and the immediate return to a policy of credit restraint in the summer and fall of 1958 can best be explained on the ground that price stability is (or was) given high priority.[13]

Fiscal Policy and Debt Management in Recession and Recovery (1957-1958)

Fiscal operations of the federal government made a substantial contribution to stabilization during the recession and recovery of 1957 and 1958, mainly through the effects of automatic stabilizers. Some destabilization resulted from the considerable decline in defense orders for aircraft and other hard goods from mid-1956 through the third quarter of 1957, and from the movement to a budgetary surplus in the latter quarter (at an annual rate of $3.4 billion). However, by the first quarter of 1958 receipts fell short of government expenditures by $6.6 billion. Three-fourths of the $10 billion turnabout was accounted for by the decline in receipts. About two-thirds of the increase in governmental outlays was accounted for by transfer payments to the unemployed. There were no anti-recessionary tax reductions, and compensatory spending action was limited to federal ex-

---

13. On a number of occasions the Federal Reserve authorities have defended their emphasis on price stability, not in terms of its ultimate primacy as an objective, but on the grounds that it is the proximate means of attaining the other objectives. Thus, in a letter to Senator Paul Douglas, Chairman Martin stated that: "My interest in a monetary policy directed toward a dollar of stable value is not based on the feeling that price stability is a more important objective than either maximum sustainable growth or a high level of employment, but rather on the reasoned conclusion that the objective of price stability is an essential prerequisite to their achievement" (*Federal Reserve Bulletin,* February 1960, p. 132.) The first point to be noted about this quotation is that it acknowledges that price stability was the immediate goal of Federal Reserve action. Second, the implication that policies to promote a stable dollar are invariably consistent with full employment and growth objectives is, to say the least, debatable.

tension of state unemployment compensation programs, an acceleration of government procurement, a salary increase for federal employees, emergency aid for housing, and suspension of certain spending limitations under the interstate highway program.

The recession and recovery of 1957-1958 brought further problems for Treasury debt management. Because of the heavy reliance on short-term issues in the preceding period of tight money, heavy refunding operations were carried out in 1958. At the same time a cash deficit of $7.3 billion and substantial net redemptions of savings bonds placed a heavy burden on Treasury financing. The decline in interest rates in late 1957 and early 1958 enabled the Treasury to engage in a modest program of debt lengthening. This was brought to a halt by the rise of interest rates in 1958 and 1959 which, for the first time, brought the Treasury up against the 4¼ per cent legal limit on interest rates on securities maturing in over five years.[14] This interest rate ceiling became the focal point of renewed controversy in which the issue, while apparently the desirability of an interest rate ceiling, was really the appropriateness of renewed tight money which brought interest rate levels to new postwar highs in 1959.

MONETARY AND FISCAL ISSUES AFTER 1958

The period after 1958 and extending into the early 1960's was characterized by continued moderate cyclical swings. The improvement in economic conditions which was already under way in 1958 was accelerated early in 1959 by expectations of a steel strike and a resultant inventory buildup. The long strike which followed reversed this advance, and investment, income, and employment declined in the second half of 1959. The expansion in GNP which followed the strike began to slow up in the second quarter of 1960 (see Table 23-1). As the weak boom of 1958-1960 drew to a close the employment rate still hovered above 5 per cent of the civilian labor force.

The recession of 1960-1961 was moderate and short. It is important to bear in mind, however, that it developed before full recovery had been achieved from the previous recession. The rate of unemployment increased from 5.1 per cent in May 1960 to 7 per cent in May 1961 and showed little improvement thereafter until near the end of 1961. Unemployment rates did not fall below 6 per cent until early in 1962.

The most volatile factor in the decline of 1960-1961 was expenditures on inventory, which changed $9.4 billion between the 1960 peak and the 1961 trough. Fixed investment declined $5.3 billion and personal consump-

---

14. The limitation was enacted during World War I in an effort to restrain the rise in yields on government obligations. The ceiling applies to the coupon rate, not to actual yield in the market. By issuing a security at a discount, therefore, the limitation could easily be evaded. This the Secretary of Treasury was unwilling, however, to do.

tion outlays only $2.2 billion. Automatic stabilizers undoubtedly played a significant role in maintaining consumer expenditures, with transfer payments increasing $3 billion and personal tax liabilities falling $700 million.

The recovery in 1961 and 1962 was sparked by an upturn in inventory investment and substantial increases in government spending, particularly on national security. Private fixed investment increased during 1961, but not by enough to bring this component up to the level attained at the cyclical peak in 1960. The expansion of outlays by the federal government was "probably the principal driving force" in the recovery.[15]

The years after 1958 focused attention upon a number of major policy issues. Some of these questions had been present in greater or less degree throughout all of the postwar period. Others, such as those relating to international monetary problems, while not new, assumed a different or more acute form in these years.

Choice of Objectives

Perhaps the most persistent and perplexing issue is one to which attention was directed earlier, that of the choice to be made among different policy objectives. Broadly speaking, this problem applies to the appropriate balance to be established among all major goals. More narrowly, during most of the period after the Accord it concerned the emphasis to be given price stability in relation to other policy objectives. The difficulty derives in part from legitimate difference of opinion as to whether one objective should take precedence over another. It derives also from the fact that the objective of price stability on the one hand, for example, and the objectives of full employment and maximum sustainable growth on the other may call for quite different monetary or fiscal action (or for a different "mix" of monetary, fiscal, and direct controls from what the authorities are prepared to put into effect).

The choice, moreover, is not between one objective or another in absolute terms but between degrees of each. Thus in 1959, for example, a major question was how much unemployment and retardation of economic growth we should be prepared to accept in order to avoid varying degrees of price level increase during the year. But even this choice presupposes that we can make dependable estimates of the degree of sacrifice of one set of objectives required in order to attain some other objective: the threat of inflation in 1959, as an example, now appears to have been considerably less serious than was then generally believed. A second major question is how much sacrifice because of conflict of objectives we should accept before resorting to other measures (fiscal policy, selective instruments, and direct controls) that might improve our ability to achieve multiple goals.

It is now widely acknowledged that during the 1950's the Federal Re-

---

15. *Economic Report of the President*, January, 1962, p. 59.

serve gave highest priority to the price stability objective. In the words of a foreign observer:

> "Policy appears to have been influenced by the trend of prices almost exclusively, to the disregard of indicators showing that output was well below capacity. It is, of course, easier to find signs of a coming recession with the benefit of hindsight, but even allowing for this it is reasonably clear that it was the behaviour of the price level that was the predominating factor in Federal Reserve policy."[16]

While the time specified was 1957, the statement is to be interpreted as applying to most of the decade. The emphasis given to price stability was widely challenged at the time and was subsequently somewhat abated.[17]

Adequacy of Existing Monetary Instruments

A second group of issues had to do with the adequacy of existing monetary weapons for achieving major economic objectives. Grave doubts were expressed as to whether general instruments of credit control would be either certain enough in terms of immediate impact or powerful enough in terms of total effect to achieve their purpose. Their limitations were regarded as resulting from difficulties in forecasting, lags between policy action and impact on economic activity, the disruptive side effects of large monetary changes, discriminatory effects of the general controls, and possible offsets generated by private financial institutions.

The growing problems of sectoral maladjustment seemed to call for selective controls over consumer and real estate credit as supplements to general monetary measures. And the feeling that important inflationary pressures may arise out of monopoly power supported the conclusion that more direct measures were required, such as extensive structural reorganization to reduce monopoly power or wage and price controls in key sectors of the economy.

An important question relating to the adequacy of monetary instruments is whether, in the interest of rapid economic growth, greater use should be made of fiscal means of curbing excess demand. If, so the argument runs, long-term growth requires a high rate of investment, monetary weapons to control inflation, because they tend to increase the cost of capital, are singularly inappropriate. A proper policy for stimulating growth and at the same time restraining inflationary pressures would be to stimulate investment by easy money and curb effective demand to the degree necessary by income and other taxes that will restrict consumption. This view has

---

16. A. E. Holmans, *United States Fiscal Policy, 1945-1959* (London: Oxford University Press, 1961), p. 271.

17. The same writer challenged the suitability of the emphasis placed on price stability, saying: "It is to the interest of the outside world that the United States should over-insure against deflation rather than against inflation."—*Ibid.*, p. 320.

much to recommend it, particularly in the light of the far from satisfactory performance of general monetary controls in recent years. On the other hand, fiscal methods are presently lacking in flexibility and may be unsuited to dealing with structural and market power sources of inflation. Thus supplementary devices for controlling inflation without restricting growth may still be required.

The Role of the Budget

Along with increased doubts as to the adequacy of existing monetary policies and greater stress on fiscal measures has come increasing attention to the influence exerted by the federal budget. And there was a growing realization that fiscal operations were capable of exerting a destabilizing influence. It is widely believed, for example, that the short duration of the upswing of 1959-1960 was due in considerable measure to the drastic shift in the position of the federal budget, from a cash deficit of $13.1 billion in 1959 to a surplus of $800 million in 1960.

The Council of Economic Advisers has stressed that with given government outlays and tax rates an increase in economic activity increases government revenues, bringing a reduced deficit or increased surplus budget and exerting a retarding influence. The strength of this braking effect depends on the levels of government expenditures, tax rates, and income. The surplus generated by a given budget at full employment, which may be termed the full employment surplus,[18] may be used to measure the restrictive or expansionary effect of a budget program on overall demand.

With given tax rates and levels of government outlays the surplus tends to grow over time, since economic growth tends to raise full employment tax revenues. Unless discretionary tax reductions or increases in government spending are carried out, therefore, the full-employment surplus may grow to levels that constitute a serious barrier to full utilization of resources. This is alleged to have been the case in 1959 and 1960, when the full employment surplus is estimated to have risen to a peak (in 1960) of $12.5 billion.[19]

The Problem of the Balance of Payments

In recent years the international payments position of the United States was such as to reestablish maintenance of a favorable balance of payments position as an important objective of public policy. Deficits in the United States international accounts emerged in 1950, but were relatively small until 1958. The large deficits after that time not only tended to persist; they also did not appear to rest on temporary developments that might soon

18. Council of Economic Advisers, *Economic Report of the President*, January 1962, pp. 78-79.
19. *Ibid.*, p. 81.

be expected to disappear. The shock to confidence in the dollar in 1960 and the accompanying large loss of gold and outflow of short-term capital suggested that continuance of substantial deficits might impair confidence of foreign holders of dollars in maintenance of the gold value of the dollar.

The outflow of short-term capital in 1960 was also influenced by the short-term interest rates in Canada and Europe which were higher than in the United States. In the interest of aiding our balance of payments position, the Federal Reserve attempted to carry out an anti-recessionary policy in 1960-1962 in which long-term rates were encouraged to fall but short-term rates were kept relatively high. This was accomplished by abandoning the bills-only policy and buying long-term securities and selling bills. The Treasury also helped to maintain higher short-term rates by new cash offerings of short-term issues. The ceiling rate on time deposits held for over twelve months was raised from 3 to 4 per cent by the Board of Governors and the FDIC, effective early in 1962, partly to increase the attractiveness to foreign investors of holding balances in the United States.

There is also some reason to suppose that the emphasis on a balanced budget and the restraint in pressing for increased non-defense outlays early in the Kennedy administration, despite the high unemployment rate, were influenced by the desire to persuade financial interests abroad that a weakening of confidence in the dollar was unwarranted.

* * * *

The post-Accord decade began with mounting enthusiasm for the general instruments of monetary control—the so-called "rediscovery of money." It ended with confidence in a predominantly monetary approach considerably shaken. The desirability of heavy reliance on fiscal methods was increasingly accepted, and sentiment for judicious resort to selective controls appeared to be mounting.

The shifting emphasis on particular policy aims suggested at times a reversion to earlier policy issues. Thus the preoccupation with the prevention of inflation was not unlike that of the 1920's and represented a subordination of the full-employment objective which assumed such importance in the 1930's. And concern with the balance of payments position was somewhat in the nature of a return to the earliest of central bank objectives, the maintenance of the external value of the currency.

In completing the circle, however, public policy did not return to the point from which it started. For whichever objective might take precedence —price stability, full employment, growth, the balance of payments position, or something else—the other objectives did not disappear from sight. At most they retreated slightly into the shadows, waiting for a shift in economic circumstances to throw the spotlight of attention once more upon them.

For the 1914 world is gone forever. Never again will it be possible to think in terms of a single monetary objective. Always it will be necessary to coordinate each of the recognized aims—no doubt in varying proportions —with the other accepted goals. And always it will be necessary to think in terms of an ever-changing combination, "mix," of monetary, fiscal, and debt management policies. Not only does economic stabilization embrace much more than it formerly did. Even the terms used to describe the policies carry a different content from what they did even a few years ago. A shifting, moving constellation of aims and methods is the characteristic feature of the post-Accord period. And it can be expected to characterize monetary and fiscal policies in the years ahead.

SELECTED BIBLIOGRAPHY

ACHINSTEIN, ASHER, *Federal Reserve Policy and Economic Stability 1951-1957.* S. Rep. No. 2500, 85th Congress, 2nd Session. Washington: 1958.

BATOR, F. M., *The Question of Government Spending.* New York: Harper, 1960.

"Controversial Issues in Recent Monetary Policy: A Symposium," *Review of Economics and Statistics* (August 1960), pp. 245-282.

ELLIS, HOWARD S., "Limitations of Monetary Policy." In American Assembly, *United States Monetary Policy,* 1958, Chapter 6.

HANSEN, ALVIN H., *The American Economy.* New York: McGraw-Hill, 1960, Chapters 3-4.

HOLMANS, A. E., *United States Fiscal Policy 1945-1959.* London: Oxford University Press, 1961, Chapters X-XIV.

JOINT ECONOMIC COMMITTEE, *Staff Report on Employment, Growth, and Price Levels.* 86th Congress, 1st Session. Washington: 1959, Chapters 5, 8-9.

LUCKETT, DUDLEY G., " 'Bills Only': A Critical Appraisal," *Review of Economics and Statistics* (August 1960), pp. 301-306.

RIEFLER, WINFIELD W., "Open Market Operations in Long-Term Securities," *Federal Reserve Bulletin* (November 1958), pp. 1260-1274.

SMITH, WARREN L., "Consumer Installment Credit (A Review Article)," *American Economic Review* (December 1957), pp. 966-984.

26

GOVERNMENT AND THE
BANKS: PROBLEMS OF
SUPERVISION AND CONTROL

Banking in the United States presents a curious paradox: we have a tradition of individual freedom and independence for the banker, but banks are nevertheless subject to legislation and control to a greater extent than in any other leading country of the free world. The individualistic tradition gave us the Free Banking System and other legislation copied from it, and it has been largely responsible for preventing to this day the development of nationwide (or even regional) branch banking such as is found in most other countries of the world. At the same time we have an extraordinarily voluminous body of state and federal law covering the organization and operation of banks. Regulation and supervision are carried to great lengths and there is a large, and to some extent duplicative, structure of supervisory institutions at both the state and national levels.

The individualistic tradition in American banking was one manifestation of the spirit of enterprise and independence that characterized a young and rising democracy. It expressed itself in resentment on the part of many local bankers against the higher standards imposed by the first and second Banks of the United States, in the revolt against the monopolistic practices of state legislatures in granting exclusive banking charters, and in hostility to the alleged threat of large eastern financial interests. In a society where one man was declared to be as good as the next there was a tendency to draw the dubious inference that one banker was as good as another.

The proliferation of laws, legal requirements, and supervisory organization was the natural consequence of a situation in which any citizen might demand an equal right with any other citizen to become a banker. Hence the paradox noted above: through insisting upon the maximum of individual freedom, the American banker has ended up by being perhaps the most regulated.

The present chapter is concerned mainly with the general background and characteristics of government policy toward banks, and a more detailed consideration of bank examination policy. Matters pertaining to the chartering of banks, branch banking, and mergers are reserved for the following chapter, which is devoted to questions relating to banking structure.

THE NATURE OF RELATIONS BETWEEN GOVERNMENT AND BANKING

Relations of government to banking extend far beyond matters of regulation and control. First, banks perform many services for the government, including the extension of short-term and long-term credit, the holding of deposits, and the performance of agency or brokerage functions as in the sale of Treasury bonds to the public. Second, there is a wide range of relationships where the government stands over the banks in the various roles of administrator, supervisor, umpire, policeman, or guardian. And third, they may engage in supplementary or even competitive lending activities.

It is to be observed that, in addition to the direct control which the government or its delegated representatives exercise through the chartering, examining, and regulation of banks, the central authorities exercise controls of an indirect character. These indirect measures extend from providing information to the discharge of such typical central bank functions as changes in the discount rate and open-market operations.[1] The government has also contributed greatly to improving the banking organization of the country through providing facilities for the more efficient clearing and collecting of checks, the rapid transfer of funds, and the mobilization of banking resources. The supplementary—and occasionally competing—financial institutions include such bodies as the Export-Import Bank, the Federal Intermediate Credit System for agriculture, the Postal Savings System, and the numerous lending agencies created during the 1930's and later.

Nature of Interests Which Are Involved

The desire to protect the customers of banks is the oldest and most important motive for governmental control over banking. Historically, this concern was directed first toward noteholders and later toward depositors. The creation of the Federal Deposit Insurance Corporation in 1933, about which more will be said presently, was the most conspicuous step in the direction of safeguarding bank depositors. Its establishment may be said to have reflected disillusionment with the effectiveness of regulation alone as a means of safeguarding the interests of depositors: it was designed not

1. In the present context the Federal Reserve authorities are included as part of government.

so much to prevent the abuses that would cause banks to fail as to indemnify smaller depositors in case failure does occur. In the course of time increased attention has been directed toward the prevention of failure, sometimes by the merger of a weak bank with a strong institution as a means of lessening the probability of failure.

Less effort has gone into safeguarding the interests of borrowers from banks even though they, like depositors, are also bank customers. This is probably because the failure of a bank may involve the loss to depositors of deposits which they own, while borrowers are merely deprived of a place to which they could go for loans with which to acquire deposit balances. The establishment of various lending agencies by the government, as well as chronic airing of the problem of availability of bank credit— particularly for smaller businesses—shows that the authorities are not oblivious to the interests of borrowers.

Through the officers, employees, and stockholders of banks, a large number of people have a direct and very material interest in the survival and success of the banks. Regulation is frequently designed for the protection of those who are regulated, and this is very definitely the case among banks. It is to the interest of banks to be safeguarded against destructive competition from badly run banks or banks whose affairs are in such condition as to make them disposed to pursue socially dangerous policies. There has been an increased tendency in recent years to regulate for the purpose of protecting banks against banks. The restriction of interest paid on deposits is a conspicuous example of this policy. The danger exists, where such policies are followed, that the legitimate objective of controlling injurious practices may serve as a cloak to restrict competition to a greater extent than is in the social interest. There is good reason to believe that some of the practices introduced in recent years, with the consent of the constituted authorities, may have tended to foster monopolistic practices and thereby enable banks to obtain higher profits than would be possible under more competitive conditions.

The public at large is chiefly concerned with how the banks affect the working of the economic system as a whole. A country's money supply is clearly a vital factor in the functioning of the entire economy. Indeed, there are those who see in an overexpansion or overcontraction of bank credit the principal element in booms and depressions. In surrendering to the nation's banks the task of providing the largest part of the circulating medium, the government did not divest itself of its responsibility to see that the task is effectively performed. The public's chief interest in the banking system lies in the manner in which banks discharge their function of providing the circulating medium and in the effect this has upon economic activity in general. It is this interest that governmental control in its broader aspects, such as credit control by the central bank, is primarily designed to serve.

The Effectiveness of Control

Evidence is necessarily inconclusive as to the effectiveness of governmental supervision and control. One reason for the uncertainty is that an ideal policy would be one that served to prevent a crisis from arising rather than one that efficiently restored order after it had occurred. The most effective system would be one that never seemed to have anything to do. It is not possible to say with any assurance how much has been accomplished by supervisory measures for the simple reason that one can never know what would have happened in the absence of these policies. Thus the most important achievements of bank examination may well lie in the risky operations that were never undertaken, because of the knowledge that examiners would expose them to public view. The magnitude of the preventive effects of supervision is necessarily conjectural. Nevertheless, the evidence of the quarter century before the War Between the States, when central control was virtually non-existent and banking conditions chaotic, should satisfy even the most skeptical that the preventive effects of governmental supervision of banks are probably substantial.

THE EVOLUTION OF GOVERNMENTAL POLICY TOWARD BANKS

The examination of banks appears to have originated in the desire of the authorities to make certain that the powers given to banks in their charters were not exceeded or abused. It was thus essentially a part of the right of the government, recognized from early times, to grant charters to particular types of business. A logical distinction between examination and regulation can readily enough be drawn, but when it comes to practice the two are indivisible since the one complements the other. The trend of governmental policy toward banking has been in the direction of a broadening of the scope of the objectives sought for, and a strengthening and expansion of the measures adopted to attain these objectives. The way in which the activities of regulatory authorities have broadened in the course of time is indicated by the various problems that have been their major concern.

Changing Character of Banking Problems

Quality of bank notes. At one time the principal banking problem was to improve the quality of bank note issues. For many years prior to the War Between the States—especially in the two decades just preceding it—the bank note circulation was of the most unreliable and non-descript character. The authorities of a few of the states, supplemented by certain private organizations such as the Suffolk Banking System, were more effective than the federal government in improving the quality of banking practices. With the passage of the National Banking Act and the subsequent law taxing state bank notes out of existence, the problem of defective bank note issues was at last brought under control, as was described in Chapter 11.

Inelasticity of currency and credit. Introduction of the National Banking System served to overcome the more glaring faults of bank note circulation, but it was not well adapted to accommodating the volume of circulating medium to changes in current needs. With the passage of time and the emergence of a more complex economic environment, this deficiency came to assume greater and greater importance in the eyes of business men and officials. Indeed, the inelasticity of notes and deposits was the major problem of banking before and after the turn of the century. It was believed to have contributed to seasonal disturbance in interest rates and to have been the principal cause of the panics of 1893 and 1907. The desire to remedy this defect was responsible to a greater extent than any other factor for the passage of the Federal Reserve Act.

Bank failures. After the introduction of the Federal Reserve System, inelasticity of bank credit was no longer a serious concern—but again it happened that the correction of the particular banking problem of the time failed to bring a solution to the banking problem as a whole. After 1920 we began to suffer severely from the problem of bank failures, which continued to plague the country down to the closing of the banks in 1933. The seriousness of bank failures and the attendant losses to depositors contributed to the passage of the Banking Acts of 1933 and 1935. This legislation brought about the organization of the Federal Deposit Insurance Corporation and the important changes in the Federal Reserve System described earlier.

Levels of prices and business activity. Throughout the decade of the 1930's, both before and after the passage of the bank reform laws, the most important problem of bank policy had to do with credit conditions as a whole and the effects of these conditions upon general economic activity. This was reflected both in Federal Reserve policies and in resort by the United States government to the use of fiscal policies to promote business recovery. Important modifications were introduced in open-market operations and the procedure of bank examination with a view toward promoting orderly credit conditions throughout the economy, rather than merely safeguarding the position of individual banks or their customers.

The transition from planned recovery to the period of war economy and then to reconversion and cold war, while not affecting the ultimate goal of general stability, reversed the immediate focus of governmental policy from encouraging expansion to resisting it. In the 1930's the authorities had directed their efforts toward stimulating expansion; now they sought to restrain inflationary tendencies present in the economy. This shift represented a changing phase of a consistent policy—in each instance banking policy was integrated into the general economic policy of the country. In both situations public policy had ceased to be directed primarily toward the banks or their patrons, but instead, was incorporated into the framework of economic policy as a whole.

Landmarks in the Extension of Federal Power Over Banks

For a good many years after the founding of the Republic, the power of the federal government to regulate banking remained open to question. It was not until 1819 that the Supreme Court ruled that Congress had the constitutional right to charter a bank (the second Bank of the United States) and that the states were not entitled to interfere with it by taxation or other means. Even then some doubt remained, and the principle had to be reaffirmed in 1824.

The next major development in the expansion of federal powers over banking came with the National Banking Act of 1863. As a result of this legislation, the authority of the federal government to charter, regulate, and supervise banks was extended to a significant proportion of the country's banks. Laws passed in 1865 and 1866 imposed a prohibitory tax on the notes of state banks, for the purpose of forcing banks into the national system. Aside from the importance of these laws in increasing the proportion of banks under federal charter, they were noteworthy as demonstrating that the power of the federal government over the issue of bank notes was absolute, and they showed that this authority extended to state banks as well as to those with national charters.

After the legislation of the 1860's, little change in the status of federal authority over banks occurred until the introduction of the Federal Reserve System in 1914. The effect of this step was to extend federal jurisdiction to a larger group of banks than was included in the National Banking System. The legislation of 1933 and 1935, and particularly the creation of the Federal Deposit Insurance Corporation, expanded the jurisdiction of federal authorities much further. While the degree of control exercised by the Federal Deposit Insurance Corporation over individual banks within its jurisdiction is less complete than that of either the Comptroller of the Currency or the Board of Governors of the Federal Reserve System, it is nevertheless substantial.

The organization of the Federal Deposit Insurance Corporation represents, as has been noted, the most recent stage in the extension of permanent federal jurisdiction over banking. It is worth observing, however, that federal authority over banking on a temporary or emergency basis has been carried much further. Thus in 1932 the Reconstruction Finance Corporation established the precedent of the federal government offering to lend emergency aid to any deserving bank. Moreover, the action of the President in declaring the Banking Holiday in March 1933 applied to all banks in the country. These two measures clearly demonstrate that, under certain circumstances, the acknowledged responsibility of the federal government and its powers embrace all banks.

Methods of Progress

In the development of governmental policy toward banking, the practice in this country has usually been to attack the particular problem rather than to effect a fundamental reorganization. Usually, we have adopted policies better calculated to remove the symptoms of weaknesses in our banking system than their causes. This is illustrated repeatedly in the laws we have enacted. We prevented state banks from issuing notes, instead of effecting reforms that would have assured the high quality of bank notes. We passed laws to control group and chain banking, rather than allowing a stronger and safer system of branch banking to develop as it had done in other countries. Instead of removing the causes of bank failures, we instituted a system for guaranteeing small deposits against losses resulting from failures. The list of similar measures could be expanded much further.

The rivalry between state and national systems of regulating banks has at times constituted an obstacle to the raising of banking standards. The laws governing the National Banking System were relaxed on certain occasions, for example, because of a desire to place national banks on a more equal footing with state banks. The same consideration was primarily responsible for the lowering of capital requirements for national banks and for the liberalization of regulations relating to the operation of trust departments, the holding of savings deposits, lending on real estate, and the establishment of branches. It is probable that certain of these measures were in the best interests of banking development. Nevertheless, it is an unfortunate commentary on the processes of banking evolution that even desirable innovations were brought about as deviations from what were generally regarded at the time as the highest standards of banking regulation.

A further obstacle to banking reform has been the large number of small but politically influential bankers scattered throughout the country. The opposition of this important conservative group to proposals for altering the organization of American banking was reinforced by a familiar feature of American social psychology—the attitude of suspicion and antagonism toward eastern financial interests. Both large bankers and small tend to be highly conservative.

The resistance to fundamental banking reform—or indeed to any banking reform, whether fundamental or not—has meant that it takes a major disturbance, such as war or a grave business depression, to precipitate significant action. This was true of the first important banking reform measure in the history of the country, the establishment of the second United States

Bank which owed its origin to the financial disorder that followed the War of 1812. Of the three major banking reforms in our history, the National Banking Act of 1863 was occasioned by the War Between the States while the Federal Reserve Act and the banking laws of 1933 and 1935 were the direct consequences of financial breakdowns accompanying crises and depressions. The Federal Reserve Act was drawn up and passed in a deliberate and orderly manner, but the acts of 1863 and 1933 were hurried through under considerable pressure. In view of the circumstances under which they were introduced, it is surprising that the reforms were as successful as they have been.

Although great progress has been made, the banking system of this country is still far from ideal. It makes a poor showing—whether judged abstractly or in the light of performance—in comparison with the banking systems of a number of other countries. It is good chiefly in relation to the banking organization which existed in this country in the past. We have come a great way from the banking conditions of the 1850's, or even of the 1890's or 1929's, but we still have far to go before we can look upon our banking system with any great sense of pride.

THE BASES OF EXAMINATION POLICY

The examination of banks has long been an important feature of public policy toward banks. It is concerned with the prevention and exposure of abuses, but not less with arriving at information which will be of use to the banks and to society generally. Bank examination implies the getting of facts, which may not always be easy, and also their appraisal. It is in the process of appraising the facts that the greatest possibility of error arises, since this necessarily involves value judgments on the part of examiners. The problem is made especially difficult because of certain automatic tendencies toward instability in the behavior of markets and the banking system. These tendencies relate to variations of bank credit and fluctuations in market quotations for commodities and securities.

"The Inherent Instability of Bank Credit"

The expression "inherent instability of bank credit" was coined by the British authority on banking, R. G. Hawtrey, to describe a tendency which was alleged to follow from the traditional theory of commercial banking, explained in Chapter 5. This theory, it will be remembered, assumes that deposits are created as a result of banks lending on the basis of self-liquidating commercial paper. With a greater volume of business to be transacted there will be more commercial paper and therefore more money will be created. Similarly, with a contraction of business there will be a falling off in the volume of commercial paper and a consequent reduction in circulating medium. Thus the volume of money was expected to conform to the rather vague ideal of the "needs of trade."

Unfortunately for the theory, the process of deposit expansion or contraction works the same whether the change in the volume of commercial paper results from a change in physical output or from a change in the level of prices. At a time when prices are rising there will be an increase in the volume of commercial paper, not because there is more money work to be done in real terms but because the same physical volume of goods will represent—at the increased level of prices—a larger dollar volume of business to be financed. Lending by banks on the increased volume of commercial paper results in additional deposits and these presumably allow the higher level of prices to be maintained or may even cause prices to rise still further. In such a situation, the chain of rising prices, increases in the volume of commercial paper, and expanding money supply is alleged to result in self-inflammatory process—with prices tending to go up and up. A similar sequence when prices start to fall tends to drive them down and down. This is what is meant by the "inherent instability of bank credit."[2]

This oversimplified description of the way the banking system *tends* to operate was not advanced as a criticism of banks or of bankers, although it is the basis for urging central banks and examiners to adopt appropriate policies to combat the tendency. It was intended as a logical deduction from the nature of deposit creation on the basis of commercial paper in an economy where prices are free to change.

While the concept of inherent stability as thus presented is an oversimplification, it must be recognized that during a period of expanding business activity it is to the interest of the individual bank to expand along with the rest. Yet it is precisely such action by each individual bank that allows an inflationary movement to progress to the danger point. Similarly during a downward trend, considerations of safety and profitability compel an individual bank to pursue a cautious policy. But the actions of individual banks in restricting credit, calling loans, and striving for liquidity depress business and place a strain on other financial institutions, thereby causing them to follow similarly deflationary tactics. The tendency for banks to be inflationary during periods of inflation and deflationary during periods of deflation aggravates—if it does not generate—deflation and depression. As Lord Keynes once remarked, the system tends to behave as though the idea of banks were "not to keep sober, but, in accordance with a perfect standard of manners, to enjoy just that degree of tipsiness (or sick-headache) as characterizes the country as a whole."[3]

---

2. R. G. Hawtrey, *Currency and Credit* (London: Longmans Green, 1928), Chapter 1, pp. 452-453, and *passim*.

3. J. M. Keynes, *A Treatise on Money* (London: Macmillan, 1930), Vol. II, p. 222.

Credit Instability and Examination Procedure

One of the aims of examination procedure should be to reduce if possible, and certainly not to aggravate, the destabilizing tendencies of bank credit. Fortunately, it seems likely that changes in the composition of bank portfolios since the early 1930's have somewhat lessened the inflationary and deflationary tendencies of bank credit. First, bank credit which is based to a considerable extent on government bonds and other less volatile assets is not as likely to contract suddenly as bank credit based mainly on commercial paper. Second, when contraction occurs it will probably be less deflationary in its effect on other parts of the economy since it is not so directly related to manufacturing and trading operations.

Despite the more stable basis of credit operations, however, an enlightened policy toward bank examination requires that the authorities should be fully conscious of the inflationary and deflationary potentialities in bank operations and should be prepared to adapt examination procedures to changes in business conditions. Ideally, the rule should be strictness in the expansion phase of the business cycle and liberality in the contraction phase. It is perhaps unnecessary to remark that this is exactly opposite to natural inclination, and to actual practice in the past. It is particularly difficult in a period of depression to think in terms of supplying additional capital and avoiding liquidation, yet these are necessary steps if the downward trend is to be reversed. Similarly, the idea of relaxing banking standards during a depression—at the very time when the evils of too great laxity are becoming most fully apparent—runs directly counter to normal behavior.

Nor is it easy to apply wise examination policies in the upward phase of the cycle. At a time of general optimism and expansion the role of the examining authorities would be that of a kill-joy—and this is clearly no way to attain popularity. The administrative authorities are exposed to two psychological hazards: they must avoid being swept away by the same popular psychology that infects the rest of the business community, and they must avoid being deterred by the knowledge that adherence to the indicated course of action is certain to provoke public criticism and possibly political intervention.

Aside from these basic difficulties there is also the problem of correctly diagnosing changes in business conditions. It may be difficult to determine whether a particular upward movement is of a cyclical or secular character, yet this issue may be crucial in deciding on the course of action that should be followed. A perfect handling of the problem of examining banks is hardly to be expected, but it is significant that the experience of the early 1930's brought about widespread recognition of the evil as well as the good that can be done by bank examination. It is to be hoped that bank examiners will never again attempt to evaluate bank assets by the rule-of-thumb methods often prevailing in the past.

The Valuation of Banking Assets

In addition to the alleged tendency for bank credit to behave in an unstable manner, there is the further difficulty that market prices also fluctuate widely. This is true of the prices of commodities which lie back of commercial paper, and it is also true of the prices of other securities which occupy a more important place than formerly among the earning assets of banks.

It is not surprising, in view of the complexity of their task, that bank examiners came to rely heavily upon market quotations and arbitrary rules and classifications for testing the quality of bank assets. But this recourse, while it helped to relieve individual examiners of personal responsibility for errors of judgment, constituted no solution. For, as had been shown repeatedly in our history, the quality of assets changes with economic conditions. Adherence to formal tests and rules, without regard to changing circumstances, has sometimes proved ineffective and sometimes positively harmful.[4]

There are two principal difficulties with market quotations as a standard for the valuation of bank assets. First, market prices at any given moment may be a very unreliable index of the long-run value of particular securities. One has only to consider the excessively high quotations recorded in 1929 and the excessively low quotations recorded in 1932 to recognize the disadvantages of relying on market value as the basis for appraising bank investments. Second, market price, far from providing an independent standard of valuation, may be partly determined by the policies of the bank examiners themselves. In the period after 1929, a decline in security prices was the signal for a writing down of assets and a forced liquidation of securities. The sale of securities in a market which was already weak contributed to further declines—and with every decline there was further liquidation. Thus reliance on market quotations for the valuation of assets was perfectly calculated to contribute to a downward spiral of security prices and a continuation of forced liquidations.

To rely at all times on current market quotations as a measure of asset values for the purpose of bank examination would be to aggravate both upward and downward swings in the market. Obviously, bank examination procedures should never be such as to contribute to disorderly market conditions or to impose unnecessary strains on other banks. A bank which has developed dangerous weaknesses should, of course, be taken in hand to prevent its endangering others or adding to its own losses. But it is dan-

---

4. Cf. Homer Jones, "An Appraisal of Rules and Procedures of Bank Examination," *Journal of Political Economy*, April 1940.

gerous to assume that "sound banks make a sound banking system."[5] Examination policy should be directed at all times toward preserving the credit structure as a working whole. It is a mistake to suppose that this can be accomplished by considering the individual bank alone without regard to the effect of procedures followed, when compounded throughout the nation, upon markets and the banking system in their entirety.

Nor does emphasis on the "intrinsic" value of assets, as contrasted with market price, provide a much more reliable basis of valuation. Value is not an intrinsic or inherent quality. It is a resultant of the complex of choices which enter into supply and demand, a product of the psychological reactions of human beings.

Changes in business conditions, inventions, discoveries, and many other factors may alter the bases on which those choices, i.e., those psychological reactions, rest. Reference to "intrinsic" value, far from providing an objective standard of valuation, does no more than express in a different form someone's personal appraisal of the factors entering into the determination of the value of securities. While it places emphasis on long-run considerations to a greater extent than market quotations, it still is strongly subject to personal impressions and passing influences.

Bank examination is primarily concerned with the ultimate safety of assets. The mistake of bank examination procedure in the 1930's was to apply short-run tests, such as market valuation, not to the short-run problem of liquidity to which they were adapted, but to the long-run problem of safety for which they were not suitable. The goal of examination policy should be to accommodate procedures to the particular problems, short run or long run, which are paramount and to which they are suited.

ROLE OF THE GOVERNMENT IN FINANCIAL STABILITY

Along with an extension of the relationships existing between government and banking has gone an increase in the dependence of our entire financial system upon government. As matters now stand, the government and agencies of the government are deeply committed to assuring that safety and stability for the banking system and for the economy generally are fully maintained. The chief agencies for safeguarding the nation's financial stability are the Federal Deposit Insurance Corporation, the Federal Reserve System, and the Treasury.

The Federal Deposit Insurance Corporation

Establishment of the FDIC was the Roosevelt Administration's answer to the problem of bank failures which had plagued the country for a

---

5. Board of Governors, *Banking Studies* (Washington: 1941), p. 213.

dozen years. The Corporation was set up with a three-man board of directors consisting of the Comptroller of the Currency and two members appointed by the President for six-year terms. Capital was provided jointly by the Treasury and the Federal Reserve Banks but was later returned to them out of earnings accumulated by the Corporation. All Federal Reserve member banks were required to join the FDIC, and all but a small number of the non-member commercial banks ultimately chose to do so. Insured commercial banks constitute 98 per cent of all operating commercial banks and hold well over 99 per cent of all commercial bank deposits.

Deposits are fully insured up to a maximum of $10,000 for each depositor. All deposits of insured banks are subject to an assessment of $\frac{1}{12}$ per cent a year. In view of the small losses incurred, it is now the practice to credit a large part of current assessments as a rebate on the next year's assessment. This procedure allows the traditional rate to be maintained for the sake of possible future need, while giving members the benefit of favorable current operating experience.

In case of failure the FDIC makes insured deposits immediately available, ordinarily in the form of deposits in some other bank in the vicinity. The Corporation directs its efforts primarily to preventing failures rather than taking care of depositors after failure. To this end it undertakes to bring about the merger of banks in weakened condition with other stronger banks. (Needless to say, most bank mergers are not of this character.)

The operating record of the Federal Deposit Insurance Corporation has been extraordinarily good—a fact to which the long period of business prosperity naturally contributed. From 1934 through 1960 disbursements by the Corporation amounting to $353 million were required for 440 banks. Recoveries are estimated to have reduced the actual loss to the Corporation to less than 10 per cent of the amount of disbursements.

In addition to taking charge of the affairs of failed banks, facilitating mergers, and the like, the FDIC shares in the task of examining and supervising the country's banks. Among other duties, it regulates the rate of interest paid on time deposits of insured nonmember banks.

At the inception of the FDIC, it was criticized as violating recognized principles of insurance, since the rate of assessment is not scaled to the apparent risk of loss among those insured and assessments are paid on deposits in excess of $10,000 even though they are not accorded protection. It was argued that the protection afforded depositors would make it unnecessary for banks to maintain high standards in order to attract business, thereby encouraging lax banking methods. In the course of time, opposition gradually died out, and today no serious complaint is heard, though recommendations are occasionally made for a reduction in the rate of assessment. The FDIC has become a prized and permanent feature of the country's financial structure.

The Federal Reserve and the Treasury

In a sense, the Federal Reserve Banks have become the "ultimate shiftee" for a significant proportion of banking assets. When member banks borrow from the Federal Reserve they typically do so by posting Treasury obligations as collateral, and these securities are accepted at par value. The banking system derives an important element of liquidity from the possibility of borrowing at the Federal Reserve. While the securities are not actually sold to the Federal Reserve in such a transaction, the position of net supplier of credit is, in fact, shifted from the borrowing bank to the Federal Reserve.

At one time, discussion of commercial banking operations proceeded from the assumption that financial markets were governed by the free play of supply and demand, independent of actual or potential intervention by governmental authorities. Establishment of the Federal Reserve and the gradual extension of its powers provided an important additional force in the market. And during the Great Depression legislation was enacted authorizing the Federal Reserve to lend on all types of collateral.

In the period before the Treasury-Federal Reserve Accord the assumption of non-intervention became absurdly unrealistic: the market for Treasury obligations, by that time held in large amounts by the banks, was pretty much what the Federal Reserve made it. Even when the rigidity of Federal Reserve support was greatly relaxed, the possibility of intervention in time of crisis was retained. Moreover, the Federal Reserve continued to lend at par on government securities. With the abandonment of the "bills-only policy" in 1962 the way was open again for the Federal Reserve to move fairly freely in the government bond market.

Federal Reserve policy toward the money market, it is clear, has followed an undulating course. But neither in the United States nor in any other modern country can a market free of potential intervention by the central bank be said to exist any longer. There can be no serious doubt that in the event of a major crisis the Federal Reserve would lend the full weight of its support to banks and the money market.

Finally, the United States Treasury has come to occupy a place of prime importance in financial affairs. As long ago as in its annual report for 1938 the Board of Governors declared that "the Treasury's powers to influence member bank reserves outweigh those possessed by the Federal Reserve System." At the time, this was a reflection of the diminished effectiveness of Federal Reserve instruments of control, no less than of the expanded power of the Treasury. Since then the effectiveness of Federal Reserve policy has been restored without the power of the Treasury, in any ultimate sense, having been reduced. Moreover, in addition to the part played by the Treasury through fiscal operations and debt management, the various lending agencies of the government are an important supporting factor, and one capable of great expansion in time of emergency.

In its role of lender of last resort the central bank has long been recognized as defender of the banking system's financial position. In a significant sense this aspect of the Federal Reserve's responsibilities has tended to grow less in recent years. For one thing, the economy is more stable than formerly and therefore the danger of severe financial crises is less serious. For another, the banking system is far stronger, partly because significant changes have taken place within the system and partly, it is to be supposed, because the procedures of regulation and examination are more enlightened. Finally, the power of the Federal Reserve to assist in withstanding adverse financial conditions is supplemented and re-enforced by a strong array of other governmental powers and instrumentalities.

SELECTED BIBLIOGRAPHY

BACH, G. L., *Federal Reserve Policy-Making.* New York: Knopf, 1950, Chapters VI, X and XV.

BOARD OF GOVERNORS OF THE FEDERAL RESERVE SYSTEM, *Banking Studies.* Washington: 1941, pp. 189-227.

HASTINGS, DELBERT C., AND ROSS M. ROBERTSON, "The Mysterious World of the FED," *Business Horizons* (Spring 1962), pp. 97-104.

JOINT COMMITTEE ON THE ECONOMIC REPORT, *Monetary Policy and the Management of the Public Debt.* S. Doc. No. 123, Part 2, 82nd Congress, 2nd Session. Washington: 1952, pp. 825-835, 898-910, 947-956, 967-1010.

JONES, HOMER, "An Appraisal of Rules and Procedures of Bank Examination," *Journal of Political Economy* (April 1940), pp. 183-198.

SHAW, E. S., *Money, Income, and Monetary Policy.* Homewood, Ill.: Irwin, 1950, Chapter V.

27

STRUCTURAL CHANGE AND REGULATORY POLICY

Previous chapters have traced the historical antecedents of the American banking system, the origin and development of the Federal Reserve System, and other significant institutional and legislative changes. The purpose of the present chapter is to depict the evolution of American banking as a continuous process which, while differing greatly in its successive stages, is still going on. We shall be concerned primarily with two aspects of this development, relating, respectively, to matters of structure and to the regulation of structural change.

THE CHANGING STRUCTURE OF COMMERCIAL BANKING

During the second half of the nineteenth century the number of banks in the United States grew more or less continuously with only occasional interruptions chiefly in the 1870's and 1890's. The rate of increase rose sharply after 1900 and by 1921 the total was approximately three times what it was at the turn of the century. Thereafter, and most rapidly from the start of the depression in 1929 to the closing of the banks in 1933, the number of banks declined (see Figure 27-1). By 1933 there were less than half as many banks as in 1921. The decline in number of independent banks—though not in number of banking offices—has continued to the present time. But the causes and the consequences of the movements before and after 1934, as will be seen below, were very different.

Bank Contraction, 1921-1933

The decrease in number of banks was brought about by mergers, consolidations, and, above all, failures. The record of bank failures during

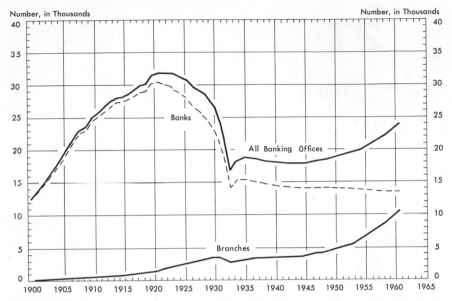

Figure 27-1.   Commercial Banking Offices in the United States, 1900-1961.

Source: Board of Governors of the Federal Reserve System.

the period from 1921 to 1933 is without parallel in this or any other country (see Figure 27-2). In the state of Florida more banks failed from 1921 to 1933 than were in existence in 1921, and the experience in many other states was hardly less calamitous. What is likely to seem strangest of all is that so many failures occurred during the 1920's, which is generally regarded as one of the most prosperous decades of our history. Nearly a thousand banks failed in 1926 alone and the total for the nine years 1921-29 was 5,411, or an average of approximately 600 a year.

A number of factors account for the bank failures of these years. First, the rise in agricultural prices and land values in the years after the depression of the 1890's stimulated a great influx of banks, with the result that in many communities, particularly in rural areas, there was an oversupply of banks—and, no less certainly, an undersupply of competent bankers. Second, the rapid improvement of transportation through the everyday use of the automobile brought the banks in rural areas into competition with stronger banks in larger towns and cities, making survival of the smaller, undiversified banks difficult. Finally, at the end of the postwar boom a great many banks found themselves overextended with loans made at a time when prices of agricultural products and farm real estate were extremely high. The collapse and subsequent further decline of these prices dissipated the values on which bankers had relied—altogether too optimistically, of course—for protection of their loans.

Changes in the number of banks are only one indication, and a somewhat misleading one, of the course of banking developments during these years. Figures of deposits and bank assets provide a very different picture. For many banks these were years of great prosperity. The growth in the average size of banks far more than offset the decrease in number of banks from 1921 to 1929. The total of bank assets increased over 40 per cent in these years despite a decline of 18 per cent in their numbers.

With the onset of the depression in 1929 the growth of deposits and bank assets was sharply reversed, and the shrinkage in number of banks was accelerated. The worsening of the general financial situation was reflected

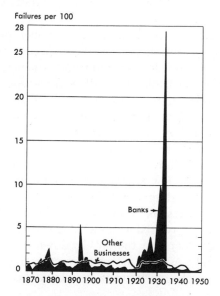

Figure 27-2. Bank and Other Business
Failures, 1867-1950.

Source: House Committee on the Judiciary,
Bank Mergers and Concentration of
Banking Facilities, 1952, p. 13.

in a decline in combined net profits of all banks in 1930 to little more than half what they were a year before. In 1931 net profits for banks as a whole all but disappeared. By that time, the principal concern of bankers was not the lack of earnings but the deterioration in quality of assets through defaults on loans and shrinkage in the market value of investments. The immediate problem was one of survival.

Banks whose difficulties became known to the public were subjected to heavy withdrawals. Forced liquidation of assets contributed to further declines in market values—thereby adding to the financial embarrassment of both banks and their customers. There was a sharp increase in the rate of bank suspensions, and the dumping of assets of failed banks exerted still another depressing influence. A decline in the number of bank failures in 1932 led the philosopher-humorist, Will Rogers, to remark that the apparent improvement did not really mean that things were getting better but just that we were running out of banks.

In the earlier years of the depression, banks in the large centers were the recipients of a flight of capital to banks believed to be stronger. The wave of cash withdrawals early in 1933, however, resulted in a liquidity crisis whose chief impact was upon banks in New York. Reserves of member banks in New York City were reduced drastically despite a large increase in borrowing at the Federal Reserve Bank. The greater pressure on New York banks was largely accounted for by the heavy withdrawals of correspondents' balances.

As the crisis spread the governors of a number of states declared a suspension of banking operations within the respective states. Then, in the opening hours of the Roosevelt Administration, a general Banking Holiday was announced. When the banks were allowed to reopen a few days later roughly a quarter found it impossible or inexpedient to do so, though several hundred of these managed to start up again within the next year or so. It is this combination of events that is depicted in the sharp downturn and slight recovery in number of banks shown in Figure 27-1.

The causes mentioned above as contributing to the 1921-29 contraction in number of banks were not without their influence on the even more rapid contraction in succeeding years. The main contributing factor, however, was the Great Depression. A falling level of deposits and bank assets was the painful corollary—related as both cause and effect—of the declining volume of national product and the steady downward pressure on prices. Not less damaging, and similarly mutually re-enforcing, was the deterioration of the psychological environment in which the credit operations of banks were carried on.

From 1921 to 1933, 21,396 banks ceased business and 6,210 banks began operations, for a net reduction of 15,186 banks. The decline in number of banks resulted mainly from suspensions and absorptions with suspensions outnumbering absorptions (which embrace mergers and consolidations) by more than two to one. Of the absorptions, a large proportion occurred as an alternative to failure or voluntary liquidation, a "life-saving job," as one writer called it. Some of the failed banks were subsequently taken over by other banks.

Structural Changes Since 1933: The Branch Banking and Merger Movements

Changes in the banking structure since 1933 have been of a very different character from those of preceding years. For one thing, the number of bank failures fell sharply in 1934 and diminished further in succeeding years. After 1942 the number of suspensions never exceeded nine in one year and in some years was as low as one or two. Most of the failures after

1933 represented a delayed response to the ravages of the depression years, although approximately a quarter were attributed to financial irregularities.[1]

A second major contrast between the period after 1933 and the preceding decade was the steady increase in the number of banking offices (but not number of banks) in the later period, as compared with the substantial decline in number of banking offices in the earlier years (cf. Figure 27-1). From 1921 through the end of 1933 there was a 45 per cent decline in the number of banking offices, while from the end of 1933 to the close of 1961 there was a 42 per cent increase in number of banking offices.

A third principal difference between structural change in banking before and after 1933 was the rapid expansion in importance of branch banking in the later period.

The growth of branch banking. Branch banking was of negligible importance in the United States at the turn of the century: there were only 119 branch offices, accounting for less than 1 per cent of total commercial banking offices. The establishment of branch offices was prohibited in a great many states. The California Banking Act of 1909, which opened the way for the expansion of the Bank of America (then called the Bank of Italy), was a landmark in the relaxing of legislative and regulatory restraints on branch banking. This process was accelerated by the high rate of bank failures in the 1920's and 1930's, which aroused widespread doubts as to the soundness of our banking structure and also created pressures for permitting the establishment of branches in areas deprived of bank facilities by failures.

By 1921 there were 1,455 branch offices, accounting for somewhat less than 5 per cent of the total number of commercial banking offices in the United States. By the end of 1933 there were 2,784 branch offices or 16 per cent of the reduced total of banking offices. By 1962 the number of branches had risen to over 11,000, or approximately 45 per cent of the total of commercial banking offices in the United States. The rapid increase in number of branches and the continued slow decline in number of banks after 1950 may be seen on Figure 27-1.

The increase in the relative importance of branch banking after 1933 reflects both a significant shift in the pattern of entry into banking and a steady process of merger and conversion of unit banks into branch offices. The organization of new banks fell to low levels in the 1930's and during World War II. After World War II, however, there was a vigorous reactivation of entry into banking, particularly after 1953. At the same time entry underwent a significant change in character, with *de novo* branches becoming predominant in the creation of new facilities and the establishment of new banks reduced again to a point where it failed to replace banks disappearing via combination or liquidation. It may be seen from Table 27-1

1. FDIC, *Annual Report for 1960*, p. 37.

TABLE 27-1. Major Structural Changes Affecting the Number of Commercial Bank Offices, 1938-1961

Year	New Banks	De Novo Branches	Consolida- tions and Absorptions	Suspensions	Voluntary Liquida- tions	Net Change No. of Banks	No. of Branches
1938	39	49	100	52	68	−179	+ 33
1939	30	47	119	41	37	−167	+ 45
1940	32	43	96	22	49	−133	+ 35
1941	53	51	59	8	40	− 54	+ 33
1942	22	28	89	9	69	−144	+ 5
1943	49	22	86	4	61	−102	+ 3
1944	69	37	72	1	35	− 39	+ 53
1945	118	65	79	—	18	+ 21	+ 91
1946	144	142	93	—	16	+ 33	+179
1947	111	146	84	1	11	+137*	+188*
1948	80	151	75	—	12	− 10	+189
1949	72	158	77	4	12	− 15	+206
1950	68	179	91	1	12	− 35	+236
1951	62	234	82	3	11	− 32	+273
1952	73	217	100	3	13	− 43	+280
1953	64	280	115	4	10	− 65	+353
1954	73	341	206	3	7	−141	+481
1955	116	442	231	4	5	−124	+602
1956	123	522	189	3	7	− 76	+652
1957	87	501	157	3	3	− 74	+606
1958	97	540	151	8	5	− 67	+645
1959	117	584	166	3	3	− 27	+775
1960	135	771	131	2	4	− 2	+828
1961	112	788	139	9	5	− 40	+861

* Includes 115 banks and 9 branches added because of revision in statistical series.

Sources: Adapted from *Monetary Policy and the Management of the Public Debt,* 1 (1952), p. 556; *Federal Reserve Bulletins.*

that in the period 1945-47 there was a net increase in the number of banks in the system. However, immediately thereafter the decline in unit banking was again renewed as a result of increased merger activity and a significant reduction in the relative importance of unit bank creation in the provision of new banking facilities. In 1946 the number of new banks and branches was approximately equal; in the early 1960's this ratio was running at about one to six. Branch banks have taken over the function of providing new banking facilities, and the establishment of new unit banks has not been sufficiently important in the recent banking expansion to prevent a net decline in the number of banks in each year after 1947.

Bank mergers. Mergers were the main source of the fairly steady decline in number of banks after 1933, in contrast with suspensions in the preceding decade. Between the end of World War II and 1962 over 2,000 banks disappeared as a result of consolidations and absorptions.[2] The pace of merger activity reached a peak in the mid 1950's, declining somewhat thereafter though remaining at levels above those of the 1940's. The further

---

2. The net reduction, of course, was much less.

decline in the early 1960's was attributable in part to the effects of the Bank Merger Act of 1960 and to a series of antitrust actions taken by the Department of Justice against bank mergers.

Merger activity after World War II was influenced by a variety of factors:

1. *The desire to expand capital and resources in order to be able to handle loans of larger size.*

The growth of the economy during the postwar period brought with it an increase in the size of business borrowers, partly as a result of internal growth and partly through combination. Most banks are limited in the amount of unsecured loans that they may make to a single borrower to 10 per cent of the bank's capital and surplus. This fact has exerted pressure to increase the size of capital accounts in order not to lose rapidly growing customers to other financial institutions able to handle their needs. Mergers have been an important means of increasing the size of bank capital.[3]

2. *The desire to adapt facilities to shifts in the location of population and business activity.*

The postwar period witnessed a major shift of both residences and business activities to the suburbs of major cities. The suburban residential trend has been in evidence for several decades; the novel feature of the postwar movement was the extent of the shift of trade and industry to outlying locations. The branch banking and merger movement of the postwar period reflected the effort of banks to follow their customers into the suburbs.

3. *The inducements of rising costs and economies of scale.*

Bank operating costs per dollar of assets rose steadily during the postwar period. The result was continued pressure on banks to find ways of improving efficiency. One manifestation of this pressure was the rapidly expanding application of computers and other automatic equipment to bank operations. Bank mergers were another.

There appear to be economies of large-scale operation in the banking business, although it may be doubted that these are indefinitely extensible with the growth in bank size.[4] The volume of business done by large banks enables them to employ high calibre administrative and technical personnel

---

3. The alternative of issuing new stock has generally not been regarded as in the interests of shareholders and is used sparingly. Bank earnings have been sustained by the maintenance of high ratios of debt to capital (high "leverage") by banks. Funds obtained by the issuance of additional shares of stock, it may be noted, would be redistributed to other banks the same as additional reserves acquired from any other source. With the funds obtained from raising $1 million of new capital, therefore, a bank could expand earning assets by only $1 million, even though its deposit-capital ratio was 15/1. Thus the earnings that would be derived from the added loans would not suffice to maintain the previously existing rate of return on shareholder investment.

4. Cf. David A. Alhadeff, *Monopoly and Competition in Banking* (Berkeley; University of California Press, 1954), Chapter VI; Lyle E. Gramley, *A Study of Scale Economies in Banking* (Federal Reserve Bank of Kansas City: 1962).

whose services may be economical despite their high money price because they can be more fully utilized in important activities. Specialization permits reduction in the unit cost of security and credit analysis, collateral supervision, public relations, law, research, personnel work, and other services. Economies of this kind mean that the ratio of expenses to assets may be reduced through merger. This assumes, of course, that there are no offsetting diseconomies of merger (the expenses of the merger itself, or losses of deposits of disaffected customers, for example) and that the merging institutions are not already so large as to have largely exhausted economies of scale.

4. *The desire to diversify bank operations.*

Safety may be enhanced by spreading a bank's activity geographically, by type of loan and borrower, or by type of business activity engaged in (lending, trust business, foreign exchange, etc.). This has generally been considered one of the stronger arguments in favor of large-area branch banking: a bank with widely dispersed branch offices is more likely to obtain a diversified loan portfolio in the servicing of its natural customers. Even if each office lends only locally, the branch system as a whole will obtain diversification roughly proportional to the size and dispersion of activity of the areas covered by the bank. Unfavorable cyclical or secular changes in the growth of specific industries and areas need not cause failures because they may be offset by favorable developments in other industries and areas served by the bank. This seems to have been the case in England prior to 1929, when several large banks were able to absorb serious losses in Lancashire caused by a severe decline in the cotton textile industry. In contrast, the agricultural depression of the 1920's spelled the ruin of numerous rural banks in the United States.[5]

Diversification may also be a product of marketing strategy. It is relatively easy for banks to sell the wide variety of financial services, such as foreign exchange and trustee services, that are demanded along with loan and deposit facilities. By offering these services banks also may be able to compete more successfully in obtaining loan and deposit business. Moreover, the speediest way of getting into, say, the trust business, is to absorb a bank with a well-established trust department.

5. *Pressure on the reserves of large urban banks.*

Under the conditions of increasingly tight money during the 1950's there was an increase in pressure on the reserves of commercial banks, particularly for larger banks in the urban centers. In general, the larger banks devoted a larger fraction of their assets to loans than did small institutions. The absorption of smaller banks by large urban institutions tended to facilitate increased

---

5. An even more enlightening comparison is afforded by the record of branch banking in Canada. In the United States, bank failures were particularly common in the agricultural sections of the West with their specialized, less developed economies and relatively sparse population. Notwithstanding even less favorable conditions, Canada with its nationwide branch banks experienced not a single failure after 1923.

lending by the big banks because of both an improved reserve position and a lower ratio of loans to assets.

6. *The low valuation of bank stocks.*

For many years before the 1960's it was common for bank shares to sell on the market at prices considerably below their liquidating value, i.e., the net value of the assets represented by the shares. (Such a company is sometimes said to be worth more dead than alive.) If the owner of bank stock were to attempt to sell in the open market, the most he could hope to get would be the current market price. Actually, he would probably realize considerably less, since selling in any sizable amount, in view of the thinness of the market, would force the price downward. If the bank were to be absorbed by another bank, on the other hand, shares would probably be valued at a price much closer to their liquidating value or even above it. This provided a continuing inducement to owners of large blocks of bank shares to sell out to a bank interested in expansion.

7. *The problem of management succession.*

A reason frequently given by absorbed banks for participation in mergers is the absence of adequate successor management. For years a major concern of many small banks in the United States has been the unattractiveness of salaries in such banks to capable young people. Consequently, as existing officers approached retirement age, there has often been no satisfactory management group groomed to take over the bank. Under these circumstances merger may be an attractive alternative, particularly as merger through an exchange of securities need not give rise to an income or capital gains tax and may make it possible for older officers to increase the liquidity of their estates.

8. *Special inducements to officers.*

Where banks are closely held by officers, premiums on their investment, accompanied by the lure of higher salaries and fringe benefits, have often combined to make them susceptible to offers from larger banks seeking to expand in suburban areas. At the same time, officers of the absorbing institutions may be influenced by the possible increase in salary and prestige associated with the enlargement of their institutions.

9. *Defensive expansion.*

In markets where there are a few dominant firms it is common for actions by one firm to induce defensive actions by its rivals to protect their relative position in the market. As we have seen, the dispersion of population and business activity into outlying regions provided strong inducements to urban banks to move into the suburbs. The move by one bank commonly led to competitive and defensive responses by big city rivals. The result frequently was merger activity carried considerably beyond what would have prevailed without such defensive reactions.

10. *Other factors.*

Merger activity in banking has been encouraged by various other considerations. Among these are the desire to eliminate competition, the spirit of empire building, and the threat of failure for such reasons as embezzlement, inadequate business volume, and unsatisfactory management.

Competition in Banking

The most familiar arguments against bank mergers and the spread of branch banking have stressed their effects on banking competition. If it could be demonstrated that specific mergers, or branch banking and merger activity in general, had a substantial adverse effect on competition so that the number of borrowers who were excluded from banking facilities or exploited was significantly larger than under a less concentrated banking structure, this would be an important and perhaps compelling consideration in their evaluation. This might be easy to demonstrate if we could assume, as is often done, that a unit banking system (one in which each bank controlled only one banking office) such as prevailed in earlier years was purely competitive and that only branch banking and merger activity resulted in conditions of fewness and monopoly power. Such a premise would be extremely dubious however, since banks usually compete only locally for the bulk of their loans and checking accounts.

In the late 1950's, for example, 6,597 or 57 per cent of all unit banks in the United States were located in communities with only a single banking office, 84 per cent were in centers with only one or two banking offices, and only 5 per cent operated in communities with more than eight banking offices.[6] Even allowing for the frequent overlap of banking markets it is difficult to avoid the conclusion from these data that fewness is characteristic of unit banking as well as branch banking.

Conditions of fewness, which have long been characteristic of most banking markets, has often made collusion practicable, and in some areas, "as one banker has happily stated, 'competition is now carried on among banks in a fine spirit of cooperation.' "[7] The nature and effectiveness of competition among banks has also been influenced by borrower ignorance of alternatives, banker distrust of borrowers shopping around, the secrecy surrounding the terms of loan contracts, the personal relationship between banker and borrower and the frequently long-term character of this relationship, and other considerations which make the product of the bank distinctive in the minds of bank customers. These characteristics have restricted the role of price as a competitive factor in the banking business; competition among banks has mainly assumed such non-price forms as advertising and the provision of special services. Thus banking markets are typically markets in which competition is limited in various ways, although it is rarely absent altogether.

---

6. FDIC, *Annual Report for 1957*, p. 96.
7. Lester V. Chandler, "Monopolistic Elements in Commercial Banking," *Journal of Political Economy* (1938), p. 22.

Given the imperfections of banking markets, it is clear that a shift from unit to branch banking, or a reduction in numbers by merger, is not a simple shift from competitive to monopolistic banking. It usually involves a decline in numbers in markets already characterized by significant elements of monopoly power and non-competitive behavior (particularly the limited application of price competition). Moreover, the reduction in numbers may go hand in hand with a transformation in the character of firm operating in banking markets: it may permit the growth of more efficient, diversified, and vigorously business oriented enterprises whose aggressiveness may enhance competition. The evidence is inconclusive, but bank behavior and performance under conditions of fairly concentrated branch organization has not shown itself to be less competitive than under unit banking.

It is not to be inferred from this that concentration cannot be carried to a point which seriously reduces the effectiveness of bank competition. This is particularly relevant when considering increases in concentration in the major urban markets: extremes of fewness have generally characterized rural areas and small towns, so that the encroachment of branch banking in these areas has tended to invigorate competition, but vigorous competition and substantial numbers of alternatives have frequently been encountered in metropolitan areas. Merger activity since the end of World War II has significantly reduced bank numbers and increased concentration in these areas of substantial competition.

In almost all major metropolitan areas concentration is higher than in 1920, although in many cases the post-World War II increases in concentration have not pushed the level of concentration to the extremes of 1934 (which was very much influenced by the failures of the previous period and the distrust of small banks in time of crisis). Whether or not banking concentration is higher than it was in the depths of the Great Depression, the fact is that the merger activity of the postwar period has been increasing concentration and reducing the number of alternatives in major banking markets. The potential which this holds for reducing competition in banking is re-enforced by the retardation in the rate of entry of new banks into the banking business. On the other hand, the improvements in communication and transport, the greater strength and vigor of many individual banks, and the growth of competitive financial institutions have offset to some degree the effects of increased concentration on competition in specific localities. There is no serious evidence that concentration since 1920 or 1945 has adversely affected competition in the banking business at large. The levels of concentration attained in urban markets, however, frequently represent substantial increases over past levels, and involve impressive aggregations of economic power (see Table 27-2). In some instances these increases in concentration may have weakened the effectiveness of banking competition.

TABLE 27-2. Concentration of Commercial Bank Deposits in 25 Metropolitan Areas, December 31, 1958.

Principal City in Metropolitan Area	Percentage of all Deposits Held by the Largest Bank or Group	Percentage of all Deposits Held by the Largest Five Banks or Groups
Birmingham, Alabama	62.1	98.8
Pittsburgh, Pennsylvania	53.1	85.8
Boston, Massachusetts	52.2	91.6
Columbus, Ohio	52.1	95.3
Buffalo, New York	48.8	95.2
Omaha, Nebraska	47.4	94.5
Rochester, New York	46.0	99.6
Minneapolis-St. Paul, Minnesota	45.3	92.2
Atlanta, Georgia	44.6	92.5
Oklahoma City, Oklahoma	44.5	83.3
Cleveland, Ohio	44.4	97.3
Milwaukee, Wisconsin	43.5	77.0
Indianapolis, Indiana	41.7	99.5
New Orleans, Louisiana	41.6	99.7
Detroit, Michigan	41.2	89.4
Richmond, Virginia	35.3	94.9
Dallas, Texas	34.8	87.8
Cincinnati, Ohio	33.0	94.9
Washington, D. C.	32.4	85.0
Kansas City, Missouri	29.7	73.9
Miami, Florida	27.5	55.1
Philadelphia, Pa.	25.1	85.1
Chicago, Illinois	22.5	59.1
New York, New York	20.5	65.8

Source: Federal Deposit Insurance Corporation, *Annual Report for 1960.*

THE REGULATION OF BANKING STRUCTURE

Changes in the structure of banking have long been subject to extensive public control through state and federal laws and regulation by the bank supervisory authorities.

Entry into Banking

Entry into the banking business is subject to minimum capital requirements fixed by law and is also contingent on the ability of promoters to obtain a charter from the relevant state supervisory authority or the Comptroller of the Currency. The standards applied by the chartering authorities and the legal criteria controlling these standards are consequently of considerable importance in determining whether entry into banking is easy or difficult.

Minimum capital requirements for entry into banking in the United States are established by state and federal banking laws and are commonly scaled to the population of the community in which the proposed banking office is to be located. Banks chartered under the authority of the federal government (national banks) must have capital of at least $50,000 if located in communities with a population of 6,000 or less; $100,000 if located in communities with a population of over 6,000 but not greater than 50,000; and $200,-000 where the bank is organized in a city with a population greater than 50,000. State banks are usually subject to similar capital requirements.

These legal minimum requirements understate to some extent the capital required for entry into banking. Cost and other advantages associated with large-scale operation in the banking business may deter entry at the legal minimum, and sometimes supervisory authorities will not permit entry without an initial capital investment substantially in excess of the minimum. Where entry is achieved at the minimum capital level the economies of size may compel rapid growth as a condition of survival.

During the period just before World War I, the Comptroller of the Currency acted favorably on over 90 per cent of the applications for bank charters submitted to him. The agricultural depression of the 1920's, the great depression of the 1930's, and the accompanying wave of bank failures led to a reassessment and reversal of the prewar trend of chartering policy.[8] During the 1920's the proportion of charters granted to applications submitted to the Comptroller sometimes fell below one-half, and in the 1930's charters were granted even more sparingly. Between 1941 and 1950 the Comptroller of the Currency approved 53 per cent of the applications submitted for permission to organize new national banks and 71 per cent of all branch applications.[9] Similar percentages applied in more recent years.

Prior to the banking legislation of the 1930's, the Comptroller in deciding on an application for a national bank charter was merely required to investigate whether the petitioning association "has complied with all the provisions of this Title required to entitle it to engage in the business of banking, . . . [and whether] the shareholders have formed the same for any other than the legitimate objects contemplated by this Title."[10] By legislation enacted following the bank holiday a national bank becomes insured from the time it is authorized to commence business, and the Comptroller is required to certify to the Federal Deposit Insurance Corporation that, in authorizing a new bank to commence operations, consideration has been given to "The financial history and condition of the bank, the adequacy of its capital structure, its future earnings prospects, the general character of its management, the convenience and needs of the community to be served by the bank, and whether or not its corporate powers are consistent with the purposes of this Act."[11]

These are highly generalized criteria and leave considerable latitude to

8. "Out of the harsh experiences of the banking troubles leading up to the bank holiday of 1933 . . . has come the realization that charters should be granted much less freely." Board of Governors, *Banking Studies* (Washington: 1941), p. 198.
9. *Monetary Policy and the Management of the Public Debt,* II (1952), pp. 929-30.
10. U.S.C., Title 12, Secs. 26-27.
11. Federal Deposit Insurance Act, Sec. 6.

administrative authority. The position of the Comptroller's office has been that "there can be no hard and fast rule in deciding upon the merits of new bank applications because of the variety of factors which must be considered in individual cases, which vary greatly in different communities. . . . It is therefore the Comptroller's policy to weigh all pertinent information developed in relation to each individual case with the view of determining whether the needs of the community for, and the prospects of successful operation of, the proposed bank under the management selected are such as to warrant favorable action on the application."[12]

Where the granting of a charter for a new banking office will increase competitive pressures on existing institutions, Comptrollers of the Currency have taken the position that this is desirable as long as it does not "jeopardize" existing institutions. The rejection of applications for charters for new national banks or permission to establish new branches has been based primarily on the estimate by the Comptroller's office that it was not "clear-cut that the community or area generates a volume of banking business amply adequate to support the existing banks and branches plus the proposed branch . . ."[13]

In dealing with applications for charters for new banks and branches, state supervisory authorities in general have also "placed greatest emphasis on prospects for profitable operation. When such prospects existed, the other factors which had to be taken into account were public convenience, the quality of management, and the competitive situation—the last in the dual sense of avoiding too much competition (i.e., enough to threaten the profitability of existing institutions) and to introduce some competition when little or none existed. There was a general anxiety to avoid the 'over-banked' condition which existed in the twenties."[14]

In sum, entry into the banking business is more difficult now than in the period before 1920. Organizational changes and competitive pressures have increased the minimum scale necessary for successful operation, and legal obstacles have contributed to a reduction in ease of entry.

The Regulation of Branch Banking

The establishment of branch offices is subject mainly to state law; federal banking legislation has largely accommodated itself to state regulation. The opening of a branch office by an insured commercial bank requires the approval of some federal authority, and uninsured banks must obtain the sanction of the appropriate state authority. The National Banking Act of 1863 said nothing about the establishment of branch offices, and for many

---

12. *Monetary Policy and the Management of the Public Debt,* II (1952), pp. 928-9.
13. Letter from Comptroller Gidney to Dr. E. Gordon Keith, dated November 8, 1956, p. 3.
14. *Monetary Policy and the Management of the Public Debt,* II (1952), p. 989.

years the Act was interpreted as prohibiting them. This attitude was modified early in this century and branching powers were increasingly granted to national banks. In 1927 the McFadden-Pepper Act granted national banks further rights to establish branches, although these were modeled after and were somewhat more restrictive than the powers granted banks subject to the authority of the individual states. The Banking Act of 1935 extended the branching rights of member banks to approximately the level permitted nonmembers by the individual states.

State branch banking laws vary widely, and still impose substantial restraints on the growth of branch banking, although by and large the restrictiveness of these laws has been considerably reduced in the present century. The relaxation of the restrictions on branches was largely due to the numerous bank failures after 1921 and the pressures for permitting the establishment of branch offices in locations where banking facilities would not otherwise be provided.

At present sixteen states permit the establishment of branches throughout the entire state, twenty permit limited area branch banking, eleven prohibit branch banking, and three have no legislation on the subject. Limited area branch banking includes instances where the law permits branch offices within the same city and county as the head office (e.g., Alabama, Indiana, and New Jersey); several where branches are permitted in the county of the head office and in counties contiguous thereto (as in Pennsylvania); several where branches may be established within a hundred mile radius of the head office (Alaska and Mississippi); and other types of restriction. Branch banking laws may limit branches according to the total number of branches, population, capital of the branch bank, whether the branch is established *de novo* or following a merger, and other criteria.

The recent rapid growth of branch banking in the United States was described earlier. The growth in importance of the *de novo* branch as compared to the *de novo* bank in the provision of new banking facilities and the history of unit banking in other countries that have allowed branch banking suggest that the development of branch banking may be a cumulative process which will inevitably engulf and supersede unit banking, at least in the absence of legal discrimination in favor of unit banking. The branch bank appears to possess certain inherent advantages in the provision of new banking facilities. A branch office has the advantage over a *de novo* bank which attaches to an established institution in any field—trained personnel, the know-how essential to efficient operation in the banking business, resources, and an established name. And as a going concern the branch bank is likely to be more alert to opportunities than outsiders; many institutions have staff exclusively devoted to the study of new banking opportunities. Finally, ability to utilize resources more effectively than a comparable group of unit banks may enable a branch bank to establish an office in a location that would be uneconomic for a unit bank. By the time the area matures to a point where a unit bank could be sustained the branch office is well established and the banking opportunity has been pre-empted. Where branch banks are important and aggressive they will tend to take advantage of conditions favorable to new facilities before inducements are sufficient to attract a *de novo* bank. The postwar incentives to growth, combined with some relaxation of obstacles to branch expansion, have thus meant that new facilities have taken the form predominantly of new branches rather than new banks.

The Regulation of Bank Mergers

Bank mergers have always required the approval of bank supervisory authorities, although for many years such sanction was more or less automatic. From 1950 to May 1, 1955, for example, the Comptroller of the Currency approved every one of 376 bank mergers submitted to his office for consideration.[15] There is additional evidence that little weight was given to the competitive effects of bank mergers in the evaluations of bank supervisory authorities. This factor, in combination with the continued rapid pace of merger activity (frequently involving large metropolitan banks), played an important part in the passage of the Bank Merger Act in May 1960.

The Bank Merger Act prohibits an insured bank from combining with another insured bank without the written consent of the Comptroller of the Currency in the case of a national bank, the Board of Governors of the Federal Reserve System in the case of a state member bank, and the FDIC in the case of an insured non-member bank. The appropriate agency is required to give explicit consideration to the effect of the proposed merger on competition in evaluating its net effect on the public interest. And the agencies involved are required (except in cases of threatened failure) to solicit an appraisal of the competitive effects of the proposed merger from the Attorney General. The three agencies are not required to follow the advice of the Attorney General, but they must publish in their annual reports descriptions of approved mergers, the assets involved in each, a resumé of the opinion of the Attorney General, and the grounds for final approval.

The greater attention to competitive factors and the increased publicity required in this area have undoubtedly exercised some restraint on merger activity in banking. This influence has been reinforced by the energetic action of the Department of Justice in the bank merger field in recent years. Although the Bank Merger Act appeared to relegate the Department of Justice to an advisory role, the Department has not hesitated to attack bank mergers independently under the Sherman and Clayton Acts when its advisory opinions were not followed. Its most successful action thus far (which

15. Cf., testimony of Comptroller Gidney, in *Current Antitrust Problems*, Hearings Before the Antitrust Subcommittee, Committee of the Judiciary, U. S. Congress, House, Serial No. 3, Part I (1955), p. 451.

preceded the Act of 1960) resulted from the attempt by the Department of Justice to block the merger of the California Bank of Los Angeles with the First Western Bank & Trust Company, a subsidiary of Firstamerica Corporation. The action, brought under the Sherman and Clayton Acts, was settled by consent under an arrangement whereby California Bank and First Western would be permitted to merge, but within six years would spin off an independent bank with deposits of $500 million and with sixty-five branches extending throughout California. After the spin-off the merged bank would still possess a statewide system of branches and deposits of almost $2 billion. Thus the Department's action contributed to the formation of an additional large statewide branch system in California.

The Department of Justice engaged in a further series of actions to prevent the completion of important bank mergers. These proceedings will have an important bearing on future merger activity and on the role that the Department of Justice will play in the bank merger field.

The Regulation of Bank Holding Companies

Mention may also be made of the regulation of bank holding companies, or what was once called "group banking" systems. Holding company systems in recent years have controlled less than 5 per cent of the number and approximately 8 per cent of the total assets of commercial banks in the United States. These percentages declined slightly following the passage of the Bank Holding Company Act of 1956.

Before 1956 corporations owning controlling interests in commercial banks (excluding other commercial banks, which are usually not permitted to own stock in banks) were subject to only minor regulatory controls by the banking authorities,[16] although the Board of Governors also possessed antitrust powers under Section 7 of the Clayton Act to prevent bank stock acquisitions that would adversely affect competition. After years of effort by the Board of Governors, impelled mainly by the rapid expansion of the Transamerica-Bank of America system, the Bank Holding Company Act of 1956 was enacted. This legislation provided that no bank holding company (defined as any company controlling at least 25 per cent of the stock of each of two banks) could acquire direct or indirect control of 5 or more per cent of the voting shares of a bank without the approval of the Board of

---

16. Under The Banking Act of 1933 bank holding companies were required to apply to the Board for a voting permit to vote the shares of banks they controlled, and companies receiving voting permits were required to submit to periodic examinations by the Board. However, the Act was applicable only where a bank in the holding company group was a member bank of the Federal Reserve System, and where the holding company urgently desired to vote the stock it owned in such bank. There were a number of devices in common use that enabled bank holding companies to maintain control while foregoing the voting of shares. See *Control of Bank Holding Companies,* Hearings on S. 880, S. 2350, and H. R. 6227, before the Senate Committee on Banking and Currency, 84th Cong., 1st Sess. (1955), pp. 55-58.

Governors. In determining whether or not to approve any acquisition under this section, the Board is instructed to take into account the financial condition and prospects of the holding company, the character of the management, the needs and welfare of the communities concerned, and "whether or not the effect of such acquisition or merger or consolidation would be to expand the size or extent of the bank holding company system involved beyond the limits consistent with adequate and sound banking, the public interest, and the preservation of competition in banking." This gave the Board the legal power which it had sought since the early 1940's to restrain the expansion of bank holding companies.

SELECTED BIBLIOGRAPHY

ALHADEFF, D. A., "A Reconsideration of Restrictions on Bank Entry," *Quarterly Journal of Economics* (May 1962), pp. 246-263.

———, *Monopoly and Competition in Banking.* Berkeley: University of California Press, 1954.

Board of Governors of the Federal Reserve System, *Recent Developments in the Structure of Banking.* Special Staff Report to the Select Committee on Small Business, U. S. Senate, 87th Congress, 2d Session. Washington: 1962.

Committee on the Judiciary, *Bank Mergers and Concentration of Banking Facilities.* Report of the Antitrust Subcommittee, House, 80th Congress, 1st Session, Washington: 1952.

———, *Corporate and Bank Mergers.* Interim Report of the Antitrust Subcommittee, 84th Congress, 1st Session. Washington: 1955, pp. 26-42, 172-188.

GRAMLEY, LYLE E., *A Study of Scale Economies in Banking.* Kansas City: Federal Reserve Bank of Kansas City, 1962.

Joint Committee on the Economic Report, *Monetary Policy and the Management of the Public Debt,* S. Doc. No. 123, Part 2, 82nd Congress, 2nd Session. Washington: 1952, pp. 925-932, 984-997.

Select Committee on Small Business, *Banking Concentration and Small Business.* Report, House, 86th Congress, 2d Session. Washington: 1960.

PART SEVEN

International Finance

28

FOREIGN EXCHANGE AND
THE BALANCE OF PAYMENTS

The international aspects of money and banking are concerned for the most part with two principal questions. The first is the problem of foreign exchange, which involves primarily the question of how an individual or business in one country is able to make payment in another country which has a different monetary unit. This is the phase of international finance which most directly concerns businessmen, bankers, investors, tourists, and others who desire to remit or receive payments across national boundaries. It involves questions of the means by which payment can be made, the market for such means of international payment, and the factors determining their price. These matters are dealt with in the present chapter.

The other phase of international finance relates to the international functions of money, broadly considered. It involves mechanisms of adjustment, including international price and income relationships, which are discussed in Chapter 29. It also concerns national and international financial policies, including the monetary standard, exchange control, clearing agreements, exchange stabilization funds, the International Monetary Fund, and other international credit institutions. These are considered in Chapter 30.

BASIC ELEMENTS OF FOREIGN EXCHANGE

An understanding of foreign exchange will be facilitated if the similarities of transactions at the domestic and the foreign level are borne in mind. Before the introduction of the Federal Reserve System, charges were commonly imposed in making monetary payments within the United States so that the outward similarity between foreign and domestic exchange transactions was closer than it is now. It is still true, however, that the process of offsetting debits and credits—which appears in the operations of clearing houses and the Interdistrict Settlement Fund, and elsewhere in domestic banking—similarly constitutes the essence of foreign exchange operations.

The Nature of Foreign Exchange

The exchange of goods and services between countries gives rise to foreign exchange, just as similar exchanges give rise to payments within a country. Such international exchanges are ordinarily not effected directly. Behind each transaction is a document expressing and representing the monetary value involved in the operation. These documents take the form of drafts, checks, letters of credit, acceptances, and similar credit instruments. They are spoken of collectively as bills of exchange or, interchangeably, as foreign exchange. They are the international financial stuff which is bought and sold in the foreign exchange markets of the world. They are expressed in terms of the domestic monetary units of the different countries. In exchanging such documents between countries it becomes necessary to relate the value of the currency of the one country to that of another. The price of one currency in terms of a foreign currency is known as the exchange rate.

The Exchange Rate as a Price

The rate of exchange, then, is a price. At any given moment, it may be regarded as the price of one currency in terms of another. It is more enlightening, however, to look upon the exchange rate as the price not of foreign money but of documents representing claims to foreign money, i.e., foreign exchange as identified above.

The supply of and demand for these foreign exchange documents originate in the items entering into the international balance of payments. They focus in, and are brought into adjustment by, a price—as with ordinary commodities.

The demand for and supply of foreign exchange are capable of great fluctuation. The volatility of particular sources of supply and demand, however, differs widely. Thus variations in the supply of commodities and services in foreign trade are relatively moderate over short periods. On the other hand, the amount of long-term securities that move across national boundaries are potentially greater. And the volume of short-term balances that move between countries may vary most of all, as the "flights of capital" during the years from 1929 to 1940 and the drain of gold from the United States in the late 1950's and early 1960's clearly demonstrated.

Sudden variations in the supply and demand of foreign exchange, and the consequent strain on the machinery of international finance, result primarily from the volatility of a few strategic items in the balance of payments.

Such variations may give rise to extreme fluctuations in exchange rates or great pressure on the mechanism for maintaining exchange rate stability.

The Markets for Foreign Exchange

The credit instruments bought and sold in foreign exchange markets show considerable diversity. At a time when foreign exchange transactions are relatively free, quotations are typically available on the following types of bills of exchange:

> Cables
> Bankers' Sight Drafts
> Commercial Sight Drafts
> 30-day, 60-day, and 90-day Bills

In addition, quotations are given for all the principal currencies in use throughout the world. Because of differences in the credit standing of the names appearing on the bills and the length of time to maturity, the various classes of bills show appreciable differences in price. For bills of the same obligor cables ordinarily command the highest price and 90-day bills the lowest. Any tendency for the rate on one type of bill to get significantly out of line with that on another would soon be corrected by arbitraging action within the market, or by converting one type of bill into another.

Bills of exchange differ, as we have seen, with respect to obligors, length of time to maturity, terms, and the currency in which they are expressed. Dealers trade in them, both as wholesalers and retailers, just as is done in the case of other economic goods. Typical of those who act as dealers are brokers who engage exclusively in operations in foreign exchange, and the foreign exchange departments of commercial banks. Both maintain deposit balances with branches or correspondents abroad. Against these they are able to draw drafts as required, building the balances up again from the proceeds of exchange transactions in the opposite directions. The margin on which dealers in foreign exchange operate, as in the case of other merchants, is the difference between the buying and selling prices of the commodity traded. The foreign exchange market so constituted is an essential part of the mechanism for effecting payments between the citizens of different countries.

Foreign exchange dealing was one of the first forms of finance to develop; it was already common by the thirteenth century and can be traced to much earlier times. Economies in time and expense, and particularly the avoidance of the risk that would have been involved in the physical transfer of gold and silver, contributed to the early development of foreign exchange operations. Over the centuries the precise nature of the economies achieved by dealings in foreign exchange have changed but their importance is undiminished.

Role of the Dealer in Foreign Exchange

As was mentioned earlier, foreign exchange operations represent an application of the principle of a clearing house to the field of international transactions. As in the domestic stages of clearing, the effect of the process is to bring about an offsetting of debits and credits, with only the balance being settled in money. Under the ordinary operation of the international gold standard, and even after the gold standard had been abandoned by most countries, the clearing process worked out in such close approximation that relatively little specie—only a small fraction of the sum total of payments effected—moved between countries. It is the role of exchange dealers to mediate this offsetting of debits and credits.

The exchange broker or dealer, then, is an intermediary. As a consequence of his intervention, an exporter may be thought of as receiving money which is turned over to the exchange dealer not by the buyer in another country but by some importer in his own country. The exporter and importer in the same country have no direct contact with one another and presumably are not even aware of each other's existence. Nevertheless, it is the pounds turned over to an exchange broker in London by a British importer of cotton from the United States which go to a British exporter of woolen textiles and thereby discharge the obligation of the merchant in New York who bought the woolen textiles. Similarly, a New York importer pays dollars to an exchange dealer in the United States and these find their way to the American exporter who shipped raw cotton to England.

The way in which the operations of the foreign exchange market enable obligations in one direction to be discharged by the transfer of money in a different direction may be illustrated diagrammatically:

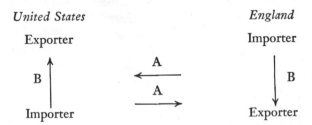

In this figure, lines A and A show how the respective obligations are discharged; lines B and B show the direction of the actual transfer. Viewing the operation as a whole, the effect of the transactions in foreign exchange is to allow the obligation of the United States for woolen textiles to be offset against the obligation of England for raw cotton, with the result that the accounts between the countries are cleared and no money has to move from one country to the other. The entire process results in a distinct gain in efficiency and safety. *Neither pounds nor dollars have to cross national frontiers.*

In real life, of course, the operations of foreign exchange dealers are much more complicated than the illustration may suggest. Individual transactions would seldom if ever exactly balance one another as to either amounts or time. Dealers would accumulate balances by means of documents arising out of transactions in the one direction and use them for drawing documents calling for payment in the other direction. Transactions with commercial bankers and with other foreign dealers would be included. Payments might involve many different countries rather than just two countries as in the example above. Despite these obvious modifications, the essential nature of the process, the character of the resulting benefits, and the role of exchange dealers as intermediaries through whom the offsetting of claims is carried out are as shown in the example.

THE TECHNIQUE OF FOREIGN EXCHANGE OPERATIONS

The details of foreign exchange operations, as of most other specialized financial operations, are rather technical and therefore likely to appear extremely complicated to the uninitiated. Numerous books are available for those who wish to pursue the subject further.[1] For present purposes it is sufficient to indicate the elementary techniques of foreign exchange as they present themselves to individual citizens and businesses.

Personal Remittances and Tourist Expenditures

If I should desire to order a book from England, I could do so by going to the post office and buying a money order payable in pounds. For larger sums, it would probably be more economical to buy a pound draft from the foreign exchange department of a bank rather than from the post office.

If I were planning to make a trip abroad, I should probably go to a bank and buy travelers' checks. These checks would be drawn in dollars and would be no different from the travelers' checks which I might buy for use within the United States. Aside from their convenience and the protection they afford against loss, such checks are so well known that they can ordinarily be cashed without difficulty anywhere in the world. When abroad, it is usual, of course, to exchange them for currency of the country where one happens to be. This is done by selling the checks at a tourist office, bank, or

---

1. Cf., for example, Franklin Escher, *Modern Foreign Exchange* (New York: Macmillan, 1932); Alan R. Holmes, *The New York Foreign Exchange Market* (New York: Federal Reserve Bank of New York, 1959); Frank A. Southard, *Foreign Exchange Practice and Policy* (New York: McGraw-Hill, 1940).

hotel for local currency at the prevailing exchange rate between dollars and that currency. For convenience in exchanging small amounts, I should also probably carry with me a certain amount of American paper money in small denominations. This is readily sold abroad for local currency, but the rate given is usually slightly less favorable than the rate on travelers' checks.[2]

From the standpoint of foreign countries, the American currency and checks which tourists from this country sell abroad constitute foreign exchange (dollar exchange). Such currency and checks are ordinarily assembled and returned to the United States where the proceeds are deposited in correspondent banks. These deposits may then provide the basis for drafts with which to settle current claims due the United States from foreign countries.

If I were expecting to be abroad for a longer time or to travel extensively I should go to my bank and purchase larger denomination bank drafts or a letter of credit. The letter of credit would ordinarily allow me to obtain a more favorable rate when cashing my dollars abroad. I should have the further advantage of being able to draw against my credit in amounts most convenient to me, and also I could arrange to have it replenished from time to time by the deposit of additional funds back home.

There are many possible variations on the foregoing procedures. For example, if I were sufficiently well known abroad or had established suitable contacts I might be able to obtain foreign currency there by offering an ordinary dollar check drawn on my account in the United States. This may be feasible even in ordering books from Canada or England, though it is likely to be less practicable in the case of other countries.

Commercial Operations

By far the largest amount of foreign exchange transactions in terms of value grow out of the movement of trade between countries. The credit instruments used in foreign trade assume various forms and differ widely as to terms, maturity, and other details, for foreign exchange operations can be handled in a variety of ways. The promissory note which is common in domestic trade in the United States is not used to any appreciable extent in international exchange.

In a typical trading operation, an American exporter agrees to ship a consignment of cotton to a British importer. He draws a draft against the British merchant payable in pounds sterling and forwards it, with bills of

---

2. In times of monetary uncertainty, the paper money of a strong currency may go to a premium over checks or drafts payable in the same currency because of demand for use for hoarding purposes. Similarly, in countries where foreign exchange operations are subject to rigid control, currency frequently commands a considerable premium over travelers' checks when sold on the black market. Early in the 1960's one of the authors was offered rubles for dollar bills on the streets of Moscow at four times the rate available through official Intourist channels.

lading attached, through his bank to some bank in England. The British importer accepts the draft in the usual manner (assuming the draft to be a time bill) and receives the bill of lading which enables him to obtain possession of the cotton. The accepted draft may be held by the American exporter until maturity or discounted for its present value. It would be even simpler for the exporter to sell the draft, bill of lading attached, to his bank at the start of the process, getting his discounted proceeds at once and allowing the bank to handle the transaction for itself from that point on.

The acceptance is presented for payment when due, as in the case of any other note or bill, and the proceeds in pounds sterling are deposited to the credit of the American exporter or bank. The sterling balance payable to American nationals can then serve as the basis for the drawing of drafts which may be sold for dollars in the United States and used for the settlement of payments due, for whatever purpose, in England.

A slight variation of this procedure occurs when the draft is drawn not against the importer in England but against the importer's bank. Such bills are employed where the credit of the importer is not well known abroad so that a more favorable rate of discount on the bill can be obtained by drawing on the importer's bank. The bank in England assumes responsibility for payment of the bill at maturity; actually, of course, it collects from the importer the funds required for settlement. The bank makes a charge for the service afforded the importer and so, in effect, derives a profit from the sale of its well-established credit.

We may think of these and similar transactions in foreign exchange as being equalized, under normal circumstances, by an offsetting series of operations representing a movement of trade and other international transactions in the opposite direction. If a balance of claims between the United States and the rest of the world should begin to accumulate on one side or the other, an adjustment must occur ultimately in which the one-sided accumulation is ended. The mechanisms by which this adjustment may be accomplished are outlined in the following chapter.

In the illustrations given, some one of the parties to the transaction—exporter, importer, or banker—would be obliged to put up money or to wait for the use of his money. This means that, in addition to his other economic functions, he would have to bear the burden of providing the financing which the carrying out of the operation entails. The ordinary functioning of the bill market makes it possible, however, for the financing to be shifted to others whose special function it is to provide short-term capital. By discounting the accepted bill at some bank which desires to hold short-term paper, or by selling it in the open market, the principals to the transaction could postpone until the date of maturity the problem of financing (i.e., of "providing the means of payment"). At that time, presumably, the completion of the selling or manufacturing operation which gave rise to the import in the first place would provide the cash with which to liquidate the accepted draft. Meanwhile, some lender of short-term capital would have found the discounted acceptance a desirable income-yielding asset.

Capital Transfers

What financial adjustments would accompany the floating of a large foreign loan in the United States? In the case of a sale of foreign bonds the net proceeds would be deposited, as in the case of domestic bond flotation, to the credit of the borrower in some large American bank or banks. The deposit would then constitute, from the standpoint of the borrowing country or foreign corporation, a stock of available foreign exchange. A draft drawn against this deposit would be foreign exchange in the same sense as the other types of foreign exchange already considered.

In terms of the balance of international payments, the loan would have added to the supply of dollar exchange available to foreigners just as an equivalent volume of commodity exports to the United States would have done. In due course, presumably, the loan would be drawn down by using the proceeds to make payments in this country for a variety of such purposes. Among them might be the export of raw materials and finished goods, the payment of interest and principal on past debts, the defraying of charges for shipping and other services, or the purchase of foreign exchange with which to make similar payments abroad. Substantially similar transactions occur in cases where the sources of the credits to foreigners are loans or grants of the United States government.

Historically the granting of short-term credit between countries has been an important source of foreign exchange. These operations ordinarily take place between banks in different countries. When exchange relations are free, it is a simple matter for banks in different countries to establish credits in banks abroad and draw bank drafts against the resulting deposit balances. Such short-term financial transactions can help to equalize interest rates between countries, to moderate exchange rate fluctuations, and to reduce strains on monetary reserves.

At times of international crisis, on the other hand, the effect of short-term capital movements can be anything but stabilizing. The phenomenon of a "flight of capital" or a "flight from the currency," which was so familiar during the 1930's, consisted primarily of a sudden transfer of short-term funds. Similar transfers are believed to have contributed to the drain of gold from the United States in the early 1960's. Such short-term capital movements, needless to say, did not represent normal operations of correspondent banks in different countries. Instead of promoting orderly international adjustment, shifts such as these, by adding suddenly to the supply of exchange payable in the currency which was weak and to demand for stronger currencies, operated to aggravate and sometimes to initiate conditions of disturbance. Not infrequently they were the prelude to currency devaluation or to the introduction of authoritarian measures to control foreign exchange operations.

Arbitrage

Foreign exchange dealers also facilitate the correction of exchange rate discrepancies by a process known as "arbitrage." Because of local supply-and-demand conditions or for other reasons, the exchange rates prevailing in one market may occasionally get out of line with those prevailing in another. If the rate between the pound and the dollar, for example, should show a substantial difference in London from the rate quoted in New York it would immediately be profitable to buy the particular currency in the market where it was low, and to sell it in the market where it was high. The effect of such operations would be to bring the quotations quickly into harmony in the two markets. While anyone can engage in arbitrage, the dealers are best situated to do so.

Arbitrage may also take place in a more roundabout way. In some third country the rate in terms of the local currency on the dollar and pound may be out of line with the quotation existing between the two countries in, say, New York and London. It would then be profitable for exchange dealers to buy the underpriced currency in the third country and sell the currency which was relatively dear there. This would continue until the opportunity for a profit through arbitrage of this character had disappeared. The currencies would then be once more in adjustment.

Forward Exchange

The service of dealers in providing a market for "forward exchange" is particularly valuable at times when exchange rates are tending to fluctuate. An exporter who expects to have foreign exchange to dispose of at some future time may fear a decline in the exchange value of the foreign currency. In order to remove this risk and to make sure of exactly what he will be able to realize on his undertaking he can go to a foreign exchange dealer and "sell forward." He does this by agreeing to deliver, at a specified future date, the foreign exchange which he is to receive at that time. An importer or other transactor having payments to make in the future in the foreign currency runs the opposite risk that the price of foreign exchange may rise in the period before the payment is to be made. He may, therefore, find it advantageous to "buy forward," that is, to contract now to buy foreign exchange in the future at a pre-established price. The additional cost to the exporter or importer of operating in the forward market represents the price of eliminating the risk of loss through exchange rate fluctuations. It is ordinarily a minor item in his cost of doing business. By dealing in forward exchange, it is usually possible to export to countries on a paper standard with as little risk from exchange losses as exist with the relatively fixed exchange rates provided by the international gold standard. However, where exchange rates are volatile, the costs of forward exchange may become so large as to burden seriously international transactions.

Foreign exchange markets provide the mechanism for pricing forward exchange just as they do for pricing spot exchange. A demand for forward sterling exchange by American importers who have to pay for British goods in sixty days may be matched, for example, with the supply of forward pounds currently offered by American exporters who will be receiving payment in sixty days. If, however, the amounts of forward exchange flowing in the two directions are unequal it is a simple matter to convert spot exchange into forward exchange by a type of arbitrage. Suppose, for example, that sixty-day forward sterling is in short supply. By acquiring spot sterling for dollars at today's price and then lending the sterling proceeds in London for sixty days, the foreign exchange dealer in the United States is assured of having the desired amount of sterling exchange sixty days hence. Accordingly, he can sell forward sterling today knowing that when the delivery of sterling is required sixty days from now the sterling to cover his obligations will be available. The difference between interest rates on sixty-day loans in New York and London would help to determine whether the quotation on forward exchange would tend to be higher or lower than on spot exchange.

THE BALANCE OF INTERNATIONAL PAYMENTS

The balance of international payments is a comprehensive summary of the international transactions of a country in a given period (usually a year). It embraces—in contrast to the balance of trade, which relates only to commodity movements—all of the items which give rise to current monetary claims between any one country and the rest of the world. The Department of Commerce regularly publishes balance of payments estimates summarizing all the economic transactions that take place between the United States and the rest of the world. Similar studies are published by other governments and international organizations. Such calculations are at once a measure of foreign exchange operations and a convenient device for identifying the various sources of supply and demand for foreign exchange.

It is essential to bear in mind that the international balance of payments includes only *current* flows between countries. In this respect it resembles an income statement showing a corporation's receipts and payments rather than a balance sheet showing assets and liabilities. Thus the cancellation of a defaulted international loan would not directly affect the balance of international payments or alter the current supply of foreign exchange. Similarly, it is impossible to say offhand what effect, if any, a transfer of territory from one country to another would have on the foreign exchange position of either country. The possible influence of such a transfer on the supply and demand of foreign exchange would be governed by the net effect which it had on the balance of current claims among the countries concerned. The country gaining territory would treat as internal certain transactions which were formerly international, and the opposite would be true for the country losing territory. But in both instances export items as well as import items, visible and invisible, would be altered. Unless it could be shown that one side, supply or demand, would be affected more than the other, it would not be possible to say whether either country would find its currency strengthened or weakened as a result of the transfer.

In parallel columns of Table 28-1 are shown the principal factors contrib-

TABLE 28-1. Sources of Supply and Demand for Foreign Exchange

Sources of Supply	Sources of Demand
1. Goods exported: Exports of commodities, including gold and silver.	1. Goods imported: Imports of commodities, including gold and silver.
2. Services performed by Americans for foreigners: Air and ocean shipping. Financial and other services, such as banking, insurance, and counseling. Services provided for foreign tourists, students, businessmen, etc. Use of American capital (for which interest and dividends are paid by foreigners).	2. Services performed by foreigners for Americans: Air and ocean shipping. Financial and other services, such as banking, insurance, and counseling. Services provided for American tourists, students, businessmen, etc. Use of foreign capital (for which interest and dividends are paid by Americans).
3. Capital transactions which place foreign exchange to the credit of Americans: Sale abroad of American securities or other property. Deposit of funds by foreigners in American banks. Repayment of principal of loans granted previously to foreigners.	3. Capital transactions which provide foreigners with credits payable in dollars: Purchase by Americans of foreign securities or other property, including short-term loans to foreigners. Repurchase of American securities owned by foreigners. Repayment of principal of loans previously extended by foreigners.
4. Unilateral or "unrequited" transactions: Gifts, remittances, and contributions by foreigners to individuals and institutions in the United States.	4. Unilateral or "unrequited" transactions: Gifts, remittances, and contributions by individuals, foundations, etc. to foreigners. Grants of financial aid by the American government to foreign countries and corporations.

uting to the demand for and supply of foreign exchange available to residents of the United States. (As was remarked in the previous section, these lists could similarly be looked upon from the standpoint of foreign nationals as sources of demand for and supply of *dollar* exchange.) The items in Table 28-1 should now be compared with those shown in Table 28-2, giving the balance of payments of the United States for 1961. Table 28-1 is designed to identify in somewhat greater detail the items shown in the official statement.

In addition, it organizes these details by logical categories, grouping them with particular reference to their role as sources of supply of and demand for foreign exchange. It remains to add a few comments with respect to the economic importance of the different items.

Exports and imports of merchandise constitute by far the largest item in the balance of payments. They are of major strategic importance not only because of their magnitude but also because they are sensitive to price and income changes between countries.

TABLE 28-2. Balance of Payments of the United States, 1961 (millions of dollars)

Credit Items		Debit Items		Net Credit (+) or Debit (−)
Exports of goods and services		Imports of goods and services		
Merchandise	19,916	Merchandise	14,524	
Transportation	1,785	Transportation	1,942	
Travel (Foreigners in United States)	961	Travel (Americans abroad)	1,743	
Miscellaneous Services		Miscellaneous Services		
Private	1,447	Private	636	
Government	562	Government	3,363	
Income on foreign investments		Income to foreigners on investments in U.S		
Private	3,284	Private	596	
Government	361	Government	275	
Total	28,316	Total	23,079	
		Balance on goods and services		+5,237
Foreign capital inflow (net)		U.S. capital outflow (net)		
Long-term	435	Private		
Short-term	1,854	Long-term	2,568	
Total	2,289	Short-term	1,383	
		Government	954	
		Total	4,905	
		Balance on capital flow		−2,616
		Unilateral transfers to foreign countries (net)		
		Private	643	
		Government	2,104	
		Total	2,747	−2,747
Export of gold	742			+ 742
Errors, omissions and other factors				− 616

Source: *Survey of Current Business*, March 1962, p. 22.

Services constitute the next largest group and embrace a diverse variety of items, some of which are relatively responsive to price and income differentials while others are governed by altogether different considerations.

Transportation and travel, for example, vary in somewhat the same manner as merchandise trade. Income on investments largely reflects investments made earlier, but varies to some extent with the current profitability of business activity. With the expansion of aid to foreign countries in recent years, the "Government" item under Miscellaneous Services has assumed major proportions. The size and behavior of this item reflect mainly humanitarian and international political considerations.

The item capital movements discloses a large outflow of private capital, of which a substantial amount consists of direct investment in plant and equipment by American corporations. Investment by the government has been largely on long term and related to foreign assistance of one kind or another. A substantial inflow of short-term funds from abroad reflects the building up of short-term balances by foreign businesses, foreign central banks and governments, and international institutions. Short-term capital, by its nature, is highly volatile. Substantial shifts may occur without necessarily being shown in the annual totals. Such movements may be of a cushioning character but at other times have been a source of serious disturbance in the balance of payments and, of course, in foreign exchange markets.

The last major category consists of gold movements. The importance of this item lies not in its magnitude, though there have been times when the amounts were rather large. The great strategic importance of gold movements lies in the role which they play as the means of settling balances on international accounts. The final entry "Errors, omissions, and other factors" is primarily an acknowledgment that even with the utmost skill and effort it is not possible to arrive at exact totals for all items entering into the international balance of payments.

It is not always easy to decide whether a particular transaction represents an addition to the supply of foreign exchange or to the demand for it. Confusion is aggravated by the terms commonly used: for example, "export of merchandise" adds to the supply of foreign exchange and therefore tends to strengthen the currency of the exporting country, but "export of capital" adds to the demand for foreign exchange and tends to depress the currency of the country making the export.

There is a simple test which will always make it clear whether a transaction is to be regarded as tending to raise or to lower the exchange value of a particular currency. The starting point is to remember that exports increase our purchasing power in foreign countries. They add to the supply of foreign exchange and, unless offset in some way, tend to raise the value of the dollar (i.e., cheapen foreign exchange in terms of the dollar). The effect of imports, on the other hand, is to increase foreign purchasing power in this country, create demand for foreign exchange, and, unless offset, to lower the foreign exchange value of the dollar.

The test of how any particular transaction tends to affect exchange rates, therefore, may be expressed in these terms:

Whatever adds to our current purchasing power abroad helps to strengthen the foreign exchange value of the dollar. It is an export (visible or invisible) and increases the supply of foreign exchange.

Whatever adds to the current purchasing power of foreign countries in the United States tends to lessen the value of the dollar in terms of foreign currencies. It is an import (visible or invisible) and increases the supply of dollar exchange payable to foreigners.

The foregoing test is merely a rule of thumb for determining whether a particular transaction is to be classified as a supply factor or a demand factor. If it falls in the supply category it tends to raise the value of domestic currency relative to foreign. If it falls in the demand category it tends to lower the value of domestic currency relative to foreign.

SELECTED BIBLIOGRAPHY

Department of Commerce, *Survey of Current Business.* March issues present balance of payments data.

HOLMES, ALAN R., *The New York Foreign Exchange Market.* New York: Federal Reserve Bank of New York, 1959.

KINDLEBERGER, CHARLES P., *International Economics.* Homewood, Ill.: Irwin, 1958, Chapters 1-4.

SOUTHARD, FRANK A., JR., *Foreign Exchange Practice and Policy.* New York: McGraw-Hill, 1940, Chapters 2-4.

29

MECHANISMS OF INTERNATIONAL ADJUSTMENT

We have seen that, by reason of the definitions and conventions of accounting, total credits or export items in the balance of payments of any country always must equal total debits or import items. The balance of payments, in other words, presents an identity. In spite of inflation, deflation, unemployment, growth, or retrogression at home or abroad the two totals are certain to be equal. The equality of the totals, therefore, tells us nothing of analytical importance.

EQUILIBRIUM IN THE BALANCE OF PAYMENTS

The Meaning of Equilibrium

Equilibrium in the balance of payments is an analytic rather than an accounting concept. It signifies that a nation's economy is so integrated with the rest of the world that there is nothing inherent in its current economic relations which requires a change in patterns of exchange with other countries. The nation, that is, is earning just enough from the sale of goods and services and long-term securities to pay for imports of goods and services and long-term securities (and possibly aid programs resulting in unilateral transfers).

It is significant that two balance of payments items are omitted from this list, namely, movements of gold and changes in short-term indebtedness. Thus movements of gold and short-term debt are to be taken as symptoms of disequilibrium in the balance of international payments. A net export of gold and short-term claims is treated as signifying a deficit in the balance of payments (which may be defined as a deficiency of supply of foreign exchange as compared with demand at the current rate, excluding the balancing gold and short-term items), and a net import of gold and short-term claims is treated as evidence of a *surplus* in the balance of payments (an excess of supply over demand at the current exchange rate, leaving out temporary items). The reason for this distinction is that the motives for movements of gold and short-term capital are essentially different from those giving rise to other elements in the balance of payments: both are *balancing* items, appearing as stopgaps, and as temporary rather than sustaining elements in the supply of or demand for exchange.[1]

The role of cash flows and changes in short-term credits may be clarified by analogy with their role in the external balance of an ordinary household. Generally, a family will expect to acquire the means to purchase goods and services from others by sales (i.e., "exports") of goods and services to others. During the stage of its life cycle in which saving occurs, equilibrium is consistent with continuous purchases of securities which, together with purchases of other commodities and services, equal sales of services. During a later stage, equilibrium is consistent with a reversal of the long-term investment flow, as during retirement. But suppose the family lives beyond its income in the sense of purchasing more goods, services, and securities than the value of sales of services. Temporarily this "deficit" in its balance of payments may be financed in two ways: (1) by drawing down ("or exporting") stocks of cash balances, or (2) by borrowing in such forms as running up department store and other trade debts or taking out installment loans. But clearly, since both are exhaustible, neither of these expedients will sustain indefinitely an excess of family imports over exports. A cash balance is limited, as is the credit that a prudent lender will provide. Eventually the household "balance of payments" must be revamped and put on a sustaining basis.

In its international transactions a nation is in a similar position. Temporarily its imports of goods and services and long-term claims can exceed similar exports, financed in part by exports of gold and in part by exporting rights to domestic demand deposits or other short-term claims. Similarly, however, both of these sources are exhaustible. There is a limit to the amount of short-term claims which foreign dealers will be willing to hold. When this limit is exceeded, short-term claims will be liquidated and withdrawn, presumably in the form of gold. Since a gold stock is also limited, a deficit in the balance of payments must ultimately lead to adjustments which will bring the disequilibrium to an end.

A surplus involves less external pressure for adjustment, but, since a surplus for one country corresponds to a deficit elsewhere, the discipline enforced on deficit countries cannot fail to affect a surplus country as well.

Causes of Disequilibrium

Assuming that a country is in balance-of-payments equilibrium, what factors could lead to a deficit or surplus in its international accounts?

---

1. Except for gold movements that correctly reflect the long-run position of a country as a producer (and exporter) or net user (and importer) of gold.

In general, any factor could do so which affects imports or exports of goods and services, or the relative profitability of investment at home and abroad, or the balance of unilateral payments. Involved are virtually all major variables in the economy, including changes in relative incomes at home and abroad, changes in relative degrees of inflation or deflation, shifts in demand as a result of product innovations or changes in fashion, discovery or depletion of sources of raw materials, crop failures or bountiful harvests, new inventions and technological changes. Some of these may result in sporadic or seasonal or cyclical dislocations, which are limited or subject to reversal within a limited period. Others, such as those resulting from shifts in access to raw materials or from technological change, may lead to deep-seated, or "fundamental," disequilibrium requiring important structural adjustments if a reasonable degree of integration with the world economy is to be achieved.

There are three major methods whereby an economy may deal with a condition of international disequilibrium. They are by means of:

1. Income changes.
2. Changes in relative prices, involving:
   a. Changes in the internal price level.
   b. Changes in exchange rates.
3. Direct controls.

Other methods, sometimes considered separately, may be subsumed in this list. Thus changes in unilateral payments may be considered to fall within the category of direct controls. Changes in international investment are influenced partly by direct controls and partly by factors such as changes in relative interest rates which accompany monetary and credit policies designed to change incomes or price levels.

These modes of coping with disequilibrium in the international accounts are not to be considered as simple alternatives, with one pattern prevailing and then another, depending on choices made. Normally they act jointly, with two or more typically operative simultaneously. Thus internal price level movements are likely to be accompanied by substantial real income changes as well, except during inflationary movements beyond full employment. Direct controls may react on internal price levels and incomes as well as on imports, and so on.

INCOME AND BALANCE-OF-PAYMENTS ADJUSTMENT

Emergence of a deficit or surplus in the balance of payments has important effects on national income, and changes in national income affect the amount of deficit and surplus. We shall examine these two relationships in turn.

Effects of the Net Export Balance on Income

Suppose a shift in demand occurs from domestic goods to imports, or a decrease in demand for exports. These changes in the net export balance not only move the balance of payments in the direction of deficit; they directly decrease expenditures on domestic output. This primary contractionary effect would then be re-enforced by secondary reactions of those receiving lower incomes, in the familiar downward multiplier process. Similarly a shift in demand from imports to domestic goods or an increase in demand for exports would result in a movement towards balance of payments surplus, with national income expanding by some multiple of the net export change. How desirable such movements would be would depend on current economic conditions. If a shift to imports or decrease in export demand were to occur under conditions of inflation, it would tend to restrain inflationary pressures. Similar movements occurring under conditions of unemployment would worsen conditions and intensify the problem of domestic stabilization.

Effects of Income Change on the Net Export Balance

As income increases or decreases, consumption expenditures, of course, may be expected to move in the same direction. In an open economy, some part of these consumption expenditures presumably will be devoted to imports from abroad. In addition, some part of the additional raw materials for domestic production must be provided by imports. Thus as income increases, imports rise, and conversely, as income decreases, imports decline. It is plausible to conceive of a *marginal propensity to import*, bearing a family resemblance to the marginal propensity to consume, to save, or to pay taxes. A marginal propensity to import of 0.1 would mean that for each one dollar change in national income, imports will vary in the same direction by ten cents.

As in the case of saving and taxes, imports are a leakage from the domestic income stream. Because of this leakage, any expansionary change, such as an increase in domestic investment, leads to a smaller increase in domestic income than would otherwise occur. The investment multiplier is reduced, and the same is true of other multipliers as well. (We may think of part of the expansionary effect as taking place abroad rather than at home.) The relationship between imports and income, reflected in the marginal propensity to import, makes income changes an important vehicle for adjustments in the balance of payments. Further examples will illustrate the process.

Let us suppose that country A experiences a decline in exports. If imports and exports were formerly in balance, the decline in exports would open an import gap. Income, as we have seen, would be directly reduced by the decline in exports, and a further decline would result from the multiplier effects. In the process, imports would decline, thus reducing the deficit in the balance of payments and moving toward external balance.

If repercussions abroad from the decline in A's imports were negligible, this would be the end of the story. But if—as a result of the induced decline in imports and reductions of income abroad—foreign demand for A's exports were to decline significantly, a further decline in income would occur in A.

If the deficit occurred as a result of an initial shift in demand from home goods to imports the results would be somewhat different. Income in A would again fall, tending to restrain the rise in imports, but income abroad would tend to rise. The rise abroad might be reflected back in some rise in exports from A, thus moderating both the fall in income in country A and the fall in imports into A.

It could be shown, similarly, that a surplus in A's balance of payments resulting from an increase in exports or decrease in imports would induce an increase in income and rise in imports. This, in turn, would tend to reduce the surplus in the balance of payments caused by the original change.

The foregoing analysis demonstrates the interactions of income changes at home and abroad, and between income and the balance of payments. Changes in income react on the balance of payments, and changes in foreign and domestic factors which affect the balance of payments also affect income. Full equilibrium requires equilibrium in income and the balance of payments at the same time.

METHODS OF PRICE LEVEL ADJUSTMENT

There are two principal methods whereby the price level of one country may be brought into adjustment with price levels in other countries. One is the method of the gold standard and the other the method of paper or "free" currencies. The essential difference between the two is this: in case the price level of one country gets out of line with price levels abroad, the gold standard mechanism involves holding exchange rates stable and bringing about a change in internal price levels. The paper standard mechanism, on the other hand, calls for a change in exchange rates without necessarily any change in internal price levels. We may think of the one as the method of fixed exchange rates with adjustment by price level changes, and of the other as the method of adjustment by way of changes in exchange rates.

To take a simplified example, let us suppose that the price index in one country has risen to 110, while in another country it is still 100. Under the gold standard, the exchange rate would remain at 1 to 1 and the price level in the first country would be brought down, say, to 105 and in the second country brought up to 105. Assuming the international position of the countries to be the same as before the original disturbance occurred, the two currencies would then be in an equilibrium relationship. Under paper standard conditions, the price levels would remain at 110 and 100, respectively, but the exchange rate would change—the quotation in terms of the currency where prices had risen would be 1.10 to 1.00, and in terms of the currency where prices had not risen it would be 0.91 to 1.00. At these exchange rates, the currencies of the two countries would again be in equilibrium (assuming still that the international economic position of the countries was unchanged). The difference between the two methods of effecting international price level adjustment is illustrated diagrammatically in Figure 29-1.

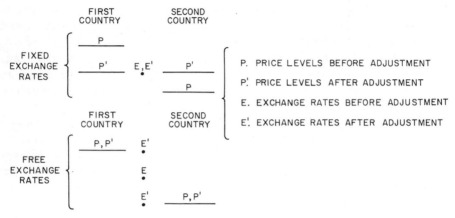

Figure 29-1.   Foreign Exchange Rates Under Fixed and Free Exchange Rate Conditions.

Both of these methods are means of achieving the same end, namely, the adjustment of relative price levels. The gold standard has the advantage of providing exchange rate stability, but it may compel a country to undergo a contraction or expansion of money and credit with accompanying deflationary or inflationary pressures. Paper standards with free exchange rates permit the pressure on price levels to be largely avoided, but only at the cost of changes in exchange rates.

No country, of course, can assure stable exchange rates with other countries by its own actions alone. Exchange rates are dependent on policies followed in the respective countries. At a time when two foreign countries are following divergent monetary policies, the preservation of exchange rate stability with one of them will presumably necessitate exchange rate instability with the other. Adherence to the gold standard assures stable exchange rates only with countries also on the gold standard. During the 1930's, the United States and later France, Switzerland, and the Netherlands found that when many countries were off the gold standard, greater stability of exchange rates was obtainable by abandoning the gold standard than by retaining it. For any particular country, maximum exchange rate stability would presumably be achieved by adapting its policies to policies followed by the majority of other countries.

The Gold Standard Mechanism

In this section and the next the gold and paper standard systems are analyzed with a view to explaining the process of international monetary adjustment. The analysis is an elaboration of the two types of adjustment sketched briefly above. The present discussion seeks to identify the essential features of the adjustment processes but is not to be regarded as giving a realistic account of how the standards actually operated.

Mint parity and the gold points. The traditional international gold standard rested on the observance by a group of countries of two essential requirements—interconvertibility between domestic currency and gold, and the free export and import of gold. The first requirement was designed to maintain equality in value between the domestic monetary unit and a given weight of gold within the country. The second was designed to maintain equality between the value of gold within the country and its value in the world market. Since things equal to the same thing are equal to each other, it follows that as long as these two conditions are satisfied, the value of the monetary unit will be equal to that of a given weight of gold in the world market.

"Going off the gold standard" consisted merely in departing from either of the two requirements. That this was regarded as abandonment of the international gold standard was tacit acknowledgment that without these two conditions parity between the value of the particular currency and a specified amount of gold in the world market could not be assured.

Under the international gold standard, exchange rates were anchored to the mint par of exchange, i.e., the ratio of the pure gold content of one monetary unit to the pure gold content of the other. To say that the par value of the pound sterling was $4.8665 simply meant that the gold pound contained 4.8665 times as much pure gold as the gold dollar. Another way of expressing the same idea is that the mint par of exchange indicates the relative amounts of the two currencies that would command an equal quantity of gold.

Exchange rates could deviate on either side of the mint par of exchange by the cost of transferring gold from the mint in one country to the mint in the other country. The limits so established were called the "gold shipping points." Exchange rates could not move beyond the gold shipping points because at those points it was possible to create foreign exchange abroad or in the home country, depending on which of the two shipping points was reached, in unlimited amounts. At the gold shipping point, that is, the demand or supply, respectively, of foreign exchange was infinitely elastic.

The gold shipped between countries was itself an item in the balance of payments. Gold movements could be an important short-run balancing factor partly because of the promptness with which they tended to take place. Another possible effect of exchange rate fluctuations within the gold points may have been to influence international trade by making the commodities of one country slightly cheaper or dearer relative to those of another. Because the range of fluctuations in relative value of currencies was so narrow, less than 1 per cent in the case of the United States and England, this influence on the balance of trade was not very significant.

Short-term capital movements. Temporary shortages in the supply of foreign exchange could also be relieved by the movement of short-term balances between countries. Such transfers could originate most expeditiously simply by a bank or exchange dealer in one country securing authorization to draw drafts against a correspondent bank or dealer in another country. Movements of short-term funds were facilitated by differences in interest rates—often with the aid of appropriate changes in the central bank discount rate.

The attraction of interest rate differentials in stimulating short-term capital movements was strongly re-enforced, at any time when the exchange rate was at or near the gold shipping points, by the prospect of an added profit through a shift of the exchange rate. A British banker who sold pounds for claims on dollars at a time when the exchange rate for the pound was $4.88 (which was close to the gold import point for England) could be confident that the dollar would not decline much farther. On the contrary, he could reasonably expect that the value of the dollar would rise. In that case the number of pounds which would be realized upon repayment would be somewhat greater than the number required to make the loan in the first place, and the British banker would have an exchange profit in addition to the interest return. Adherence to the gold standard provided assurance against any appreciable exchange loss; with the exchange rate at the gold import point there was only one direction in which the exchange rate on the dollar could move. Short-term capital movements tended to be an important short-term adjusting item—but only so long as there was confidence in the maintenance of the international gold standard.

Specie flows. The automatic drain of gold reserves that took place once the gold points had been reached was expected to have several significant consequences. First, it would add to the supply of foreign exchange in the country where exchange happened to be scarce. Second, the movement of gold between countries would furnish a guide to the type of central bank policies appropriate at that time. An outflow of gold would be a signal to raise the discount rate and otherwise to pursue a more restrictive policy. An inflow would indicate the desirability of lowering the discount rate and facilitating easier credit conditions.

Third, the flow of reserve money would also tend to bring about an expansion of the circulating medium in the country receiving gold and a contraction in the country losing gold. In accordance with the quantity theory of money, it was reasoned that the change in the volume of money would raise prices in the one country and lower them in the other. A new relationship between the price levels of different countries would thus be established, and this in turn would tend to redress the flow of trade and induce adjustments in levels of income and output corresponding to the change in the balance of exports and imports.

This is the substance of the so-called "price-specie flow analysis" which was a central feature of the traditional theory of the international gold standard. The flow of specie was regarded as providing a mechanism for inducing compensating changes in foreign trade. But it involved the sacrifice of stability of incomes and price levels.

Potentiality for disturbance. Under normal conditions, gold flows and short-term capital movements were counted on to exercise a stabilizing influence. In times of severe stress, however, the drain of gold reserves had an unsettling effect on public psychology. Fear of resulting devaluation might actually exaggerate the existing disequilibrium in the balance of payments by leading to flights of capital. In addition, the countries receiving gold did not always allow the growth of reserve balances to bring about a corresponding expansion in incomes and in the volume of money in circulation. In part, these were faults in the conduct of the international gold standard system, rather than flaws in the theoretical pattern. The effect, however, was the same, and in the end led to the worldwide abandonment of the gold standard during the 1930's.

In substance, the fixity of exchange rates decreed by the gold standard was dependent, as the condition of its survival, upon confidence in the permanence of the mint parity relationships. When confidence was shaken, the very rigidity of exchange rates became a source of weakness. Far from encouraging stabilizing movements of capital the fear that exchange rate stability would be abandoned generated destabilizing movements. There was then a powerful inducement to sell domestic currency at the existing rate in expectation that it would soon be worth considerably less. Such sales aggravated the imbalance of supply and demand for foreign exchange, making the currency weaker still. Thus fears that fixed exchange rates would be abandoned operated to produce the very results that were feared.

Stricter discipline or adjustments elsewhere might have enabled the international gold standard system to recover, but these the members of the system eventually proved unwilling to undergo. In the 1940's and 1950's, reluctance to subordinate domestic policies for full employment and economic growth to the requirements of the gold standard was sufficient to block any attempt to restore an international gold standard of the traditional type. Few would question that the choice is a proper one, but fewer still would deny a certain nostalgia for the neat and simple, if somewhat illusory, adjustment mechanism of the traditional gold standard.

The Paper Standard Mechanism: Purchasing Power Parity

Abandonment of the international gold standard signifies the surrender of fixed gold shipping points as the limits of exchange rate movements, but does not mean that exchange rates are free from all natural restraints. Even under paper standard conditions market forces impose significant limitations on exchange rate fluctuations. The limitations are by no means as definite and firm as under gold—a fact which explains why some prefer the paper standard method of adjustment—but under normal circumstances they are very real.

The concept of a "market par of exchange." The anchor for exchange rates between paper standard currencies (or between a paper and a gold standard currency) is what is technically known as "purchasing power parity." This represents the ratio between two currencies which would equalize their relative purchasing power over goods. It might also be called the "market par of exchange." Because purchasing power parity theoretically reflects equality in command over goods it is directly analogous to the mint par of exchange which represents equality in command over gold.

The basic principle of the adjusting mechanism is that as exchange rates move away from purchasing power parity it becomes more and more attractive to import from one of the countries and less and less attractive to import from the other. (For the sake of simplicity the explanation is again confined to two countries only.) The resulting shift in exports and imports will affect the supply and demand for foreign exchange and the exchange rate. Ideally, supply and demand will reach equilibrium and the exchange rate will be stabilized near purchasing power parity, the point where purchasing power over goods and services is supposedly equal.

There are both similarities and differences in the adjustment mechanism of paper standards as compared with gold. While the limits to exchange rate movements are analogous, they are wider and less definite. In place of being held within sharply defined gold points which reflect the cost of shipping *gold* in sufficient volume to equilibrate the supply of and demand for foreign exchange, exchange rates under paper are only loosely confined within a broad range which reflects the cost of transferring *goods* in sufficient volume to equalize supply and demand. Paper standard adjustments are assumed to take place almost wholly in the movement of goods and services. There is nothing to correspond to the specie flow with its impact on both balance of payments and price levels. Nor do capital movements play a comparable role.

Deviations from purchasing power parity. Purchasing power parity is calculated on the basis of price indexes in the two countries concerned, the idea being that these measure changes in the respective domestic purchasing power of the two currencies. On the assumption that purchasing power of the two currencies was equal at the exchange rate prevailing in some base year, that rate is adjusted to make it conform to relative changes which have taken place in the two indexes since that year. For example, assume that the exchange rate in the base year was $2.80 = £ and that the price level index stood at 100 in each country. If later on the indexes stood at 150 and 200, respectively, the rate which would equalize the purchasing power of the two currencies would be 150 ÷ 200 × $2.80, or $2.10. This rate would constitute purchasing power parity, the theoretical norm about which the actual exchange rate would presumably tend to fluctuate.

To expect that purchasing power parity would hold as an absolute guide to exchange rate movements under paper standard conditions it would have to be assumed that:

1. The two currencies were in an equilibrium relationship in the base year.
2. Index numbers are an accurate measure of changes in purchasing power since the base year and these changes affect domestic and foreign trade equally.
3. Commodity trade dominates the supply and demand of foreign exchange and, therefore, purchasing power over goods is the main determinant of exchange rates.
4. No change in the international economic position of the two countries, such as might result from the erection of tariff barriers or other controls or a shift from a debtor to a creditor position, has occurred since the base year.
5. Different income effects stemming from different cyclical movements or rates of growth are not large enough to be significant.

Assumptions such as these, especially the last two, are too extreme to be taken seriously. It must be concluded, therefore, that deviations from purchasing power parity will be the rule rather than the exception.

The theory of monetary adjustments under paper may be seen to turn on the role of exchange rates as the regulator of exports and imports. It is hardly realistic to suppose either that exports and imports wholly govern the supply and demand for foreign exchange or that relative price levels perfectly control international trade. Nevertheless, in the absence of unsettling influences such as sudden movements of capital, commodity trade does constitute the most important sector of the supply and demand of foreign exchange. For that reason, relative command over commodities, which purchasing power parity is designed to measure, is ordinarily a major factor influencing exchange rates between paper standard currencies. For all its limitations, purchasing power parity is an essential tool for understanding the processes of monetary adjustment.

Other Monetary Systems

The gold and paper monetary systems explained above are to be looked upon as types of monetary mechanisms and not as standards actually in use, at least in the pure form in which they are described. What we typically find is some modified monetary system embodying, for the most part, features drawn from these two types. For many years gold, silver, and paper standards existed alongside one another, not to mention variants such as the gold-exchange standard and even paper-exchange standards. We also have had the phenomenon of "currency blocs." This refers to groups of countries whose currency systems are bound together by means of a loose association or understanding. It has been customary to speak of the Scandinavian countries and various British Commonwealth nations as being in the "Sterling bloc" and of Canada and several Latin American countries as belonging to the "Dollar bloc." Such blocs ordinarily have their origin in strong political or economic ties among the members. The satellite countries, whose currencies are sometimes legally tied to that of the mother country, tend to follow the monetary lead of the major partner when it comes to such matters as devaluation and the imposition of strong controls over exchange operations. They may, it is true, also adopt such measures on their own initiative.

Where countries are on different commodity standards, or where one is on paper and the other on gold, price level relationships are likely to be adjusted mainly through changes in exchange rates. The process is somewhat like that under paper currencies except that the commodity basis may introduce some of the specie-flow and price-adjustment elements that exist under the international gold standard mechanism. Presumably the movement of a particular monetary metal would affect the reserves of one of the countries but not of the other. The case for international bimetallism, which was a lively issue in the late nineteenth century, rested mainly on the argument that it would assure stable exchange rates not only among members of the bimetallic system but also—by preserving a stable ratio between gold and silver—between countries on monometallic gold and silver standards.

Monetary standards at the present time are a far remove from the stereotypes described above. Where gold standards exist they are substantially modified, with little of the free regulation of money supply by means of specie flows. Where paper standards exist great efforts are likely to be made to hold the exchange rate fluctuations within what are regarded as reasonable bounds. The financial mechanisms centering in the International Monetary Fund, however, do embody, as will be seen later, major elements of the gold and paper standard techniques of price level adjustment. And these techniques are still representative of the basic principles of monetary adjustment between countries.

DIRECT CONTROLS AND THE BALANCE OF PAYMENTS

A country experiencing a deficit in its balance of payments might be unwilling to accept either of the adjustment methods described above. It might not want to permit automatic declines in income, because of conditions of reasonable domestic stability or actual unemployment, nor to impose contractionary monetary and fiscal policies. On various grounds it might also rule out devaluation It might then resort, instead, to direct controls as a means of forcing equality between the demand for and the supply of foreign exchange at existing exchange rates and with no change in internal price levels or income. Such controls normally would serve to restrict demand. They might take the form of tariffs or quotas to affect demand by controlling trade, or resort might be had to exchange controls operating on the demand for foreign exchange directly. The uses of such devices as these are discussed in the following chapter.

Direct restrictions on imports or on access to the foreign exchange with which to purchase them will divert expenditures from imports to domestic production. In this way, direct controls tend to be expansionary at home and contractionary abroad. Under inflationary circumstances they tend to exaggerate domestic inflation; with domestic unemployment they tend to strengthen, in the short run, other employment generating policies.

INTERNAL STABILITY AND EXTERNAL BALANCE

To review the impact on the domestic economy of the three types of policies we have examined, let us assume a country seeking to overcome a deficit in its balance of payments. Such a deficit would call for policies that would bring about a downward adjustment in income levels. The price level adjustment required also would be downward. Both of these would be consistent with a domestic full-employment policy only if inflation were dominant on the domestic scene. The use of exchange rate devaluation and direct controls to overcome the deficit, on the other hand, would be expansionary.

If a country seeks to combine full employment at home and liberal trade relations with the rest of the world, income changes and direct controls are not well suited to bear a major share of the burden of ensuring external balance. Major reliance will have to be placed on adjustments of relative price levels by means of changes in internal price structures or exchange rates as described above.

The choice between exchange depreciation, on the one hand, and the credit controls and fiscal policies necessary to exert a downward influence on prices, on the other, may depend substantially on the state of the economy. Under conditions of full employment and inflation, monetary and fiscal restraints are well adapted to facilitate both domestic stability and external balance. During conditions of unemployment, however, exchange depreciation would better facilitate both domestic expansion and external balance. But dilemmas are bound to arise (see Chapter 25) where we have, at the same time, unemployment *and* inflation, or as happened in the United States in 1960-61, where recession is accompanied by a deficit in the balance of payments but exchange depreciation is ruled out because of the necessity of maintaining the dollar as a key currency of the Western Alliance. Clearly, those who formulate monetary policy have no easy task.

SELECTED BIBLIOGRAPHY

BLOOMFIELD, ARTHUR I., *Monetary Policy Under the International Gold Standard, 1880-1914*. New York: Federal Reserve Bank of New York, 1959.

CASSEL, GUSTAV, *Money and Foreign Exchange After 1914*. New York: Macmillan, 1922, pp. 137-62.

DAY, A. C. L., and S. T. BEZA, *Money and Income*. New York: Oxford University Press, 1960, Chapters 30-32, 37-39.

FRIEDMAN, MILTON, "The Case for Flexible Exchange Rates." In *Essays in Positive Economics*. Chicago: University of Chicago Press, 1953.

KENEN, PETER B., *British Monetary Policy and the Balance of Payments, 1951-1957*. Cambridge: Harvard University Press, 1960, Chapter 2.

MACHLUP, FRITZ, "The Theory of Foreign Exchanges." *Economica* (November 1939 and February 1940). (Reprinted in American Economic Association, *Readings in the Theory of International Trade*.)

MEADE, JAMES E., *The Balance of Payments*. London: Oxford University Press, 1951, Chapters 5-6.

NURKSE, RAGNAR, "Domestic and International Equilibrium." In S. E. Harris (ed.), *The New Economics*. New York: Knopf, 1947.

30

INTERNATIONAL
FINANCIAL POLICY

International financial policies in the present century have been dominated by developments associated with two World Wars, a great depression, and the cold war. The experience with monetary disturbance and reconstruction during and following the two wars provides interesting and significant contrasts. The distinguishing feature of the period after World War I was the strength of the world's attachment to the international gold standard. While the war led to widespread departures from gold, these departures were regarded as of an emergency character and therefore only temporary. In fact, the monetary disturbances during and soon after the war, particularly the extreme German inflation, emphasized in the public mind the importance of restoring the gold standard as speedily as possible. The few voices that were raised in dissent attracted little attention until later.

Monetary reconstruction as generally understood after World War I signified little more than a return to the gold standard with its provisions for free interconvertibility between gold and domestic currency. By the latter 1920's the return to gold was general. But the conditions under which the international gold standard operated were different from those prevailing before 1914, particularly with respect to the increased rigidity of prices and wages, unwise lending abroad, obstructive trade policies including the raising of tariffs by the United States which interfered with the payment of debts, speculative excesses in the United States, and chronic unemployment in Great Britain and elsewhere.

Strains and stresses proved too great and the restored gold standard collapsed in the Great Depression. There followed a period of monetary disorder and experimentation that lasted throughout the 1930's. For the most part it was a time of nationalistic monetary policies with countries trying to go their own way and then patching up international monetary relationships with hastily improvised and often conflicting measures.

When the world again found itself faced with the problem of international monetary reconstruction toward the end of World War II there was no common desire to return to a gold standard of the traditional type. The determination was not less strong, however, to avoid a relapse into the chaotic monetary conditions of the Thirties. The contrast with the attitude that prevailed after the previous war is indicated by the fact that the only hope of finding a common monetary basis was to attempt to construct an entirely new and different monetary system. This was accomplished at the Bretton Woods Conference in 1944 in the form of the International Monetary Fund, which will be described below along with other major institutional developments.

The important moves toward convertibility, the liberalization of international trade, and the attainment of relatively stable exchange rates were substantial achievements of the period after World War II. At the same time, chronic imbalances beset the channels of international finance. For the first dozen years after the war the prevailing conception, shared even by many experts in the field, was that the dollar was permanently too strong relative to most other currencies. Even before this period ended there were signs (a persistent erosion of United States gold reserves and the accumulation of short-term balances due to foreigners) that conditions were changing. Subsequently, the situation did reverse itself and then the prevailing conception, likewise shared by many experts, was that the dollar was chronically in a weak position relative to currencies abroad. Attention which had been directed earlier toward solving the alleged problem of dollar shortage shifted to means of bolstering the position of the dollar by providing supplementary sources of reserves and of short-term credit for the United States.

A notable lesson of the years since 1914 and particularly since 1950 is the suddenness with which an existing situation in international finance can reverse itself. The rags-to-riches or riches-to-rags (or both) experiences of the French franc in the 1920s, of the Canadian dollar after World War II, and even of the United States dollar illustrate the need for adequate perspective. A further lesson is that contemporary opinions, particularly those of an extreme sort, must be received with reservation even when put forward by prominent business leaders and financial experts. Current interpretations, however convincing they appear at the moment, have not infrequently turned out to be no more than shortsighted rationalizations of transient influences.

To offer these observations is not to deny, be it noted, that significant problems have arisen and presently exist in international balances of payments, or that the same will be true in the future. Nor is it to suggest that serious efforts should not be made to strengthen and improve the machinery of international finance.

We turn now to some of the more typical and controversial international financial policies of the past half century. It may be remarked that governmental interferences with foreign exchange operations are particularly likely to flourish in periods of political disturbance or economic strain. They were widespread during World Wars I and II and in the period between. Many of the controls were carried over into the years after World War II. By the end of the 1950s economic recovery and rising prosperity had contributed to a general relaxation of international financial controls among the western nations. It is hardly to be doubted, however, that a recurrence of severe political or economic stress would once again lead to large-scale intervention in foreign exchange operations. Such measures must, therefore, be reckoned with in any realistic appraisal of international financial policies.

EXCHANGE RATE POLICIES

Intervention in international financial affairs is typically the result of real or imagined failures in the operation of monetary standards. At times, however, the malfunctioning of monetary systems has probably been as much the result as the cause of such intervention. Practices adopted usually involve attempts to influence the supply and demand of foreign exchange by some kind of control over items entering into the balance of payments. Often the measures are in the direction of maintaining artificial exchange rate quotations. Sometimes, however, their purpose is to correct abnormal exchange relationships and sometimes to reduce erratic deviations from the norm.

Exchange Stabilization

Various countries have undertaken to limit exchange rate fluctuations without going to extremes such as those described below. Perhaps the best known attempt of this sort was the Exchange Equalization Fund established by the British at the time of their departure from the gold standard in 1931. In 1933 the United States followed their example by creating the Exchange Stabilization Fund out of part of the profits resulting from dollar devaluation. The apparent need for such measures arises from the fact that under paper-standard conditions there is no automatic cushioning item such as gold movements, and movements of short-term balances, instead of being equilibrating, may sometimes be a source of disturbance. Consequently, the exchange value of paper currency may exhibit erratic fluctuations which, far from promoting orderly adjustments, tend to impair confidence and encourage speculation.

A stabilization fund for reducing exchange rate fluctuations operates on a simple supply-and-demand basis: if the exchange rate tends to move in the wrong direction the fund seeks to alter supply and demand in such a way as to offset the disturbing element. An exchange stabilization fund consists of two parts, a supply of foreign exchange and a supply of domestic funds. The stabilization operation consists of selling foreign exchange when the value of foreign exchange is tending to rise unduly and purchasing foreign exchange when its value is tending to fall unduly.

The procedure of buying or selling is similar to what would have to be done in order to stabilize the price of any ordinary commodity, such as wheat or cotton, in the domestic market. The limits of the ability of a stabilization fund to accomplish the purpose for which it is intended are governed by the adequacy of the fund's resources and the willingness of the authorities to employ them to that end. The justification for such measures lies, needless to say, in their being used to restrain erratic or disturbing fluctuations in exchange rates and not in their use to perpetuate artificial currency values.

Exchange Control

The term "exchange control" refers to the regulation of transactions involving foreign exchange with a view to relieving pressure on the exchange value of a particular currency. In its milder forms it consists of moderate measures—such as the restriction of non-essential imports—for reducing the demand for foreign exchange until some temporary strain on the balance of payments has passed. In the more extreme forms which have led to its unfavorable reputation, it involves maintaining, for an indefinite period, an artificial exchange value of the currency by means which may be damaging to economic relations with other countries.

Exchange control came into disrepute during the 1930's partly because of the extremes to which it was carried and the abuses that flourished under it. Applied on a more moderate scale after World War II, it came to be accepted as an unfortunate but sometimes justifiable means of dealing with balance of payments difficulties. In particular, Canada, Great Britain, and other countries found it necessary to economic reconstruction, and India and other countries have looked upon the rationing of scarce foreign exchange resources as an indispensable instrument for economic development.

Exchange control assumes an almost infinite variety of forms, but the basic idea is very simple, that is, the regulation of sources of demand and supply of foreign exchange. One of the most familiar exchange control practices is the resort to "blocked accounts," which result when restrictions are placed on the withdrawal of balances payable to foreigners. By refusing to allow such funds to be converted into foreign currency the current demand for foreign exchange is cut down. Gradual release of the blocked accounts may make it possible to transfer the funds abroad without the disturbing effects that would have followed their sudden withdrawal.

In the more extreme forms of exchange control, foreign exchange is rationed by an elaborate system of priorities designed to ensure satisfaction of ends given highest priority by the government. Travel abroad may be prohibited except for business purposes likely to provide additional exchange.

Capital transfers may be impeded or stopped. Imports are subjected to license in order to exclude luxuries and give preference to necessities and to raw materials required in producing for export. Strenuous efforts are made to detect and combat evasion of these controls, though never with complete success.

With full-scale exchange control, foreign exchange proceeds must be turned over to the control authorities. Moreover, various devices may be employed to force an expansion of the supply of foreign exchange. For example, simple export subsidies may be used, or elaborate systems may be devised whereby receipts from domestic and export sales are pooled to enable losses on export operations to be recouped out of profits on domestic sales. In the 1930's Germany established a system of multiple quotations for the mark with different rates corresponding to different uses.[1] Similar methods were used by Argentina and other countries much more recently.

A familiar feature of exchange control systems is the use of so-called "clearing agreements," negotiated to permit large-scale barter transactions with foreign countries or for other purposes. Sometimes commercial bargaining is backed up by a certain amount of political or even military pressure. Again, when an agreement is about to come up for reconsideration, a country may find itself maneuvered into a position where it must renew on more or less the other country's terms if it is to receive payment on balances already due.

In these and other ways, control of foreign exchange opens the door to all manner of abuses. There can be no doubt that Germany employed exchange control to facilitate the accumulation of stockpiles of war materials, to cement alliances, to weaken possible enemies, and to acquire information. Control of foreign exchange was a powerful instrument for regimenting the domestic economy as well, since the directing of imports could often be used to stimulate or retard particular types of production. It was even alleged that Germany employed exchange restrictions to drive down the market price of German bonds owned abroad and then diverted foreign exchange to the purchase of these securities at a depressed value.

Exchange control involves discrimination among the different uses to which foreign exchange resources may be put (e.g., for payment of debts or for one type of import or another), and this is very likely to entail the appearance and perhaps the reality of discrimination among countries. As practiced in the 1930's, exchange control tended to reduce the total volume of international transactions through restricting the demand for foreign exchange to the available supply. In the 1950's and 1960's, on the other hand, exchange control was less a means of restricting totals than of altering the composition of international transactions. Notwithstanding its continuing

---

1. "Travel marks" for the use of tourists visiting Germany were obtainable at a substantial reduction from the official rate. The lowest rate of all was available to persons in foreign countries desiring to make gifts in Germany.

use by a good many countries, it is generally looked upon as an uncomfortable necessity in what it is hoped will be a temporary situation of strain on the international balance of payments.

Currency Warfare vs. Corrective Adjustment of Exchange Rates

Countries may attempt to gain a competitive advantage over other countries in foreign trade by establishing a lower foreign exchange value for their currencies. Ordinarily the expectation is that this will enable them to undersell producers in other countries, especially in common export markets. The names "currency warfare," "exchange dumping," and "competitive devaluation" have been given to the use of exchange depreciation as a means of securing a competitive advantage in foreign trade.

The condition on which the success of such a policy depends is that the external value of the currency should be low relative to its internal value, that is, that money buys more inside the country than outside. As long as this relationship exists, exports will tend to be stimulated and imports, relatively speaking, will tend to be restricted. But a policy directed toward this end may find itself circumvented in a number of different ways. Some countries may retaliate by depreciating their currencies also. Others may impose import restrictions such as higher tariffs, quotas, and licensing provisions. Some countries may do both. Even in the absence of these measures, the disparity between internal and external purchasing power of the currency would tend to be closed by rising domestic prices and a strengthening of the value of the currency in foreign exchange markets.

Trade advantages gained from depressing the foreign exchange value of a currency materially below the level which corresponds to its internal value are likely to be short-lived. The possible stimulus to exports would have to be weighed against the worsening of the terms of trade of the country initiating currency depreciation. There would also be accompanying disadvantages in the form of mounting trade barriers, retaliation abroad, and the threat of inflation at home. Competitive exchange depreciation has proved damaging both to the world economy and to the individual countries practicing it.

It is not to be inferred, however, that all instances of currency devaluation are objectionable. A desire to obtain an advantage over other countries in export trade is by no means the only possible motive which may inspire a country to allow its currency to depreciate. Lowering the foreign exchange value of a previously overvalued currency to a level corresponding to its internal purchasing power is altogether different from competitive devaluation. Instead of attempting to set an artificially low exchange value for the currency, its effect is to correct a previous abnormality. Where this is the basis of devaluation the action should not be condemned but strongly endorsed.

It was for this reason that the devaluation of the French franc in 1936 was not only welcomed but even abetted by authorities in the United States and England. By the official "use of appropriate available resources" to prevent undue fluctuations in franc quotations, they undertook to facilitate the transition to a new level of exchange rates. It was their general belief that establishment of a new pattern of exchange rates for currencies which had held out against devaluation up to that time would contribute to the relaxation of quotas and removal of restrictive exchange control policies. A later report of the Bank for International Settlements commented on the "distinction between a currency adjustment likely to produce a more stable basis for international economic relations and the reduction of the foreign exchange value of a currency to such a low point as to be regarded as a measure of competitive exchange depreciation."

The devaluation of the pound in the autumn of 1949 was also strongly favored by officials in the United States. The desire to have the exchange value of the pound lowered apparently reflected a belief that the pound was overvalued relative to its internal purchasing power and that a corrective readjustment would therefore help to overcome the continuing scarcity of dollar exchange. In cases such as these the basic presumption is that a lowering of the exchange rate may be the most effective means of correcting a condition of what has come to be called "fundamental disequilibrium" in the balance of payments.[2]

Of the four types of exchange rate practices examined above, two, currency warfare and corrective adjustments, are directed toward changing exchange rates and two, exchange control and exchange stabilization, toward preventing exchange rate changes. Two of the four, corrective adjustment and exchange stabilization, are generally looked upon as desirable and the other two as undesirable. The contrast suggests a significant conclusion, namely, that the test of what is desirable turns not so much on whether or not there is intervention as upon the circumstances under which it occurs and the lengths to which it is carried.

INTERNATIONAL FINANCIAL INSTITUTIONS

As was noted earlier, the problem of international monetary reconstruction after World War I was construed to be that of restoring, in the main, the financial and economic institutions that existed in 1914. Well before the end of World War II, on the other hand, it was evident that the international gold standard could not be revived and therefore that a new international monetary structure would have to be created. In addition, new credit institutions were required which would make possible the flow of capital for rehabilitation and development in a world where confidence in traditional methods of investing abroad had been undermined. The changed circum-

---

2. See above, pp. 565-567.

stances and public attitudes here and abroad made the problem of postwar financial policy one not of restoration but of reconstruction, and more particularly of reconstruction along new and untried lines. All this had to be accomplished in the face of worldwide political insecurity and ideological differences, and with available financial resources largely confined to the United States.

The problem of international financial reconstruction was simplified, in a sense, by its very gravity. The seriousness of the obstacles to be overcome contributed to a willingness to work together in studying mutual difficulties and agreeing to solutions with a promptness that might have been lacking under less difficult circumstances. Moreover, the period after World War I had taught some pointed lessons; the experience of those earlier years enabled us, for example, to avoid the troublesome issue of war debt by the simple expedient of canceling Lend-Lease obligations. Finally, the absence of accord with Russia was perhaps as responsible as anything else for getting us to supply badly needed financial assistance to hard-pressed countries of Europe after the war and later to underdeveloped countries in other parts of the world.

The International Monetary Fund

The world had had experience with three main types of monetary arrangements—the international gold standard, relatively free and independent paper standard currencies, and the type of inconvertible currency with controlled exchange rates of which the German reichsmark under the Nazis furnished the best known example. Each of these systems is noteworthy for a feature peculiar to it. The international gold standard is distinguished by *stability* of exchange rates among the different countries adhering to the standard. The relatively free paper standard system is characterized by *flexibility* of exchange rates. Currencies operated under a system of exchange control are distinguished by the high degree of administrative *regulation* to which they are subject, regulation which may extend to the exercise of supervision and control—as by rationing, licensing, and the like—over most or all of the country's economic transactions.

None of these three methods was acceptable to those charged with drawing up international monetary plans for the postwar world. The gold standard was regarded by many countries as unduly rigid. The British in particular, but other countries as well, blamed the gold standard in large measure for their troubles during the depression of the 1930's and were disposed to think of it as "a device for exporting unemployment." Free paper standards were associated in the minds of many with disorder and chaos in foreign exchange relationships—exchange rate movements were often thought of as destabilizing and disruptive rather than as equilibrating. Most criticized of all was the system of exchange controls. These controls had not only been resorted to most extensively by Fascist governments, but, in addition, they lent themselves to discriminatory trade practices and tended toward economic warfare.

The International Monetary Fund was developed as an alternative to any one of these three monetary systems. It represents a blending of the distinctive features of all of them with, of course, many structural details of its own. The manner in which it embodies stability, flexibility, and—under exceptional and presumably rare circumstances—a certain degree of authoritarian control is the most important fact to bear in mind concerning the International Monetary Fund.

The International Monetary Fund has two primary purposes—to promote exchange rate stability by facilitating the adjustment of minor inequalities in the supply and demand of foreign exchange and to permit orderly changes in exchange rates when "fundamental disequilibrium" in exchange rates arises. To meet the first of these objectives a revolving fund was created through subscriptions by participating countries on the basis of assigned quotas. Member countries are allowed to draw upon the Fund to meet temporary shortages of foreign exchange, the amount each country is entitled to draw being governed by the size of its quota. Payments into and out of the Fund to meet temporary discrepancies in the supply and demand of foreign exchange operate in substantially the same way as the exchange stabilization funds which were established during the 1930's. The bulk of foreign exchange transactions, however, are handled through ordinary channels.

A shortage or excess of foreign exchange may be the result not of seasonal or other temporary factors but of a continuing unrealistic valuation of a country's currency. In case of such a "fundamental disequilibrium"—a meaningful though operationally somewhat indefinite concept—a member country is allowed to alter the exchange value of its currency by 10 per cent. It was provided that the Fund should be consulted when this change is made, but its consent was not required. Additional or larger changes, however, were to be made only after concurrence by the Fund.

The provision for promoting stability of exchange rates represented an adaptation of the gold standard's technique for promoting stable exchange rates between countries. The provision for allowing official exchange rates to be altered with or without the consent of the Fund's officers constituted an adaptation of the mechanism afforded by paper standards for effecting price level adjustments between countries.

The third distinctive feature of foreign exchange policy, that of administrative control of international exchange operations, was embodied in a provision for rationing scarce currencies.[3] In the event that the demand for a particular currency threatens to exhaust the available supply of that cur-

---

3. This authority has never officially been invoked.

rency or to precipitate a scramble among members for the limited supply, the Fund may notify members of the danger of a scarcity and recommend means of meeting the shortage. In case the stringency continues, the Fund may declare that the currency is scarce and undertake to apportion the existing supply among member countries. The various members are then allowed to limit transactions in that currency in accordance with their supply of the currency. This authorization of what amounts in substance to exchange control, far from according approval to the methods which were adopted during the 1930's, was designed to eliminate the possibility of a general return to such conditions. The purpose of the provision for rationing scarce currency was to prevent a reckless bidding up of exchange rates in case of a shortage of foreign exchange.

The accomplishments of the International Monetary Fund have not been as great as was expected at the time it was established—the difficulty of the task of monetary reconstruction at the end of the war was greatly underestimated. Changes in exchange rates much greater than the law stipulated have occurred, often with little regard for approval by the Fund. Exchange control and other trade restrictions were not removed as quickly or as widely as was hoped. Despite these disappointments, it is reasonable to suppose that in the absence of the Fund, exchange conditions would have been far worse. Not the least of the Fund's achievements was to provide its members with a forum for the discussion of mutual problems.

The Bank for Reconstruction and Development

Although the operations of the Fund possess some of the characteristics of a loan of foreign currency, it is a basic principle of the plan that the Fund should not be used for permanent financing, and numerous safeguards were included to assure that this would not happen. A separate institution, the International Bank for Reconstruction and Development or, more familiarly, the World Bank, was created to promote long-term investment for productive purposes. The membership of the Bank is similar to that of the Fund. Members were required to subscribe to specified amounts of capital in the Bank, corresponding closely to the quotas established for the Fund. Of the total amount subscribed, 20 per cent was paid in soon after the start of operations and the other 80 per cent remains subject to call if needed to meet losses or to fulfill guarantees. Total loans by the Bank from 1946 to the end of fiscal 1961 amounted to well over 5½ billion dollars.

The Bank acts through the Treasury, central bank, or other fiscal agency of the country where it is lending money. With the aid of these agencies, credit may be extended or guaranteed to private enterprises. The declared purposes of the Bank are to facilitate productive investments abroad by means of guarantees and participations to assist private foreign investment, and to provide a source of loans when private capital is not forthcoming on reasonable terms.

In considering applications for loans, the Bank makes extensive use of survey missions. These consist of groups of experts drawn from inside and outside the Bank's staff. A secondary but significant purpose of the studies conducted has been to improve administrative efficiency, raise the level of technical education, and make the results of scientific research more available in the developing countries.

Lending policy is on a business basis. Loans are made only if the success of the undertaking and full repayment of the loan seem assured. Early loans were largely for reconstruction, particularly in France, Holland, and Denmark, and capital came largely from the United States. Subsequent loans were mainly developmental, as for financing electric power and transportation in Latin America, Asia, and Africa. Capital has been drawn from a variety of sources in the United States and Europe.

International Finance Corporation

Accomplishments of the World Bank within its first decade, despite a rather slow start, were substantial. Attention thereupon turned increasingly toward another problem, that of helping to finance private ventures where a considerable element of risk was present. The result was the establishment of the International Finance Corporation which began operations in 1956. The relatively small capital was subscribed by member countries of the World Bank.

The IFC was organized to lend to private enterprises only, and without government guarantee. Its intended role was described as "catalytic" in the sense of promoting the flow of private capital into such undertakings. This was to be accomplished in two ways. The first was by other investors joining in to provide the initial investment in particular undertakings. It was found that in some cases private investors in Europe and the United States and Canada were willing to participate simply because of the fact that the Corporation had studied the project carefully and was investing its own funds. The other means of facilitating the flow of outside capital was by the Corporation selling all or part of its investment after the enterprise had demonstrated its worth. Thus the Charter stipulated that the IFC should "revolve its funds by selling its investments to private investors whenever it can appropriately do so on satisfactory terms." It was expected that participation by investors within the countries themselves would also be encouraged.

Lending terms reflect the venture element in the undertakings. The usual credit instrument is an unsecured long-term obligation, often subordinated to other creditors. The average interest charge has been about 7 per cent. In some instances all or part of the investment has been free of any mandatory interest charge, with payments contingent upon earnings. Certain of the loans, though made in dollars, have been repayable in other currencies, e.g., the pound sterling or the Italian lira. The contractual rates of return, though high relative to rates in the lending countries, are generally low compared with what would have to be paid in the borrowing countries.

Loans were few in the first years. By September 1960, however, the Corporation had made thirty-six loans amounting to nearly $45 million in seventeen countries distributed among all continents including Australia. The size of loans ranged from $90,000 to $3,660,000. Private participations amounted to another $6,411,000.

What makes the IFC and its affiliated undertakings chiefly noteworthy is that they constitute an attempt to supplement existing international financial machinery by facilitating the flow of venture, as contrasted with ordinary loan, capital. In the long run, the success of the IFC will be measured not in terms of the capital provided directly by it but in terms of the extent to which private investment capital has been encouraged to go into the desired ventures.[4]

PROBLEMS AND POLICIES OF THE POSTWAR PERIOD

As was to be expected, the task of postwar reconstruction imposed severe burdens on international balances of payments. Despite the efforts of the International Monetary Fund and the financial assistance supplied by the World Bank and the United States government, countries found it impossible to dispense with controls over trade and foreign exchange. For the most part, the purpose of the restrictions was to prevent exchange resources from being dissipated by luxury spending and withdrawals of capital. They were an adjunct to policies of survival and recovery. To some extent, also, they tended to become instruments of social and economic reform.

The principal international financial problems of the postwar period—problems such as the restoration of convertibility, shortage of dollars, international liquidity, and the status of gold—were closely interrelated. They were also closely connected with the goal of removing, or at least relaxing, the various impediments to free markets in foreign exchange. Moreover, the extension of massive foreign aid was a major factor in relieving the balance of payments difficulties of recipient countries—but not without, at times, creating fairly serious exchange difficulties for donor countries.

Currency Convertibility

Formerly "convertibility" signified the redeemability of a country's currency in gold. By the 1950's it meant the freedom to exchange one

---

4. The Export-Import Bank, established in 1934, has participated extensively in foreign lending but is not discussed here since it is a United States rather than an international institution. See below, pp. 600-601.

currency for another. The shift in meaning is symptomatic of the diminished importance attached to gold and the great importance attached to freedom from exchange restrictions.

The difficulty of achieving general convertibility in even this limited sense resulted from a variety of causes. Basically, of course, it reflected the absence of an effective means—such as was provided by the international gold standard and by exchange rate movements under paper standards—for bringing the exchange rates of the various countries into an equilibrium relationship. Countries were unable or unwilling to accept either the gold or the free paper mechanism for adjusting conditions of fundamental disequilibrium; instead they relied upon control devices for regulating the supply of and demand for foreign exchange. And it is probable that to some extent officials found in the control devices a means of escape from the discipline as well as the uncertainties which either of the other systems would have imposed.

Those who favored a return to convertibility, on the other hand, presumably wanted to reduce red tape and restrictiveness and to allow greater freedom for the operation of market influences. Refusal of the authorities to accede to the demand for restoration of convertibility implied their judgment that basic market conditions were still too abnormal and unstabilizing to be allowed to govern dealings in foreign exchange. The process of monetary rehabilitation after the war ran into such difficulties as the premature attempt to make the pound convertible in 1947, military crises in Korea and Suez, and recurrent incidents in the cold war.

Economic aid supplied by United Nations institutions, the United States, and others helped to ease balance of payments difficulties directly by providing needed foreign exchange and indirectly by contributing to reconstruction and development. Advances once made helped to supply the sinews for further advance, as the dramatic economic achievements of Germany and other countries clearly demonstrated. Not least important, the International Monetary Fund assumed an active role, providing substantial support to England in 1956 and to France in 1957. In 1958, sooner than would have been expected only a year or two before, it was possible to announce a major step in the restoration of convertibility. Most of the countries of Europe as well as some others agreed to the free interchange of currencies for all but a limited number of transactions.[5] Because of the impact which they have on items in the balance of payments, political and economic developments can be expected, however, to influence the success of efforts to maintain and to extend currency convertibility in the future.

---

5. The principal exception was to restrict transfer of domestic balances by citizens of the country while allowing such transfers, sometimes on a gradual basis, by foreigners.

The Dollar Problem

For a number of years after World War II a great deal of attention was directed toward the alleged "chronic dollar shortage." Countries feared that removal of controls would lead to undue demand to exchange local currency for dollars. It was believed by some that this would result in a further shift to the purchase of American goods; by others that it might proceed to a demoralized dumping of foreign currencies in a scramble for the comparative safety and security afforded by dollar balances.

There were those who contended that the superiority of American productive capacity and methods was so great and America's need for foreign goods was so limited as to cause an imbalance in the supply and demand for dollar exchange regardless of the price of foreign currencies. The foundations of the problem of dollar shortage were alleged to go back for many years. It was primarily because of the fear of dollar shortage that the "scarce currency provision" of the International Monetary Fund was introduced, giving official sanction to the imposition of quantitative restrictions on transactions with countries whose currencies were in continuing short supply.

On the other hand, there were those who argued that fears were exaggerated and that the free play of market forces could be counted on to establish rates which would produce equilibrium. It was intimated that continuance of controls was perpetuating the disequilibrium situation and tending to stifle production throughout the world.

The Anglo-American Loan of 1946 was designed to assist in relieving the shortage of dollars. Belief that it was sufficient to do so was reflected in the provision of the loan agreement that the British would remove existing restrictions on international financial operations. When this was attempted in the summer of 1947 the switching from pounds to dollars by foreign nationals was so immediate and heavy that dollar resources were threatened with exhaustion. The attempt was quickly abandoned and exchange dealings again subjected to control.

The 1947 experience tended to confirm the worst fears of dollar shortage. Devaluation of the pound in 1949, which officials in the American government strongly endorsed, was intended to relieve the situation by making the dollar dearer in terms of currencies within the sterling area. This undoubtedly helped as did the dollars supplied by the various types of foreign assistance.

The Marshall Plan, moreover, aided in establishing the European Payments Union in 1950. This was essentially an organization for the clearing of foreign exchange transactions among member countries. These included Turkey as well as most of the non-communist countries of Europe. Despite certain difficulties the plan was a distinct success and served as a pattern for other regional clearing organizations. From the standpoint of member countries it helped to relieve the problem of dollar scarcity and to afford, within a limited area, the advantages of currency convertibility. From the standpoint of the United States, its chief advantage lay in any contribution which it might make to the recovery of foreign countries; its disadvantage, that we were the principal excluded country and the system could lend itself to direct discrimination against dollar transactions. Fortunately, it did not, in fact, become an agency of serious discrimination.

With the continuance of substantial foreign aid by the United States and steady economic progress abroad the problem of dollar shortage became less acute. The restoration of currency convertibility in 1958 was a dramatic demonstration of the improvement which had taken place. Nevertheless,

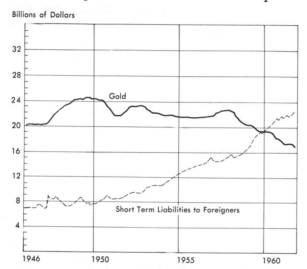

Figure 30-1.   U.S. Gold Stock and Short-Term Liabilities to Foreigners, 1946-1961.

Source: Data from *Federal Reserve Bulletin*.

concern over the problem of dollar shortage was still being expressed in influential quarters. And the United States was repeatedly petitioned to raise the price of gold in order, among other things, to make it easier for foreign countries to acquire dollars.

A net outflow of gold amounting to approximately $2½ billion occurred in 1958 (see Figure 30-1). This movement, along with the rising volume of foreign balances in the United States, indicated that dollars were no longer in short supply. In fact, the growing concern over the outflow of gold and the growth of short-term claims against the United States was tantamount to saying that the problem was now one of dollar surplus rather than dollar scarcity! This turn of events suggested that the problem of international liquidity, which had long been looked upon as something only foreigners had to worry about, had now become a matter of deep concern to Americans.

International Liquidity and the Problem of Payments Imbalances

Gold and Liquidity. The monetary role of gold has a long and varied history with the latest stage perhaps the most confused of all. Originally, of course, it was chiefly important as circulating medium. Later it combined this function with that of the regulator of the money supply. This was its traditional role under the pre-1914 international gold standard. Gold reserves were thought of as a regulator fund: changes in the volume of reserves would presumably result in more or less proportional changes in the money supply. An extension of the same idea was that movements of gold between countries served as a guide to central bank policies designed to facilitate appropriate adjustments in the money supply. The use of gold as a medium for settling balances between countries was, of course, a central feature of this gold standard mechanism. The use of gold as circulating medium, while generally present still, assumed distinctly secondary importance.

In the *Treatise on Money* published in 1930, J. M. Keynes described a somewhat different role for gold. It was that reserves should provide "liquidity." That is, they should serve as a cushioning device, enabling countries to avoid disturbances to their monetary systems that might otherwise result from temporary fluctuations in the balance of international payments. In conformity with this idea he reasoned that the size of gold reserves should be related to anticipated deficits in the trade balance. A country exporting raw materials subject to fluctuations in output and to wide swings in price was presumed to require relatively larger gold reserves than a country with more stable exports.[6]

Two points are particularly to be noted in the argument advanced by Keynes. First, gold reserves were viewed not as the regulator of monetary policies but as a liquidity cushion which would help to insulate domestic policies from the full impact of international disturbances. This implied that domestic monetary goals should not be unduly subordinated to international monetary aims. Second, the international disturbances were conceived of in terms of fluctuations in the balance of trade, the commodity items being assumed to dominate fluctuations in the balance of payments.

The position of gold in the monetary system of the United States today is markedly different from what it was under the pre-1914 international gold standard. As in practically every other country of the world, gold no longer circulates. Even gold certificates are available only to the Federal Reserve Banks. More significantly, gold movements between countries no longer influence to the extent that they once did the volume of monetary circulation in the respective shipping and receiving countries. In fact, changes in the

---

6. J. M. Keynes, *A Treatise on Money* (London: Macmillan, 1930), Vol. II, pp. 272, 276-78.

volume of our gold reserves have had virtually no recognizable connection with the money supply as may be seen from Figure 30-2. Thus the traditional role of gold movements as the regulator of money and guide to central bank policy seems almost entirely to have disappeared.

Reflecting the changed position of gold, prevailing conceptions of the role of gold have undergone corresponding changes. Concern over gold movements has been based on the thought that they might interfere with monetary and fiscal policies, especially those directed toward maintenance of full employment and economic growth. This view of the gold problem was not unlike that suggested earlier by Keynes, except that the objectives

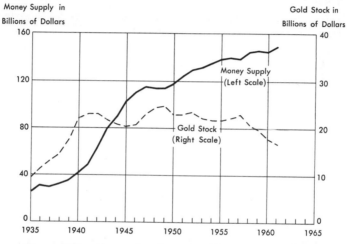

Figure 30-2. Money Supply and Gold Stock, 1935-1961.

Source: Adapted from the Federal Reserve Historical Chart Book.

of the monetary policies contemplated were somewhat different. In contrast with the earlier period, however, the pressure on the balance of payments was now primarily thought of as arising not out of fluctuations in commodity items but in the invisibles, particularly foreign aid and short-term capital movements.

The most striking difference is that throughout the period after World War II dollar balances occupied a position equivalent to that of gold in the monetary reserves of most countries. Obviously this constituted a significant dwindling in the dominant, independent status formerly ascribed to gold. It also implied a merging of the dollar problem and the gold problem. They became dual aspects of the problem of international liquidity. And upon the monetary authorities of the United States was placed a double responsibility for wisdom in the policies pursued.

The problem that aroused greatest public notice in this country was the persistent drain of gold reserves from the United States during the late 1950's and early 1960's.[7] Little or no recognition was given to the possibility that the movement was in the nature of a redistribution of the gold which had flowed to the United States in excessive quantities before and after World War II, or to the fact that holdings were still high relative to the share held in the days of the old gold standard. Nor was there any disposition to see in the outward movement of gold a reflection of the success of American efforts throughout the postwar years to strengthen foreign economic systems and improve international security. It might well have been argued that the acquistion of gold by foreign countries was a natural consequence of their economic rehabilitation and a necessary step in establishing the stability of their currencies.

Instead, forebodings were expressed as to the serious consequences to the United States of a continued drain of gold. Alarm reached national proportions when the price of gold in the London market suddenly spurted to $41 an ounce during the presidential campaign of 1960. The brief flurry was influenced by highly volatile short-term capital movements of the sort referred to earlier.[8] At the very time that the dollar experienced this apparent deterioration in terms of gold, it continued to maintain its full value in the far more significant exchange markets of the world. The fact that a sudden rise in the price of gold could occur at all, as well as the fact that similar fluctuations had taken place at various times before, was an indication of the extent to which gold, in some markets at least, had lost its basic monetary character and became just another commodity, a prey to speculators and (possibly) manipulators.

Short-run Measures for Relieving the Pressure on Liquidity. A considerable element of irrationality was undoubtedly present in the fears aroused by the outflow of gold from the United States. And the problem of international liquidity may have become something of an obsession. Nevertheless, the outflow was real, and it was persistent. In an effort to calm public fears, the newly elected President announced that the dollar would be firmly defended. Moreover, the conservative tendencies of subsequent Kennedy policies may have been dictated in some measure by the desire to dispel the view that a Democratic Administration might jeopardize the dollar.

Measures of a more concrete character were also adopted for meeting the apparent threat to international liquidity. Lending quotas of the International Monetary Fund were increased in 1961. Early in 1962 a plan was announced for expanding still further the facilities for borrowing from the Fund. In this instance it was provided that authorization for such loans must also be obtained from members of the Organization for Economic Cooperation and Development. This stipulation was apparently designed to make

---

7. "Drain" is something of a misnomer if interpreted literally. The major part of the movement consisted of a shift of title without the gold physically leaving the country. Gold held in this country subject to foreign ownership is said to be under earmark.

8. See above, pp. 552-553, 558.

sure that the additional resources should be used only for meeting genuine liquidity needs.

The most interesting innovation was the introduction, also in 1962, of arrangements with a number of foreign central banks whereby the Federal Reserve Bank of New York swapped dollars against their respective currencies. The agreements were combined with appropriate guarantees in the event of devaluation of any of the currencies concerned. The effect was to supply currencies with which to engage in exchange stabilization operations. And it was an ingenious and effective means of quickly expanding the volume of internationally liquid assets.

The gold drain was also partly responsible for another innovation in Federal Reserve policy. Early in 1961 the authorities found themselves confronted with a policy dilemma. A substantial spread between short rates in Europe and this country seemed to call for raising rates here to check the flow of gold abroad. On the other hand, recovery was lagging from a recession and the rate of economic growth was considerably slower than desired. This seemed to call for lower rates.

Faced with this conflict, the authorities undertook to push up the short rate (presumably more important with respect to short-term capital movements) while holding down the long rate (presumably more important for recovery and growth). The bills-only policy which had been in effect for many years was obviously incompatible with such a complicated maneuver and was abandoned, though not solely for this reason.

Following the adoption of the new policy the spread between long and short rates was narrowed and the drain of gold slowed down. It would be too much to give the change in Federal Reserve policy full credit for the improvement. But it is significant that a new dimension, a new element of flexibility, was thus introduced into Federal Reserve policy.

Proposals for Raising the Price of Gold. Repeatedly in the postwar period proposals were advanced for raising the price of gold in terms of the dollar. Strongest support for these proposals came, not surprisingly, from gold-producing countries, particularly South Africa. They were joined by producing interests in the United States and at times by others abroad and in this country.

The case for raising the price of gold frequently proceeded from the observation that the price of gold was the same as in 1934 even though commodity prices had greatly increased. No mention was made of the fact that the price established for gold in 1934 was exceptionally high while 1934 commodity prices were exceptionally low. Furthermore, the fact that the price of gold was raised at that time in the hope of causing commodity prices to rise would imply that in the postwar years when the problem was just the opposite (that of trying to prevent inflation) the price should be lowered rather than raised.

From a strictly monetary standpoint, proposals for increasing the price of gold are inconsistent with the basic conception of gold as a standard. The first requirement of the gold standard was always a fixed and unchanging relationship between gold and the monetary unit. This was an essential precondition of the operation of gold in promoting stable monetary and exchange values. The status of gold as a sovereign metal was violated when the tradition of a fixed price of gold was abandoned in 1931 and 1933. Proposals for changing the official price of gold, no less than actual day-to-day changes in market quotations for gold, are a measure of the degree to which gold has lost its position as a monetary standard and become just another commodity. Recommendations such as these—even though they are advanced by those who regard themselves as friends of gold—have the tendency, far from helping to rehabilitate the monetary prestige of gold, to undermine it further.

A higher price for gold was also advocated on the ground that it would help to relieve the dollar shortage by raising the dollar value of existing gold stocks and by enabling gold producers to obtain more dollars for a given quantity of gold. The idea of dispensing aid to foreign countries on the basis of present stocks of gold and of the gold they would be able to produce appeared singularly unenlightened.[9] Subsequently, the somewhat more convincing argument was advanced that the higher price would help to relieve an impending shortage of internationally acceptable liquid assets, an issue touched upon briefly below.

The Proposal for an International Central Bank. Numerous plans were advanced in the 1950's and 1960's for relieving the alleged problem of international liquidity. The most widely discussed was one set forth with great vigor by Professor Triffin.[10] It was pointed out that foreign trade was increasing at the rate of 3 or 4 per cent a year and gold supplies at less than 2 per cent. Expansion in dollar balances available to foreign countries had supplied liquid assets after the war but this could not continue without jeopardizing the position of the dollar. Consequently, it was said, an impending shortage of internationally acceptable liquid assets threatened to stifle economic growth not only in the United States but throughout the world.

Professor Triffin's suggestion was for central banks to pool their gold reserves with one central institution which would then become, in prototype, a central bank for central banks. Like other banks it would have the power to create credit. These credits would constitute legal reserves for the central banks. By providing this new source of internationally acceptable liquid assets the international liquidity problem could be ameliorated.

---

9. Especially at a time when Russia, whom we were certainly in no mood to assist in this way, was reputed to be the second largest producer of gold in the world and the holder of the second largest supply of gold.

10. R. Triffin, *Gold and the Dollar Crisis* (New Haven: Yale University Press, 1960), esp. pp. 3-14, 102-20; O. L. Altman, "Professor Triffin on International Liquidity and the Role of the Fund," International Monetary Fund. *Staff Papers*, May 1961; and R. Triffin, "After the Gold Exchange Standard?," *Weltwirtschaftliches Archiv*, Vol. 87, No. 2, 1961.

The case for an international central bank of this kind is not to be regarded as resting solely on an impending *long-run* shortage of reserves. Such an emphasis tends to exaggerate the relation of gold supply to volume of trade. It seems more important that severe pressure on balances of payments are likely to come not from the trade items but from short-term capital movements. Historically, crises of international liquidity—as in the 1930's, at the time of the Suez incident, and, on a smaller scale, during the gold scare toward the end of 1960—were seldom if ever associated with trade expansion (often just the opposite) but with capital movements and a weakening of public confidence. A plan geared to the trade items rests on an inadequate foundation: demands for liquidity arising from this source could probably be met in other ways, including possibly a reduction of the Federal Reserve's gold certificate reserve requirements as was done in 1945. The greater need is for an institution able, in the *short run*, to serve as lender of last resort on an international scale, as central banks traditionally do on a domestic scale.

A practical objection to adoption of an international central bank was the unwillingness of countries to surrender their gold reserves to—and presumably to subject their monetary policies to the authority of—a vast supranational organization such as the plan would set up. This is not to deny either the logical appeal or perhaps the ultimate wisdom of a central bank for central banks. But the obstacles to its adoption are none the less formidable because they are parochial rather than conceptual.

The Imbalance Issue in Perspective. It is probably safe to say that there has been no year since 1914 when some, at least, of the leading countries of the world were not concerned over possible pressure on the international balance of payments. At times the strains were acute and occasionally they were general. The United States, which most of the time was in a uniquely easy position in terms of its international accounts, came later to share the feeling of concern over payments imbalance.

A variety of reasons have been offered to explain the conditions of international monetary strain, especially as they apply to the United States. Some of the explanations doubtless possessed merit. Others were mistaken or out of focus, and some appeared inconsistent with a simple reading of monetary history.

Those who emphasized the threat of insufficient international monetary resources advanced, among others, the following reasons for their fears:

a. The supply of monetary reserves (gold and the reserve currencies, dollars and pounds sterling) have increased less than the volume of international trade. Productivity is continuing to rise rapidly throughout the world.
b. The increased liberalization of trade accentuates the need for reserves.
c. Where formerly the need for reserves was based on uneven timing of cyclical fluctuations among countries, now it is more the result of structural imbalance which takes longer to correct.

d. The commitment by advanced countries to assist underdeveloped countries and to provide military aid to allies requires that sufficient reserves be available to meet sudden demands upon them.

e. Shortages of reserves, actual and prospective, are responsible for growing pressures to adopt restrictive policies with respect to trade, money, and foreign assistance.

Those who feel that the need for additional reserves is exaggerated make the following points, among others:

a. Reserve requirements are not necessarily proportional to the total volume of trade. Britain operated at one time with minimal gold reserves, under liberal trade policies, with trade expanding, and when the pound was hardly less a key currency than the dollar is today. The rise in output and trade throughout the world is more likely to ease than to aggravate the main sources of balance of payments strain.

b. When liquidity crises have occurred in the past it was as a consequence of sudden demand arising out of the fear of economic collapse or war and not of the starvation of reserves. These fears are not to be overcome by piling up more and more reserves.

c. Cyclical dislocations have become less acute, thus reducing a major source of strain and loss of confidence. Economic developments of recent years, including measures to control cyclical fluctuations, the strengthening of economic systems of the west, and advances in underdeveloped areas have been in the direction of greater stability, improved confidence, and a lessening rather than an aggravation of the sources of international strain.

d. A certain amount of pressure for restrictive measures always exists but is mainly attributable to influences and attitudes other than those related to the balance of payments position. Actually, international economic policies are far more liberal than in the past, as the trade program of the United States and the rise of the Common Market demonstrate.

e. Demand for reserves to aid foreign countries are relatively controllable and are not subject to sudden expansion. In case of war, exchange problems would have to be dealt with by other means.

Foreign Assistance by the United States

The magnitude, coverage, and continuity of international economic assistance that has been forthcoming year after year since 1945 are without historical precedent. The contribution of the United States to these efforts may be thought of as falling into three principal divisions. The first relates to reconversion and rehabilitation after the war, the second to economic growth and development, and the third to military ends.

The Anglo-American Loan of 1946 was designed to remove existing uncertainty concerning the intergovernmental indebtedness resulting from the war and to assist Great Britain in meeting the difficult financial problems associated with reconversion to peace. Among other provisions, it called for the cancellation of Lend-Lease obligations amounting in the case of Great Britain to nearly $25 billion, by far the largest operation of the sort ever recorded. Its main purpose, however, was to grant a 50-year loan of $3.75 billion to the British. It was provided that payments on interest (though not on principal) would be waived in case of a shortage of foreign exchange.

The grant of the loan and the accompanying cancellation of Lend-Lease were described by Winston Churchill at the time as "the most unsordid act in history." It was in pleasant contrast with our policy after World War I when we attempted to enforce repayment of the loans made to our allies during the war.

Loans to other countries to assist in their reconversion to peacetime conditions were arranged through the Export-Import Bank, whose lending power was substantially increased to meet the added burden (to $3.5 billion in 1945 and by 1954 to $5 billion). The expanded activities of the Export-Import Bank immediately after the war reflected the assumption by the United States government of major responsibility for facilitating postwar rehabilitation. Assistance in recovering from the effects of the war was subsequently provided through the work of the United Nations Relief and Rehabilitation Administration, the Truman policy of providing help in resisting the spread of Communism as in the case of Greece and Turkey, and the Marshall Plan.

In the course of time, foreign assistance by the United States increasingly took on the form of economic and technical assistance and of military aid. The so-called Point Four Program announced in 1949 included provision for helping to increase the productivity of underdeveloped areas. Some of the projects initiated for this purpose also had military significance, as in the development of facilities for the production of strategic minerals. Assistance for economic development was supplemented by grants of food, notably wheat to India and Pakistan.

After the start of the Korean War there was a distinct shift from technical and economic assistance to aid of a military character. Under the Offshore Procurement program large orders were placed with European countries to enable them to earn dollars by producing military equipment for the forces of the North Atlantic Treaty Organization. Distribution of contracts was said to be influenced by a desire to improve economic conditions in the respective countries as well as to contribute to mutual security in a directly military way. A further modification of the program of economic and military assistance was illustrated in the action of the United States government in turning over to the French government for use in Indo-China, military supplies purchased in France with Offshore Procurement funds. Later, a comparable sum of money was given directly to the French government as a contribution to the ill-fated French military effort in the Far East.

TABLE 30-1. United States Net Foreign Aid 1945-1960 (millions of dollars)

	Military	Economic	Total
1945 (July-December)	615	1,363	1,978
1946	110	5,355	5,465
1947	43	5,622	5,665
1948	326	4,859	5,185
1949	216	5,346	5,563
1950	524	3,608	4,132
1951	1,479	3,143	4,622
1952	2,673	2,331	5,004
1953	4,268	2,084	6,352
1954	3,431	1,750	5,181
1955	2,672	2,184	4,856
1956	2,634	2,281	4,915
1957	2,483	2,604	5,087
1958	2,368	2,518	4,886
1959	2,031	1,888	3,920
1960	1,881	2,606	4,487
Total	27,842	49,939	77,781

Source: Derived from *Statistical Abstract.*

The character and amounts of foreign financial assistance by the United States are summarized in Table 30-1. From July 1945 to December 1960 the total amounted to nearly $78 billion. The average of $5 billion per annum reflected a range of from under $4 billion in 1959 to well over $6 billion in 1953. The shifts in emphasis with respect to the character of foreign assistance are indicated by the fact that grants for military purposes represented roughly 6 per cent of net credits and grants to the end of 1950, rose to two-thirds in 1953, and ranged from approximately a half to a third of the total thereafter.

The Common Market

The common market (officially the European Economic Community) was created by the Treaty of Rome signed by France, West Germany, Italy, Holland, Belgium, and Luxemburg in January 1958. While the monetary clauses of the document have been obscured by the attention directed toward provisions for reducing trade barriers, they have important long-run implications.

The declared objectives of the common market include the coordination of monetary and fiscal policies with a view to promoting full employment, stable price levels, and balance of payment equilibrium in the member countries. The short-run accomplishments of the common market in the way of economic expansion, trade liberation, and strengthening of currencies were substantial. The long-run effects are necessarily conjectural. Among the leading possibilities (of varying degrees of likelihood) would seem to be the following:

Continued expansion in the volume of trade within and between countries comprising the common market, and with outside countries.

An extension of the membership of the common market.[11]

Adoption of unified credit policies.

Establishment of a common money and capital market.

Adoption of a uniform monetary standard and currency system.

Creation of an international central bank or comparable supranational monetary authority.

The monetary provisions of the Treaty of Rome received little notice in the early years of the common market. But they were nevertheless significant as indicating, along with the proposal for an international central bank, the broadening of monetary horizons.

International financial measures adopted after World War II reflect a pronounced change both in the policy of the United States in world affairs and in the role played by the federal government. They also represent official acceptance of an important lesson from fundamental economics (and no less fundamental world politics) that the economic well-being of foreign countries is of major concern to the United States. The close integration of commercial with financial provisions in both the Fund and the Bank constitutes recognition that international trade and international finance are indivisible.

The changed attitude toward international financial reconstruction after World War II offers hope that the policies adopted will be more successful in achieving long-term objectives than were the measures taken after World War I. It signifies that society, both national and international, learns from experience; and, furthermore, that what happened earlier cannot be accepted as a reliable precedent in drawing conclusions for a later period.

It is evident, finally, that attitudes on international financial problems, even more than the problems themselves, are subject to substantial and unexpected change. Moreover, the volatility of public opinion and the volatility of international short-term capital movements are mutually re-enforcing. This is a situation that has lent itself to unwarranted generalizations as to the permanence of dollar shortage, the possibility of a dangerous loss of gold, the burden of foreign aid, and the menace of Japanese and other foreign competition. Exaggerated fears as to the consequences of particular developments such as these have been influenced by insularity of outlook and by misconceptions as to the existing monetary status of gold. It is likely that similar delusions in the future will be avoided only by the perspective which an understanding of both theory and history can alone provide.

---

11. As early as 1962 the addition of members from the European Free Trade Association seemed a certainty, with participation by Great Britain a probability and by the United States a possibility.

SELECTED BIBLIOGRAPHY

CAIRNCROSS, ALEC, *The International Bank for Reconstruction and Development*. Essays in International Finance, No. 33. Princeton: 1959.

Federal Reserve Bank of New York, "International Development Lending Institutions," *Monthly Review*, September 1961. (For current information consult the monthly issues of this publication.)

FOUSEK, PETER, *Foreign Central Banking*. New York: Federal Reserve Bank of New York, 1956, Chapter VII.

HARRIS, S. E., (ed.), *The Dollar in Crisis*. New York: Harcourt Brace, 1961. (See especially "Professor Triffin, International Liquidity, and the International Monetary Fund," by Oscar L. Altman.)

International Bank for Reconstruction and Development, *Annual Reports*.

International Monetary Fund. *Annual Reports on Exchange Restrictions*.

Joint Economic Committee, *International Payments Imbalances*. Report of the Subcommittee on International Exchange and Payments. Washington: 1961, pp. 1-26.

TRIFFIN, ROBERT, *Gold and the Dollar Crisis*. New Haven: Yale University Press, 1960, Chapters I, V.

INDEX